Frommer's 97

Paris

**by Darwin Porter
and Danforth Prince**

Macmillan • USA

ABOUT THE AUTHORS

Veteran travel writers **Darwin Porter** and **Danforth Prince** have written numerous best-selling Frommer guides, notably England, France, the Caribbean, Italy, and Germany. Porter, a bureau chief for the *Miami Herald* at the age of 21, has lived in Paris periodically and written about the city for many years. Prince also has lived in the city for many years as a member of the Paris bureau for the *New York Times.*

MACMILLAN TRAVEL

A Simon & Schuster Macmillan Company
1633 Broadway
New York, NY 10019

Find us online at **http://www.mgr.com/travel**
or on America Online at **Keyword: Frommer's.**

ISBN 0-02-861134-9
ISSN 0899-3203

Editor: Philippe Wamba
Production Editor: Phil Kitchel
Map Editor: Douglas Stallings
Design by Michele Laseau
Digital Cartography by Ortelius Design and Peter Bogaty

SPECIAL SALES

Bulk purchases (10+ copies) of Frommer's and selected Macmillan travel guides are available to corporations, organizations, mail-order catalogs, institutions, and charities at special discounts, and can be customized to suit individual needs. For more information write to Special Sales, Macmillan General Reference, 1633 Broadway, New York, NY 10019.

Manufactured in the United States of America

Contents

List of Maps

AN INVITATION TO THE READER

In researching this book, we discovered many wonderful places—hotels, restaurants, shops, and more. We're sure you'll find others. Please tell us about them, so we can share the information with your fellow travelers in upcoming editions. If you were disappointed with a recommendation, we'd love to know that, too. Please write to:

Darwin Porter/Danforth Prince
Frommer's Paris '97
Macmillan Travel
1633 Broadway
New York, NY 10019

AN ADDITIONAL NOTE

Please be advised that travel information is subject to change at any time—and this is especially true of prices. We therefore suggest that you write or call ahead for confirmation when making your travel plans. The authors, editors, and publisher cannot be held responsible for the experiences of readers while traveling. Your safety is important to us, however, so we encourage you to stay alert and be aware of your surroundings. Keep a close eye on cameras, purses, and wallets, all favorite targets of thieves and pickpockets.

WHAT THE SYMBOLS MEAN

✪ Frommer's Favorites

Hotels, restaurants, attractions, and entertainment you should not miss.

⑤ Super-Special Values

Hotels and restaurants that offer great value for your money.

ABBREVIATIONS IN HOTEL & OTHER LISTINGS

The following abbreviations are used for credit and charge cards:

AE	American Express	EU	Eurocard
CB	Carte Blanche	JCB	Japan Credit Bank
DC	Diners Club	MC	MasterCard
DISC	Discover	V	Visa
ER	enRoute		

Paris at a Glance

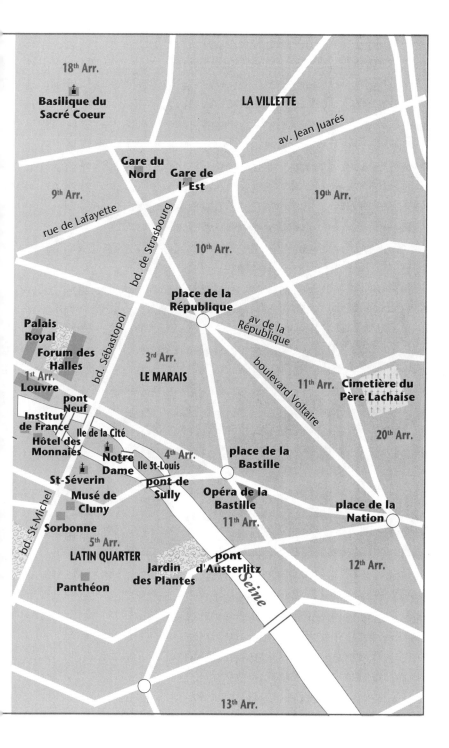

Paris By Arrondissement

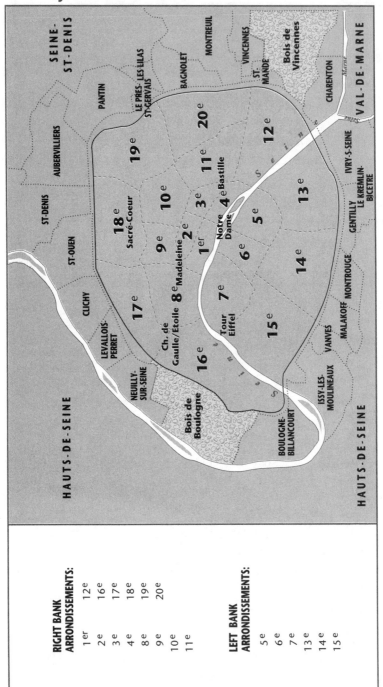

Introducing the City of Light

Whether you see it for the 1st or the 50th time, the discovery of Paris, and the experience of making it your own, is and always has been the most compelling reason to visit. Neighborhoods such as Montmartre and Montparnasse, St-Germain and Le Marais, are waiting to be explored for the first time, or to be rediscovered by a returning visitor. In some ways they remain the same, as if etched in stone, but after a second look it's obvious that they have changed. Everything is new and different—not always better, but always fresh and exciting.

Rich in history and cultural implications, the Seine, an inspiration for painters and lovers, flows through Paris, undulating in a gentle S-shaped curve, sheltering amid its current that pair of islands, Ile de la Cité and Ile St-Louis, upon which Paris was born.

Right away, this river that divides the city geographically and culturally forces you to make a choice. Are you a Right Bank (Rive Droite) or a Left Bank (Rive Gauche) type of person?

All *quartiers* are different, and since your experiences will likely be formed by where you choose to stay, so will your memory of Paris. Do you prefer a hotel deep in the heart of St-Germain, sleeping in a room where Jean-Paul Sartre and Simone de Beauvoir might have spent the night, or are you more Rive Droite, preferring to sleep in sumptuous quarters at the Crillon Hotel? Do you like looking for that special French curio in a dusty shop on the Left Bank's rue Jacob, or inspecting the latest haute-couture line of Karl Lagerfeld, Jean Patou, or Guy Laroche in a Right Bank boutique along avenue Montaigne?

If you're a first-timer, everything in Paris, of course, is new. But if you've been away for a long time, expect changes: Taxi drivers may no longer correct your fractured French, but address you in English—and that's tantamount to a revolution. More Parisians than ever have rudimentary knowledge of English, and the country, at least at first glance, seems less hysterically xenophobic than ever. Part of this derives from Parisians' interest in the cultural creations of foreign countries, music, videos, and films; part also derives from France's growing awareness of its role within a united Europe.

Yet France has never been more concerned about the loss of its unique identity within a landscape that's increasingly filled with immigrants from its former colonies. True, there's always the legitimate concern that France will continue to lose in its battle to keep French a pure tongue unadulterated by foreign influences. But as the country approaches the millennium, foreign tourists spending much-needed cash are no longer perceived as foes and antagonists. *Au contraire*—the rancor of France's collective xenophobia has been increasingly redirected toward the many immigrants seeking better lives in Paris, where the infrastructure has already been stretched almost to its limits.

Though Paris is clearly a city in constant cultural and social flux, it's still an excellent visitor's choice for all the reasons it has been for centuries. The grand old sights such as the Tour Eiffel are still there, as is the spruced up Champs-Elysées, both as crowded as ever. The beauty of Paris is still overwhelming, especially when dramatically illuminated at night. The City of Light, one of the premier tourist destinations in the world, always provides for entertaining, enlightening, and memorable experiences.

1 Frommer's Favorite Paris Experiences

- **A Walk along the Faubourg St-Honoré:** In the 1700s the wealthiest of Parisians resided in the Faubourg St-Honoré; today this *quartier* is home to the stores that cater to the rich. Even if you don't buy anything, it's great to window-shop all the big names—Hermès, Larouche, Courrèges, Cardin, Saint-Laurent.
- **An Afternoon of Café-Sitting:** The café is integral to life in Paris. Whether you have one small coffee or the most expensive cognac in the house, nobody will hurry you.
- **Afternoon Tea at Angélina:** Drinking tea in London has its charm, but the Parisian *salon de thé* is unique. Skip over those cucumber-and-watercress sandwiches and delve into the rich, luscious desserts, like Mont Blanc, a creamy purée of sweetened chestnuts once beloved by the Aga Khan. Try the grandest Parisian tea salon of them all, Angélina, 226 rue de Rivoli, 1er (Métro: Concorde).
- **A Night at the Ballet:** Renoir may have detested the **Opéra Garnier,** at place de l'Opéra, for its opulence, which he felt bordered on vulgarity, but since its opening it has been the center for ballet in Paris. An evening here takes you back to the Second Empire world of marble and gilt and grand staircases, all sheltered under a controversial ceiling by Chagall. Dress with pomp and circumstance.
- **A Day at the Races:** Paris has eight tracks for horse racing. The most famous and the classiest is **Longchamp,** in the Bois de Boulogne, 16e. It's the site of the Prix de l'Arc de Triomphe and the Grand Prix. These and other top races are major social events, so you'll have to dress up, of course. Take the Métro to Porte d'Auteuil, then a special bus from there to the track. *Paris Turf,* a racing newspaper, and other weekly entertainment magazines have details about racing times.
- **A Stroll Along the Seine:** Painters such as Sisley, Turner, and Monet have fallen under the River Seine's spell. Lovers still walk hand in hand alongside it, and anglers still cast their lines here. The *clochards* still seek a home for the night under its bridges, and on its banks the *bouquinistes* still peddle their postcards, perhaps some 100-year-old pornography or a tattered edition of an old history of Indochina. Some athletic visitors walk the full 7-mile stretch of the river through the city, but you may want to confine your stroll to central Paris, passing the Louvre, Notre-Dame, and the pont Neuf.
- **An Ice Cream at Bertillion:** A landmark on Ile St-Louis, Bertillion is said to offer the world's best selection of ice creams. Try rhubarb, fresh melon, kumquat, black currant, or any exotic fresh fruit in season—more than 50 flavors to choose

from and nothing artificial. Parisians have flocked to this place in such numbers that *gendarmes* have been called out to direct the traffic of ice cream aficionados.

- **An Evening at the Folies-Bergère:** Though often attacked and denounced, this Parisian showcase has been pleasing audiences since 1868, even though classic acts like Chevalier, Mistinguett, and Josephine Baker, who performed her famous banana dance here, are long gone. The Tour Eiffel cancan is a bit corny, and the show has gone more Latin, but those ladies in their sequins, feathers, and pompoms are still *au naturel.* Manet immortalized the Folies-Bergère on canvas, and the show, tacky or not, seems to go on forever.

- **An Evening of Opera:** The Opéra Bastille was inaugurated in July of 1989 to compete with the *grand dame* of the Paris musical scene, the Opéra Garnier. With 2,700 seats in its main hall, the Bastille is the largest opera house in France, and features opera and symphony performances in four different concert halls. Wear your most elegant evening clothes and soak up the glorious music in an opulent atmosphere that is very, very cultured and very, very French.

- **Discovering Hidden Montmartre:** This district has earned a reputation as the most touristy part of Paris. It's true that in the area surrounding Sacré-Coeur busloads of tourists descend; yet, far removed from there, another neighborhood unfolds—that of the true Montmartrois. To discover it, wander on any of the backstreets away from the souvenir shops. Many Parisian families have lived in the neighborhood for generations; other homes are being restored by actors, producers, newspaperpeople, and directors. Arm yourself with a good map and seek out such streets as rue Lepic (refresh yourself at the Lux Bar at no. 12), rue Constance, rue Tholozé (with its view over the rooftops of Paris), the lively rue des Abbesses, or rue Germain-Pilon—none of these streets is famous or celebrated, none receives hordes of visitors, but each is flanked with buildings whose detailing shows the pride and care that permeates Paris's architecture. You'll discover dozens of other streets on your own.

- **Checking Out the Marchés:** A daily Parisian ritual is to amble through one of the open-air markets to purchase fresh food to be consumed that day—the ripe and properly creamy Camembert, that pumpkin-gold cantaloupe at its peak when consumed before sundown. Even if you're staying in a hotel room with no kitchen facilities, you can partake of this time-honored French tradition and gather the supplies for a picnic in one of the city's parks. Like the artists they are, the vendors arrange their wares into a mosaic of vibrant colors. Sanguine, an Italian citrus whose juice is the color of a brilliant orange sunset; ruby-red peppers; golden-yellow bananas from Martinique—all dazzle the eye. Our favorite market? The one on rue Montorgeuil, beginning at rue Rambuteau, 1er (Métro: Les Halles). On mornings at this grubby little cluster of food stalls, we've spotted some of France's finest chefs adding to the larders of their restaurants in anticipation of a day at their stoves.

- **Cocktails at Willi's:** Back in the early 1970s, the first-time visitor to Paris might have arrived with a copy of Hemingway's *A Moveable Feast* and, taking the author's endorsement to heart, might have headed first for Harry's Bar at *Sank roo doe Noo.* Harry's is still there and now draws an older, conservative clientele. Today's young, chic crowd heads for Willi's, currently in vogue; it's found at 13 rue des Petits-Champs, 1er (Métro: Bourse, Louvre, or Palais-Royal). The young, long-haired bartenders are mostly English, as are the waitresses, dressed in Laura Ashley garb. The place, which gained popularity through word of mouth, is like an informal club for Brits, Australians, and Yanks—especially in the afternoon. Some 300 wines await your choice.

- **A Chic Place to Improve Your Tan:** Not all Parisians head to St-Tropez in the summer to get a tan. The chic place to go in the city is **Piscine Deligny,** 5 quai Anatole-France, 7e (☎ 01-45-51-72-15). Virtually a Parisian institution since the early 1840s—when people wore a lot more clothes for bathing—this large outdoor pool is surrounded by chaises longues. On one recent visit we spotted at least three young women who looked like Brigitte Bardot did in 1957 and at least two or three young men who resembled Alain Delon, circa 1962. Don't forget to bring your microbikini. Open only in summer.

- **The Ultimate in Cheese:** If France truly has 265 *spécialitiés de fromages* (kinds of cheese), you can sample virtually all of them at **Androuët,** 41 rue d'Amsterdam, 8e (Métro: St-Lazare or Liège). At this restaurant of cheese, started by Henri Androuët in 1914, the main dishes are cheese steaks and cheese scallops. Beginning in 1920, Henri invited customers into his vaulted cellars, where by candlelight, with a loaf of bread and a glass of wine, they could taste cheese ripened to perfection. One American woman reportedly sampled 86 different types of cheese all in one night, but this daring feat is not recommended. The selection is amazing, everything from the delicate and unfermented white cheese to the powerful, blue-veined, "penicillin" variety.

- **A Day at Fauchon:** "I'd much rather spend a day at Fauchon than a night at the Comédie-Française," a Frenchman confided to us. Perhaps he's right. An exotic world of food, Fauchon has a vast array of treasures. More than 20,000 products from the far corners of the globe are sold here. It has been called a "supermarket for millionaires," but it democratically maintains a reasonably priced self-service cafeteria for those who aren't. Whatever you've dreamed about in a foodstuff is here in aisle after aisle of coffees, spices, pastries, fruits, vegetables, and rare armagnacs. Take your pick: Toganese mangoes, smoked Scottish salmon, preserved cocks' combs, rose petal jelly from Romania, blue-red pomegranates from India, golden brown dates from Tunisia (only from the most famous oasis, of course), larks stuffed with foie gras, dark morels from the rich earth of France, reindeer's tongue from Finland, century-old eggs from China, and a Créole punch from Martinique that's reputed to be the best on earth.

- **Sneaking Away from It All:** When the glory and pomp of Paris become all too much, we slip away to **St-Germain-en-Laye,** 13 miles to the northwest. (Take the RER line A1.) This trendy suburb was once the residence of the kings of France, everybody from François I to Louis XIV ("The Sun King"), who was born here. Visitors often overlook this area, but Parisians adore it and often come here to escape the summer heat. You can visit the **Château Vieux** where Louis XIV lived, but mostly you'll want to wander around, inspecting the streets, parks, and gardens. A meal at the **Pavillon Henri-IV,** a hotel with a restaurant, would make the day perfect. It's named for the king who in the 1500s built a home on this site for his illegitimate children. Dumas wrote *The Three Musketeers* here at the pavillon in 1843, and earlier, the Sun King romped (among other things) with Madame de Montespan. Of course, whatever your main dish, you'll want to order it with béarnaise sauce, which is said to have been invented here.

2 The City Today

A medley of races and people from all over the world characterizes today's Paris. In many ways Paris is more international than French. Waves of immigrants from the far stretches of a former empire, including Vietnam and North Africa, have flooded

Paris in recent years, and this, combined with the millions of visitors who pour in annually from all over the world, has forever altered the legend and lore of the city. You can no longer separate Paris from its visitors: They have almost become one and the same.

What hasn't changed is the Parisian emphasis on the primacy of French culture. While it may be true that the average Parisian of today prefers watching an old Jerry Lewis movie at home on TV to sitting in a café sipping an apéritif, the good things of life are still appreciated in the City of Light: food, sex, and fashion—entirely in that order.

Celebrities have also always fascinated Parisians, and they still do, as the stars of the past are succeeded by new talents who become cultural icons in their own right. While the intense aura of Bardot and Deneuve may have faded, actress Isabelle Adjani now glows in the Parisian galaxy. This Paris-born beauty of Turkish and German descent achieved fame in Truffaut's *Adèle* (1975) and James Ivory's *Quartet* (1981). And although Yves Saint-Laurent doesn't quite create the stir in the fashion world that he did in the 1960s, Tunisian designer Azzadine Alaïa, who first opened a Marais boutique promoting skintight high-fashion clothing in the late 1970s, has become a sensation in international fashion.

Other current stars include Carole Bouquet, a Chanel model turned actress; Sophie Marceau, "the epitome of French womanhood," whose career recently got a boost when she co-starred with Mel Gibson in *Braveheart;* and Philippe Noiret, a new French leading man whose films, *Le Facteur* and *Le Vieux Fusil,* have met with critical acclaim. In the fashion world, bad boy Jean-Claude Gaultier's sartorial oddities ("kinky aliens from outer space discover the appeal of S&M and leather") continue to shake up the presuppositions of the French fashion establishment, while Christian LaCroix, a *grande couture* traditionalist, continues to produce popular designs.

Legendary Paris style and chic are changing, too. Unless you frequent upscale watering holes, you see very few Parisians dressed quite as alluringly as they did a few years ago. The city's dress code has become less formal. In fact, some young Parisians are as sloppily attired as their American counterparts in blue jeans and jogging suits. Despite these slouchily dressed Parisians parading along the boulevards, Paris remains the fashion capital of the world, but it now faces stiff competition from New York, Tokyo, Milan, and London. The old *haute couture* houses have experienced rough times, but *prêt-à-porter* designers are flourishing.

The city's architecture also exhibits a uniquely Parisian sense of culture and its importance. During his 14-year "reign," the late president François Mitterand, although a Socialist, set out to leave an architectural legacy to rival or surpass that of the autocratic "Sun King," Louis XIV. Mitterand's dream was to make Paris—not Berlin—the undisputed capital of the European Union. To do this, he virtually painted Paris in gold (well, gilt at least), and ran up a $6-billion tab as he built, restored, or recast monuments and buildings all over the city.

The most famous, and most controversial, of these Mitterand-sponsored *grands projects* was I. M. Pei's metal-and-glass pyramid for the Louvre, a design that was personally selected by the president himself. A number of other projects have also come off the drawing boards and into reality, from the Opéra Bastille in the east to La Grande Arch de la Défense in the west. Under Mitterand, regilting was the rule of the day, and Paris is now more golden than ever, from the 18 rostral columns ringing place de la Concorde to the 555,000 sheets of 24-karat leaf covering the dome of the Invalides. Even the angels at the approach to the Tuileries Gardens have been regilded.

In keeping with the quintessentially French emphasis on culture, French governments have traditionally strongly supported artistic and cultural production. In Washington, D.C., funding for the arts is currently being threatened; in contrast to this, the French government, although bankrupt, continues to subsidize the arts, including music, theater, opera, and the visual arts. Funding is given even if the art is controversial or offensive to some audiences. Art and culture are viewed as inherent to French civilization, and the government continues to honor and respect those who create. Nonetheless, in ways that imitate virtually every government in the Western world, France has indeed been forced to trim some of the excess fat from its budget; but the country still spends an awesome amount of money on the preservation of *la culture française*—more per capita than most countries of Europe.

Despite the French government's historically popular role in the promotion of culture, it has recently been the focus of tremendous criticism. Louis XV, who spent a life in lavish splendor surrounded by mistresses, is said to have uttered this very accurate prediction: *Après moi, le déluge* (After me, the flood). In Louis's case the *déluge* came in the shape of a revolution in 1789 that overthrew the monarchy. Mitterand didn't repeat these words, but it would have been prophetic if he had: Shortly after Mitterand's death in 1995, Paris became the center of a rash of antigovernment upheavals nationwide.

Mitterand's successor, Jacques Chirac, and his prime minister, Alain Juppé, are often described as the most unpopular men in France. To them has fallen the unpleasant task of stewarding a bankrupt country that must be weaned from the French brand of cradle-to-grave socialism that has increasingly proven economically unsound, a system that includes medical benefits unheard of in the rest of the Western world. Parisians took the news of possible cuts in services and benefits in traditional fashion: They took it to the streets. On October 10, 1995, a general strike paralyzed France and turned Paris into a giant parking lot as transportation strikes forced Parisians into their cars. During the strike, traffic in Paris literally couldn't move. In addition, planes were grounded, trains were idled, cars were set on fire, and unemployed young people tossed rocks or, even worse, Molotov cocktails. The strike was eventually settled and everything is now running normally, but the unrest exposed an ugly and volatile underside to French society.

Forget all those images of friendly *gendarmes* waving American movie stars through traffic lights in the films of the 1950s. Today's police are more likely to patrol the ghettos surrounding Paris (*les banlieus*)—especially the North African population centers—in armored cars. In some of these districts, 40% of the population is unemployed, and they're restless and angry. Paris, and France itself, no longer assimilates immigrants as it so easily did in its past. Many French now fear the growing Muslim ghettos surrounding Paris and other French cities. In fact, the issue has taken center stage in French politics: On an anti-immigration backlash, Jean-Marie Le Pen has risen to prominence in France as the leader of the National Front (FN). His platform is unashamedly racist, with the slogan *La France pour le français* ("France for the French") intended as a protest against Arab, black African, and Third World immigration from former French colonies. The National Front is France's main working-class party, and it blames immigrants for stealing "French jobs." In the first round of the 1995 presidential elections, it scored twice as much as the communists, and is clearly the premier party of the right wing.

Compounding matters, terrorist bombings, blamed on Muslim militants from Algeria, also plagued Paris in 1995, leading to trip cancellations on the part of some prospective visitors. In some ways, Paris in 1995 resembled a city under siege.

In the wake of the bombings, newly elected president Jacques Chirac created a radical program named *Vigi-Pirate* to steel Paris against further attacks. The result was horrendously expensive for the French government, which was probably secretly relieved when measures were relaxed late in 1995. The program vastly increased the military presence in Métro stations, in the large department stores, in the city's railway stations and airports, and inside the city's monuments to French culture, especially the Louvre. Automobiles were forbidden to park outside schools and other major public buildings, and soldiers in battle dress with assault rifles were seen along the Champs-Elysées and near the Opéra Garnier. Most cultural organizations, including some theaters and museums, began conducting pre-entry body searches and instituted airport-style surveillance, complete with x-ray machines, acts motivated by government fears that terrorists would strike at the country's most visible symbols of power, culture, and tradition.

One of the most bizarre aspects of the program involved the perception that any garbage can might make a worthwhile repository for a bomb. As a precaution, all garbage cans in certain high-profile neighborhoods were removed, citizens were ordered to deposit their litter and trash in easier-to-monitor plastic bags, and the city's *ébouers* (sanitation staff) worked overtime, making more frequent garbage pickups. Though these measures were eventually relaxed, the French government insists it will re-initiate them in the event of future terrorist attacks on Paris.

Paris today is obviously a city in disarray. Designer Philippe Starck painted this gloomy portrait: "I feel a sense of decline. The energy is draining, a negative atmosphere growing." There are those who fear that the glory of Paris "is another day," that its famed lifestyle is increasingly unaffordable. Each day even middle-class life in Paris becomes more costly.

While still a dreamy, romantic city, Paris is on the brink of major change and upheaval. The city now presides over a country facing a serious economic crisis and a great cultural decline (Matisse, for example, died in 1954 and there has not been a great French painter since), but most of these problems lurk beneath the surface. What does all this mean for the average visitor? To be honest, unless there's a strike or a street protest during your stay, you may not notice the underlying turmoil (though you'll certainly notice the high prices). Thanks to Mitterand, Paris looks more glamorous than ever. And lovers still walk arm in arm along the Seine.

3 History 101

HOW IT ALL BEGAN   Paris emerged at the crossroads of three major traffic arteries on the muddy island that today is known as the Ile de la Cité.

By around 2000 B.C., the island served as the fortified headquarters of the Parisii tribe, who referred to it as Lutetia. The pair of crude wooden bridges that connected the island to the left and right banks of the river were among the most strategically important in the region, and the settlement attracted the attention of the Roman empire. In his *Commentaries,* Julius Caesar described the Roman conquest of Lutetia, recounting how its bridges were burned during the Gallic War of 52 B.C., and how the town on

Dateline

- 2000 B.C. Paris (ancient Lutetia) thrives along a strategic crossing of the Seine, the fortified headquarters of the Parisii tribe.

- 52 B.C. Julius Caesar conquers Paris during the Gallic Wars.

- A.D. 150 Lutetia flourishes as a Roman colony, expanding to Paris's Left Bank.

continues

- **200** Barbarian Gauls force the Romans to retreat to the fortifications on Ile de la Cité.
- **300** "Paris" officially named as such; Roman power weakens in northern France.
- **350** Beginnings of Paris's Christianization.
- **400s** Frankish invasions of Paris, with social transformation from Roman to Gallo-Roman culture.
- **466** Birth of Clovis, founder of the Merovingian dynasty, first non-Roman ruler of Paris since the Parisii.
- **800** Coronation of Charlemagne, founder of the Carolingian dynasty and first Holy Roman Emperor, who rules from Aachen in modern Germany.
- **987** Hugh Capet, founder of France's foremost early medieval dynasty, rises to power; he and his heirs rule from Paris.
- **1100** The Université de Paris attracts scholars from throughout Europe.
- **1200s** Paris's population and power grow, although frequently unsettled by plagues and feudal battles.
- **1422** Paris invaded by England during the Hundred Years' War.
- **1429** Joan of Arc tries unsuccessfully to regain Paris for the French; the Burgundians later capture and sell her to the English, who burn her at the stake in Rouen.
- **1500s** François I, considered first of the French Renaissance kings, embellishes Paris but chooses to maintain his court in the Loire Valley.
- **1549** Henri II rules France from Paris; construction of public and private residences begins, many of them in the Marais neighborhood.

continues

the island was pillaged, sacked, and transformed into a Roman-controlled stronghold.

Within a century, Lutetia had become a full-fledged Roman town, and some of the inhabitants abandoned the frequently flooded island in favor of higher ground on what is today the Left Bank. By the year A.D. 200, barbarian invasions increasingly threatened the stability of Roman Gaul, and the populace from the surrounding hills flocked to the fortified safety of the island.

Within about 50 years a Christian community gained a tenuous foothold on the island. According to legend, St. Denis served as the city's first bishop (beginning around 250). Although the political power of the Roman Empire had begun to wane in the region by this time, the cultural and religious attachment of the community to the Christian bishops of Rome grew even stronger.

During the 400s, with the great decline of the Roman armies, Germanic tribes from the east (the Salian Franks) were able to successfully invade the island, founding a Frankish dynasty there and prompting a Frankish-Latin cultural fusion in the growing town. The first of these Frankish kings, Clovis (466–511), founder of the Merovingian dynasty, embraced Christianity as his tribe's official religion and spearheaded an explicit rejection of Roman cultural imperialism by encouraging the adoption of Parisii place names like "Paris," which came into common usage during this time.

The Merovingian dynasty was replaced by the Carolingians, whose heyday began with the coronation of Charlemagne in 800. The Carolingian empire sprawled over western Germany and eastern France, but Paris was never considered its capital. The city did remain a commercial and religious center, sacred to the memory of St. Geneviève, who reputedly protected Paris when it was repeatedly attacked by the Huns in the final days of the Roman Empire.

The Carolingian dynasty came to an end in 987, when the empire fragmented because of the growing regional, political, and linguistic divisions between what would eventually become modern France and modern Germany. Paris became the seat of a new dynasty, the Capetians, whose kings would rule France throughout the Middle Ages. Hugh Capet, the first of this line of kings, ruled as count of Paris and duke of France from 987 to 996.

THE MIDDLE AGES   Around 1100 Paris began to emerge as a great city, with a university established on what is today known as the Left Bank. It attracted scholars from all over Europe. Meanwhile, kings and bishops began building the great Gothic cathedrals of France, one of the greatest of which became Paris's Notre-Dame, a soaring ecclesiastical monument rising from the very heart of the city. The population of Paris increased greatly, as did the city's mercantile activity. During the 1200s a virtual building explosion transformed the skyline with convents and churches (including the jewel-like Sainte-Chapelle, completed in 1249 after just 2 years of work). During the next century the increasingly powerful French kings added dozens of monuments of their own.

As time passed, the fortunes of Paris became closely linked to the power struggles between the French monarchs in Paris and the various highly competitive feudal lords of the outlying provinces. Because of this tug-of-war, Paris was dogged by civil unrest, a series of plagues (including the famous Black Death), takeovers by one warring faction after another, and a dangerous alliance between the English and the powerful rulers of Burgundy during the Hundred Years' War. To the everlasting humiliation of the French monarchs, the city was invaded by the English army in 1422. Joan of Arc (ca. 1412–31) tried unsuccessfully to reconquer Paris in 1429, and 2 years later the English burned her at the stake in Rouen (Normandy). Paris was reduced to poverty and economic stagnation and its embittered and greatly reduced population turned to banditry and street crime to survive.

Despite Joan's ignominious end, the revolution she inspired continued in protracted form until Paris was finally taken from the English armies in 1436. During the several decades that followed, the English retreated to the Channel port of Calais, abandoning their once-mighty territories in France. France, under the leadership of Louis XI, witnessed an accelerating rate of changes that included the transformation of a feudal and medieval social system into the nascent beginnings of a modern state.

THE RENAISSANCE & THE REFORMATION   The first of the Renaissance monarchs, François I, began an extensive enlargement of Paris's Louvre (which had begun its life as a warehouse storing the archives of Philippe Auguste before being transformed into a Gothic fortress by Louis IX in the 1100s) to make it suitable as a royal residence. Despite the building's embellishment, and the continued designation of Paris as the French capital, he

- **1564** Construction of Catherine de Médicis's Tuileries Palace; building facades in Paris transform from half-timbered to more durable chiseled stonework.
- **1572** The Wars of Religion reach their climax with the massacre of Protestants on St. Bartholomew's Day.
- **1598** Henri IV, the most eccentric and enlightened monarch of his era, endorses the Edict of Nantes, granting tolerance to Protestants, for which a crazed monk fatally stabs him 12 years later.
- **1615** Construction of the Luxembourg Palace by Henri IV's widow, Marie de Médicis.
- **1636** The Palais-Royal launched by Richelieu; soon thereafter, two marshy islands in the Seine are connected and filled in to create the Ile St-Louis.
- **1643** Rise to power of Louis XIV, "the Sun King," the most powerful ruler since the Caesars; he moves his court to the newly constructed Versailles.
- **1776** American Declaration of Independence from Britain strikes a revolutionary chord in France.
- **1789** Outbreak of the French Revolution.
- **1793** Louis XVI and his Austrian-born queen, Marie Antoinette, are publicly guillotined.
- **1799** Napoléon Bonaparte crowns himself Master of France; Paris is further embellished with neoclassical splendor.
- **1803** Napoléon abandons French overseas expansion and sells Louisiana to America.
- **1812** Defeat of Napoléon in the Russian winter campaign.

continues

- **1814** Aided by a military coalition of France's enemies, especially England, the Bourbon monarchy, under Louis XVIII, is restored.
- **1821** Death of Napoléon Bonaparte.
- **1824** Death of Louis XVIII; Charles X accedes.
- **1830** Charles X is deposed and the more liberal Louis-Philippe is elected king; Paris prospers as it industrializes.
- **1848** Violent working-class revolution deposes Louis-Philippe, who is replaced by the autocratic Napoléon III; forced redesigning of Paris's landscapes by Baron Haussmann.
- **1863** Birth of impressionism.
- **1870** Franco-Prussian War ends with a defeated France; Paris threatened with bombardment by Prussian cannons; after the defeat, a revolution destroys the Tuileries palace and over-throws the government; rise of the Third Republic and its elected president, Marshal MacMahon.
- **1878–1937** A series of international expositions adds many enduring monuments to the Paris skyline, including the Eiffel Tower.
- **1914–18** World War I.
- **1940** German troops invade Paris; the official French government, under Pétain, evacuates to Vichy, while the French Resistance under de Gaulle maintains symbolic headquarters in London.
- **1944** Paris liberated by U.S. troops; de Gaulle returns from London in triumph.
- **1948** Revolt in French colony of Madagascar costs 80,000 French lives; France's empire continues to collapse in Southeast Asia and Equatorial Africa.

continues

spent much of his time at other châteaux amid the fertile hunting grounds of the Loire Valley. Many later monarchs would share his opinion that the narrow streets and teeming commercialism of Paris were unhealthy and upsetting and choose to reside elsewhere.

In 1549, however, Henri II triumphantly established his court in Paris and successfully ruled France from within the city's boundaries, thus solidifying Paris's role as the nation's undisputed capital. Responding to their ruler's initiative, fashionable aristocrats quickly began to build private residences on the Right Bank, in a low-lying marshy area known as Le Marais (the swamp).

Paris as the world knows it today came into existence during this period. The expansion of the Louvre continued, and Catherine de Médicis began building her Tuileries palace in 1564. From the shelter of dozens of elegant urban residences, the aristocracy of France imbued Paris with their sense of architectural and social style, as well as the mores and manners of the Renaissance. Stone quays were added to the banks of the Seine, defining their limits and preventing future flood damage, and royal decrees were passed establishing a series of building codes. To an increasing degree, Paris adopted the planned perspectives and visual grace of the preferred residence of an absolute monarchy.

During the late 1500s and 1600s, Protestants were brutally persecuted by the French monarchs. Under Henri III the bloodletting reached a high point during the St. Bartholomew's Day massacre of 1572.

Henri III's tragic and eccentric successor, Henri IV, ended the wars of religion in 1598 by endorsing the Edict of Nantes, which offered religious freedom to the Protestants of France. Henry IV also laid out the lines for one of the memorable plazas of Paris—place des Vosges. As a reward for his political leniency, Henry IV was stabbed in 1610 by a deranged monk who was infuriated by his emforcement of religious tolerance.

After Henri IV's death, his second wife, Marie de Médicis (acting as regent), planned the Luxembourg Palace (1615), whose gardens have functioned ever since as a rendezvous for Parisians. In 1636 Cardinal Richelieu, who virtually ruled France during the minority of Louis XIII (the period in which the boy king was still too young to rule), built the sprawling premises of the Palais-Royal.

Under Louis XIII (1601–43) two uninhabited islands in the Seine were joined together with land-fill, connected to the Ile de la Cité and also to the mainland with bridges, and renamed the Ile St-Louis. Also laid out were the Jardin des Plantes, whose flowers and medicinal herbs were arranged according to their scientific and medical category.

LOUIS XIV & THE FRENCH REVOLUTION

Louis XIV was crowned king of France when he was only 9 years old. The government in Paris was almost completely dominated during Louis's minority by his Sicilian-born chief minister, Mazarin (1602–61).

This era marked the emergence of the French kings as absolute monarchs. As if to symbolize their power, the face of Paris was embellished with many of the monuments that still serve as symbols of the city. These included new alterations to the Louvre, and construction of the Pont-Royal, quai Peletier, place des Victoires, place Vendôme, the Champs Elysées, and the Hôtel des Invalides. Meanwhile, Louis XIV preferred to absent himself from the city center, constructing—at staggering expense—the palace at Versailles, 13 miles southwest of Paris. Today its echoing and sometimes tiresome splendor is the single most visible monument to the most flamboyantly ostentatious era of French history.

Meanwhile, the rising power of England, particularly its navy, represented a serious threat to France, which was otherwise the most powerful nation in the world. One of the many theaters of the Anglo-French conflict was the American war for independence, during which the French kings supported the American revolutionaries in their struggle against the

- **1954–62** War in, and eventual loss of, Algeria; Paris flooded with refugees and the nation bitterly divided over its North African policies.
- **1958** France's Fourth Republic collapses; General de Gaulle called out of retirement to head the Fifth Republic.
- **1968** General revolt by Paris's students and factory workers; the French government overhauled in the aftermath.
- **1981** François Mitterrand elected France's first socialist president since the 1940s, and reelected in 1988.
- **1989** Paris celebrates the bicentennial of the French Revolution.
- **1990–91** France joins the U.S., Britain, and other allies in a successful war against Iraq's invasion of Kuwait.
- **1992** Euro Disney opens on Paris's outskirts.
- **1994** François Mitterrand and Elizabeth II take a ride together *under* the English Channel.
- **1995** Mitterand dies; Chirac elected; Paris crippled by general strike; terrorists bomb Paris; France rejoins NATO military alliance.

British Crown. Ironically, within 15 years the same revolutionary fervor would cross the Atlantic and destroy the French monarchy.

None of this occurred in a philosophical vacuum. For years before the outbreak of hostilities between the American revolutionaries and the British, the Enlightenment and its philosophers, usually formulating their views in the sophisticated salons of Paris, had been fostering a new generation of thinkers who opposed absolutism, religious fanaticism, and superstition. Revolution had been brewing for almost 50 years, and after the French Revolution's explosive and world-shaking events, Europe was completely changed.

Beginning in 1789 with moderate aims, the Revolution soon became dominated by the radical Jacobins, led by Robespierre. On August 10, 1792, troops from Marseilles, aided by a Parisian mob, threw Louis XVI and his Austrian-born queen, Marie Antoinette, into prison. Several months later, after countless humiliations and a bogus trial, they were guillotined at place de la Révolution (later renamed place de la Concorde) on January 21, 1793. The Reign of Terror continued for another 18 months, and Parisians of all political persuasions feared for their lives.

THE RISE OF NAPOLEON It required the militaristic fervor of Napoléon to unite France once again. Considered then and today a strategic genius with almost limitless ambition, he restored to Paris and to France a national pride that had been diminished during the horror of the Revolution. In 1799, at the age of 30, after many impressive political and military victories he entered Paris and crowned himself First Consul and Master of France.

A brilliant politician, Napoléon moderated the atheistic rigidity of the early adherents of the Revolution by establishing peace with the Vatican. Soon thereafter, the legendary love of Parisians for their amusements began to revive; boulevard des Italiens became the rendezvous point of the fashionable, while boulevard du Temple, which housed many of the capital's vaudeville and cabaret theaters, became the favorite watering hole of the working class. In his self-appointed role as a French Caesar, Napoléon continued to alter the face of Paris with the construction of the neoclassical arcades of rue de Rivoli (1801), the triumphal arches of the Arc du Carrousel and place de l'Etoile, and the neoclassical grandeur of the Church of the Madeleine. On a less grandiose scale, the city's slaughterhouses and cemeteries were sanitized and moved away from the center of town, and new industries began to crowd workers from the countryside into the cramped slums of a newly industrialized Paris.

Napoléon's victories had made him the envy of Europe, but his infamous retreat from Moscow during the winter of 1812 reduced his formerly invincible army to tatters as 400,000 Frenchmen lost their lives. After a complicated series of events that included his return from exile, Napoléon was defeated at Waterloo by the combined armies of the English, the Dutch, and the Prussians. Exiled to the British-held island of St. Helena in the remote reaches of the South Atlantic, he died in 1821, probably the victim of an unknown poisoner. Some time later his body was interred in a massive porphyry sarcophagus inside Louis XIV's monument in Paris to the ailing and fallen warriors of France, Les Invalides.

In the power vacuum that followed the expulsion and death of Napoléon, Paris became the scene of intense lobbying concerning the future fate of France. The Bourbon monarchy was soon reestablished, but with reduced powers. In 1830 the regime was overthrown. Louis-Philippe, duke of Orléans and the son of a duke who had voted in 1793 for the death of Louis XVI, was elected king under a liberalized constitution. His calm, prosperous reign lasted for 18 years, during which England and France more or less collaborated on matters of foreign policy.

Paris reveled in its new prosperity, grateful for the funds and glamour that had elevated it to become one of the top cultural and commercial centers of the world. As a fringe benefit of France's campaigns in the Egyptian desert, Paris received the Luxor obelisk as a gift from the caliphs of Egypt. Transporting it across the Mediterranean and reerecting it on a granite plinth in place de la Concorde was a major triumph of engineering in 1836. Continuing to move into the modern age, Paris received its first railway line in 1837 (running from the center of town to a suburb near St-Germain), and shortly thereafter the first gas-fed streetlights. It was a time of

Impressions

Paris (in each shape and gesture and avenue and cranny of her being) was continuously expressing the humanness of humanity. Everywhere I sensed a miraculous presence, not of mere children and women and men, but of living human beings.

—e.e. cummings

Paris is a sphinx. I will drag her secret from her.

—Mirabeau

wealth, grace, and the expansion of the arts for some French people, although the industrialization of certain working-class districts of Paris produced horrible poverty. The era also witnessed the development of French cuisine to the high art form that still prevails, while a newly empowered *bourgeoisie* reveled in its attempts to create the good life.

THE SECOND EMPIRE   In 1848 a series of revolutions spread from one European capital to the next. The violent upheaval in Paris revealed the increasing dissatisfaction of many members of the working class. Fueled by a financial crash and scandals within the government, the revolt forced Louis-Philippe out of office. That year, on the dawn of the Second Republic, Emperor Napoléon's nephew, Napoléon III, was elected president by moderate and conservative elements. Appealing to the property-owning instinct of a nation that hadn't forgotten the violent revolution of less than a century before, he established a right-wing government and eventually assumed complete power—as emperor—in 1851.

In 1853 Napoléon III undertook the largest urban redevelopment project in the history of Europe. He commissioned Baron Haussmann (1809–91) to redesign the city of Paris. Haussmann created a vast network of boulevards that cut across old neighborhoods connecting a series of squares (*places*). While this reorganization process greatly improved the capital and gave it the look for which it's famous today, screams of outrage sounded throughout most of France.

By 1866 the entrepreneurs of an increasingly industrialized Paris began to regard the Second Empire as a hindrance to its development. In 1870, during the Franco-Prussian War, the Prussians defeated Napoléon III at Sedan and held him prisoner along with 100,000 of his soldiers. Paris was threatened with bombardment by German cannons—by far the most advanced of their age—that were set up on the city's eastern periphery.

Agitated diplomacy encouraged a Prussian withdrawal, although the event's legacy of international humiliation and perceived military incompetence sparked a revolt in Paris. One of the immediate effects of the revolt was the burning of one of Paris's historic palaces, the Tuileries. Today only the sprawling gardens of this once-great palace remain. The tumultuous events of 1870 ushered in the Third Republic and its elected president, Marshal MacMahon, in 1873.

Under the Third Republic, peace and prosperity gradually returned and Paris regained its glamour. A series of Universal Expositions held in 1878, 1889, 1900, and 1937 was the catalyst for the construction of such enduring Paris monuments as the Trocadéro, the Palais de Chaillot, the Eiffel Tower, both the Grand and the Petit Palais des Champs-Elysées, and the neo-Byzantine church of Sacré-Coeur in Montmartre. Simultaneously, the *réseau métropolitain* (the Métro, or Paris subway) was constructed, providing a model for subsequent subway systems throughout Europe.

WORLD WAR I   International rivalries and conflicting alliances led to World War I, which, after decisive German victories for 2 years, degenerated into the mud-slogged horror of trench warfare. Industrialization during and after the war transformed Paris and its outlying boroughs into one vast interconnected whole, by now one of the largest metropolitan areas in Europe and undisputed ever since as the center of France's intellectual and commercial life.

Immediately after the Allied victory, grave economic problems, coupled with a populace demoralized from years of fighting, encouraged the rise of socialism and the formation of a Communist party, movements that were centered in Paris. Also from Paris, the French government, led by the almost obsessively vindictive Clemenceau, occupied Germany's Ruhr Valley, then and now one of the most profitable and industrialized regions of Germany, and demanded every *centime* of reparations it could wring from its humiliated neighbor, a policy that contributed to the outbreak of World War II.

THE 1920s—AMERICANS IN PARIS   The so-called Lost Generation, led by American expatriates Gertrude Stein and her longtime companion, Alice B. Toklas, led the list of celebrities who would "occupy" Paris after the war, ushering in one of its most glamorous eras, the 1920s. The living was cheap in Paris—for example, if you had a scholarship worth about $1,000, two people could manage for about a year, providing they could scrape up another $500 or so in extra earnings. Thus came the *littérateur,* the *bon viveur,* and drifter, along with such writers as Henry Miller, Ernest Hemingway, and F. Scott Fitzgerald. Even Cole Porter arrived, living first at the Ritz, then later at 13 rue de Monsieur (7e). James Joyce, half blind and led around by Ezra Pound, arrived in Paris and went to the salon of Natalie Barney, leading exponent of "Amazon Love." She became famous for pulling off such stunts as inviting Mata Hari to perform a Javanese dance, completely nude, at one of her parties—labeled "for women only, a Lesbian orgy." Colette was barred, although she begged her husband to let her go. With the collapse of Wall Street, many Americans returned home, except some hard-core artists such as Henry Miller, who wandered around smoking Gauloise cigarettes and formulating several pages a day of *Tropic of Cancer,* which would be banned in America for decades. "I have no money, no resources, no hopes. I am the happiest man alive," Miller said. Eventually, he met the narcissistic diary writer, Anaïs Nin, and they began to live a life that gave both of them material for their prose. Miller read Nin's diaries and proclaimed, "The whole thing is a bloody emission, the orgasm of a monster." But even such diehards as Miller and Nin eventually realized that their Paris of the 1930s was collapsing as war clouds loomed. Gertrude and Alice remained in France as other American expatriates fled to safer shores.

THE WINDS OF WAR   Thanks to an array of alliances, France had no choice but to declare war on Germany in 1939 when Germany invaded France's ally, Poland. Within only a few months, on June 14, 1940, Nazi armies marched arrogantly down the Champs-Elysées. Newsreel cameras recorded the French openly weeping at the sight. The city suffered little from the war materially, but for 4 years it survived in a kind of half-life, cold, dull, and drab, fostering scattered pockets of fighters who resisted sometimes passively and sometimes with active sabotage.

During the Nazi occupation of Paris, the French government, under Marshal Pétain (1856–1951), moved to the quiet and isolated resort of Vichy and cooperated (or actually collaborated, depending on your point of view) with the Nazis. Tremendous internal dissension, the memory of which still simmers today, pitted many factions against one another. The Free French Resistance fled for its own safety to London, where it was headed by Charles de Gaulle (1880–1970), who after the war became president of France's Fourth Republic.

POSTWAR PARIS   Despite its gains in both prestige and prosperity after the end of World War II, Paris was rocked many times by internal dissent as domestic and international events embroiled the French government in dozens of controversies. In 1951 Paris forgot its cares by celebrating the 2,000th anniversary of its founding and poured much of its energy into rebuilding its image as a center of fashion, lifestyle, and glamour. Paris became internationally recognized as both a touristic staple in the travel diets of many North Americans and as a beacon for art and artists.

The War of Algerian Independence (1954–58), in which Algeria sought to go from being a French *département* (an integral extension of the French nation) to being an independent country, was an anguishing event, more devastating than the earlier loss of France's colonies. The population of France (and Paris in particular) ballooned immediately as French citizens, fleeing Algeria with few possessions and much bitterness, returned home. In 1958, as a result of the enormous loss of lives, money, and prestige in the Algerian affair, France's Fourth Republic collapsed and de Gaulle was called out of retirement to form a new government—the Fifth Republic.

In 1962 the Algerian war of liberation ended with victory for Algeria, as France's colonies in Central and Equatorial Africa became independent one by one. The sun had finally set on an empire that had transformed Paris, during the period of its most spectacular construction, into a mighty city.

In 1968 a general revolt by students in Paris, whose activism mirrored that of their militant counterparts in the United States, turned the capital into an armed camp, causing a near-collapse of the national government and the very real possibility of total civil war. Though the crisis was averted, for several weeks it seemed as if French society was tottering near the brink of anarchy.

CONTEMPORARY PARIS   Paris today struggles with additional social unrest in Corsica and from Muslim fundamentalists residing both in and outside France. In 1981 François Mitterrand (with a very close margin of victory of 51%) was elected the first socialist president of France since World War II. The flight of massive amounts of capital held by French millionaires slowed somewhat after initial jitters, although many wealthy Parisians still prefer to invest their money elsewhere. Although much feared by the rich, Mitterrand was reelected in 1988 and (according to many of his critics) soon thereafter adopted a kind of imperial demeanor better suited to a French monarch than to a duly elected president.

In 1989 Paris celebrated the bicentennial of the French Revolution with much fanfare. In the winter of 1990–91, France joined with the United States, Great Britain, and other Allies in a successful war against Iraq, in response to that country's invasion of Kuwait. On the architectural front, new and daring designs (including I. M. Pei's iconoclastic glass pyramid in the courtyard of the Louvre, and the construction of a series of new museums and urban attractions) continued to give Paris the controversial zest for which it has traditionally been famous.

The postwar passion for exhibiting French culture has included the opening or renovation of such museums as the Musée d'Orsay, the Centre Pompidou at place Beaubourg, and the Musée Picasso. Other newly constructed or improved sites include the Orangerie of the Tuileries, the Opéra Bastille, the Forum des Halles, the Cité des Sciences et de l'Industrie at La Villette, and new residences in the newly gentrified Marais district.

In the mid-1990s racial tensions continued to nag at France as the debate over immigration raged. Many right-wing political parties have created a racial backlash against North Africans and against "corruptive foreign influences" in general. The government has recently tried to ban the use of Anglicisms in the French language. For his efforts, critics nicknamed Culture Minister Jacques Toubon "Mr. All-Good" (a rough but literal translation of his name into the dreaded English). The conflict in Bosnia and an 11% rate of unemployment also continued to plague French politics, but when Mitterrand and Elizabeth II opened the Chunnel under the English Channel in 1994, it marked the first time since the Ice Age that France and England had been joined.

When former French President François Mitterand died of cancer in 1995, France embarked upon a new era. Jacques Chirac won the presidential election in May of 1995 with 52% of the vote in his third and finally charmed attempt at the office, bringing the conservative Republic party to power. The neo-Gaulist's popularity soon faded, however, in the wake of unrest caused by an 11.5% unemployment rate, an unpopular—seemingly nepotistic—prime minister, a barrage of terrorist attacks by Algerian Muslims, and a stressed economy struggling to meet European Monetary Union entry requirements.

Chirac was hard pressed to come up with creative answers to France's continuing job crisis. The former mayor of Paris quickly became mired in his country's turmoil, chairing the government from a smoldering hot seat. Nicknamed "Bulldozer," Chirac proved the moniker apt, leveling his cabinet by ordering all 41 ministers to quit. The task of forming a new government was left to Prime Minister Alain Juppé, himself no stranger to intense public scrutiny after it was revealed that in 1993 he used his position as deputy mayor of Paris to procure his son a rent reduction.

A wave of terrorist attacks from July to September of 1995 brought an unfamiliar wariness to Paris and did little to quell French fears of a crumbling Republic. In all, six bombs were planted, 7 people were killed, and 115 were injured. In light of this rising body count, Parisians proved cautious if not fearful. Trash cans were sealed and security beefed up, but the undaunted *sang-froid* of Paris's inhabitants still pervades to this day. Algerian Islamic militants, the suspected culprits, may have brought military guards to the Eiffel Tower but they failed to throw France into panic.

Perhaps Chirac's greatest threat is not the prospect of physical violence, but rather lies in the intangible archaic monster of the French economy. The French are averse to giving up the posh benefits their society affords them and, as yet, are unable to make the tough choices necessary to cut the deficit to 3% of the Gross National Product by 1997, as required by the proposed European Monetary Union that would establish a common European currency by the millennium.

Finally, France's recent history is also marked by a return to the past. The nation has returned to NATO following a 30-year absence, an act that signals an abandonment, or at least a deferral, of the belief France had held before the Bosnia conflict that Europe would adopt a more independent defense structure after the Cold War.

4 Famous Parisians

Josephine Baker (1906–75)   Although born in an African-American ghetto in St. Louis, this singer and cabaret entertainer became the toast of *tout Paris* with sensuously scintillating performances like her famous "Danse Sauvage." Dubbed "La Baker" by her adoring French public, she was granted French citizenship in 1937 and served her adopted country as a member of the French Resistance during World War II.

Honoré de Balzac (1799–1850)   This French novelist dropped out of law school and became the greatest chronicler of the mores and values of 19th-century French society. Always in debt, he produced more than 350 lengthy works. Among his most famous works—collectively called *La Comédie humaine*—are *Eugénie Grandet, La Cousine Bette,* and *Père Goriot.*

Charles Baudelaire (1821–67)   The work of this French impressionist poet was condemned by mainstream critics as obscene and decadent. One of the world's first modern poets, he ended his life in abject poverty, hopelessly addicted to opiates. His most famous work is *Les Fleurs du mal* (Flowers of Evil, 1857).

Simone de Beauvoir (1908–86)   A French essayist and novelist, she was the leading female writer of the existentialist movement and the on-again, off-again lover of Jean-Paul Sartre. Awarded the Prix Goncourt in 1945 for her novel *The Mandarins,* she was also one of the most articulate spokespersons for the postwar feminist movement. Her most influential feminist books are *The Second Sex* and *La Vieillesse* (Old Age). *Memoirs of a Dutiful Daughter* is her life story.

Louis Braille (1809–52)   French musician and educator of the blind, he invented a reading and writing system for the blind using a system of embossed dots. Himself blind from the age of 3, Braille became a noted organist and cellist, and during his lifetime was far more famous as a musician than as the inventor of braille. Braille died impoverished and alone.

Gabrielle ("Coco") Chanel (1883–1971)   This French image-maker and designer created chic, simple women's clothing, the classic lines of which have endured longer than those of any other designer in the world. Establishing her career from a shop on the boardwalk of Deauville, she promoted small and pert hats to replace the garlands of fruit, swaths of veils, and masses of straw or linen that were fashionable during the Edwardian age. In the 1950s she introduced her famous "little black dress."

Jean Cocteau (1889–1963)   A multimedia French artist, Cocteau was a stylesetter and *enfant terrible.* After experimenting in the surrealistic and avant-garde movements of the 1910s and 1920s, Cocteau wrote novels, poems, film scripts, essays, and scenarios for plays; painted church murals; designed restaurant menus; invented costumes; choreographed parties; and directed films. *Blood of a Poet, Beauty and the Beast,* and *Orphée* are three of his best-known films. His important writings include *Les Enfants terribles, Journal d'un inconnu,* and *La Difficulté d'être.* He was buried with full honors from the Académie Française.

Marie Curie (1867–1934)   A French physicist and chemist, born Marie Slodowska in Poland, she and her French-born husband, Pierre Curie, discovered radium and determined its radioactive properties in 1898. Winner of two Nobel Prizes for her experimentation with the curative effects of radiation, she died in 1934, worn out and exhausted, from radium poisoning.

Georges Jacques Danton (1759–94)   A revolutionary and political philosopher, Danton established policies of relative moderation that evoked the rage of more radical factions, who had him guillotined. At his most powerful point, he served as minister of justice and president of the Committee of Public Safety shortly after the fall of Louis XVI.

Honoré Daumier (1808–79)   Cartoonist, caricaturist, and painter, Daumier was the most acerbic and accurate cartoonist of the 19th century, exposing in his more than 4,000 cartoons the smugness, corruption, arrogance, and silliness of the 19th-century French bourgeoisie.

Christian Dior (1905–57)   This fashion designer helped revolutionize the French fashion industry with the "New Look" after establishing his own couture business in 1947. The recognition, prestige, and money his work brought to a France ravaged by the traumas of World War II eventually earned him a membership in the French Legion of Honor.

Jean-Honoré Fragonard (1732-1806)   His paintings, more than anyone else's, capture the illusionary sweetness of upper-class life during the *ancien régime.* His best-known work, *The Swing,* is an unabashedly rococo portrayal full of ribbons, flowers, and blue satin, of fey and perhaps fickle young lovers joyously appreciating the airborne rhythms of a swing in a highly idealized garden.

Yves Montand (1921–91)   The last of the great French entertainers, Montand symbolized every American's idea of a debonair Frenchman, even though he was born in Italy. He had great success in such films as *The Wages of Fear* in the 1950s and later in Costa-Gavras's *Z.* Montand's scandalous love affair with Marilyn Monroe during the filming of *Let's Make Love* attracted international publicity, since at the time he was married to actress Simone Signoret. Signoret died of cancer in 1985, and Montand was buried next to her at Père-Lachaise Cemetery in 1991.

Edith Piaf (1915–63)   The quintessential Parisian singer, who could move listeners to tears, was born Edith Gassion, the daughter of a circus acrobat. She was raised by her grandmother, who owned and operated a brothel. Piaf began singing in the streets at age 15 and later began appearing in cafés. Beautiful only when her plain features were illuminated while singing, Piaf was nicknamed "The Little Sparrow" by her ardent admirers. Companion of pimps, thieves, prostitutes, and drug addicts, she led a life filled with tragedy, illness, despair, and lost love. Her best-loved songs include "Milord," "A quoi ça sert, l'amour," "La Foule," and "La Vie en rose."

Cardinal Richelieu (Armand Jean du Plessis, duc de Richilieu; 1585–1642)   A French financier and prelate, Richelieu effectively controlled France after the death of Louis XIII's mother, Marie de Médicis. Merciless in his hatred and persecution of Protestants, Richelieu starved and destroyed the Huguenot strongholds of France, most notably La Rochelle. He founded the Académie Française to impose linguistic and grammatical rules on the then loosely defined language that we now know as French.

Marquis de Sade (Donatien Alphonse Françoise, comte de Sade; 1740–1814) Sade, a French soldier and libertine, wrote the sexually explicit novels *Justine* and *Juliette,* which so outraged the religious and political authorities of his era that he was thrown into prisons and mental asylums for most of his life. He was, in modern times, the first to advocate inflicting pain on others for the enhancement of one's own pleasure. Sade has the dubious distinction of having the psychological tendencies and the sexual acts that he encouraged (sadism) named after him. The painful techniques he pioneered included sexual experimentation with chains, whips, nails and knives, and other inventive torture devices.

Madame de Staël (Anne-Louise-Germaine-Necker, baronne de Staël-Holstein; 1766–1817)   This French writer maintained the most sought-after salon in Paris prior to, during, and after the French Revolution. She popularized and praised German romanticism in her most widely read book, *De l'Allemagne,* which, although at first supressed by Napoléon, later encouraged the Romantic movement in France.

5 La Ville des Beaux-Arts

Paris is arguably the premier artistic capital of Europe. The city has produced, and been home to, countless great artists and artistic movements, and is still a hotbed of artistic creativity and an important center for the international art world. And its role as a world artistic capital is centuries old.

Paris's true artistic flowering began around 1150, when the city's active trade, growing population, and struggles for political and ecclesiastic power added dozens of new buildings to the city's skyline. Between 1200 and 1400 the city flowered into the Gothic explosion whose legacy includes the city's architectural symbol, the

Americans Who Bombed in Paris

Carson McCullers, arriving with her husband, Reeves, in Paris in 1946, following success from *The Heart Is a Lonely Hunter* (1940), met the literary greats of the city: Gide, Colette, Simone de Beauvoir, André Malraux, and Albert Camus. Since she couldn't speak French, she nodded *oui, oui* to everything. To her horror one day, she discovered she'd agreed to speak at the Sorbonne on French literature. She knew nothing of the subject but appeared anyway and read one of her poems.

The Café de la Rotonde, founded in 1911, included among its patrons Picasso, Max Jacob, and Apollinaire. In the spring of 1922, **Edna St. Vincent Millay** dined here almost daily with her mother. Writing home, she recorded her first impression of French food: "Mummie & I about live in this here kafe. We feed on *choucroute garnie,* which is fried sauerkraut trimmed with boiled potatoes, a large slice of ham & a fat hot dog,—yum, yum, werry excillint. Mummie & I come every day & eat the stinkin' stuff, & all our friends hold their noses & pass us by til we've finished."

Living in Paris in an apartment in 1925, **Scott Fitzgerald** owed $6,200 to his publisher, Scribner's. Even though *The Great Gatsby* had sold 20,000 copies (a huge total back then), the sales had disappointed the author. At the height of his fame and after having published his one masterpiece, Fitzgerald launched the year with "1,000 parties and no work." His drunken bouts sometimes lasted for a week. He'd show up at the *Chicago Tribune* office on rue Lamartine, staggering and shouting for reporters to get out "the goddamn paper." After he was evicted from the offices, he'd visit bars until he went into a coma. One couple reported taking him home only to hear Zelda yell down: "You bastard. Drunk again!"

Newspaper tycoon **William Randolph Hearst** visited Paris in September 1928 with his mistress, actress Marion Davies. Upon his return to America, Hearst revealed a confidential memorandum exposing a Franco-British pact to increase the strength of their navies. When he returned again in 1930, along with Ms. Davies and a dozen of her girlfriends from Hollywood, a French official greeted him and asked him—"as an enemy of France"—to leave the country at once. Hearst and his entourage hastened over to the Savoy in London. The yellow press baron later wrote that he could endure being persona non grata in France "without loss of sleep."

Cathedral of Notre-Dame, as well as the Cathedral of St-Denis on the city's eastern outskirts. In these and other Gothic buildings, the medieval sculptures on the facades and inside the buildings became less incidental to the structures they adorned and more fully developed as artistic expressions in their own right. Secondary crafts, such as the manufacture and installation of stained glass (as represented by the windows in Paris's Sainte-Chapelle), became art forms in their own right, and French glass of this age attained an intensity of blues and reds that has never been duplicated.

Gothic painters became adept at the miniaturization of religious and secular scenes that art lovers (in an era without corrective lenses for myopia) could richly appreciate close at hand. The most famous of these, Pol de Limbourg's *Les très riches heures du duc de Berri* and Fouquet's *Heures d'Etienne Chevalier,* showed occasional scenes of medieval Paris in a charmingly idealized celebration of the changing of the seasons. Around 1360 Paris provided the setting for the painting of what is usually credited by art historians as the first (known) portrait, that of Jean le Bon (artist unknown), and the weaving of one of the most famous tapestries in history, the *Angers Apocalypse.*

The evolution of French art slowed during much of the 1400s. By the 1500s, however, Paris enjoyed a great rebirth in the arts, thanks to a military campaign into Italy and the subsequent fascination with all things Italian. Two of that era's main sculptors, who embellished the facades and fountains of Paris, were Jean Goujon (1510–85), whose inspiration came mainly from the ancient Greeks as reinterpreted by Renaissance themes, and Germain Pilon (1535–90), whose carvings at St-Denis of the French kings followed mostly religious, rather than neoclassical, themes. By the late 1500s, under the auspices of the Renaissance King, François I, the royal château at Fontainebleau, 37 miles south of Paris, became a caldron of the arts, eventually producing a style of painting known later as the school of Fontainebleau.

The arts in and around Paris during the 1600s so permeated French culture that the century has been known ever since as *Le Grand Siècle* (the grand century). France's monarchy by now was so entrenched and society sufficiently stable and centralized that the arts flourished as Paris was embellished with hundreds of aristocratic mansions in Le Marais district. Important painters included Philippe de Champaigne (1602–74), famous for his severe portraits; Charles le Brun (1619–90), who painted the Galerie d'Apollon at the Louvre; and his rival, Pierre Mignard (1610–95), painter of the interior of the cupola in the church of Val-de-Grâce. Simultaneously, the art of tapestry weaving was given a tremendous boost thanks to the establishment and royal patronage of the Manufacture Royale des Gobelins.

During the early 1700s the taste for the grandiose in France was profoundly influenced by the personality of the Sun King, Louis XIV. His construction and furnishing of Versailles called for mind-boggling quantities of art and decoration, providing lavish commissions to sculptors and craftsmen of every kind. In furnishing the thousands of salons and apartments in the palace, the techniques of fine cabinetry reached their apogee under such cabinetmakers as André-Charles Boulle (1642–1732). Boulle's writing tables, secretaries, and *bombé*-fronted chests, either ebonized or inlaid with tortoiseshell, mother-of-pearl, and gilded bronze ornaments (ormolu), are today among the finest pieces of cabinetry in European history, and command appropriately stratospheric prices. Boulle was supplanted by Crescent and Oeben, under Louis XV, who were themselves replaced by such neoclassically inspired masters as Weisweiler and Kiesner during the reign of Louis XVI.

Painters from the era of Louis XIV and XV include Largilière and Rigaud and the skilled portraitists La Tour (1704–66) and Perronneau (1715–88), whose coloring techniques have been likened to those used by the impressionists more than a century later. Also noteworthy, both as an artist and as a sociological phenomenon, was the female artist Vigée-Lebrun (1755–1842), whose lavish but natural style won her a position as Marie Antoinette's preferred painter. Especially famous paintings from this era are those of Fragonard (1732–1806) and Boucher (1703–70), whose canvases captured the sweetness and whimsy of aristocratic life during the *ancien régime*.

In sculpture, painting, and furniture, the 18th century in Paris began with an allegiance to the baroque curve and a robustly sensual kind of voluptuousness, and ended with a return to the straight line and the more rigid motifs of the classical age. Especially indicative of this return to sobriety was Houdon (1741–1828), who is well remembered for his extraordinarily lifelike portrait busts such as that of Voltaire.

The French Revolution, whose first violence had erupted in 1789, brought a new politicization to the arts. Noteworthy was David (1748–1825), whose painting *Oath of the Horatii* has been credited as one of the most revolution-inducing catalysts in the history of Europe. To reward his zeal, David was appointed director of the Arts of the Revolution, an incentive that helped produce such richly idealized paintings as *The Murder of Marat.* Always in control of his own political destiny, David was later appointed court painter to Napóleon.

Meanwhile, as France grew wealthy from the fruits of the industrial revolution and the expansion of its colonial empire, Paris blossomed with the paintings of Ingres (1780–1867) and his bitter rival, Delacroix (1798–1863). Primary among their academic disputes were allegiances to the beauty of line (Ingres) and the subtleties of color (Delacroix).

Between 1855 and 1869 the partial demolition of medieval Paris and its reconstruction into the series of panoramic plazas and monuments that the world today knows as the City of Light was engineered by Napóleon III's chief architect, Baron Haussmann.

The birth of impressionism generally began with the 1863 Paris exhibition of the Salon des Refusés. There, the works of such painters as Manet—rejected by the mainstream art establishment—were shown. One of the most memorable paintings seen there was Manet's then-scandalous and still-riveting *Déjeuner sur l'herbe*. Prior to that, the subtle colorings of landscape artist Corot (1796–1875) had presaged impressionism by several years. Soon after, such artists as Sisley, Pissarro, Degas, Renoir, and the immortal Monet painted in the open air, often evoking the everyday life and cityscapes of Paris and its surroundings.

Later, the best scenes ever painted of Paris would be credited to Utrillo (1883–1955) and, to a lesser degree, Marquet (1875–1947). Utrillo in particular concentrated on the unpretentious, often working-class neighborhoods (especially Montmartre) rather than the city's more famous monumental zones. Marquet, whose work helped to establish the definition of the fauve school of painting, often executed his stylized and brightly colored works from the balcony of his Paris apartment.

Though many of them never made a career out of painting Paris itself, other 20th-century painters who for the most part made Paris their home included Vlaminck, Derain, Vuillard, Bonnard, Braque, Picasso, Dufy, and Matisse. Many of these artists used their canvases as rebellions against the restrictions of "official" art as defined at the time by the aesthetic hierarchies of France. Several movements that emerged from this artistic rebellion have, since their origins, been classified among the most potent and evocative schools of art in the world. Included among them were fauvism, a technique that employed vivid and arbitrary use of color in ways that paved the way for the nonfigurative perceptions of the movements that were to follow. Cubism, a favorite style of early Picasso and Cézanne, developed as a means of breaking subject matter into a stylized version of their basic geometric forms. Dadaism, an elaboration of the avant-garde movements that developed out of cubism and fauvism, managed to permeate painting with some of the absurdist moral and political philosophies then pervasive in the arts scene of Paris. Most stylized of all was surrealism, a movement that carried realism to boundaries never before explored, twisting everyday objects into bizarre, sometimes terrifying permutations that only a slightly mad genuis, such as Salvador Dalí, could have perceived.

Among sculptors, Paris's greatest contribution to the art of the late 19th century was Auguste Rodin (1840–1917), whose figures added new dimensions to the human form. Especially famous was the raw power emanating from his rough-surfaced sculptures *The Thinker* and *The Kiss.*

French artists today struggle in the shadow of the great modernists who transformed the artistic perceptions of the world during the early decades of the 20th century. Although the *oeuvre* of these contemporary artists will doubtless not surpass the fame, notoriety, and price levels of, say, Matisse, Braque, or Monet, they are enjoying popularity and even energetic biddings whenever their works are presented at expositions. Oliver DeBré (born in Paris in 1920), for example, whose early studies in architecture and literature influenced his role as the most important abstract artist in France today, has garnered a significant reputation through a recent retrospective of his work at the Jeu de Paume. And there are many others.

Gérard Garouste (born in Paris in 1926), who does much of his painting in a studio in the Normandy countryside, is considered one of Europe's contemporary masters of the postmodern still-life.

Ernest Pignon-Ernest (born in Nice in 1942), on the other hand, has succeeded in taking contemporary art directly to the streets. Inspired by the canvases of the 17th-century Italian master Caravaggio, Pignon-Ernest executes "neo-Renaissance" serigraphs, produced cheaply and abundantly, which he then plasters over hundreds of buildings as an artistic statement. Although based in Paris throughout most of the year, his "decoration" of the walls of Naples was widely publicized in the art world and brought a new appreciation of Caravaggio even to Italy.

Pierre Soulages's detractors compare him to a Gallic version of Mark Rothko; his fans praise his all-black canvases as "sumptuous" and claim that he can imbue shades of the color black with more meaning and subtlety than most artists can evoke with a full palette. He is probably the most controversial of France's contemporary artists, and is also possibly the most depressing.

Whatever the personal stylistic idiosyncracies of this new generation of Paris artists, all of them are part of an artistic tradition that has endured in the City of Light for centuries. Art is, and has been, a vital and integral part of Parisian society since its humble beginnings, and Paris's current artistic sophistication is the product of centuries of development. The city's current art scene pays tribute to the legacy of all who came before, and is as diverse and volatile as ever. Whatever your artistic tastes, Paris offers something to suit them.

6 French Architecture Through the Ages

Not only is Paris a world art capital—the city itself *is* art, an organic collection of beautifully designed and constructed buildings that represent diverse architectural styles and periods. Walking through Paris can be like excavating layers of sediment at an archeological dig: Each edifice bears the characteristic signatures of the period in which it was built—Paris's buildings are not only ornate and elegant, they tell the tale of the city's long and impressive architectural history.

Despite its role as an outpost of ancient Rome, the development of Paris into a bustling community of traders, merchants, and clerics didn't really come to pass until the 1100s. Historians cite the abandonment of Romanesque building techniques in the Ile de France at around 1150. Because of that, the city has surprisingly few Romanesque buildings, good examples of which are more common in such French provinces as Burgundy. Identified by their thick walls, barrel and groined vaults, small windows, and minimal carvings, the city's most important Romanesque buildings include the Churches of St-Germain-des-Prés, St-Pierre-de-Montmartre, St-Martin-des-Champs, and—in the suburbs—the Church of Morienval.

The genius of Paris's architects, however, erupted during the Gothic age, which was signaled early in the 1200s with the construction of the Cathedrals of St-Denis, in Paris's eastern suburbs; Chartres, 60 miles to the city's southwest; and Notre-Dame of Paris, situated on the Ile de la Cité. Before the mid-15th century, Gothic architecture would transform the skyline of Paris as dozens of new churches, chapels, and secular buildings outdid their neighbors in lavishness, beauty, and intricacy of design.

Although Gothic architecture was firmly rooted in the principles of the Romanesque, it differs from its predecessor in its penchant for complicated patterns of vaulting and columns, and walls that became increasingly thinner as the weight of ceilings and roofs were transferred onto newly developed systems of abutment piers (flying buttresses). Because of the thinner walls, larger openings became architecturally feasible. Churches became filled with light filtered through stained glass, and enormous rose windows awed their observers with the delicate tracery of their stonework.

During the Renaissance, beginning around 1500, influences from Italy rendered the Gothic style obsolete. In its place arose the yearning for a return to the aesthetics of ancient Greece and Rome. Massive arcades, often decorated with bas-relief sculpture of symbols of triumph, as well as Corinthian, Doric, and Ionic pediments, added grandeur to the Paris of the Renaissance kings. All links of royal residences to feudal fortresses vanished as the aristocrats of Paris competed with one another to construct elegant town houses and villas filled with sunlight, tapestries, paintings, music, and fine furniture.

During the early 17th century many of Paris's distinctive Italianate baroque domes were created. Louis XIV employed such Italian-inspired architects as Le Vau, Perrault, both Mansarts, and Bruand for his buildings and Le Nôtre for the rigidly intelligent layouts of his gardens at Versailles. Paris and the surrounding region flourished with the construction of the lavishly expensive château of Vaux-le-Vicomte and the even more elaborate royal residence of Versailles. Meanwhile, wealthy entrepreneurs encouraged the development of new expressions of artistic and architectural beauty from the many literary and artistic salons sprouting up throughout the city.

By the early 19th century a newly militaristic Paris, flushed with the titanic changes of the Revolution and the subsequent victories of Napoléon, returned to a restrained and dignified form of classicism. Modeling their urban landscape on an idealized interpretation of imperial Rome, buildings such as the Church of the Madeleine evoked the militaristic rigidity and grandeur of the classical age.

By 1850, enjoying a cosmopolitan kind of prosperity, Paris grew bored with things Greek and Roman. Despite a brief flirtation with Egyptology (based on Napoléon's campaign in the Egyptian desert and the unraveling of the secrets of hieroglyphics with the discovery of the Rosetta stone), a new school of eclecticism added controversial but often elegant touches to the Paris landscape. Among them were the voluptuous lines of the art nouveau movement, whose aesthetic was inspired by the surging curves of the botanical world. Stone, cast iron, glass, and wood were carved or molded into forms resembling orchids, vines, laurel branches, and tree trunks, each richly lyrical and based on new building techniques made possible by the industrial age. Youthful and creative architects began to specialize in the use of iron as the structural support of bridges, viaducts, and buildings—such as the National Library (1860). These techniques opened the way for Gustave Eiffel to design and erect the most frequently slurred building of its day, the Eiffel Tower, for the Paris Exposition of 1889.

During the 1920s and 1930s a newly simplified aesthetic was highly refined and greatly appreciated in Paris. Art deco, a style reflecting the newly developed materials and decorative techniques of the machine age, captured sophisticated sensibilities around the world. After Braque defined cubism, the angular simplicity of the new artistic movement influenced architectural styles as well. Le Corbusier, a Swiss-born architect who settled in Paris in 1917, eventually developed his jutting, gently curved planes of concrete, opening the doors for a new, but often less talented, school of modern French architects.

In recent years, critics have not been kind to the exposed, rapidly rusting structural elements of Paris's Centre Pompidou, and the new Opéra Bastille has also aroused opposition. The most recent controversial structure in a city where everyone presumably has an architectural opinion is undoubtedly I. M. Pei's glass pyramid in the courtyard of the Louvre.

Despite the dozens of often captivating architectural influences that have converged on Paris, all but a handful of buildings constructed in the center in the past 150 years have been designed at roughly the same height, giving the city an evenly spaced skyline and helping to justify its claim to be the most beautiful city in the world.

Planning a Trip to Paris

This chapter is designed to provide most of the nuts-and-bolts information you'll need before setting off for Paris. We've put everything from information sources to the major airlines at your fingertips.

1 Visitor Information & Entry Requirements

VISITOR INFORMATION

BEFORE YOU GO   Your best source of information before you go—besides this guide—is the **French Government Tourist Office,** which can be reached at the following addresses.

In the U.S.: 444 Madison Ave., 16th floor, New York, NY 10022; 645 N. Michigan Ave., Suite 630, Chicago, IL 60611; 2305 Cedar Springs Blvd., Dallas, TX 75201; 9454 Wilshire Blvd., Beverly Hills, CA 90212-2967. To request information, call the **"France on Call" hotline** (☎ **900/990-0040**); each call costs 95¢ per minute.

In Canada: Write or phone Maison de la France/French Government Tourist Office, 1981 Ave. McGill College, Suite 490, Montréal, PQ H3A 2W9 (☎ **514/288-4264**); or 30 St. Patrick St., Suite 700, Toronto, ON M5T 3A3 (☎ **416/593-4723**).

In Great Britain: Write or phone Maison de la France/French Government Tourist Office, 178 Piccadilly, London, W1V 0AL (☎ **0891/244-123**).

In Australia: Write or phone the French Tourist Office, B.N.P. Building, 12th Floor, 12 Castlereagh St., Sydney, NSW 2000 (☎ **02/231-52-44**).

In Ireland: Write or phone Maison de la France/French Government Tourist Office, 35 Lower Abbey St., Dublin 1, Ireland (☎ **01/703-4046**).

At present there is no representative in New Zealand, so New Zealanders should contact the representative in Australia.

IN PARIS   You need never be totally alone in Paris. There's always someone who speaks your language standing ready to provide assistance, give you information, and help you solve problems. The **Office de Tourisme et des Congrès de Paris** (or Welcome Offices) in the center of the city will give you free maps, informative booklets, and "Paris Monthly Information," an English-language listing of all current shows, concerts, and theater. At 127 Champs-Elysées, 8e (☎ 01-49-52-53-54), you can get information regarding both Paris and the provinces. The office is open daily (except May 1) from 9am to 8pm. Métro: Charles-de-Gaulle–Etoile.

ENTRY REQUIREMENTS

ENTRY DOCUMENT   In recent years Americans and Canadians traveling to France were required to obtain a visa in advance. However, since July 1989 only special groups, such as journalists on assignment and students enrolling in French schools, must still obtain visas. For tourism or business visits of less than 90 days, all you need now is a valid passport.

With today's ever-changing political climate, it's always a good idea to confirm the situation. Contact the **Embassy of France,** 4101 Reservoir Rd. NW, Washington, DC 20007 (☎ 202/944-6000), or the **French Consulate,** 10 E. 74th St., New York, NY 10021 (☎ 212/606-3689), to find out the latest on French entry requirements.

Swiss and Japanese citizens, and citizens of EU countries, such as Britain and Ireland, are exempt from any visa requirement, but check with your nearest French consulate because the situation can change overnight. Citizens of Australia need a visa to enter France, but citizens of New Zealand require only a valid passport.

DRIVING DOCUMENTS   U.S. and Canadian driver's licenses are valid in France, but if you're touring Europe by car, you may want to invest in an **International Driver's License** just to be on the safe side. Apply at a branch of the **American Automobile Association (AAA).** You must be 18 years old and include two 2- by 2-inch photographs, a $10 fee, and your valid U.S. driver's license with your application. If the AAA doesn't have a branch in your hometown, send a photograph of your driver's license (both the front and the back) with the fee and photos to AAA, 1000 AAA Dr., Heathrow, FL 32746-5063 (☎ 407/444-4300). You should always carry your original license with you to Europe, however.

In Canada, you can get the address of the **Canadian Automobile Club** closest to you by calling its national office (☎ 613/226-7631).

You must also have an **international insurance certificate,** called a green card (*carte verte* in French), to drive. The car-rental agency will provide one if you're renting. If you drive your own car into France, your car dealer can arrange to have a temporary *carte verte* issued along with the title, but you're responsible for arranging insurance coverage. If you borrow a car, make sure that you carry a photocopy of the original *carte verte* among your documents. Proof of insurance should appear on the inside of the windshield on the driver's side.

CUSTOMS   Customs restrictions differ for citizens of the European Union and for citizens of non–EU countries. Non–EU nationals can bring in duty free 200 cigarettes, 100 cigarillos, 50 cigars, or 250 grams of smoking tobacco. This amount is doubled if you live outside Europe. You can also bring in 2 liters of wine and either 1 liter of alcohol over 38.80 proof or 2 liters of wine under 38.80 proof. In addition you can bring in 50 grams (1.75 oz.) of perfume, a quarter liter of eau de toilette, 500 grams (1 lb.) of coffee, and 200 grams (half a pound) of tea. Visitors 15 years of age and over may also bring in other goods totaling 300 F ($60), whereas the allowance for those 14 and under is 150 F ($30). (Customs officials tend to be lenient about general merchandise, realizing that the limits are unrealistically low.)

If you're arriving from an EU country, there is no longer a Customs tariff or limit placed on goods carried between countries of the union.

2 Money

CURRENCY   French currency is based on the **franc (F),** which consists of 100 **centimes** (c). Coins come in units of 5, 10, 20, and 50 centimes; and 1, 2, 5, and 10 francs. Notes come in denominations of 20, 50, 100, 500, and 1,000 francs.

All banks are equipped for foreign exchange, and you'll find exchange offices at the airports and airline terminals. Banks are open Monday to Friday from 9am to noon and 2 to 4pm. At major bank branches the exchange departments are also open on Saturday between 9am and noon.

When converting your home currency into French francs, be aware that rates vary. Your hotel will probably offer the worst rate of exchange. In general, banks offer the best rate, but even banks charge a commission for the service, often $2 or $3, depending on the transaction. Whenever you can, stick to the big banks of Paris, like Crédit Lyonnais, which usually offer the best exchange rates and charge the lowest commission. Always make sure you have enough francs for the weekend.

If you need a check denominated in French francs before your trip, say, to pay a deposit on a hotel room, you can contact **Ruesch International,** 700 11th St. NW, 4th Floor, Washington, DC 20001-4507 (☎ **800/424-2923**). Ruesch performs a wide variety of conversion-related services, usually for $2 per transaction. You can also inquire at a local bank.

TRAVELER'S CHECKS   Although it's now perfectly easy to find ATM machines in Paris and get cash as you would at home, some travelers still like the security of carrying traveler's checks so that they'll be able to get a refund in the event of theft.

Most large banks sell traveler's checks, charging fees that average between 1% and 2% of the value of the checks you buy. The American Automobile Association (AAA) does not charge its members a fee for traveler's checks.

Sometimes you can purchase traveler's checks in the currency of the country you're planning to visit, thereby avoiding a conversion fee, which could amount to as much as $5. Note, also, that you sometimes get a better rate if you cash traveler's checks at the institutions that issued them: Visa at a branch of Thomas Cook, American Express at American Express, and so forth.

For more information, contact the following companies: **American Express** (☎ **800/221-7282** in the U.S. and Canada); **Citicorp** (☎ **800/645-6556** in the U.S. and Canada, or 813/623-1709 collect from other parts of the world); or **Thomas Cook** (☎ **800/223-7373** in the U.S. and Canada, or 609/987-7300 collect from other parts of the world).

CREDIT & CHARGE CARDS   Both American Express and Diners Club are widely recognized. The French equivalent for Visa is Carte Bleue. If you see the Eurocard sign on an establishment, it means that it accepts MasterCard.

You may purchase something with a credit or charge card thinking you'll be charged at a certain exchange rate, only to find that the dollar has declined by the time your bill arrives, and so you're actually paying more than you had bargained for, but those are the rules of the game. It can also work in your favor if the dollar should rise after you make your purchase.

Some automatic-teller machines in Paris accept U.S. bank cards such as Visa or MasterCard. The exchange rates are often good, and the convenience of obtaining cash on the road is without equal. Check with your credit/charge-card company or bank before leaving home.

MONEYGRAM   If you find yourself out of money, a new wire service provided by American Express can help you tap willing friends and family for emergency funds.

The French Franc, the British Pound & the U.S. Dollar

For American Readers: At this writing, $1 = approximately 5 F (or 1 F = 20¢), and this was the rate of exchange used to calculate the dollar values given in this book.

For British Readers: At this writing, £1 = approximately 7.70 F (or 1 F = 13p), and that was the rate of exchange used to calculate the pound values in the table below.

Note: Because the exchange rate fluctuates from time to time, this table should be used only as a general guide:

F	U.S.$	U.K.£	F	U.S.$	U.K.£
1	0.20	0.13	150	30.00	19.50
2	0.40	0.26	175	35.00	22.75
3	0.60	0.39	200	40.00	26.00
4	0.80	0.52	250	50.00	32.50
5	1.00	0.65	300	60.00	39.00
6	1.20	0.78	350	70.00	45.50
7	1.40	0.91	400	80.00	52.00
8	1.60	1.04	450	90.00	58.50
9	1.80	1.17	500	100.00	65.00
10	2.00	1.30	600	120.00	78.00
15	3.00	1.95	700	140.00	91.00
20	4.00	2.60	800	160.00	104.00
25	5.00	3.25	900	180.00	117.00
50	10.00	6.50	1,000	200.00	130.00
75	15.00	9.75	1,250	250.00	162.50
100	20.00	13.00	1,500	300.00	195.00

Through **MoneyGram,** 6200 S. Québec St. (P.O. Box 5118), Englewood, CO 80155 (☎ 800/926-9400), money can be sent around the world in less than 10 minutes. Senders should call AMEX to learn the address of the closest outlet that handles MoneyGrams. Cash, credit/charge card, or the occasional personal check (with ID) are acceptable forms of payment. AMEX's fee for the service is $10 for the first $300 with a sliding scale for larger sums. The service includes a short telex message and a 3-minute phone call from sender to recipient. The recipient must present a photo ID at the outlet where the money is received.

ATM NETWORKS   Plus, Cirrus, and other networks connecting automated-teller machines operate in Paris. For **Cirrus** locations abroad, call 800/424-7787; for **Plus** locations, call **800/843-7587.** And if your credit card has been programmed with a PIN (Personal Identification Number), it's likely that you can use your card at Paris ATMs to withdraw money as a cash advance. Check to see if your PIN code must be reprogrammed for usage in Paris. Discover cards are accepted only in the United States.

What Things Cost in Paris	U.S. $
Taxi from Charles de Gaulle Airport to the city center	40.00
Taxi from Orly Airport to the city center	34.00
Public transportation for an average trip within the city from a Métro *carnet* (packet) of 10	.82
Local telephone call	.40
Double room at the Ritz (very expensive)	670.00
Double room at Lord Byron (moderate)	160.00
Double room at Hotel Opal (budget)	96.00
Lunch for one, without wine, at Chez Georges (moderate)	52.00
Lunch for one, without wine, at Le Drouot (inexpensive)	14.00
Dinner for one, without wine, at Le Grand Véfour (very expensive)	150.00
Dinner for one, without wine, at Chez André (moderate)	36.00
Dinner for one, without wine, at Chartier (inexpensive)	10.40
Glass of wine	3.00
Coca-Cola	3.50
Cup of coffee	3.10
Roll of ASA 100 film, 36 exposures	7.75
Admission to Louvre	9.00
Movie ticket	9.75
Theatre ticket (at the Comédie-Française)	5.00–34.00

3 When to Go

In August Parisians traditionally leave for their annual holiday and put the city on a skeleton staff to serve visitors. Now, however, July has also become a popular vacation month, with many a restaurateur shuttering up for a month-long respite.

Hotels, especially first-class and deluxe ones, are easy to come by in July and August when so many visitors are away. Budget hotels, on the other hand, are likely to be full in July and August, because those are the months of the greatest student invasion. You might also try to avoid the first 2 weeks in October when the annual motor show attracts thousands of boy-at-heart enthusiasts.

Paris is now a city of all seasons, as regards to hotels. However, if you're coming for the weather, it's somehow more romantic in the spring and autumn.

THE CLIMATE   Balmy weather in Paris has prompted more popular songs and love ballads than weather conditions in any other city in the world. The main characteristic of the city's weather is its changeability. Rain is much more common than snow throughout the winter, prompting many longtime residents to complain about the occasional bone-chilling dampness.

In recent years, Paris has had only about 15 snow days a year, and there are only a few oppressively hot days (that is, over 86°F) in midsummer. Perhaps the most disturbing aspect of Parisian weather is the blasts of rapidly moving air—perhaps the result of a wind-tunnel effect caused by the city's long boulevards being bordered by buildings of uniform height. Other than the occasional winds and rain (which add an undeniable drama to many of the city's panoramas), Paris offers one of the most pleasant weather conditions of any capital in Europe, with a highly tolerable average temperature of 53°F.

Paris's Average Daytime Temperature & Rainfall

	Jan	Feb	Mar	Apr	May	June	July	Aug	Sept	Oct	Nov	Dec
Temp. (°F)	38	39	46	51	58	64	66	66	61	53	54	40
Rainfall (in.)	3.2	2.9	2.7	3.2	3.5	3.3	3.7	3.3	3.3	3.0	3.5	3.1

HOLIDAYS   In France, holidays are known as *jours fériés*. Shops and banks are closed, as well as many (but not all) restaurants and museums. Major holidays include January 1, Easter, Ascension Day (40 days after Easter), Pentecost (seventh Sunday after Easter), May 1, May 8 (V-E Day), July 14 (Bastille Day), August 15 (Assumption of the Virgin Mary), November 1 (All Saints' Day), November 11 (Armistice Day), and December 25 (Christmas).

PARIS CALENDAR OF EVENTS

January
- **International Ready-to-Wear Fashion Shows** (Le Salon International de Prêt-à-Porter), Parc des Expositions, Porte de Versailles, Paris, 15e (Métro: Porte de Versailles). Various couture houses, such as Lanvin and Courrèges, present their own shows at their respective headquarters. See what the public will be wearing in 6 months. Mid-January to mid-February.

March
- **Foire du Trône,** on the Neuilly Lawn of the Bois de Vincennes. This mammoth amusement park operates daily from 2pm to midnight. End of March to June.

April
- **Paris Marathon.** Runners compete from around the world. Weekend of April 2.
- **City of Paris Festival of Sacred Art.** A dignified series of concerts held in five of the oldest (or most recognizable) churches of Paris. For information, call 01-45-61-54-99.

May
- **End of World War II.** The capitulation of the Nazis was signed on May 7, 1945. The celebration lasts 3 days in Paris, and with even more festivity in Reims. May 5–8.
- **French Open Tennis Championship,** Stade Roland-Garros. World-class tennis on Paris's famous clay courts. May 29 to June 11.
- **Les Grandes Eaux Musicales**. This event at Versailles is presented every Sunday afternoon between 3:30 and 5:30pm and features loud music by French-born composers (Couperin, Charpentier, Lully) and others (Mozart and Haydn) whose music was contemporaneous with the construction of the palace of Versailles. All the fountains of the parks around the palace are turned on, and people promenade in the garden. May to September.

June
- **Festival de Musique de St-Denis.** Music in the burial place of the French kings. Call 01-48-13-12-12 for information. Throughout June.
- **Festival Juin.** A month of music, art exhibitions, and drama set for the most part in Paris's well-heeled 16th arrondissement. For information, call 01-40-72-16-16.

- **Le Prix du Jockey Club,** Hippodrome de Chantilly. Call 01-44-62-41-00 for information on this and on all other equine events in this calendar. June 4.
- **Prix Diane-Hermès,** Hippodrome de Chantilly. Call 01-44-62-41-00 for information on this and on all other equine events in this calendar. June 11.
- **Paris Air Show,** at Le Bourget Airport. Early June in alternate years only (next air show is 1997).
- **Festival Chopin.** Everything you ever wanted to hear from the Polish exile who lived most of his life in Paris. Piano recitals in the Orangerie de Bagatelle. For information, call 01-40-67-96-10. June 16 to July 14.
- **Grand Steeplechase de Paris,** at the Auteuil racetrack in the Bois de Boulogne. Mid-June.
- **Grand Prix de Paris,** at Longchamp racetrack. Late June.

July

○ **Bastille Day**   Celebrating the birth of modern-day France, the nation's festivities reach their peak in Paris with street fairs, pageants, fireworks, and feasts. The day begins with a parade down the Champs-Elysées and ends with fireworks at Montmartre. Wherever you are, before the end of the day you'll hear Piaf warbling "La Foule" (The Crowd), the song that celebrated her passion for the stranger whom she met and later lost in a crowd on Bastille Day.

   When: July 14. **Where:** Bars, restaurants, streets, and private homes throughout Paris. **How:** Hum "La Marseillaise"; outfit yourself with a beret, a pack of Gauloises, and a bottle of cheap wine; leave your hotel; and stamp around the neighborhood.

- **Paris Quartier d'Eté.** A moveable feast of concerts, art exhibitions, and dance recitals held at four locations in and around central Paris. For information, call 01-44-83-64-40. July 15 to August 15.
- **Le Grand Tour de France.** Europe's most visible bicycle race decides its winner at a finish line drawn across the Champs-Elysées. Late July.

September

- **Festival d'Automne.** One of the most famous festivals in France, this is also one of the most eclectic, concentrating mainly on modern music, ballet, theater, and modern art. Depending on the event, tickets cost 100 to 300 F ($20 to $60). For details throughout the year, write or phone the Festival d'Automne, 156 rue de Rivoli, 75001 Paris (☎ 01-42-96-12-27). During the festival itself, call 01-42-96-96-94 to reserve tickets for any of the cultural events. Mid-September to just after Christmas.
- **International Ready-to-Wear Fashion Shows** (Le Salon International de Prêt-à-Porter), Parc des Expositions, Porte de Versailles, Paris, 15e (Métro: Porte de Versailles). Mid-September.

October

- **Festival d'Automne.** All month.
- ○ **Paris Auto Show**   Glistening metal, glitzy women, lots of hype, and the latest models from world auto makers, this is the showcase for European car design.

   Where: Parc des Expositions, near the Porte de Versailles in western Paris. **When:** 10 days in early October. **How:** Check *Pariscope* for details or contact the French Government Tourist Office (see the addresses and telephone numbers in "Visitor Information & Entry Requirements," earlier in this chapter).

- **Prix de l'Arc de Triomphe.** France's answer to the horsey set at Ascot is the country's most prestigious horse race. Early October.

November
- **Festival d'Automne.** All month.
- **Armistice Day.** The signing of the controversial document that ended World War I is celebrated with a military parade from the Arc de Triomphe to the Hôtel des Invalides. November 11.

December
- **Festival d'Automne.** Through late December.
- **Salon Nautique International de Paris** (The Boat Fair), Parc des Expositions, Porte de Versailles, Paris, 15e (Métro: Porte de Versailles). Europe's most visible exposition of what's afloat. Late November–early December.
- **Fête de St-Sylvestre** (New Year's Eve). It's most boisterously celebrated in the *quartier latin* around the Sorbonne. At midnight, the city explodes. Strangers kiss strangers; boulevard St-Michel becomes a virtual pedestrian mall, as does the Champs-Elysées. December 31.

4 Tips for Travelers with Special Needs

FOR TRAVELERS WITH DISABILITIES

Facilities in Paris for persons with disabilities are certainly better than you'll find in most cities. Every year the French government does more and more to help ease life for persons with disabilities in using the public facilities of the country.

In France, most high-speed trains can deal with wheelchairs. Guide dogs ride free. Older trains have special compartments built for wheelchair boarding. On the Paris Métro, handicapped persons can sit in wider seats provided for their comfort. Some stations don't have escalators or elevators, however, and this may present problems.

Nearly all modern hotels in France now have rooms designed especially with persons with disabilities in mind. Older hotels, unless renovated, may not provide such important features as elevators, special toilet facilities, or ramps for wheelchair access. For a list of hotels in Paris offering facilities for persons with disabilities, contact the **APF Evasion (Association des Paralysés de France)**, 17 bd. Auguste Blanqui, 75013 Paris (☎ **01-40-78-69-00**).

There are many agencies that provide advance data to help you plan your trip. One is the **Travel Information Service** at Philadelphia's MossRehab Hospital (☎ **215/456-9603**), which provides information to telephone callers only: Call for assistance with your travel needs.

You may also want to consider joining a tour for travelers with disabilities. The names and addresses of operators of such tours can be obtained from the **Society for the Advancement of Travel for the Handicapped,** 347 5th Ave., Suite 610, New York, NY 10016 (☎ **212/447-7284**; fax 212/725-8253). Yearly membership in this society is $45 ($25 for senior citizens and students). Send a self-addressed stamped envelope.

One specialized French travel agency is **I. Care,** Forum Du Pont Services 69–73, avenue du Général-Leclerc (BP 304), 9920102 Boulogne CEDEX (☎ **01-46-20-04-56**).

For the blind or visually impaired, the best source is the **American Foundation for the Blind,** 11 Penn Plaza, Suite 300, New York, NY 10001 (☎ **212/502-7600**, or 800/232-5463 to order information kits and supplies). The organization offers information on travel and various requirements for the transport and border formalities for Seeing Eye dogs. It also issues identification cards to those who are legally blind.

Finally, a bimonthly publication, the ***Handicapped Travel Newsletter,*** keeps you current on accessible sights worldwide for the disabled. Call or fax to order an annual subscription for $15 (☎ **903/677-1260**; fax 903/677-1260).

IN THE U.K. In the United Kingdom, the **Royal Association for Disability and Rehabilitation (RADAR),** Unit 12, City Forum, 250 City Rd., London ECIV 8AF (☎ **0171/250-3222**), publishes holiday "fact packs" (three in all), which sell for £2 each or £5 for the set of all three. The first one provides general information, including planning and booking a holiday, insurance, finances, and useful organization and holiday providers. The second outlines transport and equipment, transportation available when going abroad, and equipment for rent. The third deals with specialized accommodations.

Another good resource is the **Holiday Care Service,** Imperial Buildings, 2nd Floor, Victoria Road, Horley, Surrey RH6 7PZ (☎ **01293/774-535**; fax 01293/784-647), a national charity that advises on accessible accommodations for elderly and disabled people. Annual membership costs £25. Once a member, you can receive a newsletter and access to a free reservations network for hotels throughout Britain and—to a lesser degree—Europe and the rest of the world.

FOR GAY & LESBIAN TRAVELERS

"Gay Paree," with one of the world's largest homosexual populations, has dozens of gay clubs, restaurants, organizations, and services. Other than publications (see below), one of the best sources of information on gay and lesbian activities is the **Centre Gai & Lesbien,** 3 rue Keller, 11e (☎ **01-43-57-21-47;** Métro: Bastille). Well equipped to dispense information and to coordinate the activities and meetings of gay people from virtually everywhere, it's open daily from 2 to 8pm. On Sunday it adopts a format known as *Le Café Positif,* and features music, cabaret, and information about AIDS and the care for and prevention of sexually transmitted diseases.

SOS Ecoute Gay (☎ **01-44-93-01-02**) is a gay hotline, theoretically designed as a way to creatively counsel individuals with gay-related problems. A phone counselor responds to calls Monday to Friday from 6 to 10pm. **SOS Homophobie** (☎ **01-48-06-42-41**) is a separate hotline specifically intended for victims of homophobia or gay-related discrimination; calls are received by a panel of French-trained lawyers and legal experts who offer advice and counsel Monday to Friday from 8am to 10pm.

Another helpful source is **La Maison des Femmes,** 8 Cité Prost, 11e (☎ **01-43-48-24-91;** Métro: Charonne), offering information about Paris for lesbians and bisexual women and sometimes sponsoring informal dinners and get-togethers. Call any Monday, Wednesday, or Friday from 3 to 8pm for further information.

A publication, Gai Pied's *Guide Gai* (revised annually) is the best source of information on gay and lesbian clubs, hotels, organizations, and services—even restaurants. Lesbian or bisexual women might also like to pick up a copy of *Lesbia,* if only to check out the ads. These publications and others are available at Paris's largest and best-stocked gay bookstore, **Les Mots à la Bouche,** 6 rue Ste-Croix-de-la-Bretonnerie, 4e (☎ **01-42-78-88-30**), open Monday to Saturday from 11am to 11pm and on Sunday from 3 to 8pm. Both French- and English-language publications are available.

France is one of the world's most tolerant countries toward gays and lesbians, and there are no special laws that discriminate against them. Technically, sexual relations are legal for consenting partners age 16 and over. However, one doesn't come of legal age in France until 18, so there could still be legal problems with having sex with anyone under 18. Paris, of course, is the center of gay life in France, although gay and lesbian establishments exist through the provinces as well.

The following information may be helpful before you leave home.

PUBLICATIONS Before going to France, men can order *Spartacus,* the international gay guide ($29.95) or the brand-new *Paris Scene* ($10.95), a guidebook published in London but available in the United States. Also helpful is *Odysseus, the International Gay Travel Planner* ($25). Both lesbians and gay men might want to pick up a copy of the *Ferrari Travel Planner* ($16). *Gay Europe,* published by David Andrusia, a Perigee book (1995), earned the très-gay praise of usually bitchy Michael Musto, a columnist for the *Village Voice.* It includes France in its Europe survey, but lacks details and specifics. These books and others are available from **Giovanni's Room**, 1145 Pine St., Philadelphia, PA 19107 (☎ 215/923-2960).

Our World, 1104 N. Nova Rd., Suite 251, Daytona Beach, FL 32117 (☎ 904/441-5367), is a magazine devoted to gay and lesbian travel worldwide. It costs $35 for 10 issues. *Out & About,* 8 W. 19th St., Suite 401, New York, NY 10011 (☎ 800/929-2268), has been hailed for its "straight" reporting about gay travel. It profiles the best gay or gay-friendly hotels, gyms, clubs, and other places, with coverage ranging from Key West to Paris. Its cost is $49 a year for 10 information-packed issues. It's aimed at the more upscale gay traveler and has been praised by everybody from *Travel & Leisure* to the *New York Times.*

ORGANIZATIONS The **International Gay Travel Association (IGTA),** P.O. Box 4974, Key West, FL 33041 (☎ 305/292-0217, or 800/448-8550 for voice mailbox), is an international network of travel industry businesses and professionals who encourage gay/lesbian travel worldwide. With around 1,000 members, it offers quarterly newsletters, marketing mailings, and a membership directory that's updated four times a year. Membership often includes gay or lesbian businesses, but is open to individuals as well for $125 yearly, plus a $100 administration fee for new members. Members are kept informed of gay or gay-friendly hoteliers, tour operators, airline and cruise-line representatives, and also ancillary businesses such as the contacts at travel guide publishers and gay-related travel clubs.

TRAVEL AGENCIES **Our Family Abroad,** 40 W. 57th St., Suite 430, New York, NY 10019 (☎ 212/459-1800, or 800/999-5500), operates escorted tours that include about a dozen itineraries through Europe. Tour guides serve on a volunteer basis and are gay-sensitive.

In California, a leading gay-friendly option for travel arrangements is **Above and Beyond,** 300 Townsend St., Suite 107, San Francisco, CA 94107 (☎ 415/284-1666 or 800/397-2681).

Also in California, **Skylink Women's Travel,** 2953 Lincoln Blvd., Santa Monica, CA 90405 (☎ 310/452-0506 or 800/225-5759), runs about six international trips for lesbians yearly.

FOR STUDENTS

Students can usually obtain a number of travel discounts. The most wide-ranging travel service for students is **Council Travel,** a subsidiary of the Council on International Educational Exchange (CIEE), 205 E. 42nd St., New York, NY 10017 (☎ 212/661-1450; fax 212/972-3231), which provides details about budget travel, study abroad, work permits, and insurance. It also publishes a variety of helpful materials and issues an International Student Identity Card (ISIC) to bona-fide students for $18. For a copy of its *Student Travels* magazine, with information on all of the council's services and CIEE's programs and publications, send $1 in postage. Council Travel offices are located throughout the United States. Call 800/GET-AN-ID to find an office near you. There's also a Council Travel Office in France at 16 rue de Vaugirard (☎ 01-43-26-79-65).

For true budget travelers it's worth joining **Hostelling International/IYHF** (International Youth Hostel Federation). For information, contact Hostelling International American Youth Hostels (HI-AYH), 733 15th St. NW, Suite 840, Washington, DC 20005 (☎ **202/783-6161**). Membership costs $25 annually, $10 for those under 18, and $15 for those over 54.

In the United Kingdom, **Campus Travel,** 52 Grosvenor Gardens, London SW1W 0AG (☎ **0171/730-3402**), provides information for student travelers. The International Student Identity Card (ISIC), which is recognized internationally, will entitle you to savings on flights, sightseeing, food, and accommodations throughout Europe and the world. It costs only £5 and is well worth the money. Youth hostels are the place to stay if you're a student or traveling on a shoestring. You'll need an International Youth Hostels Association Card, which you can purchase from the **youth hostel store** at 14 Southampton St., London WC23 7HY (☎ **0171/836-4739**), or at Campus Travel (see above).

One privately run establishment catering to students most of the year is the **Maison d'Etudiants J. de Rufz de Lavison,** 18 rue Jean-Jacques-Rousseau, 75001 Paris (☎ **01-45-08-02-10**). It offers inexpensive lodgings for about 50 male students, usually French-born men from the provinces, ages 18 to 23, during the academic year. In summer, from July to late August, it opens its doors to nonstudents, male and female, and houses them in simple rooms with one or two beds. (In summer, about 70 beds are available, and the minimum stay is reduced to 4 nights.) Breakfast included, overnight rates are 200 F ($40) for a single and 280 F ($56) for a double. After 15 days rates are reduced to 150 F ($30) per person. Advance reservations are essential. The building is owner-managed by Mme Michelle Besnier, and has a small but charming garden in the back. Métro: Louvre or Palais-Royal.

The **Foyer International des Etudiantes,** 93 bd. St-Michel, 5e (☎ **01-43-54-49-63**), stands across from the Jardin du Luxembourg, welcoming students from all over the world. From October to June it accepts women only, charging 160 F ($32) in a single or 90 F ($18) per person in a double, including breakfast. From July to September both men and women are accepted, paying 165 F ($33) in a single or 115 F ($23) per person in a double, including breakfast. This place is popular and you must write at least 2 months in advance for the reservation and pay a 200-F ($40) deposit if space is confirmed. Facilities are available for cooking and laundry, and there's a TV lounge. Some accommodations have their own balconies. Métro: Luxembourg.

FOR FAMILIES

On airlines, you must request a special menu for children at least 24 hours in advance. If baby food is required, however, bring your own and ask a flight attendant to warm it to the right temperature.

Arrange ahead of time for such necessities as a crib, bottle warmer, and car seat. Find out if the place where you're staying stocks baby food. If it doesn't, take some with you and plan to buy more abroad in supermarkets. Baby-sitters can be found for you at most hotels.

Family Travel Times is published quarterly by Travel With Your Children (TWYCH), 40 5th Ave., New York, NY 10011 (☎ **212/477-5524**). The $40 annual subscription fee includes a weekly call-in service for subscribers.

TWYCH also publishes a nitty-gritty information guide, *Cruising with Children,* which sells for $22, and is discounted to newsletter subscribers. An information packet, which describes TWYCH's publications and includes a recent sample issue, can be purchased by sending $3.50 to the above address.

Families Welcome!, in the Woodcraft Shopping Center, 4711 Hope Valley Rd., Durham, NC 27707 (☎ 919/489-2555, or 800/326-0724), is a travel company specializing in worry-free vacations for families, offering "City Kids" packages to Paris that feature accommodations in family-friendly hotels or apartments. Some hotels include a second room for children free or at a reduced rate (depending on house count, availability, etc.) during certain time periods. Individually designed family packages can include car rentals, train and ferry passes, and special air prices. A welcome kit is distributed, containing "insider's information" for families traveling in Paris—such as reliable baby-sitters, where to buy Pampers, and a list of family-friendly restaurants.

5 Special-Interest Travel Programs

LEARNING VACATIONS   The **Alliance Française,** 101 bd. Raspail, 75270 Paris CEDEX 06 (☎ **01-45-44-38-28**)—a state-appointed, nonprofit organization with a network of 1,300 establishments in more than 131 countries—offers French-language courses to some 385,000 students annually. The international school in Paris is open all year, and you can enroll for a minimum of a month-long session. Fees tend to be reasonable, and the school offers numerous activities and services. Write for information and application forms at least a month before your departure for Paris. In some cases it's wise to request information from any of the Alliance Française's North American branches, the largest of which is at 22 E. 60th St., New York, NY 10022 (☎ **212/355-6100**).

The **National Registration Center for Studies Abroad (NRCSA),** 823 N. 2nd St., Milwaukee, WI 53203 (☎ **414/278-0631**), has a catalog ($2) of schools in France, including the Sorbonne in Paris. The organization will register you at the school of your choice, arrange for room and board, and make your airline reservations, all for no extra charge. Ask for a (free) copy of their newsletter.

A clearinghouse for information on French-based language schools is **Lingua Service Worldwide,** 216 E. 45th St., 17th Floor, New York, NY 10017 (☎ **212/ 867-1225,** or 800/394-LEARN; fax 212/867-7666). Its programs cover not only Paris, but Antibes, Aix-en-Provence, Avignon, Bordeaux, Cannes, Juan-les-Pins, Megève, Montpellier, Nice, Strasbourg, Tours, and other places as well. Courses can be either long- or short-term, the latter consisting of 20 lessons per week.

SAILING UP THE SEINE   The river that winds through the heart of Paris is the third longest of the four great rivers of France, yet its role in French history is greater than that of the other three waterways combined. Sailing between its banks, with the architecture of the most beautiful city in the world passing on either side of you, is one of the most rewarding experiences in France.

For a description of the glass-sided *bateaux-mouches* that offer short-term river excursions through the monumental zone of Paris, see Chapter 6. Some visitors, however, prefer longer excursions along the river that gave rise to the French nation. **Paris Canal** (☎ **01-42-40-96-97**) requires advance reservations for 3-hour waterborne tours that begin either at the quays in front of the Musée d'Orsay (Métro: Solférino) or in front of the Musée des Sciences et de l'Industrie at Parc de la Villette (Métro: Porte de la Villette). Excursions negotiate the waterways and canals of Paris, including the Seine, an underground tunnel below place de la Bastille, and the Canal

La Gastronomie 101

In a nation devoted to the pursuit of gastronomic excellence, you'll find a wide array of chefs (skilled and otherwise) eager to impart a few of their culinary insights—for a fee. A knowledge of at least rudimentary French is a good idea before you enroll, although a visual demonstration of any culinary technique is often more valuable than reading or hearing about it. The cooking schools listed below will send you information in English or French if you write to them in advance; their courses might be attended by professional chefs and serious or competitive connoisseurs.

Ritz-Escoffier Ecole de Gastronomie Française, 38 rue Cambon, 1er, 81 Paris (☎ **01-43-16-30-50,** or 800/966-5758 in the U.S.). Letters should be addressed to 15 Place Vendôme, CEDEX 75401 Paris. Famed for his titanic rages in the kitchens of the French and English aristocrats who engaged him to prepare their banquets, and also for his well-publicized culinary codifications, Georges-Auguste Escoffier (1846–1935) taught the Edwardian Age how to eat. Today the Ritz Hotel, site of many of Escoffier's meals, maintains a school that offers demonstration classes daily of the master's techniques. Courses last 1 to 12 weeks and are taught in French and English.

Le Cordon Bleu, 8 rue Léon-Delhomme, 15e Paris (☎ **01-53-68-22-50,** or 800/457-2433 in the U.S.). Originally established in 1895, this is the most famous French cooking school. Call for a brochure. Cordon Bleu's most famous courses last 10 weeks, at the end of which certificates of competence are issued—highly desired within the restaurant world. Many readers of this guidebook, however, prefer a less intense immersion into the rituals of French cuisine, and opt for either a 4-day workshop or a 3-hour demonstration class. Enrollment in either of these is on a first-come, first-served basis; the cost is around 220 F ($44) for a demonstration and around 4,590 F ($918) for the 4-day workshop. Also of interest to professional chefs (or wannabes) is the 5-week course in catering, which attracts avid business hopefuls. Any of these programs, even the 3-hour quickies, offer unexpected insights into the culinary subculture of Paris.

St-Martin. The cost is 95 F ($19). With the exception of excursions on Sunday and holidays, prices are usually reduced to 70 F ($14) for passengers 12 to 25, to 55 F ($11) for children 4 to 12, and to nothing for children 3 and under. Tours are offered daily, March to November; only on Sunday after November 11.

6 Getting There

BY PLANE
FLYING FROM NORTH AMERICA

The flying time to Paris from New York is about 7 hours; from Chicago, 9 hours; from Los Angeles, 11 hours; from Montréal, about 6^1/$_2$ hours; and from Toronto, about 7^1/$_2$ hours.

One of the best choices for passengers flying to Paris from both the southeastern United States and the Midwest is **Delta Airlines** (☎ **800/241-4141**), whose network greatly expanded after its acquisition of some of the former Pan Am routes. From such cities as New Orleans, Phoenix, Columbia (S.C.), and Nashville, Delta flies to Atlanta, connecting every evening with a nonstop flight to Orly Airport in Paris. Delta also operates flights to Orly from Cincinnati four times a week nonstop, and seven flights a week that stop briefly en route in Atlanta. There are also daily flights to Paris's Orly from New York's JFK. All these flights depart late enough in the day to permit easy transfers from much of Delta's vast North American network.

Another excellent choice for Paris-bound passengers is **United Airlines** (☎ 800/538-2929), with nonstop flights from Chicago, Washington, D.C. (Dulles), Los Angeles, and San Francisco to Paris's Charles de Gaulle Airport. United also offers attractive promotional fares—especially in the low and shoulder seasons—to London's Heathrow from five major North American hubs. From London, it's an easy train and Hovercraft or Chunnel connection to Paris, a fact that tempts many passengers to spend a weekend in London either before or after their visit to Paris.

Another good option is **Continental Airlines** (☎ 800/231-0856), which services the Northeast and much of the Southwest through its busy hubs in Newark and Houston. From both those cities, Continental provides nonstop flights to Orly Airport. Flights from Newark depart daily, while flights from Houston depart between four and seven times a week, depending on the season.

TWA (☎ 800/892-4141) operates daily nonstop service to Charles de Gaulle Airport from Boston, New York's JFK, and in summer, several nonstop flights a week from Washington, D.C.'s Dulles airport. In summer, TWA also flies to Paris from St. Louis several times a week nonstop, and to Paris from Los Angeles three times a week nonstop. In winter, flights from Los Angeles and Washington, D.C., are suspended, and flights from St. Louis have brief touchdowns in New York or Boston en route to Paris.

American Airlines (☎ 800/433-7300) provides daily nonstop flights to Paris (Orly) from Dallas/Fort Worth, Chicago, Miami, and New York's JFK.

USAir (☎ 800/428-4322) offers daily nonstop service from Philadelphia International Airport to Paris's Charles de Gaulle Airport.

The French flag carrier, **Air France** (☎ 800/237-2747) offers daily or several-times-a-week flights between Paris's Orly Airport and Newark (N.J.), Washington, D.C.'s Dulles, Miami, Chicago, Houston, San Francisco, Los Angeles, Montréal, Toronto, Mexico City, and Los Angeles. Flights to Paris from Los Angeles originate in Papeete, French Polynesia, very far from *la France métropolitaine*.

Canadians usually choose flights from Toronto and Montréal to Paris on **Air Canada** (☎ 800/776-3000 in the U.S. and Canada). For most of the year, nonstop flights from Montréal depart every evening for Paris, while flights from Toronto to Paris are nonstop 6 days a week and direct (with a touchdown in Montréal en route) 1 day a week. Two of the nonstop flights from Toronto are shared with Air France and feature Air France aircraft.

FLYING FROM THE U.K.

From London, **Air France** (☎ 0181/742-6600) and **British Airways** (☎ 0181/897-4000) fly regularly and frequently from London to Paris (trip time is only 1 hour). Air France and British Airways alone operate up to 17 flights daily from Heathrow, one of the busiest air routes in Europe. Many commercial travelers also use regular flights originating from the London City Airport in the Docklands. There are also direct flights to Paris from such major cities as Manchester, Birmingham, Glasgow, Edinburgh, and Southampton.

Flying from England to France is often quite expensive, even though the distance is short. That's why most Brits rely on a good travel agent to get them the lowest possible airfare. Good values are offered by a number of companies, including **Nouvelles Frontières**, 2–3 Woodstock St., London W1R 1HE (☎ 0171/629-7772).

There are no hard-and-fast rules about where to get the best deals for European flights, but do bear the following points in mind: (1) Daily papers often carry advertisements for companies offering cheap flights. Highly recommended companies include **Trailfinders** (☎ 0171/937-5400), which offers discounted fares, and **Avro Tours** (☎ 0181/715-0000), which operates charters. (2) In London, there are many ticket consolidators (who buy inventories of tickets from airlines and then resell them) in the neighborhood of Earl's Court and Victoria Station that offer low fares. For your own protection, make sure that the company you deal with is a member of the IATA, ABTA, or ATOL. (3) CEEFAX, a British television information service (received by many private homes and hotels), presents details of package holidays and flights to Europe and beyond.

PARIS AIRPORTS

Paris has two major international airports: **Aéroport d'Orly** (☎ 01-49-75-15-15), $8^1/2$ miles south, and **Aéroport Roissy–Charles de Gaulle** (☎ 01-44-04-24-24), $14^1/4$ miles northeast of the city. A shuttle operates between the two airports about every 30 minutes, taking 50 to 75 minutes to make the journey.

CHARLES DE GAULLE AIRPORT (ROISSY)   At Charles de Gaulle Airport, foreign carriers use Aérogare 1 and Air France uses Aérogare 2. From Aérogare 1 you take a moving walkway to the passport checkpoint and the Customs area. The two terminals are linked by a shuttle bus.

The **free shuttle bus** (*navette*) connecting Aérogare 1 with Aérogare 2 also transports passengers to the Roissy rail station, from which fast **RER trains** leave every 15 minutes to such Métro stations as Gare-du-Nord, Châtelet, Luxembourg, Port-Royal, and Denfert-Rochereau. The train fare from Roissy to any point in central Paris is 43 F ($8.60). You can also take an **Air France shuttle bus** to central Paris for 55 F ($11). It stops at the Palais des Congrès (Port Maillot), then continues on to place de l'Etoile, where underground lines can carry you farther along to any other point in Paris. That ride, depending on traffic, takes between 45 and 55 minutes. The shuttle departs about every 12 minutes between 5:40am and 11pm.

Taxis from Roissy into the city will cost about 200 F ($40). At night (from 8pm to 7am), fares are 35% higher. Long lines of both taxis and passengers form outside each of the airport's terminals in a surprisingly orderly fashion.

An option for **returning to the airport,** the **Roissybus** (☎ 01-48-04-18-24), departs from a point near the corner of rue Scribe and place de l'Opéra every 15 minutes from 5:45am to 11pm. The cost for the 45- to 50-minute bus ride is 40 F ($8).

ORLY AIRPORT   Orly has two terminals: Orly Sud (south) for international flights and Orly Ouest (west) for domestic flights. They're linked together by a free shuttle bus. **Passenger information in English** is available daily from 6am to 11:45pm (☎ 01-49-75-15-15).

Air France buses leave Exit E of Orly Sud, and from Exit F of Orly Ouest, every 12 minutes between 5:45am and 11pm, heading for the Gare des Invalides in central Paris. Other buses depart for place Denfert-Rochereau in the south of Paris. Passage on any of these buses costs 40 F ($8).

An alternative method for reaching central Paris involves taking a **free shuttle bus** that leaves both of Orly's terminals at intervals of approximately every 15 minutes for the nearby Métro and RER train station (Pont-de-Rungis/Aéroport-d'Orly), from which **RER trains** take 30 minutes for rides into the city center. A trip to Les Invalides, for example, costs 40 F ($8).

A **taxi** from Orly to the center of Paris costs about 170 F ($34), more at night. Don't take a meterless taxi from Orly Sud or Orly Ouest—it's much safer (and usually cheaper) to hire a metered cab from the lines, which are under the scrutiny of a police officer.

Returning to the airport, buses to Orly Airport leave from the Invalides terminal for either Orly Sud or Orly Ouest every 15 minutes, taking about 30 minutes.

BY TRAIN

If you're already in Europe, you might decide to travel to Paris by train, especially if you have a Eurailpass. Even if you don't, the cost is relatively low. For example, the one-way fare from London to Paris by train (including the Channel crossing) is $117 to $172 in first class and $68 to $121 in second class; from Rome to Paris, depending on the route the train takes and the time of travel, the one-way fare ranges from $191 to $251 in first class and $125 to $161 in second class; and from Madrid to Paris, the one-way fare is $172 in first class and $119 in second class.

Visitors from London may want to consider a British/French joint rail pass, linking the two most popular vacation spots in Europe—Britain and France. Called the **BritFrance Railpass,** it's available to North Americans and provides unlimited train travel in both Britain and France. (Unlike previous years, it does not include passage by boat or Hovercraft across the English Channel.) The pass comes in two options: 5 days of travel within any consecutive month, or 10 days of travel within any consecutive month on both the British and French rail networks. Adult first-class fares for the 5-day option are $359 in first class and $259 in second class. For the 10-day option the price is $539 in first class and $399 in second class. When they're accompanied by adult holders of either of the passes described above, children 4 to 12 travel for half the adult fare, and those age 3 and under travel free. The pass is activated the first time you use it, but be warned that holders must validate their pass at a railway station's ticket counter prior to boarding a train. Rail passes as well as individual rail tickets within Europe are available at most travel agencies, at any office of **RailEurope** (☎ **800/848-7245** in the U.S.), or at **BritRail Travel International** (☎ **800/677-8585**, or 212/575-2667 in New York City).

In London, an especially convenient place to buy railway tickets to virtually anywhere is just opposite Platform 2 in Victoria Station, where **Wasteels Ltd.** (☎ **0171/ 834-6744**) provides railway-related services and discusses the pros and cons of various types of fares and rail passes. Occasionally Wasteels charges a £5 fee for its services, but the information provided warrants the fee and the company's staff do spend a generous amount of time with a client while planning an itinerary. Some of the most popular passes, including Inter-Rail and EuroYouth, are available only to those under 26 years of age for unlimited second-class travel in 26 European countries.

THE PARIS TRAIN STATIONS

There are six major train stations in Paris: **Gare d'Austerlitz**, 55 quai d'Austerlitz, 13e (serving the southwest with trains to the Loire Valley, the Bordeaux country, and the Pyrénées); **Gare de l'Est**, place du 11 Novembre 1918, 10e (serving the east, with trains to Strasbourg, Nancy, Reims, and beyond to Zurich, Basel, Luxembourg, and Austria); **Gare de Lyon**, 20 bd. Diderot, 12e (serving the southeast, with trains to the Côte d'Azur, Provence, and beyond to Geneva, Lausanne, and Italy); **Gare Montparnasse**, 17 bd. Vaugirard, 15e (serving the west, with trains to Brittany); **Gare du Nord**, 18 rue de Dunkerque, 15e (serving the north, with trains to Holland, Denmark, Belgium, and the north of Germany); and **Gare St-Lazare**, 13 rue d'Amsterdam, 8e (serving the northwest, with trains to Normandy).

For **general train information** and to make reservations, call **01-45-82-50-50** from 7am to 8pm daily. Buses operate between rail stations.

Note: The stations and the surrounding areas are usually seedy and frequented by pickpockets, hustlers, prostitutes, and drug addicts. Be alert, especially at night.

Each of these stations also has a Métro stop, making the whole city easily accessible. Taxis are also available at every station at designated stands. Look for the sign that says TÊTE DE STATION.

BY BUS

Bus travel to Paris is available from London as well as many other cities throughout the Continent. In the early 1990s the French government established strong incentives for long-haul buses not to drive into the center of Paris. Now most buses arrive at **Gare Routière Internationale du Paris–Gallieni**, avenue du Général-de-Gaulle, Bagnolet (☎ **01-49-72-51-51;** Métro: Gallieni), a 35-minute Métro ride from central Paris at the terminus of Métro Line 3, in the eastern suburb of Bagnolet. Despite this inconvenience, many people prefer bus travel. Europe's largest bus operator, **Eurolines France,** is located at 28 av. du Général-de-Gaulle, 93541 Bagnolet (☎ **01-49-72-51-51**).

Long-haul buses are equipped with toilets and stop at mealtimes for rest and refreshment. The price of a round-trip ticket between Paris and London (a 7-hour trip) is 540 F ($108) for passengers 26 and over, and 390 to 510 F ($78 to $102) for passengers 25 and under, depending on the restrictions. A round-trip ticket from Rome to Paris (a trip time of 22¹/₂ hours) costs 680 F ($136) for passengers 26 or over and 610 F ($122) for passengers 25 and under. The price of a round-trip ticket from Stockholm to Paris (a trip time of almost 28 hours) is 1,290 F ($258) for passengers 26 and over and 1,190 F ($238) for passengers 25 and under.

Because Eurolines does not have a U.S.–based sales agent, most people wait until they reach Europe to buy their tickets. Any European travel agent can arrange these purchases. If you're traveling to Paris from London, you can contact **Eurolines U.K.,** Victoria Coach Station at the continental check-in desk (☎ **01582/40-45-11** for information, or 0171/73-03-499 for credit/charge-card sales). In Frankfurt, contact **L'Agence Wasteels**, Am Hauptbahnhof 18, 6000 Frankfurt (☎ **069/232385**).

BY CAR

Driving a car in Paris is definitely not recommended unless you have lots of experience with European traffic patterns, nerves of steel, and lots of time and money. Parking is difficult, traffic is dense, and networks of one-way streets make navigation, even with the best of maps, a problem. If you do drive, remember that Paris is encircled by a ring road called the *périphérique.* Always obtain detailed directions to your destination, including the name of the exit you're looking for on the périphérique (exits are not numbered). Avoid rush hours.

Few hotels, except the luxury ones, have garages, but the staff will usually be able to direct you to one nearby.

The major highways into Paris are A1 from the north (Great Britain and Benelux); A13 from Rouen, Normandy, and other points of northwest France; A10 from Bordeaux, the Pyrénées, France's southwest, and Spain; A6 from Lyon, the French Alps, the Riviera, and Italy; and A4 from Metz, Nancy, and Strasbourg in eastern France.

BY FERRY FROM ENGLAND

For many visitors, crossing the English Channel offers a highly evocative insight into European culture and history. If your plans call for water travel to France, there are three main carriers. The most frequently used are **SuperFerry** (conventional ferry-boat service) and **Hoverspeed catamarans** (motorized catamarans—**Sealynx**—which skim along a few inches above the surface of the water). Despite the difference in speed (the catamarans are considerably faster), transportation with a car aboard either mode of transport costs the same: $136 to $248 each way to transport a car with two to nine passengers. Cars with just a driver are charged $104 to $248 each way, depending on the service. Not all the catamarans offer car service, and since those that do have only a limited capacity for vehicles, it's probable that your means of transport with a car will be aboard one of the conventional ferryboats. Foot passengers (travelers without cars) pay $36 each way on the SuperFerry and $39 on the catamarans, regardless of which points of embarkation and disembarkation are involved.

The shortest and busiest route between London and Paris is the one from Dover to Calais. By ferryboat, the trip takes about 90 minutes, although a Sealynx can make the run in about 45 minutes. The Sealynx also crosses from Folkestone to Boulogne in about 60 minutes, but that route caters only to foot passengers.

Each crossing is carefully timed to coincide with the arrival and departure of trains from London and Paris, which disgorge passengers and their luggage a short walk from the piers. The U.S. sales agent for the above-mentioned lines is **BritRail** (☎ **212/575-2667,** or 800/677-8585).

Another opportunity to travel by ferryboat from England to France is offered by **P&O Channel Lines** (☎ **099/0980-980** in London). It maintains 20 to 25 ferry-boat crossings a day, depending on the season, between the busy harbors of Dover and Calais in northeastern France. The crossing can take as little as $1\,^{1}/_{4}$ hours, depending on the craft.

If you plan to take a rented car across the Channel, research license and insurance requirements with the rental company before you leave.

UNDER THE CHANNEL

Queen Elizabeth and the late French President François Mitterrand officially opened the Channel Tunnel in 1994, and the **Eurostar Express** now has twice-daily passenger service between London and both Paris and Brussels. The $15-billion tunnel, one of the great engineering feats of all time, is the first link between Britain and the Continent since the Ice Age. The 31-mile journey takes 35 minutes, although the actual time spent in the Chunnel is only 19 minutes. (Chunnel train traffic is roughly competitive with air travel, if you calculate door-to-door travel time. Trains leave from London's Waterloo Station and arrive in Paris at Gare du Nord.)

Eurostar tickets, for train service between London and Paris or Brussels, are available through **Rail Europe** (☎ **800/94-CHUNNEL** for information). The round-trip fare between London and Paris is $312 in first class and $258 in second class. But you can cut costs to $140 with a nonrefundable second-class, 15-day-advance-purchase round-trip fare. You can make **Eurostar reservations** by phone (☎ **01345/300003** in the U.K., 01-47-42-50-00 in France, and 800/387-6782 in the U.S.).

The tunnel also accommodates passenger cars, charter buses, taxis, and motorcycles, transporting them under the English Channel from Folkestone, England, to Calais, France. It operates 24 hours a day, 365 days a year, running every 15 minutes during peak travel times and at least once an hour at night. Tickets may be purchased at the toll booth at the tunnel's entrance. With **"Le Shuttle,"** gone are the days of weather-related delays, seasickness, and advance reservations.

Before boarding Le Shuttle, motorists stop at a toll booth and then pass through British and French Immigration services at the same time. They then drive onto a half-mile-long train and travel through an underground tunnel built beneath the sea-bed through a layer of impervious chalk marl and sealed with a reinforced-concrete lining. During the ride, motorists stay in bright, air-conditioned carriages, remaining inside their cars or stepping outside to stretch their legs. When the trip is completed, they simply drive off toward their destinations—in our case, Paris. Total travel time between the French and English highway systems is about an hour. Once on French soil, British drivers must remember to drive on the right-hand side of the road.

Stores selling duty-free goods, restaurants, and service stations are available to travelers on both sides of the Channel. A bilingual staff is on hand to assist travelers at both the French and British terminals.

PACKAGE TOURS

Booking a package can save you a lot of money. Through volume purchases of hotel rooms, airlines and travel agents can arrange affordable visits to Paris (and elsewhere in Europe) that are geared to either first-timers or seasoned travelers. Tours can range from fully escorted excursions with trained guides to independent and unsupervised trips (just booking airfare, transfers, and accommodations).

Delta Air Lines, for example, through its tour division, Delta Dream Vacations (☎ 800/872-7786), offers a land package (without airfare) to the Ile de France that includes 6 nights at a good hotel in Paris, guided tours of the city's monuments, outings to Versailles, breakfasts, taxes, a 5-day pass for public transport in the city, and a 3-day museum pass. The cost varies from $989 to $1,379 per person, double occupancy, depending on the hotel you stay in. (Single occupancy for the same package costs $1,609.) Other packaged trips to the Riviera, Geneva, and the rest of Europe can save you a bundle compared to independently coordinated trips.

The French Experience, 370 Lexington Ave., New York, NY 10017 (☎ 212/986-1115), offers tours including inexpensive airline tickets to Paris on most scheduled airlines. Several car-dependent tours use varied types and categories of country inns, hotels, private châteaux and bed-and-breakfasts. It takes reservations for about 30 small hotels in Paris and arranges short-term apartment rentals in the city or farmhouse rentals in the countryside. It also offers all-inclusive packages in Paris as well as prearranged package tours of various regions of France. Any tour can be adapted to suit individual needs.

American Express Vacations (operated by Certified Vacations, Inc.), P.O. Box 1525, Fort Lauderdale, FL 33302 (☎ 800/446-6234 in the U.S. and Canada), is the most instantly recognizable tour operator in the world. Its offerings in France and the rest of Europe are more comprehensive than those of many other companies. More than 40 "go-any-day" city packages, 13 freelance vacations, and 23 escorted tours highlight their unparalleled variety.

3 Getting to Know Paris

Ernest Hemingway referred to the many splendors of Paris as a "moveable feast" and wrote, "There is never any ending to Paris, and the memory of each person who has lived in it differs from that of any other." It is this personal discovery of the city that has always been the most compelling reason for coming to Paris. And perhaps that's why France has been called *le deuxième pays de tout le monde*—everybody's second country.

The Seine not only divides Paris into a Right Bank (Rive Droite) and a Left Bank (Rive Gauche), but it also seems to split the city into two vastly different sections and ways of life. Depending on your time, interest, and budget, you may quickly decide which section of Paris interests you the most.

1 Orientation

VISITOR INFORMATION

The main Paris **tourist information office** is at 127 av. des Champs-Elysées, 8e (☎ **01-49-52-53-54**), where you can secure information about both Paris and the provinces. The office is open daily (except May 1) from 9am to 8pm.

Welcome Offices, situated in each of the city's railway stations (except Gare St-Lazare) will also give you free maps, brochures, and a copy of *Paris Selection,* a French-language listing of all current events and performances, which is published monthly.

CITY LAYOUT

Paris is surprisingly compact. Occupying 432 square miles (6 more than San Francisco), it's home to more than 10 million people. As mentioned, the River Seine divides Paris into the Right Bank (Rive Droite) to the north and the Left Bank (Rive Gauche) to the south. These designations make sense when you stand on a bridge and face downstream, watching the waters flow out toward the sea—to your right is the north bank, to your left the south. In all, 32 bridges link the Right and Left banks, some providing access to the two small islands at the heart of the city, Ile de la Cité—the city's birthplace and site of Notre-Dame—and Ile St-Louis, a moat-guarded oasis of sober 17th-century mansions. These islands can cause some confusion to walkers who think they've just crossed a bridge from one bank to the other, only to find themselves caught up in an almost medieval maze of narrow streets and old buildings.

Impressions

Paris is still monumental and handsome. Along the rivers where its splendours are, there's no denying its man-made beauty. The poor, pale little Seine runs rapidly north to the sea, the sky is pale, pale jade overhead, greenish and Parisian, the trees of black wire stand in rows, and flourish their black wire brushes against a low sky of jade-pale cobwebs, and the huge dark-grey palaces rear up their masses of stone and slope off towards the sky still with a massive, satisfying suggestion of pyramids. There is something noble and man-made about it all.

—D. H. Lawrence

Paris is the greatest temple ever built to material joys and the lust of the eyes.

—Henry James

The kid will come from Nebraska or Heidelberg, from Poland or Senegal, and Paris will be born again—new, brand new and unexpected, and the Arch of Triumph will rise again, and the Seine will flow for the first time, and there will be new areas, unknown and unexplored, called Montmartre and Montparnasse . . . and it will all be for the first time, a completely new city, built suddenly for you and you alone.

—Romain Gary

MAIN ARTERIES & STREETS   Between 1860 and 1870 Baron Haussmann forever changed the look of Paris by creating the legendary boulevards: St-Michel, St-Germain, Haussmann, Malesherbes, Sébastopol, Magenta, Voltaire, and Strasbourg.

The "main street" on the Right Bank is, of course, the **Champs-Elysées**, beginning at the Arc de Triomphe and running to place de la Concorde. Haussmann also created avenue de l'Opéra (as well as the Opéra), and the 12 avenues that radiate starlike from the Arc de Triomphe, giving it its original name, place de l'Etoile (renamed place Charles-de-Gaulle following the general's death). Today it's often referred to as place Charles-de-Gaulle–Etoile.

Haussmann also cleared the Ile de la Cité of its medieval buildings, transforming it into a showcase for Notre-Dame. Finally, he laid out the two elegant parks on the western and southeastern fringes of the city: Bois de Boulogne and Bois de Vincennes.

FINDING AN ADDRESS   Paris is divided into 20 municipal wards called *arrondissements,* each with its own mayor, city hall, police station, and central post office. Some even have remnants of market squares. Most city maps are divided by arrondissement, and all addresses include the arrondissement number (written in Roman or Arabic numerals and followed by "e" or "er"). Paris also has its own version of a ZIP Code. Thus the proper mailing address for a hotel is written as, say, 75014 Paris. The last two digits, 14, indicate that the address is in the 14th Arrondissement, in this case, Montparnasse.

Building numbers on streets running parallel to the River Seine usually follow the course of the river—that is, east to west. On perpendicular streets, numbers on buildings begin low closer to the river.

STREET MAPS   If you're staying more than 2 or 3 days, purchase an inexpensive, pocket-size book that includes the *plan de Paris* by arrondissement available at all major newsstands and bookshops. Most of these guides provide you with a Métro map, a foldout map of the city, and indexed maps of each arrondissement, with all streets listed and keyed. And check out the free full-color foldout map in the back of this guide.

ARRONDISSEMENTS IN BRIEF

Each of Paris's 20 arrondissements possesses a unique style and flavor. You'll want to decide which district appeals most to you and then find accommodations there. Later on, try to visit as many areas as you can.

1st Arr. (Musée du Louvre/Les Halles) "I never knew what a palace was until I had a glimpse of the Louvre," wrote Nathaniel Hawthorne. One of the world's greatest art museums (some say *the* greatest), the **Louvre**, a former royal residence, still lures all visitors to Paris to the 1st arrondissement. Here are many of the elegant addresses of Paris, like rue de Rivoli, with the Jeu de Paume and Orangerie on raised terraces. Walk through its **Jardin des Tuileries,** the most formal garden of Paris (originally laid out by Le Nôtre, gardener to Louis XIV). Pause to take in the classic beauty of **place Vendôme,** opulent, wealthy, and home of the Ritz Hotel. Jewelers and art dealers are in plentiful supply, and the memories of Chopin are evoked on the square where he died. Zola's "the belly of Paris" (Les Halles) is no longer the food and meat market of Paris (traders moved to a new, more accessible suburb, Rungis), but is today **Forum des Halles,** a center of shopping, entertainment, and culture.

2nd Arr. (La Bourse) Home to the **Bourse** (stock exchange), this Right Bank district lies mainly between the Grands Boulevards and rue Etienne-Marcel. Monday to Friday the shouts of brokers—*J'ai!* or *Je prends!*—echo across place de la Bourse until it's time to break for lunch, when the movers and shakers of French capitalism bring their hysteria into the restaurants of the district. Much of the eastern end of the arrondissement (**Le Sentier**) is devoted to the wholesale outlets of the Paris garment district, where thousands of garments are sold (usually in bulk) to buyers from clothing stores throughout Europe. "Everything that exists elsewhere exists in Paris," wrote Victor Hugo in *Les Misérables,* and if you take on this district, you'll find ample evidence to support his bold claim. Little nuggets of true beauty and value do exist amid the often overwhelming commercialism—none finer than the **Musée Cognacq-Jay**, 25 bd. des Capucines. Ernest Cognacq created the Samaritaine chain of stores, but also had time to collect some of the world's most exquisite art. His collection is a jewel box brimming with treasures, featuring work by every artist from Watteau to Fragonard.

3rd Arr. (Le Marais) This district embraces much of **Le Marais** (the swamp), one of the best loved of the old Right Bank neighborhoods. Allowed to fall into decades of seedy decay, Le Marais has now made a comeback, although perhaps it will never again enjoy the grand opulence of its aristocratic heyday during the 17th century. Over the centuries, kings have called Le Marais home, and its salons have resounded with the witty, often devastating remarks of Racine, Voltaire, Molière, and Madame de Sévigné. One of the district's chief attractions today is the **Musée Picasso,** stuffed with treasures that the Picasso estate had to turn over to the French government in lieu of the artist's astronomical death duties. Forced donation or not, it's one of the world's great repositories of 20th-century art.

4th Arr. (Ile de la Cité/Ile St-Louis & Beaubourg) At times it seems as if the 4th has it all: Not only **Notre-Dame** on the **Ile de la Cité,** but the **Ile St-Louis,** with its aristocratic town houses, courtyards, and antiques shops. The Ile St-Louis, a former cow pasture and dueling ground, is home to dozens of 17th-century mansions and 6,000 lucky *louisiens,* its permanent residents. Voltaire found it "the second-best" address in all the world, citing the straits of the Bosporus separating Europe from Asia as number one. Of course, the whole area is touristy and overrun. Forget the "I Love

Paris" bumper stickers and seek out the Ile St-Louis's two gems of Gothic architecture, **La Sainte-Chapelle** and Notre-Dame, a majestic and dignified structure that, according to the poet e. e. cummings, doesn't budge an inch for all the idiocies of this world.

The heart of medieval Paris, the 4th evokes memories of Danton, Robespierre, and even of Charlotte Corday, who stabbed Marat in his bath. Here you not only get France's finest bird and flower markets, but the nation's law courts. Though Balzac described the courts as a "cathedral of chicanery," they have a long tradition of dispensing justice, French style: It was here that Marie Antoinette was sentenced to death in 1793. If all this weren't enough, the 4th is also home to the **Centre Georges-Pompidou,** now one of the top three tourist attractions of France, partly because of its National Museum of Modern Art. Finally, after all this pomp and glory, you can retreat to **place des Vosges,** a square of perfect harmony and beauty where Victor Hugo lived from 1832 to 1848 and penned many of his famous masterpieces.

5th Arr. (Latin Quarter)   The **Quartier Latin** (Latin Quarter) is the intellectual heart and soul of Paris. Bookstores, schools, churches, smoky jazz clubs, student dives, Roman ruins, publishing houses, and, yes, expensive and chic boutiques characterize the district. Discussions of Artaud or Molière over long, lingering cups of coffee are not just a cliché—they really happen. Beginning with the founding of the **Sorbonne** in 1253, the *quartier* was called Latin because all students and professors spoke the scholarly language. As the traditional center of what was called "bohemian Paris," it formed the setting for Henri Murger's novel *Scènes de la vie de Bohème* (later the Puccini opera *La Bohème*).

You'll follow in the footsteps of Descartes, Verlaine, Camus, Sartre, James Thurber, Elliot Paul, and Hemingway as you explore this historic district. For sure, the old Latin Quarter is gone forever. Changing times have brought Greek, Moroccan, and Vietnamese immigrants, among others, hustling everything from couscous to fiery-hot spring rolls and souvlaki. The 5th also borders the Seine, and you'll want to stroll along **quai de Montebello,** inspecting the inventories of the *bouquinistes* who sell everything from antique Daumier prints to yellowing copies of Balzac's *Père Goriot* in the shadow of Notre-Dame. The 5th also stretches down to the **Panthéon,** which was constructed by a grateful Louis XV after he'd recovered from the gout and wanted to do something nice for Ste-Geneviève. It's the dank, dark resting place of Rousseau, Gambetta, Emile Zola, Louis Braille, Victor Hugo, Voltaire, and Jean Moulin, the World War II Resistance leader who was tortured to death by the Gestapo.

6th Arr. (St-Germain/Luxembourg)   This is the heartland of Paris publishing and, for some, the most colorful quartier of the Left Bank, where waves of earnest young artists still emerge from the famous **Ecole des Beaux-Arts.** To stroll the boulevards of the 6th, including St-Germain, has its own rewards, but the secret of the district lies in discovering its narrow streets and hidden squares as well as the Jardin du Luxembourg, a classic French garden overlooked by Marie de Médici's Italianate Palais du Luxembourg. Of course, to be really "authentic," you'll stroll these streets with an unwrapped loaf of country sourdough bread from the wood-fired ovens of Poilâne, the world's most famous baker, at 8 rue du Cherche-Midi. Everywhere you turn in the district, you encounter famous historical and literary associations, none more so than on rue Jacob. At 7 rue Jacob, Racine lived with his uncle as a teenager; Richard Wagner resided at 14 rue Jacob from 1841 to 1842; Ingres once lived at 27 rue Jacob (now it's the offices of the French publishing house Editions du Seuil); and Hemingway once occupied a tiny upstairs room at no. 44. Today's "big name" is likely to be filmmaker Spike Lee checking into his favorite, La Villa Hôtel, at 29 rue Jacob.

Delacroix—whom Baudelaire called "a volcanic crater artistically concealed beneath bouquets of flowers"—kept his atelier in the 6th, and George Sand and her lover, Frédéric Chopin, used to visit him there to have their portraits done. His studio is now open to the public. **Rue Monsieur-le-Prince** has historically been a popular street for Paris's resident Americans, once frequented by Martin Luther King, Jr., Richard Wright, James McNeill Whistler, Henry Wadsworth Longfellow, and even Oliver Wendell Holmes. The 6th even takes in the **Luxembourg Gardens,** a 60-acre playground where Isadora Duncan went dancing in the predawn hours and a destitute writer, Ernest Hemingway, went looking for pigeons for lunch while pushing a baby carriage to carry his hunting trophies back to his humble flat for cooking.

7th Arr. (Eiffel Tower/Musée d'Orsay)   Paris's most famous symbol, the **Eiffel Tower**, dominates Paris and especially the 7th, a Left Bank district of respectable residences and government offices. Part of the **St-Germain neighborhood** is included here as well. The tower is now one of the most recognizable landmarks in the world, despite the fact that many Parisians (most notably some of its nearest neighbors) hated it when it was unveiled in 1889. Many of the most imposing monuments of Paris are in the 7th, including the **Hôtel des Invalides**, which contains both Napoléon's Tomb and the Musée de l'Armée. But there's much hidden charm here as well. Who has not walked these often narrow streets before you? Your predecessors include Picasso, Manet, Ingres, Baudelaire, Wagner, Simone de Beauvoir, Sartre, even Truman Capote, Gore Vidal, and Tennessee Williams.

Rue du Bac was home to the swashbuckling heroes of Dumas's *The Three Musketeers,* and to James McNeill Whistler, who, after selling *Whistler's Mother,* moved to 110 rue du Bac, where he entertained the likes of Degas, Henry James, Manet, and Toulouse-Lautrec. Auguste Rodin lived at what is now the **Musée Rodin** at 77 rue de Varenne until his death in 1917.

Even visitors with no time to thoroughly explore the 7th at least rush to its second major attraction (after the Eiffel Tower), the **Musée d'Orsay**, the world's premier showcase of 19th-century French art and culture. The museum is housed in the old Gare d'Orsay, which Orson Welles used in 1962 as a setting for his film *The Trial,* based on the book by Franz Kafka.

8th Arr. (Champs-Elysée/Madeleine)   The 8th is the heart of the Right Bank and its prime showcase is the **Champs-Elysées**, which links the **Arc de Triomphe** with the delicate obelisk on **place de la Concorde**. Here you'll find the fashion houses, the most elegant hotels, expensive restaurants and shops, and the most fashionably attired Parisians. Stretching grandly from the Arc de Triomphe to place de la Concorde, the Champs-Elysées has long been cited as the perfect metaphor of the Parisian love of symmetry. However, by the 1980s it had become a garish strip, with too much traffic, too many fast-food joints, and too many panhandlers. In the 1990s the Gaulist mayor of Paris, Jacques Chirac, launched a massive cleanup. The major change has been in broadened sidewalks, with new rows of trees planted. The old glory? Perhaps it's gone forever, but what an improvement.

Whatever it is you're looking for, in the 8th it will be the city's "best, grandest, and most impressive:" It has the best restaurant in Paris (Taillevent), the sexiest strip joint (Crazy Horse Saloon), the most splendid square in all of France (place de la Concorde), the best rooftop café (at La Samaritaine), the grandest hotel in France (the Crillon), the most impressive triumphal arch on the planet (the Arc de Triomphe), the world's most expensive residential street (avenue Montaigne), the world's oldest Métro station (Franklin-D-Roosevelt), and the most ancient monument in Paris (the Obelisk of Luxor, 3,300 years old). Also here is the Madeleine church, looking like a Greek temple. It stands at the junction of the boulevards at place de la Madeleine, reached from place de la Concorde by walking along rue Royale.

9th Arr. (Opéra Garnier/Pigalle) Everything from the **Quartier de l'Opéra** to the strip and clip joints of **Pigalle** (the infamous "Pig Alley" for the GIs of World War II) falls inside the 9th. When Balzac was writing his novels, the author considered the most elitist address for his socially ambitious characters as the 9th's chaussée d'Antin. The 9th was radically altered by the 19th-century urban redevelopment projects of Baron Haussmann, whose *grands boulevards* radiating through the district are among the most obvious of his labors. Although the chaussée d'Antin is no longer particularly elegant, having been supplanted by some of Paris's largest department stores, the 9th endures, even if fickle fashion now prefers other addresses. Over the decades the 9th has been celebrated in literature and song for the music halls that brought gaiety to the city. Marie Duplessis, known as Marguerite Gautier, heroine of *La Dame aux camélias* by Alexandre Dumas the younger (1824–95) (a character made famous by Greta Garbo's portrayal in the film *Camille*), died at 17 bd. de la Madeleine. Boulevard des Italiens is the site of the Café de la Paix, opened in 1856 and once the meeting place of the Romantic poets, including Théophile Gautier and Alfred de Musset. Later, Charles de Gaulle, Marlene Dietrich, and two million Americans started showing up.

At place Pigalle, gone is the café La Nouvelle Athènes, where Degas, Pissarro, and Manet used to meet. Today you're likely to encounter a few clubs where the action gets really down and dirty. Other major attractions include the **Folies Bergère,** where cancan dancers have been high-kicking it since 1868, and French entertainers such as Mistinguett, Edith Piaf, and Maurice Chevalier have appeared along with Josephine Baker, once hailed as "the toast of Paris." More than anything, it was the **Opéra Garnier** (Paris Opera House) that made the 9th the last hurrah of Second Empire opulence. Renoir hated it, but several generations later Chagall did the ceilings. Pavlova danced *Swan Lake* here, and Nijinsky took the night off to go cruising.

10th Arr. (Gare du Nord/Gare de l'Est) The **Gare du Nord** and **Gare de l'Est**, along with movie theaters, porno houses, and dreary commercial zones, make the 10th one of the least desirable arrondissements for living, dining, and sightseeing in Paris. We always try to avoid the 10th, except for two longtime favorite restaurants, Brasserie Flo at 7 cour des Petites-Ecuries (go there for its *la formidable choucroute,* a heap of sauerkraut garnished with everything), and Julien, 16 rue du Faubourg St-Denis (called the poor man's Maxim's because of its belle époque interiors and moderate prices).

11th Arr. (Opéra Bastille) For many years this quartier seemed to sink lower and lower into poverty and decay, overcrowded by working-class immigrants from the far reaches of the former French Empire. The opening of the **Opéra Bastille**, however, has given the 11th new hope and new life. The facility, called the "people's opera house," stands on the landmark place de la Bastille where, on July 14, 1789, 633 Parisians stormed the fortress and seized the ammunition depot as the French Revolution swept across the city. Over the years the prison held Voltaire, the Marquis de Sade, and the mysterious "Man in the Iron Mask."

Even when the district wasn't fashionable, visitors flocked to Bofinger, at 5–7 rue de la Bastille, to sample its Alsatian *choucroute.* (Technically, Bofinger lies in the 4th arrondissement, although its fans have always associated it with place de la Bastille.) Established around 1864, it's perhaps the most famous brasserie in Paris. The 11th has its charms, but they need to be sought out; *Le Marché* at place d'Aligre, for example, is surrounded by a Middle Eastern food market and is a good place to hunt for second-hand bargains: Everything is cheap, and although you must search hard for treasures, they often appear.

12th Arr. (Bois de Vincennes/Gare de Lyon)   Very few out-of-towners came here until a French chef opened a restaurant called Au Trou Gascon. Then *tout le monde* started showing up at the door (see Chapter 5, "Dining," for more details). In addition to this eatery, the 12th's major attraction remains the **Bois de Vincennes,** a sprawling park on the eastern periphery of Paris. It has been a longtime favorite of French families, who enjoy its zoos and museums, its royal château and boating lakes, and most definitely, the Parc Floral de Paris, a celebrated flower garden whose springtime rhododendrons and autumn dahlias are among the major lures of the city. The dreary **Gare de Lyon** also lies in the 12th, but going there is worthwhile even if you don't have to take a train, because Le Train Bleu, a restaurant in the station, features ceiling frescoes and art nouveau decor that are classified as national artistic treasures. The food's good, too.

The 12th arrondissement, once a depressing urban wasteland, has been singled out for multi-million-dollar resuscitation, and will soon sport new housing, shops, gardens, and restaurants. Many of these new structures will occupy the site of the former Reuilly railroad tracks.

13th Arr. (Gare d'Austerlitz)   Centered around the grimy **Gare d'Austerlitz,** the 13th might have its devotees, but we've yet to meet one. British snobs who flitted in and out of the train station were among the first of the district's foreign visitors, and they in essence wrote the 13th off as a dreary working-class district reminiscent of London's East End. Certainly there are far more fashionable places to see, but there's at least one reason to visit the 13th: The **Manufacture des Gobelins** at 42 av. des Gobelins, the tapestry factory that made the word "Gobelins" internationally famous. Some 250 Flemish weavers, under the reign of Louis XIV, launched the industry to compete with the tapestries being produced in southern Belgium (Flanders), and in time they became the preferred suppliers of the French aristocracy—many of the walls of the Sun King's palace at Versailles were covered with Gobelins.

14th Arr. (Montparnasse)   The northern end of this large arrondissement is devoted to **Montparnasse,** home of the "lost generation" and former stomping ground of Stein, Toklas, Hemingway, and other American expatriates who gathered here in the 1920s. After World War II it ceased to be the center of intellectual life in Paris, but the memory lingers on in its cafés. One of it most visible monuments, one that helps set the tone of the neighborhood, is the Rodin statue of Balzac at the junction of boulevard Montparnasse and boulevard Raspail. At this corner are some of the world's most famous literary cafés, including La Rotonde, Le Select, La Dôme, and La Coupole. Though Gertrude Stein probably avoided this corner (she loathed cafés), all the other American expatriates, including Hemingway and Scott Fitzgerald, had no qualms about enjoying a drink here (or quite a few of them, for that matter). Henry Miller, plotting *Tropic of Cancer* and his newest seduction of Anaïs Nin, came to La Coupole for his morning porridge. So did Roman Polanski, Josephine Baker (with a lion cub on a leash), James Joyce, Man Ray, Matisse, Ionesco (ordering *café liègeois*), Jean-Paul Sartre, and even the famous Kiki as she worked on her memoirs. Though she shunned the cafés, Stein amused herself at home (27 rue de Fleurus) with Alice Toklas, collecting paintings, including those of Picasso, and entertaining the likes of Max Jacob, Apollinaire, T. S. Eliot, and Matisse. At its southern end, the 14th arrondissement contains pleasant residential neighborhoods filled with well-designed apartment buildings, many of them built between 1910 and 1940.

15th Arr. (Gare Montparnasse/Institut Pasteur)   A mostly residential district beginning at **Gare Montparnasse,** the 15th stretches all the way to the Seine. In size and population, it's the largest quartier of Paris, but it attracts few tourists and has few attractions, except for the **Parc des Expositions** and the **Institut Pasteur.** In the early 20th century, many artists—Chagall, Léger, and Modigliani—lived in this arrondissement in a shared atelier known as "The Beehive."

16th Arr. (Trocadéro/Bois de Boulogne)   Originally the village of Passy, where Benjamin Franklin lived during most of his time in Paris, this district is still reminiscent of Proust's world. Highlights include the **Bois de Boulogne,** the **Jardin du Trocadéro,** the **Musée de Balzac,** the **Musée Guimet** (famous for its Asian collections), and the **Cimetière de Passy,** resting place of Manet, Talleyrand, Giraudoux, and Debussy. One of the largest of the city's arrondissements, it's known today for its well-heeled bourgeoisie, its upscale rents, and some rather posh (and, according to its critics, rather smug) residential boulevards. Prosperous and suitably conservative addresses include avenue d'Iéna and avenue Victor-Hugo. Also prestigious is avenue Foch, the widest boulevard in Paris, with homes that at various periods were maintained by Onassis, the shah of Iran, composer Charles Debussy, and Prince Rainier of Monaco. The arrondissement also includes what some visitors consider the best place in Paris from which to view the Eiffel Tower: **place du Trocadéro.**

17th Arr. (Parc Monceau/Place Clichy)   Flanking the northern periphery of Paris, the 17th incorporates neighborhoods of conservative bourgeois respectability in its western end and less affluent, more pedestrian neighborhoods in its eastern end. Regardless of its levels of prosperity, most of the arrondissement is residential, and most of it, at least to habitués of glamour and glitter, is rather dull. Highlights include the **Palais des Congrès,** which is of interest only if you're attending a convention or special exhibit, and the **Porte Maillot Air Terminal,** no grand distinction. More exciting than either of those are two of the greatest restaurants of Paris, Guy Savoy and Michel Rostang (see Chapter 5).

18th Arr. (Montmartre)   The 18th is the most famous outer quartier of Paris, containing **Montmartre,** the **Moulin Rouge,** the **Basilica of Sacré-Coeur,** and **place du Tertre.** Utrillo was its native son, Renoir lived here, and Toulouse-Lautrec adopted the area as his own. The most famous enclave of artists in Paris's history, the Bateau-Lavoir, of Picasso fame, gathered here. Max Jacob, Matisse, and Braque were all frequent visitors. Today place Blanche is known for its prostitutes and Montmartre is filled with honky-tonks, too many souvenir shops, and terrible restaurants. Go for the attractions and the *mémoires.* The city's most famous flea market, **Marché aux Puces de Clignancourt,** is another landmark.

19th Arr. (La Villette)   Today visitors come to what was once the village of La Villette to see the angular, much-publicized **Cité des Sciences et de l'Industrie,** a spectacular science museum and park built on a site that for years was devoted to the city's slaughterhouses. Mostly residential, and not at all upscale, the district is one of the most ethnically diverse in Paris, the home of people from all parts of the former French Empire. A highlight is **Les Buttes–Chaumont**, a park where kids can enjoy puppet shows and donkey rides.

20th Arr. (Père-Lachaise Cemetery)   The 20th's greatest landmark is **Père-Lachaise Cemetery**, the resting place of Edith Piaf, Marcel Proust, Oscar Wilde, Isadora Duncan, Sarah Bernhardt, Gertrude Stein, Colette, and many, many others.

Otherwise, the 20th arrondissement is a dreary and sometimes volatile melting pot comprising residents from France's former colonies. Although nostalgia buffs sometimes head here to visit Piaf's former neighborhood, Ménilmontant-Belleville, it has been almost totally bulldozed and rebuilt since the bad old days when she grew up there. Parts of the 20th won't correspond to your vision of the legendary Paris of yesteryear in any way: The district contains many Muslims (the turbaned man selling dates and grains on the street presents a scene directly out of northern Africa) and hundreds of deeply entrenched members of Paris's Sephardic Jewish community, many of whom fled their former homes in Algeria or Tunisia, fearing for their safety. It's grimy and shunned by many residents of more upscale Parisian neighborhoods, and sometimes there's a palpable sense of discontent here, but the 20th provides an interesting cultural contrast to some of Paris's other quartiers.

2 Getting Around

Paris is a city for strollers whose greatest joy in life is rambling through unexpected alleyways and squares. Given a choice of conveyance, make it your own two feet whenever possible. Only when you're dead tired and can't walk another step, or in a roaring hurry to reach an exact destination, should you consider the following swift and prosaic means of urban transport.

BY PUBLIC TRANSPORTATION

DISCOUNT PASSES   You can purchase a *Paris-Visite* pass, a tourist pass valid for 2, 3, or 5 days of travel within clearly defined zones of the city's public transportation system. For travel within the inner three zones of the transport system—an area that includes everything within Paris's 29 arrondissements and some of the suburbs as well—the price for a two-day pass costs 70 F ($14), a three-day pass costs 105 F ($21), and a five-day pass costs 165 F ($33). If you want to extend your hunting grounds to the outer suburbs of Paris with the purchase of a pass that includes all five zones of the city transport system, two-day, three-day, and five-day passes cost 170 F ($34), 230 F ($46), and 315 F ($63), respectively. The pass includes unlimited access during the designated number of days to the Métro, city buses, and RER (Réseau Express Régional) trains. (The RER has both first- and second-class compartments, and the pass lets you travel in the first class.) As a special bonus, the funicular ride to the top of Montmartre is also included. The card is available at RATP (Régie Autonome des Transports Parisiens), tourist offices, and at most Métro stations. For information, call **01-44-68-20-20.**

What is basically the same pass, but with a validity of only one day is the *Formulae 1* pass, which allows unlimited travel on each of the transit networks that apply to the above-mentioned Paris-Visite. A *Formulae 1* pass costs 30 F ($6) for transit within two zones (i.e., all of inner Paris plus some of the inner suburbs), and 40 F ($8), 60 F ($12), and 100 F ($20) for unlimited one-day transport within 3, 4, and 5 zones, respectively. Ask for it at any Métro station. There are other discount passes as well, although most are available only to French residents with government ID cards and proof of taxpayer status.

BY SUBWAY (MÉTRO)

The **Métro** (☎ **01-43-46-14-14** for information) is the most efficient means of transportation, and it's easy to use. Each line is numbered and the final destination of each is clearly marked on subway maps, on the trains themselves, and in the underground passageways. Most stations display a map of the system at the entrance.

Figure out the route from where you are to your destination, noting the stations where you'll have to change. To make sure you catch the right train, find your destination, then visually follow the line it's on to the end of the route and note its name. This is the *direction* you follow in the stations and see on the train. Transfer stations are known as *correspondances*. (Note that some require long walks—Châtelet is the most notorious.)

Most trips will require only one transfer. Many of the larger stations have maps with pushbutton indicators that will help you plot your route more easily by lighting up automatically when you press the button for your destination. A ride on the urban lines costs 7.50 F ($1.50) to any point within the 20 arrondissements of Paris, as well as to many of its near suburbs. A bulk purchase of 10 tickets (which are bound together into what the French refer to as a **carnet**) costs 44 F ($8.80). Métro fares to far-flung, outlying suburbs on the Sceaux, the Noissy–St-Léger, and the St-Germain-en-Laye lines cost more, and are sold on an individual basis based on the distance you travel.

At the entrances to the Métro station, insert your ticket into the turnstile and pass through. At some exits, tickets and their validity are checked by uniformed police officers, so hold onto your ticket. There are occasional ticket checks on the trains, platforms, and passageways, too.

If you're changing trains, get out and determine which *direction* (final destination) on the next line you want, and follow the bright-orange CORRESPONDANCE signs until you reach the proper platform. Don't follow a SORTIE sign, which means "exit," or else you'll have to pay another fare to resume your journey.

The Métro starts running daily at 5:30am and closes down around 1:15am. It's reasonably safe at any hour, but beware of pickpockets.

BY BUS

Bus travel is much slower than the subway. Most buses run from 7am to 8:30pm (a few operate until 12:30am, and 10 operate during the early-morning hours). Service is limited on Sunday and holidays. Bus and Métro fares are the same and you can use the same *carnet* tickets on both.

At certain bus stops, signs list the destinations and numbers of the buses serving that point. Destinations are usually listed north to south and east to west. Most stops along the way are also posted on the sides of the buses. To catch a bus, wait in line at the bus stop. Signal the driver to stop the bus and board in order. During rush hours you may have to take a ticket from the dispensing machine, indicating your position in the line.

In the mid-1990s Paris initiated the **Batobus** (☎ 01-44-11-33-44), a series of passenger ferryboats inspired by the gondolas that glide along the canals of Venice. Every day from April to September they sail along the Seine from east to west, stopping at five points of touristic interest: the Hôtel de Ville–Georges Pompidou Centre, Notre-Dame, the Louvre, the Musée d'Orsay, and the Eiffel Tower, in that order. They are equipped with large windows for viewing the passing riverfront. Transport between any two stops costs 12 F ($2.40) (if you travel the distance between 4 stops, you'll pay 48 F), and departures are about every 30 minutes between 10am and 7pm. If you want to hang out on the boat for a full day, no one will stop you, but in that event, it's wise to buy an all-day pass for unlimited time aboard. That pass is priced at 50 F ($12). Unlike the Bateaux-Mouches, which are run by an entirely separate outfit, there is no recorded commentary aboard the Batobus. These boats were not technically conceived as a sightseeing attraction (although the views are panoramic and inspiring), and were instead designed to offer an easy way to move from one sightseeing attraction to another without heading into the bowels of the Métro or braving the roaring traffic of Paris's streets.

Another service, **Le Balabus** (☎ **01-36-68-77-14**), is a fleet of orange-and-white motorcoaches that also take visitors to the main tourist sites in Paris. You can board a Balabus at most bus stops, and you'll recognize the bus and its route by the **"Bb"** symbol emblazoned across its side and on signs posted along its route. The whole trip of the city's scenic highlights lasts only 50 minutes but includes stops at the Gare de Lyon, Saint-Michel, the Musée d'Orsay, the Louvre, place de la Concorde, the Champs-Elysées, Porte Maillot, and Neuilly. The Balabus runs from mid-April to September on Sunday afternoon from 1:30 to 7:30pm, and on the afternoons of some national holidays. Three Métro tickets will carry you along the entire route.

If you intend to use the buses frequently, pick up a RATP bus map at the office on place de la Madeleine, 8e; at the tourist offices at RATP headquarters, 55 quai des Grands-Augustins, 75006 Paris; or write to them ahead of time. Call for detailed information on **bus and Métro routes** (☎ **01-43-46-14-14**).

BY CAR

Don't even think about driving in Paris. The streets are narrow, with confusing one-way designations, and parking is next to impossible. Besides, most visitors don't have the nerve, skill, and ruthlessness required to survive in Parisian traffic.

If you insist on ignoring our advice, here are a few tips: Get an excellent street map and ride with a copilot because there's no time to think at intersections. Carry plenty of coins (1-, 5-, and 10-franc denominations) for parking meters. Depending on the neighborhood, the cost of an hour's parking beside a coin-operated meter can vary from 3 to 10 F (60¢ to $2) an hour. Some out-of-the-way neighborhoods still rely on the increasingly old-fashioned "Blue Zones," where parking Monday to Saturday requires a "parking disc" obtainable from garages, police stations, and hotels. Parking is unrestricted in these zones on Sunday and holidays. Attach the disc to your windshield, setting its clock to show the time of your arrival. Between 9am and noon and from 2:30 to 5pm you may park for 1 hour; from noon to 2:30pm, for 2$^1\!/_2$ hours.

Watch for the gendarmes, who lack patience and consistently countermand the lights. Horn-blowing is absolutely forbidden except in dire emergencies.

RENTALS   The major car-rental companies usually try to match one another's price schedules and rental conditions, although, depending on circumstances, one or another sometimes offers rates that rival the cost of touring the French countryside by train. Of the major worldwide competitors, the cheapest weekly arrangements, as of this writing—and subject to change—were offered by **Budget,** followed (often in hot pursuit) by **Avis, Hertz,** and **National.** These relative advantages change (sometimes radically) for luxury-category cars, but usually the best deal is a weekly rental with unlimited mileage and an advance reservation *made from North America* between 2 days and 2 weeks in advance. Shop around at least 14 days before your departure, knowing that it pays to ask questions and make comparisons.

Warning: All car-rental bills in France are subject to an 18.6% tax, one of the highest in Europe. In some cases, the tax will be factored into the rate quoted to you over the phone. Be sure to ask.

Renting a car in Paris (and France) is easy. All you need is a valid driver's license, a passport, and (unless the rate is prepaid in dollars in North America) a valid credit or charge card. In some cases, the rental company will require that your driver's license has been valid for 1 to 2 years prior to your rental, depending on the value of the car you want to rent. Usually it isn't obligatory, but small companies may require an international driver's license as well. To rent the cheapest cars, Budget requires that drivers be at least 23; Hertz, at least 25; Avis and National, at least 21.

Unless it's already factored into the rental agreement, an optional collision-damage waiver (CDW) carries an additional charge of between 72 and 95 F ($14.40 and $19) a day for the least expensive cars. Buying this additional insurance will usually eliminate all except 1,000 F ($200) of your responsibility in the event of accidental damage to the car. Because most newcomers are not familiar with local driving customs and conditions, we highly recommend that you buy the CDW, although certain credit/charge-card issuers will compensate a renter for any accident-related liability to a rented car if the imprint of their card appears on the original rental contract. At some of the companies (including Hertz) the CDW will not protect you against the theft of a car, so if this is the case, ask about buying additional theft protection. This costs 38 F ($7.60) extra per day.

At all four car-rental companies, the least expensive car will probably be either a Ford Fiesta, a Renault Clio, a Peugeot 106, or an Opel Corsa, usually with manual transmission, no air conditioning, and few frills. Depending on the company and the season, prices may range from $186 to $201 per week, with unlimited mileage (but not including tax or CDW) included. Discounts are sometimes granted for rentals of 2 weeks or more. Automatic transmission is regarded as a luxury in Europe, so if you want it you'll have to pay dearly for it.

Budget Rent-a-Car (☎ **800/527-0700**) maintains about 30 locations in Paris, including its largest branch at 81 av. Kléber, 16e (☎ **01-47-55-61-00**). For rentals of more than 7 days, cars can be picked up in one French city and dropped off in another with no additional charge. Drop-offs in cities within an easy drive of the French border (including Geneva and Frankfurt, for example) incur no additional charges either, and drop-offs in other non-French cities can be arranged for a reasonable surcharge. Its rates are among the most competitive and its cars are well maintained, but be aware that Budget does not allow its French cars to be driven anywhere in Britain.

Hertz (☎ **800/654-3001**) maintains about 15 locations in Paris, including the city's airports. The company's main office is at 27 rue St-Ferdinand, 17e (☎ **01-45-74-97-39**). Be sure to ask about any promotional discounts the company might offer.

Avis (☎ **800/331-1084**) has offices at both city airports, as well as an inner-city headquarters at 5 rue Bixio, 7e (☎ **01-44-18-10-50**), near the Eiffel Tower.

National Car Rental (☎ **800/227-3876**) is represented in Paris by Europcar, whose largest office is at 145 av. Malakoff, 16e (☎ **01-45-00-08-06**). It also has offices at both Paris airports and at about a dozen other locations throughout the city. Any of its offices can rent you a car on the spot, but to qualify for the lowest rates it's usually best to reserve in advance from North America.

GASOLINE   Gasoline—or *essence,* as it's known in France—is extraordinarily expensive for the visitor who's used to North American prices. All except the cheapest European cars require an octane rating that the French classify as *super,* which costs around 6.15 F ($1.25) per liter, which works out to around 23.30 F ($4.65) per North American gallon. Depending on your car, you'll need either unleaded gasoline (*sans plomb*), or—less frequently—leaded gasoline (*avec plomb*). What this means is that filling up the tank of a medium-sized car can cost between $40 and $65. Plan your finances accordingly.

DRIVING RULES   Everyone in the car, in both the front and back seats, must wear seat belts. Children 11 and under must ride in the back seat. Drivers are supposed to yield to the car on their right, except where signs indicate otherwise (for instance, at traffic circles). If you violate the speed limits, expect a large fine. Speed limits are usually 130 kmph (80 m.p.h.) on expressways, about 100 kmph (60 m.p.h.) on major national highways, and 90 kmph (56 m.p.h.) on small country roads. In towns, don't exceed 60 kmph (37 m.p.h.).

MAPS Before setting out from Paris on a tour of that city's environs, pick up a good regional map of the district you plan to explore. If you're visiting a town, ask at the local tourist office for a town plan. They're usually free.

For France as a whole, most motorists prefer the Michelin map 989. For regions, Michelin publishes a series of yellow maps that are quite good. Large travel bookstores in North America carry these maps, but they're commonly available in France and at lower prices. One useful feature of the Michelin map (in this age of congested traffic) is its designations of alternative *routes de dégagement,* which let you skirt big cities and avoid traffic-clogged highways.

BREAKDOWNS/ASSISTANCE A breakdown is called *une panne* in France, and it's just as frustrating there as anywhere else. Call the police by dialing 17, anywhere in France, and they'll put you in touch with the nearest garage. Most local garages have towing services. If your breakdown should occur on an expressway, find the nearest roadside emergency phone box, pick up the phone, and put a call through. You'll be connected immediately to the nearest breakdown service facility.

BY TAXI

It's impossible to get one at rush hour, so don't even try. Taxi drivers are organized into an effective lobby to keep their number limited to 14,300.

Watch out for the common rip-offs. Always check the meter to make sure you're not paying the previous passenger's fare. Beware of cabs without meters, which often wait for tipsy patrons outside nightclubs—always settle the tab in advance. Regular cabs can be hailed on the street when their signs read LIBRE. Taxis are easier to find at the many stands near Métro stations.

The basic fee (*prix en charge*) is 11 F ($2.20). Additional charges, ranging from 5 to 10 F ($1 to $2), are imposed for luggage weighing more than 5 kilograms (11 lb.), a fourth adult in the cab, or for cabs leaving from train stations and marked taxi stops. Tip 12% to 15%—the latter usually elicits a *merci.* For **radio cabs**, call 01-45-85-85-85, 01-42-70-41-41, or 01-42-70-00-42, although you'll be charged from the point where the taxi begins the drive to pick you up.

BY BICYCLE

To ride a bicycle through the streets and parks of Paris, perhaps with a *baguette* tucked under your arm, might have been a fantasy of yours since you saw your first Maurice Chevalier film. If the idea appeals to you, you won't be alone: The city in recent years has added many miles of right-hand lanes specifically designated for cyclists, and hundreds of bike racks. (When these aren't available, many Parisians simply chain their bike to the nearest available fence or lamppost.) Cycling is especially popular in Paris's larger parks and gardens.

One of the largest companies in Paris for renting a bicycle is the **Bicy-Club,** 8 place de la Porte-de-Champerret, 17e (☎ **01-47-66-55-92** or 01-45-20-60-33; Métro: Porte-de-Champerret); it maintains at least a half-dozen rental outlets in the parks and gardens of the Paris region, usually on weekends and holidays between March and November. Two of the company's most popular outlets include a kiosk behind the Relais du Rois, route de Suresnes, in the Bois de Boulogne, and another kiosk

in the Bois de Vincennes near the entrance to the Parc Floral, near Esplanade du Château. Rates start at 25 F ($5) per hour, 100 F ($20) per day. Deposits of 1,000 to 2,000 F ($200 to $400) must be mailed. Bikes can be rented July to September, daily from 9am to 7pm; October to June, Monday to Friday from 9am to 7pm and on Saturday from 9am to 1pm and 2 to 7pm.

FAST FACTS: Paris

American Express   There's an office located at 11 rue Scribe, 9e (☎ 01-47-77-70-07), which is close to the Opéra (also the Métro stop), open Monday to Friday from 9am to 6:30pm; the bank window is open on Saturday from 9am to 6:30pm, but you can't pick up mail until Monday. Other offices are at 5 rue de Chaillot, 16e (☎ 01-47-23-72-15; Métro: Alma-Marceau), and 38 av. de Wagram, 8e (☎ 01-42-27-58-80; Métro: Ternes), both open Monday to Friday from 9am to 1pm and 2 to 5:30pm.

Area Code   There isn't one. In 1996, each of France's 8-digit phone numbers were lengthened to 10-digit numbers, each digit of which must be entered into your telephone keypad regardless of the distances within France between you and the number you are trying to reach. Beginning in October of 1996, the former prefix, 16, which was required before the composition of the intra-France long distance calls for many, many years, is no longer used.

Auto Clubs   The Association Française des Auto Clubs "Automobile Club," 14 av. de la Grande Armée, 17e (☎ 01-40-55-43-00), provides limited information to members of U.S. auto clubs such as AAA.

Baby-Sitters   Students of the Institut Catholique, 21 rue d'Assas, 6e (☎ 01-45-48-31-70), offer a baby-sitting service for 32 F ($6.40) an hour plus 10 F ($2) for insurance. The main office is open from 9am to noon and 2 to 6pm Monday to Saturday only. *Tip:* It's advisable to verify that the sitter and your child speak the same language before you commit yourself.

Banks   American Express may be able to meet most of your banking needs. If not, banks in Paris are open Monday to Friday from 9am to 4:30pm, and a few are open on Saturday. Ask at your hotel for the location of the bank nearest you. Shops and most hotels will cash your traveler's checks, but not at the advantageous rate a bank or foreign-exchange office will give you, so make sure you've allowed enough funds for *le weekend.*

Bookstores   Paris has several English-language bookstores carrying American and British books, maps, and guides to the city and other destinations. Try the century-old Brentano's, 37 av. de l'Opéra, 2e (☎ 01-42-61-52-50; Métro: Opéra), open Monday to Saturday from 10am to 7pm, and on Thursday evening until 8:30pm; or Galignani, 224 rue de Rivoli, 1e (☎ 01-42-60-76-07; Métro: Tuileries), open Monday to Saturday from 10am to 7pm. Most famous of all is Shakespeare and Company, 37 rue de la Bûcherie, 5e (☎ 01-43-26-96-50; Métro or RER: St-Michel). It's open daily from 11am to midnight.

Business Hours   French business hours are erratic, as befits a nation of individualists. Most museums close 1 day a week (often Tuesday), and they're generally closed on national holidays. Usually hours are 9:30am to 5pm. Some museums, particularly the smaller and less-staffed ones, close for lunch from noon to 2pm. Most French museums are open on Saturday, but many are closed Sunday morning,

opening in the afternoon. Refer to the individual museum listings. Generally, offices are open Monday to Friday from 9am to 5pm, but don't count on it—always call first. Stores are open from 9 or 9:30am (often 10am) to 6 or 7pm without a break for lunch. Some shops, particularly those operated by foreigners, open at 8am and close at 8 or 9pm. In some small stores the lunch break can last 3 hours, beginning at 1pm.

Cameras/Film   See "Photographic Needs," below.

Car Rentals   See "Getting Around," earlier in this chapter.

Climate   See "When to Go" in Chapter 2.

Currency   See "Visitor Information & Entry Requirements" in Chapter 2.

Currency Exchange   For the best exchange rate, cash your traveler's checks at banks or foreign-exchange offices, not at shops and hotels. Most post offices will also change traveler's checks or convert currency, and Paris's airports and train stations are equipped with currency-exchange desks. Every foreign-exchange office seems to have its own rate—and the differences can be dramatic. Some with a better exchange rate end up charging more because of a higher service fee. Obviously, the more money you're exchanging, the better it is to get a high rate and pay a single service fee.

One of the most central currency-exchange branches in Paris is at 103 av. des Champs-Elysées, 8e (☎ 01-42-25-93-33; Métro: George-V). It's open Monday to Friday from 9am to 5pm and on Saturday and Sunday from 10:30am to 6pm. A small commission is charged.

Another conveniently positioned moneychanger considers its favorable rates an incentive for visitors to purchase its other products, which include an array of guided tours through Paris and nearby regions of France. Paris Vision, 214 rue de Rivoli, 1er (☎ 01-42-86-09-33; Métro Tuileries), a travel agency, also maintains a mini-banque that performs currency exchanges. It's open daily from 9am to 2:30pm and 3:30 to 6pm, and provides exchange rates that are only a fraction less favorable than those offered for very large blocks of money as listed by the Paris stock exchange.

Dentists   If a toothache strikes you at night or in the early hours of the morning (and doesn't it always?), telephone 01-43-37-51-00 anytime from 8am to 11:40pm daily. You can also call or visit the American Hospital, 63 bd. Victor-Hugo, Neuilly (☎ 01-46-41-25-41, Métro: Pont-de-Levallois or Pont-de-Neuilly; Bus: 82). A bilingual (English-French) dental clinic is on the premises.

Doctors   Some large hotels have a doctor attached to their staff. If yours doesn't, we recommend the American Hospital, 63 bd. Victor-Hugo, Neuilly (☎ 01-46-41-25-41; Métro: Pont-de-Levallois or Pont-de-Neuilly; Bus: 82). The emergency room is open 24 hours daily with 43 outpatient and inpatient specialists housed under one roof.

Documents Required   See "Visitor Information & Entry Requirements" in Chapter 2.

Driving Rules   See "Getting Around," earlier in this chapter.

Drug Laws   A word of warning: Penalties for illegal drug possession in France are more severe than those in the United States or Canada. You could go to jail or be deported immediately. By law, the police can stop you and search you at will. *Caveat:* Drug pushers often turn in their customers to the police.

Drugstores   Go to the nearest *pharmacie*. If you need a prescription during off-hours, have your concierge get in touch with the nearest commissariat de police.

An agent there will have the address of a nearby pharmacy open 24 hours a day. French law requires that the pharmacies in any given neighborhood designate which one will remain open all night. The address of the one that will stay open for that particular week will be prominently displayed in the windows of all other drugstores. One of the most centrally located pharmacies is 24-hour Pharmacy "les Champs," 84 av. des Champs-Elysées, 8e (☎ 01-45-62-02-41; Métro: George-V).

Electricity   In general, expect 200 volts, 50 cycles, although you'll encounter 110 and 115 volts in some older establishments. Adapters are needed to fit the sockets. Many hotels have two-pin (in some cases, three-pin) sockets for electric razors. It's best to ask at your hotel before plugging in any electric appliance.

Embassies/Consulates   If you lose your passport or have some such emergency, the consulate can usually handle your individual needs. (An embassy is more often concerned with matters of state between France and the home country represented.) Hours and offices of the various foreign embassies and consulates follow:

The embassy of the **United States,** 2 av. Gabriel, 75008 Paris (☎ **01-43-12-22-22**), is open Monday to Friday from 9am to 6pm. Passports are issued at its consulate at 2 rue St-Florentine (☎ 01-42-96-12-02, ext. 2531; Métro: Concorde), which is situated off the northeast section of place de la Concorde. To get a passport replaced costs $55. In addition to its embassy and consulate in Paris, the United States also maintains the following consulates: 22 cours du Maréchal Foch, 33080 Bordeaux (☎ 01-56-52-65-95); 12 bd. Paul-Peytral, 13286 Marseille (☎ 01-91-54-92-00); and 15 av. d'Alsace, 67082 Strasbourg (☎ 01-88-35-31-04).

The embassy of **Canada** is at 35 av. Montaigne, 75008 Paris (☎ **01-47-23-01-01;** Métro: F-D-Roosevelt or Alma-Marceau), open Monday to Friday from 9am to noon and 2 to 5pm. The Canadian consulate is located at the embassy.

The embassy of the **United Kingdom** is at 35 rue du Faubourg St-Honoré, 75383 Paris (☎ **01-42-66-91-42;** Métro: Concorde or Madeleine), open Monday to Friday from 9:30am to 1pm and 2:30 to 6pm. The British consulate is at 35 rue du Faubourg St-Honoré (☎ 01-44-51-31-00; Métro: Concorde or Madeleine); it's open Monday to Friday from 9:30am to 12:30pm and 2:30 to 5pm.

The embassy of **Australia** is at 4 rue Jean-Rey, 75015 Paris (☎ **01-45-59-33-00;** Métro: Bir-Hakeim), open Monday to Friday from 9am to 1pm and 2:30 to 5:30pm.

Emergencies   For the **police,** call 17; to **report a fire,** 18. For an **ambulance,** call the fire department at 01-45-78-74-52; a fire vehicle rushes patients to the nearest emergency room. For S.A.M.U., an independently operated, privately owned ambulance company, call 15. If you need a **doctor,** call SOS Médecins (☎ 01-63-77-77-77). For non-emergency situations, you can reach the police at 9 bd. du Palais, 4e (☎ 01-53-71-53-71 or 01-53-73-53-73; Métro: Cité).

Eyeglasses   Lissac Brothers (Frères Lissac) is one of the city's largest chains, with at least 14 branches in greater Paris. On the Right Bank, go to 114 rue de Rivoli, 1e (☎ 01-42-33-44-77; Métro: Châtelet), and on the Left, to 207 bd. St-Germain, 7e (☎ 01-45-48-16-76; Métro: Rue-du-Bac). There's a surcharge for same-day service. Always carry an extra pair.

Hairdressers/Barbers   In France they're known as *coiffeurs,* and enormous emphasis is placed on their talents. One of the most famous is Alexandre de Paris, 3 av. Matignon, 8e (☎ 01-42-25-57-90; Métro: F-D-Roosevelt). Everybody from royalty to French film stars comes here for that elegant look. Always call for an appointment at least a day in advance. If you're a woman, count on spending

150 F ($30) and up for a cut, 60 F ($12) for a shampoo, and 300 to 1,000 F ($60 to $200) for coloring. Men pay 310 F ($62) for a cut and shampoo. Much more popular and more avant-garde is Mod's Hair, 24 rue St-Denis, 1er (☎ 01-42-33-61-36; Métro: Châtelet). The team of 20 services many clients from the nearby garment district—a crowd who knows and appreciates the nuances of fashion. A shampoo, haircut, and blow-drys will cost 178 F ($35.60) for men, 290 F ($58) for women, with a 20% discount offered to students. An advance appointment is recommended.

Holidays   See "When to Go" in Chapter 2.

Hospitals   The American Hospital, 63 bd. Victor-Hugo, Neuilly (☎ 01-46-41-27-37), operates 24-hour emergency service. There's a direct line to its **emergency service** (☎ **01-47-47-70-15;** Métro: Pont-de-Levallois or Pont-de-Neuilly; Bus: 82).

Information   See "Visitor Information & Entry Requirements" in Chapter 2.

Language   In the wake of two world wars and many shared experiences, not to mention the influence of English-language movies, TV, and records, the English language has made major inroads and is almost a second language in some parts of Paris. An American trying to speak French might even be understood. The world's best-selling phrase books are published by Berlitz—*French for Travellers* has everything you'll need.

Laundry/Dry Cleaning   Ask at your hotel for the nearest laundry or dry-cleaning establishment—they appear in virtually every neighborhood. Expensive hotels provide this service, but it's expensive. Instead, consult the yellow pages under *laveries automatiques.* For dry cleaning, look under *nettoyage à sec.* If you're staying in the Latin Quarter, take your clothes for machine washing, dry cleaning, or pressing to Pressing des Ecoles, 34 rue des Ecoles, 5e (☎ 01-46-33-47-13; Métro: Maubert-Mutualité), open Monday to Saturday from 8:30am to 7:30pm. If you drop them off in the morning, most normal washloads can be retrieved that evening.

Libraries   There are many. The American Library, 10 rue du Général-Camou, 7e (☎ 01-45-51-46-82; Métro: Alma-Marceau), founded in 1920 as a nonprofit membership library, allows nonmembers to read for 70 F ($14) per day. It's open Tuesday to Saturday from 10am to 7pm. The Bibliothèque Publique Information, Centre Pompidou, place Georges-Pompidou, 4e (☎ 01-44-78-12-33; Métro: Rambuteau), has books in English. There are also records, videos, CDs, a software library, and a data-base service. You can read on the premises but can't check out books. It's open Monday and Wednesday to Friday from noon to 10pm and on Saturday and Sunday from 10am to 10pm; closed Tuesday.

Legal Aid   This may be hard to come by in Paris. The French government advises foreigners to consult their embassy or consulate (see "Embassies/Consulates," above) in case of a dire emergency, such as an arrest. Even if a consulate or embassy declines to offer financial or legal help, the staff will generally offer advice as to how you can obtain help locally. For example, they can furnish a list of attorneys who might represent you. Most visitor arrests are for illegal possession of drugs, and the U.S. embassy and consular officials cannot interfere with the French judicial system in any way on your behalf. A consulate can only advise you of your rights.

Liquor Laws   Visitors will find it easier to get a drink—wine, beer, or other spirits—in France than in England or some other countries. Supermarkets, grocery stores, and cafés all sell alcoholic beverages. The legal drinking age is 16, but those under that age can be served an alcoholic drink in a bar or restaurant if accompanied by a parent or legal guardian. Wine and liquor are sold every day of the week, all year round.

Café hours vary throughout the country and with local restrictions. Some open at 6am, serving drinks until 3am; others are open 24 hours a day. Bars and nightclubs may stay open as they wish.

The Breathalyzer test is in use in France, and a motorist is considered "legally intoxicated" with 0.8 grams of alcohol per liter of blood (the more liberal U.S. law is 1 gram per liter.) If convicted, a motorist faces a stiff fine and a possible prison term of 2 months to 2 years. If bodily injury results from a drunk-driving incident, the judge might throw the book at a convicted offender.

Lost Property   Frankly, there isn't much chance of retrieving lost property in Paris. Go to (don't call) the Bureau des Objets Trouvés, 36 rue des Morillons, 15e (☎ 01-55-76-20-20; Métro: Convention), open Monday to Friday from 8:30am to 6pm.

Luggage Storage/Lockers   Your best bet is your hotel, especially if you plan to return to Paris after a tour of the provinces. Otherwise try the *consignes* at the railroad stations.

Mail   Most post offices in Paris are open Monday to Friday from 8am to 7pm and on Saturday from 8am to noon. Allow 5 to 8 days to send or receive mail from your home. To send an *aerogramme* to the United States or Canada costs 4.30 F (85¢). To send a letter weighing 40 grams (about an ounce) costs 7.90 F ($1.60). A postcard to the U.S. or Canada is 4.30 F (85¢). Letters to the U.K. cost 2.80 F (55¢) for up to 20 grams.

If you don't have a hotel address in Paris, you can receive mail 5 American Express (see above). However, you may be asked to show an American Express card or traveler's check when you go to pick up your mail.

Another option is to have your mail sent *poste restante* (general delivery) in care of the major post office in whatever town you plan to visit. You'll need to produce a passport to pick up mail, and you may be charged a small fee for the service. The poste restante system works within any post office in France. In Paris, however, it's important to specifiy the arrondissement no. you want the mail directed to. You can also exchange money at post offices.

Many hotels sell stamps.

Maps   See "Getting Around," earlier in this chapter.

Medical Emergencies   If you're ill and need medicine at night or on Sunday, the local commissariat de police will tell you the location of the nearest drugstore that's open or the address of the nearest doctor on duty. The police or fire department will also summon an ambulance if you need to be rushed to a hospital. Seek assistance first at your hotel desk if language is a problem. Or call the **emergency services** department at the American Hospital (☎ **01-47-47-70-15**) (see "Hospitals," above).

Money   See "Money" in Chapter 2.

Newspapers/Magazines   English-language newspapers are available at nearly every kiosk (newsstand) in Paris. Published Monday through Saturday, the *International Herald Tribune* is the most popular paper with visiting Americans and Canadians. Kiosks are generally open daily from 8am to 9pm.

Pets   If you have certificates from a vet and proof of antirabies vaccination, you can bring most house pets into France.

Photographic Needs   All types of film are available in Paris at fairly modest prices. Ask at your hotel for the nearest camera shop.

Police   Call 17 for emergencies. Most problems are handled by the police precinct of the arrondissement in which a crime or conflict occurs. Anyone will direct you to the nearest *préfet de police,* although a good place to begin gathering information for whatever problem you need solved is at the most central of them all, the préfet of the 4th arrondissement, place Baudoyer, 4e (☎ **01-53-71-53-71;** Métro: Hôtel-de-Ville).

Post Office   The main post office (PTT) for Paris is the Bureau de Poste, 52 rue du Louvre, 75001 Paris (☎ 01-40-28-20-00; Métro: Louvre). Your mail can be sent here *poste restante* (general delivery) for a small fee. Take an ID, such as a passport, if you plan to pick up mail. It's open daily from 8am to 7pm for most services, 24 hours a day for telegrams and phone calls. Stamps can also usually be purchased at your hotel reception desk and at *café-tabacs* (tobacconists).

Radio/TV   The major TV channels in France are France 2 (also known as FR2), TF1, FR3, Canal+ (accessed by switching to "4" on the TV set), ARTE (French/German—many programs are in German with French subtitles), and M6. Though most programming is obviously in French, after a day of sightseeing you might be able to catch a foreign film late at night in English with French subtitles. In the summer months the domestic radio France-Inter broadcasts daily news and important traffic conditions in English, usually at 8am and 1 and 7pm. Short- or medium-wave radios allow you to tune in to BBC programs.

Rest Rooms   If you're in dire need, duck into a café or brasserie to use the lavatory; it's customary to make some small purchase if you do so. Paris Métro stations and underground garages usually have public lavatories, but the degree of cleanliness varies. France still has many "hole-in-the-ground" toilets, so be forewarned.

Safety   In Paris, be especially aware of child pickpockets. They roam the French capital, preying on tourists around attractions such as the Louvre, Eiffel Tower, and Notre-Dame, and they also often strike in the Métro, sometimes blocking a victim off from the escalator. A band of these young thieves can clean your pockets even while you try to fend them off. Their method is to get very close to a target, ask for a handout (sometimes), and deftly help themselves to your money or passport.

As in every world metropolis in the 1990s, public safety is more and more on people's minds, and the general perception in Paris is that urban life is increasingly dangerous. Although public safety concerns are not as prevalent in Paris as they are in such cities as Los Angeles and New York, concerns are growing. Robbery at gun or knife-point is not common, but it's definitely not unheard of either. Be careful.

Shoe Repairs   Ask at your hotel for a nearby repair shop or try Central Crepins, 48 rue de Turbigo, 3e (☎ 01-42-72-68-64; Métro: Arts-et-Métiers), which performs at least some of its sewing by hand and does very competent repair work. It's open Monday to Friday from 8am to 2:30pm and 3:30 to 7pm and on Saturday from 8am to 1pm. Or try La Cordonnerie Pulin, 5 rue Chauveau-LaGarde, 8e (☎ 01-42-65-08-57; Métro: Madeleine), open Monday to Saturday from 9am to 7pm.

Taxes   Watch it: You could get burned. As a member of the European Union, France routinely imposes a value-added tax (VAT) on many goods and services. This standard VAT on merchandise is 20.6%, and is applied to clothing, appliances, liquor, leather goods, shoes, furs, jewelry, perfumes, cameras, and even caviar.

Refunds on certain goods and merchandise are made—but not on services. The minimum purchase is 2,000 F ($400) in the same store for nationals or residents of countries outside the European Union.

To get a refund, ask the store you purchased from for a completed VAT form and a stamped, self-addressed envelope. The cashier will ask you how you wish to be refunded: (1) in cash at the airport (international airports in France only, where the bank handling the refund is close to the Customs desk), (2) by crediting your credit/charge card, (3) by bank transfer, or (4) by check in French francs.

When exiting the country, for example, at the airport you must go to the Detaxe TVA/VAT refund counter with the merchandise you purchased to get the form stamped by a Customs official. The Customs officer can ask to see the merchandise as proof that you're taking it out of the country. After getting stamped, one copy of the form stays with Customs, one is for you, and the third should be immediately mailed back to the store (there's a mailbox at the Customs counter). After filing with the government, the store will then mail a check in francs to the buyer (unless a different method of payment was specified).

If the store accepts credit/charge cards, we recommend that you ask that the refund be credited to your card. Otherwise, ask the store to indicate that you wish to receive a cash refund at the airport—a U.S. bank usually charges a $10 to $15 fee to process a French check or bank transfer.

Taxis   See "Getting Around," earlier in this chapter.

Telegrams/Telex/Fax   Since the late 1980s virtually every hotel in Paris has maintained its own **fax** line, and will probably consider sending your faxes as part of its normal services, though you'll be charged a small fee (the price of the fax transmission plus a modest surcharge). **Telegrams** may be sent from any Paris post office during the day (see "Post Office," above) and anytime from the 24-hour central post office. In sending telegrams, you're charged for each word in the address as well as for each word in the message. There are no discounts for exceeding a certain number of words, but telegrams sent during the night usually cost a bit less.

The 24-hour **telex and telegram office** in Paris is at 103 rue de Grenelle, 7e (☎ 01-42-60-34-34; Métro: Rue-du-Bac or Invalides). You can dictate a telex or telegram by phone, in English or in French, by dialing toll free (within the borders of France only) 01-05-33-44-11 for messages being sent within France or 01-05-33-36-55 for messages destined for other countries. Although the cost of the phone call to either number is free, the charges for the message you send will be billed directly to whatever phone you're calling from, and not all phones will accept the charges. If for whatever reason the phone you're using is blocked from accepting charges, you can always send telex, telegram, and fax messages from the main post office of each arrondissement of Paris.

Telephone   Public **phone booths** are found in cafés, restaurants, Métro stations, post offices, airports, train stations, and occasionally on the streets. Finding a coin-operated telephone in France may be an arduous task. A simpler and more widely accepted method of payment is the *télécarte,* a prepaid calling card. These debit cards are priced at 40 and 80 F ($8 and $19.20) for 50 and 120 *unités,* respectively. A local call costs 1 *unité,* which provides you with 6 to 18 minutes of conversation depending on the rate (and where you're calling). *Télécartes* are available at most post offices and Métro stations.

If possible, avoid making calls from your hotel, which might double or triple the charges.

For **information,** dial 12.

When you're calling **long distance within France,** pick up the receiver, wait for the dial tone, and them dial the 10-digit number of the person or place you're calling. Use of the prefix "16," formerly an essential part of dialing long distance within France, is no longer valid.

To make an **international call** to the United States or Canada, first dial 19, listen for the tone, then slowly dial 1, the area code, and the seven-digit number. To place a collect call to North America, dial 01-19-33-11 and an English-speaking operator will assist you. Dial 01-19-00-11 for an American AT&T operator.

Television   See "Radio/TV," above.

Time   French summer time lasts from around April to September, and clocks are set 1 hour ahead of French winter time. Depending on the time of year, France is 6 or 7 hours ahead of eastern standard time in the United States.

Tipping   Tipping is practiced with flourish and style in France, and, as a visitor, you're expected to play the game. All bills, as required by law, show *service compris,* which means that the tip is included; customary practices of additional gratuities are as follows:

Cloakroom attendants: Often the price is posted; if not, give them 5 F ($1).

Guides: In museums, guides expect 5 to 10 F ($1 to $2).

Hairdressers: The service charge is most often included; otherwise, tip at least 15%, more in swankier places.

Hotels: The service charge is added, but tip the bellboy extra—6 to 10 F ($1.20 to $2) per bag (more in deluxe and first-class hotels). A lot depends on how much luggage he has carried and the class of the establishment. Tip the concierge based entirely on how many requests you've made. Give the maid about 20 F ($4) if you've stayed for 3 or more days. The doorman who summons a cab expects another 6 F ($1.20), likewise your room-service waiter, even though you've already been hit for 15% service. Most small services around the hotel should be rewarded with a 5-F ($1) tip.

Porters: Usually a fixed fee is assessed, about 5 to 10 F ($1 to $2) per piece of luggage. You're not obligated to give more; however, many French people do, ranging from 1 to 2 F (20¢ to 40¢).

Theater ushers: Give at least 2 F (40¢) for seating up to two persons.

Waiters: In restaurants, cafés, and nightclubs, service is included; however, it's customary to leave something extra, especially in first-class and deluxe establishments, where 10% to 12% extra is often the rule. In inexpensive places, 8% to 10% will suffice.

Toilets   See "Rest Rooms," above.

Transit Information   For information on the city's public transportation, stop in at the office of the Services Touristiques de la RATP at 55 quai des Grands-Augustins, 6e (☎ 01-44-68-20-20; Métro: St-Michel). For recorded information, in French, about stoppages, subway or bus breakdowns, or exceptionally heavy traffic on any particular bus or Métro line, call 01-43-46-14-14.

Useful Telephone Numbers   Police, 17; fire, 18; emergency medical assistance, 15.

Visas   See "Visitor Information & Entry Requirements" in Chapter 2.

Water   The drinking water is generally safe, although it has been known to cause diarrhea in some unaccustomed stomachs. If you ask for water in a restaurant it will be bottled water (for which you'll pay) unless you specifically request tap water (*l'eau du robinet*).

Weather   Call 01-36-68-00-75.

Yellow Pages   As in North America, the yellow pages are immensely useful. Your hotel will almost certainly have a copy, but you'll need the help of a French-speaking resident before tackling the French Telephone Company's (PTT's) yellow pages.

Some words aren't too different from the English. *Pharmacie* (pharmacy), *antiquités* (antiques), *théâtres* (theaters), and *objets d'art* may be easy to decipher. But other words, such as *cordonniers* (shoemakers and shoe-repair shops) and *horlogerie* (watch-repair shop), might be less obvious. Ask someone at the reception desk of your hotel for translations if needed.

Don't ever assume that someone on the other end of the phone speaks English. You may have to ask a French-speaking person to make the call for you.

4 Accommodations

In 1996 it was estimated (no one really knows for sure) that Paris had some 2,000 hotels—a total of some 80,000 bedrooms—spread across 20 arrondissements. These range from palaces with belle époque interiors to dives so seedy that the late George Orwell, author of *Down and Out in Paris and London,* wouldn't even have considered checking in. (Of course, none of those are in this guide!)

Though there are so many hotels in Paris, it isn't always easy to get a room. In fact, while there used to be a hotel "low season" during the cold, rainy period from November to February, when tourism slowed and rooms were plentiful, nowadays hotels can be completely packed in those months. If there's a low season at all, it might be in July and August, which is the "peak" season throughout most of Europe. Parisians are likely to be away on vacation at that time, and trade fair and convention people are wherever that crowd goes in summer. This leaves far more empty rooms waiting in the heat of a Paris summer.

We've tried to focus our 1997 recommendations mainly on central Paris, touching only very lightly on the outlying arrondissements, the 10th to the 15th and the 18th to the 20th. (As for the 20th, few would want to stay there.) These outer districts may be too far removed from the central action of Paris to attract the average visitor, but some do relish the opportunity to stay in a hotel off the beaten track in areas that are not usually frequented by tourists. As one reader writes, "Every year I go to Paris, and every year I seek out a neighborhood in some relatively unknown district. To me, this is the true joy of discovering Paris." You will need to decide what type of neighborhood you want to be based in, keeping in mind that your choice of hotel in Paris can greatly influence the perspective you get on the city.

Not only must you make a decision about lodging in central Paris or an outlying district, you must also answer the Right Bank or Left Bank hotel question.

If you have to have chic surroundings, choose a Right Bank hotel. That puts you close to all the most elegant shops—Dior, Cardin, Saint-Laurent—and within walking distance of such important sights as the Arc de Triomphe, place de la Concorde, the Tuileries Gardens, and the Louvre. And for relaxing after sightseeing during the day or for an apéritif at night, you have all the glittering cafés along the Champs-Elysées.

The best Right Bank hotels are in the 8th arrondissement (home of the Arc de Triomphe), and many first-class ones are found in the 16th (near the Trocadéro and Bois du Boulogne) and 17th arrondissements (near the Palais des Congrès). If you'd like to be near place Vendôme, then try for a hotel in the 1st arrondissement.

Other Right Bank hotel sections include the increasingly fashionable Marais and Bastille districts, comprising the 3rd and 4th arrondissements, and Les Halles/Beaubourg, mainly in the 3rd arrondissement, which is the home of the Centre Pompidou and Les Halles shopping mall, site of the former marketplace of Paris.

If you want more informality, more local flavor, and more bohemian surroundings, then head for the Left Bank, where prices are traditionally lower. Hotels here are mainly in the 5th and 6th arrondissements, which is the area of the Sorbonne, café life, and bookstores. Many hotels in this district cater to students. The 7th arrondissement provides a touch of the avant-garde lifestyle of St-Germain.

The 1990s have seen major changes in hotels in Paris. More and more have been upgraded. Old-fashioned charm—or at least an attempt at it—characterizes many of the newer hotels, which have turned their back on the sterility and unfortunate architectural and design trends of the 1960s and 1970s.

Since the hot weather doesn't last long in Paris, most hotels, except the deluxe ones, don't provide air-conditioning. If you're trapped in a Paris garret on a hot summer night, you'll have to sweat it out. You can always open your window to get some fresh cooler air, but then you'll encounter a major nuisance plaguing many hotels: noise pollution. To try to avoid this, you may wish to request a room in the back when making a reservation.

While in Paris, you may often be prompted to wonder, "When is a hotel not a hotel?" The answer is when it's another kind of building. The word *hôtel* in French has several meanings. It means a lodging, of course, but it also means a large mansion or town house, such as the Hôtel des Invalides, once a home for disabled soldiers, now the most important military museum in the world. *Hôtel de ville* means town hall; *hôtel des postes* refers to the general post office; and *hôtel-dieu* is a hospital. So be warned.

It's important to remember that the last two numbers of the postal code indicate the arrondissement. For example, a postal code of 75008 Paris means that the hotel lies in the 8th arrondissement; 75005 indicates that the hotel is in the 5th arrondissement. These can also be represented as 8e and 5e, respectively.

Hotel breakfasts are fairly uniform and include your choice of coffee, tea, or chocolate, a freshly baked croissant and roll, plus limited quantities of butter and jam or jelly. It can be at your door moments after you call for it, and can be served at almost any hour requested. When a breakfast charge is given for an individual listing, it's always a continental breakfast. Breakfasts with eggs, bacon, ham, or other items will have to be ordered from the à la carte menu. For a charge, larger hotels serve the full breakfast—called "English breakfast"—but smaller hotels typically serve only the continental variety.

PRICE CATEGORIES

Classifying Paris hotels by price is a long day's journey into madness. For example, it's possible many times to find a moderately priced room in an otherwise "very expensive" hotel or an "expensive" room in an otherwise "inexpensive" property. That's because most hotel rooms—at least in the older properties—are not standardized; therefore, the range of rooms goes from super-deluxe suites to the "maid's pantry," now converted into a small bedroom. At some hotels, in fact, you'll find rooms that are **moderate, expensive,** and **very expensive,** all under one roof.

The following price categories are only for a quick general reference. When we've classified a hotel as "moderate," it means that the *average* room is moderately priced—not necessarily *all* the rooms. It should also be noted that Paris is one of the most expensive cities in the world for hotels. Therefore, what might be viewed as expensive in your hometown could very likely be classified as inexpensive in Paris.

In general (and don't hold us to this), hotels rated "very expensive" in this guide charge from a low of 2,000 F ($400) for a double room to a high of 4,500 F ($900)—and far beyond that for suites. Doubles in "expensive" hotels might begin at 1,155 F ($231) and go up to 2,400 F ($480), the latter only for their most select rooms, which would push them into the "very expensive" category. Hotels considered "moderate" have doubles beginning at around 600 F ($120) and climbing all the way up to 1,600 F ($320), into the expensive category. At "inexpensive" hotels, doubles begin at 450 F ($90) and climb fast to 1,000 F ($200). But be warned: Even in some of these "inexpensive" hotels a room or two—obviously the best they've got—might cost as much as 700 F ($140), which would make them "moderate," not "inexpensive," at least by the standards of Paris hotel pricing.

1 Best Bets

- **Best for the Business Traveler:** Businesspeople from all over the world converge at **Le Grand Hôtel Inter-Continental,** 2 rue Scribe, 9e (☎ **01-40-07-32-32**), a grand monument ordered built by Napoléon III in the 1860s. The best hotel business center in Paris is here, and you can always take a client to the Café de la Paix for a drink.
- **Best for Families:** One of the best hotels of the Novotel chain, the **Novotel Paris Les Halles,** place Marguerite-de-Navarre, 1er (☎ **01-42-21-31-31**), is also the most family-friendly hotel in Paris. All rooms are arranged to accommodate families. The breakfast buffet is one of the most generous in the town, and kids delight in the fountains and the carousel at the nearby Forum des Halles.
- **Best for Value:** Near the Champs-Elysées (but not that close), the **Résidence Lord-Byron,** 5 rue de Chateaubriand, 8e (☎ **01-43-59-89-98**), is a classy little gem that's far from opulent, but is clean, comfortable, and a good buy. Unlike so many of the grander places surrounding it in the 8th, it's totally lacking in pretension.
- **Best Location:** A chic, elegant 17th-century mansion, **Le Pavillon de la Reine,** 28 place des Vosges, 3e (☎ **01-42-77-96-40**), not only has a garden courtyard, but also opens onto the most harmonious and beautiful square of Paris, place des Vosges, of Victor Hugo fame.
- **Best View:** In the small **Hôtel Le Colbert,** 7 rue de l'Hôtel-Colbert, 5e (☎ **01-43-25-85-65**), a private home of the 18th century, you can take in the view of Notre-Dame while ordering breakfast in bed. Not the most luxurious accommodations in Paris, Le Colbert is still one of our favorite secrets.
- **Best for Nostalgia:** Offering the most panoramic views of the Seine and the Tuileries of any hotel in Paris, the **Hôtel du Quai Voltaire,** 19 quai Voltaire, 7e (☎ **01-42-61-50-91**), is a venerated old inn that was once frequented by the likes of Oscar Wilde, Richard Wagner, Jean Sibelius, and Charles-Pierre Baudelaire.
- **Best for Prestige:** Those California tycoons, legendary stars, and platinum mistresses of yesterday—Douglas Fairbanks and Mary Pickford, William Randolph Hearst and Marion Davies—knew where to stay back then. Tom Cruise and his ilk know it's still true today. The **Hôtel de Crillon,** 10 place de la Concorde, 8e (☎ **01-44-71-15-00**), is *the* address of Paris. If you want its grandest suite and have a taste for the macabre, ask for the Marie Antoinette Apartment; it exhibits

classic Antoinette-style elegance, and its namesake was beheaded practically at the doorstep of this deluxe citadel.

- **Best for Discretion:** If you're not a splashy Hôtel de Crillon type, yet still crave luxury and elegance, then follow in the footsteps of Lauren Bacall and Raquel Welch to a fashionable town house filled with antiques and paintings: the **Hôtel San Régis,** 12 rue Jean-Goujon, 8e (☎ 01-44-95-16-16). What you do here is your own affair, provided you don't advertise it.
- **Best for Opulence: Le Ritz,** 15 place Vendôme, 1er (☎ 01-43-16-30-30), has been a center of wealth, luxury and decadence since it was opened by César Ritz in 1898. Barbara Hutton, Coco Chanel, and Marcel Proust are just a few names from its glorious guest list of yesteryear. Join the parade of oil-rich Saudi princes, divas from Milan, and movie stars.
- **Best Unknown Hotel in Paris:** Constructed in 1913 and long in a seedy state, the fully restored **Terrass Hôtel,** 12–14 rue Joseph-de-Maistre, 18e (☎ 01-46-06-72-85), is now the only four-star choice in Montmartre, an area not known for its luxury accommodations. Its rooms take in far-ranging views: the Tour Eiffel, the Arc de Triomphe, the Paris Opéra. You can even go over to the nearby Cimetière de Montmartre to pay your respects to yesterday's legends: Degas, Zola, Stendhal, Dumas, and Fragonard.
- **Best Historic Hotel:** The **Hôtel Meurice,** 228 rue de Rivoli, 1er (☎ 01-44-58-10-10), has housed everyone from Dalí to the German commanders of Paris during World War II. Few contenders can match its 18th-century authenticity.

---

⑨ Budget Bests

Since Paris hotels are so expensive, we've decided to highlight our favorite budget finds here. Of course you can't expect Ritz-level trappings, but these places are great for those looking to save money.

The **Hôtel des Deux Acacias,** 28 rue de l'Arc de Triomphe, 75017 Paris (☎ 01-43-80-01-85; fax 01-40-53-94-62; Métro: Charles-de-Gaulle/Etoile), is named after two gnarled acacia trees sprouting from its garden and rents 50 rooms with bath, TV, and phone. Built circa 1905, the building was modernized in 1991. Some vestiges (travertine floors, hardwood paneling) of its belle époque grandeur still remain, though most of what you'll see has been streamlined and simplified. The rates are 310 to 350 F ($62 to $70) double. MC, V.

A four-story two-star walkup, the **Hôtel Navarin et d'Angleterre,** 8 rue Navarin, 75009 Paris (☎ 01-48-78-31-80; fax 01-48-74-14-09; Métro: St-Georges or Notre-Dame-de-Lorette), is managed by the charming Maylin family. Each of the 26 rooms is unique (24 with bath, 2 with toilet only). In summer, breakfast is served in a small garden with an acacia tree and fountain. The rooms were modernized in 1995, but the sitting room and lounge still radiate a *fin-de-siècle* atmosphere. Rates are 250 F ($50) double with toilet only and 340 F ($68) double with bath. MC, V.

North of the grand monuments of central Paris, the **Hôtel de Parme,** 61 rue de Clichy, 75009 Paris (☎ 01-48-74-40-41; fax 01-53-21-91-84; Métro: Place-Clichy, Trinité, or Liège), has a kindly English-speaking manager on site, M. Cornilleau, and 36 cheerfully decorated rooms (16 with bath, 11 with shower only). Because of its location away from the usual tourist traffic, it often has vacancies when other hotels are booked. Rates are 180 F ($36) double without bath, 230 F ($46) double with shower only, and 250 to 280 F ($50 to $56) double with bath. MC, V.

- **Best for a Romantic Getaway:** Until the 1970s **L'Hôtel,** 13 rue des Beaux-Arts, 6e (☎ **01-44-41-99-00**), was a run-down fleabag for drunks and addicts. Millions of francs' worth of renovations later, rooms that once were cramped and claustrophobic are now ravishingly romantic, outfitted like small jewelboxes of the decorator's art.
- **Best Trendy Hotel:** The **Hôtel Montalembert,** 3 rue de Montalembert, 7e (☎ **01-45-49-68-68**), has an impeccable pedigree: France's leading architectural designers enhanced an already illustrious frame into one of the most stylish hotel venues of Paris's Left Bank. An upscale but offbeat gem, it boasts rooms with individualized decors that range from conservative French Empire style to Bauhaus and postmodern.
- **Best Moderately Priced Hotel:** Set in one of the most evocative neighborhoods of Old Paris, the Ile St-Louis, the **Hôtel de Lutèce,** 65 rue St-Louis-en-l'Ile, 4e (☎ **01-43-26-23-52**), resembles a Breton country house, despite its continued refusal to raise its prices. Its tasteful bedrooms, decorated with antiques and fine reproductions, provide the visitor affordable elegance.
- **Best Service:** Although no Parisian can fault the **George V,** 31 av. George-V, 8e (☎ **01-47-23-54-00**), for its flawless decor, the billionaires check in because of the sophisticated, laissez-faire indulgence of the jaded but ever-so-polite staff. Nestled in an upscale neighborhood between the Seine and the Champs-Elysées, the George V offers service that is, quite simply, impeccable.

2 On the Right Bank

We'll begin with the most centrally located arrondissements on the Right Bank, then work our way through the more outlying neighborhoods.

1ST ARRONDISSEMENT (LOUVRE / LES HALLES)
VERY EXPENSIVE

Hôtel Lotti. 7–9 rue de Castiglione, 75001 Paris. ☎ **01-42-60-37-34,** or 800/221-2626 in the U.S., 800/237-0319 in Canada, 800/282729 in the U.K. Fax 01-40-15-93-56. 127 rms, 6 suites. A/C MINIBAR TV TEL. 1,900–2,600 F ($380–$520) double; 4,900 F ($980) junior suite; 6,500 F ($1,300) suite. AE, DC, MC, V. Parking 160 F ($32). Métro: Opéra or Tuileries.

Would you believe that the oldest luxury property in Paris is perennially maintained as state-of-the-art? The classic seven-story structure occupied by the Hôtel Lotti is a grand 19th-century building. With elegant trappings of marble, gilt, tapestries, and crystal, this hotel has sometimes been compared to the Ritz, although the Lotti is much smaller; it lacks the pretension but not the grandeur. The staff is dignified and attentive. The accommodations have the ambience of a 19th-century Paris town house; they're outfitted with rosewood, mahogany, tambour desks, and damask. Top-story attic rooms with their sloping ceilings have a certain idiosyncratic charm and are reserved for nonsmokers. Since the early 1980s the Lotti has been administered by Jolly Hotels, a well-known chain based in Italy.

Dining/Entertainment: Le Lotti may not offer the most innovative cuisine, but the hotel restaurant is still distinguished as one of the best in town. Its admirably accurate cooking features fragrant, feather-light sauces.

Services: Room service, laundry, baby-sitting.

Hôtel Meurice. 228 rue de Rivoli, 75001 Paris. ☎ **01-44-58-10-10,** or 800/325-3535 in the U.S. and Canada. Fax 01-44-58-10-15. 152 rms, 28 suites. A/C MINIBAR TV TEL. 2,550–3,650 F ($510–$730) double; 5,000–8,000 F ($1,000–$1,600) suite. For stays of 2 or more nights (including breakfast): 2,300 F ($460) double. AE, DC, MC, V. Parking 100 F ($20). Métro: Tuileries or Concorde.

The Meurice envelops guests in its 18th-century French aura. Its gilded salons were copied from those in the château at Versailles, complete with monumental crystal chandeliers, ornate tapestries, and furnishings from the periods of Louis XIV, XV, and XVI. Built in 1907, the hotel is just off rue de Rivoli and the Tuileries Gardens and within walking distance of the Louvre (you can see the museum from the upper floors). The lounge has a circular "star"-studded ceiling. In its category, it's not as elegant or grand as the Ritz, but we still find it far superior to the fading Inter-Continental, and even like it better than the Lotti, which we also recommend. The staff is slightly haughty, but this is Paris, after all.

Soundproof windows effectively keep out noise from the street; however, the voices from adjacent rooms are still as audible as the cantankerous plumbing. The rooms are richly furnished with some period and modern pieces. Fit for a king, they're more likely to house diplomats, industrialists, and successful authors. The self-proclaimed "mad genius" Salvador Dalí made the Meurice his headquarters, beginning in the post–World War II years until near the end of his life, occupying Suite 108 whenever he came to Paris. The same suite was used in the 1930s by the deposed and exiled king of Spain, Alfonso XIII. Suite 108 also served as the office of German General von Choltitz, who was in charge of Paris during the Nazi occupation from 1940 to 1945.

Dining/Entertainment: The Meurice Restaurant serves true French haute cuisine. The Pompadour cocktail lounge is ideal for cocktails and tea, and the elegantly renovated Meurice Bar offers drinks in a warm atmosphere. Formal service amid an elegant setting, the Meurice's enlightened culinary classics are more discreet than daringly creative.

Services: "Solve-everything" concierge, room service (24 hours), laundry/valet, telex, fax.

✪ **Le Ritz.** 15 place Vendôme, 75001 Paris. ☎ **01-43-16-30-30,** or 800/448-8355 in the U.S. and Canada. Fax 01-43-16-36-68. 142 rms, 45 suites. A/C MINIBAR TV TEL. 3350–4,250 F ($670–$850) double; from 5,500 F ($1,100) suite. AE, DC, MC, V. Parking 180 F ($36). Métro: Opéra or Madeleine.

Unequivocally, the Ritz is the greatest hotel in Europe. The Plaza Athénée and the Crillon mount the only challenges to its imminence. This enduring symbol of elegance is located on one of the most beautiful and historic squares in Paris. César Ritz, the "little shepherd boy from Niederwald," converted the Lazun Mansion into this lavish hotel; it opened in 1898. César hired the legendary culinary master Escoffier to be the hotel's chef. The Ritz had the world's first shopping gallery. This lap of luxury has attracted some of the most celebrated people of the world, including Edward VII of England.

In 1979 the Ritz family sold the hotel to Egyptian businessman Mohamed al-Fayed, who has refurbished it and added a cooking school. All the hotel's drawing rooms, salons, three gardens, and courtyards were preserved. The salons are furnished with museum-caliber antiques: gilt pieces, ornate mirrors, Louis XV and Louis XVI furnishings, and 10-foot-high candelabra. The decor of the bedrooms is impeccably French, with antique chests, desks with bronze trimmings, and crystal light fixtures.

The battle rages between the Ritz crowd and the Crillon crowd. Fans of the Ritz often dub the Crillon "too American," while Crillon regulars retort that the Ritz has no soul. The Ritz has an abundance of soul and almost *ancien régime* manners. Many guests arrive with security guards and in limos with bullet-proof windows.

Right Bank Accommodations

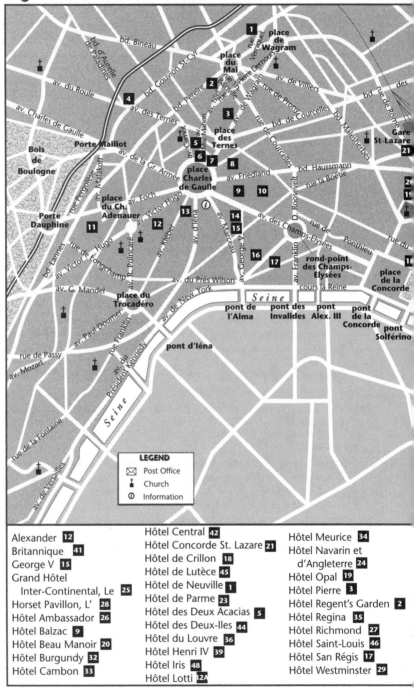

LEGEND
⊠ Post Office
† Church
ⓘ Information

Alexander **12**
Britannique **41**
George V **15**
Grand Hôtel
  Inter-Continental, Le **25**
Horset Pavillon, L' **28**
Hôtel Ambassador **26**
Hôtel Balzac **9**
Hôtel Beau Manoir **20**
Hôtel Burgundy **32**
Hôtel Cambon **33**

Hôtel Central **42**
Hôtel Concorde St. Lazare **21**
Hôtel de Crillon **18**
Hôtel de Lutèce **45**
Hôtel de Neuville **1**
Hôtel de Parme **23**
Hôtel des Deux Acacias **5**
Hôtel des Deux-Iles **44**
Hôtel du Louvre **36**
Hôtel Henri IV **39**
Hôtel Iris **48**
Hôtel Lotti **32A**

Hôtel Meurice **34**
Hôtel Navarin et
  d'Angleterre **24**
Hôtel Opal **19**
Hôtel Pierre **3**
Hôtel Regent's Garden **2**
Hôtel Regina **35**
Hôtel Richmond **27**
Hôtel Saint-Louis **46**
Hôtel San Régis **17**
Hôtel Westminster **29**

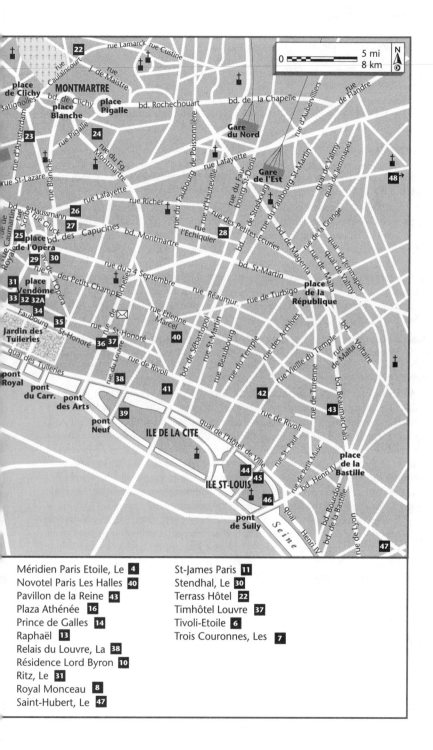

Méridien Paris Etoile, Le **4**
Novotel Paris Les Halles **40**
Pavillon de la Reine **43**
Plaza Athénée **16**
Prince de Galles **14**
Raphaël **13**
Relais du Louvre, La **38**
Résidence Lord Byron **10**
Ritz, Le **31**
Royal Monceau **8**
Saint-Hubert, Le **47**

St-James Paris **11**
Stendhal, Le **30**
Terrass Hôtel **22**
Timhôtel Louvre **37**
Tivoli-Etoile **6**
Trois Couronnes, Les **7**

Dining/Entertainment: The Espadon is one of the finest restaurants in Paris. The Ritz Club has a bar, a salon with a fireplace, and a dance floor. In the paneled Le Bar Vendôme, one of the world's most elegant, you can have a drink or lunch and enjoy a garden view.

Services: Concierge, room service (24 hours), laundry, valet.

Facilities: Luxury health club (with swimming pool, squash courts, and massage parlor), florist, shops.

EXPENSIVE

Hôtel Cambon. 3 rue Cambon, 75001 Paris. ☎ **01-42-60-38-09.** Fax 01-42-60-30-59. 42 rms, 6 junior suites. A/C MINIBAR TV TEL. 1,480 F ($296) double; 1,980 F ($396) suite. AE, MC, V. Parking in nearby lot 170 F ($34) per 24-hour period. Métro: Concorde.

On a stylish street conveniently located for sightseeing, this 19th-century hotel was renovated completely and given a contemporary decor that some find a bit sterile and antiseptic. The Louvre (below) has a lot more atmosphere and style, although the Cambon's location is excellent, right in the chic heart of Paris. The public rooms display 19th- and 20th-century paintings and sculptures. The bedrooms are individually decorated and have fabric wallcoverings, marble bathrooms, and much exposed wood. The staff here seems especially helpful, and many of them speak English. In the cozy street-level bar, guests can sometimes converse with the genial owners, the Siméon family.

Hôtel du Louvre. Place André-Malraux, 75001 Paris. ☎ **01-44-58-38-38,** or 800/888-4747 in the U.S. and Canada. Fax 01-44-58-38-01. 178 rms, 22 suites. A/C MINIBAR TV TEL. 1,350–1,950 F ($270–$390) double; 3,000 F ($600) suite. AE, DC, MC, V. Midwinter promotions available. Métro: Louvre.

When this hotel was inaugurated in 1855 by Napoléon III, a French journalist described it as "a palace of the people, rising adjacent to the palace of kings." The hotel has a decor of soaring marble, bronze, and gilt decor. The bedrooms are quintessentially Parisian—cozy and filled with souvenirs of *la belle époque.* They've recently been renovated and soundproofed against the roar of traffic. Although the views of the inner courtyard have their own understated charm, the sweeping panoramas down avenue de l'Opéra are among the best in the world. This hotel gives all the other similarly priced hotels in the neighborhood major competition, especially the Westminster and the declining Inter-Continental.

Dining/Entertainment: Le Bar "Defender" is a cozy, luxurious, and masculine hideaway; it has overtones of Scotland and an impressive collection of single-malt whiskies. A pianist plays after dusk. The elegant Brasserie du Louvre is a bistro done in the style of the French Empire; during fine weather, tables are set up on the terrace beneath the hotel's sandstone arcades.

Services: Concierge, room service (24 hours), baby-sitting, laundry/valet, filtered tap water.

Facilities: Business center.

Hôtel Regina. 2 place des Pyramides, 75001 Paris. ☎ **01-42-60-31-10.** Fax 01-40-15-95-16. 121 rms, 14 suites. A/C MINIBAR TV TEL. 1,820 F ($364) double; 2,620–3,820 F ($524–$764) suite. AE, DC, MC, V. Métro: Pyramides or Tuileries.

Until a radical renovation restored its old-fashioned grandeur in 1995, the Regina slumbered in peaceful obscurity in a prime location in central Paris, adjacent to rue de Rivoli's gilded equestrian statue of Joan of Arc. Built about a century ago, the hotel was known for its high-ceilinged, richly paneled lobby, impeccably mannered staff, and antique-strewn rooms; some of its regular clients compared it to a dowdy but endlessly genteel hotel in London.

All that changed when the management poured funds into the site's recent renovation, retaining the patina and beeswax of the art nouveau interior and adding hundreds of thousands of francs' worth of historically appropriate decorative flourishes. The hotel is filled with Oriental carpets, Louis-style furniture from every period, and 18th-century paintings and bowls of flowers; it also features a flagstone-covered courtyard with fountains.

Dining/Entertainment: Conservative French cuisine is served in a well-managed restaurant, Pluvinel, with a deliberately nostalgic art deco ambience. Pluviel is closed on weekends, forcing clients to satisfy themselves at a less appealing bistro-style snack bar.

Services: 24-hour room service, a concierge who acquires theater tickets, guides, secretarial and translation services, baby-sitters from outside sources and agencies, dry cleaning and laundry.

Facilities: Access to the facilities of a health club/gym next door, private salons for conferences.

MODERATE

Hôtel Burgundy. 8 rue Duphot, 75001 Paris. ☎ **01-42-60-34-12.** Fax 01-47-03-95-20. 90 rms. MINIBAR TV TEL. 890 F ($178) double. AE, DC, MC, V. Métro: Madeleine.

The Burgundy is one of the best values in an outrageously expensive neighborhood. This frequently renovated building stands in one of the city's most stylish business districts; it's a former run-down *pension* where impressionist poet Charles Baudelaire wrote some of his eerie poetry in the 1860s. Radically renovated in 1992, and the frequent nesting place for clients from throughout North and South America, the hotel features conservatively decorated and very comfortable bedrooms, and a restaurant (Le Charles Baudelaire) that's open for lunch and dinner Monday to Friday. There's no bar on the premises, but drinks can be served in the lobby during restaurant hours.

Novotel Paris Les Halles. Place Marguerite-de-Navarre, 75001 Paris. ☎ **01-42-21-31-31,** or 800/207-2542 in the U.S. and Canada. Fax 01-40-26-05-79. 271 rms, 14 suites. A/C MINIBAR TV TEL. 915 F ($183) double; 1,200–1,500 F ($240–$300) suite. Buffet breakfast 60 F ($11.40) extra. AE, DC, MC, V. Métro: Les Halles.

At the edge of the beaux-arts lattices of place des Halles, this is one of the best Novotels in its worldwide network. It is part of a chain, however, so it's short on quirky Parisian charm and character. Its cubist-inspired, mirror-sheathed facade and sloping skylights mimic the most daring of the Beaubourg neighborhood's futuristic architecture. Built in 1986, the hotel has a sunny lobby and a small-scale copy of the Statue of Liberty, along with a stylish bar on a dais above the ground floor.

Each room offers an efficient but comfortable decor, with one double bed and one single (which can serve as a couch or a bed), and a streamlined private bath. All units have the same floor plan and furnishings, but the most sought-after rooms overlook Le Forum des Halles, with its fountains, shrubbery, and carousel. The greenhouse restaurant, Le Sun Deck, opens onto the ancient Church of St-Eustache on the opposite side of the square.

Le Relais du Louvre. 19 rue des Prêtres, 75001 Paris. ☎ **01-40-41-96-42.** Fax 01-40-41-96-44. 18 rms, 2 suites. MINIBAR TV TEL. 820 F ($164) double; 1,280–1,450 F ($256–$290) suite. AE, DC, DISC, MC, V. Parking 70 F ($14). Métro: Louvre or Pont-Neuf.

Opened in 1991, this hotel has what the French call *charme et caractère.* Many visitors from the provinces seek it out—it does suggest rural France—because it lies between the Louvre and Notre-Dame and within walking distance of the pont Neuf

---

ⓜ Family-Friendly Hotels

Novotel Paris Les Halles *(see page 75)*   Every room is suitable for a family "doubling up." The hotel overlooks Les Halles shopping complex, and children love the carousel there.

Résidence Lord Byron *(see page 86)*   The Byron is not only a good value and a family-oriented place for the swanky 8th arrondissement, but is only a 10-minute walk from many of the city's major monuments.

Hôtel Saint-Louis *(see page 79)*   The family atmosphere that descends from proprietor Guy Record and his wife, Andrée, has become a precious commodity in Paris these days. This 17th-century town house is fashionably located on the historic Ile Saint-Louis and priced with families in mind.

---

in the historic heart of Paris. Le Relais has a lot more atmosphere than the more antiseptic Novotel Paris Les Halles (see above) and more style and glamour than one of its major competitors, the less expensive Britannique (see below). Nostalgia buffs are usually impressed with this building's history: Once Voltaire and Victor Hugo frequented the legendary Café Momus, which was located here on the street level. One of the pivotal scenes of Puccini's *La Bohème* also takes place at this café. The hotel's bedrooms are painted in bright, strong hues; they're decorated with reproductions of antique French furniture and have soundproofed windows and modern conveniences.

INEXPENSIVE

Britannique. 20 av. Victoria, 75001 Paris. ☎ **01-42-33-74-59.** Fax 01-42-33-82-65. 40 rms. MINIBAR TV TEL. 720–830 F ($144–$166) double. AE, DC, MC, V. Parking 90 F ($18). Métro: Châtelet.

This is a terrific location near the Louvre. The soundproof rooms come replete with amenities such as satellite TV, a hair dryer, and a safe. The best chances for a discount come during the months of February, July, August, and December. Although the 1st arrondissement has far superior hotels, the Britannique is a superior value.

Hôtel Henri IV. 25 place Dauphine, 75001 Paris. ☎ **01-43-54-44-53.** 22 rms, 2 with shower only. 155–200 F ($31–$40) double without bath, 230–260 F ($46–$52) double with shower only. Rates include continental breakfast. No credit cards. Métro: Pont-Neuf.

Some 400 years ago this narrow, decrepit building housed the printing presses used for the edicts of Henri IV. Today one of the most famous, and one of the most consistently crowded, budget hotels in Europe sits at this dramatic location, the northernmost tip of the Ile de la Cité, beside a formal and unexpected park lined with orderly rows of trees. The clientele is mostly bargain-conscious academics, journalists, and francophiles, many of whom reserve their accommodations as much as 2 months in advance. The low-ceilinged lobby, one flight above street level, is cramped and bleak; the creaky stairway leading to the bedrooms is almost impossibly narrow. The rooms are considered romantically threadbare by many, run-down and substandard by others. Each contains a sink, and the management is rather reluctantly planning to add increasing numbers of showers to selected bedrooms during the lifetime of this edition. Despite its awesome sense of history, the hotel is too bareboned for many, but has its diehard fans—including lots of American backpackers who flock here during midsummer.

Hotels: 1st & 2nd Arrondissements

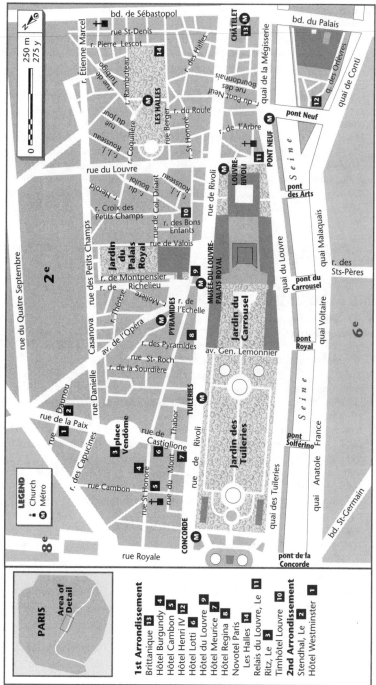

LEGEND
† Church
Ⓜ Métro

PARIS

Area of Detail

1st Arrondissement
Brittanique **13**
Hôtel Burgundy **4**
Hôtel Cambon **5**
Hôtel Henri IV **12**
Hôtel Lotti **6**
Hôtel du Louvre **9**
Hôtel Meurice **7**
Hôtel Regina **8**
Novotel Paris **14**
Relais du Louvre, Le **11**
Ritz, Le **3**
Timhôtel Louvre **10**

2nd Arrondissement
Stendhal, Le **2**
Hôtel Westminster **1**

Timhôtel Louvre. 4 rue Croix-des-Petits-Champs, 75001 Paris. ☎ **01-42-60-34-86.** Fax 01-42-60-10-39. 56 rms. A/C TV TEL. 550 F ($110) double. AE, DC, MC, V. Métro: Palais-Royal.

This hotel and its sibling, the Timhôtel Bourse (see below), are mirror images of one another, at least from the inside; both are good examples of a new breed of two-star, business-oriented hotels cropping up around France. Both Timhôtels share the same manager and the same temperament, and although bedrooms at Timhôtel Bourse are larger than those at Timhôtel Louvre, the Louvre branch is so close to the museum as to be almost irresistible to anyone wishing to spend lots of time in its galleries. Both were conversions of venerable but decrepit older hotels (the Hôtel du Globe and the Hôtel de Normandie) that functioned for years as expatriate homes of writers, art lovers, and tourists. Today the ambience is bland and standardized, but modern and comfortable, with tiled bathrooms, monochromatic (blue and gray) bedrooms, and wall-to-wall carpeting. Breakfasts are served rather anonymously from self-service cafeterias, but room service is available either from a local delicatessen or a simple restaurant nearby, depending on what you're hungry for and when you want it. If you spend any 10 nights in any combination of Timhôtels, you'll get the 11th night free.

The **Timhôtel Bourse** is located at 3 rue de la Banque, 75002 Paris (☎ **01-42-61-53-90;** fax 01-42-60-05-39), has 46 rooms, and charges the same price. Métro: Bourse.

2ND ARRONDISSEMENT (LA BOURSE)
VERY EXPENSIVE

Hôtel Westminster. 13 rue de la Paix, 75002 Paris. ☎ **01-42-61-57-46,** or 800/344-1212. Fax 01-42-60-30-66. 84 rms, 18 suites. A/C MINIBAR TV TEL. 2,400 F ($480) double; 3,700–5,500 F ($740–$1,100) suite. AE, DC, MC, V. Métro: Opéra.

The Westminster was built during Baron Haussmann's redesigning of Paris in 1846, and it incorporated an old convent. At the turn of the century the hotel was purchased by Monsieur Bruchon, who installed its now-famous collection of clocks. The recently renovated guest rooms feature individual designs that effectively combine modernity and tradition. Even though we find parts of the 2nd arrondissement rather tacky, the Westminster is still very conveniently located between the Opéra and place Vendôme. This converted hotel doesn't quite match the style of the Lotti, but has a lot more charm and character than the famed Warwick in the 8th Arrondissment, which is under the same ownership.

Dining/Entertainment: The hotel restaurant, Le Céladon, is one of the finest hotel dining rooms in Paris. It's not only noted for its celadon porcelain collection on display but for food that's traditional and also light. A varied and imaginative menu is embellished by professional service.

Services: Room service, laundry, valet.

EXPENSIVE

Le Stendhal. 22 rue Danielle-Casanova, 75002 Paris. ☎ **01-44-58-52-52.** Fax 01-58-52-00. 17 rms, 3 suites. A/C MINIBAR TV TEL. 1,580–1,780 F ($316–$356) double; 1,800–2,000 F ($360–$400) suite. AE, DC, MC, V. Métro: Opéra.

Established in 1992, this hotel mixes a young and hip style with a more traditional one. Its location, close to the glamorous jewelry stores on place Vendôme, couldn't be more grand. The bedrooms, accessible via a tiny elevator, have vivid color schemes. The red-and-black Stendhal Suite pays homage to the most famous novel of the hotel's namesake, *Le Rouge et le Noir.* The author died here in 1842. Breakfast is served in the stone cellar, which has a vaulted ceiling. Simple meals can be ordered and are served in the bedrooms or at the bar, 24 hours a day.

3RD ARRONDISSEMENT (LE MARAIS)
EXPENSIVE

✪ **Le Pavillon de la Reine.** 28 place des Vosges, 75003 Paris. ☎ **01-42-77-96-40.** Fax 01-42-77-63-06. 30 rms, 17 duplexes, 15 suites. A/C MINIBAR TV TEL. 1,700 F ($340) double; 2,100 F ($420) duplex for one or two; 2,700–3,200 F ($540–$640) suite. AE, DC, MC, V. Free parking. Métro: Bastille.

Lovers of Le Marais long lamented the absence of a hotel on this square where Victor Hugo lived, but the inauguration of this hotel in 1986 assuaged that. The entrance is through a tunnel leading under the northern side of the square. At the end of the tunnel, flanked with vine-covered lattices and a small formal garden, is a cream-colored villa, a simple neoclassical facade that blends perfectly into the neighborhood.

This hotel reigns supreme in the 3rd arrondissment. Its main competitor in classic tradition is the Relais Christine in the Latin Quarter, but the Pavillon de la Reine is more stylish. Romantics seeking a traditional French atmosphere that's not quaint and creaky gravitate here to the most beautiful square in Paris. The furniture is either antique or a fool-the-eye reproduction.

4TH ARRONDISSEMENT (ILE DE LA CITE / ILE ST-LOUIS & BEAUBOURG)
MODERATE

Hôtel des Deux-Iles. 59 rue St-Louis-en-l'Ile, 75004 Paris. ☎ **01-43-26-13-35.** Fax 01-43-29-60-25. 17 rms. A/C TV TEL. 840 F ($168) double. V. Métro: Pont-Marie.

The Hôtel des Deux-Iles occupies a restored 17th-century mansion on this most charming of Seine islands. It's the most elaborate establishment opened by interior designer/hotelier Roland Buffat to date. A garden of plants and flowers off the lobby sets the tone; bamboo and reed are used extensively in both the public and private rooms. A rustic tavern on the lower level is a favorite gathering place; in cool weather a fire is lit in the open fireplace.

Deux-Iles is absolutely comparable to the Hôtel de Lutèce (same ownership; see below). Both the Lutèce and des Duex-Iles are the style-setters for Ile Saint-Louis.

Hôtel de Lutèce. 65 rue St-Louis-en-l'Ile, 75004 Paris. ☎ **01-43-26-23-52.** Fax 01-43-29-60-25. 23 rms. A/C TV TEL. 840 F ($168) double; 990 F ($198) triple. AE, DC, MC, V. Métro: Pont-Marie.

This hotel has a sparkling style. It's located on the historic Ile St-Louis, where it seems everybody wants to live although there's just not enough room. You pass through the glass entrance doors into what resembles the inviting living room of a Breton country house. Down-filled couches and armchairs are set around a stone fireplace in the salon. All this is the creation of interior designer/hotelier Roland Buffat. The floors are done with *naif* decorated tiles. Antiques are interspersed with fine reproductions in the tasteful bedrooms.

The hotel is comparable in style and amenities with the Deux-Iles (same ownership; see above).

INEXPENSIVE

⊖ **Hôtel Saint-Louis.** 75 rue St-Louis-en-l'Ile, 75004 Paris. ☎ **01-46-34-04-80.** Fax 01-46-34-02-13. 21 rms. TEL. 695 F ($139) double. MC, V. Métro: Pont-Marie.

Proprietor Guy Record and his wife, Andrée, maintain a charming family atmosphere—which is becoming harder and harder to find in Paris—at this small hotel in a 17th-century town house. It's an incredible value considering its historic location on the highly desirable but crowded island of Saint-Louis. The small reception lounge is filled with antiques. Many of the rooms on the upper levels offer views over

Hotels: 3rd & 4th Arrondissements

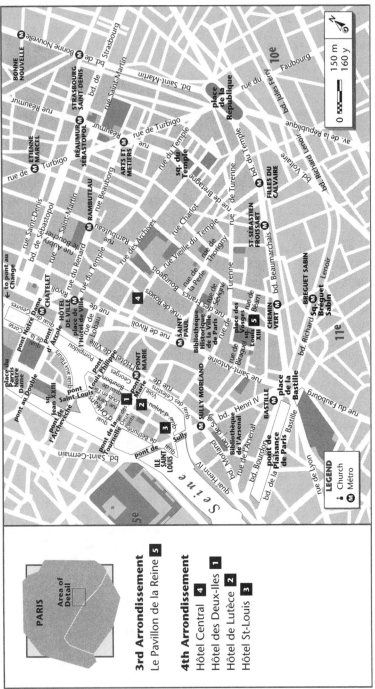

3rd Arrondissement
Le Pavillon de la Reine **5**

4th Arrondissement
Hôtel Central **4**
Hôtel des Deux-Iles **1**
Hôtel de Lutèce **2**
Hôtel St-Louis **3**

the rooftops of Paris. We prefer the rooms on the fifth floor, which have old wood trim and attractive pieces of furniture. The breakfast room lies in the cellar; its stone vaulting dates from the 17th century.

8TH ARRONDISSEMENT (CHAMPS-ELYSEES / MADELEINE)
VERY EXPENSIVE

George V. 31 av. George-V, 75008 Paris. ☎ **01-47-23-54-00,** or 800/224-5843 in the U.S. and Canada. Fax 01-47-20-40-00. 228 rms, 40 suites. A/C MINIBAR TV TEL. 2,800–3,900 F ($560–$780) double; from 5,700 F ($1,140) suite. AE, DC, MC, V. Parking 100 F ($20). Métro: George-V.

Built in 1928, the art deco George V has sumptuous architectural details and a lot of glitz. While certainly swanky and ostentatious, the George V is not quite the prestigious address that the Plaza Athénée and Crillon are, but it aspires to be. It certainly was in 1944, when General Eisenhower made it his headquarters during the liberation of Paris. Major efforts have been expended to keep this hotel among the best. It lies in a relentlessly upscale neighborhood midway between the Champs-Elysées and the Seine. Sometimes referred to as the "French Waldorf Astoria," it has a luxurious and mysterious aura. (Reportedly, the management keeps a "black file" on the whims and preferences of many of its regulars.) It was acquired in the 1980s by the British Trusthouse Forte chain, which lavished money on its renovations in 1993. The staff is almost faultless.

The public lounges are adorned with tapestries and 100- and 200-year-old paintings. Inlaid marble walls in the Pompeian style add a touch of staid dignity. The preferred rooms overlook the courtyard; those with terrace balconies are simply perfection.

Dining/Entertainment: In good weather, haute cuisine luncheons are served in the courtyard's garden-style outdoor café/restaurant. The two formal restaurants of the hotel are Les Princes and Le Grill.

Services: Concierge, room service (24 hours), CBS news service, in-room movies, laundry, valet.

Facilities: Seven conference rooms, tearooms, gift shop.

✪ **Hôtel de Crillon.** 10 place de la Concorde, 75008 Paris. ☎ **01-44-71-15-00,** or 800/241-3333 in the U.S. and Canada. Fax 01-44-71-15-02. 120 rms, 43 suites. A/C MINIBAR TV TEL. 3,200–3,500 F ($640–$700) double; from 4,900 F ($980) suite. AE, DC, MC, V. Parking 150 F ($30). Métro: Concorde.

Only the Ritz can boast a classier address. The Crillon is superior to such frontrunners as the Plaza Athénée and the Bristol, and this national monument is not only fit for a king but has actually housed a few. It offers the most dramatic setting in Paris, overlooking place de la Concorde, where the guillotine claimed the lives of such celebrated victims as Louis XVI, Marie Antoinette, Madame du Barry, Madame Roland, and Charlotte Corday. Designed by the famed Gabriel, the building was the former home of the duke of Crillon. Although more than 200 years old, it has been a hotel only since 1909.

Restored, the hotel still evokes the 18th century, with parquet floors, crystal chandeliers, sculpture, 17th- and 18th-century tapestries, gilt moldings, antiques, and paneled walls. If you get a room at the front, you'll be treated to a view of one of the most beautiful plazas in the world. Don't expect all bedrooms to be spacious; many are a good size but hardly large. The styling, in the words of one critic, is Sonia Rykiel's "take on Louis XV." Soundproofing keeps out the street noise but not necessarily sounds from next door. All the bathrooms are fresh and well maintained, lined with travertine or pink marble.

Dining/Entertainment: Les Ambassadeurs is truly the formal dining room of ambassadors, with classic French food and superb service. Less formal is L'Obélisque, where the food isn't as grand (but at least it allows you to dine at the Crillon without going broke). The hotel encircles a large, formal 18th-century courtyard and garden, one of the ideal places in Paris for afternoon tea.

Services: Room service (24 hours), secretarial and translation services.

Facilities: Meeting and conference rooms, garden-style courtyard with restaurant service, elevators, shops.

Hôtel San Régis. 12 rue Jean-Goujon, 75008 Paris. ☎ **01-44-95-16-16.** Fax 01-45-61-05-48. 34 rms, 10 suites. A/C MINIBAR TV TEL. 2,200–2,850 F ($440–$570) double; 3,200–5,500 F ($640–$1,100) suite. AE, DC, MC, V. Métro: F-D-Roosevelt.

It's often said that this is the most discreet hotel in Paris, the ideal place to have an affair. The Hôtel San Régis, the ultimate boutique hotel of Paris—small, personalized, and private—resides on the swankest street in Paris: avenue Montaigne. This is just about the only place in the neighborhood for understated traditional style; the hotel seems like a private club. A fashionable town house until 1922, the San Régis enjoys, in a quiet and modest way, its position as one of the best hotels in Paris in its price bracket. Just off the Champs-Elysées and just a short walk from the Seine, it's in a neighborhood of embassies and exclusive boutiques (Christian Dior is across the street). The rooms are individually decorated with style and taste, although they tend to be small. A few rooms have a separate sitting room, and many overlook a side garden. Thirty-five units have air-conditioning. An attentive staff quickly learns guests' fancies and makes them feel at home.

Dining/Entertainment: The hotel has an elegantly decorated restaurant in the classic style, serving formal French cuisine. There's also a winter garden.

Services: Room service (24 hours), laundry/valet, baby-sitting.

Facilities: Car-rental desk.

✪ Plaza Athénée. 23–27 av. Montaigne, 75008 Paris. ☎ **01-47-23-78-33.** Fax 01-47-20-20-70. 211 rms, 42 suites. A/C MINIBAR TV TEL. 4,000–4,650 F ($800–$930) double; 6,500–13,500 F ($1,300–$2,700) suite. AE, DC, MC, V. Parking 150 F ($30). Métro: F-D-Roosevelt.

The Plaza Athénée, though a slight tier below the Ritz and the Crillon, is a landmark of discretion, style, and elegance—even more so than the George V and the Royal Monceau, its two major competitors. The nine-story stone edifice is refurbished constantly over a 6-year cycle.

A palace of gilded luxury, the Plaza Athénée has been a celebrity haunt since the days when Mata Hari checked in. It's said that the hotel has two employees for each guest and spends more on flowers than on its electric bill. A citadel dedicated to the good life, it has arched windows and ornate balconies. The hotel's high style is exemplified by the Montaigne Salon, with its mellow wood-grain paneling and marble fireplace. The rooms have huge beds, fine antique mahogany pieces, and elegant taffeta draperies. The marble bathrooms are especially large. Rooms facing avenue Montaigne have a view of the Eiffel Tower rising up from the chestnut trees. Service is of the highest standard.

Dining/Entertainment: Meals are an occasion. The preferred choice for dining is La Régence, with its large curvy-topped windows opening onto the garden courtyard. It's known for its lobster soufflé. With its bright colors and decoration, the Grill Relais Plaza is the meeting place of *tout Paris,* especially at lunch, drawing dress designers and personalities from the world of publishing, cinema, and art. The Bar Anglais is a favorite spot for a late-night drink (it's open until 1:30am).

Hotels: 8th Arrondissement

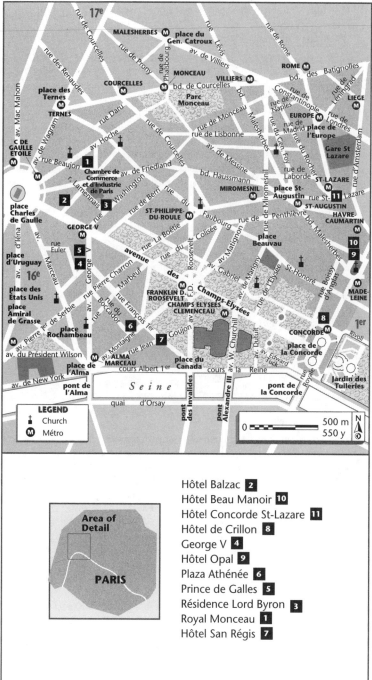

Hôtel Balzac **2**
Hôtel Beau Manoir **10**
Hôtel Concorde St-Lazare **11**
Hôtel de Crillon **8**
George V **4**
Hôtel Opal **9**
Plaza Athénée **6**
Prince de Galles **5**
Résidence Lord Byron **3**
Royal Monceau **1**
Hôtel San Régis **7**

Services: Concierge, room service (24 hours), laundry, Reuters telex with international stock quotes.

Facilities: Conference rooms, beauty parlor and hairdresser, massage parlor.

Prince de Galles. 33 av. George-V, 75008 Paris. ☎ **01-47-23-55-11,** or 800/323-3535 in the U.S. and Canada. Fax 01-47-20-06-61. 140 rms, 30 suites. A/C MINIBAR TV TEL. 2,250–3,100 F ($450–$620) double; 3,650–12,000 F ($730–$2,400) suite. AE, DC, MC, V. Parking 80 F ($16). Métro: George-V.

This quiet, discreet, and tranquil deluxe hotel thankfully lacks the showbiz glitz of other Paris luxury hotels. A renowned hotel from the Roaring Twenties, it no longer attracts the glitterati, but doesn't need such flash. It may not be quite up there with the Bristol, Crillon, Plaza Athénée, and the gaudy George V, but it remains a prestigious hotel and solid choice. It occupies a platinum location, only a short stroll from the Champs-Elysées, the Arc de Triomphe, and the glamorous boutiques of avenue Montaigne.

In 1994 new owners ITT Sheraton spent millions of dollars on a complete, historically authentic restoration. The public areas, bars, and accommodations were upgraded. They installed "acres" of beige or gray marble.

Guests are greeted at the front door by a team of uniformed attendants. The elegantly furnished bedrooms are equipped with in-room movies and radios, and receive plenty of sunshine.

Dining/Entertainment: The paneled bar, with its leather replicas of 18th-century armchairs, is one of the great hotel bars of Paris. The Restaurant Jardin des Cygnes provides flavorful, albeit expensive, cuisine. The once-stuffy menu now reflects a lightness, style, and taste that only the finest ingredients can provide.

Services: Concierge, room service (24 hours), baby-sitting.

Facilities: Conference rooms, fitness room.

Royal Monceau. 37–39 av. Hoche, 75008 Paris. ☎ **01-45-61-98-00,** or 800/888-1199 in the U.S. and Canada. Fax 01-42-99-88-90. 180 rms, 39 suites. A/C MINIBAR TV TEL. 2,600–3,200 F ($520–$640) double; 3,500–13,000 F ($700–$2,600) suite. AE, DC, MC, V. Métro: Charles-de-Gaulle/Etoile.

The Royal Monceau isn't quite in a league with the Plaza Athénée and the Crillon, but is comparable in style and luxury to the Prince de Galles, attracting the same "carriage trade" as that fine hotel. Foreign businesspeople, politicians, and international entertainers who like to keep it quiet when they're in Paris are attracted here. This graceful hotel from 1928 combines the best of French restraint with Gallic flair. After the occupying Nazi officers fled, General Eisenhower used the hotel as his base in 1944 for planning his final assault on Germany. In an upscale neighborhood, it has a view of the Arc de Triomphe. The facade is intricately carved, and the entrance is below a translucent art nouveau canopy. In the center of the airy lobby is an oval dome covered with murals of heavenly skies and fluffy clouds. The grand scale of the bedrooms was maintained in a sympathetic restoration completed in 1992. Some of the accommodations are the largest hotel bedrooms in Paris. Some rooms have an elegant four-poster bed set in an alcove. Other rooms have walls hung with moiré silk, carved-wood bedsteads, and marble fireplaces. The bathrooms are done in marble. Thin walls make room-to-room calls seem superfluous.

Dining/Entertainment: Le Jardin restaurant is a glassed-in gazebo with rounded walls combining space-age construction with French neoclassicism. In the surrounding courtyard are double tiers of plants, including a 20-foot magnolia and dozens of flowering shrubs. In addition, guests can dine at Le Carpaccio, one of the best restaurants of Paris, with one of the most acclaimed chefs. It's a very chic place for a dinner rendezvous. The candy-pink of the restaurant walls may make you want to skip straight to dessert, but don't miss out on the cuisine here—it has a flavorful, provincial flair.

Services: Concierge, room service (24 hours), secretarial service, laundry, valet.

Facilities: State-of-the-art health club/gym with sauna, swimming pool, balneotherapy (hydrotherapy), squash court, and massage parlor; solarium; hairdressing salon; conference rooms.

EXPENSIVE

Hôtel Balzac. 6 rue Balzac, 75008 Paris. ☎ **01-44-35-08-00,** or 800/457-4000 in the U.S. and Canada. Fax 01-42-25-24-82. 70 rms, 14 suites. A/C MINIBAR TV TEL. 1,850–2,200 F ($370–$440) double; 3,200–6,000 F ($640–$1,200) suite. AE, DC, MC, V. Parking 150 F ($30). Métro: George-V.

A boutique hotel, the Balzac is intimate and full of charm. It attracts an affluent, style-conscious clientele and is a haven of tranquillity in a bustling district near the Arc de Triomphe, just off the Champs-Elysées. The hotel opened in 1986 in a belle époque town house. Then in 1994 the famous English designer Nina Campbell redecorated all the rooms and suites individually. Each bedroom is outfitted with soundproof windows, tasteful upholstery, and a marble bathroom. For royal guests, the hotel has a royal suite; there's also a slightly less grand presidential suite.

Dining/Entertainment: The Balzac has an offshoot of the famous Restaurant Bice—under the direction of Mama Bice—that opened in Milan in 1926. Some of the finest Italian cuisine in Paris is served there.

Services: Room service (24 hours), dry cleaning, express laundry.

Hôtel Beau Manoir. 6 rue de l'Arcade, 75008 Paris. ☎ **01-42-66-03-07,** or 800/528-1234 in the U.S. and Canada. Fax 01-42-68-03-00. 29 rms, 3 suites. A/C MINIBAR TV TEL. 1,155 F ($231) double; 1,465 F ($293) suite. Rates include breakfast. AE, MC, V. Métro: Madeleine.

Open since 1994, this four-star hotel prides itself on its 19th-century nostalgia and decorative zest. The lobby boasts the trappings of a private living room, with walnut reproductions of 18th- and 19th-century antiques, Aubusson tapestries, and fresh flowers. Breakfast is served beneath the chiseled stone vaults of a very old cellar, and the guest rooms are charming and very French. Each contains a safe for valuables, soundproofing, a marble bath, and the conveniences you'd expect. The suites often have exposed beams and/or sloping garret-style ceilings.

Hôtel Concorde St-Lazare. 108 rue St-Lazare, 75008 Paris. ☎ **01-40-08-44-44,** or 212/752-3900 in New York State, 800/888-4747 in the U.S. and Canada 0171/630-1704 in London. Fax 01-42-93-01-20. 277 rms, 23 suites. A/C MINIBAR TV TEL. 1,260–1,960 F ($252–$392) double; 3,500–6,000 F ($700–$1,200) suite. AE, DC, MC, V. Parking 100 F ($20). Métro: St-Lazare.

This is the best hotel in the Gare St-Lazare area. After a careful restoration, its *fin-de-siècle* style has come back. Its granite-pillared lobby is a French national monument. The St-Lazare was built in 1889 to accommodate the thousands of visitors who flocked to Paris for the Exposition Universelle. It's situated across from the Gare St-Lazare. A turn-of-the-century palace, it was inspired by British and Spanish models. Its architects designed the hotel to appeal to the tastes of France's emerging merchant class. Along with gilded-age details of bronze, white marble, mosaics, and mirrors, they combined Scottish granite, soaring ceilings, and the newfangled inventions of electricity and telephones.

All the bedrooms were soundproofed and elegantly redecorated. Done in floral fabrics of blue and yellow tones, the rooms are well maintained and very French. The staff is proud and motivated.

Dining/Entertainment: Worthy of J. P. Morgan, a gilt-and-russet room is exclusively devoted to French billiards—it's the only room of its kind in Paris. An American bar, Le Golden Black, bears Sonia Rykiel's signature decor of black lacquer with touches of gold and amber. The Café Terminus, accessible directly from the nearby railway station, bristles with turn-of-the-century accessories and daily brasserie service from noon to 11pm. The very Parisian Bistrot 108 offers provincial dishes along with great vintages, which can be ordered by the glass.

Services: Concierge, room service (24 hours), baby-sitting, laundry/valet, currency exchange.

MODERATE

Résidence Lord Byron. 5 rue de Chateaubriand, 75008 Paris. ☎ **01-43-59-89-98.** Fax 01-42-89-46-04. 31 rms, 6 junior suites. MINIBAR TV TEL. 800–900 F ($160–$180) double; from 1,250 F ($250) junior suite. AE, MC, V. Métro: George-V. RER: Etoile.

The Lord Byron may not be as grand as other hotels in the neighborhood, but it's affordable. No style setter—nor does it claim to be—it's solid and reliable and maybe a little stuffy. It remains a good value and a family-oriented place for the upscale 8th arrondissement. Some of the city's major monuments are only a 10-minute walk away. Just off the Champs-Elysées on a curving street of handsome buildings, the Lord Byron sports fine antique reproductions and framed prints of butterflies and scenes in France. The bathrooms are as attractively decorated as they are functional. If you choose to have breakfast at the hotel, you can order it in the dining room or in a shaded inner garden. Six junior suites with two beds and one bath are available.

INEXPENSIVE

Hôtel Opal. 19 rue Tronchet, 75008 Paris. ☎ **01-42-65-77-97.** Fax 01-49-24-06-58. 36 rms. MINIBAR TV TEL. 480–610 F ($96–$122) double. Second bed 100 F ($20) extra. AE, MC, V. Parking 120 F ($24). Métro: Madeleine.

In the heart of Paris, behind the Madeleine church and within an easy walk of the Opéra, this spruced-up hotel is a real find. Decorated with style and taste, it offers entirely renovated but small bedrooms. Some people especially enjoy the closet-size bedrooms on the top floor, reached by a narrow staircase—these are really attic rooms. The Opal promises visitors a warm welcome and an intimate atmosphere.

9TH & 10TH ARRONDISSEMENTS (OPÉRA GARNIER / GARE DU NORD)
VERY EXPENSIVE

Le Grand Hôtel Inter-Continental. 2 rue Scribe, 75009 Paris. ☎ **01-40-07-32-32,** or 800/327-0200 in the U.S. and Canada. Fax 01-42-66-12-51. 494 rms, 20 suites. A/C MINIBAR TV TEL. 2,100–2,800 F ($420–$560) double; from 3,500 F ($700) suite. AE, DC, MC, V. Parking 150 F ($30). Métro: Opéra.

In the 1860s Le Grand Hôtel was conceived by Napoléon III as an appropriate neighbor to the Paris Opéra, whose foundation was already being laid across the street. Napoléon had admired the massive hotels of London and strived to duplicate their size and grandeur in a redesigned Paris. The hotel rose in beaux arts glory, one of the few in Paris to fill an entire city block. Its cost at the time would exceed $60 million in today's currency. Empress Eugénie presided over its inauguration. There's nothing in the neighborhood to equal it.

Millions of dollars' worth of steel, marble, gilt, and fabrics were used to restore the hotel to its original style. Guests are welcomed into shimmering Second Empire elegance. The high-ceilinged bedrooms are luxurious. Done in pastel colors, they're filled with plush upholsteries and equipped with electronic amenities needed by the business traveler.

Dining/Entertainment: Le Restaurant Opéra is recommended separately in Chapter 5. Less formal is the Café de la Paix—the celebration site for countless cultural and military victories since its construction in the 1860s (see Chapter 5). Perfect for breakfast, light lunch, afternoon tea, and conversation over drinks, La Verrière is sheltered from street noise in what was originally planned as an open courtyard.

Services: Room service (24 hours), laundry/dry cleaning, beauty parlor, tour desk.

Facilities: Le Gym Club offers exercise equipment and a view over the copper-sheathed domes of the adjacent Opéra that's almost mystical. A business center offers all related services, including secretarial and translation.

EXPENSIVE

Hôtel Ambassador. 16 bd. Haussmann, 75009 Paris. ☎ **01-44-83-40-40,** or 800/888-4747 in the U.S. and Canada. Fax 01-40-22-08-74. 289 rms, 9 suites. MINIBAR TV TEL. 1,350–1,710 F ($270–$342) double; 1,810–3,510 F ($362–$702) suite. AE, DC, MC, V. Parking 90 F ($18). Métro: Richelieu-Drouot or Chaussée-d'Antin.

This hotel, the most appealing first-class choice in the neighborhood, hosted the reception that celebrated Charles Lindbergh's historic flight across the Atlantic, but the pilot managed to find lodging elsewhere: After the party, the exhausted hero spent the night at the U.S. ambassador's residence. When the Ambassador opened in 1927 with its 600 rooms and seven elevators, it was the biggest and most modern hotel in Paris, an anchor on the legendary *grands boulevards.* Today many rooms still have their original art deco built-in wardrobes. Floral curtains and pastel-colored carpets and upholstery were installed in the early 1990s. About 80% of the rooms are air-conditioned.

Dining/Entertainment: The hotel contains an award-winning restaurant, Venantius. There's also an appealingly nostalgic bar, Le Bar des Aigles, in a cubbyhole at one end of the grandly eclectic hotel lobby.

Services: Concierge, room service (24 hours), baby-sitting, laundry, dry cleaning.

Facilities: Some of the largest conference and convention facilities in Paris, duty-free shop.

MODERATE

L'Horset Pavillon. 38 rue Echiquier, 75010 Paris. ☎ **01-42-46-92-75.** Fax 01-42-47-03-97. 92 rms. MINIBAR TV TEL. 850–950 F ($170–$190) double. AE, MC, V. Métro: Bonne-Nouvelle.

Imposing and dignified, this hotel occupies what in 1593 was the hunting pavilion of Henri IV; a little later it became a convent. During the Revolution the building was confiscated by the government, and in 1850 it was transformed into the first hotel of the Horset Group, which now operates five hotels scattered throughout Paris.

Vestiges of the hunting lodge remain, such as the semiconcealed columns in the lobby level's cloak room. More obvious in their charms are the art nouveau restaurant (1900) and art deco bar (1925), both of which haven't been altered since their installation. The bedrooms are conservative and contemporary, with masculine accents of bordeaux and emerald. The staff speaks English.

INEXPENSIVE

Hôtel Richmond. 11 rue du Helder, 75009 Paris. ☎ **01-47-70-53-20.** Fax 01-48-00-02-10. 58 rms. MINIBAR TV TEL. 737 F ($147.40) double; 950 F ($190) triple. AE, DC, MC, V. Métro: Opéra.

This three-star hotel is a short walk from the Opéra, near American Express, the Café de la Paix, and many fine shops. There are a lot of tacky hotels in the neighborhood, but this one has a bit of style and class. Behind the attractive facade is a pleasant lounge with sofas, marble columns, and a Roman-style fountain—all contributing to an Empire-style aura. The rooms are comfortably and traditionally furnished in Louis XV style, with hair dryers and personal safes.

11TH & 12TH ARRONDISSEMENTS (OPERA BASTILLE / BOIS DE VINCENNES)
MODERATE
Le Pavillon Bastille. 65 rue de Lyon, 75012 Paris. ☎ **01-43-43-65-65.** Fax 01-43-43-96-52. 23 rms, 1 suite. A/C MINIBAR TV TEL. 955 F ($191) double; 1,375 F ($275) suite. AE, DC, V. Métro: Bastille.

For those who want to stay in the increasingly fashionable Bastille district, this is the finest choice. Opened in 1991, this town-house hotel is situated across from the Bastille Opera House and about a block south of place de la Bastille. Hardly your cozy little backstreet Paris digs, it's a bold, brassy, and innovative hotel with a clever color scheme. A 17th-century fountain graces the courtyard that sets the hotel off from the street. The rooms provide twin or double beds, mirrored walls, and comfortable contemporary built-in furniture. The English-speaking staff is friendly and efficient, offering room, baby-sitting, laundry, and valet service. Breakfast is served in a dining room set beneath the ceiling vaults of the cellar. Business travelers make up 90% of the hotel's clientele. The well-stocked minibar is complimentary.

INEXPENSIVE
Résidence Alhambra. 11 bis, 13 rue de Malte, 75011 Paris. ☎ **01-47-00-35-52.** Fax 01-43-57-98-75. 58 rms. TEL. 330–360 F ($66–$72) double; 390–530 F ($78–$106) triple. MC, V. Métro: Oberkampf.

Named for the famous cabaret and vaudeville theater that once stood nearby, the Alhambra was built in the 1800s. A radical renovation in 1989 gave the hotel its now comfortable, contemporary format. The hotel rises five stories (10 rooms per floor); in the rear garden, its two-story chalet offers eight additional bedrooms. The rather small accommodations are done in a monochromatic pastel color scheme, which differs from floor to floor. Many Dutch and Italian tour groups stay here. Other than breakfast, no meals are served on the premises. Au Métro, a notable brasserie, is next door, and the nearest RER station (Nation) for Paris Disneyland is only five stops from the hotel.

16TH ARRONDISSEMENT (TROCADERO / BOIS DE BOULOGNE)
VERY EXPENSIVE
Raphaël. 17 av. Kléber, 75116 Paris. ☎ **01-44-28-00-28,** or 800/447-7463 in the U.S. Fax 01-45-01-21-50. 53 rms, 35 suites. MINIBAR TV TEL. 2,520–4,020 F ($504–$804) double; from 7,040 F ($1,408) suite. AE, DC, MC, V. Métro: Kléber or Charles-de-Gaulle/Etoile.

Elite and exclusive—too much so for some—the Raphaël is a celebrity favorite. Near the Arc de Triomphe, it's an oasis of stately dignity. The tone of the hotel is set by the main hallway, with its dark-paneled walnut walls, oil paintings framed in gilt, and lavish bronze torchères. The rich wood paneling continues into the music salon, with its opera-red carpeting and marble fireplace. The bedrooms are impressive, luxuriously furnished with brass-trimmed chests, tables of inlaid wood, armoires, and silk draperies. Some units are air-conditioned. Prices depend on the view. When you pay your bill, you can admire an original Turner (the orange-and-gold painting to the right of the cashier).

Dining/Entertainment: Be sure to have a meal in the formal dining room, La Salle à Manger, with its gold-and-red carpeting, white paneled walls, and arched windows with rich draperies, or enjoy your favorite drink in the wood-paneled English Bar.

Services: Room service, laundry, baby-sitting.

Facilities: Car-rental desk.

EXPENSIVE

Alexander. 102 av. Victor-Hugo, 75016 Paris. ☎ **01-45-53-64-65,** or 800/843-3311 in the U.S. and Canada. Fax 01-45-53-12-51. 60 rms, 2 suites. MINIBAR TV TEL. 1,190 F ($238) double; from 1,870 F ($374) suite. AE, DC, MC, V. Parking 100 F ($20) across the street. Métro: Victor-Hugo.

This is where you might send a very staid relative on a first trip to Paris. It's correct and conservative with a few elegant touches, such as chandeliers in each room. A wrought-iron stairwell winds around the elevator. The rooms are carpeted and rather frilly, half of them facing a well-planted, quiet courtyard. One-day laundry service is provided, and room service is available daily from 7am to 9pm.

St-James Paris. 43 av. Bugeaud, 75116 Paris. ☎ **01-44-05-81-81,** or 800/223-5652 in the U.S. and Canada. Fax 01-44-05-81-82. 14 rms, 5 junior suites, 27 suites, 2 garden pavilions. A/C MINIBAR TV TEL. 1,800 F ($360) double; 2,400 F ($480) jr. suite; 3600 F ($720) suite or garden pavilion. AE, DC, MC, V. Free parking. Métro: Porte-Dauphine.

The only château hotel in Paris, the St-James offers exceptional luxury. In a residential area close to avenue Foch, the 1892 château once housed a foundation for the most brilliant scholars from all over France. The famous French designer Andrée Putman revitalized the art deco interior of the guest rooms. On the third floor 10 rooms open onto a winter garden. At first the St-James Paris required membership, but it's now open to all. Accommodations include penthouse suites (two with their own garden), deluxe suites, and deluxe bedrooms.

Dining/Entertainment: The hotel has a restaurant open daily for lunch serving classic French cuisine. The unique bar is a library with polished oak and some 10,000 leather-bound books.

Services: Room service (24 hours).

Facilities: Health club with Jacuzzi and sauna, billiard room.

17TH ARRONDISSEMENT (PARC MONCEAU / PLACE CLICHY)

EXPENSIVE

Le Méridien Paris Etoile. 81 bd. Gouvion-St-Cyr, 75017 Paris. ☎ **01-40-68-34-34,** or 800/223-0888 in the U.S. and Canada. Fax 01-40-68-31-31. 989 rms, 17 suites. A/C MINIBAR TV TEL. 1,450–1,850 F ($290–$370) double; from 3,800 F ($760) suite. AE, DC, MC, V. Parking 100 F ($20). Métro: Porte-Maillot.

The largest hotel in France, and one of the most visible buildings in the Porte Maillot development northwest of the center of Paris, this megahotel is owned and managed by Air France and caters to groups as well as to individuals. It's functional, not charming. The location is opposite the Porte Maillot Métro stop on the Neuilly–Vincennes line. The setting of the hotel is contemporary French, and the overscale lobby chandelier is an eye-catcher. The bedrooms are designed to provide convenience and comfort, and often you get a good view as well. The rooms on the 8th and 9th floors are particularly luxurious, and are serviced by a private concierge and private receptionist.

Dining/Entertainment: The four restaurants feature everything from traditional French cuisine (Le Clos Longchamp) to Japanese specialties (Yamato). Other dining choices include Le Café Harlequin. There's a musical apéritif hour at 6pm and a 10pm jazz session at the Lionel Hampton Jazz Club.

Services: Room service, laundry, baby-sitting, express checkout.

Facilities: Foreign-currency exchange, business office with English-language secretarial services, photocopies.

MODERATE

Hôtel de Neuville. 3 rue Verniquet, 75017 Paris. ☎ **01-43-80-26-30.** Fax 01-43-80-38-55. 28 rms. TV TEL. 700 F ($140) double. Second bed 100 F ($20) extra. AE, DC, MC, V. Parking 90 F ($18). Métro: Pereire.

The Hôtel de Neuville has retained the symmetrical facade of the 19th-century private house it occupies. The wrought-iron balconies are adorned with potted plants in the summer. The lobby has Ionic columns and warm tones and textures. Furnished in typical French provincial style, this hotel is part of the Minotel chain, which is well-known for value. It may not be particularly glamorous, but it's perfectly respectable, and offers amenities including a garden and tennis court. The rooms are small with pink-and-beige decor, and were renovated as recently as 1994.

Hôtel Regent's Garden. 6 rue Pierre-Demours, 75017 Paris. ☎ **01-45-74-07-30.** Fax 01-40-55-01-42. 39 rms. MINIBAR TV TEL. 710–960 F ($142–$192) double. AE, DC, MC, V. Parking 50 F ($10). Métro: Ternes or Charles-de-Gaulle/Etoile.

The Regent's Garden has a proud heritage: Napoléon III built this stately château for his physician. It's near the convention center and minutes from the Arc de Triomphe. In its price range, this hotel has more traditional French styling and ambience than the Hôtel de Neuville. There are two gardens, one with ivy-covered walls and umbrella tables—a perfect place to meet other guests. The interior resembles a country house with classic touches. The entryway has fluted columns, and the lobby has a casual mixture of comfortable furniture. The rooms are outfitted with flower prints on the walls and bedspreads; the furniture is mostly traditional French. The tall windows are soundproof and have light, airy curtains. Hair dryers are provided.

INEXPENSIVE

Tivoli-Etoile. 7 rue Brey, 75017 Paris. ☎ **01-42-67-12-68.** Fax 01-47-64-01-21. 30 rms. A/C MINIBAR TV TEL. 575–835 F ($115–$167) double. Rates include continental breakfast. AE, DC, MC, V. Métro: Charles-de-Gaulle/Etoile.

Rue Brey is a side street branching off avenue de Wagram, one of the spoke avenues of the Etoile. This street has a number of reasonably priced hotels (all of which seem to be full all year), but the Tivoli-Etoile offers the best value for its mid-city location. The hotel has a contemporary lobby with a mural and a quiet inner patio. The rather cramped bedrooms are all equipped with radios, modern but unremarkable furnishings, hair dryers, air-conditioning, and individual safes.

Les Trois Couronnes. 30 rue de l'Arc-de-Triomphe, 75017 Paris. ☎ **01-43-80-46-81.** Fax 01-46-22-53-96. 20 rms. MINIBAR TV TEL. 350–598 F ($70–$119.60) double. AE, DC, MC, V. Parking 75 F ($15). Métro: Charles-de-Gaulle/Etoile.

This prestigious older hotel is located near the Etoile, where many important Paris streets intersect in a star-shaped network of boulevards—Etoile is the center of the tourist district and business center of Paris, and affords easy access to the Métro and to many of the city's attractions. The hotel, with its blend of art deco and art nouveau, was redecorated in 1995 and is under new management. The hotel staff takes pleasure in assisting guests with their needs. The rooms are cheerfully decorated with a view of the surroundings, and the hotel has a security system for protection and an elevator for convenience. Laundry service is available.

18TH ARRONDISSEMENT (MONTMARTRE)

Terrass Hôtel. 12–14 rue Joseph-de-Maistre, 75018 Paris. ☎ **01-46-06-72-85,** or 800/
528-1234 in the U.S. and Canada. Fax 01-42-52-29-11. 91 rms, 10 suites. MINIBAR TV TEL.
1,110 F ($222) double; 1,550 F ($310) suite. AE, DC, MC, V. Rates include breakfast. Métro:
Place-de-Clichy or Blanche.

Originally built in 1913, and richly renovated into a plush but traditional style in
1991, this is the only four-star hotel on the Butte Montmartre. In an area filled with
some of the seediest hotels in Paris, this place outclasses all others. Its main advantage is its location in Montmartre, a decent address for those who want to soak up
the bohemian atmosphere (or what's left of it). Staffed with English-speaking employees and its owner-managers, it offers a large, marble-floored lobby ringed with blond
oak paneling and accented with 18th-century antiques and even older tapestries. The
bedrooms are high-ceilinged, cozy, well upholstered, and very French, often with
views.

Dining/Entertainment: There's an elegant street-level restaurant and a seventh-
floor summer-only garden/terrace with bar and food service and sweeping views over
many of the most important monuments of Paris. For colder weather, the hotel's
Lobby Bar, with its own fireplace, offers charm and live piano music.

Services: Foreign exchange, car rentals, tour desk, laundry/dry cleaning.
Facilities: Conference facilities.

3 On the Left Bank

We'll begin with the most centrally located arrondissements on the Left Bank, then
work our way through the more outlying neighborhoods.

5TH ARRONDISSEMENT (LATIN QUARTER)
MODERATE

Hôtel le Colbert. 7 rue de l'Hôtel-Colbert, 75005 Paris. ☎ **01-43-25-85-65,** or 800/
448-8355 in the U.S. and Canada. Fax 01-43-25-80-19. 36 rms, 2 suites. MINIBAR TV TEL.
1,010 F ($202) double; 1,630–1,930 F ($326–$386) suite. AE, DC, MC, V. Métro: Maubert-
Mutualité or St-Michel.

How can you miss by staying at this little 18th-century inn? Not only is it on the Left
Bank, just a minute's walk from the Seine, but many of its rooms have a fine view
of Notre-Dame, too. Bordered by a wrought-iron fence, a small courtyard with
evergreens sets the hotel apart from the narrow street and the bustle of Rive Gauche
life.

Visitors entering the hotel find themselves in a tastefully decorated lobby with
marble floors and antiques. Gilt-accented furniture fills a sunny bar area. The guest
rooms are well designed; most have comfortable chairs and a breakfast area. Those
on the fifth floor, the uppermost *étage*, evoke a garret. The suites feature very old
beams. The beds are inviting. Plenty of towels and efficient maid service are provided.
Some rooms are suitable for persons with disabilities.

Hôtel Moderne St-Germain. 33 rue des Ecoles, 75005 Paris. ☎ **01-43-54-37-78.** Fax 01-
43-29-91-31. 45 rms. TV TEL. 840 F ($168) double. AE, DC, MC, V. Parking 170 F ($34). Métro:
Maubert-Mutualité or St-Michel.

Near Notre-Dame and the Panthéon, in the heart of the Latin Quarter, the Hôtel
Moderne St-Germain was completely renovated in 1992. Its charming owner,
Madame Gibon, welcomes guests warmly. The comfortably furnished bedrooms are
spotlessly maintained. In the rooms fronting rue des Ecoles, double-glazed aluminum
windows create a quieter atmosphere. The hotel also has a sauna and Jacuzzi, along

Left Bank Accommodations

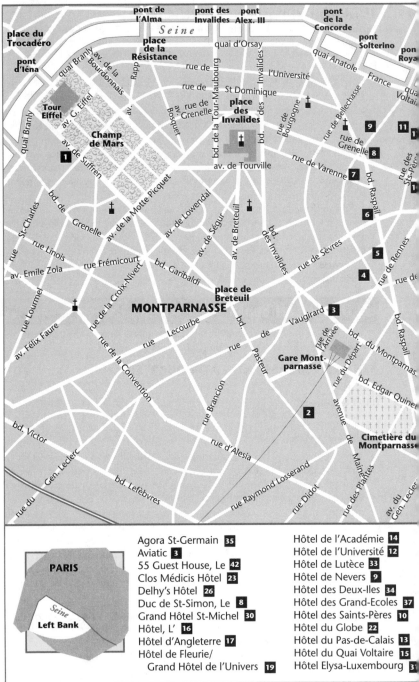

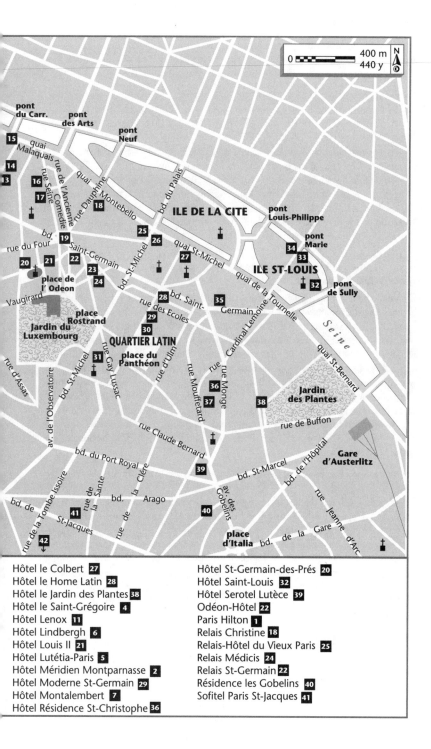

Hôtel le Colbert **27**
Hôtel le Home Latin **28**
Hôtel le Jardin des Plantes **38**
Hôtel le Saint-Grégoire **4**
Hôtel Lenox **11**
Hôtel Lindbergh **6**
Hôtel Louis II **21**
Hôtel Lutétia-Paris **5**
Hôtel Méridien Montparnasse **2**
Hôtel Moderne St-Germain **29**
Hôtel Montalembert **7**
Hôtel Résidence St-Christophe **36**

Hôtel St-Germain-des-Prés **20**
Hôtel Saint-Louis **32**
Hôtel Serotel Lutèce **39**
Odéon-Hôtel **22**
Paris Hilton **1**
Relais Christine **18**
Relais-Hôtel du Vieux Paris **25**
Relais Médicis **24**
Relais St-Germain **22**
Résidence les Gobelins **40**
Sofitel Paris St-Jacques **41**

with an indoor swimming pool, a rarity for a hotel of this price range. The rooms are small, but this is still one of the better three-star hotels in the neighborhood. Traditional cuisine is served at Le Clos Bruneau, the hotel restaurant.

INEXPENSIVE

✪ **Agora St-Germain.** 42 rue des Bernardins, 75005 Paris. ☎ **01-46-34-13-00.** Fax 01-46-34-75-05. 39 rms. MINIBAR TV TEL. 720 F ($144) double; 820 F ($164) triple. AE, DC, MC, V. Parking 110 F ($22). Métro: Maubert-Mutualité.

This is a good choice for travelers seeking that little St-Germain hotel of charm and character. It's the best of the many neighborhood hotels in its price range. The Agora St-Germain was originally built in the early 1600s to house a group of guardsmen protecting the brother of the king at his lodgings in the nearby rue Monsieur-le-Prince. The hotel offers compact but soundproof rooms, each comfortably furnished and equipped with an alarm clock, hair dryer, and safe-deposit box. Room service is provided every morning, from 7:30 to 10:30am.

Grand Hôtel St-Michel. 19 rue Cujas, 75005 Paris. ☎ **01-46-33-33-02.** Fax 01-40-46-96-33. 61 rms. TV TEL. 400–500 F ($80–$100) double. AE, DC, JCB, MC, V. Métro: Cluny–La Sorbonne. RER: Luxembourg.

Originally built during the 19th century, this hotel, with 61 rooms, is larger and more businesslike than many of the smaller town-house–style inns in the same neighborhood. It basks in the reflected glow of Brazilian dissident Georges Amado, whose memoirs—released in 1996—recorded his 2-year literary sojourn in one of the bedrooms of this hotel. The hotel has systematically renovated all but a handful of its accommodations, and hopes to eventually move from two- to three-star status, in which event the prices will probably become a bit higher than those recorded above. The renovated bedrooms have lower ceilings and more modern-looking accessories than those that await renovations. Many bedrooms have small balconies overlooking the street scenes below, and those on the sixth floor have interesting views over the nearby rooftops. Each room has a private shower and toilet. Overall, the hotel offers good value and cleanliness.

Hôtel des Grands-Ecoles. 75 rue Cardinal-Lemoine, 75005 Paris. ☎ **01-43-26-79-23.** Fax 01-43-25-28-15. 50 rms. TEL. 520 F ($104) double. MC, V. Métro: Cardinal-Lemoine or Monge.

This hotel, which has the feel of a private home in the French countryside, incorporates three separate 18th-century buildings, connected via a pleasantly landscaped garden, in a historic and rather conservative neighborhood. In 1996 massive renovations were completed, including improvements to the bedrooms in one of the three buildings (the other two had already been renovated) and an underground parking lot beneath the garden. Breakfast can be served in any bedroom, in a communal breakfast room, or in the garden. The bedrooms have floral-patterned wallpapers and cheerful color schemes, and each comes with a private shower and toilet. The staff is usually very helpful.

Hôtel Elysa-Luxembourg. 6 rue Gay-Lussac, 75005 Paris. ☎ **01-43-25-31-74.** Fax 01-46-34-56-27. 30 rms. MINIBAR TV TEL. 560–720 F ($112–$144) double; 820 F ($164) triple. AE, MC, V. Parking 50 F ($10). Métro: Odéon or St-Michel; RER: Luxembourg.

One of the best choices in the heart of the Latin Quarter, the Elysa-Luxembourg is near the Luxembourg Gardens. The completely renovated rooms in this 19th-century structure are charming, spacious, and soundproof. Some accommodations are reserved for nonsmokers.

Hôtel le Home Latin. 15–17 rue du Sommerard, 75005 Paris. ☎ **01-43-26-95-15.** Fax 01-43-29-87-04. 55 rms. TV TEL. 430–495 F ($86–$99) double. AE, MC, V. Métro: St-Michel or Maubert-Mutualité.

It's one of the most famous budget hotels of Paris, known since the 1970s for inexpensive, clean, and uncomplicated lodgings. Countless numbers of foreign students have stayed here over the years. The hotel originally consisted of two separate side-by-side buildings that the management unified in the 1970s, retaining the hotel's two original entrances. Renovations in 1992 transformed the bedrooms into blandly functional lodgings, some of which have small balconies overlooking the street. Bedrooms facing the courtyard are quieter than those fronting the street, and the elevator doesn't go beyond the fifth floor. Guests on the sixth floor, *chambres mansardées,* tend to appreciate their romantic location under the eaves and the better views over the surrounding rooftops. Each room contains a hair dryer, plus a private bath.

Hôtel le Jardin des Plantes. 5 rue Linne, 75005 Paris. ☎ **01-47-07-06-20.** Fax 01-47-07-62-74. 33 rms. MINIBAR TV TEL. 510–640 F ($102–$128) double. DC, DISC, MC, V. Métro: Jussieu. Bus: 67 or 89.

Opened in 1986, the two-star Hôtel le Jardin des Plantes lies near the Panthéon and across from the Jardin des Plantes, the botanical gardens created by order of Louis XIII's doctors in 1626 and first called the Jardin Royal des Plantes Médicinales. There are still some 15,000 medicinal herbs in the gardens. Some of the well-equipped bedrooms open onto flowered, sunny terraces. A vaulted lounge in the basement, a sauna, and ironing facilities are provided. Equipped with an elevator, the hotel has a small roof terrace and a brasserie and snack bar where breakfast is served.

Hôtel Résidence Saint-Christophe. 17 rue Lacépède, 75005 Paris. ☎ **01-43-31-81-54.** Fax 01-43-31-12-54. 31 rms. MINIBAR TV TEL. 550–750 F ($110–$150) double. AE, DC, MC, V. Métro: Place-Monge.

In one of the most charming but lesser-known parts of the Quartier Latin, a short walk east of the Botanical Gardens, the Saint-Christophe was created in 1987 by combining a derelict hotel with an adjacent butcher shop. With millions spent on the restoration, the resulting hotel is clean and warmly comfortable. The rooms have tall sunny windows, traditional furniture, wall-to-wall carpeting, and marble baths. In its category it's absolutely comparable—no better, no worse—to the Elysa-Luxembourg (see above). Only breakfast is served here; the gracious English-speaking staff offers good advice on neighborhood restaurants.

Hôtel Serotel Lutèce. 2 rue Berthollet, 75005 Paris. ☎ **01-43-36-26-30.** Fax 01-43-31-08-21. 48 rms, 1 suite. MINIBAR TV TEL. 690–720 F ($138–$144) double; 1,400 F ($280) suite. AE, MC, V. Métro: Censier-Daubenton.

Set near Pont-Royal, in a quiet, charming residential neighborhood, the Hôtel Serotel Lutèce was built in the 19th century. A complete renovation in the early 1990s modernized many of the bedrooms, equipping them with comfortable beds, simple furniture, and wall-to-wall carpeting. The bathrooms have slightly cramped but adequate shower stalls and a handful of amenities and extras. Some of the bedrooms overlook a courtyard dotted with jardinières and potted flowers. Breakfast (the only meal offered) is served in a basement-level room that resembles a clean and well-lighted cave.

6TH ARRONDISSEMENT (ST-GERMAIN / LUXEMBOURG)
EXPENSIVE

✪ **L'Hôtel.** 13 rue des Beaux-Arts, 75006 Paris. ☎ **01-44-41-99-00**. Fax 01-43-25-64-81. 24 rms, 3 suites. A/C MINIBAR TV TEL. 1,000–1,700 F ($200–$340) small double;

2,300–2,800 F ($460–$560) large double; from 3,600 F ($720) suite. AE, DC, MC, V. Métro: St-Germain-des-Prés.

In the 19th-century this was a fleabag called the Hôtel d'Alsace, whose major distinction was that Oscar Wilde, broke and in despair, died here in 1900. Today guests at L'Hôtel aren't exactly on poverty row. Many fashion and show business personalities march through the lobby. French actor Guy-Louis Duboucheron has created an intimate, super-sophisticated jewel box. A Texas architect, Robin Westbrook, gutted the core of the Alsace and designed a circular courtyard and an interior that reminds us of the Tower of Pisa. You'll feel like a movie star yourself when you take a bath; at the edge of your rosy-pink Italian marble tub sits a delicate vase holding a single rose. Antiques are used with discretion throughout the hotel; the eclectic collection has pieces from the periods of Louis XV and Louis XVI, as well as Empire and Directoire. The rooms are small, but everything is impeccably maintained.

Dining/Entertainment: Breakfast is served in a winter garden, which in the evening becomes a restaurant for intimate dinners. Le Bélier is a luxurious piano bar/restaurant.

Services: Concierge, room service (24 hours), baby-sitting, laundry/valet.

Hôtel Lutétia-Paris. 45 bd. Raspail, 75006 Paris. ☎ **01-49-54-46-46,** or 800/888-4747 in the U.S. and Canada. Fax 01-49-54-46-00. 241 rms, 29 suites. A/C MINIBAR TV TEL. 1,150–1,950 F ($230–$390) double; from 3,500 F ($700) suite. AE, DC, MC, V. Parking 120 F ($24). Métro: Sèvres-Babylone.

This eight-story, carved-stone building stands at a Left Bank crossroads. No more prestigious an address exists in the 6th arrondissement, nor does a better hotel. It doesn't quite have the antique charm of the Relais Christine or Relais Saint-Germain, but, then, not many do. Richly associated with the city's literary history, this is the largest and one of the most unusual hotels on the Left Bank. Built in 1910 in the art deco style, it has been restored to its original splendor. Early in its history the Lutétia attracted such luminaries as Cocteau, André Gide, Picasso, and Charles de Gaulle, who spent part of his honeymoon here. The comfortable bedrooms, with a distinct flavor of the Roaring Twenties, are tastefully subdued and high-ceilinged. The hotel attracts a knowledgeable clientele of repeat visitors, many of them diplomats.

Relais Christine. 3 rue Christine, 75006 Paris. ☎ **01-43-26-71-80.** Fax 01-43-26-89-38. 38 rms, 13 duplexes. A/C MINIBAR TV TEL. 1,680–1,790 F ($336–$358) double; 2,550–3,100 F ($510–$620) duplexes. AE, DC, MC, V. Free parking. Métro: Odéon.

This is generally cited as the "second-best" hotel in the 6th, ranked under the Lutétia, which has far better facilities and services. It is, however, an equal to the Relais Saint-Germain (see below). We've only received one complaint about this hotel, from a woman who claimed that her bedroom was "from hell," although we've yet to see that particular chamber. The rooms are fair-sized, a mix of rustic and traditional. The best accommodations open onto the central lawn. The Relais Christine welcomes an international clientele into what was formerly a 16th-century Augustinian cloister. You enter from a narrow cobblestone street, first into a symmetrical courtyard and then into an elegant reception area dotted with baroque sculpture, plushly upholstered chairs and sofas, and a scattering of Renaissance antiques.

Each bedroom is individually decorated with Louis XII–style furnishings. Accents might include massively beamed ceilings and luxurious wall-to-wall carpeting. The bathrooms are done in marble.

Dining/Entertainment: There's a paneled sitting room and bar area ringed with 19th-century portraits and comfortable leather chairs. In the breakfast room in the

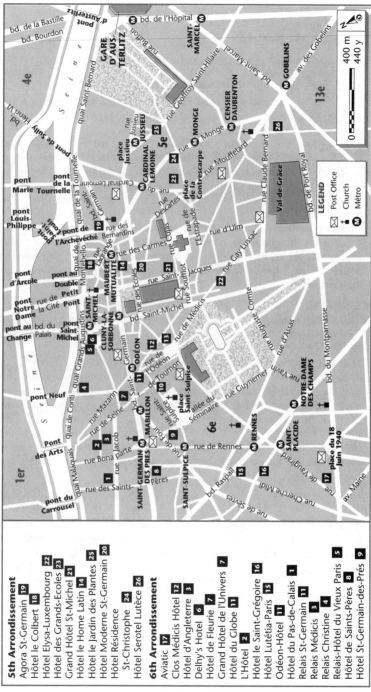

97

vaulted cellar, the ancient well and the massive central stone column were part of the cloister's former kitchen.

Services: Room service (24 hours), laundry, baby-sitting, private garage.

Relais Saint-Germain. 9 carrefour de l'Odéon, 75006 Paris. ☎ **01-43-29-12-05.** Fax 01-46-33-45-30. 22 rms, 4 suites. A/C MINIBAR TV TEL. 1,530–1,700 F ($306–$340) double; from 1,950 F ($390) suite. Rates include breakfast. AE, DC, MC, V. Métro: Odéon.

The Relais Saint-Germain is an oasis of charm and comfort. But keep it a secret. Comparable to the Relais Christine, its nearest rival, the Saint-Germain was skillfully converted from a 17th-century edifice and is now one of the most charming of all Left Bank hostelries. The owner is a well-known designer, and his influence and decorating skill show at every turn. The rooms are named after French writers. Each is individually decorated with style and flair. Of course, all the necessary amenities were tucked in under the beams as well, including soundproofing, private safe, and hair dryer. Four bedrooms feature kitchenettes, and two of the suites are complete with terraces.

Dining/Entertainment: The hotel operates a bistro/wine bar, the Comptoir du Relais, that's a delightful little retreat. Here you can order such oh-so-French dishes as potted goose pâté, pork-and-pistachio sausage, or any number of sandwiches with traditional French bread, including "Rosette" sausage from Lyon or smoked salmon from Norway.

MODERATE

Le Clos Médicis Hôtel. 56 rue Monsieur-le-Prince, 75006 Paris. ☎ **01-43-29-10-80.** Fax 01-43-54-26-90. 37 rms, 1 duplex. A/C MINIBAR TV TEL. 786–892 F ($157.20–$178.40) double; 1,212 F ($242.40) duplex. AE, DC, MC, V. RER: Luxembourg.

Once a private home (1860), then a bookstore and run-down boardinghouse, Le Clos Médicis opened in 1994 to become one of the Latin Quarter's newest hotels. If you want the charm and elegance of the Relais Christine or the Relais Saint-Germain at a more reasonable price, this hotel provides it. Its location, adjacent to the Luxembourg Gardens, is one of its advantages. A multilingual staff runs the hotel. Simple Provençal furniture decorates the lobby. Outside, a garden has lattices and is bordered by stone walls. The bedrooms, done in warm tones and in an uncomplicated style, are comfortable but not overly large. A buffet breakfast is the only meal served here.

Hôtel d'Angleterre. 44 rue Jacob, 75006 Paris. ☎ **01-42-60-34-72.** Fax 01-42-60-16-93. 27 rms. TV TEL. 800–1,250 F ($160–$250) double. AE, DC, MC, V. Métro: St-Germain-des-Prés.

Situated amid antique shops and art galleries, this quaint 1650 building remains a solid and reliable (if not terribly stylish) choice. The rooms are individually decorated, and although many of them are quite spacious, some are quite small and others are downright plain. Nevertheless, this remains a somewhat snobbish Left Bank address. Many visitors to Paris who return year after year would stay nowhere else.

Hôtel des Saints-Pères. 65 rue des Sts-Pères, 75006 Paris. ☎ **01-45-44-50-00.** Fax 01-45-44-90-83. 39 rms, 3 suites. MINIBAR TV TEL. 500–550 F ($100–$110) double with shower, 720–980 F ($144–$196) double with bathttub; 1,620 F ($324) suite. AE, MC, V. Métro: St-Germain-des-Prés or Sèvres-Babylone.

This hotel just off boulevard St-Germain is comparable to the Odéon, attracting people who love Paris or, more specifically, love traditional Left Bank hotels. The best recommendation for this old favorite is its long list of guests who return again and again. The late Edna St. Vincent Millay enjoyed the camellia-trimmed garden. The hotel, designed by Louis XIV's architect, is decorated in part with antique paintings, tapestries, and mirrors. Many of the bedrooms face a quiet courtyard accented in summer with potted plants. The most sought-after room is the *chambre à la fresque,* which has a 17th-century painted ceiling. The hotel's plumbing has been updated and the rooms replastered and repainted. Some rooms now have air-conditioning. Breakfast is served outside in the courtyard, weather permitting.

Hôtel le Saint-Grégoire. 43 rue de l'Abbé-Grégoire, 75006 Paris. ☎ **01-45-48-23-23.** Fax 01-45-48-33-95. 20 rms, 1 suite. A/C TV TEL. 790–1,390 F ($158–$278) double; 1,390 F ($278) suite. AE, DC, MC, V. Parking 70 F ($14). Métro: St-Placide.

This well-run hotel in a restored town house has been awarded three stars. The well-decorated rooms are often dotted with antiques. White damask bedspreads and chintz curtains add a graceful decorative tone. Double glazing helps keep down some of the street noise. The breakfast is of the perfect continental variety, and the staff is always thoughtful and helpful. In winter, a cozy fire warms the intimate salon.

Hôtel St-Germain-des-Prés. 36 rue Bonaparte, 75006 Paris. ☎ **01-43-26-00-19.** Fax 01-40-46-83-63. 28 rms, 2 suites. MINIBAR TV TEL. 750–900 F ($150–$180) double; 1,300–1,600 F ($260–$320) suite. Rates include breakfast. MC, V. Métro: St-Germain-des-Prés.

After renovations overhauled its beautiful and traditional interior, this hotel shot ahead of its nearby competitors in offering traditional French style and grace. Much of this hotel's attractiveness comes from its enviable location in the Latin Quarter— near many shops and behind a well-known Left Bank street. Janet Flanner, a legendary correspondent for *The New Yorker* in the 1920s, lived at this hotel for a while. All the bedrooms, capped with antique ceiling beams, are small but charming. The severely elegant public rooms have dentil moldings and Louis XIII furnishings. Some of the building's original stonework is exposed. Air-conditioning is available in most of the bedrooms; all rooms have safes and trouser presses.

Odéon-Hôtel. 3 rue de l'Odéon, 75006 Paris. ☎ **01-43-25-90-67.** Fax 01-43-25-55-98. 34 rms. TV TEL. 850–1,000 F ($170–$200) double. AE, DC, MC, V. Métro: Odéon.

Conveniently located near both the Théâtre de l'Odéon and boulevard St-Germain, the Odéon stands on the first street in Paris to have pavements and gutters (it was first paved in 1779). By the turn of this century this area, which had the bookshop Shakespeare and Company no. 12 rue de l'Odéon, began attracting such writers as André Gide, Paul Valéry, James Joyce, T. S. Eliot, F. Scott Fitzgerald, Ernest Hemingway, and Gertrude Stein. Today the hotel is reminiscent of a modernized Norman country inn. Exposed beams, rough stone walls, high crooked ceilings, tapestries, and wallpaper with swirling designs (like that found on the endpapers of antique books) are mixed with bright contemporary fabrics, mirrored ceilings, and black leather furniture. After modern plumbing was installed, each room was individually redesigned.

Le Relais Médicis. 23 rue Racine, 75006 Paris. ☎ **01-43-26-00-60.** Fax 01-40-46-83-39. 16 rms. A/C MINIBAR TV TEL. 995–1,495 F ($199–$299) double. Rates include breakfast. AE, DC, MC, V. Métro: Odéon.

Until its radical overhaul in 1991, this place next to the Théâtre de l'Odéon was a well-worn two-star hotel favored by students, indigent artists, and visiting professors from abroad. It attempted to reinvent itself as a four-star property, but the anticipated business didn't materialize. Now the Relais is a standard three-star hotel with reduced services and reduced rates attempting to attract more business. It's a lavishly decorated romantic hideaway. The richly upholstered rooms have a stylishly cluttered and old-fashioned patina reminiscent of a family homestead in Provence. Fabric covers the walls. The wide price difference of the rooms is based on their size; some are quite large. There's a small bar, private safes, and cable TV. Old oil portraits and antique lithographs hang in the public room.

INEXPENSIVE

Aviatic. 105 rue de Vaugirard, 75006 Paris. ☎ **01-45-44-38-21.** Fax 01-45-49-35-83. 43 rms. MINIBAR TV TEL. 750–780 F ($150–$156) double. AE, DC, MC, V. Parking 100 F ($20). Métro: Montparnasse-Bienvenue.

A bit of Old Paris, the Aviatic has been a family-run hotel of character and elegance for more than a century. A modest inner courtyard has vine-covered lattices on its walls. Both the reception lounge and a petit salon provide traditional settings, with marble columns, brass chandeliers, and antiques. It doesn't have grand decorative style and flair, but it offers good comfort, a warm ambience, and a welcoming English-speaking staff. Completely remodeled, the hotel is situated in an interesting section of Montparnasse, with cafés frequented by artists, writers, and jazz musicians.

Delhy's Hotel. 22 rue de l'Hirondelle, 75006 Paris. Tel. **01-43-26-58-25.** Fax 01-43-26-51-06. 21 rms, 7 with shower only. TV TEL. 356 F ($71.20) double without shower, 436 F ($87.20) double with shower only; 579 F ($115.80) triple with shower only; 682 F ($136.40) quad with shower only. Rates include breakfast. AE, DC, MC, V. Métro: St-Michel.

This six-story urban antique was built around 1400, and later was bought by François I as a home for one of his mistresses. It lies on a narrow and crooked alleyway, one end of which runs into a point adjacent to no. 6 place St-Michel, in the heart of the densest and most frenetic part of the Latin Quarter. Don't expect Shangri-La here, but look for certain touches of charm that help compensate for the lack of an elevator. If you get a room without a shower, you'll have to go down to the ground floor for access to the public facilities. The building's staircase is listed as a French national relic, and most of the compact bedrooms still have the building's original, almost fossilized, timbers and beams. The hotel has been owned for many years by Mme Kenneche, who leaves the day-to-day management of the place to a hardworking North African staff while spending much of her day maintaining a Mexican bistro in the 5th arrondissement.

Grand Hôtel de l'Univers. 6 rue Grégoire-de-Tours, 75006 Paris. ☎ **01-43-29-37-00.** Fax 01-40-51-06-45. 34 rms. A/C MINIBAR TV TEL. 850 F ($170) double. AE, DC, MC, V. Métro: Odéon.

In the 1400s this was home to a family of the then-emerging bourgeoisie. The hotel's main competitor—right on the same street near the Luxembourg Palace—is the Hôtel de Fleurie (see below), which has a slight edge. But de l'Univers is the epitome of a Left Bank hotel of charm and tranquillity. The rooms are cramped but well maintained. Some of the pleasantly renovated rooms enjoy a panoramic view over the crooked rooftops of the surrounding neighborhood. La Bonbonnière (the Candy Box) is an all-pink confection of a bedroom. All rooms are equipped with satellite TV reception, private safe, and a hair dryer. Breakfast is served in the cellar beneath the 500-year-old stone vaults. For reasons known only to them, Michelin consistently ignores this hotel even though it's a worthy choice.

Hôtel de Fleurie. 32–34 rue Grégoire-de-Tours, 75006 Paris. ☎ **01-53-73-70-00.** Fax 01-53-73-70-20. 29 rms. A/C MINIBAR TV TEL. 850–1,200 F ($170–$240) double. Children 11 and under stay free in parents' room. AE, DC, MC, V. Métro: Odéon.

When de Fleurie opened it was one of the most exciting renovations in the neighborhood in years. So many hotels, such as the St-Germain-des-Prés, have opened to challenge de Fleurie that the excitement has dimmed. But de Fleurie is still going strong, despite newer and more stylish competitors. In the reception salon, stone walls peek out behind elaborate latticework, and beams support the ceiling. An elevator ascends to the well-furnished, modern bedrooms. A spiral staircase descends to the breakfast room. Safes are found in the accommodations. Each room is equipped with a modem plug.

☉ **Hôtel du Globe.** 15 rue des Quatre-Vents, 75006 Paris. ☎ **01-46-33-62-69.** Fax 01-46-33-17-29. 15 rms, 14 with bath (tub or shower). 250 F ($50) double with toilet only, 350–450 F ($70–$90) double with bath. No credit cards. Métro: Mabillon, Odéon, or St-Sulpice.

This 17th-century building occupies a historically evocative street in one of the oldest neighborhoods of Paris. Inside you'll find most of the original stonework and dozens of the original timbers and beams that a team of craftspeople labored to restore. Each bedroom is decorated with individual flair in an old-fashioned style, a rarity in hotels as inexpensive as this. The rooms with a bathtub are almost twice as large as those with a shower, so for the extra expense you'll usually get a lot more than just an improvement in the plumbing. There's no elevator (you'll have to lug your suitcases up a very narrow, very inconvenient antique staircase) and no breakfast area (breakfast trays are brought to your room). The largest and most desirable rooms are nos. 1, 12 (which has a baldaquin-style bed), 14, 15, and 16.

Hôtel du Pas-de-Calais. 59 rue des Sts-Pères, 75006 Paris. ☎ **01-45-48-78-74.** Fax 01-45-44-94-57. 41 rms. TV TEL. 620–790 F ($124-$158) double. AE, MC, V. Métro: St-Germain-des-Prés or Sèvres-Babylone.

The five-story Pas-de-Calais was built in the 17th century by the Lavalette family. Its elegant facade, complete with massive wooden doors, has been retained. The romantic novelist Chateaubriand lived here from 1811 to 1814. Its most famous guest of literary distinction was Jean-Paul Sartre, who struggled with the play *Les Mains Sales* (called *The Red Gloves* on Broadway) in Room 41 during the hotel's pre-restoration days. The hotel is a bit weak on style, unlike those previously reviewed, but as one longtime guest confided, in spite of the updates and renovations "we still stay here for the memories."

The guest rooms are modern with large baths. The inner rooms surround a modest courtyard, which has two garden tables and several trellises. All rooms have TVs, safe-deposit boxes, and hair dryers. Off the somewhat sterile lobby is a comfortable, carpeted sitting room.

Hôtel Louis II. 2 rue St-Sulpice, 75006 Paris. ☎ **01-46-33-13-80.** Fax 01-46-33-17-29. 22 rms. MINIBAR TV TEL. 525–750 F ($105–$150) double; 920 F ($184) triple. AE, DC, MC, V. Métro: Odéon.

Housed in what was a neglected 18th-century building, this hotel provides rustic accommodations that are a bit threadbare but acceptable. Afternoon drinks and morning coffee are served in the reception salon, where gilt-framed mirrors, fresh flowers, and well-oiled antiques give the room a provincial feel. Upstairs, the rooms boast exposed beams but the beds are not the most comfortable. Many repeat visitors request the romantic attic rooms. TVs are available upon request. The street outside tends to be noisy.

7TH ARRONDISSEMENT (EIFFEL TOWER / MUSEE D'ORSAY)
EXPENSIVE

Le Duc de Saint-Simon. 14 rue de St-Simon, 75007 Paris. ☎ **01-44-39-20-20.** Fax 01-45-48-68-25. 29 rms, 5 suites. TEL. 1,050–1,450 F ($210–$290) double; 1,850–1,900 F ($370–$380) suite. No credit cards. Métro: Rue-du-Bac.

Set on a quiet residential street on the Left Bank, this is the only hotel in the 7th arrondissement to seriously challenge the Montalembert (see below). This small villa has a tiny front garden and an 1830s decor with *faux-marbre* trompe-l'oeil panels and a frescoed elevator. Its courtyard is graced with climbing wisteria. The two famous cafés, Les Deux Magots and Le Flore, are only a few steps away. Each bedroom is unique and sure to include at least one antique. The service, the best reflection of the owner's extensive training, is welcoming.

✪ Hôtel Montalembert. 3 rue de Montalembert, 75007 Paris. ☎ **01-45-49-68-68**, or 800/447-7462 in the U.S. and Canada. Fax 01-45-49-69-49. 51 rms, 5 suites. A/C MINIBAR TV TEL. 1,625–2,080 F ($325–$416) double; 2,750 F ($550) junior suite; 3,650 F ($730) suite. AE, DC, MC, V. Parking 120 F ($24). Métro: Rue-du-Bac.

The Montalembert's beaux arts style (1926) made it the darling of France's intellectual *crème de la crème* and serious fashion types. There's no finer address in all the 7th arrondissement. This is one of the most appealing small hotels of Paris, rivaled only in the 6th by the Relais Christine and the Relais Saint-Germain. In 1989, much in need of renovation, the hotel was bought by the Leo group, a Hong Kong–based chain. One of France's premier architectural designers, Christian Liaigre, directed a well-publicized overhaul. After millions of dollars' worth of discreet improvements, the hotel reopened in 1990 and was immediately hailed as one of the capital's most successful and imaginative restorations.

Unusually elegant for a Left Bank hotel, the public rooms—done in a palette of honey beiges, creams, and golds—borrow elements of Bauhaus design and postmodernism. Half the bedrooms are conservatively decorated in French Empire style and the rest are modern. All have VCRs and safes. The bathrooms are sheathed in gray Portuguese marble. The in-house Restaurant Montalembert is noteworthy.

MODERATE

Hôtel de l'Académie. 32 rue des Sts-Pères, 75007 Paris. ☎ **01-45-48-36-22.** Fax 01-45-44-75-24. 34 rms. A/C MINIBAR TV TEL. 490–1,290 F ($98–$258) double. AE, DC, MC, V. Métro: St-Germain-des-Prés.

The exterior walls and old ceiling beams are all that remain of this 17th-century residence for the private guards of the duc de Rohan. The hotel now has an elegant marble and oak reception area. With views over the 18th- and 19th-century buildings in the immediate neighborhood, the comfortably up-to-date rooms are done in soft colors; they have Directoire beds and an "Ile de France" ambience. By American standards the rooms are rather small, but they're quite normal as Parisian bedrooms go. The staff speaks English.

✪ Hôtel de l'Université. 22 rue de l'Université, 75007 Paris. ☎ **01-42-61-09-39.** Fax 01-42-60-40-84. 28 rms. A/C TV TEL. 800–1,300 F ($160–$260) double. AE, MC, V. Métro: St-Germain-des-Prés.

L'Université is the love child of Madame Bergmann, who has a flair for restoring old places and a collector's eye for assembling antiques. She has completely renovated this 300-year-old town house and decorated it with unusually fine antiques. It long ago became the preferred little place to stay for those who want a St-Germain-des-Prés atmosphere (reservations are imperative). No. 54 is a favorite room, with a rattan bed, period pieces, and a marble bath. Opening onto a courtyard, no. 35, with a fireplace and a provincial armoire, is another charmer. A small, bistro-style breakfast room opens onto a tiny courtyard with a fountain. Everything is personal.

INEXPENSIVE

Hôtel de Nevers. 83 rue du Bac, 75007 Paris. ☎ **01-45-44-61-30.** Fax 01-42-22-29-47. 11 rms. MINIBAR TEL. 410–440 F ($82–$88) double. No credit cards. Métro: Rue-du-Bac.

Hotels: 7th Arrondissement

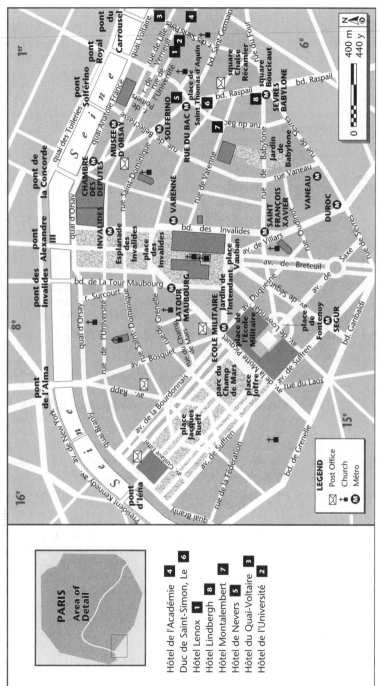

LEGEND
⊠ Post Office
† ■ Church
Ⓜ Métro

PARIS
Area of
Detail

Hôtel de l'Académie **4**
Duc de Saint-Simon, Le **6**
Hôtel Lenox **1**
Hôtel Lindbergh **8**
Hôtel Montalembert **7**
Hôtel de Nevers **5**
Hôtel du Quai-Voltaire **3**
Hôtel de l'Université **2**

Named after a famous Romanesque town in Burgundy, this building is one of the most historic choices in a very old neighborhood. Between 1627 and 1790 it was a convent for the Soeurs de la Recollettes before they were disbanded by the French Revolution (look for the religious plaque on the stone wall opposite the reception desk). The building, brought to its present level of modernization in 1983, is presently *classé*, which means that any restoration must respect the original architecture. That precludes an elevator, so you'll have to climb the never-ending but very beautiful white staircase. The rooms, cozy and pleasant, contain a mishmash of antique and reproduced furniture. Two rooms (nos. 10 and 11) are especially sought-after because of their terraces that overlook either a corner of rue du Bac or a rear courtyard. Each room contains a shower or tub and a toilet.

Hôtel du Quai Voltaire. 19 quai Voltaire, 75007 Paris. ☎ **01-42-61-50-91.** Fax 01-42-61-62-26. 32 rms. TV TEL. 600-690 F ($120-$138) double; 800 F ($160) triple. AE, DC, MC, V. Parking 120 F ($24) nearby. Métro: Palais-Royal.

This is an inn with a rich past and one of the most panoramic views in all Paris. The hotel occupies a prime site on the Left Bank quays of the Seine, halfway between the pont Royal and the pont du Carrousel. Twenty-nine of its rooms—many of them renovated—gaze over the Louvre, directly across the river. Through the years, Charles Baudelaire, Jean Sibelius, Richard Wagner, and Oscar Wilde have stayed here, and photos of Wagner and Baudelaire hang in the small, plush sitting room. The rooms are a bit dowdy but pleasantly furnished and arranged. The focal point of every front room is that view—seen through floor-to-ceiling double French windows.

Hôtel Lenox. 9 rue de l'Université, 75007 Paris. ☎ **01-42-96-10-95.** Fax 01-42-61-52-83. 30 rms, 2 duplex suites. TV TEL. 590–780 F ($118–$156) double; 960 F ($192) duplex suite. AE, DC, MC, V. Métro: Rue-du-Bac.

The Lenox has long been a favorite for those seeking a reasonably priced nest in St-Germain-des-Prés. T. S. Eliot spent the hot summer of 1910 here on "the old man's money." Once a rather basic little pension, this much improved hotel now offers small and snug, comfortably furnished bedrooms. Some rooms have elaborate ceiling moldings. All have floral draperies and a view over an inner courtyard or the busy street. Some returning guests request an attic duplex, which has a tiny balcony and a skylight. The lobby has a pair of marble fireplaces, and the staff is helpful. A bar off the main reception area is open daily from 5:30pm to 1:30am.

Hôtel Lindbergh. 5 rue Chomel, 75007 Paris. ☎ **01-45-48-35-53.** Fax 01-45-49-31-48. 26 rms. TV TEL. 470–600 F ($94–$120) double; 700 F ($140) triple; 760 F ($152) quad. AE, DC, MC, V. Parking 164 F ($32.80). Métro: Sèvres-Babylone or St-Sulpice.

The Hôtel Lindbergh honors the late American aviator whose nonstop solo flight across the Atlantic electrified Paris and the world in 1927. Until a complete renovation in 1995, this hotel looked as if nothing had changed since Charles landed. Now it sports an elegant modern exterior. On a somewhat hidden-away Left Bank street, it's just a 2-minute walk from St-Germain-des-Prés. Breakfast is the only meal served. The hotel is next to a good budget restaurant, Le Cigale, down the street on rue Chomel, off boulevard Raspail.

13TH & 14TH ARRONDISSEMENTS (GARE D'AUSTERLITZ / MONTPARNASSE)
EXPENSIVE

Hôtel Méridien Montparnasse. 19 rue du Commandant-Mouchotte, 75014 Paris. ☎ **01-44-36-44-36,** or 800/225-5843 in the U.S. and Canada. Fax 01-44-36-67-00. 928 rms,

25 suites. A/C MINIBAR TV TEL. 1,700 F ($340) double for stay of 1 night, 960 F ($192) double for stay of 2 nights or more; 3,500 F ($700) suite. AE, DC, MC, V. Parking 90 F ($18) per day with direct access to the hotel hall. Métro: Montparnasse-Bienvenue.

In a 25-story skyscraper that dominates Montparnasse (and much of Paris, too), this is the largest hotel on the Left Bank. It rises almost immediately above the Montparnasse-Bienvenue network of Métro, railway, and RER lines. The main reason to stay here is the Méridien's location in Montparnasse, once the art capital of the world in the 1920s and 1930s and still a district of great appeal to many visitors. The hotel offers the best (if not the most romantic) accommodations in the 14th arrondissement. The hotel caters to large groups, as well as frequent corporate travelers and individual tourists. The accommodations are soundproof, color coordinated, and very modern, with international furnishings and an anonymous but soothing kind of comfort. Each has a cable color TV with video movies, and an alarm clock; some have panoramic views.

Dining/Entertainment: Montparnasse '25, on the building's uppermost observation platform, serves high-quality French cuisine and takes its look from the 1920s (black lacquered furniture, gold-leaf sculptures, and reproductions of works by Modigliani and van Dongen). The glass-enclosed Restaurant Justine overlooks the gardens and serves both a buffet and à la carte specialties. Justine is open daily from 7am to 11pm. Before-dinner drinks are available in the Platinum Bar and Café Atlantic in the lobby.

Services: Room service (24 hours), laundry/valet, baby-sitting.

Facilities: Shopping boutiques.

MODERATE

Sofitel Paris St-Jacques. 17 bd. St-Jacques, 75014 Paris. ☎ **01-40-78-79-80.** Fax 01-45-88-43-93. 797 rms, 14 suites. A/C MINIBAR TV TEL. 1,500 F ($300) double; 2,000 F ($400) suite. AE, DC, MC, V. Parking 70 F ($14). Métro: St-Jacques.

This very modern, 14-story glass-and-steel hotel is refreshingly stylish and very French. It's not a good choice if you want to be close to the monuments of the heart of Paris but it's convenient for catching early-morning flights at Orly. Renovated in 1994, all the bedrooms have a color scheme of browns, beiges, and golds. A busy stream of business travelers and tourists passes through the lobby, which has a marble fountain and sometimes features live music. The good-sized rooms come attractively furnished with blackout blinds to help recent arrivals recover from jet lag.

Dining/Entertainment: Le Français is a re-creation of a turn-of-the-century brasserie, with bentwood chairs, 1890s posters, potted palms, and belle époque lighting fixtures.

Services: Room service (24 hours), laundry/valet, baby-sitting.

Facilities: Business center, shopping boutiques.

INEXPENSIVE

Résidence les Gobelins. 9 rue des Gobelins, 75013 Paris. ☎ **01-47-07-26-90.** Fax 01-43-31-44-05. 32 rms. TV TEL. 400–455 F ($80–$91) double; 585 F ($117) triple; 700 F ($140) quad. AE, MC, V. Métro: Gobelins.

This hotel lies far south of the Ile St-Louis and the Latin Quarter. It's an offbeat choice, but many savvy visitors seek out hotels such as this, refusing to pay the prices charged in the more expensive and more central arrondissements. The plain rooms, with modern furnishings and simple accessories, are well maintained. The hotel has an elevator and cable TV. The breakfast room overlooks a small plant-filled courtyard.

15TH ARRONDISSEMENT
(GARE MONTPARNASSE / INSTITUT PASTEUR)

Paris Hilton. 18 av. Suffren, 75015 Paris. ☎ **01-44-38-56-00,** or 800/445-8667 in the U.S. and Canada. Fax 01-44-38-56-10. 455 rms, 28 suites. A/C MINIBAR TV TEL. 1,695 F ($339) double; 3,700–5,800 F ($740–$1,160) suite. Parking 115 F ($23). RER: Champ-de-Mars.

The Hilton chain built this hotel on a tract of land near the Eiffel Tower in the 15th arrondissement, shattering the Right Bank's monopoly on grand hotels. Today the Paris Hilton has become a focal point of social life in this part of the city. Having all the usual Hilton comforts—to the maximum degree—the hotel rises 11 stories and has strong accents of Parisian flavor. The soundproofed rooms are well furnished. The bathrooms have oversize sinks, terrycloth bathrobes, toiletries, and dozens of towels. A computer-age security system is in place. The emphasis throughout is on personal service provided by a professional staff. A bustle of international business permeates the public areas of this always-crowded hotel.

Dining/Entertainment: A breakfast buffet is served on La Terrasse (one of the best in Paris). There are three bars and Le Western, a Tex-Mex steak house with a cowboy theme and a definite sense of humor.

Services: Room service (24 hours), same-day laundry and dry cleaning, babysitting, travel services, beauty parlor.

Facilities: Nearby underground garage, several chic boutiques.

4 Near the Airports

AT ORLY

Hilton International Orly. Aéroport Orly, 267 Orly Sud, 94544 Val-de-Marne. ☎ **01-45-12-45-12,** or 800/445-8667 in the U.S. and Canada. Fax 01-45-12-45-00. 347 rms, 12 suites. A/C MINIBAR TV TEL. 1,090–1,300 F ($218–$260) double; 1,500 F ($300) suite. AE, DC, MC, V. Parking 90 F ($18). Free shuttle bus between the hotel and both Orly terminals; 40-minute taxi ride from central Paris, (longer during rush hours).

Built in the 1960s, this hotel lies midway between the two terminals at Orly Airport. It's one of the most comfortable airport hotels anywhere. Dining, registrations, arrivals, and departures seem to continue around the clock. Catering mostly to business executives, the hotel is efficient and very international. Each of the bedrooms has soundproof walls and windows, multilanguage radio, and TV with in-house movies. Each year a different floor of rooms is renovated to keep the hotel up to date.

Dining/Entertainment: The hotel has two restaurants, one of them in the Louisiana plantation style, and a bar area.

Services: Room service (24 hours), laundry.

Facilities: Nearby tennis courts.

AT CHARLES DE GAULLE

Hôtel Sofitel Paris Aéroport CDG. Aéroport Charles-de-Gaulle, Zone Central (B.P. 20248), 95713 Roissy. ☎ **01-48-62-23-23,** or 800/221-4542 in the U.S. and Canada. Fax 01-49-19-29-39. 344 rms, 8 suites. A/C MINIBAR TV TEL. 850–1,250 F ($170–$250) double; 1,700 F ($340) suite. AE, DC, MC, V. Parking 52 F ($10.40). Free shuttle bus service to/from the airport.

Rising nine floors above an industrial landscape near the airport, this is a bustling, somewhat anonymous hotel where the staff is accustomed to departures and arrivals at all hours of the day and night. There's a straightforward but comfortable restaurant, and on the uppermost (ninth) floor, a dramatically lit piano bar, Neuvième Ciel. The bedrooms are soundproofed and bland but comfortable. Facilities include a swimming pool and sauna, and a business center. Laundry service, 24-hour room service, and video movies in several different languages are available. The prices listed above apply throughout most of the year, although singles or doubles can go for as much as 1,400 F ($280) each during conventions and periods of peak demand.

5 Gay-Friendly Hotels

Virtually any hotel receptionist in Paris will register a same-sex couple as a matter of course, and will usually perform the required paperwork with courtesy and the smooth nonchalance for which the French are famous. So although any hotel recommended in this guidebook is considered friendly (or at least tolerant) of same-sex couples, the hotels that follow are especially welcoming of gay guests.

✪ Le 55 Guest House. 55 av. Reille, 75014 Paris. ☎ **01-45-89-91-82.** Fax 01-45-89-91-83. 2 suites. TV TEL. 900–1,200 F ($180–$240) suite for two. Rates include breakfast. No credit cards. Métro: Porte-d'Orléans. RER: Cité Universitaire.

Its owners consider it the smallest luxury hotel in Paris, although it's better described as an upscale B&B with exceptionally tasteful furnishings. It's set on the southern periphery of Paris, between the trees of the Parc Montsouris and an expansive lawn, in a quiet and respectable residential neighborhood scattered with buildings from the 1920s. (Georges Braque lived in this house for a while, and Le Corbusier designed the house next door.) Jean-Marc Perry, a half-French, half-Irish linguist of great charm who maintains the suites in good form, has owned the Le 55 since 1993. Breakfast is served either in your suite or on a flower-covered terrace, weather permitting. The suites are accented with oak paneling, monochromatic colors, and art deco furnishings. Each suite has cable TV and a telephone-answering machine, and a fax can be installed if you want it. The minibar is stocked with complimentary soft drinks. Many clients are repeat visitors, often in Paris on business.

Hôtel Central. 33 rue Vieille-du-Temple, 75004 Paris. ☎ **01-48-87-99-33.** Fax 01-42-77-06-27. 7 rms, 1 with bath. TEL. 485 F ($97) double. MC, V. Métro: Hôtel-de-Ville.

This is the most famous gay hotel in Paris. The bedrooms are on the third, fourth, and fifth floors of the 18th-century, five-story building that contains Le Central, the leading gay bar in the Marais. If you arrive between 8:30am and 3pm, you'll find a registration staff one floor above street level; if you arrive any time other than that, you'll have to retrieve your room keys and register at the street-level bar. Frankly, many visitors prefer Le Central much more for its bar than for its bedrooms, but if you want a hotel that will really put you smack in the middle of the gay scene, this is definitely it. The bedrooms are simple, serviceable, and durable. Women are welcome, but rare. The downstairs bar, incidentally, is open Sunday to Thursday from 2pm to 1am and on Friday and Saturday from 2pm to 2am.

Hôtel Pierre. 25 rue Théodore-de-Banville, 75017 Paris. ☎ **01-47-63-76-69.** Fax 01-43-80-63-96. 50 rms. MINIBAR TV TEL. 50 F ($161.50) double. AE, DC, MC, V. Parking 80 F ($15.20). Métro: Péreire.

The Pierre was named as a facetious counterpoint to the owner's favorite North American hotel, the Pierre in New York City. To create it, the owners combined a trio of five-story 19th-century buildings into a clean, modern hotel with art deco styling. Opened in 1986, and renovated in 1995, it sits at the end of a residential street a short walk from the Arc de Triomphe. Each stylish accommodation has a TV with video movies and a safe with a combination lock. Most are outfitted with conservative modern furnishings. There's no restaurant or bar, but room service is available from 6:30am to midnight daily.

Iris Hôtel. 80 rue de la Folie-Regnault, 75011 Paris. ☎ **01-43-57-73-30.** Fax 01-47-00-38-29. 33 rms. TV TEL. 400–460 F ($80–$92) double. MC, V. Métro: Père-Lachaise.

The neighborhood could never be called glamorous, but the price is right at the Iris, and the Marais is just a 15-minute walk west. About a quarter of the clients here are gay men and women; the remainder are straight folks looking for clean accommodations at reasonable prices. Set behind a simple, cream-colored facade, the place has functioned as some kind of hotel since the 1930s, but in 1988 it was radically modernized, and the beige-colored bedrooms were given a no-nonsense face-lift. There's an elevator on the premises, and breakfast is served in the cellar.

Relais-Hôtel du Vieux Paris. 9 rue Gît-le-Coeur, 75006 Paris. ☎ **01-43-54-41-66.** Fax 01-43-26-00-15. 13 rms, 7 suites. A/C MINIBAR TV TEL. 1,070–1,370 F ($214–$274) double; 1,470–1,650 F ($294–$330) suite. AE, MC, V. Métro: St-Michel.

Tucked away within a maze of medieval streets in the heart of Paris, this stone and timbered building was erected in 1480 as the home of the ducs de Luynes. Later it was the elegantly appointed home of Pierre Séguier, one of Richelieu's advisers. In the 1600s it was notorious as a hideaway for Henri IV and one of his mistresses. In the 1950s the Beats (Allen Ginsberg, W. S. Burroughs, and Jack Kerouac themselves) made it their Paris headquarters when it was a simple (relatively battered) two-star hotel. The only person disappointed by the wholesale renovation of this hotel was Ginsberg himself. In the early 1990s he showed up, asking for his tiny bedroom on the top floor, only to discover that it doesn't exist anymore. Over the years the hotel has welcomed so many gay guests that sexual orientation hardly matters around here. The rooms are elegantly furnished with upholstered walls and copies of 19th-century antiques, and about 15 have the massive beams and timbers of the building's original construction. Each accommodation is furnished with a "massage shower" (Jacuzzi baths in the suites), hair dryer, and individual safe. Two of the suites have mezzanines overlooking the rooftops of Paris, and some of the rooms offer views of the Conciergerie.

Le Saint-Hubert. 27 rue Traversière, 75012 Paris. ☎ **01-43-43-39-16.** Fax 01-43-43-35-32. 15 rms. TEL TV. 315–335 F ($63–$67) double. AE, MC, V. Métro: Gare-de-Lyon.

This hotel occupies a five-story 19th-century town house on a quiet but unremarkable residential street. The bedrooms have salmon-colored walls, simple accessories, and not a great deal of extra room, but each is very clean. Because the building doesn't contain an elevator, rooms on the fourth and fifth floors are less expensive than those closer to the street-level reception area and breakfast room. The eastern edge of the Marais lies within a 10-minute walk (west). According to the management, about 40% of the clients here are gay men and women, traveling alone or as couples.

Welcome to the city that prides itself on being the culinary capital of the world. Only in Paris can you turn onto the nearest side street, enter the first ramshackle hostelry you see, sit down at the bare and wobbly table, glance at an illegibly hand-scrawled menu—and get a memorable meal.

LA GASTRONOMIE FRANÇAISE

Modern French cuisine owes a great debt to Auguste Escoffier, the renowned 19th-century chef who commanded the kitchens of some of Paris's most famous restaurants. He forged various regional French cooking styles into what we now regard as classic French cookery, elaborate feasts featuring rich sauces, exotic ingredients, and painstaking culinary techniques. Escoffier's emphasis on creams and sauces has, in recent years, made French cuisine unpopular with increasingly health-conscious diners, and the French food industry has experienced a backlash against this classic, fattening style of cooking (haute cuisine) in favor of healthier dishes that nonetheless seek to retain some French culinary styles and flavors (nouvelle cuisine). Now, however, the revolution against Escoffier has been raging for so long that many of the early rebels are returning to the old style of cookery, as exemplified by the reappearance and resurgent popularity of dishes like *boeuf bourguignon, blanquette de veau,* and *pot-au-feu.*

The battle between haute cuisine and nouvelle cuisine didn't begin in Paris. One would like to imagine that it started when Michel Guérard's beautiful Christine murmured in his ear, "*Tu sais,* Michel, if you would lose some weight, you'd look great."

For a man who loved food as much as Guérard, this was a formidable challenge. But he set to work and, ultimately, invented *cuisine minceur,* which is a way to cook good French food without the calories. The world now makes its way to Guérard's restaurant, at Eugénie-les-Bains in the Landes, just east of the Basque country. His *cuisine minceur* became a best-seller in North America, and food critic Gael Greene hailed Guérard as "the brilliant man who is France's most creative chef."

Cuisine minceur is more a diet cuisine than the nouvelle cuisine that thrived in the 1980s. When its early disciple, the great chef Paul Bocuse, pronounced nouvelle cuisine dead, many French chefs started calling their food *cuisine moderne* or any other name they wanted to give it—anything but "nouvelle." This "modern cuisine," like *cuisine minceur,* represents a major break with haute cuisine, while still being based on the classic principles of French cookery. Rich sauces, for example, have been eliminated. Cooking times that can destroy the best of fresh ingredients have been reduced. The aim is to release the natural flavor of food without covering it with heavy layers of butter and cream. New flavor combinations in this widely expanding repertoire are often inspired.

Paris borrows from the other provinces, all of which have distinctive cuisines. Even if you don't venture outside the city limits, you can get a good sampling of the diversified regional cooking of France because all French kitchens are represented in Paris. Some restaurants specialize in one cuisine—such as that of Normandy— whereas others offer a selection that might range from Brittany to Provence.

And increasingly the cuisine of Paris today is likely to be foreign—from Vietnam, Morocco, Tunisia, Algeria, Martinique, Guadeloupe, Greece, Cambodia, or even America—instead of French. Foreign restaurants now abound in every *quartier* of the city.

WINE

French cookery achieves perfection only when accompanied by wine, which is not considered a luxury or even an addition, but rather an integral part of every meal. Certain rules about wine drinking have been long established in France, but no one except traditionalists seems to follow them anymore. "Rules" would dictate that if you're having a roast, steak, or game, a good burgundy should be your choice. If it's chicken, lamb, or veal, you would choose a red from the Bordeaux country, certainly a full-bodied red with cheese such as Camembert, and a *blanc-de-blanc* with oysters. A light rosé can go with almost anything, especially if enjoyed on a summer terrace overlooking the Seine.

Let your own good taste—and your pocketbook—determine your choice of wine. Most wine stewards, called *sommeliers,* are there to help you in your choice, and only in the most dishonest of restaurants will they push you toward the most expensive selections. Of course, if you prefer only bottled water or perhaps a beer, then be firm and order either without embarrassment. Some restaurants include a beverage in their menu rates (*boisson compris*), but that's only in the cheaper places. Nevertheless, some of the most satisfying wines we've drunk in Paris came from unlabeled house bottles or carafes, called a *vin de la maison.* In general, unless you're a real connoisseur, don't worry about labels and vintages.

When in doubt, you can rarely go wrong with a good burgundy or bordeaux, but you may want to be more adventurous than that. That's when the *sommelier* can help you, particularly if you tell him or her your taste in wine (semidry or very dry, for example). State frankly how much you're willing to pay and what you plan to order for your meal. If you're dining with others, you may want to order two or three bottles with an entire dinner, selecting a wine to suit each course. However, Parisians at informal meals—and especially if there are only two people dining—select only one wine to go with all their platters, from hors d'oeuvres to cheese. As a rule of thumb, expect to spend about one-third of the restaurant tab for wine.

WINE LABELS   Since the latter part of the 19th century, French wines sold in France (and sometimes elsewhere) have been labeled. The general labeling term is *appellations contrôlées.* These controls, for the most part, are by regions such as Bordeaux and the Loire. The wines so labeled are the simple, honest wines of the district. They can be blended from grapes grown at any place in the region. Some are composed of the vintages of different years.

In most cases, the more specific the label, the better the wine. For example, instead of a bordeaux, the wine might be labeled "Médoc" (pronounced *May*-doc), which is the name of a triangle of land extending some 50 miles north from Bordeaux. Wine labels can be narrowed down to a particular vine-growing property, such as a Château Haut-Brion, one of the most famous and greatest of red wines of Bordeaux (this château produces only about 10,000 cases a year).

On some burgundies you're likely to see the word *clos* (pronounced *cloe*). Originally that meant a walled or otherwise enclosed vineyard, as in Clos-de-Bèze, which is a celebrated Burgundian vineyard producing superb red wine. *Cru* (pronounced *croo,* and meaning "growth") suggests a wine of superior quality when it appears on a label as *vin-de-cru.* Wines and vineyards are often divided into crus. A grand cru or premier cru should, by implication, be an even superior wine.

Labels are only part of the story. It's the vintage that counts. Essentially vintage is the annual grape harvest and the wine made from those grapes. Therefore, any wine can be a vintage wine unless it is a blend. But there are good vintages and bad vintages. The variation between wine produced in a "good year" and wine produced in a "bad year" can be great, and even noted by the neophyte.

Finally, champagne is the only wine that can be correctly served through all courses of a meal—but only to those who can afford its astronomical cost.

DINING WITH CHILDREN

Meals at the grand restaurants of Paris are rarely suitable for young children. Nevertheless, many parents drag their children to these deluxe citadels, often to the annoyance of other diners. If you want to dine at a fancy restaurant, consider leaving the kids with a baby-sitter. However, if you prefer to dine with your children, then you may have to make some compromises. Perhaps you'll have to dine earlier than most Parisians. **Hotel dining rooms** can be another good choice for family dining. They usually have children's menus, or at least one or two *plats du jour* cooked for children, such as spaghetti with meat sauce.

If you take your child to one of the moderately priced or budget restaurants, ask if the restaurant will serve a child's plate. If not, order a *plat du jour* or *plat garni,* which will be suitable for most children, particularly if a dessert is to follow.

Most **cafés** welcome children throughout the day and early evening. At a café, children always seem to like the sandwiches (try a croque-monsieur), the omelets, and especially the *pommes frites* (crispy french fries). Although we have listed a number of cafés later in this chapter (see Section 6), one that particularly appeals to children is **La Samaritaine,** 75 rue de Rivoli (☎ **01-40-41-20-20;** Métro: Pont-Neuf). The snack bar down below doesn't have a panoramic view, but the restaurant on the fifth floor does. You can take children to the top and order ice cream for them at tea time daily from 3:15 to 6pm.

Les Drug Stores (at 149 bd. St-Germain-des-Prés, 6e, and at Publicis Champs-Elysées, 133 av. des Champs-Elysées, 8e) also welcome children, especially in the early evening, as do most **tearooms,** and you can tide the kids over with pastries and ice cream if dinner will be late. Try a **picnic** in the park. Also, there are lots of fast-food eateries, such as **Pizza Hut** and **McDonald's,** all over the city.

For a run-down of more kid-friendly establishments, see "Family-Friendly Restaurants."

1 Today's Restaurant Scene

Paris has more restaurants than it can support. These temples of *haute gastronomie* include the legendary Alain Senderens and Michel Rostang, although the legends of yesterday—Taillevent, Lasserre, and La Tour d'Argent—are still there, still dispensing their ever-changing cuisines to the faithful. Only the faces in some of these places have changed. Franklin Roosevelt, Greta Garbo, the Aga Khan, Onassis (with either Jackie or Maria), and Cole Porter have given way to Tom Cruise, Madonna, Paul McCartney, or the latest computer millionaire.

What about belle époque Maxim's, arguably the most famous restaurant in the world? Still going strong, it's just as overrated and overpriced as ever. Colette and Cocteau no longer occupy its tables—more likely a rich Saudi prince and his blonde date for the night.

If your wallet tells you yes, try to splurge on at least one memorable meal in one of the city's most renowned restaurants, perhaps chef-owner Bernard Pacaud's tiny, romantic L'Ambroisie on the patrician place des Vosges.

The big change on the restaurant scene in Paris in the late 1990s, in addition to the growing abundance and popularity of "ethnic" restaurants serving Asian, African, and Middle Eastern food, is that you might actually get a reservation. Blame it on *le crise,* the economic recession that hit Paris hard. In the heady late 1980s if you spoke only English, or else an English-accented French, you were likely to be turned away. On a phone call from New York to Taillevent, the maître d' informed us that he couldn't get us a table "even if we were Mitterrand calling from the Palais de l'Elysée."

Taillevent remains one of the most difficult-to-get dining reservations in Paris, but many readers have reported good luck lately in getting tables at acclaimed restaurants on short notice. Places such as Le Tour d'Argent and Taillevent have traditionally operated on a "quota season"—that is, deliberately limiting the number of tables assigned to Americans every night. Of course, the way around that was to get a cultured French person to call and reserve a table for you. Today if you're willing to shell out at least 900 F ($180) per person, you can dine almost anywhere you choose.

Savvy visitors, including Parisians as well, confine their trips to these *luxe* establishments to special occasions. An array of other choices await, including simpler restaurants dispensing every cuisine from every province of France and from all the former colonies such as Morocco and Algeria. Paris now has hundreds of restaurants serving exotic fare from all over the world, reflecting the changing complexion of Paris itself and the city's increasing appreciation for food from other cultures. Your most memorable Paris meal may turn out to be Vietnamese or West African instead of French.

Hundreds of bistros and brasseries also await you. Many bistros can be chic and elegant, but others dispense gutsy, time-tested fare including the *pot-au-feu* that the chef's *grand-mère* prepared for him as a kid. Brasseries, including those in the Alsatian tradition that serve sauerkraut with an array of pork products, are often open 24 hours a day. Cafés, too, are not just places for a *café au lait* and a croissant, or perhaps an apéritif. Many serve rib-sticking fare as well, certainly entrecôte with *pommes frites* but often such classics as *blanquette* of veal.

More attention in the 1990s has focused on the wine bar. Originally these wine bars concentrated on their lists of wines, perhaps featuring many esoteric choices and ignoring the food except for some *charcuterie* (cold cuts) and cheeses. Today you're likely to be offered various *plats du jour* as well, ranging from homemade foie gras to *boeuf à la mode.*

One question often asked, is this: Can you dine badly in Paris? The answer is an emphatic yes, and increasingly so. The mailbox fills up with complaints from visitors who cite rude, haughty service, and bland, mediocre food—all dispensed at outrageous prices.

Often these complaints are directed at restaurants catering almost solely to tourists. To avoid them, follow along with our selections, including making your own discoveries, and do as the Parisians do. Take your choice of a restaurant seriously. Considering the prices charged, view the culinary pursuit as a bit of an investment. While the tourists are fighting it out for a table at one of the tacky places along the Champs-Elysées, you might be enjoying finer fare at some well-recommended choice farther away—truffle-studded foie gras served on Limoges china at Grand Véfour or the eponymous pig's feet at Pied de Cochon where the chefs follow the same recipes they used back at its founding in 1946.

Other changes are in the air. Today it's considered "provincial" to request *l'addition* (the bill). Chic Parisians ask for *la note*.

Although prices in even "cheap" places remain high for many visitors from other parts of the world, Paris is increasingly seeing the emergence of informal, moderately priced eateries, and we'll recommend several of these.

In years gone by no one thought of dining out, even at the neighborhood bistro, without a suit and a tie for men or a smart dress for a woman. That dress code is more relaxed now, except in first-class and *luxe* establishments. Relaxed doesn't mean sloppy jeans and jogging attire, however. Parisians still value style, even when dressing informally.

Establishments are still required by law to post their menus outside, so peruse them carefully. The *prix-fixe menu* (fixed-price menu) still remains an admirable choice if you want to have some vague idea of what your final *la note* will be when presented by the waiter.

A final trend on the dining scene is the opening of "baby bistros"—reasonably priced spinoffs from some of Paris's ultra-deluxe restaurants. For details, see the box "The Baby Bistro Boom" later in this chapter.

WHAT'S NEW & HOT   The hottest news in 1996 was the retirement of the brilliant Joël Robuchon, creator of *cuisine actuelle,* and the hiring of culinary star Alain Ducasse, chef/owner of the renowned Louis XV in Monaco, to replace him. Robuchon attracted the attention of *le tout* Paris in the early 1990s when he pioneered a form of modern cuisine called *cuisine actuelle* (what is being cooked right now). He's credited with redefining modern cuisine in Paris, using imagination and originality without the excesses of nouvelle.

On his retirement, Robuchon's restaurant, located in a 1912 town house adjacent to and loosely affiliated with Hôtel Le Parc, underwent architectural changes and now boasts a colonial "out of Africa" ambience in a conservatory setting, with a garden terrace for summer dining. It's also now much more closely tied to the hotel. Amid much mystery about what he planned to do, Ducasse took command of Restaurant Alain Ducasse soon after, promising to make creative statements here far different from those at his Monaco restaurant. Since all this was happening at press time, we were unable to visit the restaurant and provide you with a full review, but we're sure it'll be a smashing success and that you should check it out while you're in Paris— but be aware that reservations will be needed weeks in advance. **Restaurant Alain Ducasse** is at 59 av. Raymond-Poincaré, 16e (☎ **01-47-27-12-27**; Métro: Trocadéro).

WHAT THE LISTINGS MEAN   Restaurants classified as "Very Expensive" charge 550 F ($110) and up, plus drinks, for dinner. That's per person, too. In **Expensive** restaurants, dinner for one ranges from 300 to 550 F ($60 to $110); **Moderate,** 175 to 300 F ($35 to $60). Anything under 175 F ($35) per person is considered **Inexpensive,** although such a price tag is luxurious dining in most parts of the world.

Frédéric [Frédéric Delair, former owner of La Tour d'Argent] was preparing the duck in a special way. He got two servings (and two lots of profit) out of it, one pressed, the other grilled. Although they are both equally delicious, I think I still prefer the grilled version. Frédéric was really quite a sight, with his lorgnon, his graying side-whiskers and his imperturbably serious expression, as he cut up his plump quack-quack, already trussed and flambéed, threw it into the saucepan and made his sauce, salting and peppering just as Claude Monet painted.

—Léon Daudet, Paris Vécu (1929)

The Closerie des Lilas had once been a café where poets met more or less regularly and the last principal poet had been Paul Fort whom I had never read. But the only poet I ever saw there was Blaise Cendrars, with his broken boxer's face and his pinned-up empty sleeve, rolling a cigarette with his one good hand. He was a good companion until he drank too much and, at that time, when he was lying, he was more more interesting than many men telling a story truly.

—Ernest Hemingway, A Moveable Feast (1964)

Service compris or *prix nets* (the tax and tip) are included in all prices. In simple bistros, the small change is left on the table; in *luxe* or first-class establishments, patrons often add another 5% to the bill.

In the addresses listed, such designations as "1er" and "12e," which follow the name of the street, refer (in French form) to the arrondissement in which the establishment is located.

In France, lunch (as well as dinner) tends to be a full-course meal with meat, vegetables, salad, bread, cheese, dessert, wine, and coffee. It may be difficult to find a restaurant that serves the type of light lunch that North Americans are accustomed to. Cafés, however, may be the answer, since they offer sandwiches, soup, and salads in a relaxed setting.

Coffee, in France, is served after the meal and carries an extra charge. The French consider it absolutely barbaric to drink coffee during the meal, and, unless you specifically order it with milk (*au lait*), the coffee will be served black. In the more conscientious establishments it's prepared as the traditional *filtre*, a rather slow but rewarding filtered style that takes a bit of manipulating.

2 Best Bets

- **Best Decor: Bofinger**, 5–7 rue de la Bastille, 4e (☎ **01-42-72-87-82**), is an Alsatian brasserie resplendent with shiny brass. This much-restored dining palace looks better than ever. The setting at **Au Gourmet de l'Ile,** 42 St-Louis-en-l'Ile, 4e (☎ **01-43-26-79-27**), is also beautiful, with a beamed ceiling and candlelit tables.
- **Best View: La Tour d'Argent,** 15–17 quai de la Tournelle, 5e (☎ **01-43-54-23-31**), is a penthouse restaurant owned by shrewd ex-playboy Claude Terrail, who pays part of Notre-Dame's electric bill to illuminate the cathedral at night for his diners' pleasure. At **Auberge des Deux Signes,** 46 rue Galande, 5e (☎ **01-43-25-46-56**), you can enjoy Auvergne cuisine and a floodlit Notre-Dame without paying the prices charged by La Tour d'Argent. **Le Jules Verne,** Tour Eiffel, Champ-de-Mars, 7e (☎ **01-45-55-61-44**), on the second platform of the Eiffel Tower, looks out over a twinkling Paris panorama that seems to enter the restaurant itself. The

food on the **Bateaux-Mouches,** pont de l'Alma, place de l'Alma, 8e (☎ **01-42-25-96-10**), the glass-topped boats that sail up and down the Seine, may not be as inspired as that prepared by conventional restaurants, but the view is much, much better.

- **Best Wine Bar: Willi's Wine Bar,** 13 rue des Petit-Champs, 1er (☎ **01-42-61-05-09**), named after owner Mark Williamson, is the closest Paris has to a typical London wine bar. Excellent quality wines are available by the glass. Meet that strange creature, the tweedy French Anglophile.
- **Best Wine Cellar:** The sophisticated **Jacques Cagna,** 14 rue des Grands-Augustins, 6e (☎ **01-43-26-49-39**), has more than 500 varieties of wine in its world-class cellar. The wine list at **L'Arpège,** 84 rue de Varenne, 7e (☎ **01-47-05-09-06**), is also something to write a postcard home about. And **Carré des Feuillants,** 14 rue de Castiglione, 1er (☎ **01-42-86-82-82**), offers an exciting wine selection that includes a fabulous collection of armagnacs along with some little-known wines.
- **Best Value:** Is there still a good, cheap restaurant in Paris? Yes, at least one— **L'Etoile Verte,** 13 rue Brey, 17e (☎ **01-43-80-69-34**). This utterly plain old standby has been feeding familiar favorites to hungry customers longer than anyone here cares to remember—especially the no-nonsense waitresses.
- **Best American Cuisine: Joe Allen,** 30 rue Pierre-Lescot, 1er (☎ **01-43-36-70-13**), is a little bit of New York in Les Halles. The burgers are the finest in the city. Desserts include real New York cheesecake, pecan pie with fresh pecans imported from the States, and brownies made with French chocolates (unrivaled in the States).
- **Best Cuisine Bourgeoise:** Should Joyce, Verlaine, Valéry, or even Hemingway return today to the **Crémerie-Restaurant Polidor,** 41 rue Monsieur-le-Prince, 6e (☎ **01-43-26-95-34**), he wouldn't notice any change, not even on the menu. He'd still ask for his napkin locked in a cabinet in back with his name on it.
- **Best Kosher Food:** If the idea of corned beef, pastrami, schmaltz herring, and dill pickles excites you, then head out to rue des Rosiers in the 4th arrondissement (Métro: St-Paul). This street is in one of the most colorful neighborhoods of Paris. The blue-and-white Star of David is prominently displayed. John Russel wrote that rue des Rosiers is the "last sanctuary of certain ways of life; what you see there in miniature is Warsaw before the ghetto was razed." North African overtones also reflect the arrival, long ago, of Jews from Morocco, Tunisia, and especially Algeria. The best time to go is Sunday morning, when many parts of Paris are still sleeping. You can wander the streets eating as you go—apple strudel, Jewish rye bread, pickled lemons, smoked salmon, and *merguez,* a typical smoked from Algeria. Many spots offer proper sit-down meals. At **Chez Jo Goldenberg,** 7 rue des Rosiers, 4e (☎ **01-48-87-20-16**), the carpe farcie (stuffed carp) is a preferred selection, but the beef goulash is also good.
- **Best Vegetarian Cuisine: Aquarius,** 54 rue Ste-Croix-de-la-Bretonnerie, 4e (☎ **01-48-87-48-71**), is one of the best-known veggie restaurants in the Marais. Choose from their array of soups and salads, a galette of wheat served with crudités, and mushroom tarts. **Le Grain de Folie,** 24 rue de la Vieuville, 18e (☎ **01-42-58-15-57**), serves simple, wholesome, and unpretentious vegetarian cuisine inspired by France, Greece, California, and India. Wine or vegetable juice can accompany your meal.
- **Best Beer: Pub Saint-Germain-des-Prés,** 17 rue de l'Ancienne-Comédie, 6e (☎ **01-43-29-38-70**), the largest pub in France, offers 24 draft beers and 500 international beers.

- **Best Champagne Julep:** While you wait for a table at the **Closerie des Lilas,** 171 bd. du Montparnasse, 6e (☎ 01-43-26-70-50), have the best champagne julep in the world at the bar.

- **Best Cheese:** Cheese is king at **Androuët,** 41 rue d'Amsterdam, 8e (☎ 01-48-74-26-93). Many cheese lovers opt for a bottle of wine, a green salad, and all-you-can-eat choices from the most sophisticated *dégustation de fromages* in the world.

- **Best Fresh Mint Souffle:** **Escargot-Montorgueil,** 38 rue Montorgueil, 1er (☎ 01-42-36-83-51), the "golden snail" of Les Halles, is as golden as ever. And its fresh mint soufflé, served with chocolate sauce, is a perennial dessert favorite.

- **Best Ice Cream:** Try **Bertillion,** 31 rue St-Louis-en-l'Ile, 4e (☎ 01-43-54-31-61), a *salon de thé* that after three dozen years in the business still sells 30 of the most delectable ice cream flavors ever concocted. It's open Wednesday to Sunday from 10am to 8pm.

- **Best Late-Night/24-Hour Dining:** Check out **Café le Départ,** 1 place St-Michel, 5e (☎ 01-43-54-24-55), where the most popular order among the late-night regulars is entrecôte with french fries. And only at the famous **Au Pied de Cochon** (the "Pig's Foot"), 6 rue Coquillière, 1er (☎ 01-42-36-11-75), can you be assured of a good meal at 3am.

- **Best Tea:** Try **Angélina,** 226 rue de Rivoli, 1er (☎ 01-42-60-82-00), for excellent tea and light fare and a view of the lionesses of haute couture, in an ambience that is at once glittery, bourgeois and hysterical. Other noteworthy teahouses include **The Tea Caddy,** 14 rue St-Julien-le-Pauvre, 5e (☎ 01-43-54-15-56), (renowned for its homemade marmalade), and **Ladurée,** 16 rue Royale, 8e (☎ 01-42-60-21-79), where you'll sip tea in turn-of-the-century grandeur at tables barely big enough to hold a napkin.

- **Best Brunch:** The **Hôtel Méridien Paris Etoile,** 81 bd. Gouvion-St-Cyr, 17e (☎ 01-40-68-34-34), hosts "Le Sunday Jazz Brunch," where you can eat smoked salmon and excellent roasts while jazz artists entertain you.

- **Best Picnic Fare:** For the most elegant picnic fixings in town, go to **Fauchon,** 26 place de la Madeleine, 8e (☎ 01-47-42-60-11). Here you'll find a complete charcuterie and famous pastry shop. It's said to offer 20,000 kinds of imported fruits, vegetables, and other exotic delicacies, snacks, salads, and canapés—all packed to take out. Another gourmet supplier, **Peltier,** 66 rue de Sèvres, 7e (☎ 01-47-34-06-62; Métro: Sèvres-Babylone), has been one of the city's leading pâtisseries since 1961. Try its delectable tarte au chocolate. A section of the shop is devoted to take-out items, including salads, sandwiches, pastries, terrines, cheeses, quiches, and bottles of wine, of course. Peltier also has a *salon de thé;* many people consider this a simple yet elegant venue for lunch.

- **Best All-Around: Taillevent,** 15 rue Lamennais, 8e (☎ 01-45-63-39-94), named for a chef of the 14th century who wrote one of the oldest-known books on French cookery, is the most outstanding all-around restaurant in Paris.

- **Best Place to Experiment:** Tripe is a delicacy at **Pharamond,** 24 rue de la Grande-Truanderie, 1er (☎ 01-42-33-06-72). If you're at all experimental, you'll find no better introduction to it than here in Les Halles.

- **Best on the Champs-Eylsées:** The specialties of Denmark are served with flair at the **Copenhague/Flora Danica,** 142 av. des Champs-Elysées, 8e (☎ 01-43-59-20-41). In summer you can dine on the terrace of this "Maison du Danemark."

- **Best Chef:** Simple and elegant, Bernard Pacaud's cuisine has drawn the world's attention to **L'Ambroisie,** 9 place des Vosges, 4e (☎ 01-42-78-51-45). Diners come back again and again to see where his imagination will take him next.

- **Best Atmosphere:** A favorite of Colette and Cocteau, the world-famous **Grand Véfour,** 17 rue de Beaujolais, 1er (☎ 01-42-96-56-27), at the Palais-Royal has an interior that's classified as a historical monument. It serves some of the most refined cuisine in Paris.
- **Best for Opulence:** Although "Pierre Cardin's place," as it's called, has an ever-growing list of detractors, **Maxim's,** 3 rue Royale, 8e (☎ 01-46-65-27-94), is still the ultimate choice in art nouveau grandeur, just as it was decades ago when Leslie Caron dined here in *Gigi.*
- **Best Presentation:** Always count on high drama at **Lasserre,** 17 av. Franklin-D-Roosevelt, 8e (☎ 01-43-59-53-43). The presentation is imaginative and winning.
- **Best for Big Appetites:** Go to **La Taverne du Sergent Recruteur,** 41 rue St-Louis-en-l'Ile, 4e (☎ 01-43-54-75-42), a romantic dive on Ile St-Louis, for a fixed-price menu that begins with a big salad, an entire basket of sausage, and a crock of pâté. And that's only the beginning.
- **Best Underappreciated Restaurant:** Once hailed as the best restaurant in Paris by some critics, **Le Vivarois,** 192–194 av. Victor-Hugo, 16e (☎ 01-45-04-04-31), the domain of eccentric chef-patron Claude Peyrot, no longer enjoys such acclaim. Yet we think his cuisine is better than ever. He's not flashy, inventive, or pretentious—a strong classic chef and a master that Escoffier would have blessed.
- **Best Unkept Secret:** The **Restaurant Paul,** 15 place Dauphine, 1er (☎ 01-43-54-21-48), on the historic Ile de la Cité, is too good a secret to keep.
- **Best Pizza:** The **Chicago Pizza Pie Factory,** 5 rue de Berri, 8e (☎ 01-45-62-50-23), is devoted to the almighty pizza pie. The chef creates endless delicious variations on eight different themes.
- **Best Italian Cuisine: Bice Ristorante,** in the Hôtel Balzac, 6 rue Balzac, 8e (☎ 01-45-61-97-22), is the greatest Italian restaurant in Paris, an authentic off-shoot of the Bice in Milan. It serves up the finest antipasti, market-fresh grilled fish, and assorted meat dishes.
- **Best Burgers & Beer:** The **Hard Rock Cafe,** 14 bd. Montmartre, 9e (☎ 01-42-46-10-00), is a carnivorous rock fan's paradise. Still going strong since its establishment in London in 1971, the Hard Rock Cafe network is perhaps the most successful restaurant chain in the world. Despite the hype, they really do flip a mean burger.
- **Best Outdoor Dining:** Set in Paris's largest park, **La Grande Cascade**, Bois de Boulogne, 16e (☎ 01-45-27-33-51), is a calm and nostalgic retreat from the bustling urban scene. The *grand bourgeois* menu meshes favorably with the belle époque sentimentality, luring visitors with wafting scents and ambience.
- **Best People Watching:** Spend an afternoon on the terrace of the **Café de la Paix,** place de l'Opéra, 9e (☎ 01-40-07-30-20), and watch the world go by. See-and-be-seen or settle back into anonymity while enjoying the vast variety of faces in this international mingling joint.

3 Restaurants by Cuisine

ALSATIAN
Bofinger (4e, *M*)
Brasserie Flo (10e, *M*)

AMERICAN
Chicago Pizza Pie Factory (8e, *M*)
Hard Rock Cafe (9e, *I*)
Joe Allen (1er, *I*)

Key to Abbreviations: *VE* = Very Expensive, *E* = Expensive, *M* = Moderate, and *I* = Inexpensive.

CAFÉS

Brasserie Lipp (6e, *M*)
Café Beaubourg (4e, *I*)
Café de Flore (6e, *M*)
Café de la Paix (9e, *I*)
Café Marly (1er, *I*)
Coupole, La (14e, *M*)
Deux-Magots, Les (6e, *I*)
Fouquet's (8e, *M*)
Mandarin, Le (6e, *I*)
Rotonde, La (6e, *M*)
Select, Le (6e, *I*)

CENTRAL EUROPEAN

Chez Jo Goldenberg (4e, *I*)

DANISH

Copenhague/Flora Danica (8e, *E*)

FRANCHE COMTÉ/JURA

Chez Maître Paul (6e, *I*)

FRENCH

Amazonial, L' (1er, *M*)
Ambassade d'Auvergne, L' (3e, *I*)
Ambroisie, L' (4e, *VE*)
Ami Louis, L' (3e, *E*)
Androuët (8e, *M*)
Arpège, L' (7e, *VE*)
Auberge Basque, L' (7e, *I*)
Auberge des Deux Signes (5e, *M*)
Au Gourmet de l'Ile (4e, *I*)
Au Pactole (5e, *M*)
Au Pied de Cochon (1er, *M*)
Au Rendez-vous des Camionneurs
    (1er, *M*)
Au Trou Gascon (12e, *E*)
Aux Charpentiers (6e, *I*)
Bateaux-Mouches (8e, *E*)
Bistrot de Paris, Le (7e, *I*)
Bofinger (4e, *M*)
Brasserie Balzar (5e, *I*)
Brise-Miche, Le (4e, *I*)
Café du Commerce, Le (15e, *I*)
Café le Départ (5e, *I*)
Cafetière, La (6e, *I*)
Chartier (1er, *I*)
Chez André (8e, *M*)
Chez Edgard (8e, *M*)
Chez Georges (2e, *M*)
Chez René (5e, *I*)

Ciel de Paris, Le (15e, *E*)
Closerie des Lilas (6e, *E*)
Crémerie-Restaurant Polidor (6e, *I*)
Drouot, Le (2e, *I*)
Escargot-Montorgueil (1er, *E*)
Etoile Verte, L (17e, *I*)
Faugeron (16e, *VE*)
Fermette Marbeuf, La (8e, *M*)
Gai Moulin, Le (4e, *I*)
Grande Cascade, La (16e, *E*)
Grand Véfour, Le (1er, *VE*)
Grand Zinc, Le (9e, *I*)
Guy Savoy (17e, *VE*)
Imprimerie, L' (3e, *M*)
Incroyable, L' (1er, *I*)
Jacques Cagna (6e, *VE*)
Jules Verne, Le (7e, *VE*)
Julien (10e, *M*)
Lasserre (8e, *VE*)
Lescure (1er, *I*)
Lucas-Carton (Alain Senderens)
    (8e, *VE*)
Marc-Annibal de Coconnas (4e, *M*)
Maxim's (8e, *VE*)
Michel Rostang (17e, *VE*)
Nuit de Saint Jean (7e, *I*)
Petite Chaise, La (7e, *I*)
Petit Vatel, Le (6e, *I*)
Pharamond (1er, *M*)
Procope, Le (6e, *I*)
Pub Saint-Germain-des-Prés
    (6e, *M*)
Restaurant des Beaux-Arts (6e, *I*)
Restaurant Opéra (9e, *E*)
Restaurant Paul (1er, *M*)
Rose de France, La (1er, *I*)
Rôtisserie d'en Face, La (6e, *I*)
Rôtisserie du Beaujolais (5e, *M*)
Taillevent (8e, *VE*)
Taverne du Sergent Recruteur, La
    (4e, *I*)
Tour d'Argent, La (5e, *VE*)
Train Bleu, Le (12e, *M*)
30 (Chez Fauchon), Le (8e, *M*)
Trumilou (4e, *I*)
Vaudeville, Le (2e, *I*)
Vivarois, Le (16e, *E*)

GASCONY

Au Trou Gascon (12e, *E*)
Carré des Feuillants (1er, *VE*)

INDIAN
Yugaraj (6e,*E*)

ITALIAN
Bice Ristorante (8e, *E*)

JAPANESE
Inagiku (5e, *M*)

JEWISH
Chez Jo Goldenberg (4e, *I*)
Goldenberg's (17e, *M*)

KOREAN
Shing-Jung (8e, *I*)

LIGHT FARE
Angélina (1er, *I*)

LYONNAIS
Moissonnier (5e, *I*)
Carré des Feuillants (1er, *VE*)

PROVENÇAL
Campagne et Provence (5e, *I*)

SEAFOOD
Goumard-Prunier (1er, *VE*)
Paul Minchelli (7e, *E*)

SOUTH AMERICAN
Amazonial, L' (1er, *M*)

SPIT-ROASTED FOODS
Rôtisserie du Beaujolais (5e, *M*)

TEA
Angélina (1er, *I*)

VEGETARIAN
Aquarius (4e, *I*)
Grain de Folie, Le (18e, *I*)

VIETNAMESE
P'tite Tonkinoise, La (10e, *I*)

4 On the Right Bank

We'll begin with the most centrally located arrondissements on the Right Bank, then work our way through the more outlying neighborhoods.

1ST ARRONDISSEMENT (MUSEE DU LOUVRE / LES HALLES)
VERY EXPENSIVE

✪ **Carré des Feuillants.** 14 rue de Castiglione, 1er. ☎ **01-42-86-82-82.** Reservations required. Main courses 198–240 F ($39.60–$48); fixed-price menu 285 F ($57) at lunch, 600 F ($120) at dinner. AE, DC, MC, V. Mon–Fri noon–2:30pm and 7:30–10:30pm, Sat 7:30–10:30pm. Closed Aug. Métro: Tuileries, Concorde, Opéra, or Madeleine. FRENCH.

Alain Dutournier, one of France's leading chefs, established his reputation as a leading chef de cuisine at Au Trou Gascon, now run by his wife, Nicole. His new showcase is this restaurant in a beautifully restored 17th-century convent near place Vendôme and the Tuileries. It immediately became an overnight sensation. The interior is like a turn-of-the-century bourgeois house, with several small salons that have *faux-bois* painted walls. The salons open onto an inviting skylit interior courtyard, across which you can view the glass-walled kitchen (no secrets here).

Monsieur Dutournier likes to call his food *cuisine du moment*. He has a whole network of little farms that supply him with the fresh produce on which he casts his magic spell. He's especially known for using beef from one of the oldest breeds of cattle in France, the *race Châlosse* of western France. Flavor, tradition, and regional specialties of Gascony dominate the cuisine, as exemplified by the traditional thick, grilled ewe chops. Justly famous dishes include knuckle of veal en cocotte with eggplant, and lobster in white gazpacho.

The wine list has an exciting selection, including several little-known wines and a fabulous collection of armagnacs.

Goumard-Prunier. 9 rue Duphot, 1er. ☎ **01-42-60-36-07.** Reservations recommended. Main courses 210–380 F ($42–$76); fixed-price lunch 295 F ($59); *menu gastronomique* 750 F

Right Bank Restaurants

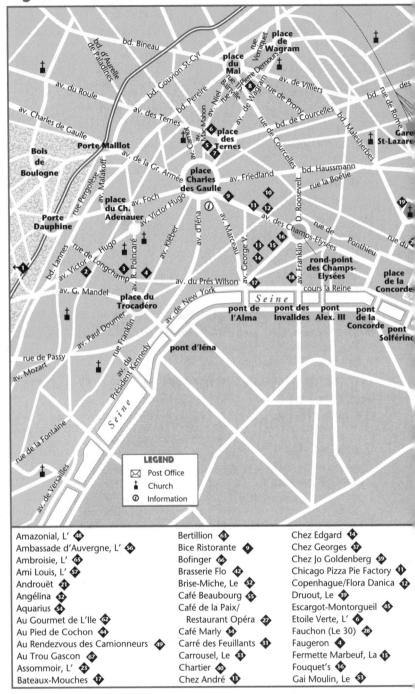

Amazonial, L' **48**
Ambassade d'Auvergne, L' **56**
Ambroisie, L' **65**
Ami Louis, L' **57**
Androuët **21**
Angélina **32**
Aquarius **54**
Au Gourmet de L'Ile **62**
Au Pied de Cochon **44**
Au Rendezvous des Camionneurs **49**
Au Trou Gascon **67**
Assommoir, L' **23**
Bateaux-Mouches **17**

Bertillion **63**
Bice Ristorante **9**
Bofinger **66**
Brasserie Flo **42**
Brise-Miche, Le **52**
Café Beaubourg **55**
Café de la Paix/
   Restaurant Opéra **27**
Café Marly **34**
Carré des Feuillants **31**
Carrousel, Le **43**
Chartier **40**
Chez André **13**

Chez Edgard **14**
Chez Georges **37**
Chez Jo Goldenberg **59**
Chicago Pizza Pie Factory **11**
Copenhague/Flora Danica **12**
Druout, Le **39**
Escargot-Montorgueil **45**
Etoile Verte, L' **6**
Fauchon (Le 30) **28**
Faugeron **4**
Fermette Marbeuf, La **15**
Fouquet's **16**
Gai Moulin, Le **53**

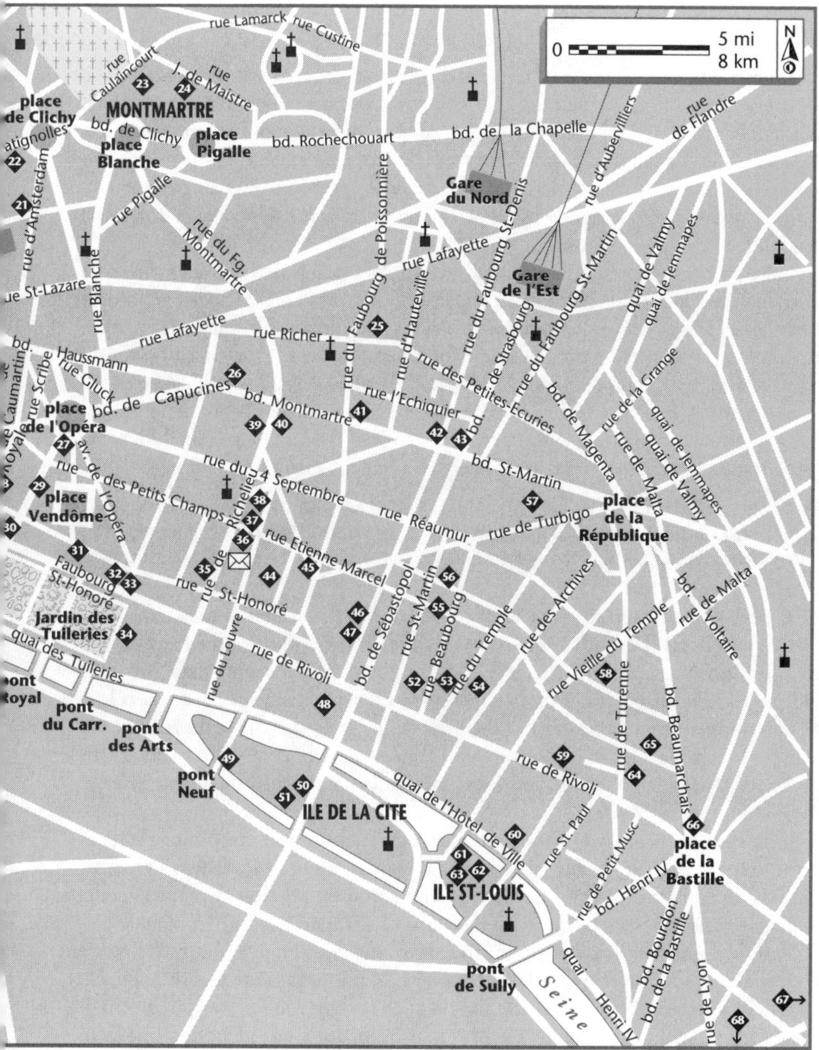

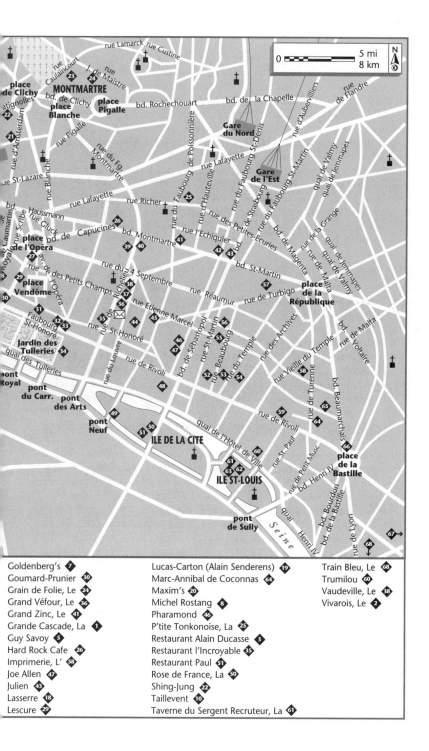

Goldenberg's 7
Goumard-Prunier 30
Grain de Folie, Le 24
Grand Véfour, Le 36
Grand Zinc, Le 41
Grande Cascade, La 1
Guy Savoy 5
Hard Rock Cafe 26
Imprimerie, L' 58
Joe Allen 47
Julien 43
Lasserre 18
Lescure 29
Lucas-Carton (Alain Senderens) 19
Marc-Annibal de Coconnas 64
Maxim's 20
Michel Rostang 8
Pharamond 46
P'tite Tonkonoise, La 25
Restaurant Alain Ducasse 3
Restaurant l'Incroyable 35
Restaurant Paul 51
Rose de France, La 50
Shing-Jung 22
Taillevent 10
Taverne du Sergent Recruteur, La 61
Train Bleu, Le 68
Trumilou 60
Vaudeville, Le 38
Vivarois, Le 2

($150). AE, DC, MC, V. Mon–Sat noon–2:30pm and 7:15–10:30pm. Closed 2 weeks in Aug and Mon Oct–Mar. Métro: Madeleine or Concorde. SEAFOOD.

Established in 1872, Goumard-Prunier is the forerunner of the staid, very bourgeois, and very famous Prunier found in the 16th arrondissement. The restaurant is done in tones of greens and warm golds. A most unusual collection of Lalique crystal fish is displayed in "aquariums" that line the walls. (Even more unusual are the men's and women's toilets, now classified as a *monument historique* by the French government. The commodes were designed by the art nouveau master cabinetmaker Majorelle around the turn of the century.)

Some of the freshest and best seafood in Paris is served here. It's usually flown in directly from suppliers in Brittany. Examples include a craquant of crayfish in its own herb salad of baby rouget prepared with onions and tomatoes in the Catalán style, Breton lobster prepared with a herbed beurre-blanc sauce, filet of grilled turbot on a bed of artichokes with tarragon, and a canot of grilled seawolf with a daube of basil-seasoned vegetables. In all of these dishes nothing—no excess butter, spices, or salt—is allowed to interfere with the natural flavor of the sea. Be prepared for some very unusual food here—the staff will help translate the menu items for you.

✪ **Le Grand Véfour.** 17 rue de Beaujolais, 1er. ☎ **01-42-96-56-27.** Reservations required. Main courses 230–380 F ($46–$76); fixed-price menu 325–750 F ($65–$150) at lunch, 750 F ($150) at dinner. AE, DC, MC, V. Mon–Fri 12:30–2:15pm and 7:30–10:15 pm. Métro: Louvre. FRENCH.

Le Grand Véfour, amid the arcades of the Palais Royal, has been a restaurant since the reign of Louis XV, and it has had its ups and downs. Although the exact date of its opening as the Café de Chartres is not precisely known, it's more than 200 years old and is classified as a historical treasure. It got its present name in 1812, when Jean Véfour, former chef to a member of the royal family, owned it. Since that time it has attracted such notables as Napoléon and Danton and a host of writers and artists, such as Victor Hugo, Colette, and Jean Cocteau (who designed the menu cover in 1953).

Jean Taittinger, of the Taittinger Champagne family, and the Concorde hotel group purchased the restaurant, and it has now recaptured—perhaps even surpassed—its former glories. At Le Grand Véfour, you eat off elegant Limoges china at a table bearing a brass plaque with the name of a famous former occupant.

The chef, Guy Martin, a native of the Savoy region of France, will surely please even the most discriminating palates. Monsieur Martin brings originality to French classics in a near-perfect blend of classical tradition and the robust flavors of his childhood. Try his foie gras ravioli in a light truffle-cream sauce, or a delicate white-bean soup flavored with truffles. Some newer dishes are pigeon in the style of Rainier of Monaco, or parmentier of oxtail with truffles. Fresh roasted sole and sea scallops in a velvety pumpkin sauce are other specialties. He also brings in omble chevalier, or char, a troutlike fish from Lake Geneva, which he feels is so delectable that he prepares it simply, merely sautéeing it and serving it meunière.

EXPENSIVE

Escargot-Montorgueil. 38 rue Montorgueil, 1er. ☎ **01-42-36-83-51.** Reservations required. Main courses 115–150 F ($23–$30); fixed-price menu 180 F ($36) at lunch, 190–250 F ($38–$50) at dinner. AE, DC, MC, V. Daily noon–2:30pm and 7:30–11pm. Closed 2 weeks in Aug. Métro: Les Halles. FRENCH.

The "golden snail" of Les Halles has long been deserted by fickle fashion—and the guidebooks—but those in search of nostalgic Paris still go here for the memories. Even if the famous market has moved elsewhere, the Escargot-Montorgueil is housed

Restaurants: 1st Arrondissement

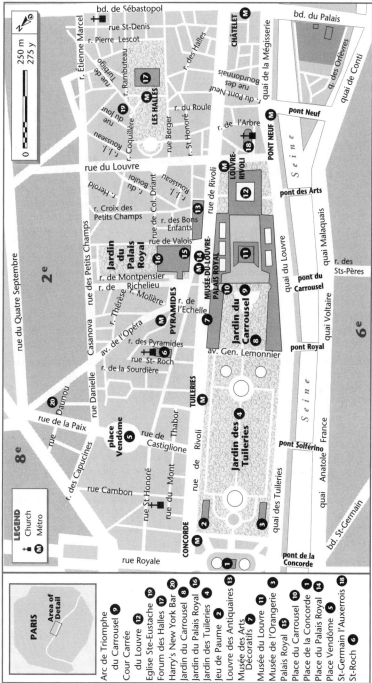

LEGEND
+ Church
Ⓜ Métro

Arc de Triomphe du Carrousel **9**
Cour Carrée du Louvre **12**
Eglise Ste-Eustache **19**
Forum des Halles **17**
Harry's New York Bar **20**
Jardin du Carrousel **8**
Jardin du Palais Royal **16**
Jardin des Tuileries **4**
Jeu de Paume **2**
Louvre des Antiquaires **13**
Musée des Arts Décoratifs **7**
Musée du Louvre **11**
Musée de l'Orangerie **3**
Palais Royal **15**
Place du Carrousel **10**
Place de la Concorde **1**
Place du Palais Royal **14**
Place Vendôme **5**
St-Germain l'Auxerrois **18**
St-Roch **6**

123

in a building dating from the days of Catherine de Médicis. The restaurant opened its doors in the 1830s—and inside it looks it. The decor has been described as "authentic Louis Philippe." The greats, such as Sarah Bernhardt, have paraded through here. The food—in the grand bistro tradition—remains consistently good.

Everyone but the regulars appears to order escargots, but this dish doesn't seem to get much attention from the chef. We recommend instead the pieds de porcs (pig's feet), duckling in orange sauce, and turbot Montorgueil (a delectable version of fresh seafish gratinéed and served in a form resembling a soufflé). A perennial dessert favorite is a fresh mint soufflé served with chocolate sauce.

MODERATE

Au Pied de Cochon. 6 rue Coquillière, 1er. ☎ **01-42-36-11-75.** Reservations recommended for lunch but not accepted for dinner after 8:30pm. Main courses 78–150 F ($15.60–$30); fixed-price menu 180 F ($36). AE, DC, MC, V. Daily 24 hours. Métro: Les Halles. FRENCH.

Although the great market that used to surround this restaurant has moved to Rungis, near Orly Airport, traditions die hard. Au Pied de Cochon's famous onion soup still lures visitors, and besides, where else in Paris can you be assured of getting a good meal at 3am? The house specialty (in addition to its classic onion soup) is the restaurant's namesake: pig's feet grilled and served with béarnaise sauce. Both dishes are as good—or in the view of some, as bad—as they always were. Try the suckling pig St-Eustache or another well-known specialty, andouillette (chitterling sausage) with béarnaise sauce.

Outside on the street you can buy some of the freshest oysters in town. The attendants will even give you slices of lemons to accompany them, so you can down them right on the spot.

Pharamond. 24 rue de la Grande-Truanderie, 1er. ☎ **01-42-33-06-72.** Reservations required. Main courses 90–150 F ($18–$30); fixed-price menu 180 F ($36) at lunch, 250 F ($50) at dinner. AE, DC, MC, V. Mon 7:30–10:45pm, Tues–Sat 12:30–2:30pm and 7:30–10:45pm. Métro: Les Halles or Châtelet. FRENCH.

On a street in Les Halles, Pharamond occupies part of a neo-Norman building from 1832. For an appetizer, work your way through half a dozen Breton oysters (available between October and April). Next, the main dish to order here is tripes à la mode de Caen, served in charcoal-fired brass braziers. Tripe is a delicacy, and if you're at all experimental you'll find no better introduction to it anywhere. If you're not up to tripe, try the coquilles St-Jacques au cidre (scallops in cider), available from mid-October to April. Other main-dish specialties include grillade au feu de bois, as well as filets de sole normande. The food remains competently prepared as the restaurant itself remains an enduring favorite. Most guidebooks have long passed it by, except for Michelin, which still awards it a coveted star.

INEXPENSIVE

L'Amazonial. 3 rue Ste-Opportune, 1er. ☎ **01-42-33-53-13.** Reservations recommended. Main courses 75–120 F ($15–$24); fixed-price menus 75–120 F ($15–$24). AE, MC, V. Daily noon–3pm and 7pm–1am (last order). Métro: Châtelet. SOUTH AMERICAN/FRENCH.

Established a decade ago in the heart of the Marais, this is one of Paris's busiest and most popular gay restaurants, with an estimated 80% gay clientele (male and female). Set in a 19th-century building, with a flowered terrace extending out onto the pavement outside, it features a decor that incorporates elements from ancient Egypt, ancient Greece, and the Amazon basin into one large dining room. Menu items include codfish cooked in coconut milk, prawns grilled in the style of Barbados, ostrich steak with white peppercorns, Bahia (Brazil)-style lamb curry, tacos, guacamole, and Brazilian-style feijoada.

Angélina. 226 rue de Rivoli, 1er. ☎ **01-42-60-82-00.** Reservations accepted for lunch, not for teatime. Pot of tea for one 32 F ($6.40); sandwiches and salads 35–58 F ($7–$11.60); *plats du jour* 80–95 F ($16–$19). AE, MC, V. Daily 9:30am–7pm (lunch served 11:45am–3pm). Closed most of Aug. Métro: Tuileries. TEA/LIGHT FARE.

In the high-rent district near the Inter-Continental Hotel, this *salon de thé* has an ambience that manages to combine glitter, bourgeois respectability, and frantic hysteria all at the same time. The ceilings are high, and the gilded interior has been worn to just the right patina. In contrast, the carpets, tables, and chairs by well-known designer Jean-Michel Wilmotte and the computer-generated artwork by Francis Giacobetti are deliberately modern. For a view of the lionesses of *haute couture* having their tea and delicate sandwiches, the place is without equal. Bearing silver trays, overwrought waitresses serve light platters, pastries, coffee, drinks, and tea at tiny marble-topped tables. The claustrophobic charm here seems a part of the commercial whirl of central Paris. Lunches usually consist of a salad and a *plat du jour*, such as chicken salad, sole meunière, filet of barbue (brill) on a bed of braised fennel, and poached salmon. There are two drawbacks, however: This neighborhood is not as nice as it used to be, and the service here can be a bit snooty.

Au Rendez-vous des Camionneurs. 72 quai des Orfèvres, 1er. ☎ **01-43-54-88-74.** Reservations recommended on weekends. Main courses 78–98 F ($15.60–$19.60); fixed-price dinner 120 F ($24). AE, MC, V. Daily noon–2:30pm and 7–11:30pm (last order). Métro: Pont-Neuf. FRENCH.

Set on the Ile de la Cité adjacent to the pont Neuf, this restaurant has the look, feel, and service of a traditional Parisian or Lyonnais bistro. It was founded in 1870, and many of the original mirrors and banquettes—and even the burgundy, olive, and khaki color scheme—remain. The food, traditional bistro fare, is reasonably priced and well prepared. Options include terrine of rabbit, crottin de chavignol (a traditional appetizer layered with goat's cheese), snails with garlic-cream sauce, a ragoût of mussels and shrimp with a fondée of leeks, blanquette de veau (veal in white sauce), and filet mignon. The staff is intelligent and charming, and the majority of the regular crowd is gay.

Chartier. 7 rue du Faubourg Montmartre, 1er. ☎ **01-47-70-86-29.** Reservations not accepted. Main courses 32–52 F ($6.40–$10.40). MC, V. Daily 11am–3pm and 6–9:30pm. Métro: Montmartre. FRENCH.

Established in 1896, this unpretentious *fin-de-siècle* restaurant lies near the Montmartre and is now a historic monument. Chartier has long been a favorite budget place offering good value in authentic French surroundings. The focal point—a whimsical mural with trees, a flowering staircase, and an early depiction of an airplane—was painted in 1929 by a then-penniless artist who executed the painting in exchange for food. The menu items respect conservative brasserie-style traditions, using recipes that haven't changed very much since the original commission of that mural. They include dishes most foreigners almost never order (including boiled veal's head, tripe, tongue, sweetbreads, and lamb's brains) as well as some old-timey tempters that never lose their popularity. The waiter will advise you, and you'll do well with beef bourguignon, pot-au-feu (one of the best-sellers, combining beef, turnips, cabbage, and carrots on a savory platter), pavé of rumpsteak, and at least five kinds of fish. The prices are low enough that a three-course repast is easy on the budget, a fact appreciated by as many as up to 320 diners at a time.

L'Incroyable. 26 rue de Richelieu or 23 rue de Montpensier, 1er. ☎ **01-42-96-24-64.** Reservations recommended Fri–Sat night. Four-course *menu du jour* 70 F ($14) Mon–Fri at lunch, 80 F ($16) Sat at lunch and Mon–Sat at dinner. No credit cards. Daily noon–2:30pm and 6:30–9pm (last order) Closed Jan. Métro: Palais-Royal/Musée-du-Louvre (then walk up either rue de Richelieu or rue de Montpensier behind the Comédie-Française). FRENCH.

This little place, open since the turn of the century, is justly named "the Incredible"— it offers four-course meals in appealing old-fashioned surroundings at unbelievable prices. The restaurant lies beside a narrow alleyway behind the Palais Royal, and is outfitted with dark bentwood furniture, old plaques, pictures, and an assortment of knickknacks belonging to the Burgundy-born owners, the Breyers. Their family pieces add to the general coziness of the place. When weather is good, a few small tables out in the passageway make this restaurant truly French. The food is old-fashioned, with a roster of attractive *plats du jour*. L'Incroyable features dishes well known to anyone born inside the borders of France, including a pavé of salmon, calves' liver with cassis sauce, confit of duckling, beef bourguigon, and a *petit salé* of pork made by reheating boiled salt pork in a kettle of richly seasoned white beans or lentils.

Joe Allen. 30 rue Pierre-Lescot, 1er. ☎ **01-42-36-70-13.** Reservations recommended for dinner. Main courses 72–140 F ($14.40–$28). AE, MC, V. Daily noon–2am. Métro: Les Halles. AMERICAN.

The last place in the world you'd expect to find Joe Allen is Les Halles, that once-legendary Paris market. But the New York restaurateur long ago invaded Paris with an American hamburger that easily wins as the finest in the city.

Joe Allen's "little bit of New York"—complete with imported red-checked tablecloths, a green awning over the entrance, and waiters who speak English—was made possible by "grants" from such fans as Lauren Bacall, whose poster adorns one of the walls. The decor is in the New York saloon style, complete with brick walls, oak floors, and movie stills. A chalkboard lists such menu items as black-bean soup, chili, and apple pie. A spinach salad makes a good beginning, although some food critics have claimed that this popular dish is "not serious." The barbecued ribs are succulent as well, but Joe Allen is getting more sophisticated in its menu, catering to modern tastes with such dishes as grilled salmon with coconut rice and sun-dried tomatoes.

Joe Allen's also claims that it's the only place in Paris where you can have real New York cheesecake or pecan pie made with pecans imported from the United States. Thanks to French chocolate, Joe claims, "we make better brownies than those made in the States." Giving the brownies tough competition is the California chocolate-mousse pie, along with the strawberry Romanoff and the coconut-cream pie.

Lescure. 7 rue de Mondovi, 1er. ☎ **01-42-60-18-91.** Reservations not accepted. Main courses 38–90 F ($7.60–$18); four-course fixed-price menu 100 F ($25). MC, V. Mon–Fri noon–2:15pm and 7–10:15pm. Closed 2 weeks in Aug. Métro: Concorde. FRENCH.

Lescure is a small, inexpensive restaurant in the high-priced place de la Concorde district. Right off rue de Rivoli, the restaurant has been serving simple French bourgeoise cookery since 1919. In fair weather a few sidewalk tables are placed outside; inside the decor is rustic, with an exposed kitchen. You might begin with duckling pâté. Main courses include a hearty filet of duckling in a green-pepper sauce and a brochette of lamb kidneys in a wine sauce. The classic beef bourguignon seems to have been served here since the place opened. Our favorite dessert is one of the chef's fruit tarts.

Restaurant Paul. 15 place Dauphine, 1er. ☎ **01-43-54-21-48.** Reservations required. Main courses 98–155 F ($19.60–$31). AE, MC, V. Tues–Sun noon–2:30pm and 7:30–10:15pm. Métro: Pont-Neuf. FRENCH.

This place has what's vanishing from the Paris restaurant scene—an authentic decor. A shiny mustard-yellow ceiling and matching walls, old red-leather banquettes, speckled fiberboard paneling that's mellowed to a honey tone, and murals of Paris street scenes lend real charm to this narrow bistro that opens onto the Seine and the historic place Dauphine on Ile de la Cité. Le filet mignon de veau en papillote (veal cooked in parchment) is a specialty of the house, and most dinners finish with one of the tartes du jour. The chef seems to believe that if a dish was good 20 years ago, why wouldn't it be good today? Restaurant Paul used to be an unknown bistro where no foreigner ever set foot, but it's too good a secret to keep.

La Rose de France. 24 place Dauphine, 1er. ☎ **01-43-54-10-12.** Reservations recommended. Main courses 78–99 F ($15.60–$19.80); menu du jour 135 F ($27); menu gastronomique 310 F ($62). MC, V. Mon–Fri noon–2pm and 7–10pm. Closed last 3 weeks in Aug and 15 days at the end of Dec. Métro: Cité or Pont-Neuf. FRENCH.

This restaurant is located in the old section of Ile de la Cité near Notre-Dame, just around the corner from the old pont Neuf. You'll dine with a crowd of young Parisians who know that they can expect a good meal at reasonable prices. In warm weather the sidewalk tables overlooking the Palais de Justice are most popular.

Main dishes include sweetbreads, veal cutlet flambéed with calvados (French apple brandy), filet of beef en croûte, and lamb chops seasoned with the herbs of Provence. For dessert, try the fruit tart of the day, a sorbet, or iced melon (in summer only). This place is similar to Restaurant Paul (see above) in that it offers a dependable variety of fresh food at affordable prices. Although the tables are crowded together, the noise level is rarely deafening.

2ND ARRONDISSEMENT (LA BOURSE)
MODERATE

Chez Georges. 1 rue du Mail, 2e. ☎ **01-42-60-07-11.** Reservations required. Main courses 100–150 F ($20–$30). AE, MC, V. Mon–Sat 12:30–2pm and 7:30–10pm. Closed 3 weeks in Aug. Métro: Bourse. FRENCH.

This bistro, which has thrived here since 1964, is a local landmark, and the food critics (ourselves included) always claim that the atmosphere is more interesting than the cuisine. At lunch it's packed with Parisian stockbrokers (the stock exchange is about a block away). The owner serves what he calls "food from our grandmother in the provinces." Waiters bring around bowls of appetizers, such as celery rémoulade, to get you started. Then you can follow with such favorites as filet of duckling with flap mushrooms, sweetbreads with morels, veal kidneys in the style of Henri IV (with béarnaise sauce), and filet of fish with a crème fraîche (fresh thick cream) sauce. You can also enjoy a classic cassoulet (the famed meat, poultry, and white-bean stew of Gascony). Beaujolais goes well with this hearty food.

INEXPENSIVE

☉ Le Drouot. 103 rue Richelieu, 2e. ☎ **01-42-96-68-23.** Reservations recommended Sat night. Main courses 34–57 F ($6.80–$11.40). MC, V. Daily 11:45am–3pm and 6:30–10pm. Métro: Richelieu-Drouot. FRENCH.

Le Drouot was established in 1938, as a downscale version of a grand French restaurant, in a frequently remodeled building that was once the site of Louis XIII's hunting lodges. In honor of the building's historical function, a plaster statue of a naked Diana, in her role as huntress presiding over a fireplace, decorates one edge of the sprawling and very loud dining room. Many local office workers come here in droves for lunch. Service is wryly amused and efficient; the setting is traditional with few intrusions of glitter or plastic, and the clientele is loyal. The cuisine is unabashedly French and unashamedly old-fashioned, the kind of rock-solid fare that has contributed to this place's success since it was established. Menu items include boeuf à la mode braised in madeira sauce, blanquette of veal, salmon with béarnaise sauce, leg of lamb with white beans, trout amandine, and beef bourguignon. Don't confuse

Restaurants: 2nd Arrondissement

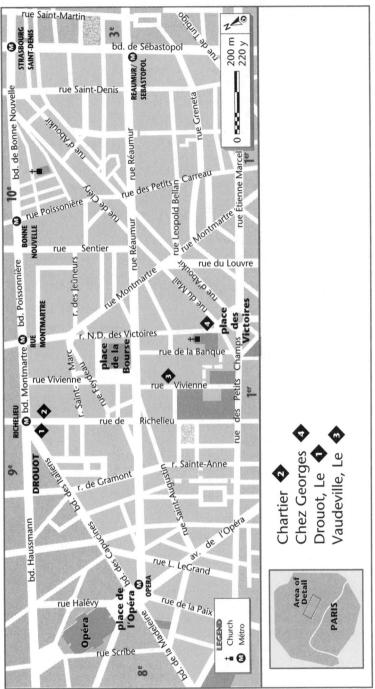

Chartier **2**
Chez Georges **4**
Drouot, Le **1**
Vaudeville, Le **3**

this place, which lies one floor above street level, with the simple street-level café below it.

Le Vaudeville. 29 rue Vivienne, 2e. ☎ **01-40-20-04-62.** Reservations recommended in the evenings. Main courses 85–175 F ($17–$35); fixed-price menu 112–189 F ($22.40–$37.80). AE, DC, MC, V. Daily 11:30am–3pm and 7pm–4am. Métro: Bourse. FRENCH.

Adjacent to the Paris stock exchange (La Bourse), this bistro has retained its original marble walls and art deco carvings since 1918. It has the same nostalgic atmosphere as the fabled La Coupole on the Left Bank, but is much more convivial and a lot smaller. In summer tables are placed on a terrace in front, amid banks of geraniums. Any time of year the place is boisterous and informal, often welcoming groups of six or eight diners at a time to its closely spaced tables. A bar near the entrance provides a place to perch if your table reservation is delayed.

The bountiful roster of bistro-style platters includes snails in garlic butter, smoked salmon, steak au poivre, sole meunière, sauerkraut, and several kinds of grilled meats. This is the type of fare familiar to French bistro-goers for decades. This is not a place for innovation, and not every dish on the menu inspires rave reviews. Its main dining value lies in its fixed-price menus.

3RD ARRONDISSEMENT (LE MARAIS)
MODERATE

L'Ami Louis. 32 rue de Vertbois, 3e. ☎ **01-48-87-77-48.** Reservations required. Main courses 190–270 F ($38–$54). AE, DC, MC, V. Wed–Sun noon–2pm and 8–11pm. Closed July 10–Aug 25. Metro: Temple. FRENCH.

L'Ami Louis is in one of the least fashionable neighborhoods of Paris, and its facade has seen better days. Nonetheless, this bistro preserves something magical from the prewar years. It's always luring in well-heeled French politicians and business moguls, who could be accused of slumming if it were any cheaper.

The bistro was established in 1924 by someone named Louis, who sold it in the 1930s to "Monsieur Antoine," who became a legend for intimidating (and at times, deliberately insulting) the grandest of his guests. Under his direction, L'Ami Louis became one of the most famous brasseries in all of Paris, thanks to its excellent food, its copious portions, and its earthy, ostentatiously old-fashioned decor. The master died in 1987, yet his traditions are fervently maintained by a new generation of more polite directors. Amid a "brown gravy" decor—the walls retain a smoky patina that no one has scrubbed off since the 1920s—you'll dine at marble-topped tables. Menu items include suckling lamb, pheasant, venison, confit of duckling, and endless slices of foie gras. The super-large portions continue to attract the gourmand who doesn't seem to mind that the ingredients aren't as select or as high quality as they were in the restaurant's heyday. The sauces are thick and viscous, as they were "between the wars." Don't save room for dessert!

INEXPENSIVE

L'Ambassade d'Auvergne. 22 rue de Grenier-St-Lazare, 3e. ☎ **01-42-72-31-22.** Reservations recommended. Main courses 86–120 F ($17.20–$24). MC, V. Daily noon–2pm and 7:30–11pm. Closed Aug 1–15. Métro: Rambuteau. FRENCH.

Located in an obscure district of Paris, this rustic tavern serves the hearty *cuisine bourgeoise* of Auvergne, the heartland of France. You enter through a busy bar decorated with ceramic plates; hams and sausages hang from its heavy oak beams. Rough wheat bread is stacked in baskets, and rush-seated ladderback chairs are placed at tables covered with bright cloths. Stem glassware, mills to grind your own salt and pepper, and a jug of mustard are on each table.

The chef follows the authentic classic traditions. One American guidebook called the cuisine "innovative," which must have elicited mirth in the kitchen. It's as innovative as smoky bacon, cabbage soup, and lentil stew. Specialties include cassoulet with lentils, pot-au-feu, confit de canard, codfish casserole, and stuffed cabbage. Some of these specials are only featured once a week. For a side dish, we recommend aligot, a medley of fresh potatoes, garlic, and Cantal cheese.

Le Gai Moulin. 4 rue St-Merri, 4e. ☎ **01-42-77-60-60.** Reservations recommended. Fixed-price menu 99 F ($19.80). MC, V. Daily 7:30–11pm. Métro: Hôtel-de-Ville. FRENCH.

This is a good place for a convivial night out, not a quiet conversation. A tiny space that's outfitted with gray walls and tables with almost no space between them, it lies near the Centre Beaubourg, attracts a clientele that's almost 99% gay (many of whom seem to have known one another for decades), and offers meals that are about as reasonably priced as anything else you'll find in the neighborhood. Only set menus are offered, each a three-course affair that can be served to only 28 diners at a time. Menu items include such time-tested dishes as a confit of duckling, a magret of duckling, shrimp flambéed in calvados, and tournedos in a peppered cream sauce.

4TH ARRONDISSEMENT
(ILE DE LA CITE / ILE ST-LOUIS & BEAUBOURG)
EXPENSIVE

✪ **L'Ambroisie.** 9 place des Vosges, 4e. ☎ **01-42-78-51-45.** Reservations required. Main courses 300–500 F ($60–$100). AE, MC, V. Tues–Sat noon–1:30pm and 8–9:30pm. Métro: St-Paul. FRENCH.

Bernard Pacaud is one of the most talented chefs in Paris, and his cuisine has drawn world attention with his strikingly vivid flavors and expert culinary skill. He trained at the prestigious Vivarois before deciding to strike out on his own, first on the Left Bank and now at this early 17th-century town house in Le Marais, a former goldsmith's shop. You'll dine in one of the two high-ceilinged salons with a decor vaguely inspired by an Italian *palazzo*. In summer there's outdoor seating as well.

Pacaud's tables are nearly always filled with satisfied diners, who come back again and again to see where his imagination will take him next. His cooking has a certain elegant and harmonious simplicity. The dishes change with the seasons. Perhaps on your visit they'll include a feuillantine of crayfish tails with sesame seeds and curry sauce; or filet of turbot braised with celery and celeriac, served with a julienne of black truffles; or one of our favorite dishes in all of Paris, poulard de Bresse demi-deuil hommage à la Mère Brazier, chicken roasted with black truffles and truffled vegetables in a style invented by a Lyonnais matron (La Mère Brazier) after World War II. An award-winning dessert is a tarte fine sablée served with bitter chocolate and mocha-flavored ice cream.

MODERATE

Bofinger. 5–7 rue de la Bastille, 4e. ☎ **01-42-72-87-82.** Reservations recommended. Main courses 100–150 F ($20–$30). AE, DC, MC, V. Daily noon–3pm and 6:30pm–1am. Métro: Bastille. FRENCH/ALSATIAN.

Bofinger was founded in the 1860s and is the oldest Alsatian brasserie in town—and it's certainly one of the best. It's actually a belle époque dining palace, resplendent with shiny brass and stained glass. After a thorough restoration, it looks better than ever. If you prefer, you can dine on an outdoor terrace, weather permitting.

Fashionable types make their way here at night through the Marais district, right off place de la Bastille. In their floor-length white aprons, the waiters bring dish

Restaurants: 3rd & 4th Arrondissements

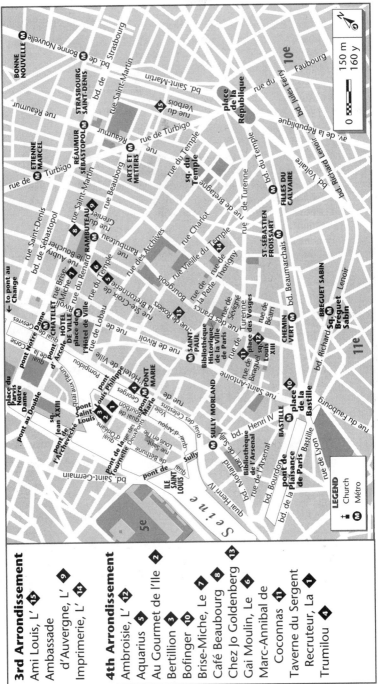

3rd Arrondissement

Ami Louis, L' **15**
Ambassade
d'Auvergne, L' **9**
Imprimerie, L' **14**

4th Arrondissement

Ambroisie, L' **12**
Aquarius **5**
Au Gourmet de l'Ile **2**
Bertillion **3**
Bofinger **10**
Brise-Miche, Le **7**
Café Beaubourg **8**
Chez Jo Goldenberg **13**
Gai Moulin, Le **6**
Marc-Annibal de
Coconnas **11**
Taverne du Sergent
Recruteur, La **1**
Trumilou **4**

after dish of satisfying fare at reasonable prices. For those not watching waistlines or bulges, choucroute (sauerkraut) is the preferred dish, accompanied by a vast array of bacon, sausages, and a pork chop. Look for the chef's specials; he features a different one each day, including a superb cassoulet. The food is honest, tasty, and good—nothing more, nothing less.

Marc-Annibal de Coconnas. 2 bis place des Vosges, 4e. ☎ **01-42-78-58-16.** Reservations required. Main dishes 90–150 F ($18–$30); fixed-price menu 170 F ($34). AE, DC, MC, V. Wed–Sun noon–2pm and 7:45–10:45pm. Métro: Bastille or St-Paul. FRENCH.

Chef Claude Terrail (who also owns La Tour d'Argent) serves superb cuisine in this restaurant, which is located in a historic district (Henri II was mortally wounded nearby, and Victor Hugo lived in an apartment on place des Vosges). Named after the legendary French rake whose peccadilloes with members of the royal family once scandalized the residents of place des Vosges, the restaurant features a Louis XIII decor of high-backed chairs and elegantly rustic accessories. Menu items change frequently but might include a soup of scallops with anise; foie gras; a pastillade of crayfish; a rack of veal en papillote (in parchment) with crème fraîche, white wine, and mushrooms; and turbot poached in an essence of almonds and served on a bed of fennel. None of these items sets off culinary fireworks, but the ingredients are fresh and the flavors are in perfect harmony.

INEXPENSIVE

Aquarius. 54 rue Ste-Croix-de-la-Bretonnerie, 4e. ☎ **01-48-87-48-71.** Reservations not required. Main courses 32–50 F ($6.40–$10); fixed-price lunch 56 F ($11.20). No credit cards. Mon–Sat noon–9:45pm. Closed 2 weeks in Aug. Métro: Hôtel-de-Ville. RER: Châtelet–Les Halles. VEGETARIAN.

In a 17th-century building whose original stonework forms part of the rustic, earthy decor, this is one of the best-known vegetarian restaurants of the Marais. Neither wine nor spirits are served, and smoking is strictly prohibited. The meals are flavorful and healthfully prepared and come in generous portions. Choose from an array of soups and salads; a galette of wheat served with crudités and mushroom tarts; or an assiette paysanne, composed of fried mushrooms, fried potatoes, garlic, and goat cheese, and served with a salad.

☉ Au Gourmet de l'Ile. 42 rue St-Louis-en-l'Ile, 4e. ☎ **01-43-26-79-27.** Reservations required. Fixed-price menus 85–130 F ($17–$26). MC, V. Wed–Sun noon–2pm and 7–10pm. Métro: Pont-Marie. FRENCH.

Local regulars swear by the cuisine at Au Gourmet de l'Ile. Its fixed-price meals are one of the dining bargains of Paris. The setting is beautiful, with a beamed ceiling and candlelit tables. Many Parisian restaurants approach its level of decor, but where other establishments in this popular tourist area fall short in the food they serve, this little "Gourmet Island" succeeds.

In the window you'll see a sign emblazoned with A.A.A.A.A., which, roughly translated, stands for the Amiable Association of Amateurs of the Authentic Andouillette. These chitterling sausages are soul food to the French. Popular and tasty, too, is la charbonnée de l'Ile, a savory pork with onions. An excellent appetizer is the stuffed mussels in shallot butter. The fixed-price menus include a choice of 15 appetizers, 15 main courses, salad or cheese, and a choice of 15 desserts.

Le Brise-Miche. 10 rue Brise-Miche, 4e. ☎ **01-42-78-44-11.** Reservations recommended. Main courses 62–87 F ($12.40–$17.40). AE, DC, MC, V. Daily 8am–midnight (full menu available daily noon–midnight.) Métro: Rambuteau, Hôtel-de-Ville, or Châtelet–Les Halles. FRENCH.

Whimsical and sometimes chaotic, this appealing, inexpensive restaurant shares something of the avant-garde aesthetic of its neighbor, the Centre Pompidou. Named after the bread rations (*les brise-miches*) that were issued from its premises during World War II, it occupies an enviable location next to the medieval Church of St-Merri and the neighborhood's most charming fountain. In nice weather tables and chairs overlook about a dozen spinning, spitting, and bobbing fountains, which were beautifully sculpted by Jean Tingueley and Niki de Saint-Phalle. Each table is provided with a round loaf of bread, crayons, and paper place mats for doodlings (if your impromptu artwork is good enough, it will be framed and proudly displayed as part of the restaurant's permanent decor).

No one will mind if you order just a glass of wine. The menu choices include a range of "maxi salads," tagliatelle with smoked salmon, filet of duckling with peaches, a half chicken roasted à l'ancienne, steaks in pepper sauce, and tarte Tatin with crème fraîche, which (if you choose) can be flambéed in calvados.

Chez Jo Goldenberg. 7 rue des Rosiers, 4e. ☎ **01-48-87-20-16.** Reservations recommended. Main courses 70–90 F ($14–$18). AE, DC, MC, V. Daily noon–1am. Métro: St-Paul. JEWISH/ CENTRAL EUROPEAN.

The distinctive regional decor here comes complete with a collection of samovars and kitsch from central Europe. Interesting paintings and strolling musicians add to the ambience. The carpe farcie (stuffed carp) is our favorite choice, but the beef goulash is also good. We also like the eggplant moussaka, and the pastrami is one of the most popular items. The menu also offers Israeli wines, but M Joseph Goldenberg, the proprietor, admits that they're not as good as French labels.

L'Imprimerie. 101 rue Vieille-du-Temple, 3e. ☎ **01-42-77-93-80.** Reservations recommended. Main courses 77–97 F ($15.40–$19.40); fixed-price menus 139–179 F ($27.80– $35.80). AE, MC, V. Daily noon–3pm and 8pm–1am (last order). Métro: Filles-du-Calvaire. FRENCH.

In a building that in the 19th century functioned as a printing press (*imprimerie*) for the National Archives (which lie a few steps away), this restaurant welcomes a largely gay clientele from the arts community of the Marais. The setting reminds some newcomers of a brick-lined bistro in New York's Greenwich Village, particularly because of the changing array of paintings (some for sale) that decorate the walls. Menu items include a conservative array of French-inspired dishes that include an effeullantine of avocado with shrimp and fresh basil, a ravioli of goat cheese, magret of duckling with a honey-coriander sauce and braised cabbage, and Norwegian salmon prepared with recipes that vary according to the season.

La Taverne du Sergent Recruteur. 41 rue St-Louis-en-l'Ile, 4e. ☎ **01-43-54-75-42.** Reservations recommended. All-you-can-eat menu 185 F ($37). AE, MC, V. Mon–Sat 7pm–midnight (last order). Métro: Pont-Marie. FRENCH.

La Taverne du Sergent Recruteur, like many restaurants on the historic Ile St-Louis, occupies a historic 17th-century building. What sets La Taverne apart from all the others is its all-you-can-eat meal. You more or less make your own salad with the items placed before you, including black radishes, fennel, celery, cucumbers, green pepper, hard-boiled eggs, and carrots. After that, a huge basket of sausages is brought around, and you can slice as you wish, sampling one or all. The carafe of wine, either red, white, or rosé, is bottomless. *Plats du jour,* ranging from beef to veal, change daily. You usually select from three different items. Next, a large cheese board makes the rounds, and, if you're still standing, you can select chocolate mousse or ice cream for dessert. Come here for the big fill-up—not haute cuisine.

Trumilou. 84 quai de l'Hôtel-de-Ville, 4e. ☎ **01-42-77-63-98.** Reservations recommended Sat–Sun. Fixed price menus 65–102F ($13–$20.40). MC, V. Daily noon–3pm and 7–11pm. Métro: Hôtel-de-Ville. FRENCH.

It's one of the most popular of the many restaurants surrounding Paris's Town Hall (Hôtel de Ville), and as such has welcomed most of France's politicians, including George Pompidou, who came here frequently before his election as president of France. ("As soon as they become president they opt for grander restaurants," say the good-natured owners, the Drumond family.) The name comes from the hamlet in Auvergne, Trumilou, where the Drumonds were born, a *lieu-dit* with no more than three houses that' now famous thanks to this restaurant. The decor is provincial and countrified, and includes a rustic collection of farm implements and family memorabilia. Tables are crowded together, and the staff is jovial. Most diners remain on the street level, although additional seating is available in the cellar. The food is tried, true, and well known to every French grandmother. The menu rarely changes, regardless of whomever happens to rule France from nearby City Hall. Examples include poulet provençal, sweetbreads grand-mère, duckling with plums, and the inevitable blanquette de veau (veal in white sauce).

8TH ARRONDISSEMENT (CHAMPS-ELYSEES / MADELEINE)
VERY EXPENSIVE

✪ **Lasserre.** 17 av. Franklin-D-Roosevelt, 8e. ☎ **01-43-59-53-43.** Reservations required. Main courses 260–300 F ($52–$60). AE, MC. V. Mon 7:30–10:30pm, Tues–Sat 12:30–2:30pm and 7:30–10:30pm. Closed Aug. Métro: F-D-Roosevelt. FRENCH.

This elegant restaurant was a simple bistro before World War II—a "rendezvous for chauffeurs." Then along came René Lasserre, who bought the dilapidated building and set out to create his dream. He succeeded in creating a legend that now attracts gourmets from around the world.

Two white-painted front doors lead to the dining rooms and a reception lounge with Louis XVI–style furnishings and brocaded walls. The main salon is two stories high; on each side is a mezzanine. Tall arched windows draped with silk open onto the street. The tables are set with fine porcelain, crystal glasses edged in gold, a silver candelabrum, and even a silver bird and a ceramic dove. You study the menu sitting on a Louis XV–style salon chair.

Overhead, the ceiling is painted with lamb-white clouds and a cerulean sky, but in fair weather the staff slides back the roof to reveal the real sky, letting moonlight or sunshine pour into the room.

The food is a combination of French classicism and originality. The presentation of dishes is one of the most winning and imaginative aspects of Lasserre. Always count on high drama. Michelin only awards this restaurant two stars, as opposed to three for Lucas-Carton or Taillevent, but we've never understood why it's not at the very top.

Lasserre's appetizers are among the finest in Paris, including an unusual serving of a bouillabaisse in gelatin or a salad of truffles. You might also be tempted by a trio of terrines. The fish selections are excellent, including lobster from Brittany and a sole soufflé. A hallmark dish is filets de sole Club de la Casserole. Meat and poultry selections are also outstanding, including veal kidneys flambé and steak de Charolais au Bourgueil, one of the tenderest and most succulent choices of beef offered in Paris. The desserts are also spectacular and can include soufflés or a soothing sabayon. The cellar, with some 180,000 bottles of wine, is among the most remarkable in Paris; red wines are decanted into silver pitchers or ornate crystal.

Restaurants: 8th Arrondissement

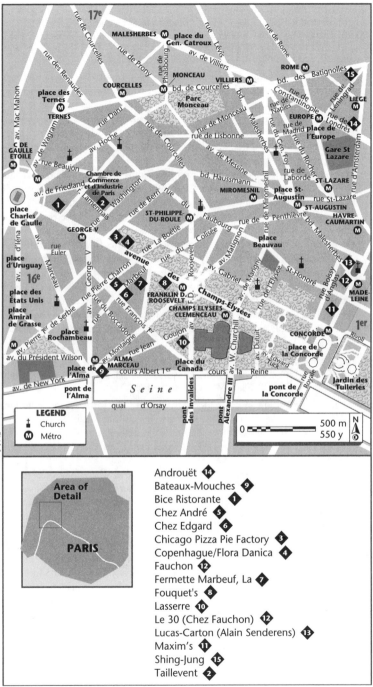

LEGEND
† Church
Ⓜ Métro

0 ━━━━━ 500 m
━━━━━ 550 y

Area of Detail

PARIS

Androuët ⑭
Bateaux-Mouches ⑨
Bice Ristorante ❶
Chez André ⑤
Chez Edgard ⑥
Chicago Pizza Pie Factory ❸
Copenhague/Flora Danica ❹
Fauchon ⑫
Fermette Marbeuf, La ⑦
Fouquet's ⑧
Lasserre ⑩
Le 30 (Chez Fauchon) ⑫
Lucas-Carton (Alain Senderens) ⑬
Maxim's ⑪
Shing-Jung ⑮
Taillevent ❷

Lucas-Carton (Alain Senderens). 9 place de la Madeleine, 8e. ☎ **01-42-65-22-90.** Reservations required several days ahead for lunch and several weeks ahead for dinner. Main courses 300–700 F ($60–$140); fixed-price lunch 395 F ($79); *menu dégustation* 1,500–1,900 F ($300–$380). AE, DC, MC, V. Mon–Fri noon–2:30pm and 8–10:15pm, Sat 8–10:15pm. Closed 3 weeks in Aug and 2 weeks in Dec (dates vary). Métro: Madeleine. FRENCH.

This landmark restaurant, dating from the belle époque, was designed by an Englishman named Lucas and a talented French chef, Francis Carton. Since Senderens has taken over as restaurateur, he has added some welcome modern touches to the historic restaurant, along with a brilliantly realized culinary repertoire. The two dining rooms downstairs and the private rooms upstairs are decorated with mirrors, fragrant bouquets of flowers, and wood paneling that has probably been polished every week since its original installation in 1900.

French food critics always divide into two camps: those who claim that Lucas-Carton is the best restaurant in Paris and those who instead favor Taillevent. The battle of the toques may never really be settled—the race is too close to call.

Every dish here is influenced by the creative flair of Alain Senderens. The menu items change with the seasons, but the food presentation always makes an artistic statement on its own. Examples include ravioli aux truffes (ravioli with truffles), foie gras with cabbage, vanilla-flavored lobster, duckling Apicius (roasted with honey and spices), a pastillade of rabbit, sweetbreads with acidified carrot juice, and a dessert that critics unanimously declare wonderful: a mille-feuille with vanilla sauce. However, Senderens is constantly creating and experimenting, so by the time you visit there will probably be a fresh addition to his innovative menu. His *menu dégustation,* although lethally priced, includes a selection of major and very grand French wines—hence the high tab.

Maxim's. 3 rue Royale, 8e. ☎ **01-42-65-27-94.** Reservations required. Main courses 225–300 F ($45–$60) at lunch, 265–460 F ($53–$92) at dinner. AE, DC, MC, V. Mon–Sat 12:30–2:30pm and 7:30–10:30pm. Métro: Concorde. FRENCH.

Maxim's is the world's most legendary restaurant. The Michelin guide no longer even bothers to recommend it, much less give it stars, but Maxim's carries on in its overpriced way. It even has clones in New York, Beijing, and Tokyo. Maxim's has preserved its belle époque decor—during that era, it was a favorite dining spot of Edward VII, then the prince of Wales.

The restaurant was the setting for *The Merry Widow,* where John Gilbert dipped and swayed with Mae Murray. You can always be sure the orchestra will play that tune at least once each evening. Much later in film history, Louis Jourdan—at that time considered "the handsomest man in the world"—took Leslie Caron to dine here in the musical *Gigi.*

Today rich tourists from around the world are likely to occupy once-fabled tables where Onassis wooed Callas. Clothing-industry giant Pierre Cardin took over the restaurant in 1981. Although not always available, billiby soup—made with mussels, white wine, cream (of course), chopped onions, celery, parsley, and coarsely ground pepper—is a classic opener. Another favorite, sole Albert, named after the late famous maître d'hôtel, is flavored with chopped herbs and breadcrumbs, plus a large glass of vermouth. For dessert, try the tarte Tatin.

✪ **Taillevent.** 15 rue Lamennais, 8e. ☎ **01-44-95-15-01.** Reservations required weeks, even months, in advance for both lunch and dinner. Main courses 240–380 F ($48–$72.20). AE, DC, MC, V. Mon–Fri noon–2:30pm and 7–10pm. Closed Aug. Métro: George-V. FRENCH.

Taillevent dates from 1946, and it has climbed steadily in the ranks of excellence since then. Today it's recognized as the most outstanding all-around restaurant in Paris.

In the highly competitive 8th arrondisement, with its temples of haute cuisine, Taillevent surfaces at the top, challenged only by Lucas-Carton and Lassere.

The setting is a grand 19th-century town house off the Champs-Elysées, once inhabited by the duc de Morny. The rooms are paneled and have crystal chandeliers; the predominant color scheme is blue. The restaurant is named after a famous chef of the 14th century (Guillaume Tirel Taillevent) who wrote one of the oldest known books on French cookery. The place is not huge, but that's as the owner wishes, since it permits him to give personal attention to every facet of the operation and maintain a discreet club atmosphere. You might begin with a boudin (sausage) of Breton lobster à la nage, red snapper with black olives, duck liver with spice bread and ginger, duck rouennais with mild spices, or Scottish salmon cooked in sea salt with a sauce of olive oil and lemons. Dessert might be a nougatine glacé with pears. The wine list is among the best in Paris.

Although Monsieur Vrinat likes Americans, it isn't always easy for visitors from the States and other countries to book a table, since the owner prefers that about 60% of his clients be French.

EXPENSIVE

Bateaux-Mouches. Pont de l'Alma, place de l'Alma, 8e. ☎ **01-42-25-96-10.** Reservations required. Fixed-price cruise and lunch 300 F ($60) Tues–Fri, 350 F ($70) Sat–Sun; fixed-price cruise and dinner 500–650 F ($100–$130). AE, DC, MC, V. Lunch cruise Tues–Sun 1–2:45pm; dinner cruise daily 8:30–10:45pm. Métro: Alma-Marceau. FRENCH.

These glass-topped boats carry passengers on sightseeing excursions along the Seine, and also function as floating restaurants. The food is definitely not as inspired as that prepared by conventional restaurants, but the view is much, much better. During the dinner cruise live music is provided, and men are requested to wear jackets and ties. At dinner two different menus are offered, both of which include wine. Children 11 and under 12 are accepted on the luncheon cruises but not the dinner cruises.

Bice Ristorante. In the Hôtel Balzac, 6 rue Balzac, 8e. ☎ **01-45-61-97-22.** Reservations recommended. Main courses 120–150 F ($24–$30). AE, DC, MC, V. Mon–Sat 12:30–4pm and 8–11:30. Closed the first 3 weeks of Aug. Metro: George-V. ITALIAN.

The greatest Italian restaurant in Paris is actually an offshoot of the most famous Bice in Milan, which was created in 1926 and has now crossed the seas to New York, Tokyo, and other major capitals. Located at the Hôtel Balzac since 1990, it has become one of the most fashionable restaurants in Paris. Bice, with its sleek art deco decor by Adam Tihany, caters to the Italian elite of Paris. Before being seated at your table you can have a drink in the chic little bar. The well-prepared and well-received cuisine concentrates on specialties of northern Italy. Offering the town's finest antipasti, the chef turns out one delectable opener after another, including smoked sturgeon with caviar. The fish and meat courses are wisely limited, but include our favorite—a delectable assortment of grilled mixed fish, selected fresh at the market that very day. Meat-lovers might fancy the superb ossobuco with saffron rissoto or the classic veal cutlet milanese. The veal liver Venetian style with grilled polenta is another savory selection.

Copenhague/Flora Danica. 142 av. des Champs-Elysées, 8e. ☎ **01-43-59-20-41.** Reservations recommended. Main dishes 70–180 F ($14–$36); fixed-price menus 148–240 F ($29.60–$48). AE, DC, MC, V. Restaurant Copenhague, Mon–Sat noon–2pm and 7:15–10:30pm (closed Jan 1–7 and Aug). Flora Danica, daily noon–2pm and 7:15–11pm. Métro: George-V. DANISH.

The specialties of Denmark are served with flair at the "Maison du Danemark," which functions as a quasi-official Danish goodwill ambassador. In many ways it's the best restaurant along the Champs-Elysées, with an outside terrace for midsummer dining. There are two dining areas to choose from: the Flora Danica, on the street level, and the somewhat more formal Restaurant Copenhague, upstairs.

To be thoroughly Danish, order an apéritif of aquavit and ignore the wine list in favor of Carlsberg. Menu items include a terrine of reindeer, foie gras, smoked salmon, a selection of fresh shrimp, or any of an elegant array of open-face sandwiches. The house specialty is a platter of *délices Scandinaves,* composed of the many seafood and dairy specialties that the Danes prepare exceptionally well. Our preferred dish here is grilled Norwegian salmon cooked on one side only. The cookery is forever competent here—not "forever boring," as one critic suggested.

MODERATE

Chez André. 12 rue Marbeuf (at rue Clement-Marot), 8e. ☎ **01-47-20-59-57.** Reservations recommended. Main courses 89–150 F ($17.80–$30). AE, DC, MC, V. Daily 11:30am–1am. Métro: F-D-Roosevelt. FRENCH.

Chez André is one of the neighborhood's favorite bistros. Its major drawback is that you'll feel a bit left out in the cold if you're not one of the regulars. Outside, a discreet red awning stretches over an array of shellfish on ice; inside, an art nouveau decor includes etched glass and masses of flowers. The old-style cuisine on the menu includes pâté of thrush, Roquefort in puff pastry, several kinds of omelets, calves' head vinaigrette, a potage du jour, and an array of fresh shellfish, along with several reasonably priced wines. Desserts might be rum baba, chocolate cake, or a daily pastry. Dishes are all prepared with skill and care, but the menu remains faithful to old-fashioned bistro fare. But that's the way the regulars seem to like it.

Chez Edgard. 4 rue Marbeuf, 8e. ☎ **01-47-20-51-15.** Reservations not accepted. Main courses 80–160 F ($16–$32). AE, DC, MC, V. Mon–Sat noon–3pm and 7pm–12:30am. Métro: F-D-Roosevelt. FRENCH.

A chic crowd of neighborhood residents regard this belle époque restaurant as their favorite local spot, and ebullient owner Paul Benmussa makes a special point of welcoming them on their frequent visits as if they were members of his family. This fashionable bistro serves the same kind of food and attracts the same type of clients as Chez André (see above). Customers include politicians, journalists, and show-business personalities such as Roman Polanski and Sydney Pollack. The noise level sometimes reaches quite a din.

Specialties include breast of duckling, red mullet with basil in puff pastry, and several terrines, including one made from scallops. Also offered is a range of well-prepared meat dishes. Although it's a cliché of French bistro cookery, the menu remains reliably delicious. In winter, seafood and oysters are shipped in from Brittany. The ice-cream sundaes (listed with other desserts on a special menu) are particularly delectable. There's a small outdoor terrace, but most guests prefer to eat inside on one of the semiprivate banquettes.

Chicago Pizza Pie Factory. 5 rue de Berri, 8e. ☎ **01-45-62-50-23.** Reservations accepted only Mon–Fri, and only for groups of eight or more. Pizza for two, 86–189 F ($17.20–$37.80); pizza for four, 129–195 F ($25.80–$39); fixed-price lunch 51 F ($10.20), 62 F ($12.40), and 71 F ($14.20). AE, DC, MC, V. Daily noon–1am. Métro: Champs-Elysées–Clemenceau. AMERICAN/PIZZA.

On a side street of the Champs-Elysées, you'll find a busy tribute to the city of Chicago in a former garage. The bar is outfitted with anything and everything to do with Chicago—hotos, sports banners, kitsch. The dining room is as large and raucous as the Windy City itself. Although rather dull platters of chicken, lasagne, and salads are served, you come here for pizza, prepared in endless variations on eight basic themes. It's the best in Paris. There's also cheesecake, pecan pie, and garlic bread. The management proudly refuses, except under dire circumstances, to serve burgers of any kind. No one will mind if you bypass the food altogether in favor of a drink at the bar. Happy hour is from 6 to 8pm and 11:30pm to 1am, when some drinks (but not beer) are reduced in price.

La Fermette Marbeuf. 5 rue Marbeuf, 8e. ☎ **01-53-23-08-00.** Reservations recommended. Main courses 85–150 F ($17–$30); fixed-price dinner 169 F ($33.80). AE, DC, MC, V. Daily noon–3pm and 7:30–11:30pm. Métro: F-D-Roosevelt or Alma. FRENCH.

La Fermette has a turn-of-the-century decor, reasonable prices, fine cuisine, and a location just a short distance from the Champs-Elysées. You might rub shoulders with French TV or film stars. The hand-painted tiles and stained-glass windows of the twin dining rooms have earned this place a designation as a national historic monument, but don't think that means La Fermette is stodgy—guests come here for the fun of it all, too.

The fresh fish is shipped in directly from Concarneau or Boulogne sur Mer. Brill filet is subtly flavored with sesame, and grilled sole is so good it needs only a white-butter sauce. An exceptionally tasty dish is roast guinea fowl with fresh herbs, although the duck filet with fresh figs and rosemary is equally enticing.

Le 30 (Chez Fauchon). 30 place de la Madeleine, 8e. ☎ **01-47-42-56-58.** Reservations recommended, especially at lunch. Main courses 125–220 F ($25–$44). AE, DC, MC, V. Mon–Sat 12:15–2:30pm and 7:30–10:30pm. Métro: Madeleine. FRENCH.

In 1990 Fauchon, one of Europe's most legendary delicatessens, transformed one of its upper rooms into an airy and elegant pastel-colored showplace dotted with neo-Grecian columns and accessories. It caught on immediately as a lunch spot for the many bankers, stockbrokers, and merchants who work nearby. The menu selections are prepared with the freshest ingredients available from the food emporium down-stairs, and might include a cassoulet of lobster served with a basil-flavored shellfish sauce, a curried version of fried sweetbreads, suprême of sea bass with fennel, and a luscious assortment of cheeses and pastries.

Le 30 is our personal favorite of the four restaurants that Fauchon operates along place de la Madeleine. Other choices include **La Trattoria,** 26 place de la Madeleine, for upscale Italian food; and **Le Bistro du Caviar,** 30 place de la Madeleine, where a chariot de caviar dispenses epicurean samples of foie gras and smoked salmon, as well as every imaginable type of caviar. Fauchon also operates a seafood bistro, **Bistro de la Mer,** at 6 place de la Madeleine. The Bistro de la Mer shares a phone with Le 30. The other two restaurants can be reached by calling 01-47-42-60-11.

INEXPENSIVE

Shing-Jung. 7 rue Clapeyron, 8e. ☎ **01-45-22-21-06.** Reservations recommended at dinner. Main courses 75–100 F ($15–$20); fixed-price menus 100–200 F ($20–$40). MC, V. Mon–Sat noon–2:30pm and 7–10:30pm. Métro: Rome. KOREAN.

This is one of about two dozen Korean restaurants in all of Paris, and it's known for its low prices and generous portions. Its sashimi is comparable to the versions served in competing Japanese restaurants, although the portions of the fresh tuna, salmon, and daurade tend to be more generous. A specialty is the Korean barbecue called bulgoogi, cooked according to age-old traditions, which seems more authentic thanks to a clever interior decor that juxtaposes Korean chests and paintings by Korean artists.

Le Grand Fromage

Cheese is king at **Androuët,** 41 rue d'Amsterdam, 8e (☎ **01-48-74-26-93**). True, it's a novelty restaurant, but if you're devoted to cheese, there's nothing like it in Europe. A boutique on the street level sells a mind-boggling array of virtually every dairy product made in France. True aficionados, however, climb a flight of stairs to a windowless restaurant with a modern decor and pink napery, where most of the dishes are concocted with a base of—you guessed it—cheese. A savory and impressive array of wines, well-prepared green salads, and ultra-fresh bread is available to accompany whatever you order. Examples include a fondue of three cheeses, a filet de boeuf contentin (beef filet with Roquefort sauce flambéed with calvados), grilled chateaubriand, and magret de canard (duckling). Many cheese lovers, however, opt for just a bottle of wine, a green salad, and all-you-can-eat choices from the most sophisticated *dégustation de fromages* in the world. Six platters, each loaded with a different category of cheese (one with goat cheeses, another with triple crèmes, etc.), are brought to your table, allowing you to select random samples. Reservations are required. Main courses are 100 to 130 F ($20 to $26); the set-price lunch is 175 F ($35), and the set-price dinner is 195 F ($39); the *dégustation des fromages* is 250 F ($50). AE, DC, MC, V are accepted. Androuët is open Monday to Saturday from noon to 3pm and 7:30 to 10pm. Métro: St-Lazare or Liège.

9TH ARRONDISSEMENT (OPERA GARNIER / PIGATELLE)
EXPENSIVE

Restaurant Opéra. In the Grand Hôtel Inter-Continental, place de l'Opéra, 9e. ☎ **01-40-07-30-10.** Reservations recommended. Main courses 140–225 F ($28–$45); fixed-price menu 230–335 F ($46–$67). AE, DC, MC, V. Mon–Fri noon–2:30pm and 7–11pm. Métro: Opéra. FRENCH.

This elegant and prestigious restaurant is situated in the historic Grand Hôtel Inter-Continental. We no longer recommend it for accommodations, but there's no denying that it has played an important role in Parisian history since its construction in 1860. If you dine here, your predecessors will have included Salvador Dalí, Harry S Truman, Josephine Baker, Marlene Dietrich, Maurice Chevalier, Maria Callas, and Marc Chagall, who often came here while working on the famous ceiling of the nearby Opéra. On August 25, 1944, Charles de Gaulle placed this famous restaurant's first food order in a newly freed Paris—a cold plate to go.

Today you can enjoy a before-dinner drink in a lavishly ornate bar before heading for a table in the gilded jewel box of a dining room. Menu choices change with the seasons. The menu is not a prisoner of some culinary past, but is fairly inventive and reaches out to various provinces of France and to the world for its repertoire. Start with a warm filet of squab and truffle pie, or perhaps sautéed veal head and veal foot ravioli. Follow with one of the perfectly prepared fish dishes such as braised turbot with celery, or a thick rack of veal for two. The roasted veal kidney with green cabbage displays the chef's talent at its best.

INEXPENSIVE

🟢 **Le Grand Zinc.** 5 rue du Faubourg Montmartre, 9e. ☎ **01-47-70-88-64.** Reservations not required. Main courses 80–150 F ($16–$30); fixed-price menu 100 F ($20). AE, DC, MC, V. Mon–Sat noon–3pm and 7pm–1am. Metro: Rue-Montmartre. FRENCH.

Paris of the 1880s lives on here, as exemplified by the spirit lamps hanging inside. You make your way into the restaurant past baskets of seafood in which you can inspect the bélons (brown-fleshed oysters) from Brittany, a traditional favorite that's available year round. The atmosphere is bustling in the tradition of a typical French brasserie.

Specialties include steak au poivre (pepper steak), magret de canard (duck) with grilled peppers, côte de boeuf for two, confit de canard prepared in the style of Toulouse and served with ratatouille, and grilled filet of turbot with beurre blanc (white-butter sauce). Nothing ever changes, certainly not the time-tested recipes.

Hard Rock Cafe. 14 bd. Montmartre, 9e. ☎ **01-42-46-10-00.** Reservations not accepted. Sandwiches, salads, and platters 62–99 F ($12.40–$19.80). AE, MC, V. Daily 11:30am–2am. Métro: Rue-Montmartre or Richelieu-Drouot. AMERICAN.

Like its counterparts, which now stretch from Hong Kong to Reykjavik, the Hard Rock Cafe offers a collection of musical memorabilia as well as musical selections from 35 years of rock 'n' roll classics. These are pumped out at reasonable levels during lunchtime, and at slightly less reasonable levels every evening, much to the delight of the crowd, which appreciates both the music and the juicy steaks, hamburgers, veggie burgers, salads, and heaping platters of informal, French-inspired food. As you dine, scan the high-ceilinged room for such venerated objects as the stage tuxedo worn by Buddy Holly, Jim Morrison's leather jacket, Jimi Hendrix's psychedelic vest, or the black-and-gold bustier sported by Madonna during one of her concerts in Paris.

10TH ARRONDISSEMENT (GARE DU NORD / GARE DE L'EST)
MODERATE

Brasserie Flo. 7 cour des Petites-Ecuries, 10e. ☎ **01-47-70-13-59.** Reservations recommended. Main courses 70–100 F ($14–$20); fixed-price menu 112 F ($22.40) at lunch, 185 F ($37) at dinner; fixed-price late-night supper (served only after 10pm) 112 F ($22.40). AE, DC, MC, V. Daily noon–3pm and 7pm–1:30am. Metro: Château-d'Eau or Strasbourg–St-Denis. ALSATIAN.

The Brasserie Flo is a remembrance of things past. You walk through an area of passageways, stumbling over garbage littering the streets, then come upon this sepia world of turn-of-the-century Paris: old mahogany, leather banquettes, and brass-studded chairs. Some of the most sophisticated Parisian diners come here.

The thing to order, of course, is the delicious *la formidable choucroute* (sauerkraut), but don't expect just a heap of sauerkraut: The mound is surrounded by ham, bacon, and sausages. It's bountiful in the best tradition of Alsace. The onion soup is always good, as is guinea hen with lentils. Look for the *plats du jour*, ranging from roast pigeon to fricassée of veal with sorrel.

Julien. 16 rue du Faubourg St-Denis, 10e. ☎ **01-47-70-12-06.** Reservations required. Main courses 80–130 F ($16–$26); fixed-price lunch (and after 10pm) 112 F ($22.40). AE, DC, MC, V. Daily noon–3pm and 7pm–1:30am. Métro: Strasbourg–St-Denis. FRENCH.

🅐 Family-Friendly Restaurants

Moissonnier *(see p. 151)*   Give the kids a taste of real French home-cooking, served in big portions.

Le Brise-Miche *(see p. 132)*   The ideal choice when visiting the Pompidou Museum. Diners are encouraged to doodle on the place mats; crayons are provided.

Bertillion *(see p. 2)*   When they're screaming for ice cream, Bertillion is *the* place to go.

"The poor man's Maxim's," Julien offers an opportunity to dine in one of the most sumptuous belle époque interiors in Paris. Located near Les Halles, it began life at the turn of the century as an elegant and acclaimed restaurant, but declined after World War II to become a cheap and unremarkable eatery; the lavish decor, however, remained, although grimy and unappreciated. From a dingy working-class dive, the Julien has now been restored to its former elegance. The dirt has been cleaned off and the magnificence of its dining room brought back to life. Of special interest are four murals representing the four seasons, and a sometimes very fashionable clientele.

The food served here is *cuisine bourgeoise,* but without the heavy sauces formerly used. Excellently prepared dishes include eggplant caviar and wild-mushroom salad. Among the main courses are cassoulet (a stew of Gascony), fresh salmon with sorrel, and chateaubriand béarnaise. The wine list is extensive and reasonably priced.

INEXPENSIVE

La P'tite Tonkinoise. 56 rue du Faubourg-Poissonière, 10e. ☎ **01-42-46-85-98.** Reservations recommended. Main courses 80–120 F ($16–$24); fixed-price lunch 133 F ($26.60). DC, MC, V. Tues–Sat noon–2:15pm and 7:30–10:15pm. Métro: Poissonière or Bonne-Nouvelle. VIETNAMESE.

Paris has hundreds of Vietnamese restaurants, but this is our favorite. Named after the old, diminutive matriarch of the family that has run this restaurant since 1972, La P'tite Tonkinoise provides an exceptional opportunity to learn more about Tonkin (the 19th-century Asian province later renamed North Vietnam), its culture, and its cuisine. The decor mimics a Vietnamese hut, with walls almost completely sheathed in bamboo. Reservations in advance are a good idea, as the dining room can only accommodate about 30 diners at a time. The menu items, usually based on seafood, chicken, or pork, are less spicy than you might expect. A perennial favorite is my sao, a medley of stir-fried vegetables served on a crispy rice cake and garnished with shrimp. Few tourists venture into this neighborhood, but you'll be rewarded if you do.

11TH & 12TH ARRONDISSEMENTS (OPERA BASTILLE / BOIS DE VINCENNES)
EXPENSIVE

✪ **Au Trou Gascon.** 40 rue Taine, 12e. ☎ **01-43-44-34-26.** Reservations required. Main courses 158–168 F ($31.60–$33.60); fixed-price menu 220 F ($44) at lunch, 280 F ($56) at dinner. AE, DC, MC, V. Mon–Fri noon–2pm and 7:30–10pm, Sat 7:30–10pm. Closed Aug. Métro: Daumesnil. GASCONY.

One of the most acclaimed chefs in Paris today, Alain Dutournier launched his cooking career in the Gascony region of southwest France. His parents mortgaged their own inn to allow Dutournier to open a turn-of-the-century bistro in an unfashionable part of the 12th arrondissement. At first he got little business, but word soon spread that this man was a true artist in the kitchen who knew and practiced authentic *cuisine moderne.* Today he has opened another restaurant in Paris, and he has shared his secret recipes with his kitchen staff. The owner's wife, Nicole, is the welcoming hostess, and the wine steward has distinguished himself for his exciting *cave* containing several little-known wines along with a fabulous collection of armagnacs. It's estimated that the cellar has some 750 varieties of wine.

Here you can enjoy the true and authentic cuisine of Gascony. Start with fresh duck foie gras cooked in a terrine, or Gascony cured ham cut from the bone. Favorite main dishes include veal head with spring vegetables, and the best cassoulet (a local white-bean stew with traditional preserved duck, lamb, pork, and homemade sausage) in town. The poultry and foie gras come exclusively from Châlosse farms in the southwest of France.

MODERATE

Le Train Bleu. In the Gare de Lyon, 12e. ☎ **01-43-43-09-06.** Reservations recommended. Main courses 110–185 F ($22–$37); fixed-price menu (including wine) 250 F ($50). AE, DC, MC, V. Daily noon–2pm and 7–9:45pm (last order). Métro: Gare-de-Lyon. FRENCH.

To reach this restaurant, climb the ornate double staircase that faces the grimy platforms of the Gare de Lyon. Both the restaurant and the station were built simultaneously with the Grand Palais, pont Alexandre-III, and the Petit Palais, as part of the World Exhibition of 1900. As a fitting sequel to a train ride from anywhere in the south of France, the station's architects designed a restaurant whose decor is now classified as a national artistic treasure. Inaugurated by the French president in 1901 and renovated and cleaned at great expense in 1992, the restaurant displays an army of bronze statues, a lavishly frescoed ceiling, mosaics, mirrors, old-fashioned banquettes, and 41 belle époque murals. Each of these celebrates the distant corners of the French-speaking world, which are linked to Paris by its rail network.

Service is fast, attentive, and efficient, in case you're about to catch a train to someplace. A formally dressed staff will bring steaming platters of soufflé of brill, escargots in chablis sauce, calves' head ravigote, steak tartare, loin of lamb provençal, veal kidneys in mustard sauce, rib of beef for two, and rum baba. The food is standard French fare and a bit overpriced. The setting, however, makes it worthwhile.

16TH ARRONDISSEMENT (TROCADERO / BOIS DE BOULOGNE)
VERY EXPENSIVE

✪ **Faugeron.** 52 rue de Longchamp, 16e. ☎ **01-47-04-24-53.** Reservations required. Main courses 185–260 F ($37–$52); fixed-price menu 295–650 F ($59–$130) at lunch, 550–650 F ($110–$130) at dinner. AE, MC, V. Mon–Fri 11:30am–2pm and 7:30–10pm, Sat 7:30–10pm. Closed Aug and Sat May–Sept. Métro: Trocadéro. FRENCH.

Henri Faugeron is an inspired chef who many years ago established this restaurant as an elegant yet unobtrusive backdrop for his superb cuisine, which he calls "revolutionary." He is viewed as a culinary researcher, and his menu always includes one or two platters from the classic French cookery canon—perhaps a leg of lamb baked 7 hours, or a rack of hare in the traditional French style. Much of his zesty cuisine depends on the season and on his market selections; he purchases only the freshest ingredients available. Game dishes, frogs' legs, oysters, scallops, whatever—Henri Faugeron and his chefs prepare food with style. He is aided in his endeavors by Jean-Claude Jambon, one of the premier sommeliers of France—indeed, of the world. Service is reassuring and discreet.

EXPENSIVE

La Grande Cascade. Bois de Boulogne, 16e. ☎ **01-45-27-33-51.** Reservations required. Main courses 200–280 F ($40–$56); *menu d'affaires* (served at lunch Mon–Fri) 285 F ($57). AE, DC, MC, V. Daily noon–3pm and 7:30–10:30pm. Closed Dec 20–Jan 14. You must take a taxi or drive; there's no Métro stop nearby. FRENCH.

Set amid the trees of Paris's largest park (the Bois de Boulogne), this is where even the most jaded of Parisians can find a calm and nostalgic retreat from the urban congestion of the city's core. It was originally designed in 1865 by Baron Haussmann, the architect who rearranged the boulevards of Paris, as a private hunting lodge for Napoléon III. Around 1900 it was converted into a restaurant, and attracted the chic and theatrical patrons of its day, including Colette.

In warm weather you might want a table on the terrace; otherwise there's a suitably grand gilt-with-crystal dining room. Soft lights and 19th-century references create an undeniably romantic appeal.

The menu is as traditional and *grand bourgeois* as the setting, although not bogged down in the past. Sauces are lighter and the fresh, high-quality ingredients aren't overcooked as they were in the past. Specialties include warm foie gras of duckling, Atlantic lobster served whole with truffle oil, and a rosette of beef Rossini filet, served with a nugget of foie gras in its center. A spectacular finish is provided by crêpes soufflés à l'orange.

✪ **Le Vivarois.** 192–194 av. Victor-Hugo, 16e. ☎ **01-45-04-04-31.** Reservations required. Main courses 245–300 F ($49–$60); fixed-price lunch 360 F ($72). AE, DC, MC, V. Mon–Fri noon–2pm and 8–10pm. Closed Aug. Métro: Pompe. FRENCH.

Food critics have called Le Vivarois "a revelation." *Gourmet* magazine once hailed it as "a restaurant of our time . . . the most exciting, audacious, and important restaurant in Paris today." Le Vivarois still maintains its standards, but it no longer occupies such a lofty position in the culinary world.

Le Vivarois is the personal statement of its supremely talented owner-chef, Claude Peyrot. The tasteful modern decor is accented by slabs of marble and polished cherrywood, and the food is equally impressive. Peyrot's menu is constantly changing. One food critic once said, and quite accurately, "the menu changes with the marketing and his genius." He does a most recommendable lobster ravioli and coquilles St-Jacques (scallops). To many his most winning dish is rognons de veau (veal kidneys).

Madame Peyrot is one of the finest maîtres d'hôtel in Paris. She'll guide you through wine selections so you'll end up with the right complement to her husband's superlative cuisine.

17TH & 18TH ARRONDISSEMENT (PARC MONCEAU / MONTMARTRE)
VERY EXPENSIVE

✪ **Guy Savoy.** 18 rue Troyon, 17e. ☎ **01-43-80-40-61.** Reservations required 1 week in advance. Main courses 240–400 F ($48–$80); *menu dégustation* 840 F ($168). AE, MC, V. Mon–Fri noon–2pm and 7:30–10:30pm, Sat 7:30–10:30pm. Métro: Charles-de-Gaulle–Etoile. FRENCH.

Guy Savoy serves the kind of food that Monsieur Savoy himself likes to eat, and it's prepared with consummate skill. When the five or six hottest chefs in Europe are named today, his name is on the list, and deservedly so. His nearest rival is Michel Rostang (see below), over whom we think he has a very slight edge. Both have earned two stars from Michelin. Though the food is superb and meals comprise up to nine courses, the portions are small; you won't necessarily be satiated before the meal has run its course.

The menu changes with the seasons, but at the time of your visit might include a light cream soup of lentils and crayfish, foie gras of duckling with aspic of duckling and gray salt, or red snapper with a liver-and-spinach sauce served with crusty potatoes. If you visit in the right season, you may have a chance to order such masterfully prepared game as mallard, venison, or even game birds. Savoy is fascinated with the champignon (mushroom) in all its many varieties, and has been known to serve as many as a dozen different types, especially in the autumn.

✪ **Michel Rostang.** 20 rue Rennequin, 17e. ☎ **01-47-63-40-77.** Reservations required. Main courses 198–290 F ($39.60–$58); set menus 540–720 F ($108–$144); fixed-price lunch 298 F

($59.60). AE, MC, V. Mon–Fri 12:30–2:30pm and 8–10:30pm, Sat 8–10:30pm. Closed 2 weeks in Aug. Métro: Ternes. FRENCH.

Monsieur Rostang is one of the most creative chefs in Paris. He's the fifth generation of one of the most distinguished French "cooking families," who have been connected with the famed Bonne Auberge at Antibes on the French Riviera.

The restaurant is composed of four different dining rooms, each paneled in mahogany, cherry, or pearwood, and in some cases accented with frosted panels of Lalique crystal. One contains collages of broken musical instruments crafted by the contemporary French artist Armand. Another features a collection of 19th-century liqueur bottles (*Robj*) crafted in the shape of famous figures from French history, and a glassed-in view of the kitchen where Mr. Rostang or his assistants can be observed preparing their highly nuanced cuisine.

The menu changes every 2 months and features modern improvements on France's *cuisine bourgeoise.* In midwinter, truffles are the dish of choice; in spring, you'll find racks of suckling lamb from the salt marshes of France's western seacoasts; and in game season, look for sophisticated preparations of pheasant and venison. Three staples that are usually available year round include quail eggs with a coque of sea urchins, a fricassée of sole, or a young chicken from Bresse (the finest in France) served with a chervil sauce.

MODERATE

Goldenberg's. 69 av. de Wagram, 17e. ☎ **01-42-27-34-79.** Reservations required. Main courses 70–160 F ($14–$32); fixed-price menus 138 F ($27.60). MC, V. Daily 9am–midnight. Métro: Ternes or Charles-de-Gaulle–Etoile. JEWISH/DELI.

This is a Jewish delicatessen-restaurant in the Champs-Elysées area. Its founder, Albert Goldenberg, was known as the dean of Jewish restaurateurs in Paris, and rightly so, since he opened his first delicatessen in Montmartre in 1936. The deli, like many of its New York counterparts, has the front half reserved as the specialty take-out section and the back half for in-house dining. The menu features such old-world specialties as carpe farcie (stuffed carp), blini, cabbage borscht, and pastrami, one of the most popular items. Naturally, everything tastes better if accompanied by Jewish rye bread. For those who want to really get in the spirit, the menu offers Israeli as well as French wines.

INEXPENSIVE

⑤ **L'Etoile Verte.** 13 rue Brey, 17e. ☎ **01-43-80-69-34.** Reservations recommended. Main courses 45–98 F ($9–$19.60); fixed-price menus 69–145 F ($13.80–$29). AE, DC, MC, V. Daily 11am–3pm and 6:30–11pm. Métro: Charles-de-Gaulle–Etoile. FRENCH.

This "Green Star" is synonymous with no-nonsense dining at a reasonable price. In fairly simple surroundings, a large array of hearty foods emerges from the kitchen in back, and the staff is helpful. The cookery is that of a typical French bistro of long ago: rabbit pâté, veal Marengo, fresh oysters, coq (chicken) au vin in Cahors, sweetbreads with sautéed endive, mussels ravigote, chateaubriand béarnaise, and ris de veau (sweetbreads). Its least expensive menu, with drink included, is served from 11:30am to 3pm and 6:30 to 8pm.

Le Grain de Folie. 24 rue de la Vieuville, 18e. ☎ **01-42-58-15-57.** Reservations recommended. Main courses 80–100 F ($16–$20); fixed-price menus 80–100 F ($16–$20). No credit cards. Mon–Fri 11am–2:30pm and 6–11 pm, Sat–Sun 11am–midnight. Métro: Abbesses. VEGETARIAN.

Simple, wholesome, and unpretentious, the cuisine at this vegetarian restaurant has been inspired by France, Greece, California, and India. The menu includes an array of salads, cereal products, tarts, terrines, and casseroles. Dessert selections might include an old-fashioned tart or a fruit salad. The decor includes potted plants, exposed stone, and a collection of masks from around the world. You can choose from an array of wines or a frothy glass of vegetable juice to accompany your meal.

5 On the Left Bank

We'll begin with the most centrally located arrondissements on the Left Bank and then survey the outlying neighborhoods.

5TH ARRONDISSEMENT (LATIN QUARTER)
VERY EXPENSIVE

✪ **La Tour d'Argent.** 15–17 quai de la Tournelle, 5e. ☎ **01-43-54-23-31.** Reservations required. Main courses 255–500 F ($51–$100); fixed-price lunch 395 F ($79). AE, DC, MC, V. Tues–Sun noon–2:30pm and 8–10:30pm. Métro: Maubert-Mutualité or Pont-Marie. FRENCH.

La Tour d'Argent is a national institution. The view over the Seine and of the apse of Notre-Dame from this penthouse restaurant is panoramic. Although this restaurant's long-established reputation as "the best" in Paris has been eclipsed by such restaurants as Taillevent, dining at this temple of gastronomy remains unsurpassed as a theatrical event.

La Tour d'Argent traces its history back to 1582, when a restaurant of some sort stood on this site. Madame de Sévigné refers to the café in her celebrated letters, and Dumas set part of one of his novels here. The fame of the La Tour d'Argent spread during its ownership by Frédéric Delair, who bought the fabled wine cellar of Café Anglais to supply his restaurant. It was Delair who started the practice of issuing certificates to diners who ordered the house specialty—caneton (pressed duckling). The birds, incidentally, are numbered, and the first one was served to Edward VII in 1890. As of April 28, 1996, La Tour d'Argent had served 844,646 canetons, and they're still counting.

Under the sharp eye of its current owner, Claude Terrail, the cooking is superb and the service impeccable. Dresden china adorns each table. Although part of the menu is devoted to the various ways you can order duck, we assure you that the kitchen *does* know how to prepare other dishes. We especially recommend the ravioli with foie gras, the salmon and turbot à la Sully, and, to begin your meal, the pheasant consommé.

MODERATE

Auberge des Deux Signes. 46 rue Galande, 5e. ☎ **01-43-25-46-56.** Reservations required for dinner. Main courses 136–192 F ($27.20–$38.40); fixed-price menu 150 F ($30) at lunch, 230 F ($46) at dinner. AE, DC, MC, V. Mon–Fri 12:30–2pm and 7:30–10:30pm, Sat 7:30–10:30pm, Sun 12:30–2pm. Closed Aug. Métro: Maubert-Mutualité or St-Michel. FRENCH.

This restaurant was once the chapel of St-Blaise. In the evening you'll enjoy the view of floodlit Notre-Dame (without having to pay the prices charged by La Tour d'Argent) and the Church of St-Julien-le-Pauvre. Try to get a table upstairs with a view of the garden, but be prepared for a wait.

The kitchen draws its inspiration from the ancient French province of Auvergne. The food is packed with robust flavor and is well crafted into delectable combinations. Choices are wisely limited to keep everything fresh. Try the potted goose with cèpes (flap mushrooms) or the slices of veal sweetbreads au gratin. And the sole soufflé with crayfish tails is well worth a trip across Paris.

Au Pactole. 44 bd. St-Germain, 5e. ☎ **01-46-33-31-31.** Reservations recommended. Main courses 130–190 F ($26–$38); fixed-price menu 149–285 F ($29.80–$57). AE, MC, V. Sun–Fri noon–2:45pm and 7:15–10:45pm, Sat 7:15–10:45pm. Closed May 1 and Dec 25. Métro: Maubert-Mutualité. FRENCH.

The late French president Mitterand no longer drops in for dinner (he once accompanied German chancellor Helmut Kohl), and even Jacques Chirac isn't seen around here anymore, but Au Pactole has survived without the big names. It consistently remains one of the best restaurants of the 5th arrondissement and continues to offer good value. Roland Magne, whose gracious wife, Noëlle, is Au Pactole's hostess, is not as celebrated as some Paris chefs, but his is an award-winning cuisine nonetheless. His ravioli d'escargots is exceptional, and he also prepares the best beef ribs, roasted in a crust of salt, you're likely to be served in the 5th. His cabillaud (a large North Atlantic cod) is also excellent: The flesh is white and flaky, and he seasons it perfectly with green olive oil and herbs.

Brasserie Balzar. 49 rue des Ecoles, 5e. ☎ **01-43-54-13-67.** Reservations recommended. Main courses 90–115 F ($18–$23). AE, MC, V. Daily noon–midnight. Métro: Cluny–La Sorbonne. FRENCH.

Established in 1898, the Brasserie Balzar is a bit battered, yet made cheerful by some of the friendliest waiters in Paris. The menu makes almost no concessions to *nouvelle cuisine,* and includes steak au poivre (pepper steak), sole meunière, sauerkraut garnished with ham and sausage, pigs' feet, and calves' liver. The food is decently prepared, and who would want to come up with anything new when these dishes still keep people happy? Be warned that if you just want coffee or a drink, you probably won't get a table during meal hours. But the staff will be happy to serve you if you want to have a full dinner in the midafternoon, accustomed as they are to the nonstandard schedules of many loyal members of their clientele.

If you select this place, you'll be in good company: Former patrons have included both Sartre and Camus (who often got into arguments), William Shirer, Elliot Paul, James Thurber, countless professors from the nearby Sorbonne, and a bevy of English and American journalists.

Inagiku. 14 rue de Pontoise, 5e. ☎ **01-53-54-70-07.** Reservations not required. Main courses 168–188 F ($33.60–$37.60); fixed-price menus 148–348 F ($29.60–$69.60). AE, MC, V. Mon–Sat noon–2:30 and 7–11pm. Métro: Maubert-Mutualité. JAPANESE.

Come here for the best Japanese food in Paris. Inagiku brought a dose of Asian authenticity to the Latin Quarter. Three culinary themes run rampant here: sushi, sashimi, and teppanyaki, for which you'll observe the cooking ritual as performed by a chef with his own sense of drama and flair. There are no *tatami* mats here, and you won't have to sit cross-legged on the floor, because the tables are conventional, European-style. There are other more expensive Japanese restaurants—some outrageously expensive—but this one is just as good and a lot more reasonable. The menu items include flash-fried pork, chicken, steak, shrimp, and scallops. And if you love sashimi and sushi, look for it on the set-price menus.

⑤ Rôtisserie du Beaujolais. 19 quai de la Tournelle, 5e. ☎ **01-43-54-17-47.** Reservations recommended. Main courses 85–115 F ($17–$23). MC, V. Tues–Sun noon–2:30pm and 7:30–10:30pm. Métro: Pont-Marie. FRENCH/SPIT-ROASTED.

You may be surprised to learn that this place, with its straightforward, no-nonsense cuisine and reasonable prices, was founded by Claude Terrail, owner of the stratospherically expensive Tour d'Argent, which occupies the top floor of a building across the street. Set at the edge of the Seine overlooking the Ile St-Louis, the

Left Bank Restaurants

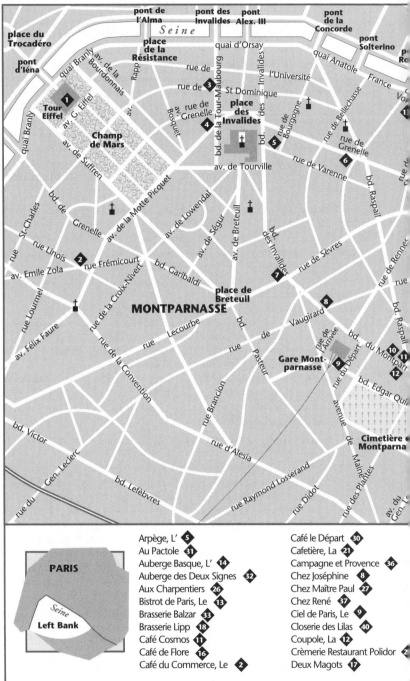

PARIS

Seine

Left Bank

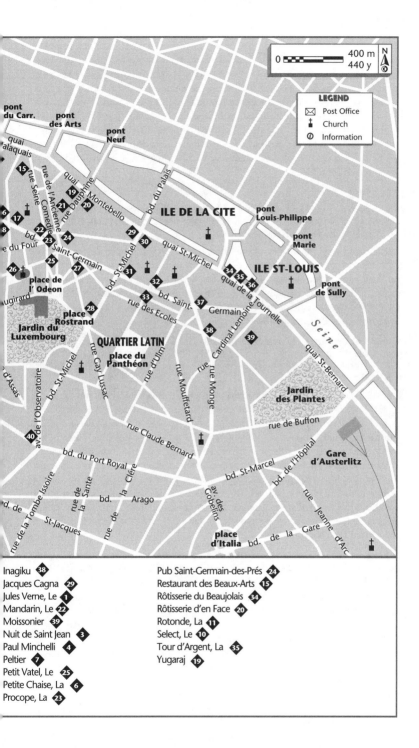

LEGEND

- ⊠ Post Office
- ✝ Church
- 𝑶 Information

pont du Carr.
pont des Arts
pont Neuf
pont Louis-Philippe
pont Marie
pont de Sully

quai Malaquais
rue Seine
rue de l'Ancienne Comédie
rue Dauphine
quai Montebello
bd. du Palais
quai St-Michel
quai de la Tournelle
quai St-Bernard

ILE DE LA CITE

ILE ST-LOUIS

rue du Four
bd. Saint-Germain
bd. St-Michel
place de l' Odeon
place Rostrand
Jardin du Luxembourg
place du Panthéon
rue des Ecoles
bd. Saint-Germain
rue Cardinal Lemoine
Seine
quai St-Bernard

QUARTIER LATIN

rue Gay Lussac
bd. St-Michel
rue d'Ulm
rue Mouffetard
rue Monge

Jardin des Plantes

rue de Buffon
rue Claude Bernard
av. de l'Observatoire
bd. du Port Royal
bd. St-Marcel
bd. de l'Hôpital

Gare d'Austerlitz

d'Assas
rue de la Tombe Issoire
rue de la Santé
bd. Arago
rue de St-Jacques
av des Gobelins
rue Jeanne d'Arc
bd. de la Gare

place d'Italia

Inagiku ⟨38⟩
Jacques Cagna ⟨29⟩
Jules Verne, Le ⟨1⟩
Mandarin, Le ⟨22⟩
Moissonier ⟨39⟩
Nuit de Saint Jean ⟨3⟩
Paul Minchelli ⟨4⟩
Peltier ⟨7⟩
Petit Vatel, Le ⟨25⟩
Petite Chaise, La ⟨6⟩
Procope, La ⟨23⟩

Pub Saint-Germain-des-Prés ⟨24⟩
Restaurant des Beaux-Arts ⟨15⟩
Rôtisserie du Beaujolais ⟨34⟩
Rôtisserie d'en Face ⟨20⟩
Rotonde, La ⟨11⟩
Select, Le ⟨10⟩
Tour d'Argent, La ⟨35⟩
Yugaraj ⟨19⟩

149

Rôtisserie contains a stone, zinc, and wood-inlaid antique bar imported from the Beaujolais region of France. The tasteful decor is completed by comfortable banquettes; everything is deliberately unpretentious and designed to evoke a brasserie in the French provinces. Appetizers include a fricassée of wild mushrooms, a gâteau of chicken livers, and salads. Main courses are usually roasted on spits in the kitchen, and are served, savory and steaming, with a garnish of mashed potatoes in the old-fashioned style. Examples include spit-roasted chicken, duck, or pigeon, as well as nonspit dishes such as coq au vin (chicken in wine) or côte de boeuf prepared for two. The wine list is deliberately unpretentious, with—you guessed it—many different vintages from Beaujolais.

INEXPENSIVE

Café le Départ. 1 place St-Michel, 5e. ☎ **01-43-54-24-55.** Reservations not accepted. Platters 27–67 F ($5.40–$13.40); sandwiches 18–45 F ($3.60–$9); crêpes 18–50 F ($3.60–$10). AE, DC, MC, V. Daily 24 hours. Métro: St-Michel. FRENCH.

One of the most popular cafés on the Left Bank, Le Départ is open 24 hours a day. On the banks of the Seine, it has a view of both the steeple of the Sainte-Chapelle and the dragon statue of place St-Michel. The decor is warmly modern, with etched mirrors. The menu offers warm and cold snacks, including sandwiches. The most popular late-night order is a grilled entrecôte with french fries, and eating it at 3 in the morning is a Parisian tradition.

Campagne et Provence. 25 quai de la Tournelle, 5e. ☎ **01-43-54-05-17.** Reservations recommended. Main courses 89–99 F ($17.80–$19.80); fixed-price lunch 99 F ($19.80). AE, MC, V. Mon 8–11pm, Tues–Fri 12:30–2pm and 8–11pm, Sat 8–11pm. Métro: Maubert-Mutualité. PROVENÇAL.

This restaurant, set beside a quay across from the Ile de la Cité, celebrates the traditions of Provence. Its cream-colored walls are garnished with bouquets of dried flowers, and the upholstery is the blue of the Provençal sky. The waiters are likely to speak with the modulated accents of southern France. Prices are kept deliberately modest. Among the savory foods of the south offered here are a brandade of codfish with aïoli, a very ethnic dish known as pieds et paquet (lamb's feet served with lamb tripe in a white-wine sauce), a ragoût of stockfish, and roasted rabbit stuffed with olives. But the best item on the menu is bouillabaisse of lobster and red mullet. Dessert might include a spice-flavored savarin served with fennel-flavored ice cream. Most Americans probably won't recognize the names or faces of some of the starlets of French cinema who dine here.

Chez René. 14 bd. St-Germain, 5e. ☎ **01-43-54-30-23.** Reservations recommended. Main courses 74–162 F ($14.80–$32.40); fixed-price lunch 153 F ($30.60). MC, V. Mon–Fri 12:15–2:15pm and 7:45–11pm. Métro: Cardinal-Lemoine. FRENCH.

Restaurants like this used to be much more widespread—particularly on the Left Bank—but many of them were transformed into pizzerias. Established in 1957, Chez René maintains its allegiance to the tried-and-true tenets of French cuisine. The staff is often more than a bit harassed, and the seating is cramped in the sometimes charming way that only a bistro can be. The dining room certainly isn't fancy, but its clients return loyally, often several nights a week, for the steady and reliable stream of food and the frequently changing *plats du jour.*

For an appetizer, if featured, try fresh wild mushrooms laced with butter and garlic and perhaps a platter of country-style sausages. You'll find such reliable old-time French fare as boeuf bourguignon and a dish of the day that might be pot-au-feu (beef simmered with vegetables) or blanquette de veau (veal in white sauce). Enjoy it all with a bottle of beaujolais.

Moissonnier. 28 rue des Fossés-St-Bernard, 5e. ☎ **01-43-29-87-65.** Reservations required for dinner. Main courses 80–140 F ($16–$28); fixed-price menu (Tues–Fri) 150 F ($30). MC, V. Tues–Sat noon–2:30pm and 7–9:15pm, Sun noon–2:30pm. Closed Aug. Métro: Jussieu or Cardinal-Lemoine. LYONNAISE.

Come here for real French home-cooking from the provinces. Big portions of solid old-style food are served, beginning with saladiers, large glass salad bowls filled with a selection of charcuterie. You might also select some excellent terrines, perhaps of Lyonnais sausages. The specialties, from Burgundy and Lyons, include such main dishes as pike quenelles, duck with turnips, and rack of herb-flavored lamb. Try to get a seat in the ground-floor dining room.

6TH ARRONDISSEMENT (ST-GERMAIN / LUXEMBOURG)
VERY EXPENSIVE

✪ **Jacques Cagna.** 14 rue des Grands-Augustins, 6e. ☎ **01-43-26-49-39.** Reservations required. Main courses 210–360 F ($42–$72); fixed-price menu 270 F ($54) at lunch, 490 F ($98) at dinner. AE, DC, MC, V. Mon–Fri noon–2pm and 7:30–10:30pm, Sat 7:30–10:30pm. Closed 3 weeks in Aug. Métro: St-Michel. FRENCH.

There's no finer dining in all the 6th arrondissement than at Jacques Cagna, a sophisticated restaurant set in a 17th-century town house with massive timbers, done in a delectable color scheme of pinkish beige and decorated with 17th-century Flemish paintings. The main dining room is located one flight above street level.

Jacques Cagna is one of the best-trained classic chefs in Paris, but some of his dishes offered today are more in the *cuisine moderne* style—for example, the delectable carpaccio of pearly sea bream with a céleri rémoulade lavished with caviar. As tempting as that is, Cagna can masterfully prepare tried-and-true favorites as well; his specialty is Aberdeen Angus beef, aged for a full 3 weeks, then imbued with a fragrant shallot-flavored sauce, rich with herbs and seasonings. The menu is forever changing, but hopefully he'll offer his lobster and bay scallops in puff pastry at the time of your visit.

EXPENSIVE

Closerie des Lilas. 171 bd. du Montparnasse, 6e. ☎ **01-43-26-70-50.** Reservations required. Main courses 190–250 F ($38–$50) in the restaurant, 90–130 F ($18–$26) in the brasserie. AE, DC, MC, V. Restaurant, daily 12:30–2:30pm and 7:30pm–12:30am; brasserie, daily noon–1am. Métro: Port-Royal or Vavin. FRENCH.

The famous people who have sat in the Closerie watching the falling leaves blow along the streets of Montparnasse are almost countless: Gertrude Stein, Ingres, Henry James, Chateaubriand, Picasso, Hemingway, Apollinaire, Lenin and Trotsky (at the chess board), and Whistler, who would expound on the "gentle art" of making enemies. Established in 1847, "the Pleasure Garden of the Lilacs" has been a social and culinary monument to the avant-garde ever since. Today the crowd is likely to include a sprinkling of French film stars and the starstruck.

It's tough to get a seat in what's called the *bateau* section of the restaurant, but you can make the wait a lot more enjoyable by ordering the best champagne julep in the world at the bar. What does it matter that the fickle guidebooks, including Michelin, have turned elsewhere with their recommendations? The food here is better than it was when the place was highly touted. By pushing open the door to Closerie you gain access to nearly a century and a half of French history and good cuisine as well. You can order such dishes as poached haddock, beef with a salad, or even steak tartare. The cooking is classic. Try the escargots façon de La Closerie (snails removed from their shells and presented with butter, herbs, and wine sauce) or ribs of veal in a cider sauce.

Yugaraj. 14 rue Dauphine, 6e. ☎ **01-43-26-44-91.** Reservations recommended. Main courses 98–118 F ($19.60–$23.60); fixed-price menus 250–270 F ($50–$54). AE, DC, MC, V. Mon 7–11pm, Tues–Sun noon–2:15pm and 7–11pm. Métro: Odéon. INDIAN.

On two floors of an old building in the Latin Quarter, this restaurant serves flavorful, moderately priced food based on the recipes of northern and, to a lesser degree, southern India. In rooms outfitted in vivid shades of "Indian pink," with formally dressed staff and lots of intricately carved Kashmiri panels and statues, you can sample the spicy, aromatic tandoori dishes that are becoming all the rage in France. Seafood specialties are usually concocted from warm-water fish imported to Rungis from the Seychelles, including species such as merou, capitaine, and bourgeois, prepared in the style of Calcutta, with tomatoes, onions, cumin, coriander, ginger, and garlic. The flavors are spicy and earthy, rich with mint and, sometimes, touches of yogurt.

INEXPENSIVE

Aux Charpentiers. 10 rue Mabillon, 6e. ☎ **01-43-26-30-05.** Reservations required. Main courses 90–180 F ($18–$36); fixed-price menu 122 F ($24.40) at lunch, 153 F ($30.60) at dinner. AE, DC, MC, V. Mon–Sat noon–3pm and 7:30–11:30pm. Métro: Mabillon. FRENCH.

This bistro, established more than 130 years ago, was once the rendezvous of the master carpenters, whose guild was next door. Nowadays it's where the young men of St-Germain-des-Prés take their dates. Although not especially imaginative, the food is well prepared in the best tradition of *cuisine bourgeoise:* traditional and hearty, not refined. Appetizers include pâté of duck and rabbit terrine. Especially recommended as a main course is the roast duck with olives. Time-tested French home-cooking is offered as the *plats du jour:* salt pork with lentils, pot-au-feu (beef simmered with vegetables), or stuffed cabbage. The restaurant also offers platters of fresh fish daily. The wine list has a large selection of Bordeaux wines direct from the châteaus, including Château Gaussens.

La Cafetière. 21 rue Mazarine, 6e. ☎ **01-46-33-76-90.** Reservations recommended. Main courses 65–120 F ($13–$24); fixed-price lunch 100 F ($20). AE, MC, V. Mon–Sat noon–2:30pm and 7:30–11pm. Métro: Odéon. FRENCH.

This tiny neighborhood bistro is located in the heart of the Odéon district, and sports two floors of slightly cramped pale-yellow dining rooms that display hundreds of antique *cafetières* (coffeepots). Service is excellent and usually charming, under the direction of co-owner Jean Romestant. The food is dependable and well cooked. Menu items include tenderloin of beef in a mustard-and-pepper sauce, scallops Provençal, mussels in white-wine sauce, rack of lamb with Provençal herbs, filet of duck with baked apples, veal chops with lemon sauce, and sautéed veal kidneys.

Chez Maître Paul. 12 rue Monsieur-le-Prince, 6e. ☎ **01-43-54-74-59.** Reservations recommended Sat–Sun. Main courses 120–220 F ($24–$44); three-course fixed-price meal 155 F ($31) without wine, 190 F ($38) including half a bottle of wine. AE, DC, MC, V. Daily noon–2:30pm and 7–10:30pm. Métro: Odéon. FRENCH/JURA.

This restaurant has changed very little since it was originally established in 1945 by a restaurateur (Maître Paul) who served specialities he prepared from his native district, the Jura region of eastern France. Since then, only three owners have tried their hand here, all from the same region, all devoted to retaining the provincial integrity of the hearty, tried-and-true country French cuisine. Try the saucisson chaude avec pommes à l'huile (hot sausage with potatoes in oil) or a terrine maison to start. Follow it with poulet sauté au vin rouge d'Arbois (chicken sautéed in red wine with mushrooms and tomatoes). The tables are attractively outfitted with starched napery, and a secondary dining room, half the size of one on the restaurant's street level, is upstairs.

Restaurants: 5th & 6th Arrondissements

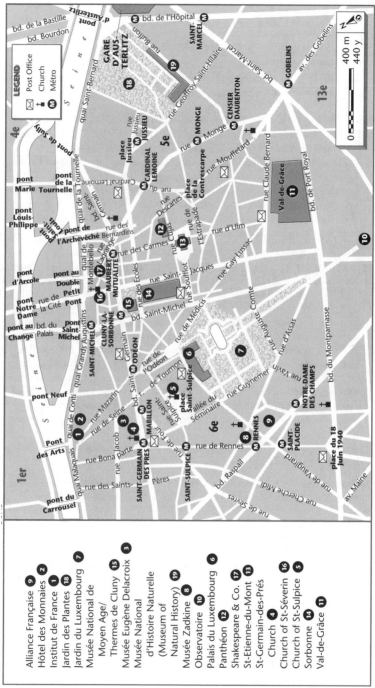

LEGEND
⊠ Post Office
✝ Church
Ⓜ Métro

Alliance Française ❾
Hôtel des Monnaies ❷
Institut de France ❶
Jardin des Plantes ⓲
Jardin du Luxembourg ❼
Musée National de
  Moyen Age/
  Thermes de Cluny ⓯
Musée Eugène Delacroix ❸
Musée National
  d'Histoire Naturelle
  (Museum of
  Natural History) ⓳
Musée Zadkine ❽
Observatoire ⓾
Palais du Luxembourg ❻
Panthéon ⓬
Shakespeare & Co. ⓱
St-Etienne-du-Mont ⓭
St-Germain-des-Prés
  Church ❹
Church of St-Séverin ⓰
Church of St-Sulpice ❺
Sorbonne ⓮
Val-de-Grâce ⓫

Crémerie-Restaurant Polidor. 41 rue Monsieur-le-Prince, 6e. ☎ **01-43-26-95-34.** Reservations not accepted. Main courses 40–69 F ($8–$13.80); fixed-price lunch (Mon–Fri) 50 F ($10); fixed-price menu 100 F ($20). No credit cards. Mon–Sat noon–2:30pm and 7pm–12:30am, Sun noon–2:30pm and 7–11pm. Métro: Odéon. FRENCH.

Crémerie Polidor is the most traditional bistro in the Odéon area, serving *cuisine familiale.* Its name dates back to the early part of this century when the restaurant specialized in frosted cream desserts, but the restaurant itself can trace its history back to 1845.

The Crémerie is one of the Left Bank's oldest and most established literary bistros. In fact, it was André Gide's favorite, and Hemingway, Valéry, Artaud, Charles Boyer, Joyce, and Kerouac have also dined here.

The atmosphere is one of lace curtains, polished brass hat racks, and drawers in the back where repeat customers lock up their cloth napkins. It's frequented largely by students and artists, who always seem to head for the rear. Overworked but smiling waitresses serve such old-timey dishes as pumpkin soup, snails from Burgundy, rib of beef with onions, beef bourguignon, and veal in white sauce, followed by such desserts as chocolate, raspberry, and lemon tarts, the best in Paris. The menu changes daily.

⑤ Le Petit Vatel. 5 rue Lobineau, 6e. ☎ **01-43-54-28-49.** Reservations not required. Main courses 45–55 F ($9–$11); two-course fixed-price lunch 61 F ($12.20). AE, MC, V. Mon–Fri noon–3pm and 7pm–midnight. Closed Dec 25–Jan 1. Métro: Mabilion (then walk up rue Mabilion and turn left onto rue Lobineu) or Odéon. FRENCH.

One of Paris's most charming eateries and best buys, Le Petit Vatel has 22 seats (plus a few more on the sidewalk in the summer) in a pocket-sized dining room where tables and chairs jostle each other for position. Marie Bosquet is the amusing and hard-working owner. Until 1990 she prepared most of her meals in the dining room on a pink-sided cookstove made in 1914. (Fire authorities ordered her to remove it, although its role in the restaurant's life is commemorated in framed photos.) The daily specials may be stuffed cabbage, rice sautéed with seafood, moussaka, or roast chicken, all served with a vegetable or salad. The food is plain but good-tasting and home-cooked. The two-course lunch consists of a choice of an appetizer, cheese or dessert, and a choice of the daily special or a *plat garni.* A candlelit meal at this jewel is something you'll remember for a long time.

Le Procope. 13 rue de l'Ancienne-Comédie, 6e. ☎ **01-43-26-99-20.** Reservations recommended. Main courses 82–148 F ($16.40–$29.60); fixed-price menu 99 F ($19.80) 11:30am–8pm, 169 F ($33.80) all day, 119 F ($23.80) after 11pm. AE, DC, MC, V. Daily 11:30am–1am. Métro: Odéon. FRENCH.

Le Procope, originally opened in 1686 by a Sicilian named Francesco Procopio dei Coltelli, is the oldest café in Paris. Now more restaurant than café, it's sumptuously decorated with gilt-framed mirrors, antique portraits of former illustrious clients, crystal chandeliers, banquettes of bordeaux-colored leather, and marble-topped tables.

Voltaire, Benjamin Franklin, Rousseau, Anatole France, Robespierre, Danton, Marat, a youthful Bonaparte, Balzac (who drank endless cups of very strong coffee), and Verlaine (who preferred the now-illegal absinthe) all dropped by in their day. There are two levels for dining: two rooms downstairs, five rooms upstairs. Fresh oysters and shellfish are served from a chilled display. A well-chosen selection of classic French dishes is presented, including baby duckling with spices and "green coffee," filet of beef with peppercorns, and "drunken chicken." The food is typical brasserie fare—but few places have the nostalgia of this old and venerated café. Its major drawback is that it's too tourist trodden and too famous.

Pub Saint-Germain-des-Prés. 17 rue de l'Ancienne-Comédie, 6e. ☎ **01-43-29-38-70.** Reservations not required. Meals 48–150 F ($9.60–$30); bottle of beer 28–75 F ($5.60–$15). AE, DC, MC, V. Daily 24 hours. Métro: Odéon. FRENCH.

For late-night drinking and snacking, this is one of the most popular spots on the Left Bank. The pub offers one of the best beer selections in France, with 26 varieties on tap and 500 international beers by the bottle. There are nine different rooms and 500 seats, making it the largest pub in France. Sit in one of the leather booths and enjoy a great late-night snack. Live music—rock and variety bands—is presented every night from 10:30pm to at least 3:30am.

Restaurant des Beaux-Arts. 11 rue Bonaparte, 6e. ☎ **01-43-26-92-64.** Reservations not accepted. Fixed-price menu (including wine) 75 F ($15). No credit cards. Daily noon–2:30pm and 7–10:45pm. Métro: St-Germain-des-Prés. FRENCH.

Located across from Paris's Ecole Nationale Supérieure des Beaux-Arts (School of Fine Arts), this is the most famous budget restaurant in Paris. Does it please everyone? Hardly. Are there complaints about bad food and service? Some. Is it packed every day with hungry patrons? Inevitably so. That means it must please literally thousands of diners every year, drawn to its low prices, large portions, and hearty, stick-to-the-ribs dishes, all featured on a set menu. The place still captures the old "starving student" lifestyle of the Latin Quarter.

The best tables are upstairs, but if you can get a place on the main floor you can see the steaming pots in the open kitchen. This is what a provincial French family might cook at home—bourguignon navarin d'agneau (lamb chops cooked with carrots, onions, and tomatoes), lapin sauce moutarde (rabbit leg with mustard sauce), cod fish filet with garlic sauce, fish soup, and a popular French staple that doesn't always appeal to foreigners, blanquette de veau (veal with white sauce).

⑤ La Rôtisserie d'en Face. 2 rue Christine, 6e. ☎ **01-43-26-40-98.** Reservations recommended. Lunch main course 98 F ($19.60); fixed-price dinner 198 F ($39.60). AE, MC, V. Mon–Fri noon–2:30pm and 7–11pm, Sat 7–11pm. Métro: St-Michel. FRENCH.

This is the most frequented "chef-bistro" in Paris. And well it should be, because the food, although simply prepared, is very good, using high-quality ingredients. The place features a postmodern decor with high-tech lighting and black lacquer chairs; it's informal, and at times very, very busy. Menu items include several types of ravioli, a pâté of duckling en croûte with foie gras, a friture d'éperlans (tiny fried freshwater fish), smoked Scottish salmon with spinach, and several different types of fresh fish and grilled meats. Dessert might be profiteroles stuffed with pistachio ice cream. It's operated by Jacques Cagna, whose vastly more expensive restaurant, which bears his name (see above), is across the street.

7TH ARRONDISSEMENT (EIFFEL TOWER / MUSEE D'ORSAY)
VERY EXPENSIVE

L'Arpège. 84 rue de Varenne, 7e. ☎ **01-47-05-09-06.** Reservations required. Main courses 280–380 F ($56–$76); fixed-price lunch 390 F ($78); *menu dégustation* 790 F ($158). AE, DC, MC, V. Mon–Fri noon–1:30pm and 7:30–9:45pm, Sun 7:30–9:45pm. Métro: Varenne. FRENCH.

One of the most talked-about and super-expensive restaurants in Paris is L'Arpège, where chef Alain Passard prepares many of his adventurous and charming culinary specialties. No restaurant in the 7th serves better food, except perhaps for the seafood restaurant Le Divellec, which is unfortunately also known for its chilly reception. The restaurant is in a prosperous residential neighborhood, across from the Rodin Museum on the site of what for years was the world-famous L'Archestrate, where Passard once worked in the kitchens.

A Few of Our Dining Favorites

- **Peltier,** 66 rue de Sèvres, 7e. ☎ **01-47-34-06-62.** The best tarte au chocolat in Paris. Métro: Vaneau or Duroc.
- **Le Carrousel,** 194 rue de Rivoli, 1er. ☎ **01-42-60-63-28.** We think its croque-monsieur is the most authentic in Paris. Métro: Palais-Royal.
- **Chez Joséphine,** 117 rue du Cherche-Midi, 6e. ☎ **01-45-48-52-40.** A 19th-century bistro with an omelette aux truffes (omelet with truffles) worth crossing town to eat. Métro: Croix-Rouge.
- **L'Assommoir,** 12 rue Girardon, 18e. ☎ **01-42-64-55-01.** Under threat from the patron that if we published his name in a travel guide, we'd never be allowed back, we still mention his establishment, L'Assommoir. It's the most authentic bistro in touristy Montmartre. It takes its name from the novel by Emile Zola. The tripes (tripe) à 1a mode de Caen is almost as good as that served at Pharamond in Les Halles. The owner makes the terrine de foies de volailles (chicken-liver terrine) himself. Don't even ask him to give you the recipe for his fondant au chocolat.
- **Café Cosmos,** 101 bd. du Montparnasse, 6e. ☎ **01-43-26-74-36.** Does today's generation have a café to equal the Lost Generation's Select or Coupole? Perhaps it's the Cosmos, with an ultramodern interior. Today you might rub elbows with a French film star or executive ("no one writes novels anymore"). The café features black tables, black leather chairs, and black clothing in winter—just the backdrop for smoked salmon with toast. Métro: Vavin.

Amid an intensely cultivated modern decor of etched glass, burnished steel, monochromatic oil paintings, and pearwood paneling, you can enjoy specialties that have been heralded as being among the most innovative to emerge in recent culinary history. These might include, for example, cream of flap mushrooms and truffle soup, sweet-and-sour scallops, grilled sweetbreads with licorice sauce, or John Dory with celery juice and asparagus flavored with sage. The wine list is also something to write home about. It's usually advisable to make reservations 3 or 4 days in advance.

Le Jules Verne. On the second level of the Tour Eiffel, Champ-de-Mars, 7e. ☎ **01-45-55-61-44.** Reservations required. Main courses 210–430 F ($42–$86); fixed-price lunch (Mon–Fri) 290 F ($55.10); *menu dégustation* 690 F ($138). AE, DC, MC, V. Daily 12:15–2pm and 7:30–9:30pm. Métro: Trocadéro, Ecole-Militaire, or Bir-Hakeim. FRENCH.

Today the tradition of drinking and dining inside the monument that symbolizes Paris is still alive and well. The menu may not be as refined as that at L'Arpège, but no restaurant in Paris has a better view. Many visitors see the elevator ride to the second platform of the Eiffel Tower as one of the highlights of their Paris experience. After the ride, you're ushered into a room as dark as the Parisian night outside, with only strategically placed spotlights set on each of the minimalist tables. The sparse lighting seems to bring the twinkling Paris panorama into the restaurant itself.

All of this would be merely a trip into a fantasy world were it not for the simple fact that a gifted culinary team is at work in the kitchen. The menu changes with the season, but might include fricassée of squid with chives and sautéed foie gras, filet of turbot with seaweed and buttered sea urchins, an Alsatian-style baeckoffe of red snapper with potatoes and meat drippings, veal chops with truffled vegetables, and a cassolette of fresh hot oysters with cucumbers.

Restaurants: 7th Arrondissement

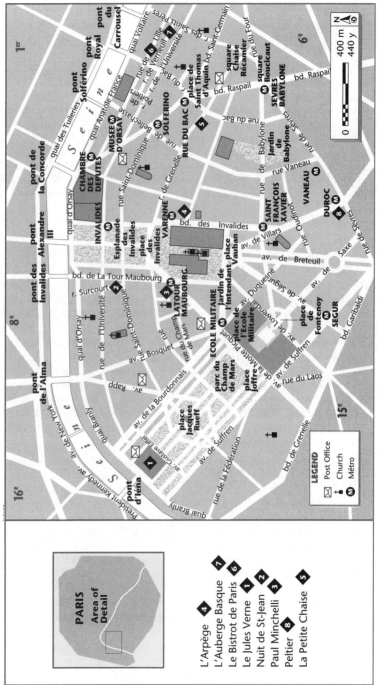

LEGEND

⌧ Post Office
✝ Church
Ⓜ Métro

PARIS
Area of
Detail

L'Arpège ◆4
L'Auberge Basque ◆7
Le Bistrot de Paris ◆6
Le Jules Verne ◆1
Nuit de St-Jean ◆2
Paul Minchelli ◆3
Peltier ◆8
La Petite Chaise ◆5

EXPENSIVE

Paul Minchelli. 54 bd. de la Tour-Maubourg, 7e. ☎ **01-47-05-89-86.** Reservations required. Main courses 200–300 F ($40–$60). MC, V. Tues–Sat noon–3pm and 8–11pm. Métro: La-Tour-Maubourg. SEAFOOD.

Opened in 1994, this restaurant had an immediate and powerful impact on the Paris dining scene. The chef is said to have reinvented fish by stripping away its extra sauces and conflicting flavors to reveal its true "taste of the sea." Much of this restaurant's appeal derives from its deliberate earthiness, its refusal to indulge in the gratuitously pretentious rituals of some of its competitors. Its namesake is Marseille-born Paul Minchelli, whose cuisine is described even by his financial backers as "marginal," having abandoned the tried-and-true methods of many other Parisian chefs. Minchelli uses the old-fashioned Provençal techniques he learned from his parents over the bouillabaisse pots of his childhood. Very little meat is offered. Some of the shellfish is so fresh it might have been scooped from an aquarium just moments before it was cooked.

In a yellow-walled dining room outfitted with modern furniture and round sea-scapes evocative of the portholes on a ship, you can order such dishes as raw salt-water fish served only with olive oil, salt, and pepper; an old-fashioned recipe known as merlan Colbert; grilled John Dory; and filet of bar steamed in seaweed.

INEXPENSIVE

L'Auberge Basque. 51 rue de Verneuil, 7e. ☎ **01-45-48-51-98.** Reservations recommended. Main courses 80–120 F ($16–$24); fixed-price menu 120 F ($24) at lunch, 180 F ($36) at dinner. MC, V. Mon–Sat noon–2:30pm and 7:30–10:30pm. Métro: Rue-du-Bac. FRENCH/BASQUE.

Owners Monsieur and Madame Rourre come from the Basque country near the Spanish border, and their excellent meals, made from fresh ingredients selected daily at the market, reflect the rich cookery of that area. Among their satisfied diners are famous sportsmen and French TV stars. The food is good, solid and reliable, and the chef never dares to experiment. You might begin with the Basque pâté, then follow with a pipérade, the omelet of the region. The Rourres also prepare both magret and confit of canard (duck). Various fresh fish dishes are also served, along with a selection of cheese and fresh fruit tarts. The wines are well chosen.

Le Bistrot de Paris. 33 rue de Lille, 7e. ☎ **01-42-61-16-83.** Reservations recommended. Main courses 92–95 F ($18.40–$19). MC, V. Mon–Fri noon–2pm and 7:15–10:30pm, Sat 7:15–10:30pm. Métro: Rue-du-Bac. FRENCH.

In the early 1990s this well-recommended bistro made a conscious effort to lower its prices and eliminate most of the experimental cuisine that had made it famous under an earlier, much-publicized chef. The result today is an honest, no-nonsense kind of bistro, and clients seem to appreciate the new, less pretentious format. Now you can enjoy an array of the *plat de jour:* Monday might be andouillette (chitterling sausages); Tuesday, a blanquette de veau (veal in white sauce); Wednesday, a conservative version of fried rabbit; Thursday, a cassoulet in the style of Toulouse; and Friday, stuffed cabbage. Appetizers that precede any of these might include crabmeat salad with a light tomato sauce, lentil salad, watercress soup, and a parfait of chicken livers. A small garden helps ventilate the bar area.

Nuit de Saint Jean. 29 rue Surcouf, 7e. ☎ **01-45-51-61-49.** Reservations recommended. Main courses 68–130 F ($13.60–$26); fixed-price menu 120 F ($22.80). AE, DC, MC, V. Mon–Fri noon–2:30pm and 7:30–10:30pm, Sat 7:30–10:30pm. Métro: Invalides. FRENCH.

This enclave of cuisine from France's southwest is one of the smallest and most charming restaurants in the well-heeled residential neighborhood of Les Invalides.

The Baby Bistro Boom

The boom in "baby bistros," begun in the early 1990s, continues in Paris. These reasonably priced bistros were created by some of the leading chefs or restaurateurs, including Guy Savoy, Claude Terrail, and Jacques Cagna, who realized that the average visitor cannot afford the celestial prices at their deluxe restaurants. Of course these bistros don't serve *haute cuisine*—some claim they serve "food like our mothers fed us." Their mothers must've been creditable chefs to judge from the offerings of the "babies."

One of Paris's most famous baby bistros is the **Rôtisserie du Beaujolais** (see later in this chapter under "Left Bank"), operated by Claude Terrail, owner of La Tour d'Argent. It's a facsimile of a traditional bistro you might find in Lyon.

The king of these bistros is Jacques Cagna, whose cookery has been extolled for "exhaling a discreet but seductive Southern aroma." His first baby bistro success was with the **Rôtisserie d'en Face**, 2 rue Christine, 6e (☎ **01-43-26-40-98**; Métro: St-Michel or Odéon), where all the robust French favorites (like snail-stuffed ravioli) are served. Cagna followed this with the **Rôtisserie d'Armaillé**, 6 rue d'Armaillé, 17e (☎ **01-42-27-19-20**; Métro: Ternes or Charles-de-Gaulle).

A rival for the throne of king is Guy Savoy, one of Paris's hottest new chefs. He launched into the baby bistro business with **La Butte Chaillot**, 110 bis av. Kléber, 16e (☎ **01-47-27-88-88**; Métro: Trocadéro), attracting a fashionable clientele with dishes that include everything from the innovative to the plain, like spit-roasted chicken and perfect mashed potatoes. Then he went on to open the **Bistrot de l'Etoile-Niel**, 75 av. Niel, 17e (☎ **01-42-27-88-44**; Métro: Ternes), a neighborhood favorite that serves staples like *blanquette de veau* and ever-changing *plats du jour*.

With seating for only 30, it's warmly decorated in a conservative modern style. It features such dishes as andouillettes of tripe, lamb curry with rice, lime-marinated chicken, magret of duckling with honey and green peppercorns, and fondant au chocolat à la crème anglaise (a chocolate-based dessert served with a light egg-custard cream). Two dishes of which the chef is particularly proud are a savory, crispy-skinned grilled salmon served with hazelnuts, and a crème brûlée (thick cream) with ginger. Although the restaurant has been around since the early 1950s, it was given new life when owners Monsieur and Madame Krinbarg took it over in the mid-1980s.

La Petite Chaise. 36–38 rue de Grenelle, 7e. ☎ **01-42-22-13-35.** Reservations required. Fixed-price menu 180 F ($36). MC, V. Daily noon–2:15pm and 7–11pm. Métro: Sèvres-Babylone. FRENCH.

This is the oldest restaurant in Paris, established by the baron de la Chaise in 1680 as an inn at the edge of what at the time was a large hunting preserve. (According to popular lore, the baron used the upstairs bedrooms for midafternoon dalliances, which he conducted between fox and pheasant hunts.) Very Parisian, the "Little Chair" invites you into a world of cramped but attractive tables, very old wood paneling, and ornate wall sconces. The only dining option available is a four-course set menu with a large choice of dishes within each category.

A new chef has brought renewed taste and flavor to this longtime favorite. Try his thin slices of salmon—cooked simply with salt and olive oil, and all the better for it. His classic Bourgogne snails with garlic butter are perfectly prepared, as are the eggs cooked with Roquefort cheese. Roquefort appears again in a sauce with filet of beef, or you can opt for tender beef in a wine sauce. For dessert, it might be everyone's favorite, chocolate cake.

15TH ARRONDISSEMENT
(GARE MONTPARNASSE / INSTITUT PASTEUR)
EXPENSIVE

Le Ciel de Paris. In the Maine-Montparnasse Tower, 33 av. du Maine, 15e. ☎ **01-45-38-52-35.** Reservations required. Main courses 134–390 F ($26.80–$78); fixed-price menus 250–310 F ($50–$62). AE, DC, MC, V. Mon–Fri noon–2:30pm and 7–11:30pm, Sat–Sun noon–3pm and 7pm–midnight. Métro: Montparnasse-Bienvenue. FRENCH.

Dominating the Left Bank quarter of Montparnasse, this massive tower, completed in 1973, covers an entire block and houses some 80 shops, including the Galeries Lafayette and more than 200 offices. Its floors are served by rapid elevators that speed visitors from the lobby to the top floor in less than 40 seconds. The charge for the elevator is 42 F ($8.40) for adults and 25 F ($5) for children. It's open daily: from 9:30am to 11pm April to October, from 10am to 10pm off-season. Because this is one of the most crowded and consistently popular sightseeing attractions in Paris, you should have an idea of how you want to approach it. If you want an eagle's-eye panorama over the greatest possible number of architectural monuments, head for the covered, glassed-in observation deck on the skyscraper's 56th floor, where uncluttered views sweep out over Paris from every side. Your ticket includes an audiovisual presentation on the glamour of Paris, an exhibit showing how the tower was built, and highlights of the Paris skyline far above.

If you want, however, to sip coffee or a drink while you watch Paris, head for either the Belvedere bar/café or the Ciel de Paris Restaurant. You won't be able to wander as you would on the observation deck, and your view of the city might be limited to only one direction, depending on where you sit, but the ambience is exciting and the elevator ride from the street-level lobby to both the bar and its restaurant is free. The bar serves morning coffee for 18 F ($3.60), and whisky with soda for 30 to 70 F ($6 to $14) (depending on the time it's served). The bar is open daily from 9am to 7pm, and again from 10:30pm to 1am. It features live jazz every Thursday night and piano music most other nights.

Finally, the Ciel de Paris (Skies of Paris) restaurant: The food is international, and the staff is suitably accustomed to serving hordes of sightseers. Dishes are competently prepared but rather standard, and can't really compete with the awesome view. Reservations are usually advisable several days in advance. Don't expect intimacy. After you finish your meal, ask the waiter for a free pass for the observation platform, where you'll be able to see those neighorhoods that might have been blocked by the position of your individual table.

INEXPENSIVE

Le Café du Commerce. 51 rue du Commerce, 15e. ☎ **01-45-75-03-27.** Main courses 54–87 F ($10.80–$17.40); three-course fixed-price menu 90–110 F ($18–$22). AE, DC, MC, V. Daily noon–midnight. Métro: Emile-Zola, Commerce, or La Motte–Picquet. FRENCH.

Le Café is one of the best dining bargains in this area. Originally established in 1921, it was renovated in the late 1980s, its decor designed to hearken back to the glory days of the 1920s. Le Café contains dozens of verdant plants and photographs of the various writers who scribbled manuscripts on its premises. Dining tables are scattered over three different floors, illuminated with light from an overhead atrium. The menu is old-fashioned, with no attempt at modernity or high style, and it's very French.

Overall, this is a busy, high-energy emporium dispensing platters of food to hundreds of office workers and neighborhood locals. Menu items include warm goat cheese on a bed of lettuce, poulet sauce estragon (chicken tarragon), breast of duck with a green-pepper sauce, a well-prepared version of sole meunière, a croustillant de porc au miel (crispy baked pork with honey sauce), or escalope of salmon with a sage sauce. Crème caramel or chocolate mousse make for a satisfying, if not particulary imaginative, dessert.

6 The Best Cafés

It would be just about impossible to estimate how many cafés there are in Paris. A single block in the central arrondissements may have three or four. They thin out somewhat in the farther suburbs.

It's also difficult to define their precise function. Cafés aren't restaurants, although the larger ones may serve complete and excellent meals. They aren't bars, although they offer an infinite variety of beer, wine, and cocktails. And they aren't coffee shops in the American sense of the word, because they'll serve you a bottle of champagne just as readily as a café au lait.

Parisians use them as combination club/tavern/snack bars, almost as extensions of their living rooms. They're spots where you can read your newspaper or meet a friend, do your homework or write your memoirs, nibble at a hard-boiled egg or drink yourself into oblivion. At cafés you meet your dates to go on to a show or to stay and talk. Above all, cafés are for people-watching.

Perhaps their single common denominator is the encouragement of leisurely sitting. Regardless of whether you have one small coffee or the most expensive cognac in the house, nobody badgers, pressures, or hurries you. If you wish to sit there until the place closes, that's your affair. For the café is one of the few truly democratic institutions—a solitary soda buys you the same view and sedentary pleasure as an oyster dinner.

All cafés sport an outdoor area. Some have merely a few tables on the pavement, whereas others have immense terraces, glassed in and heated in winter. Both types, however, fulfill the same purpose. They offer a vantage point from which to view the passing parade.

Coffee, of course, is the chief drink. It comes black in a small cup, unless you specifically order it *au lait* (with milk). Tea (*thé,* pronounced "tay") is also fairly popular, but it's not of the same quality.

The famous apéritifs, French versions of the before-dinner drink, are the aniseed-flavored, mild-tasting Pernod, Ricard, and Pastis, all mixed with ice and water. There are also St. Raphaël and Byrrh, which taste rather like port wine, and the slightly less sweet Dubonnet. Another local favorite is the Italian Campari, drunk with soda and ice, very bitter and refreshing. Try it at least once.

If you prefer beer, we advise you to pay a bit more for the imported German, Dutch, or Danish brands, which are a lot better than the local brew. If you insist on the French variety, at least order it *à pression* (draft), which is superior. There's also a vast variety of fruit drinks, as well as Coca-Cola.

French chocolate drinks—either hot or iced—are absolutely superb and on par with the finest Dutch brands. They're made from ground chocolate, not a chemical compound.

Cafés keep flexible hours, depending on the season, the traffic, and the part of town they're in. Nearly all of them stay open until 1 or 2am, and a few are open all night.

Now just a few words on café etiquette. You don't pay when you get your order—only when you intend to leave. Payment indicates that you've had all you want. *Service compris* means that the tip is included in your bill, so it really isn't necessary to tip extra; still, feel free to leave an extra franc or so if the service has been attentive.

You'll hear the locals call the *garçon*, but as a foreigner it would be more polite to say *monsieur*. On the other hand, *all* waitresses are addressed as *mademoiselle*, regardless of age or marital status.

In the smaller cafés, you may have to share your table. In that case, even if you haven't exchanged a word with your table companions, when you leave it's customary to bid them good-bye with a perfunctory *messieurs et dames*.

Brasserie Lipp. 151 bd. St-Germain, 6e. ☎ **01-45-48-53-91.** Full meals average 220 F ($44); café au lait 18 F ($3.60). AE, DC, MC, V. Daily 9am–1am (restaurant service 11:45am–1am). AE, DC, MC, V. Métro: St-Germain-des-Prés.

On the day of Paris's liberation in 1944, former owner Roger Cazes (now deceased) spotted Hemingway, the first man to drop in for a drink. Then as now, famous people often drop by the Lipp for its beer, wine, and conversation. It's the quintessential Parisian brasserie. The food is secondary, yet quite good, providing you can get a seat (an hour and a half waiting time is customary if you're not a friend of the management). The specialty is choucroute garni, the best sauerkraut in Paris. You not only get sauerkraut, but a thick layer of ham and braised pork as well. It can be downed with the house reisling or beer. You can perch on a banquette, admiring your face reflected in the "hall of mirrors." The Lipp was opened in 1870–71, following the Franco-Prussian War, when its founder, Léonard Lipp, fled German-occupied territory for Paris. It has been a Parisian tradition ever since, with a staff known for its temperamental ways. Even if you don't go inside for a drink, you can sit at a sidewalk café table, enjoying a cognac and people-watching.

Café Beaubourg. 100 rue St-Martin, 4e. ☎ **01-48-87-63-96.** Glass of wine 22–30 F ($4.40–$6); beer 25–40 F ($5–$8); American breakfast 110 F ($22); sandwiches and platters 25–120 F ($5–$24); ice creams 35–45 F ($7–$9). AE, DC, MC, V. Sun–Thurs 8am–1am, Sat–Sun 8am–2am. Métro: Rambuteau or Hôtel-de-Ville.

Located across the all-pedestrian plaza from the Centre Pompidou, this is an avant-garde café with soaring concrete columns and a minimalist decor designed by the noted architect Christian de Portzamparc. Many of the regulars work in the neighborhood's funky shops and galleries. In warm weather, tables are set up on the sprawling outdoor terrace, providing a great place to watch the young and the restless go by.

Café de Flore. 172 bd. St-Germain, 6e. ☎ **01-45-48-55-26.** Café espresso 24 F ($4.80); glass of beer 41 F ($8.20). AE, MC, V. Daily 7am–1:30am. Métro: St-Germain-des-Prés.

Sartre, the granddaddy of existentialism, a key figure in the Resistance movement and a renowned café-sitter, often came here during World War II. Wearing a leather jacket and beret, he sat at his table and wrote his trilogy, *Les Chemins de la liberté* (The Roads to Freedom). In *A Memoir in the Form of a Novel (Two Sisters),* Gore Vidal introduces his two main characters with "I first saw them at the Café de Flore in the summer of 1948. They were seated side by side at the center of the first row of sidewalk tables, quite outshining Sartre and de Beauvoir, who were holding court nearby." Camus, Picasso, and Apollinaire also frequented the Flore. The café is still going strong, although the famous folks have moved on and the tourists have taken up all the tables.

Café de la Paix. Place de l'Opéra, 9e. ☎ **01-40-07-30-20.** Café espresso 19 F ($3.80); fixed-price menu 139 F ($27.80); daily specials 97 F ($19.40); beer 29 F ($5.80). AE, DC, MC, V. Daily 10am–1:30am. Métro: Opéra.

This hub of the tourist world virtually commands place de l'Opéra, and the legend goes that if you sit here long enough, you'll see someone you know passing by. Huge, grandiose, frighteningly fashionable, sometimes brusque, and rather anonymous, it harbors not only Parisians, but, at one time or another, nearly every visiting American—a tradition that dates from the end of World War I. Once Emile Zola sat on the terrace; later, Hemingway and Fitzgerald frequented it.

Café Marly. Cour Napoléon du Louvre, 93 rue de Rivoli, 1er. ☎ **01-49-26-06-60.** Reservations recommended. Main courses 90–130 F ($18–$26). AE, DC, MC, V. Daily noon–3pm and 8–11pm. Métro: Palais-Royal or Musée-du-Louvre. FRENCH.

In 1994 the French government gave the green light for a café and restaurant to open in one of the most historic courtyards of the Louvre. It's accessible only from a point close to the famous glass pyramid that rises above the Cour Marly, and has become a favorite refuge for Parisians trying to escape the roar of traffic just outside. Anyone is welcome to sit down for a café au lait (anytime between 8am and 2am daily, whenever meals are not being served), which costs 30 F ($6). More substantial fare is the norm here, served in one of three different Louis Philippe–style dining rooms, each outfitted in tones of burgundy, black, and gilt. Menu items include club sandwiches, fresh oysters and shellfish, steak au poivre (pepper steak), sole meunière, and an array of upscale, bistro-inspired food. In summer outdoor tables overlook views of one of the most celebrated courtyards in Europe.

La Coupole. 102 bd. du Montparnasse, 14e. ☎ **01-43-20-14-20.** Breakfast buffet 79 F ($15.80); coffee 5–15 F ($1–$3); fixed-price lunch 112 F ($22.40); set menu 112 F ($22.40) every night after 10pm. AE, DC, MC, V. Daily 7:30am–2am (breakfast buffet Mon–Fri 7:30–10:30am). Métro: Vavin.

Once a leading center of the city's artistic life, La Coupole is now a bastion of traditionalism in Montparnasse in the grand Paris brasserie style. It was born in 1927 at the height of the city's jazz age. This big, attractive café has, however, grown more fashionable through the years, attracting fewer locals—such as Sartre and de Beauvoir in the old days—and rarely a struggling artist anymore. But some of the city's most interesting foreigners show up. Former patrons have included Josephine Baker, Henry Miller, Dalí, Calder, Hemingway, Dos Passos, Fitzgerald, and Picasso. Today you might see Gérard Depardieu.

The sweeping outdoor terrace is among the finest in Paris. At one of its sidewalk tables, you can sit and watch the passing scene and order a coffee or a cognac VSOP. The food is quite good, despite the fact that the dining room resembles an enormous railway station waiting room. Try, for example, such main dishes as sole meunière, curry d'agneau (lamb), cassoulet, and some of the best steak au poivre (pepper steak) in Paris. The fresh oysters and shellfish are especially popular.

Les Deux-Magots. 6 place St-Germain-des-Prés, 6e. ☎ **01-45-48-55-25.** Café au lait 24 F ($4.80); whisky and soda 67 F ($13.40). AE, DC, V. Daily 7:30am–1:30am. Métro: St-Germain-des-Prés.

This legendary café is still the hangout for the sophisticated residents of St-Germain-des-Prés. In summer, however, it becomes a tourist favorite in summer—in fact, visitors virtually monopolize the few sidewalk tables. Waiters rush about, seemingly oblivious to your needs. It remains busy in the tourist off-season as well, when it's reclaimed by regulars from around the neighborhood.

The Deux-Magots was once a gathering place of the intellectual elite, including Sartre, Simone de Beauvoir, and Jean Giraudoux. Inside are two large Asian statues that give the café its name. The crystal chandeliers are too brightly lit, but the regulars seem to be accustomed to the glare. After all, some of them even read their daily newspapers there.

Fouquet's. 99 av. des Champs-Elysées, 8e. ☎ **01-47-23-70-60.** Glass of wine from 45 F ($9); sandwiches 45–65 F ($9–$13); fixed-price lunch 265 F ($53); average à la carte meal 450 F ($90). AE, DC, MC, V. Daily 9am–2am (restaurant, daily noon–3pm and 7pm–midnight). Métro: George-V.

Fouquet's has been collecting anecdotes and a patina since it was founded in 1901. A celebrity favorite, it has attracted Chaplin, Chevalier, Dietrich, Churchill, Roosevelt, and Jackie O. The premier café on the Champs-Elysées, it sits behind a barricade of potted flowers at the edge of the sidewalk. You can choose a table outdoors in the sunshine or retreat to the glassed-in elegance of the leather banquettes and rattan furniture of the street-level grill room. Although Fouquet's is a full-fledged restaurant, with an additional dining room with a beautiful, very formal decor on the second floor, most visitors come by just for a glass of wine, coffee, or a sandwich.

Le Mandarin. 148 bd. St-Germain, 6e. ☎ **01-46-33-98-35.** Café au lait 32 F ($6.40); crêpes 22–44 F ($4.40–$8.80); glass of wine 21 F ($4.20). MC. Sun–Thurs 8am–2am, Fri–Sat 8am–4am. Métro: Odéon or Mabillon.

This elegantly decorated corner café is thronged with young Left Bank types or visitors soaking up the atmosphere of St-Germain-des-Prés. At the brass bar you can order fine wines or a coffee. Decorated with lace-covered hanging lamps, brass trim, and lots of exposed wood, the establishment serves good food, including crêpes and onion soup.

La Rotonde. 105 bd. du Montparnasse, 6e. ☎ **01-43-26-68-84.** Glass of wine 20 F ($4); fixed-price menus 110–200 F ($22–$40). AE, MC, V. Daily 7am–2am (restaurant, daile noon–1am). Métro: Vavin.

Once patronized by Hemingway, the original Rotonde faded into history but is immortalized in the pages of *The Sun Also Rises,* in which Papa wrote, "No matter what café in Montparnasse you ask a taxi driver to bring you to from the right bank of the river, they always take you to the Rotonde." Lavishly upgraded, the reincarnation of La Rotonde has an art deco paneled elegance, and shares the once-hallowed site with a motion-picture theater. If you stand at the bar, prices are lower.

Le Select. 99 bd. du Montparnasse, 6e. ☎ **01-45-48-38-24.** Coffee 12–15 F ($2.40–$3); hard drinks from 60 F ($12). MC, V. Sun–Thurs 8am–2:30am, Fri–Sat 8am–3:30am. Métro: Vavin.

Le Select may be a notch down the social ladder from the other glittering cafés of Montparnasse, but we find it the liveliest and friendliest. It opened in 1923 and really hasn't changed very much since then. At one time it was the favorite hangout of Cocteau. It serves 60 different whiskeys and 20 different cocktails, some of which are rather exotic.

What to See & Do in Paris

Paris is one of those world-class cities where simply strolling and taking in the street life should claim as much of your time as sightseeing in churches or museums. A gourmet picnic in the Bois de Boulogne, a sunrise stroll along the Seine, an afternoon spent bargaining at the flea market—experiences like these are how you'll make Paris your own, and they're probably more important than seeing every painting in the Louvre. So don't feel guilty when the city lures you into hours of aimless rambling.

SUGGESTED ITINERARIES

These itineraries are obviously intended for the first-time visitor, but even those making their 30th trip to Paris will want to return again and again to such attractions as the Louvre. You could visit that museum every day of your life and still see something you'd missed before.

If You Have 1 Day

The most practical way to see Paris in a day is to take a guided tour, since you can't possibly master the city on your own in such a short period of time. Start the day by ordering coffee and croissants at a sidewalk café. The Cityrama tour (see "Organized Tours," later in this chapter) begins at 9:30am. A double-decker bus will take you for a fast 2-hour ride through the city, past Notre-Dame and the Eiffel Tower. After the tour, have lunch and go to the Louvre for a guided tour, in English, of its most important artworks. If you'd rather explore the museum on your own, pick up an Audioguide in English at the rental counter located in the Hall Napoléon on the mezzanine level and set out. Use what's left of the afternoon to stroll along the banks of the Seine; ideally you'll end up at Notre-Dame in time to see the sun sinking over the rooftops of the city. If you have an early dinner at a nearby bistro, you may still have the time and energy to attend the Lido or Folies Bergère (see Chapter 9).

If You Have 2 Days

Spend your first day as outlined above. Start your second day by taking a Bateaux-Mouches cruise on the Seine (see "Organized Tours," later in this chapter), with departures from pont de l'Alma, at place de l'Alma on the Right Bank (Métro: Alma-Marceau). Then go to the Eiffel Tower for lunch with a spectacular view (see our recommendation of Le Jules Verne in Chapter 5).

Next, head for the Arc de Triomphe, a perfect place to begin a stroll down the Champs-Elysées, the main boulevard of Paris, until you reach the Egyptian obelisk at place de la Concorde. This grand promenade is one of the most famous walks in the world (see Chapter 7). In the late afternoon do something uniquely Parisian— take a walk along rue des Rosiers, a narrow street that's the heart of the Jewish community. Select one of the restaurants there for dinner and cap the evening with a romantic stroll along the Seine.

If You Have 3 Days

Spend your first and second days as above. Spend your third morning exploring the Sainte-Chapelle and the Conciergerie. Have lunch, perhaps on the Ile St-Louis, and then take a walking tour (see Chapter 7). Afterward, spend 2 or 3 hours at the Musée d'Orsay. Before the day is over, head for the Cimetière du Père-Lachaise and pay your respects at the graves of Edith Piaf, Richard Wright, Oscar Wilde, Jim Morrison, and Gertrude Stein.

If You Have 4 Days

For your first 3 days, follow the itinerary above. On your fourth day, head to Versailles, 13 miles south of Paris (see Chapter 10). After viewing the palace and gardens, head back to the city for an evening stroll through the Latin Quarter, perhaps dining in a Left Bank bistro. Take along a good map, so you can wander along some of the livelier streets, such as rue de la Huchette and rue Monsieur-le-Prince.

If You Have 5 Days

Spend Days 1 to 4 as recommended above. On your fifth day, spend the morning roaming around Le Marais. Pay a visit to the Musée Picasso and have lunch near the historic place des Vosges. Afterward, you might want to head toward Montmartre (see the walking tour in Chapter 7 for specific sightseeing suggestions). Try to time your visit so you'll be at the Basilica of Sacré-Coeur at sunset. Cap the evening by heading for one of the famous cafés of Montparnasse.

1 The Top Museums

Some people find visiting museums in Paris redundant, and you might agree with this. Why sacrifice sunshine for dim museum corridors when every stroll by the Seine brings you vistas the masters have painted and every city square is a paragon of design?

If that's your view, stick with it. Of the almost 100 museums in Paris, only one is a requirement for the world traveler: the Louvre. Some say that the Musée d'Orsay should also be added to that list. But all the rest can be guiltlessly left to people with serious and specific interests, or saved up for that proverbial (and inevitable) rainy day, or for your next visit. In this section, we've listed only what we consider to be the most outstanding.

Paris museums fit into three categories: city museums, national museums, and those run by private organizations. The municipal and national museums have fairly standard hours. They're often closed on Tuesday and national holidays. Fees vary, but half-price tickets are usually provided to students, children ages 3 to 7, and extra-large families or groups. If you want to museum-hop in earnest, pick a Sunday, when most museums let you in for half price.

Attractions: 1st Arrondissement

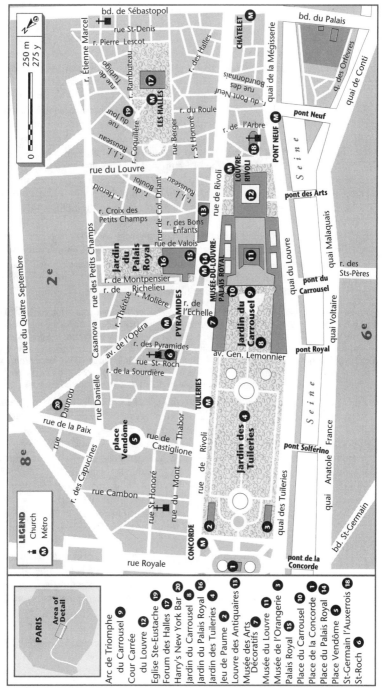

LEGEND
† Church
Ⓜ Métro

250 m
275 y

PARIS
Area of Detail

Whatever the time of year you come, Paris seems to be hosting an outstanding exhibition—keep your eyes open for huge, colorful posters hanging from the lampposts. In the halls and museum rooms across the city, at least 15 special shows are on during any given week, events such as a Chagall retrospective, a special exhibition of Giacometti sculptures, a show on Art of the Workers' Movement, or something on the public life of Napoléon. The fees charged depend on the exhibit.

To find out what's showing while you're in town, stop at the **Welcome Office,** 127 av. des Champs-Elysées (☎ **01-49-52-53-54;** Métro: Charles-de-Gaulle–Etoile), open daily from 9am to 8pm in summer, daily from 9am to 6pm in winter. Here you can pick up a free copy of the English-language booklet "Paris Weekly Information," published by the Paris Convention and Visitors' Bureau.

You can buy **Le Pass-Musée (the Museum and Monuments Pass)** at any of the museums that honor it, or at any branch of the Paris Tourist office. It offers free entrance to the permanent collections of 65 monuments and museums in Paris and the Ile-de-France. A 1-day pass is 70 F ($14); a 3-day pass is 140 F ($28); a 5-day pass is 200 F ($40).

Note: Museums require that you check shopping bags and book bags, and sometimes the lines for these can be longer than the ticket/admission lines. Visitors who value their time should leave their bags behind: The coat line at the Pompidou Center, for example, can take 30 minutes. Ask if a museum has more than one coat line, and if so, avoid the main one and go to the less frequented ones.

✪ **Musée du Louvre.** 34–36 quai du Louvre, 1er (entrance: Pyramid/cour Napoléon). ☎ **01-40-20-53-17,** or 01-40-20-51-51 for a recorded message, 01-40-20-53-17 for the information desk. Admission 45 F ($9) before 3pm, 26 F ($5.20) after 3pm and on Sun, free for children 17 and under, free for everyone the first Sun of every month. Mon (Richelieu wing only) and Wed 9am–9:45pm, Thurs–Sun 9am–6pm. 90-minute English-language tours leave Mon and Wed–Sat various times of the day for 33 F ($6.60) adults, 22 F ($4.40) children 13–18, free for children 12 and under with a museum ticket. Métro: Palais-Royal or Musée-du-Louvre.

From far and wide they come—from North Dakota to Pakistan, from Nova Scotia to Japan—all bent on seeing the wonders of the legendary Louvre. People on one of those "Paris-in-a-day" tours try to break track records to get a glimpse of the two most famous ladies of the Louvre: the *Mona Lisa* and the armless *Venus de Milo.* (The scene in front of the *Mona Lisa* is best described as a circus. Viewers push and shove, and there seems minimal supervision from the staff. Flashbulbs, which are forbidden, pop all over the place. In all this fracas, you'll have anything but a contemplative moment.) Those with an extra 5 minutes to spare go in pursuit of *Winged Victory,* that headless statue discovered at Samothrace and dating from about 200 B.C.

But then a big question looms: Which of the rest of the 30,000 works on display would you like to see?

The Louvre suffers from an embarrassment of riches. Hence, masterpieces are often ignored by the casual visitor—there's just too much of a good thing. It's the world's largest palace and the world's largest museum (some say the greatest). As a palace, it leaves us cold, except for its old section, the cour Carrée. As a museum, it's one of the greatest art collections in the world.

Between the Seine and rue de Rivoli (Métro to Palais-Royal or Louvre, the latter the most elegant subway stop in the world), the Palace of the Louvre stretches for almost half a mile. In the days of Charles V it was a fortress, but François I, a patron of Leonardo da Vinci, had it torn down and rebuilt as a royal residence. Less than a month after Marie Antoinette's head and body parted company, the Revolutionary Committee decided that the king's collection of paintings and sculpture would be opened to the public. At the lowest point in its history, in the 18th century, the

The Louvre

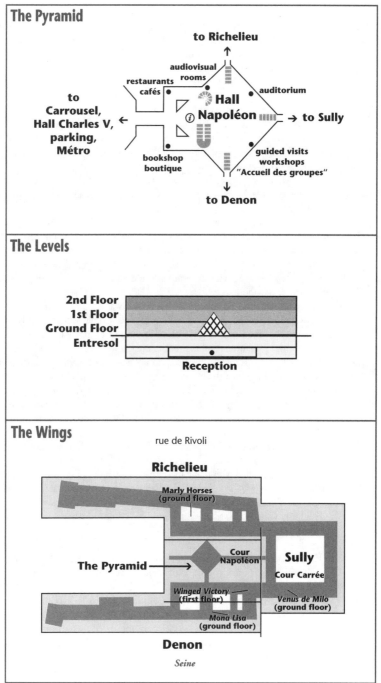

The Pyramid

to Richelieu

audiovisual rooms

restaurants cafés

auditorium

Hall Napoléon

to Carrousel, Hall Charles V, parking, Métro

to Sully

bookshop boutique

guided visits workshops "Accueil des groupes"

to Denon

The Levels

2nd Floor
1st Floor
Ground Floor
Entresol

Reception

The Wings

rue de Rivoli

Richelieu

Marly Horses (ground floor)

The Pyramid

Cour Napoléon

Sully

Cour Carrée

Winged Victory (first floor)

Venus de Milo (ground floor)

Mona Lisa (ground floor)

Denon

Seine

Louvre was home for anybody who wanted to set up housekeeping. Laundry hung out the windows, corners were literally pig pens, and each family built a fire somewhere to cook a meal during the long winter. Napoléon changed all that, chasing out the inhabitants and beginning the restoration of the palace. In fact, the Louvre became the site of his marriage to Marie-Louise.

So where did all these paintings come from? The kings of France, notably François I and Louis XIV, acquired many of them. Others have been willed to or purchased by the state. Many that Napoléon contributed were taken from reluctant donors like the church, an especially heavy and unwilling giver. Much of Napoléon's plunder had to be returned, although France hasn't seen its way clear to giving back all the booty.

To enter the Louvre, you'll pass through a controversial 71-foot-high glass pyramid in the courtyard. Commissioned by Mitterrand and completed in 1989, it has received mixed reviews. Designed by I. M. Pei to allow sunlight to shine on an underground reception area, it shelters a complex of shops and restaurants. Automatic ticket machines help relieve the long lines of yesteryear.

The collections are divided into seven departments: Egyptian antiquities; Oriental antiquities; Greek, Estruscan, and Roman antiquities; sculptures; paintings; graphics and graphic arts; and art objects. If you don't have to "do" Paris in a day, perhaps you can return to the Louvre for several visits, concentrating on different collections or schools of painting. Those with little time should go on one of the guided tours (in English), which last about 1 1/2 hours.

Da Vinci's much-traveled *La Gioconda* (*Mona Lisa*) was acquired by François I to hang above his bath. Note the guard and bullet-proof glass: The world's most famous painting was stolen in the summer of 1911 and found in Florence in the winter of 1913. At first, both Guillaume Apollinaire, the poet, and Picasso were suspected as the thieves, but it was discovered in the possession of a former Louvre employee, who had apparently carried it out of the museum under his overcoat. The *Mona Lisa* has been the source of legend and lore for centuries. Less well known (but to us even more enchanting) are Da Vinci's *Virgin and Child with St. Anne* and the *Virgin of the Rocks*.

Of the Greek and Roman antiquities, the most notable collections (aside from the *Venus de Milo* and *Winged Victory*) are fragments of the frieze from the Parthenon (located in the Denon wing). In Renaissance sculpture, you'll see two slaves by Michelangelo—originally intended for the tomb of Julius II but sold into other bondage. The Denon wing is filled with many masterpieces, including Ingres's *The Turkish Bath;* David's *Portrait of Madame Récamier* lounging on her famous sofa; the Botticelli frescoes from the Villa Lemmi; Raphael's *La Belle Jardinière;* and Titian's *Open Air Concert.* The Sully wing is also filled with gems, including Boucher's *Diana Resting After Her Bath* and Fragonard's *Bathers.*

The Richelieu wing, inaugurated in 1993, houses the museum's collection of northern European and French paintings, along with decorative arts, French sculpture, Oriental antiquities (a rich collection of Islamic art), and the salons of Napoléon III. Originally constructed from 1852 to 1857, the Richelieu wing was virtually rebuilt to add some 230,000 square feet of exhibition space. In 165 rooms and three covered courtyards, some 12,000 works of art alone are displayed in this new section. One gallery in the Richelieu wing displays 21 paintings by Rubens, done for Marie de Medici for her Luxmebourg Palace in only 2 years. This wing stacks masterpiece upon masterpiece: Dürer's self-portrait, Anthony Van Dyck's portrait of Charles I of England, Hans Holbein's (the Younger) *Portrait of Erasmus of Rotterdam*—everything combined with a wealth of art that includes Sumerian and Babylonian treasures, Assyrian winged bulls, and Persian friezes.

When you tire of strolling the galleries, you might consider a pick-me-up at **Café Marly** in the Richelieu wing. In three grandiose rooms with high ceilings and lavish 19th-century adornments, the café has a view of the museum's glass pyramid. The menu is limited to coffees, pastries (by Paris's most legendary pastry-maker, Lenôtre), salads, sandwiches, and simple platters.

✪ **Musée d'Orsay.** 1 rue de Bellechasse or 62 rue de Lille, 7e. ☎ **01-40-49-48-14.** Admission 35 F ($7) adults, 24 F ($4.80) ages 18–24 and over 60, free for children 17 and under. Tues–Wed and Fri–Sat 10am–6pm, Thurs 10am–9:45pm, Sun 9am–6pm. June 20–Sept 20, museum opens at 9am. Métro: Solférino. RER: Musée-d'Orsay.

In the middle of Paris, a defunct rail station, the handsome neoclassical Gare d'Orsay, has been transformed into one of the greatest art museums in the world. Standing across the Seine from the Louvre and the Tuileries, it's a museum of the 19th century. A detailed and wide-ranging panorama of international art is presented from the birth of the Second French Republic to the dawn of World War I (1848–1914).

The Musée d'Orsay houses thousands of pieces of sculpture and painting spread across 80 different galleries. It also displays belle époque furniture, photographs, objets d'art, and architectural models; it even contains a cinema that shows classic films.

A monument to the Industrial Revolution, the Orsay station, once called "the elephant," is covered by an arching glass roof, flooding the museum with light. The museum displays works ranging from the creations of academic and historic painters such as Ingres to romanticists such as Delacroix, to neo-realists such as Courbet and Daumier. The impressionists and postimpressionists, including Cézanne, van Gogh, and the Fauves, are displayed along with Matisse, the cubists, expressionists, and the abstract painters, in a setting once used by Orson Welles to film a nightmarish scene in *The Trial,* based on a Kafka work. You get the sunny wheatfields by Millet, works from the Barbizon School, the misty landscapes of Corot, and brilliant-hued Gauguins—all in the same hall.

Mainly it's the impressionists that keep the crowds lining up. Once the Louvre didn't want the works of these painters, although Americans appreciated them. If nothing else, the impressionists were independent, but unified in opposition to the dictatorial Académie des Beaux-Arts. They chose the world about them for their subject matter; they bathed their canvases in light, ignoring ecclesiastical or mythological scenes. They painted the Seine, Parisians strolling in the Tuileries, even railway stations such as the Gare St-Lazare (some critics considered Monet's choice of the latter an unforgivable vulgarity). The impressionists were the first to paint the most characteristic feature of Parisian life: The sidewalk café, especially those in what was then the artists' quarter of Montmartre.

Perhaps the most famous painting on view here from this era is Manet's *Picnic on the Grass,* which sent shock waves through respectable society when it was first exhibited. (Painted in 1863, it depicts a forest setting with a nude woman and two fully clothed men.) Two years later his *Olympia,* also here, created another scandal. It depicts a woman lounging on her bed and wearing nothing but a flower in her hair and high-heeled shoes, and attended by her African maid in the background. Zola called Manet "a man among eunuchs."

One of Renoir's brightest, most joyous paintings is also here—the *Moulin de la Galette,* painted in 1876. Degas is represented by his paintings of racehorses and dancers; his 1876 café scene *Absinthe,* also here, remains one of his most reproduced works. Paris-born Claude Monet was fascinated by the changing light effects on Rouen Cathedral, and in a series of five paintings, displayed here, he makes the old landmark live as never before.

One of the most celebrated works at the Orsay is by an American—Whistler's *Arrangement in Gray and Black: Portrait of the Painter's Mother,* perhaps better known as *Whistler's Mother.* It's said that this painting heralded the advent of modern art, although many critics denounced it at the time as "Whistler's Dead Mother" because of its funereal overtones. Today the painting has been hailed as a "veritable icon of our consciousness." As far as Whistler was concerned, he claimed he made "Mummy just as nice as possible."

Centre Georges Pompidou. Place Georges-Pompidou, 4e. ☎ **01-44-78-12-33.** All-day pass 70 F ($14) adults, 45 F ($9) ages 16–25 and over 60, free for children 17 and under; Museum of Modern Art only, 35 F ($7) adults, 24 F ($4.80) ages 16–24, free for children 15 and under. Mon and Wed–Fri noon–10pm, Sat–Sun 10am–10pm. Métro: Rambuteau, Hôtel-de-Ville, Châtelet, or Les Halles.

In 1969 Georges Pompidou, then president of France, decided to create a large cultural center to spotlight every form of 20th-century art. The center was finally opened in 1977 on the plateau Beaubourg, in the midst of a huge, car-free pedestrian district, east of boulevard de Sébastopol.

The structure, towering over a festive plaza, is the subject of much controversy. Parisians refer to the radical exoskeletal design as "the refinery." The Tinker Toy array of pipes and tubes surrounding the transparent shell are actually functional, serving as casings for the heating, air-conditioning, electrical, and telephone systems for the center. The great wormlike tubes crawling at angles up the side of the building contain the escalators that transport visitors from one floor to the next. Inside, no interior walls block one's view. Each floor is one vast room, divided as necessary by movable partitions.

The unique structure has already proved a favorite attraction for Parisian and foreign visitors alike, drawing more viewers each year than the Eiffel Tower. From the top of the center you can also enjoy one of the best views of the city.

In 1997, at the museum's 20th birthday, the Pompidou Center will have had completed the first major stage of an $80-million renovation of the entire structure. The exterior was done first. The interior work will be done in stages—floor by floor—and should be completed by the millennium; the museum will not close while the interiors are being redone.

The center is made up of four separate attractions:

The **Musée National d'Art Moderne** (National Museum of Modern Art) offers a large collection of 20th-century art, including French and American masterpieces. All the current trends of modern art are displayed on two floors (entrance on the fourth floor) in well-lit rooms of varying sizes. From the Fauves up to current abstract and expressionist works, the range is complete.

Featured are such artists as Max Ernst (whose contribution is a sculpture, *The Imbecile*), Kandinsky, Vuillard, Bonnard, Utrillo, Chagall, Dufy, Juan Gris, Léger, and Pollock, as well as sketches by Le Corbusier and stained glass by Rouault. Modern sculpture includes works by Alexander Calder, Henry Moore, and Jacob Epstein. A gallery of contemporary artists (Galeries Contemporaines), on the ground floor, demonstrates the trends in artistic activity today. Special exhibitions and demonstrations are constantly being staged in the Grande Galerie to acquaint the public with the significant works of the 20th century. Guided tours are available.

The center also houses the **Public Information Library,** where, for the first time in Paris's history, the public has free access to one million French and foreign books, periodicals, films, records, slides, and microfilms in nearly every area of knowledge.

Attractions: 3rd & 4th Arrondissements

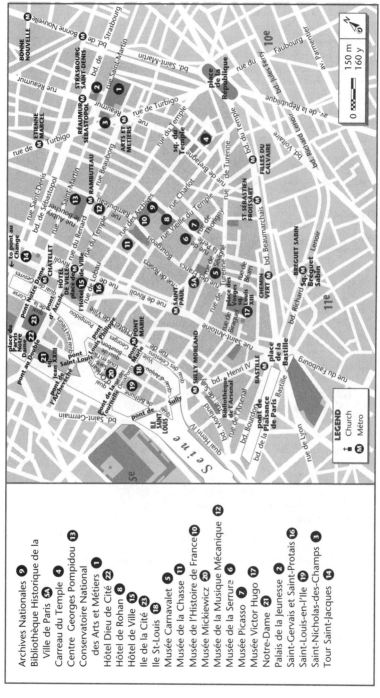

LEGEND

† Church
Ⓜ Métro

Archives Nationales ❾
Bibliothèque Historique de la
 Ville de Paris ❺ᴬ
Carreau du Temple ❹
Centre Georges Pompidou ❶
Conservatoire National
 des Arts et Métiers ㉒
Hôtel Dieu de Cité ㉓
Hôtel de Rohan ❽
Hôtel de Ville ⓯
Ile de la Cité ㉓
Ile St-Louis ⓲
Musée Carnavalet ❺
Musée de la Chasse ⑪
Musée de l'Histoire de France ❿
Musée Mickiewicz ⑳
Musée de la Musique Mécanique ⑫
Musée de la Serrure ❻
Musée Picasso ❼
Musée Victor Hugo ⑰
Notre-Dame ㉑
Palais de la Jeunesse ❷
Saint-Gervais et Saint-Protais ⑯
Saint-Louis-en-l'Ile ⑲
Saint-Nicholas-des-Champs ❸
Tour Saint-Jacques ⑭

The **Center for Industrial Design,** covering some 40,000 square feet of space, emphasizes the contributions made in the fields of architecture, visual communications, publishing, and community planning.

The **Institute for Research and Coordination of Acoustics/Music** brings together musicians and composers interested in furthering the cause of music, both contemporary and traditional. Concerts, workshops, and seminars are frequently open to the public.

In addition to its four main departments, the center also offers a **children's workshop and library** and a *cinémathèque,* which tells the history of motion pictures. The center's top-floor restaurant and cafeteria offers a panoramic view of Paris.

FYI: The coat line at the Pompidou Center can take 30 minutes. The trick here is to go to the coat line for the photo exhibit downstairs, where there's almost never a wait.

✪ **Musée Picasso.** In the Hôtel Salé, 5 rue de Thorigny, 3e. ☎ **01-42-71-25-21.** Admission 28 F ($5.60) adults, 18F ($3.60) ages 19–25, free for children 17 and under. Apr–Sept, Wed–Mon 9:30am–6pm; Oct–Mar, Wed–Mon 9:30am–5:30pm. Métro: St-Paul, Filles-du-Calvaire, or Chemin-Vert.

When it opened at the beautifully restored Hôtel Salé (salt mansion), a state-owned property in Le Marais, the press hailed this as a "museum for Picasso's Picassos." And that's what it is. Almost overnight it became—and continues to be—one of the most popular attractions in Paris.

The greatest Picasso collection in the world, acquired by the state in lieu of inheritance taxes totaling $50 million, consists of 203 paintings, 158 sculptures, 16 collages, 19 bas-reliefs, 88 ceramics, and more than 1,500 sketches and 1,600 engravings, along with 30 notebooks. These works are representative of the artist, spanning some 75 years of his life and changing styles.

The range of paintings includes a remarkable self-portrait from 1901 and goes on to embrace such masterpieces as *Le Baiser* (*The Kiss*), painted at Mougins on the Riviera in 1969. The museum also acquired another masterpiece he did a year later at the same place on the Riviera, called *Reclining Nude and the Man with a Guitar.* It's easy to stroll through the handsome museum seeking your own favorite work— perhaps a wicked one: *Jeune Garçon à la Langouste,* "young man with a lobster," painted in Paris in 1941. The Paris museum owns several intriguing studies for *Les Demoiselles d'Avignon,* the painting that launched cubism.

Many of the major masterpieces, such as *The Crucifixion* and *Nude in a Red Armchair,* should remain on permanent view. However, because the collection is so vast, temporary exhibitions, featuring such items as his studies of the Minotaur, will be held for the public at the rate of two a year.

In addition to Picasso's own treasure trove of art, works by other masters from his private collection are displayed, including the contributions of such world-class artists as Cézanne, Rousseau, Braque, André Derain, and Miró. Picasso was fascinated with African masks, and many of these are on view as well.

2 Ile de la Cité: Where Paris was Born

Medieval Paris, that architectural blending of grotesquerie and Gothic beauty, began on this island in the Seine. The venerated island, protected by the surrounding moat of the Seine, has been known as "the cradle" of Paris ever since. As Sauval once observed, "The Island of the City is shaped like a great ship, sunk in the mud, lengthwise in the stream, in about the middle of the Seine."

Few have written more movingly about 15th-century Paris than Victor Hugo, who invited the reader "to observe the fantastic display of lights against the darkness of that gloomy labyrinth of buildings; cast upon it a ray of moonlight, showing the city in glimmering vagueness, with its towers lifting their great heads from that foggy sea."

Medieval Paris was a city of legends and lovers—none more notable than Abélard, who was emasculated because of his love for Héloïse (afterward, he became a monk, she a nun)—but it was also a place of blood-curdling tortures and brutalities. Explore as much of it as you can, but even if you're in a hurry, try to visit Notre-Dame, the Sainte-Chapelle, and the Conciergerie.

THE ILE DE LA CITE'S TOP ATTRACTIONS

✪ Cathédrale de Notre-Dame. 6 place du parvis Notre-Dame, 4e. ☎ **01-42-34-56-10.** Cathedral, free; towers, 27 F ($5.40) adults, 18 F ($3.60) ages 18–24 and over 60, 15 F ($3) children 12–17, free for children 11 and under; treasury or crypt, 27 F ($5.40) adults, 18 F ($3.60) ages 18–24 and over 60, 15 F ($3) children 12–17, free for children 11 and under. Cathedral, daily 8am–6:45pm (closed Sat 12:30–2pm); towers, daily 9:30am–5pm; museum, Wed and Sat–Sun 2:30–6pm; treasury and crypt, Mon–Sat 9:30am–5:30pm. Six masses are celebrated on Sun, four on weekdays, and one on Sat. Métro: Cité or St-Michel. RER: St-Michel.

Notre-Dame is the heart of Paris, even of France itself. Distances from Paris to all parts of France are calculated from its precincts.

Although many may disagree, Notre-Dame is, in our opinion, more interesting outside than in. Hence, you'll want to walk around the entire structure to appreciate this "vast symphony of stone" more fully. Better yet, cross over the bridge to the Left Bank and view it from the quay.

The setting, on the banks of the Seine, has always been memorable. Founded in the 12th century by Maurice de Sully, bishop of Paris, Notre-Dame grew and grew. Over the years the cathedral has changed as Paris has—often falling victim to fads in decorative taste. Its flying buttresses were rebuilt in 1330.

The history of Paris and that of Notre-Dame are inseparable. Many came here to pray before going off to lose their lives in the Crusades. "Our Lady of Paris" was not spared by the revolutionaries, who destroyed the Galerie des Rois. Later, Napoléon was crowned emperor here, taking the crown from Pius VII and placing it on his own head. But carelessness, vandalism, "embellishments," and wars of religion had already demolished much that previously existed.

The cathedral was once scheduled for demolition, but a movement mushroomed to restore the cathedral to its original glory, partly because of the Victor Hugo classic *The Hunchback of Notre Dame* and the revival of interest in the Gothic. The task was completed under Viollet-le-Duc, an architectural genius.

Once the houses of old Paris crowded in on the structure, but Haussmann ordered them torn down to show off the edifice to its best advantage from the square known as *parvis.* From that vantage point you can view the trio of 13th-century sculptured portals. On the left, the Portal of the Virgin depicts the signs of the Zodiac and the coronation of the Virgin. The association of the Virgin and the cosmos is to be found in dozens of earlier and later medieval churches.

The restored central Portal of the Last Judgment is divided into three levels: The first shows Vices and Virtues; the second, Christ and his Apostles; and above that, Christ in triumph after the Resurrection. The portal is a close illustration of the Gospel according to Matthew.

Finally, the Portal of St. Anne is on the right, depicting such scenes as the Virgin enthroned with Child. It's the best preserved and probably the most perfect piece of sculpture in Notre-Dame. Over the central portal is a remarkable rose window, 31 feet in diameter, forming a showcase for a statue of the Virgin and Child.

Only in Paris

• A **stroll along the Seine** is for many visitors the most memorable and romantic way to experience Paris. The riverbanks afford some breathtaking views of the city's most important monuments. You may also stumble across the next Matisse in the clusters of young artists peddling their canvases. For a spectacular view of the Louvre, cross the pont des Arts. The first iron bridge in the city, it's one of only four pedestrian bridges in Paris. As you continue your stroll, you encounter the pont Neuf, the oldest and most famous bridge in Paris. (In the Middle Ages, Parisians came to the bridge to have their teeth pulled.) From here you have an excellent view of the Palais de Justice and Sainte-Chapelle on the Ile de la Cité.

  A fine finish to any day spent meandering with the river would include a stroll through the *marché aux fleurs,* the city's flower market. Here you can purchase rare flowers, the gems of the French Riveria, bouquets that have inspired artists throughout the centuries. From here, enter the famed *marché aux oiseaux* (bird market), where you can purchase rare birds from around the world, or at least look at them.

• If there's a literary bone in your body, you'll feel a vicarious thrill on discovering the haunts of the famous writers and artists who have lived, worked, and played in Paris. Take the Métro to place St-Michel to begin your tour. As you wander away from the Seine, you encounter **rue de la Huchette,** one of the most famous streets on the Left Bank. Its inhabitants were immortalized in Eliot Paul's *The Last Time I Saw Paris.*

  As you continue into the Left Bank, you enter territory still haunted by members of the Beat Generation. This area is home to the Café Gentilhomme, described by Jack Kerouac in *Satori in Paris.* Allen Ginsberg's favorite, the **Hôtel du Vieux-Paris,** still attracts those in search of the Beats. You must also include a stroll down **rue Monsieur-le-Prince,** the "Yankee alleyway," where Richard Wright, James McNeill Whistler, Henry Wadsworth Longfellow, and Oliver Wendell Holmes all lived at one time or another.

  A perfect end to your literary tour is a drink at the famed **Hôtel de Crillon,** where heroine Brett Ashley broke her promise to rendezvous with Jake Barnes in Hemingway's *The Sun Also Rises.* Zelda and F. Scott Fitzgerald once lifted their glasses here as well.

Equally interesting (although often missed by the scurrying visitor) is the Portal of the Cloisters (around on the left), with its dour-faced 13th-century Virgin, a unique survivor of the many that originally adorned the facade. (Unfortunately, the Child figure she is holding is decapitated.) Finally, the Portal of St. Stephen on the Seine side traces the martyrdom of that saint.

If possible, see the interior of Notre-Dame at sunset. Of the three giant medallions that warm the austere cathedral, the north rose window in the transept, dating from the mid-13th century, is best. The interior is in the typically Gothic style, with slender, graceful columns. The stone-carved choir screen from the early 14th century depicts such biblical scenes as the Last Supper. Near the altar stands the 14th-century Virgin and Child, highly venerated among the more faithful of Paris.

In the treasury is a display of vestments and gold objects, including crowns, behind glass. Exhibited are a cross presented by Haile Selassie, the former emperor of

- **Free concerts** are one of the joys of Paris. In the summer they're held all over the city, in parks and churches. The entertainment weeklies have details, or you can call a 24-hour hotline, **AlloConcert,** for information (☎ **01-42-76-50-00**), but you have to speak French.

  Some of the best concerts are held at the **American Church in Paris,** 65 quai d'Orsay (☎ **01-42-37-20-00;** RER: Luxembourg). The **Eglise St-Merri,** 76 rue de la Verrerie, 4e (☎ **01-42-71-93-93;** Métro: Châtelet), is also known for its free concerts, which are regularly featured from September to July at 9pm on Saturday and 4pm on Sunday. The **Sainte-Chapelle**, 4 bd. du Palais, 1er (☎ **01-46-61-55-41;** Métro: Cité), also stages concerts a few times per week in summer, but these concerts charge an admission ranging from 120 to 150 F ($24 to $30). Call the box office for more details; it's open daily from 1:30 to 5:30pm.

- **Place des Vosges,** Paris's oldest square, is best enjoyed on a balmy spring evening. From the center of the square a glance in every direction affords a view into ancient Paris. The square, which was originally called the Palais Royale, was constructed as the royal residence for Henri IV, though an assassin took his life before he ever lived here. Once the setting of jousts and duels, this placid square boasts some of the finest architecture in Europe.

  Although built along strict architectural plans, each residence is personalized. Each facade is garnished with different windows and balconies. The most famous resident was Victor Hugo, who lived here from 1832 to 1848, before fleeing to Guernsey in exile. His home is now the site of the Musée Victor-Hugo.

  And every evening stroll must include a walk under the square's spacious arcades. These revolutionary structures allowed shopping in fair or inclement weather, a luxury in ancient Paris.

- Even if you have only 24 hours in Paris and can't explore most of the sights recommended in this chapter, try to make it to the **Basilique du Sacré-Coeur,** at place St-Pierre in Montmartre, at dusk. There, as you sit on the top steps with the church at your back and the square Willette in front of you, nighttime Paris begins to come alive. First, a twinkle, like a firefly—then all the lights go on like magic.

Ethiopia, and a reliquary given by Napoléon. Notre-Dame is especially proud of its relic of the True Cross and the Crown of Thorns.

Finally, to visit those grimy gargoyles immortalized by Hugo, you have to scale steps leading to the twin square towers, flat on top rising to a height of 225 feet. Once there, you can closely inspect those devils (some sticking out their tongues), hobgoblins, and birds of prey. You expect to see the imaginary character of Quasimodo in one of his celluloid hunchback interpretations (Charles Laughton, Anthony Quinn, or Lon Chaney, depending on which version you saw).

Approached through a garden behind Notre-Dame is the **Le Memorial de la Déportation,** jutting out on the very tip of the Ile de la Cité. Birds chirp nowadays, the Seine flows gently by, but the memories are far from pleasant. It's a memorial to French martyrs of World War II, who were deported to such camps as Auschwitz and Buchenwald. Carved into stone in blood-red are the words (in French): "Forgive, but don't forget." The memorial can be visited daily from 10am to noon and 2 to 7pm. Admission is free.

Conciergerie. 1 quai de l'Horloge, 1er. ☎ **01-43-54-30-06**. Admission 28 F ($5.60) adults, 18 F ($3.60) children 12–17, 15F ($3) children 11 and under. Apr–Sept, daily 9:30am–6:30pm; Oct–Mar, daily 10am–5pm. Métro: Cité, Châtelet, or St-Michel. RER: St-Michel.

London has its Tower of London, Paris its Conciergerie. Although it had a long and regal history before the Revolution, it's visited today chiefly by those wishing to bask in the horrors of the Reign of Terror. The Conciergerie lives on as a symbol of infamy, recalling the days when carts pulled up daily to haul off the fresh supply of victims to the guillotine.

On the Seine, the Conciergerie is approached through its landmark twin towers, the Tour d'Argent and the Tour de César. The 14th-century vaulted Guard Room, which remains from the days when the Capets made the Palace of the Cité a royal residence, is the actual entrance to the chilling building. Also dating from the 14th century, and even more interesting, is the vast, dark, and foreboding Gothic Salle des Gens d'Armes (People at Arms), totally changed from the days when the king used it as a banqueting hall.

Architecture, however, plays a secondary role to the list of famous prisoners who spent their last miserable days on earth at the Conciergerie. Few in its history endured the tortures of Ravaillac, who assassinated Henry IV in 1610. He got the full treatment—pincers in the flesh, and hot lead and boiling oil poured on him like bath water.

During the Revolution the Conciergerie became more than a symbol of terror to the nobility or the "enemies of the State." Meeting just a short walk from the prison, the Revolutionary Tribunal dispensed "justice" in a hurry. And the guillotine fell even faster. If it's any consolation, these "freedom-loving" jurors did not believe in torturing their victims—only in decapitating them.

In failing health and shocked beyond grief, Marie Antoinette was brought here to await her trial. Only a small screen (and sometimes not even that) protected her modesty from the glare of the guards stationed in her cell. The Affair of the Carnation failed in its attempt to abduct her and secure her freedom. (In retrospect, one can perhaps feel sympathy for the broken and widowed queen. By accounts of that day, she was shy and stupid, although the evidence is that upon her death she attained the nobility of a true queen. Furthermore, historians deny that she uttered the famous quotation attributed to her, "Let them eat cake," when told the peasants had no bread.) It was shortly before noon on the morning of October 16, 1793, when her executioners came for her, grabbing her and cutting her hair, as was the custom for victims marked for the guillotine.

Later the Conciergerie housed yet more noted prisoners, including Madame Elizabeth; Madame du Barry, mistress of Louis XV; Mme Roland ("O Liberty! Liberty! What crimes are committed in thy name!"); and Charlotte Corday, who killed Marat with a kitchen knife while he was taking a sulfur bath. In time, the Revolution turned on its own leaders, such as Danton and Robespierre. Finally, even one of the most hated men in Paris, the public prosecutor Fouquier-Tinville, faced the same guillotine to which he'd sent so many others.

Among the few interned here who lived to tell the tale was America's Thomas Paine, who reminisced about his chats in English with Danton.

✪ **Sainte-Chapelle.** In the Palais de Justice, 4 bd. du Palais, 1er. ☎ **01-53-73-78-50**. Admission 28 F ($5.60) adults, 21 F ($4.20) ages 18–25, 15 F ($3) children 12–17, free for children 11 and under. Apr–Sept, daily 9:30am–6:30pm; Oct–Mar, daily 10am–5pm. Métro: Cité, St-Michel, or Châtelet. RER: St-Michel.

Countless travel writers have called this tiny chapel a jewel box. That hardly suffices. Nor will it do to call it "a light show." Go when the sun is shining and you'll need no one else's words to describe the remarkable effects of natural light on the Sainte-Chapelle.

The church is approached through the Cour de la Sainte-Chapelle of the Palais de Justice. If it weren't for the chapel's 247-foot spire, the law courts here would almost swallow it up.

Built in only 5 to 7 years, beginning in 1246, the chapel has two levels. It was constructed to house relics of the True Cross, including the Crown of Thorns acquired by St. Louis (the Crusader king, Louis IX) from the emperor of Constantinople. (In those days, cathedrals throughout Europe were busy acquiring relics for their treasuries, regardless of their authenticity. It was a seller's—perhaps a sucker's—market.) Louis IX is said to have paid heavily for his precious relics, raising the money through unscrupulous means. He died of the plague on a crusade and was canonized in 1297.

You enter through the lower chapel, supported by flying buttresses and ornamented with fleur-de-lis designs. The lower chapel was used by the servants of the palace, the upper chamber by the king and his courtiers. The latter is reached by ascending narrow spiral stairs.

Viewed on a bright day, the 15 stained-glass windows seem to glow with ruby red and Chartres blue. They vividly depict scenes from the Bible. The walls consist almost entirely of the glass, which had to be removed for safekeeping during the Revolution and again during both world wars. In them are embodied the hopes and dreams—and the pretensions—of the kings who ordered their construction.

OTHER SIGHTS AROUND THE ILE DE LA CITE

After leaving the Conciergerie, turn left and stroll along the Seine past medievalesque towers until you reach the **pont Neuf** or "New Bridge." The span isn't new, of course—actually it's the oldest bridge in Paris, erected in 1604. In its day the bridge had two unique features: It was not flanked with houses and shops, and it was paved.

At the Hôtel Carnavalet, a museum in the Marais section (see Section 9, later in this chapter), is a painting called *Spectacle of Buffons,* showing what the bridge was like between 1665 and 1669. Duels were fought on the structure, great coaches belonging to the nobility crossed it, peddlers sold their wares, and as there were no public facilities, men defecated right on the bridge. With all those crowds, it attracted entertainers, such as Tabarin, who sought a few coins from the gawkers. The pont Neuf is decorated with corbels, a melange of grotesquerie.

Finally, continue on to the "prow" of the island, the **square du Vert-Galant,** pausing first to look at the equestrian statue of the beloved Henri IV, who was killed by an assassin. A true king of his people, Henry was (to judge from accounts) also regal in the boudoir. Hence the nickname "Vert Galant," or gay old spark. Gabrielle d'Estrées and Henriette d'Entragues were his best-known mistresses, but they had to share him with countless others—some of whom would casually catch his eye as he was riding along the streets of Paris.

In fond memory of the king, the little triangular park continues to attract lovers. If at first it appears to be a sunken garden, that's because it remains at its natural level; the rest of the Cité has been built up during the centuries.

ANOTHER ISLAND IN THE SEINE: ILE ST-LOUIS

As you walk across the little iron footbridge from the rear of Notre-Dame toward the Ile St-Louis, you'll enter a world of tree-shaded quays, aristocratic town houses with courtyards, restaurants, and antiques shops. (You can also take the Métro to

Ile de la Cité & Ile St-Louis

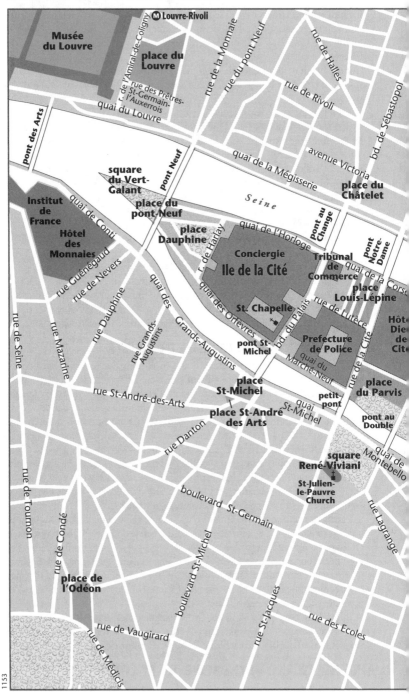

Musée du Louvre

Ⓜ Louvre-Rivoli

place du Louvre

rue de l'Amiral-de-Coligny

r. des Prêtres-St-Germain-l'Auxerrois

quai du Louvre

rue de la Monnaie

rue du pont Neuf

rue de Rivoli

rue de Halles

bd. de Sébastopol

pont des Arts

quai de la Mégisserie

avenue Victoria

square du Vert-Galant

pont Neuf

Seine

place du Châtelet

place du pont-Neuf

Institut de France

quai de Conti

place Dauphine

quai de l'Horloge

pont au Change

pont Notre-Dame

Hôtel des Monnaies

rue Guénégaud

rue de Nevers

r. de Harlay

Concierge

Ile de la Cité

Tribunal de Commerce

quai de la Corse

place Louis-Lépine

quai des Grands-Augustins

rue Dauphine

rue Mazarine

quai des Orfèvres

bd. du Palais

St. Chapelle

rue de Lutèce

Prefecture de Police

rue de la Cité

Hôtel-Dieu de Cité

rue de Seine

rue de Tournon

rue de Condé

rue St-André-des-Arts

pont St-Michel

place St-Michel

place St-André des Arts

rue Danton

quai du Marché-Neuf

quai St-Michel

petit-pont

place du Parvis

pont au Double

quai de Montebello

boulevard St-Germain

square René-Viviani

St-Julien-le-Pauvre Church

rue Lagrange

place de l'Odéon

boulevard St-Michel

rue de Vaugirard

rue de Médicis

rue St-Jacques

rue des Ecoles

1153

180

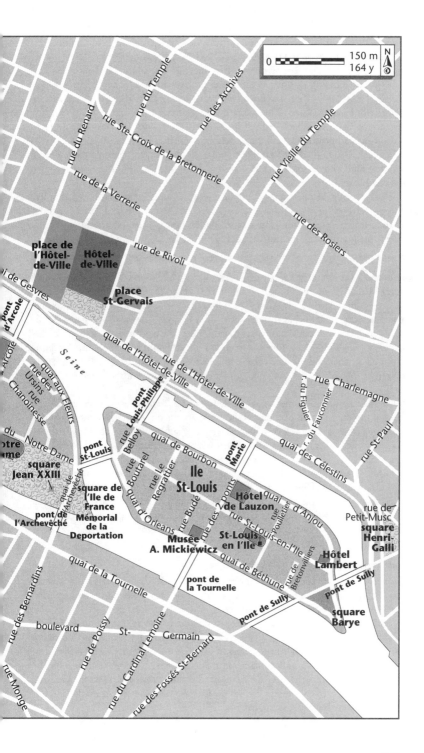

place de l'Hôtel-de-Ville

Hôtel-de-Ville

place St-Gervais

rue du Renard

rue du Temple

rue Ste-Croix de la Bretonnerie

rue des Archives

rue Vielle du Temple

rue de la Verrerie

rue de Rivoli

rue des Rosiers

quai de Gesvres

pont d'Arcole

quai de l'Hôtel-de-Ville

rue de l'Hôtel-de-Ville

rue Charlemagne

Seine

quai aux Fleurs

rue des Ursins

rue Chanoinesse

pont Louis-Philippe

rue du Figuier

r. du Fauconnier

rue St-Paul

du

Notre Dame

pont St-Louis

rue Belloy

quai de Bourbon

pont Marie

quai des Célestins

ôtre me

square Jean XXIII

quai de l'Archevêché

rue Boutarel

rue Le Regrattier

Ile St-Louis

Hôtel de Lauzon

quai d'Anjou

rue de Petit-Musc

square de l'Ile de France Mémorial de la Deportation

pont de l'Archevêché

quai d'Orleans

rue Budé

rue des 2 ponts

rue St-Louis-en-l'Ile

rue Poulletier

rue de Bretonvilliers

square Henri-Galli

Musée A. Mickiewicz

St-Louis-en l'Ile

Hôtel Lambert

quai de Béthune

pont de la Tournelle

pont de Sully

pont de Sully

square Barye

quai de la Tournelle

rue des Bernardins

boulevard

St-

Germain

rue de Poissy

rue du Cardinal Lemoine

rue des Fossés St-Bernard

rue Monge

0   150 m / 164 y   N

Sully-Morland or Pont-Marie.) The twin island of Ile de la Cité, it's primarily residential, and plaques on the facades of houses identify the former residences of the famous. Marie Curie lived at 36 quai de Béthune, near the pont de la Tournelle.

The most exciting mansion is the **Hôtel de Lauzun,** at 17 quai d'Anjou, which can be viewed only from the outside. It was the home of the duc de Lauzun, a favorite of Louis XIV, until his secret marriage angered the king and the duc was sent to the Bastille. Baudelaire lived here in the 19th century, squandering his family fortune and penning poetry that would be banned in France until 1949.

Voltaire lived in the **Hôtel Lambert,** at 2 quai d'Anjou, with his mistress, and their quarrels here were legendary. The mansion also housed the Polish royal family for over a century.

Farther along, at no. 9 quai d'Anjou, stands the house where Honoré Daumier, the painter, sculptor, and lithographer, lived between 1846 and 1863. Here he produced hundreds of lithographs satirizing the bourgeoisie and attacking government corruption. His caricature of Louis-Philippe landed him in jail for 6 months.

3 The Champs-Elysées: The Grand Promenade of Paris

In 1891 that "Innocent Abroad," Mark Twain, called the Champs-Elysées "the liveliest street in the world." It was designed for the favorite pastime of Parisians, promenading. (It's *too* innocent to rank walking as Parisians' number-one pastime, but surely it comes in second.) Nowadays tourists follow the old Parisian tradition; Americans who would normally drive half a block to the drugstore are seen doing the sprint from place Charles-de-Gaulle (Etoile) to place de la Concorde. That walk is surely a grand promenade, and you won't know Paris until you've done it. (And it's even grander at night.)

We'll start at the Tuileries and place de la Concorde and take the Champs-Elysées toward the Arc de Triomphe. Part of the boulevard is a drive through a chestnut-lined park; the other section is a commercial avenue of sidewalk cafés, automobile showrooms, airline offices, cinemas, lingerie stores, even hamburger joints. The dividing point between the park and the commercial sections is the **rond-point des Champs-Elysées.** Close to that is a philatelist's delight, the best-known open-air **stamp market** in Europe, held on Thursday and Sunday. To chronicle the people who have walked this broad avenue would be to tell the history of Paris through the last few centuries. Ever since the days of Thomas Jefferson and Benjamin Franklin, Americans have gravitated here, and even if it has lost its turn-of-the-century elegance, that's still true today.

✪ **Jardin de Tuileries.** Place de la Concorde, 1er. ☎ **01-44-50-75-01.** Métro: Tuileries.

Behind the Louvre and bordering place de la Concorde, the Tuileries are as much a part of Paris as the Seine. These statue-studded gardens were designed by Le Nôtre, the gardener to Louis XIV, who planned the grounds of Versailles.

About 100 years before that, a palace was ordered built by Catherine de Médicis. Connected to the Louvre, it was occupied by Louis XVI after he left Versailles. Napoléon I called it home. Twice attacked by the people of Paris, it was finally burnt to the ground in 1871 and never rebuilt. The gardens, however, remain. Like the orderly French mind, the trees are arranged according to designs. Even the paths are straight, as opposed to winding English gardens. To break the sense of order and formality there are bubbling fountains.

The neoclassic statuary is often insipid and is occasionally desecrated by rebellious "art critics." Seemingly half of Paris is found in the Tuileries on a warm spring day,

Attractions: 8th Arrondissement

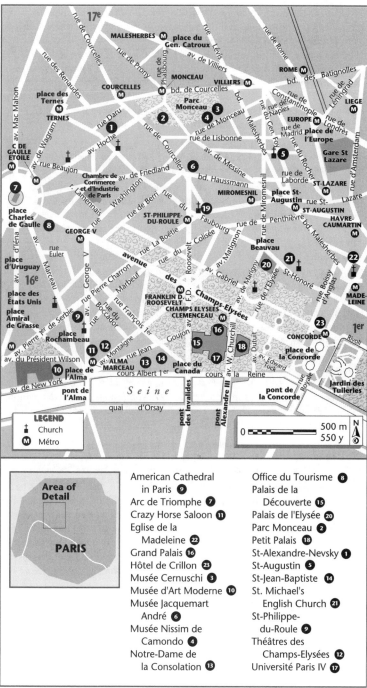

listening to the chirping birds and watching the daffodils and red tulips bloom. Fountains bubble, and mothers roll their carriages over the grounds where 18th-century revolutionaries killed the king's Swiss guards.

Also here—2 miles from place Charles-de-Gaulle (Etoile)—stands the **Arc de Triomphe du Carrousel,** at the cour du Carrousel. Pierced with three walkways and supported by marble columns, the monument honors the Grand Armée, celebrating Napoléon's victory at Austerlitz on December 5, 1805. The arch is surmounted by statuary, a chariot, and four bronze horses. "Paris needs more monuments," Napoléon once shouted. He got his wish.

Musée de l'Orangerie des Tuileries. Jardin des Tuileries, place de la Concorde, 1er. ☎ **01-42-97-48-16.** Admission 28 F ($5.60) adults, 18 F ($3.60) ages 18–24 and for everyone on Sun, free for children 17 and under. Wed–Mon 9:45am–5pm. Métro: Concorde.

In the Tuileries stands this gem among galleries. It has an outstanding collection of art and one celebrated painting on display: Claude Monet's exquisite *Nymphéas* (1915–27), in which water lilies float amorphously on the canvas. The work panels the walls of two oval rooms on the ground floor; the artist himself supervised the installation.

Creating his effects with hundreds and hundreds of minute strokes of his brush (one irate 19th-century critic called them "tongue lickings"), Monet achieved unity and harmony, as he did in his Rouen Cathedral series and his haystacks. Artists with lesser talent might have stirred up "soup." But Monet, of course, was a genius. See his lilies and evoke for yourself the mood and melancholy as he experienced them so many years ago. Monet continued to paint his water landscapes right up until his death in 1926, although he was greatly hampered by failing eyesight.

The renovated building also shelters the Walter-Guillaume collection, which includes more than 24 Renoirs, including *Young Girl at a Piano.* Cézanne is represented by 14 works, notably *The Red Rock,* and Matisse by 11 paintings. The highlight of Rousseau's nine works displayed here is *The Wedding,* and the dozen paintings by Picasso reach the pinnacle of their brilliance in *The Female Bathers.* Other outstanding paintings are by Utrillo (10 works in all), Soutine (22), and Derain (28).

Galerie Nationale du Jeu de Paume. Jardin des Tuileries / place de la Concorde, 1er. ☎ **01-47-03-12-50.** Admission 35 F ($7) adults, 25 F ($5) students, free for children 12 and under. Tues noon–9:30pm, Wed–Fri noon–7pm, Sat–Sun 10am–7pm. Métro: Concorde.

For years the national gallery in the Jeu de Paume, in the northeast corner of the Tuileries gardens, was one of the treasures of Paris, displaying some of the finest works of the impressionists. In 1986 that collection was hauled off to the Musée d'Orsay, much to the regret of many. Following a $12.6-million face-lift, this Second Empire building has been transformed into a state-of-the-art gallery with a video screening room. No permanent collection is housed here, but each 2 or 3 months a new show is mounted. Sometimes the works of little-known contemporary artists are on display; at other times an exhibit will feature "unexplored" aspects of established artists.

Originally, in this part of the gardens, Napoléon III built a ball court on which *jeu de paume,* an antecedent of tennis, was played—hence the museum's name. The most infamous period in the national gallery's history came during the Nazi occupation, when it served as an "evaluation center" for works of modern art. Paintings from all over France were shipped to the Jeu de Paume; art condemned by the Nazis as "degenerate" was burned.

Place de la Concorde. 1er. Métro: Concorde.

In the east, the Champs-Elysées begins at place de la Concorde, an octagonal traffic hub built in 1757 to honor Louis XV. The statue of the king was torn down in 1792 and the name of the square changed to place de la Révolution. Floodlit at night, it's dominated nowadays by an **Egyptian obelisk** from Luxor, considered the oldest man-made object in Paris. It was carved circa 1200 B.C. and presented to France in 1829 by the viceroy of Egypt.

In the Reign of Terror, the dreaded guillotine was erected on this spot, and claimed the lives of thousands—everybody from Louis XVI, who died bravely, to Madame du Barry, who went screaming and kicking all the way. Before the leering crowds, Marie Antoinette, Robespierre, Danton, Mme Roland, and Charlotte Corday were executed. (You can still lose your life on place de la Concorde—all you have to do is chance the traffic and cross over.)

For a spectacular sight, look down the Champs-Elysées—the view is framed by the Marly horses. On the opposite side, the gateway to the Tuileries is flanked by the winged horses of Coysevox. On each side of the obelisk are two fountains with bronze-tailed mermaids and bare-breasted sea nymphs. Gray-beige statues ring the square, honoring the cities of France. To symbolize the city's fall to Germany in 1871, the statue of Strasbourg was covered with a black drape that wasn't lifted until the end of World War I. Two of the palaces on place de la Concorde are today the Ministry of the Marine and the deluxe Hôtel de Crillon. They were designed in the 1760s by Ange-Jacques Gabriel.

✪ **Arc de Triomphe.** Place Charles-de-Gaulle (Etoile), 16e. ☎ **01-43-80-31-31.** Admission 32 F ($6.40) adults, 21 F ($4.20) ages 18–24, 15 F ($3) children 12–17, free for children 11 and under. Apr–Sept, Tues–Sat 9:30am–11pm, Sun–Mon 9:30am–6:30pm; Oct–Mar, Tues–Sat 10am–10:30pm, Sun–Mon 10am–6pm. Métro: Charles-de-Gaulle–Etoile.

At the western end of the Champs-Elysées, the Arc de Triomphe suggests one of those ancient Roman arches—only it's larger. Actually, it's the biggest triumphal arch in the world, about 163 feet high and 147 feet wide. To reach it, don't try to cross the square, the busiest traffic hub in Paris (death is certain!). Take the underground passage and live longer. With a dozen streets radiating from the "Star," the roundabout was called by one writer "vehicular roulette with more balls than numbers."

After the death of Charles de Gaulle, the French government—despite protests from anti-Gaullists—voted to change the name of the heretofore place de l'Etoile to place Charles-de-Gaulle.

The arch has witnessed some of France's proudest moments—and some of its more shameful and humiliating defeats, notably those of 1871 and 1940. The memory of German troops marching under the arch that had come to symbolize France's glory and prestige is still painful to the French. Who could ever forget the 1940 newsreel of the Frenchman standing on the Champs-Elysées openly weeping as the Nazi stormtroopers goose-stepped through Paris?

Commissioned by Napoléon in 1806 to commemorate his victories, the arch wasn't ready for the entrance of his new empress, Marie-Louise, in 1810. It served its ceremonial purpose anyway, and in fact, wasn't completed until 1836, under the reign of Louis-Philippe. Four years later the remains of Napoléon—brought from his grave on St. Helena—passed under the arch on the journey to his tomb at the

---

Impressions

To the Arc de Triomphe de l'Etoile
raise yourself all the way to the heavens, portal of victory
That the giant of our glory
Might pass without bending down.

—Victor Hugo

Invalides. Since that time it has become the focal point for state funerals. It's also the site of the permanent tomb of the unknown soldier, in whose honor an eternal flame is kept burning.

The greatest state funeral was that of Victor Hugo in 1885; his coffin was placed under the center of the arch, and much of Paris turned out to pay tribute to the author. Another notable funeral was that of Ferdinand Foch, the supreme commander of the Allied forces in World War I who died in 1929. Perhaps the Arc's happiest moment occurred in 1944, when the Liberation of Paris parade passed through. That same year Eisenhower paid a visit to the tomb of France's unknown soldier, a new tradition among leaders of state and important figures.

Of the sculptures on the monument, the best known is Rude's *Marseillaise,* also called *The Departure of the Volunteers. The Triumph of Napoléon in 1810,* by J. P. Cortot, and the *Resistance of 1814* and the *Peace of 1815,* both by Etex, also adorn the facade. The monument is engraved with the names of hundreds of generals (those underlined died in battle) who commanded French troops in Napoleonic victories.

You can take an elevator or climb the stairway to the top, where there's an exhibition hall with lithographs and photos depicting the arch throughout its history. From the observation deck you have the finest view of the Champs-Elysées and of such landmarks as the Louvre, the Eiffel Tower, Sacré-Coeur, and the new district of La Défense.

OTHER SIGHTS NEARBY

Palais de l'Elysée. Rue du Faubourg St-Honoré, 8e. Métro: Miromesnil.

A slight detour from the Champs-Elysées along avenue de Marigny takes you to the French "White House," which occupies a block along fashionable Faubourg St-Honoré. It's now occupied by the president of France and cannot be visited by the public without an invitation.

Built in 1718 for the count d'Evreux, the palace had many owners before it was purchased by the Republic in 1873. Once it was owned by Madame de Pompadour. When she "had the supreme delicacy to die discreetly at the age of 43," she bequeathed it to the king. The world première of the Voltaire play *The Chinese Orphan* was presented there. After her divorce from Napoléon, Josephine also lived there, as did Napoléon III when he was president, beginning in 1848. When he became emperor in 1852, he moved to the Tuileries. Such celebrated English visitors as Queen Victoria and Wellington have spent their nights there as well.

Included among the palace's works of art are tapestries made at Beauvais in the 18th century, Raphael and Leonardo da Vinci paintings, and Louis XVI furnishings. A grand dining hall was built for Napoléon III, as well as an orangerie for the duchess du Berry (now converted to a winter garden).

Palais Royal. Place du Palais-Royal, on rue St-Honoré, 1er. Métro: Louvre.

At the demolished Café Foy in the Palais Royal, Camille Desmoulins jumped up on a table and shouted for the mob "to fight to the death." The date was July 13, 1789. The French Revolution had begun. But the renown of the Palais Royal goes back much further. Facing the Louvre, the gardens were planted in 1634 for Cardinal Richelieu, who presented them to Louis XIII. As a child, Louis XIV played around the fountain, and once nearly drowned in it. Despite his close call so long ago, children still frolic here to this day.

In time the property became the residence of the dukes of Orléans. Philippe-Egalité, a cousin of Louis XVI, built his apartments on the grounds, and subsequently rented them to prostitutes. By the 20th century those same apartments were rented by such artists as Colette and Cocteau. Of the gardens Colette wrote, "It is as though I were living in the provinces under the shadow of the parish church! I go into the temple en passant." (A plaque at 9 rue Beaujolais marks the entrance to her apartment, which she inhabited until her death in 1954.) Today the Palais Royal contains apartments, some discreet shops, and a few great restaurants (like Le Grand Véfour—see Chapter 6).

New York–born American actor and playwright John Howard Payne wrote *Home, Sweet Home* while living in one of the apartments.

Let's turn the clock back again: As an 18-year-old lieutenant, Napoléon Bonaparte met his first prostitute in the Palais Royal. Robespierre and Danton dined here. An actress, Mlle Montansier, "knew" many of them, including the Corsican. Charlotte Corday came this way, looking for a dagger with which to kill Marat. During the Directoire, when gambling dens flourished at the Palais Royal, foreigners reported seeing Frenchmen leaving the salons without their silk breeches—they had literally lost their trousers at the tables!

Today a sleepy provincial air remains. It's hard to imagine its former life. From place Colette, you enter the Court of Honor, colonnaded on three sides. The palace is the headquarters of the Councils of State these days, and the Court of Honor is a parking lot during the day. In the center of the Palais Royal is the Galerie d'Orléans, with two fountains and many a colonnade. You can stroll through the gardens or down the Galerie Montpensier, which is filled with little shops.

Place Vendôme. 8e. Métro: Opéra.

Always aristocratic, sometimes royal, place Vendôme enjoyed its golden age in the heyday of the Second Empire. Dress designers—the great ones, such as Worth—introduced the crinoline here. Louis Napoléon lived here, wooing his future empress, Eugénie de Montijo, at his address at the Hôtel du Rhin. In its halcyon days the waltzes of Strauss echoed across the plaza. But in time they were replaced by cannon fire.

Today the most prestigious tenant on the plaza is the Ritz. Banks and offices abound. Still, place Vendôme is one of the most harmonious squares in France, evoking the Paris of Louis XIV.

Today the square is dominated by a column crowned by Napoléon. The plaza was originally planned by Mansart to honor Louis XIV—so it's a good thing he died earlier. There was a statue of the Sun King here until the Revolution, when it was replaced briefly by a statue of Liberty.

Then came Napoléon, who ordered that a sort of Trajan's Column be erected in honor of the victor at Austerlitz. That Napoléon himself won the battle was "incidental." The column was made of bronze melted from captured Russian and Austrian cannons.

After Napoléon's downfall the statue was replaced by one of Henri IV, everybody's favorite king and every woman's favorite man. Later Napoléon surmounted it once again, this time in uniform and without the pose of a Caesar.

The Communards of 1871, who detested royalty and the false promises of emperors, pulled down the statue. The artist Courbet is said to have led the raid. For his part in the drama, he was jailed and fined the cost of restoring the statue. He couldn't pay it, of course, and was forced into exile in Switzerland. Eventually the statue of Napoléon, wrapped in a Roman toga, finally won out.

The plaza is one of the best known in Paris. It has attracted such tenants as Chopin, who lived at no. 12 until his death in 1849. Who was Vendôme, you ask? He was the son (delicate writers refer to him as "the natural son") of the roving Henri IV and his best-known mistress, Gabrielle d'Estrées.

Petit Palais. Petit Palais, av. Winston-Churchill, 8e. ☎ **01-42-65-12-73.** Admission 27 F ($5.40), free on Sun; special exhibitions, 30–40 F ($6–$8). Tues–Sun 10am–5:40pm. Closed Aug. Métro: Champs-Elysées.

Built by architect Charles Girault, this small palace faces the Grand Palais (housing special exhibitions); both were erected for the 1900 exhibition.

The Petit Palais contains works of art belonging to the city of Paris. Most prominent are the Dutuit and Tuck collections. In the Dutuit collection are Egyptian, Greek, and Roman bronzes, rare ivory statues (the most prominent of which is of a Roman actor), and a series of ancient Greek porcelains. The collection also boasts enamels, sculpture, and hand-lettered and -painted manuscripts from the Middle Ages. A good collection of 17th-century Dutch and Flemish paintings are also on view, with representative artists including Breughel the Younger (*Wedding Pageant*), Rubens, Hobbema, Ruysdaël, and others.

The museum's other major collection was donated by Edward Tuck in 1930. It's composed mainly of decorative artwork of the 18th century, including tapestries, heavily gilted furniture, wood-paneled salons, and porcelains, which give a good overview of French aesthetic sense at the time of the fall of the *ancien régime*.

A number of rooms are dedicated to 19th-century French painting, including a few works by major impressionists. The collection contains canvases by Courbet, Daumier, Corot, Delacroix, Manet, Sisley, Mary Cassatt (*Le Bain*), Maurice Denis, Odilon Redon, a series of portraits (one of Sarah Bernhardt by Clairin), and art by Edouard Vuillard and Pierre Bonnard. The 19th century, as you will have seen by now, is the best represented at the museum, which has a strong emphasis on the "academic school," especially the enormous compositions of Gustave Doré. Other important artists come from the symbolist school, including Osbert, whose *Soir Antique* is an important item in the collection. Notable paintings displayed include *The Death of Seneca* by David, *Portrait of Lalande* by Fragonard, and *Young Shepherd Holding a Flower* by Greuze. The museum also has sculptures by Rodin, Bourdelle, Maillol, and Carpeaux, and glassworks by Galle and Lalique.

La Grande Arche de la Défense. 1 place du parvis de la Défense, 18e. ☎ **01-49-07-27-57.** Admission 40 F ($8) adults, 30 F ($6) children 4–18, free for children 3 and under. Daily, year-round 10am–6pm. RER: La Défense.

Designed as the architectural centerpiece of the sprawling and futuristic satellite suburb of La Défense, this massive steel-and-masonry arch rises 35 stories from the pavement. Built with the blessing of the late President François Mitterrand, the deliberately overscale archway is the latest landmark to dot the Paris skyline. Though it's removed from the other sights listed above, it extends that magnificently engineered straight line that links the Louvre, the Arc du Carroussel, the Champs-Elysées, the Arc de Triomphe, avenue de la Grande Armée to place du Porte-Maillot. The arch is ringed with a circular avenue (*périphérique*), patterned after the one that winds around the more famous Arc de Triomphe. The monument is high enough to shelter the Cathedral of Notre-Dame below its heavily trussed canopy. An elevator carries visitors to an observation platform, where they get a view of the carefully planned geometry of the surrounding streets.

4 The Eiffel Tower & Environs

Everyone visits the landmark that has become the symbol of Paris. For maximum enjoyment, however, don't just rush to it right at once. Approach it gradually.

Take the Métro to place du Trocadéro, dominated by a statue of Marshal Foch. Once you've surfaced from the underground, you'll be at the gateway to the **Palais**

de Chaillot. Replacing the 1878 Palais du Trocadéro, the new palace was built in 1937 for the International Exhibition. If you have time, try to visit at least two of the three important museums lodged in the building: one a maritime showcase, another a gallery of reproductions of many of the monuments of France, a third devoted to people.

From the palace terrace (one writer called it "Mussolinian"), you have a panoramic view across the Seine to the Eiffel Tower. The **Jardins du Palais de Chaillot,** in back sweeping down to the Seine, are noted for their fountain displays. From April to October the gardens are a babel of international tongues.

✪ **La Tour Eiffel.** Champ-de-Mars, 7e. ☎ **01-44-11-23-23.** First landing 20 F ($4), second landing 40 F ($8), third landing 56 F ($11.20); stairs to second floor 12 F ($2.40). July–Aug, daily 9am–midnight; Sept–June, daily 9:30am–11pm (in fall and winter the stairs are open only until 6:30pm). Métro: Trocadéro, Ecole-Militaire, or Bir-Hakeim. RER: Champ-de-Mars–Tour Eiffel.

Except for perhaps the Leaning Tower of Pisa, this is the single most recognizable structure in the world. Weighing 7,000 tons but exerting about the same pressure on the ground as an average-size person sitting in a chair, the tower was never meant to be permanent. It was built for the Exhibition of 1889 by Gustave Alexandre Eiffel, the French engineer whose fame rested mainly on his iron bridges. (Incidentally, he also designed the framework for the Statue of Liberty.)

The tower, including its 55-foot television antenna, is 1,056 feet high. On a clear day you can see it from some 40 miles away. An open-framework construction, the tower unlocked the almost unlimited possibilities of steel construction, paving the way for the skyscrapers of the 20th century. Skeptics said it couldn't be built, and Eiffel actually wanted to make it soar higher than it did. For years it remained the tallest man-made structure on earth, until such skyscrapers as the Empire State Building usurped its record.

We could fill an entire page of this guide with nothing but statistics on this tower. The plans for it covered 6,000 square yards of paper, it weighs 7,000 tons, and contains $2^1/_2$ million rivets. But enough of that. Just stand underneath the tower and look straight up. It's like a rocket of steel lacework shooting into the sky. If nothing else, it's a fantastic engineering achievement.

Initially, artists and writers vehemently denounced it when it went up, although later generations sang its praises. People were fond of calling it names: "a giraffe," "the world's greatest lamppost," "the iron monster." Others suggested, "Let's keep art nouveau grounded." Nature lovers feared it would interfere with the flights of birds over Paris.

In the early 1890s the tower escaped destruction because it found a new practical use: the French government installed antennae on the tower, thus enabling wireless communications throughout the city.

Although the tower contains six different platforms, only the first, second, and fourth are bona-fide visiting sites acknowledged as such by the employees who administer them. The third level, while worthwhile for its view, functions mainly as a midway point en rout to the other levels, and levels five and six, which contain radio and telecommunications equipment, are strictly off-limits to the public.

Most visitors pay homage to the tower in three stages. Taking the elevator to the first landing, you have a view over the rooftops of Paris. On the first level, a cinema museum that shows films can be visited, and restaurants and a bar are open year round. The second landing provides a panoramic look at the city. The third and final stage, on the fourth platform, gives the most spectacular view, allowing you to identify monuments and buildings that are visible. On the ground level, in the eastern and western pillars, you can visit the 1899 elevator machinery when the tower is open.

Eiffel's office has been re-created on the fourth level; wax figures depict the engineer receiving Thomas Edison.

Of course, it's the view that most people come for, and this extends for 42 miles, theoretically. In practice, weather conditions tend to limit it. Nevertheless, it's fabulous, and the best time for visibility is about an hour before sunset.

Champ-de-Mars and Ecole Militaire. 7e. Métro: Trocadéro, Ecole-Militaire, or Bir-Hakeim.

Leave some time to explore the Champ-de-Mars, the gardens between the Eiffel Tower and the Military School. Traditionally, these gardens, laid out around 1770, were the World's Fair grounds of Paris, the scene of many a military parade.

Thanks in part to one of France's best-known mistresses, Madame de Pompadour, who persuaded the king to finance the project, the Ecole Militaire (Military School) was established; the plans were drawn up by A. J. Gabriel. This classical school was founded in 1751 for about 500 young men who wanted a military career.

Napoléon entered in 1784, the year his father died of cancer. He graduated a year later as a lieutenant, aged 16. According to accounts, he wasn't popular with his classmates, many of whom openly made fun of him. One wrote, "All boots, no man." Pity those creatures when their names came up for promotion years later. Another French general, Charles de Gaulle, also studied at the school. The Military School usually only grants special permission to enter to military bodies; apply in writing to the Général Commandant Militaire, Ecole Militaire, 13, place Joffre, 75007 Paris.

Hôtel des Invalides (Napoléon's Tomb). Place des Invalides, 7e. ☎ **01-44-42-37-72.** Admission 35 F ($7) adults, 25 F ($5) children 7–18 and seniors over 60, free for children 6 and under. The ticket, valid for 2 consecutive days, covers admission to the Musée de l'Armée, Napoléon's Tomb, and the Musée des Plans-Reliefs. Oct–Mar, daily 10am–5pm; Apr–Sept, daily 10am–6pm (Napoléon's tomb open until 7pm June–Aug). Closed Jan 1, May 1, Nov 1, Dec 25. Métro: Latour-Maubourg, Varenne, or Invalides.

It was the Sun King who decided to build the "hotel" to house soldiers who'd been disabled. It wasn't entirely a benevolent gesture, since these veterans had been injured, crippled, or blinded while fighting his battles. Louvois was ordered in 1670 to launch this massive building program. When it was completed—and Louis XIV was long dead—the corridors stretched for miles. Eventually the building was crowned by a gilded dome designed by Jules Hardouin-Mansart.

The Invalides is best approached by walking from the Right Bank across the turn-of-the-century Alexander III Bridge. In the building's cobblestone forecourt is a display of massive cannons—a formidable welcome.

Before rushing on to Napoléon's tomb, you may want to take the time to visit the greatest military museum in the world, the **Musée de l'Armée,** where the glory of the French army lives on. In 1794 a French inspector started collecting weapons, uniforms, and equipment, and with the continued accumulation of war material over the centuries, the museum has become a horrifying documentary of man's self-destruction. Viking swords, Burgundian bacinets, blunderbusses from the 14th century, Balkan khandjars, American Browning machine guns, war pitchforks, salamander-engraved Renaissance serpentines, "Haute Epoque" armor, a 1528 Griffon, musketoons, grenadiers . . . if it can kill, it's enshrined in a place of honor here. As a sardonic touch, there's even the wooden leg of General Daumesnil. The museum was looted by the Germans in 1940.

Among the outstanding acquisitions are the suits of armor—especially in the new so-called Arsenal—worn by the kings and dignitaries of France, including Louis XIV. The best-known one—the "armor suit of the lion"—was made for François I. Henri II ordered his suit engraved with the monogram of his mistress, Diane de Poitiers,

Attractions: 7th Arrondissement

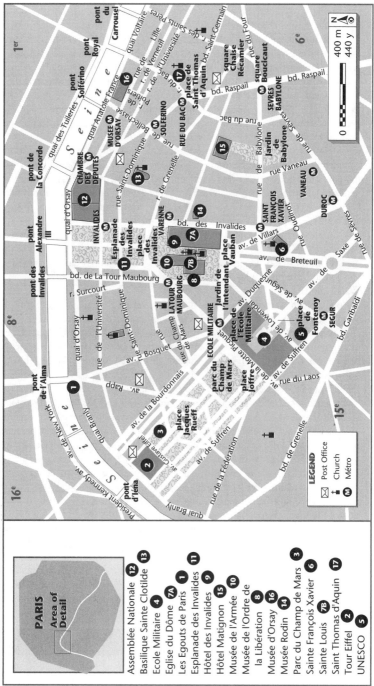

and (perhaps reluctantly) that of his wife, Catherine de Médicis. The showcases of swords are reputedly among the finest in the world.

The mementos of World War I, including those of American and Canadian soldiers, are especially interesting. Included is the Armistice Bugle, which sounded the cease-fire on November 7, 1918, before the general cease-fire on November 11, 1918.

And then there's that Corsican general who became France's greatest soldier. A plaster death mask by Antommarchi is one of the most notable pieces on display. So, too, an oil by Delaroche, painted at the time of Napoléon's first banishment (April 1814), which depicted him as he probably looked, paunch and all. In the rooms relating to the First Empire are displayed Napoléon's field bed with his tent. In the room devoted to the Restoration, the 100 Days, and Waterloo, you can see Napoléon's reconstituted bedroom at the time of his death on St. Helena. On the more personal side, you can view Vizir, a horse he owned (stuffed), as well as a saddle he used mainly for state ceremonies. The Turenne Salon contains other souvenirs of Napoléon, including the hat he wore at Eylau, his sword from his victory at Austerlitz, and his "Flag of Farewell" which he kissed before departing for Elba.

The Salle Orientale in the west wing shows arms of the Eastern world, including Asia and the Muslim countries of the Mideast, from the 16th to the 19th century. Turkish armor (see Bajazet's helmet) and weapons, and Chinese and Japanese armor and swords, are on display. Moreover, the west wing houses exhibits on World Wars I and II.

You can gain access to the **Musée des Plans-Reliefs** through the west wing. This unique collection shows French towns and monuments done in scale models.

A walk across the Court of Honor delivers you to the **Eglise du Dôme (Church of the Dome),** designed by Hardouin-Mansart for Louis XIV. The great architect began work on the church in 1677, although he died before its completion. The dome is the second-tallest monument in Paris. The hearse used at the emperor's funeral on May 9, 1821, is in the Napoléon Chapel.

To accommodate the **Tomb of Napoléon,** the architect Visconti had to redesign the high altar in 1842. First buried on St. Helena, Napoléon's remains were returned to Paris in 1840, as Louis-Philippe had demanded of England. The triumphal funeral procession passed under the Arc de Triomphe, down the Champs-Elysées, en route to the Invalides, as snow swirled through the air.

The tomb is made of red Finnish porphyry, the base from green granite. Napoléon's remains were locked away inside six coffins. Surrounding the tomb are a dozen amazonlike figures representing his victories. Almost lampooning the smallness of the man, everything is done on a gargantuan scale. You'd think a real giant was buried here, not a symbolic one. In his coronation robes, the statue of Napoléon stands 8$\frac{1}{2}$ feet high. The grave of Napoléon's son, "the King of Rome," lies at his feet.

Napoléon's tomb is surrounded by those of his brother, Joseph Bonaparte; the great Vauban; Foch, the Allied commander in World War I; Turenne; and La Tour d'Auvergne, the first grenadier of the republic (actually, only his heart is entombed here).

5 Montparnasse

For the "lost generation," life centered around the literary cafés of Montparnasse. Hangouts such as Dôme, Coupole, Rotonde, and the Select became legendary. Artists, especially American expatriates, turned their backs on Montmartre, dismissing it as too touristy.

Montparnasse

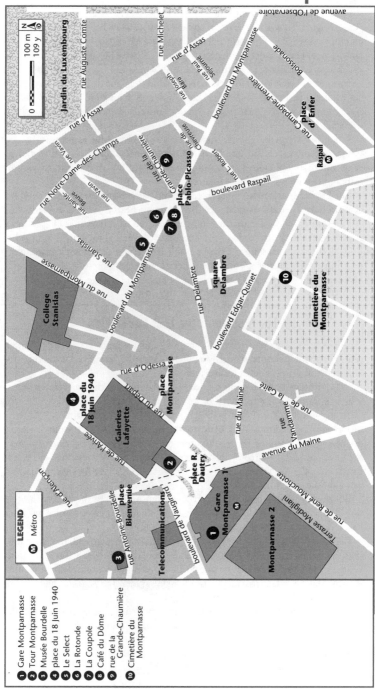

LÉGEND

Ⓜ Métro

1 Gare Montparnasse
2 Tour Montparnasse
3 Musée Bourdelle
4 place du 18 Juin 1940
5 Le Select
6 La Rotonde
7 La Coupole
8 Café du Dôme
9 rue de la Grande-Chaumière
10 Cimetière du Montparnasse

Picasso, Modigliani, and Man Ray came this way, and Hemingway was also a popular figure. So was Fitzgerald when he was poor (when he was in the chips, you'd find him at the Ritz). William Faulkner, Archibald MacLeish, Isadora Duncan, Miró, James Joyce, Ford Madox Ford, even Trotsky—all were here.

All, that is, except for Gertrude Stein, who would not frequent the cafés. To see her, you had to wait for an invitation to her salon at 27 rue de Fleurus. She bestowed her favor on Sherwood Anderson, Elliot Paul, and, for a time, Hemingway. However, Papa found that there wasn't "much future in men being friends with great women."

When not receiving guests, Miss Stein was busy buying paintings—works by Cézanne, Renoir, Matisse, and Picasso. One writer said that her salon was engaged in an international conspiracy to promote modern art. At her Saturday-evening gatherings you might have met Braque.

The life of Montparnasse still centers around its cafés and exotic nightclubs, many of them only a shadow of what they used to be. Its heart is at the crossroads of boulevard Raspail and boulevard du Montparnasse, one of the settings of *The Sun Also Rises*. Hemingway wrote that "the boulevard Raspail always made dull riding." Rodin's controversial statue of Balzac swathed in a large cape stands guard over the prostitutes who cluster around the pedestal. Balzac seems to be the only one in Montparnasse who doesn't feel the impact of time and change.

The Mother of the Lost Generation

"So Paris was the place that suited those of us that were to create the twentieth century art and literature, naturally enough." Gertrude Stein, who made this pronouncement, wasn't known for her modesty.

In the 1920s she and her lover, Alice B. Toklas, became the most famous expatriates in Paris. To get an invitation to call on Lovey and Pussy (nicknames for Gertrude and Alice) at 27 rue de Fleurus, in the heart of Montparnasse, was to be invited into the innermost circle of expatriate Paris. Though Gertrude didn't achieve popular success until the 1933 publication of her *Autobiography of Alice B. Toklas,* she was known and adored by many members of the Lost Generation—all except Ernest Hemingway, who later turned on her, libeling her in *A Moveable Feast,* which was published posthumously.

But to the young sensitive men, arriving from America in the 1920s, La Stein was "The Mother of Us All." These young fans hung on her every word, while Alice baked her notorious hash brownies in the kitchen.

On rue de Fleurus, Gertrude and Alice lived in a world filled with modern paintings, including a nude by Vallotton, and pieces by Toulouse-Lautrec, Picasso, Gauguin, and Matisse. Gertrude paid $1,000 for her first Matisse, $30 for her first Picasso. Matisse, in fact, first met Picasso at Stein's studio. The Saturday-night soirées here became a Montparnasse legend.

Not all visitors came to worship. Gertrude was denounced by many, including avant-garde magazines of the time, which called her a "fraud, egomaniac, and publicity seeking." Braque called her claim to influence art in Paris "nonsense."

In spite of the attacks, the jokes, and the lurid speculation, Stein, at least in public, kept her ego intact. Bernard Fay once told her he'd met three people in his life who ranked as geniuses: Gide, Picasso, and Stein herself.

"Why include Gide?" Stein asked.

6 The Latin Quarter

The University of Paris (the Sorbonne) lies on the Left Bank in the 5th arrondissement—this is where students meet and fall in love over coffee and croissants. Rabelais called it the Quartier Latin, because of the students and professors who spoke Latin in the classroom and on the streets. The neighborhood teems with belly dancers, exotic restaurants (from Vietnamese to Balkan), sidewalk cafés, bookstalls, *caveaux* (basement nightclubs), and assorted street characters.

A good starting point for your tour is **place St-Michel** (Métro: Pont-St-Michel), where Balzac used to get water from the fountain when he was a youth. This center was the scene of much Resistance fighting in the summer of 1944. The quarter centers around **boulevard St-Michel,** to the south (the students call it "Boul Mich").

From place St-Michel, with your back to the Seine, you can cut left down **rue de la Huchette,** the setting of Elliot Paul's *The Last Time I Saw Paris.* Paul first wandered into this typical street "on a soft summer evening, and entirely by chance," in 1923. Although much has changed since his time, some of the buildings are so old they often have to be propped up by timbers. Paul captured the spirit of the street more evocatively than anyone, writing of "the delivery wagons, makeshift vehicles propelled by pedaling boys, pushcarts of itinerant vendors, knife-grinders, umbrella menders, a herd of milk goats, and the neighborhood pedestrians." (The local bordello has closed, however.)

Branching off from Huchette is **rue du Chat-Qui-Pêche** (the "Street of the Cat Who Fishes"), said to be the shortest, narrowest street in the world, containing not one door and only a handful of windows. It's usually filled with garbage or lovers . . . or both.

Musée National du Moyen Age / Thermes de Cluny (Musée de Cluny). 6 place Paul-Painlevé, 5e. ☎ **01-43-25-62-00.** Admission 28 F ($5.60) adults, 18 F ($3.60) ages 18–25, free for children 17 and under. Wed–Mon 9:15am–5:45pm. Métro: Cluny-Sorbonne.

You stand in the cobblestoned Court of Honor, admiring the flamboyant Gothic building with its clinging vines, turreted walls, gargoyles, and dormers with seashell motifs. Along with the Hôtel de Sens in Le Marais, the Hôtel de Cluny is all that remains of domestic medieval architecture in Paris. Originally the Cluny was the mansion—built over and beside the ruins of a Roman bath—of a rich 15th-century abbot. By 1515 it was the residence of Mary Tudor, teenage widow of Louis XII and daughter of Henry VII of England and Elizabeth of York.

Seized during the Revolution, the Cluny was rented in 1833 to Alexandre du Sommerard, who adorned it with his collection of medieval works of art. Upon his death in 1842, both the building and the collection were bought back by the government.

The present-day collection of arts and crafts of the Middle Ages is the finest in the world. Most people come primarily to see the **Unicorn Tapestries,** the most acclaimed tapestries in the world. A beautiful princess and her handmaiden, beasts of prey, and just plain pets—all the romance of the age of chivalry lives on in these remarkable yet mysterious tapestries. They were discovered only a century ago in the Château de Boussac in Limousin. Five seem to deal with the five senses (one, for example, depicts a unicorn looking into a mirror held up by a dour-faced maiden). The sixth shows a woman under an elaborate tent with jewels, her pet dog resting on an embroidered cushion beside her, the lovable unicorn and his friendly companion, a lion, holding back the flaps. The background in red and green forms a rich carpet of spring flowers, fruit-laden trees, birds, rabbits, donkeys, dogs, goats, lambs, and monkeys.

The other exhibitions are wide-ranging, including several Flemish retables; a 14th-century Sienese (life-size) John the Baptist and other Italian sculptures; statues from the Sainte Chapelle, dating from 1243 to 1248; 12th- and 13th-century crosses, studded with gems; and golden chalices, manuscripts, ivory carvings, vestments, leatherwork, jewelry, coins, a 13th-century Adam, and heads and fragments of statues from Notre-Dame de Paris recently discovered. In the fan-vaulted medieval chapel hang tapestries depicting scenes from the life of St. Stephen.

Downstairs are the ruins of the Roman baths, dating supposedly from around A.D. 200. You wander through a display of Gallic and Roman sculptures. A votive pillar dates from the days of Tiberius.

The Sorbonne. Bd. St-Michel. Métro: St-Michel.

The University of Paris—everybody calls it the Sorbonne—is one of the most famous institutions in the world. Founded in the 13th century, by 100 years later it had become the most prestigious university in the West, drawing such professors as Thomas Aquinas. Reorganized by Napoléon in 1806, today the Sorbonne is the premier university of France.

At first glance from place de la Sorbonne, it seems architecturally undistinguished. In truth, it was rather indiscriminately reconstructed at the turn of the century. Not so the **Church of the Sorbonne,** built in 1653 by Le Mercier, which contains the marble tomb of Cardinal Richelieu, a work by Girardon based on a design by Le Brun. At his feet, the statue *Science in Tears* is remarkable.

The Panthéon. Place du Panthéon, 5e. ☎ **01-43-54-34-51.** Admission 32 F ($6.40) adults, 21 F ($4.20) ages 18–25, 15 F ($3) children 12–17, free for children 11 and under. Apr–Sept, daily 9:30am–6:30pm; Oct–Mar, daily 9:30am–6:15pm. Métro: Cardinal-Lemoine or Maubert-Mutualité.

Some of the most famous men in the history of France (Victor Hugo, for one) are buried here in austere grandeur, on the crest of the mount of St. Geneviève. In 1744 Louis XV made a vow that if he recovered from a mysterious illness, he would build a church to replace the decayed Abbey of St. Geneviève. Well, he recovered. Madame de Pompadour's brother hired Soufflot for the job. He designed the church in 1764, in the form of a Greek cross, with a dome reminiscent of that of St. Paul's Cathedral in London. When Soufflot died, the work was carried out by his pupil, Rondelet, who completed the structure 9 years after his master's death.

After the Revolution, the church was converted into a "Temple of Fame"—ultimately a pantheon for the great men of France. The body of Mirabeau was buried here, although his remains were later removed. Likewise, Marat was only a temporary tenant. However, Voltaire's body was exhumed and placed here—and allowed to remain.

In the 19th century the building changed roles so many times—first a church, then a pantheon, then a church—that it was hard to keep its function straight. After Victor Hugo was buried here, it became a pantheon once more. Other notable men entombed within include Jean-Jacques Rousseau, Soufflot, Emile Zola, and Louis Braille.

The finest frescoes—the Puvis de Chavannes—are found at the end of the left wall before you enter the crypt. One illustrates St. Geneviève bringing supplies to relieve the victims of the famine. The very best fresco depicts her white-draped head looking out over moonlit medieval Paris, the city whose patroness she became.

Attractions: 5th & 6th Arrondissements

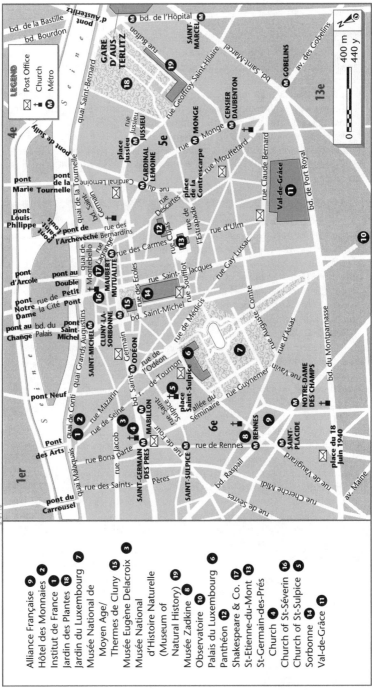

Alliance Française **9**
Hôtel des Monnaies **2**
Institut de France **1**
Jardin des Plantes **18**
Musée National de Luxembourg **7**
Musée National de Moyen Age/ Thermes de Cluny **15**
Musée Eugène Delacroix **3**
Musée National d'Histoire Naturelle (Museum of Natural History) **19**
Musée Zadkine **8**
Observatoire **10**
Palais du Luxembourg **6**
Panthéon **12**
Shakespeare & Co. **17**
St-Etienne-du-Mont **13**
St-Germain-des-Prés Church **4**
Church of St-Séverin **16**
Church of St-Sulpice **5**
Sorbonne **14**
Val-de-Grâce **11**

Church of St-Séverin. Rue des Prêtres, 5e. ☎ **01-43-25-93-63.** Free admission. Daily 11am–7:30pm. Métro: St-Michel or Maubert-Mutualité.

This flamboyant Gothic church, named for the 6th-century recluse St. Séverin, lies just a short walk from the Seine. Given to Paris in the 11th century by Henri I, it slowly began to adopt some of the architectural features of Notre-Dame, located across the river.

It was originally built from 1210 to 1230, and then it was reconstructed in 1458. The tower was completed in 1487, the chapels between 1498 and 1520. Hardouin-Mansart designed the Chapel of the Communion in 1673 when he was 27 years old.

Before entering, walk around the church to examine its gargoyles, birds of prey, and reptilian monsters projecting from the top. To the right, facing the church, is the "garden of ossuaries" of the 15th century. Inside St-Séverin, the stained glass is a stunning adornment.

7 Les Halles District

In the 19th century Zola called it "the underbelly of Paris." For eight centuries Les Halles was the major wholesale fruit, meat, and vegetable market of Paris. The smock-clad vendors, the carcasses of beef, the baskets of what many regarded as the most appetizing fresh vegetables in the world—all that belongs to the past. Today the action has moved to the steel-and-glass contemporary structure at Rungis, a suburb near Orly Airport. The original edifice, Baltard's old zinc-roofed Second Empire "umbrellas of iron," has been torn down.

Replacing these so-called umbrellas is **Les Forum des Halles,** 1er, which opened in 1979 (Métro: Les Halles; RER: Châtelet–Les Halles). This large complex, much of it underground, contains dozens of shops, plus several restaurants and movie theaters. Many of the shops aren't as good as one would wish, but others contain a wide display of merchandise that has made the complex popular with both residents and visitors alike.

For many tourists a night on the town is still capped by the traditional bowl of onion soup at Les Halles, usually at Au Pied de Cochon ("Pig's Foot") or at Au Chien Qui Fume ("Smoking Dog"), in the wee hours. One of the most classic scenes of Paris was night-owling tourists or elegantly dressed Parisians (many just released from Maxim's) standing at a bar drinking cognac with bloody butchers. Some writers have suggested that one Gérard de Nerval introduced the custom of frequenting Les Halles at such an unearthly hour. (De Nerval was a 19th-century poet whose life was considered "irregular." He hanged himself in 1855.)

A newspaper correspondent described the market scene today this way: "Les Halles is trying to stay alive as one of the few places in Paris where one can eat at any hour of the night."

Church of St-Eustache. 2 rue du Jour, 1er. ☎ **01-42-36-31-05.** Free admission. Mon–Sat 9am–7pm, Sun 9am–12:30pm and 3–7pm. Métro: Les Halles.

In our opinion, this mixed Gothic and Renaissance church completed in 1637 is rivaled only by Notre-Dame. It took nearly a century to build. Madame de Pompadour and Richelieu were baptized here, and Molière's funeral was held here in 1673. The church has been known for its organ recitals ever since Liszt played here in 1866. Inside is the black-marble tomb of Jean-Baptiste Colbert, the minister of state under Louis XIV. On top of his tomb is a marble statue of the statesman flanked by statues of *Abundance* by Coysevox and *Fidelity* by J. B. Tuby. There's a side entrance to the church on rue Rambuteau.

> ## ❓ Did You Know?
>
> - The world's oldest "grocery store," Les Halles moved in 1969—its first reloca-tion in eight centuries.
> - Rising 981 feet, the Eiffel Tower was the tallest edifice in the world in 1889.
> - Place Denfert-Rochereau, an old burial ground, was once called place d'Enfer, or the "Square of Hell"—it was stacked with millions of bones from old charnel houses to conserve space in 1785.
> - On the narrow Seine island Allée des Cygnes stands a smaller version of the Statue of Liberty.
> - At the end of the 18th century, place de Charles de Gaulle–Etoile was the world's first organized traffic circle.
> - Pont-Neuf (New Bridge) isn't new at all. Dating from 1607, it's the oldest and most famous bridge in Paris.
> - The Sorbonne began in 1253 as modest lodgings for 16 theology students who pursued their education on the site of the present-day University of Paris.
> - In 1938 workmen discovered 3,350 22-karat gold coins weighing 1.3 grams each while digging at 51 rue Mouffetard. An accompanying note said they belonged to Louis Nivelle, royal counselor to Louis XV, who mysteriously disappeared in 1757.

8 St-Germain-des-Prés

This was the postwar home of existentialism, associated with Jean-Paul Sartre, Simone de Beauvoir, Albert Camus, and an intellectual, bohemian crowd that gathered at the Café de Flore, the Brasserie Lipp, and Les Deux-Magots. Among them, the black-clad poet Juliette Greco was known as *la muse de St-Germain-des-Prés,* and to Sartre she was the woman who had "millions of poems in her throat." Her long hair, black slacks, black sweater, and black sandals launched a fashion trend adopted by young women from Paris to California.

In the 1950s new names appeared, like Françoise Sagan, Gore Vidal, and James Baldwin, but by the 1960s the tourists were just as firmly entrenched at the Café de Flore and Deux-Magots. Today St-Germain-des-Prés retains a bohemian and intel-lectually stimulating street life, full of many interesting bookshops, art galleries, *cave* (basement) nightclubs, and bistros and coffeehouses—as well as two historic churches.

Just a short walk from the Delacroix museum, **rue Visconti** was obviously designed for pushcarts and is worth a stroll today. At no. 17 is the maison where Balzac established his printing press in 1825. (The venture ended in bankruptcy—which forced the author back to his writing desk.) In the 17th century the French drama-tist Jean-Baptiste Racine lived across the street. Such celebrated actresses as Champ-meslé and Clairon were also in residence.

Church of St-Germain-des-Prés. 3 place St-Germain-des-Prés, 6e. ☎ **01-43-25-41-71.** Free admission. Daily 8am–7:30pm. Métro: St-Germain-des-Prés.

Outside it's an early 17th-century town house, and a handsome one at that. But beneath that exterior it's one of the oldest churches in Paris, dating back to the 6th century when a Benedictine abbey was founded on the site by Childebert, son of Clovis, the "creator of France." Unfortunately, the marble columns in the triforium

Attractions: St-Germain-des-Prés

1. Musée d'Orsay
2. Palais de la Légion d'Honneur
3. 2 rue de l'Université
4. Brasserie Lipp
5. Café de Flore
6. Deux-Magots
7. St-Germain-des-Prés Church
8. Place de Furstemberg
9. Musée Eugène Delacroix
10. rue Visconti
11. Ecole des Beaux-Arts
12. Buci Market
13. Cour du Commerce St-André
14. Le Procope
15. carrefour de l'Odéon
16. Galerie Regine Lussan
17. Théâtre de l'Odéon
18. Marché St-Germain
19. Church of St-Sulpice
20. rue Férou
21. Palais du Luxembourg
22. Jardin du Luxembourg

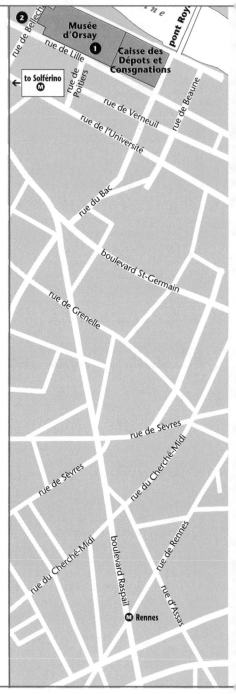

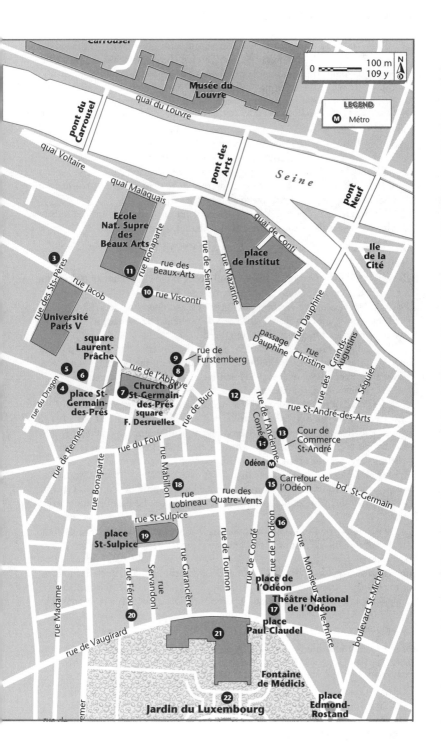

201

are all that remains from that period. At one time the abbey was a pantheon for Merovingian kings. Restoration of St. Symphorien Chapel, which is the site of the Merovingian tombs, at the entrance of the church, began in 1981. During that work, unknown Romanesque paintings were discovered on the triumphal arch of the chapel, making it one of the most interesting places of old Christian Paris.

Its Romanesque tower, topped by a 19th-century spire, is the most enduring landmark in the village of St-Germain-des-Prés. Its church bells, however, are hardly noticed by the patrons of Deux-Magots across the way.

The Normans nearly destroyed the abbey at least four times. The present building, the work of four centuries, has a Romanesque-style nave and a Gothic-style choir with fine capitals. Among the people interred at the church are Descartes and Jean-Casimir, the king of Poland who abdicated his throne.

When you leave St-Germain-des-Prés Church, just turn right onto rue de l'Abbaye and have a look at the 17th-century **Palais Abbatial,** a pink palace.

Church of St-Sulpice. Rue St-Sulpice, 6e. ☎ **01-46-33-21-78.** Free admission. Daily 7:30am–7:30pm. Métro: St-Sulpice.

Pause first on the 18th-century **place St-Sulpice.** On the 1844 fountain by Visconti are sculpted likenesses of four 18th-century bishops: Fenelon, Massillon, Bossuet, and Flechier. Napoléon, then a general, was given a stag dinner there in 1799. He liked the banquet but not the square. When he was promoted he changed it. One of the two towers of the church was never completed.

Work originally began on the church in 1646; the neoclassic facade was completed in 1745. Many architects, including Le Vau, worked on the building. Some were summarily fired; others, such as the Florentine Servandoni, were discredited.

One of the most notable treasures inside the 360-foot-long church is Servandoni's rococo Chapel of the Madonna, with a marble statue of the Virgin by Pigalle. One critic wrote that you'd have to go to Versailles to find a peer of that chapel. The church contains one of the world's largest organs, with more than 6,500 pipes. The Sunday mass concerts—made known by Charles Widor—draw many visitors. Chalgrin designed the organ case in the 18th century.

One of the largest and most prestigious churches in Paris, St. Sulpice was sacked during the Revolution and converted into the Temple of Victory. Camille Desmoulins, the revolutionary who sparked the raid on the Bastille, was married here.

But the real reason you come to St. Sulpice is to see the **Delacroix frescoes** in the Chapel of the Angels (first on your right as you enter). Seek out his muscular Jacob wrestling (or is he dancing?) with an effete angel. On the ceiling St. Michael is having his own troubles with the Devil, and yet another mural depicts Heliodorus being driven from the temple. Painted in the final years of his life, the frescoes were a high point in the career of the baffling, romantic Delacroix. If you're impressed by Delacroix, you can pay him a belated tribute by visiting the Delacroix museum previewed below.

Musée Eugène-Delacroix. 6 place de Furstenberg,6e. ☎ **01-43-54-04-87.** Admission 15 F ($3) adults, 10 F ($2) ages 18–25 and over 60, free for children 17 and under. Wed–Mon 9:30am–5pm. Closed holidays. Métro: St-Germain-des-Prés.

To art historians, Delacroix is something of an enigma. Even his parentage is a mystery. Many believed that Talleyrand had the privilege of fathering him. The Frank Anderson Trapp biography saw him "as an isolated and atypical individualist—one who respected traditional values, yet emerged as the embodiment of Romantic revolt."

By visiting his atelier, you'll see one of the most charming squares on the Left Bank and also the romantic garden of the museum. You reach the studio through a large arch on a stone courtyard.

Delacroix died in this apartment on August 13, 1863. This is no poor artist's shabby studio, but the very tasteful creation of a solidly established man. Sketches, lithographs, watercolors, and oils are hung throughout, and a few personal mementos remain, including a lovely mahogany paint box.

Note: To see the work that earned Delacroix his niche in art history, go to the Louvre for such passionate paintings as his *Liberty Leading the People on the Barricades,* or to the nearby Church of St-Sulpice (Métro: Mabillon) for the famed fresco *Jacob Wrestling with the Angel,* among others.

9 Le Marais

When Paris began to overflow the confines of the Ile de la Cité in the 13th century, the citizenry settled in Le Marais, the marsh that used to be flooded regularly by the high-rising Seine. By the 17th century the Marais had reached the pinnacle of fashion, becoming the center of aristocratic Paris. At that time many of its great mansions—many now restored or still being spruced up today—were built by the finest craftsmen in France.

In the 18th and 19th centuries, fashion deserted the Marais for the expanding Faubourg St-Germain and Faubourg St-Honoré. Industry eventually took over, and the once-elegant hotels were turned into tenements. There was talk of demolishing this seriously blighted neighborhood, but in 1962 the alarmed Comité de Sauvegarde du Marais banded together and saved the historic district.

Today the 17th-century mansions are fashionable once again. The *International Herald Tribune* called this area the latest refuge of the Paris artisan fleeing from the tourist-trampled St-Germain-des-Prés. The "marsh" sprawls across the 3rd and 4th arrondissements bounded by the grands boulevards, rue du Temple, place des Vosges, and the Seine.

The neighborhood has become the center of gay life in Paris, and is a great place for an afternoon of window-shopping in funky, chic boutiques, up-and-coming galleries, and more.

Place de la Bastille. 11e–12e. Métro: Place de la Bastille.

Here, on July 14, 1789, a mob of people attacked the Bastille and so began the French Revolution. Now nothing remains of the historic Bastille, built in 1369—it was completely torn down. A symbol of despotism, it once contained eight towers, rising 100 feet high. Many prisoners—some sentenced by Louis XIV for "witchcraft"—were kept inside its walls, the best known being "The Man in the Iron Mask." And yet, when the fortress was stormed by the revolutionary mob, only seven prisoners were discovered. (The Marquis de Sade had been transferred to the madhouse 10 days earlier.) The authorities had discussed razing it anyway, so in itself, the attack meant nothing. What it symbolized, however, and what it started will never be forgotten. Bastille Day is celebrated with great festivity each July 14.

The Colonne de Juillet memorializes the victims of the July Revolution of 1830, which marked the fall of Charles X.

To honor the bicentennial of the revolution in 1989, the government built the 3,000-seat **Opéra Bastille** on the south side of the square. Opened in 1990, the Opéra has five moving stages. The launching of this cultural center, along with major restoration of the area, has turned the formerly dreary Bastille area into a chic neighborhood.

From place de la Bastille, head up rue St-Antoine; turn right on rue des Tournelles, with its statue honoring Beaumarchais (author of *The Barber of Seville*). Take a left again onto Pas-de-la-Mule, "the footsteps of the mule," which will carry you to place des Vosges.

Place des Vosges. 4e. Métro: St-Paul or Chemin-Vert.

It's the oldest square in Paris and was once the most fashionable. Right in the heart of the Marais, it was called the Palais Royal in the days of Henri IV. The king planned to live here, but his assassin, Ravaillac, had other plans in mind for him. Henry II was killed while jousting on the square in 1559, in the shadow of the Hôtel des Tournelles. His widow, Catherine de Médicis, had the place torn down.

Place des Vosges, once the major dueling ground of Europe, is one of the first planned squares in the continent. Its *grand-siècle* rosy-red brick houses are ornamented with white stone. The covered arcades allowed people to shop at all times, even in the rain—quite an innovation at the time. In the 18th century chestnut trees were added, sparking a controversy that continues to this day: Critics say that the addition spoils the perspective.

Over the years the famous and infamous passed this way: Descartes, Pascal, Cardinal Richelieu, the courtesan Marion Delorme, Gautier, Daudet, and the most famous letter writer of all time, Madame de Sévigné, lived here. But its best-known occupant was Victor Hugo (his home, now a museum, is the only house that can be visited without a private invitation). The great writer could be seen rushing under the arcades of the square to a rendezvous with his mistress. In the center of the square is a statue of Louis XIII on horseback.

Maison de Victor Hugo. 6 place des Vosges, 3e. ☎ **01-42-72-10-16.** Admission 17.50 F ($3.50) adults, 9 F ($1.80) children 8–18, free for children 7 and under. Tues–Sun 10am–5:40pm. Closed national holidays. Métro: St-Paul, Bastille, or Chemin-Vert.

Appraisals of Hugo have been varied. Some have called him a genius. Cocteau said he was a madman, and an American composer discovered that in the folly of his dotage he carved furniture—with his teeth! From 1832 to 1848 the novelist and poet lived on the second floor at 6 place des Vosges, in the old Hôtel Rohan Guéménée, built in 1610 on what was then place Royale. His maison is owned by the city of Paris, which has taken over two additional floors.

A leading figure in the French Romantic movement, Hugo is known for such novels as *The Hunchback of Notre Dame* and *Les Misérables*. The museum owns some of Hugo's furniture as well as pieces that once belonged to Juliette Drouet, the mistress with whom he lived in exile on Guernsey, one of the Channel Islands.

Worth the visit are Hugo's drawings, more than 450, illustrating scenes from his own works. Mementos of the great writer abound: Samples of his handwriting, his inkwell, and first editions of his works. A painting of his funeral procession at the Arc de Triomphe in 1885 is on display. Portraits and souvenirs of Hugo's family are also plentiful. Of the furnishings, especially interesting is a chinoiserie salon. The collection even contains Daumier caricatures and a bust of Hugo by David d'Angers, which—when compared to Rodin's—looks saccharine.

Hôtel Carnavalet. 23 rue de Sévigné, 3e. ☎ **01-42-72-21-13.** Admission 27 F ($5.40) adults, 14.50 F ($2.90) students under age 25, free for children 17 and under and for seniors over 60. Tues–Sun 10am–5:40pm. Métro: St-Paul or Chemin-Vert.

At the Hôtel Carnavalet (now also referred to as the Musée Carnavalet), the history of Paris comes alive in intimately personal terms—right down to the chessmen

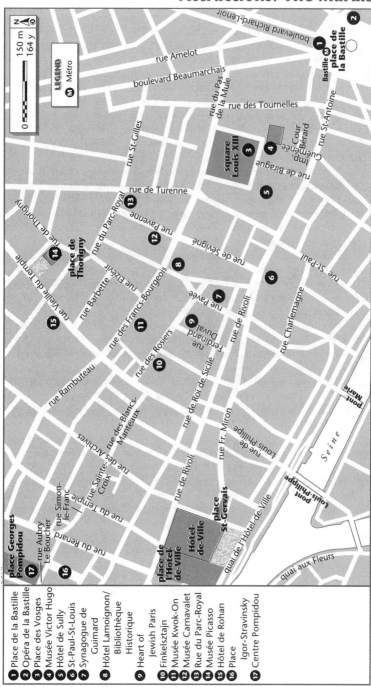

1. Place de la Bastille
2. Opéra de la Bastille
3. Place des Vosges
4. Musée Victor Hugo
5. Hôtel de Sully
6. St-Paul-St-Louis
7. Synagogue de Guimard
8. Hôtel Lamoignon/ Bibliothèque Historique
9. Heart of Jewish Paris
10. Finkelsztajn
11. Musée Kwok-On
12. Musée Carnavalet
13. Rue du Parc-Royal
14. Musée Picasso
15. Hôtel de Rohan
16. Place
17. Igor-Stravinsky
    Centre Pompidou

Louis XVI used to distract his mind in the days before he went to the guillotine. A renowned Renaissance palace, it was built in 1544 by Pierre Lescot and Jean Goujon; later it was acquired by Madame de Carnavalet. The great François Mansart transformed it between the years 1655 and 1661.

But it's probably best known because one of history's most famous letter writers, Madame de Sévigné, moved into the house in 1677. Fanatically devoted to her daughter (she ended up having to move in with her because she couldn't bear their separation), she poured out nearly every detail of her life in letters, virtually ignoring her son. A native of the Marais district, she died at her daughter's château in 1696. It wasn't until 1866 that the city of Paris acquired the mansion, eventually turning it into a museum.

Many salons depict events related to the Revolution: a bust of Marat, a portrait of Danton, and a model replica of the Bastille (one painting shows its demolition), for example. Another salon is devoted exclusively to the story of the captivity of the royal family at the Temple, including the bed in which Madame Elizabeth slept. The exercise book of the dauphin is there—the pathetic legacy he left the world before his mysterious disappearance.

There is much to see: The Bouvier collection on the first floor, façades of old apothecary shops, extensive wrought-iron works, a bust of Napoléon by Charles-Louis Corbet, a Cazals portrait of Paul Verlaine that makes him look like Lenin, Jean Beraud's parade of 19th-century opulence, and Baron François Gérard's painting of Madame Récamier—lounging, of course.

One room is crammed with signposts from the 17th and 18th centuries, designed to let the illiterate know what was in store—a tree indicated a carpenter's workshop and a pig was the symbol for a butcher's shop. An entire jewelry shop designed by Mucha in 1900 is installed here.

Exhibits continue at the Hôtel le Pelletier de St-Fargeau, across the courtyard. On display is furniture from the Louis XIV period to the early 20th century. Here, too, is a replica of Marcel Proust's cork-lined bedroom with his actual furniture, including his brass bed.

Musée de la Chasse (Hunting Museum). 60 rue des Archives, 3e. ☎ **01-42-72-86-43**. Admission 25 F ($5) adults, 12.50 F ($2.50) students and seniors, 5 F ($1) children 5–16, free for children 4 and under. Wed–Mon 10am–12:30pm and 1:30–5:30pm. Métro: Rambuteau or Hôtel-de-Ville.

Near the Hôtel Carnavalet, the Hôtel Guénégaud—also built by François Mansart—has been restored and turned into the Musée de la Chasse by the Sommer Foundation. Photographs at the entrance depict the shocking state of the building's decay before its subsequent restoration.

Mounted heads are plentiful, ranging from the antelope to the elephant, from the bushbuck to the waterbuck, from the moose to the "bush pig." Rembrandt's sketch of a lion is here, along with a collection of wild-animal portraits by Desportes (1661–1743). The hunt tapestries are outstanding and often amusing—one a cannibalistic romp, another showing a helmeted man standing eye to eye with a bear he's stabbing to death. The rifles, some inlaid with pearls, others engraved with ivory, are exceptional, many dating from the 17th century. The museum also displays other historic weapons, along with a remarkable collection of paintings, including works by Rubens, Breughel, Oudry, Chardin, and Corot.

Musée de l'Histoire de France. 60 rue des Francs-Bourgeois, 3e. ☎ **01-40-27-60-96**. Admission 15 F ($3) adults, 10 F ($2) children and seniors. Wed–Mon 1:45–5:45pm. Métro: Hôtel-de-Ville or Rambuteau.

A short walk from the hunting museum takes you to this Paris landmark, steeped in French history.

On Napoléon's orders, the Palais Soubise was made the official records depository of France. But the building, designed by the much-underrated Delamair, is as fascinating as—or even more so than—the exhibits inside. Apartments that once belonged to the prince and princess de Soubise have been turned into the Musée de l'Histoire de France.

You enter through the colonnaded Court of Honor. Before going inside, walk around the corner to 58 rue des Archives to the medieval turreted gateway to the original Clisson mansion. (The Clisson mansion gave way to the residence of the dukes of Guise, who owned the property until it was purchased by the Soubise family. The princess de Soubise was once the mistress of Louis XIV, and apparently the Sun King was very generous, giving her the funds to remodel and redesign the palace.)

The archives contain documents that go back to Charlemagne and even earlier. The letter collection is highly valued, exhibiting the penmanship of Marie Antoinette (a farewell letter), Louis XVI (his will), Danton, Robespierre, Napoléon I, and Joan of Arc. The museum possesses the only known sketch made of the maid from Orléans while she was still alive. Even the jailer's keys to the old Bastille are found here.

In 1735 Germain Boffrand designed a Salon Ovale, with *parfaites* (faultless) *expressions,* for a much later princess de Soubise. Adding to the lush decor, the gilt, and the crystal are paintings by Van Loo, Boucher, and Natoire.

10 Montmartre

Soft white three-story houses, slender, barren trees sticking up from the ground like giant toothpicks—that's how Utrillo, befogged by absinthe, saw Montmartre. On the other side of the canvas, Toulouse-Lautrec brush-stroked it as a district of cabarets, circus performers, and prostitutes. Today Montmartre remains truer to the dwarfish artist's conception than it does to that of Utrillo.

From the 1880s to the years preceding World War I, Montmartre enjoyed its golden age as the world's best-known art colony. *La vie de bohème* reigned supreme. At one time the artistic battle in La Butte was the talk of the art world. There was, for one, the bold Matisse, and his band of followers, known as "The Savage Beasts."

Following World War I the pseudo-artists flocked to Montmartre in droves, with camera-snapping tourists hot on their heels. The real artists have long gone, perhaps to Montparnasse.

Before its discovery and subsequent chic, Montmartre was a sleepy farming community, with windmills dotting the landscape. The name has always been the subject of disagreement, some maintaining that it originated from the "mount of Mars," a Roman temple that crowned the hill, others asserting that it means "mount of martyrs," a reference to the martyrdom of St. Denis, the patron saint of Paris, who was beheaded on the mountain along with his fellow saints Rusticus and Eleutherius.

The name Montmartre has spread chaos and confusion in many an unwary tourist's agenda. So just to make things clear, there are *three* of them.

The first is boulevard Montmartre, a busy commercial street nowhere near the mountain. The second is the tawdry, expensive, would-be-naughty, and utterly phony amusement belt along boulevard de Clichy, culminating at place Pigalle (the "Pig Alley" of World War II GIs). The third—the Montmartre we're talking about—lies on the slopes and the top of the actual *mont.*

The best way to get there is to take the Métro to Anvers, then walk to the nearby rue de Steinkerque and ride the curious little **funicular** to the top. It operates daily between 6am and 11pm.

The center point of Montmartre, **place du Tertre,** looks like an almost-real village square, particularly when the local band is blowing and puffing oompah music on tubas, sousaphones, trombones, and trumpets. All around the square run terrace restaurants with dance floors and colored lights. The Basilica of Sacré-Coeur gleams white through the trees.

Behind the church and clinging to the hillside below are steep and crooked little streets that almost seem to have survived the relentless march of progress. Rue des Saules has Montmartre's last vineyard and a cabaret. Rue Lepic still looks, almost, the way Renoir, the melancholy van Gogh, and the unfortunate genius Toulouse-Lautrec saw it. All this almost makes up for the blitz of portraitists and souvenir stores and postcard vendors up on top.

The traditional way to explore Montmartre is on foot, but many visitors who are not in tip-top physical shape find the uphill climb to Paris's highest elevation arduous. Those who prefer to ride can take a white-sided, diesel-powered "train," which rolls on rubber tires along the steep streets, on a 35-minute guided tour. **Le Petit Train de Montmartre** carries 55 passengers who can listen to an English commentary as they pass by the district's major landmarks. Boarding is either at place du Tertre (beside the Church of St-Pierre) or near the Moulin Rouge in place Blanche. Trains run daily throughout the year, beginning at 10am and continuing until midnight between June and September, until 7pm the rest of the year. Depending on the season, departures are scheduled every 30 to 45 minutes. The cost is 30 F ($6) for adults, half price for children. For information, call **Promotrain,** 131 rue de Clignancourt, 18e (☎ **01-42-62-24-00**).

For a more detailed look at Montmartre, see our walking tour in Chapter 7.

✪ **Basilique du Sacré-Coeur.** Place St-Pierre, 18e. ☎ **01-42-51-17-02.** Basilica, free; dome, 15 F ($3) adults, 8 F ($1.60) students 6–25; crypt, 15 F ($3) and 5 F ($1), respectively; joint ticket to both, 25 F ($5) adults. Basilica, daily 7am–10:30pm. Dome and crypt, Apr–Sept, daily 9:15am–7pm; Oct–Mar, daily 9:15am–6pm. Métro: Abbesses. Take the elevator to the surface and follow the signs to the funiculaire, which takes you up to the church for the price of one Métro ticket.

After the Eiffel Tower, Sacré-Coeur is the most characteristic landmark of the Parisian scene. Like the tower, it has always been—and still is—the subject of much controversy. One Parisian called it "a lunatic's confectionery dream." An offended Zola declared it "the basilica of the ridiculous." Sacré-Coeur has had warm supporters as well, including the poet Max Jacob and the artist Maurice Utrillo. Utrillo never tired of drawing and painting it, and he and Jacob came here regularly to pray.

In gleaming white, it towers over Paris—its five bulbous domes suggesting some Byzantine church of the 12th century, and its campanile inspired by Roman-Byzantine art. But it's not that old. After France's defeat by the Prussians in 1870, the basilica was planned as a votive offering to cure France's misfortunes. Rich and poor alike contributed money to build it. Construction was begun on the church in 1876 and it was not consecrated until 1919, but perpetual prayers of adoration have been made here day and night since 1885.

On a clear day the vista from the dome can extend for 35 miles. You can also walk around the inner dome of the church, peering down like a pigeon (one is likely to be keeping you company).

11 More Museums

Below is a partial listing of the balance of the city's museums. Be sure to refer back to Section 1, "The Top Museums," for details on where to get information.

Cité des Sciences et de l'Industrie. La Villette, 30 av. Corentine-Cariou, 19e. ☎ **01-40-05-70-00.** Cité Pass (entrance to all exhibits), 45 F ($9) adults, 35 F ($7) ages 7–25, free for children 6 and under; Géode, 57 F ($11.40) adults, 40 F ($8) children 17 and under. Tues and Thurs–Fri 10am–6pm, Wed noon–9pm, Sat–Sun and holidays noon–8pm. Show times at Géode, Tues–Sun on the hour 10am–9pm. Métro: Line 7 to Porte-de-la-Villette.

A city of science and industry has risen here. When its core was originally built in the 1960s, it was touted as the most modern slaughterhouse in the world. When the site was abandoned as a failure in 1974, its echoing vastness and unlikely location on the northern edge of the city presented the French government with a problem. In 1986 the converted premises opened as the world's most expensive ($642 million) science complex designed to "modernize mentalities" as a first step in the process of modernizing society.

The place is so vast, with so many exhibits, that a single visit gives only an idea of the scope of the Cité. It's like a futuristic airplane hangar. Busts of Plato, Hippocrates, and a double-faced Janus gaze silently at a tube-filled, space-age riot of high-tech girders, glass, and lights—something akin to what a layman might think of the interior of an atomic generator.

The sheer dimensions of the place are awesome, a challenge to the arrangers of the constantly changing exhibits. Some of the exhibits are couched in an overlay of Gallic humor, including seismographic activity as presented in the comic-strip adventures of a jungle explorer. Among others is the silver-skinned geodesic dome (called the Géode) that shows the closest thing to a 3-D cinema in Europe on the inner surfaces of its curved walls; it's a 112-foot-high sphere with a 370-seat theater.

Explora, a permanent exhibit, is spread over the three upper levels of the building; its displays revolve around four themes: the universe, life, matter, and communication. The Cité also has a multimedia library and a planetarium. An "inventorium" is designed for children.

The Cité is in **La Villette** park, the city's largest, with 136 acres of greenery—twice the size of the Tuileries. Here you'll find a belvedere, a video workshop for children, and information about exhibitions and events, along with a café and restaurant.

Manufacture des Gobelins. 42 av. des Gobelins, 13e. ☎ **01-44-08-52-00.** Admission 37 F ($7.40) adults, 30 F ($6) ages 7–24 and 65 or older, free for children 6 and under. Tours given in French (with English pamphlets) Tues–Thurs 2–2:45pm. Métro: Gobelins.

The founding father of the dynasty in question, Jehan Gobelin, came from a family of dyers and clothmakers. In the 15th century he discovered a scarlet dye that was to make him famous. By 1601 Henry IV had become interested, bringing up 200 weavers from Flanders whose full-time occupation was to make tapestries (many of which are now scattered across various museums and residences). Oddly enough, until this endeavor the Gobelin family had not made any tapestries, although the name would become synonymous with that art form.

Colbert, the minister of Louis XIV, purchased the works, and under royal patronage the craftsmen set about executing designs by Le Brun. After during the Revolution, the industry was reactivated by Napoléon.

Les Gobelins is still going strong and you can visit the studios of the craftspeople—called *ateliers.* Some of the ancient high-warp looms are still in use. Weavers sit behind huge screens of thread, patiently thrusting stitch after stitch into work that may take up to 3 years to complete.

Manufacture Nationale de Sèvres. Place de la Manufacture, Sèvres. ☎ **01-45-34-34-00.** Free admission. Mon–Sat 10am–5pm. Métro: Pont-de-Sèvres; then walk across the Seine to the Right Bank.

Madame de Pompadour loved Sèvres porcelain. She urged Louis XV to order more of it, thus ensuring its abundance among the chic people of the 18th century. Two centuries later it's still fashionable.

The Sèvres factory has been owned by the state of France for more than two centuries. It was founded originally in Vincennes, and moved to Sèvres, a riverside suburb on the western edge of Paris, in 1756. The factory's commercial service sells porcelain to the public Monday to Saturday (it's closed on holidays).

Next door, the **Musée National de Céramique de Sèvres** (☎ 01-41-14-04-20) boasts one of the finest collections of faïence and porcelain in the world, some of which belonged to Madame du Barry, Pompadour's hand-picked successor. On view, for example, is the "Pompadour rose" (which the English insisted on calling the "rose du Barry"), a style much in vogue in the 1750s and 1760s. The painter Boucher made some of the designs used by the factory, as did the sculptor Pajou (he created the bas-reliefs for the Opéra at Versailles). The factory pioneered what became known in porcelain as the *Louis Seize* style—it's all here, plus lots more, including works from Meissen (archrival of Sèvres). This museum is open Wednesday to Monday from 10am to 5pm. Admission is 20 F ($4) for adults, 13 F ($2.60) for ages 18 to 25 and over 65, and free for children 17 and under.

Musée Cernuschi. 7 av. Velàsquez, 8e. ☎ **01-45-63-50-75.** Admission 17.50 F ($3.50) adults, 9 F ($1.80) students and seniors, free for children 17 and under. Tues–Sun 10am–5:40pm. Métro: Monceau or Villiers. Bus: 30 or 94.

Bordering the Parc Monceau, this small museum is devoted to the arts of China. It's another one of those mansions whose owners stuffed them with art objects, then bequeathed them to the city of Paris. The address was quite an exclusive one when the town was built in 1885.

Inside, there is, of course, a bust of Cernuschi—a self-perpetuating memorial to a man whose generosity and interest in the East was legend in his day. Now the collections include a fine assortment of Neolithic potteries, as well as bronzes from the 14th century B.C., perhaps the most famous being the tiger-shaped vase. The jades, ceramics, and funereal figures are exceptional, as are the pieces of Buddhist sculpture. Most admirable is a Bodhisattva originating from Yun-kang (6th century). Rounding out the exhibits are some ancient paintings, the best known of which is *Horses with Grooms,* attributed to Han Kan (8th century, T'ang Dynasty). The museum also houses a good collection of contemporary Chinese paintings.

Musée d'Art Moderne de la Ville de Paris. 11–13 av. du Président-Wilson, 16e. ☎ **01-47-23-61-27.** Admission 35 F ($7) adults, 25 F ($5) ages 18–24 and over 60, free for children 17 and under. Tues–Fri 10am–5:30pm, Sat–Sun 10am–7pm. Métro: Iéna or Alma-Marceau.

Right next door to the Palais de Tokyo, this museum displays a permanent collection of paintings and sculpture owned by the city of Paris. In addition, the M.A.M. section of the city's modern art museum presents ever-changing temporary exhibitions on individual artists from all over the world or on international art trends. Bordering the Seine, the salons display works by such artists as Chagall, Matisse, Léger, Braque, Picasso, Dufy, Utrillo, Delaunay, Rouault, and Modigliani.

See, in particular, Pierre Tal Coat's *Portrait of Gertrude Stein.* Picasso wasn't the only artist to tackle this difficult subject. Other sections in the museum are ARC,

Attractions: 16th Arrondissement

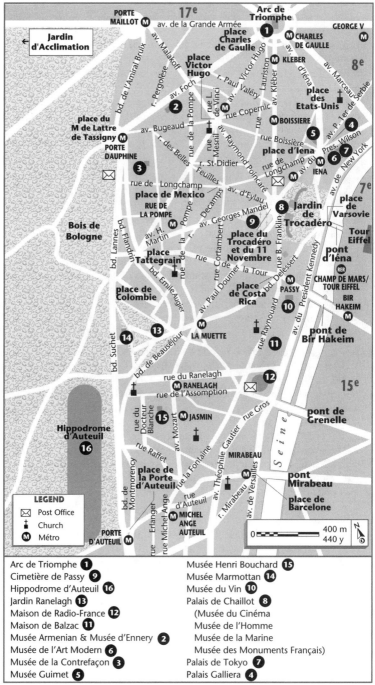

Arc de Triomphe **1**
Cimetière de Passy **9**
Hippodrome d'Auteuil **16**
Jardin Ranelagh **13**
Maison de Radio-France **12**
Maison de Balzac **11**
Musée Armenian & Musée d'Ennery **2**
Musée de l'Art Modern **6**
Musée de la Contrefaçon **3**
Musée Guimet **5**

Musée Henri Bouchard **15**
Musée Marmottan **14**
Musée du Vin **10**
Palais de Chaillot **8**
   (Musée du Cinéma
   Musée de l'Homme
   Musée de la Marine
   Musée des Monuments Français)
Palais de Tokyo **7**
Palais Galliera **4**

which shows work of young artists and new trends in contemporary art, and the Musée des Enfants, which has exhibitions and shows for children.

Musée de Baccarat. 30 bis rue de Paradis, 10e. ☎ 01-47-70-64-30. Free admission. Mon–Fri 9am–6:30pm, Sat 10am–noon and 2–5pm. Métro: Poissonnière or Château-d'Eau.

This museum resembles an ice palace, filled with crystal of all shapes and sizes. It's found in a Directoire building from the late 18th century, which houses the Baccarat headquarters. The museum contains some of the most impressive pieces produced by this crystal company through the years. Czars, royalty, and oil-rich sheiks have numbered among the best patrons of this prestigious name in crystal, established in 1764. At the entrance to the museum stands "Lady Baccarat," a chandelier in the form and size of a woman.

Musée des Arts Décoratifs. In the Palais du Louvre, 107 rue de Rivoli, 1er. ☎ 01-44-55-57-50. Admission 25 F ($5) adults, 16 F ($3.20) ages 5–24, free for children 4 and under. Wed–Sat 12:30–6pm, Sun noon–6pm. Métro: Palais-Royal or Tuileries.

In the northwest wing of the Louvre's Pavillon de Marsan, this museum holds a treasury of furnishings, fabrics, wallpaper, objets d'art, and other items displaying living styles from the Middle Ages to the present. Notable on the first floor are the 1920s deco boudoir, bath, and bedroom done for couturier Jeanne Lanvin by designer Rateau. Decorative art from the Middle Ages to the Renaissance is on the second floor, whereas rich collections from the 17th, 18th, and 19th centuries occupy the third and fourth floors. The fifth has specialized centers, such as wallpaper and drawings, and documentary centers detailing fashion, textiles, toys, crafts, and glass trends.

Musée Guimet. 6 place d'Iéna, 16e. ☎ 01-47-23-61-65. Admission 26 F ($5.20) adults, 17 F ($3.40) ages 18–25 and over 60, free for children 17 and under. Wed–Mon 9:45am–6pm. Métro: Iéna or Alma-Marceau.

Named after its founder and established originally at Lyon, the Guimet was transferred to Paris in 1889. It received in 1931 the collections of the Musée Indochinois du Trocadéro and, after World War II, the Asian collections of the Louvre. Today it's one of the world's richest museums of its genre.

The art ranges from Tibet to Japan to Afghanistan to Nepal to Java to India to China. There are even sculptures from Vietnam. The most interesting displays are on the ground floor, the exhibits encompassing Buddhas, heads of serpentine monsters, and funereal figurines. See, for example, antiquities from the temple of Angkor Wat. The Jacques Bacot gallery is devoted to Tibetan art: fascinating scenes of the Grand Lamas entwined with serpents and demons.

On the first floor is the Indian section with the remarkable Mathura Serpent-King (2nd century A.D.), the Amaravati reliefs. René Grousset, a French art historian, was impressed with the "simple paganism, the innocent pleasure in the nude form." Of a harem group from that school (3rd century), he found its sensuality "refined," its freshness "agreeable." On the same floor is the Rousset collection.

On the top floor, the Michael Calmann collection is devoted to vases, statuettes in porcelain, ceramics, and pottery, including the Grandidier collection, that run the gamut of Chinese dynasties—going back six or seven centuries before the birth of Christ and forward to the Ts'ing Dynasty (1644–1911).

Musée Jacquemart-André. 158 bd. Haussmann, 8e. Tel. **01-42-89-04-91.** Admission 45 F ($9). Daily 10am–6pm. Metro: Miromesnil or St-Philippe-du-Roule.

It's the finest museum of its type in Paris, an inspired 19th-century blend of taste and money that's unlike anything else in town. The collection used to belong to the André family, a prominent family of French Protestants who made a fortune in banking and industry in the 19th century. The family's last scion, Edouard André, spent most of his life as an officer in the French army stationed abroad, returning later in his life to marry a well-known portraitist of French governmental figures and members of the aristocracy, Nélie Jacquemart. Together they compiled a collection of rare French 18th-century decorative art and European paintings in an 1850s town house that was continually upgraded and redecorated according to the fashions of their time.

In 1912 Mme Jacquemart willed the house and its collection to the Institut de France, which paid for an extensive renovation and enlargment that was completed in 1996. The pride of the collection are works by Bellini, Carpaccio, and Uccelo, which are complemented by Houdon busts, Gobelins tapestries, Savonnerie carpets, della Robbia terra-cottas, an awesome collection of antiques, and works by Rembrandt (*The Pilgrim of Emmaus*), Van Dyck, Tiepolo, Rubens, Watteau, Fragonard, Boucher, and Mantegna. Salons drip with gilt and the ultimate in *fin-de-siècle* style.

Take a break from all this gilded age opulence with a cup of tea in Mme Jacquemart's high-ceilinged dining room, where 18th-century tapestries adorn a tearoom well suited to light lunches. Salads, tartes and tourtes (a round pastry filled with meat or fruit), and an assortment of Viennese pastries are served throughout the opening hours of the museum, and are eminently suited for a light lunch or a pick-me-up.

Musée Marmottan–Claude-Monet. 2 rue Louis-Boilly, 16e. ☎ **01-42-24-07-02.** Admission 35 F ($7) adults, 25 F ($5) children 8–18 and seniors over 60, free for children 7 and under. Tues–Sun 10am–5:30pm. Métro: La-Muette.

A town-house mansion with all the trappings of the First Empire, the Marmottan Museum is one of the many private family collections on display in Paris.

Occasionally a lone art historian would venture here, on the edge of the Bois de Boulogne, to see what Paul Marmottan donated to the Académie des Beaux-Arts. Hardly anybody else did . . . until 1966 when Michel Monet, son of Claude Monet, died in a car crash, leaving a bequest of his father's art—valued at the time at $10 million—to the little museum. The Académie des Beaux-Arts suddenly found itself heir to more than 130 paintings, watercolors, pastels, and drawings—and a whole lot of Monet lovers, who can, in one place, trace the evolution of the great man's work.

The gallery owns more than 30 pictures of his house at Giverny, and many of water lilies, his everlasting source of intrigue. The bequest included his *Willow* (1918), his *House of Parliament* (1905), even a portrait Renoir did of Monet when he was 32. The collection has been hailed as "one of the great art treasures of the world"—and that it is. Ironically, the museum had always owned Monet's *Impression,* from which the movement got its name.

Paul Marmottan's original collection includes fig-leafed nudes, First Empire antiques, assorted objets d'art, bucolic paintings, and crystal chandeliers. Many of the tapestries date from the Renaissance, and you can also see the extensive collection of miniatures donated by Daniel Waldenstein.

Musée National Auguste-Rodin. In the Hôtel Biron, 77 rue de Varenne, 7e. ☎ **01-44-18-61-10.** Admission 32 F ($6.40) adults, 22 F ($4.40) ages 18–26 and over 60, free for children 17 and under, free for everyone on Sun. Apr–Sept, Tues–Sun 9:30am–5:45pm; Oct–Mar, Tues–Sun 9:30am–4:45pm. Métro: Varenne.

These days Rodin is acclaimed as the father of modern sculpture, but in a different era his work was labeled obscene. The world's artistic taste changed, and in due course the government of France purchased the gray-stone 18th-century luxury residence in Faubourg St-Germain. The mansion was Rodin's studio from 1910 until his death in 1917. After the government bought the studio, the rose gardens were restored to their 18th-century splendor, making the garden a perfect setting for Rodin's most memorable works.

In the courtyard are three world-famous creations: *The Gate of Hell, The Thinker,* and *The Burghers of Calais.* Rodin's first major public commission, *The Burghers* commemorated the heroism of six burghers of Calais who, in 1347, offered themselves as hostages to Edward III in return for his ending the siege of their port. Perhaps the single best-known work, *The Thinker,* in Rodin's own words, "thinks with every muscle of his arms, back, and legs, with his clenched fist and gripping toes." Not yet completed when Rodin died, *The Gate of Hell,* as he put it, is "where I lived for a whole year in Dante's Inferno."

Inside the building, the sculpture, plaster casts, reproductions, originals, and sketches reveal the freshness and vitality of this remarkable man. Many of his works appear to be emerging from marble into life. Everybody is attracted to *The Kiss* (of which one critic wrote, "the passion is timeless"). Upstairs are two different versions of the celebrated and condemned nude of Balzac, his bulky torso rising from a tree trunk (Albert E. Elsen commented on the "glorious bulging" stomach). Included are many versions of his *Monument to Balzac* (a large one stands in the garden), which was Rodin's last major work and which caused a furor when it was first exhibited.

Other significant sculpture includes Rodin's *Prodigal Son* (it literally soars), *The Crouching Woman* (called the "embodiment of despair"), and *The Age of Bronze,* an 1876 study of a nude man, modeled by a Belgian soldier. (Rodin was accused—falsely—of making a cast from a living model.)

Wander back from the house through the long wooded garden where more sculptures await you under the trees.

Musée Nissim-de-Camondo. 63 rue de Monceau, 8e. ☎ 01-45-63-26-32. Admission 27 F ($5.40) adults, 18 F ($3.60) children 17 and under and seniors over 60. Wed–Sun 10am–5pm. Closed Jan 1, Dec 25. Métro: Villiers.

This museum is a jewel box of elegance and refinement, evoking the days of Louis XVI and Marie Antoinette. The pre–World War I town house was donated to the Museum of Decorative Arts by Comte Moïse de Camondo (1860–1935) in memory of his son, Nissim, a French aviator killed in combat during World War I.

Entered through a courtyard, the museum is like the private home of an aristocrat of two centuries ago—richly furnished with needlepoint chairs, tapestries (many from Beauvais or Aubusson), antiques, paintings (the inevitable Guardi scenes of Venice), bas-reliefs, silver, Chinese vases, crystal chandeliers, Sèvres porcelain, and Savonnerie carpets. And, of course, a Houdon bust (in an upstairs bedroom). The Blue Salon, overlooking the Parc Monceau, is impressive. You can wander without a guide through the gilt and oyster-gray salons.

Musée Zadkine. 100 bis rue d'Assas, 6e. ☎ 01-43-26-91-90. Admission 17 F ($3.40) adults, 9.50 F ($1.90) children. Tues–Sun 10am–5:30pm. Métro: Luxembourg or Vavin.

This museum near the Luxembourg Gardens and boulevard St-Michel was once the private residence of Ossip Zadkine, the sculptor. Now this famous artist's collection has been turned over to the city of Paris for public viewing. Included are some 300 pieces of sculpture, displayed both in the museum and in the garden, bringing a little rural charm to the heart of the city. Some drawings and tapestries are also exhibited.

12 More Churches

St-Etienne-du-Mont. Place Ste-Geneviève, 5e. ☎ **01-43-54-11-79.** Free admission. Mon–Sat 8:30am–noon and 2–7pm, Sun 8:30–noon and 3–7:15pm. Closed Mon July–Aug. Métro: Cardinal-Lemoine or Luxembourg.

Once there was an abbey on this site, founded by Clovis and later dedicated to St. Geneviève, the patroness of Paris. Such was the fame of this popular saint that the abbey proved too small to accommodate the pilgrimage crowds. Now part of the Lycée Henri IV, the **Tower of Clovis** is all that remains of the ancient abbey (you can see the Tower from rue Clovis).

Today the task of keeping alive the cult of St. Geneviève has fallen on the Church of St-Etienne-du-Mont, on place Ste-Geneviève, practically adjoining the Panthéon. The interior is in the Gothic style, unusual for a 16th-century church. Construction on the present building began in 1492 and was plagued by delays before the structure was finally finished in 1626.

Besides the patroness of Paris, such men as Pascal and Racine were entombed in the church. Incidentally, the tomb of the saint was destroyed during the Revolution. However, the stone on which her coffin rested was discovered later, and the relics were gathered for a place of honor at St-Etienne.

The church possesses a remarkable rood screen, built in the first part of the 16th century. Across the nave, it's unique in Paris—uncharitably called spurious by some, although others have hailed it as a masterpiece. Another treasure is a carved-wood pulpit, held up by a seminude Samson who clutches a bone in one hand, having slain the lion at his feet. The fourth chapel on the right (when entering) contains most impressive stained glass, from the 16th century.

St-Germain-l'Auxerrois. 2 place du Louvre, 1er. ☎ **01-42-60-13-96.** Free admission. Daily 8am–8pm. Métro: Louvre.

Once it was the church for the Palace of the Louvre, drawing an assortment of courtesans, men of art and of law, artisans from the *quartier,* even royalty. Sharing place du Louvre with Perrault's colonnade, the church contains only the foundation stones of its original belfry built in the 11th century. It was greatly enlarged in the 14th century by the addition of side aisles. The little primitive chapel that had stood on the spot eventually gave way to a great and beautiful church, with 260 feet of stained glass, including some rose windows from the Renaissance.

The saddest moment in its history was on August 24, 1572, the evening of the St. Bartholomew Massacre. On that night the bells rang in the tower, signaling the supporters of Catherine de Médicis, Marguerite of Guise, Charles IX, and the future Henri III to launch a slaughter of thousands of Huguenots, who had been invited to celebrate the marriage of Henri of Navarre to his cousin, Marguerite of Valois. There is little evidence of the blood-bath now, of course. The church-wardens' pews are outstanding, with intricate carving, based on designs by Le Brun in the 17th century. Behind the pew is a 15th-century triptych and Flemish retable (so badly lit you can hardly appreciate it). The organ was originally ordered by Louis XVI for the Sainte-Chapelle. In that architectural melange, many famous men were entombed, including the sculptor Coysevox and Le Vau, the architect. Around the chancel is an intricate 18th-century grille.

Val-de-Grâce. 1 place Alphonse-Laveran, 5e. ☎ **01-40-51-45-75.** Free admission. Mon–Sat 9am–noon and 2–5pm. Touring prohibited during services. Métro: Port-Royal. Bus: 38.

According to an old proverb, to understand the French you must like Camembert cheese, the pont-Neuf, and the dome of Val-de-Grâce.

After 23 years of a barren marriage to Louis XIII, Anne of Austria gave birth to a boy who would one day be known as the Sun King. In those days, if monarchs wanted to express gratitude, they built a church or monastery. On April 1, 1645, 7 years after his birth, the future Louis XIV laid the first stone of the church. At that time Mansart was the architect. To him we owe the facade in the Jesuit style. Le Duc, however, designed the dome, and the painter Mignard decorated it with frescoes. Other architects included Le Mercier and Le Muet.

The origins of the church go back even further, to 1050, when a Benedictine monastery was founded on the grounds. In 1619 Marguerite Veni d'Arbouze was appointed abbess by Louis XIII. She petitioned Anne of Austria for a new monastery, as the original one was decaying. Then came Louis XIV's church, which in 1793 was turned into a military hospital and in 1850 an army school. Since even today it is a chapel of a military hospital, Val-de-Grâce may be closed at times because the French government fears it may be a target for a terrorist bomb.

13 Gardens & Parks

See Section 3, "The Champs-Elysées: The Grand Promenade of Paris," for details on the **Tuileries,** perhaps the most famous gardens in Paris.

Hemingway told a friend that the ✪ **Jardin du Luxembourg,** 6e; (Métro: Odéon; RER: Luxembourg) "kept us from starvation." He related that in his poverty-stricken days in Paris, he wheeled a baby carriage (the vehicle was considered luxurious) and child through the gardens because it was known "for the classiness of its pigeons." When the *gendarme* went across the street for a glass of wine, the writer would eye his victim, preferably a plump one, then lure him with corn and. . ."snatch him, wring his neck," then flip him under Bumby's blanket. "We got a little tired of pigeon that year," he confessed, "but they filled many a void."

Before it became a feeding ground for struggling Montparnasse artists of the 1920s, Luxembourg knew greater days. But it has always been associated with artists, although students from the Sorbonne and children predominate nowadays. Watteau came this way, as did Verlaine. Balzac, however, didn't like the gardens at all. In 1905 Gertrude Stein would cross the gardens to catch the Batignolles-Clichy-Odéon omnibus pulled by three gray mares across Paris, to meet Picasso in his studio at Montmartre, where she sat while he painted her portrait.

The gardens are the best on the Left Bank (some say in all of Paris). Marie de Médicis, the much-neglected wife and later widow of the roving Henri IV, ordered a palace built on the site in 1612. She planned to live there with her "witch" friend, Leonora Galigal. A Florentine by birth, the regent wanted to create another Pitti Palace, or so she ordered the architect, Salomon de Brossee. She wasn't entirely successful, although the overall effect is most often described as Italianate.

The queen didn't get to enjoy the palace for very long after it was finished. She was forced into exile by her son, Louis XIII, after it was discovered that she was plotting to overthrow him. Reportedly, she died in Germany in poverty, quite a step down from the luxury she had once known in the Luxembourg. Incidentally, the 21 paintings she commissioned from Rubens that glorified her life were intended for her palace, but are now in the Louvre. You can visit the palace the first Sunday of each month at 10:15am, for 45 F ($9). However, you must call 01-44-33-99-83 to make a reservation.

But you don't come to the Luxembourg to visit the palace, not really. The gardens are the attraction. For the most part, they're in the classic French tradition: well groomed and formally laid out, the trees planted in designs. A large water basin in the center is encircled with urns and statuary on pedestals—one honoring St. Geneviève the patroness of Paris, depicted with pigtails reaching to her thighs. Another memorial is dedicated to Stendhal.

Crowds throng the park on May Day, when Parisians carry their traditional lilies of the valley. Birds sing, and all of Paris (those who didn't go to the country) celebrates the rebirth of spring.

One of the most spectacular parks in Europe is the ✪ **Bois de Boulogne,** Porte Dauphine, 16e (☎ **01-40-67-90-80;** Métro: Les-Sablons, Porte-Maillot, or Porte-Dauphine). The Bois is often called the "main lung" of Paris. Horse-drawn carriages traverse it, but you can also take your car through. Many of its hidden pathways, however, must be discovered by walking. If you had a week to spare, you could spend it all in the Bois de Boulogne and still not see everything.

Porte Dauphine is the main entrance, although you can take the Métro to Porte Maillot as well. West of Paris, the park was once a forest kept for royal hunts. In the late 19th century it was in vogue. Carriages containing elegantly attired and coiffured Parisian damsels with their foppish escorts rumbled along avenue Foch. Nowadays it's more likely to attract picnickers from the middle class. (And at night, hookers and muggers are prominent, so be duly warned.)

When Emperor Napoléon III gave the grounds to the city of Paris in 1852, they were developed by Baron Haussmann. Separating Lac Inférieur from Lac Supérieur is the Carrefour des Cascades (you can stroll under its waterfall). The Lower Lake contains two islands connected by a footbridge. From the east bank you can take a boat to these idyllically situated grounds, perhaps stopping off at the café-restaurant on one of them.

Restaurants in the Bois are numerous, elegant, and expensive. The Pré-Catelan contains a deluxe restaurant of the same name and a Shakespearean theater in a garden said to have been planted with trees mentioned in the bard's plays.

The **Jardin d'Acclimation,** at the northern edge of the Bois de Boulogne, is for children, with a small zoo, an amusement park, and a narrow-gauge railway. (See "Especially for Kids," later in this chapter, for more details.)

Two **racetracks,** Longchamp and the Auteuil, are in the park. The annual Grand Prix is run in June at Longchamp (the site of a medieval abbey). The most fashionable people of Paris turn out, the women gowned in their finest *haute couture.* Directly to the north of Longchamp is Grand Cascade, the artificial waterfall of the Bois de Boulogne.

In the 60-acre **Bagatelle Park,** the comte d'Artois (later Charles X), brother-in-law of Marie Antoinette, made a bet with her—he could erect a small palace in less than 3 months—and won. If you're in Paris in late April, go to the Bagatelle to look at the tulips, if for no other reason. In late May one of the finest and best-known rose collections in all of Europe is in full bloom.

Note: Beware of muggers and prostitutes at night.

Much of the **Parc Monceau,** 8e (☎ **01-42-27-39-56;** Métro: Monceau or Villiers), is ringed with 18th- and 19th-century mansions, some of them evoking Proust's *Remembrance of Things Past.* The park was opened to the public in the days of Napoléon III's Second Empire. It was built in 1778 by the duke of Orléans, or Philippe-Egalité, as he became known. Carmontelle designed the park for the duke, who was at the time the richest man in France. "Philip Equality" was noted for his debauchery and his pursuit of pleasure. No ordinary park would do.

Monceau was laid out with an Egyptian-style obelisk, a dungeon of the Middle Ages, a thatched alpine farmhouse, a Chinese pagoda, a Roman temple, an enchanted grotto, various chinoiseries, and of course a waterfall. These fairytale touches have largely disappeared except for a pyramid and an oval *naumachie* fringed by a colonnade. Many of the former fantasies have been replaced with solid statuary and monuments, one honoring Chopin. In spring, the red tulips and magnolias are worth the air ticket to Paris.

14 Cemeteries

The cemeteries of Paris are often viewed by sightseers as being somewhat like parks, suitable places for strolling. The graves of celebrities past also lure the sightseers. Père-Lachaise, for example, is a major sightseeing goal in Paris; the other cemeteries are of much lesser importance. Some of the burial sites, such as de Montrouge and Saint-Pierre, are only of very minor interest.

✪ **Cimetière du Père-Lachaise.** 16 rue du Repos, 20e. ☎ **01-43-70-70-33.** Free admission. Mar 15–Nov 5, Mon–Fri 8am–6pm, Sat 8:30am–6pm, Sun 9am–6pm; Nov 6–Mar 14, Mon–Fri 8am–5:30pm, Sat 8:30am–5:30pm, Sun 9am–5:30pm. Métro: Père-Lachaise.

When it comes to name-dropping, this cemetery knows no peer; it has been called the "grandest address in Paris." Everybody from Madame Bernhardt to Oscar Wilde (his tomb by Epstein) was buried here. So were Balzac, Delacroix, and Bizet. The body of Colette was taken here in 1954, and in time the little sparrow, Piaf, would follow. The lover of George Sand, Alfred de Musset, the poet, was buried here under a weeping willow. Napoléon's marshals, Ney and Masséna, were entombed here, as were Chopin and Molière. Marcel Proust's black tombstone rarely lacks a tiny bunch of violets. Colette's black granite slab always sports flowers, and legend has it that the cats replenish the red roses.

Some tombs are sentimental favorites; the grafitti-covered tomb of Jim Morrison draws devoted Doors fans. The great dancer Isadora Duncan is reduced to a "pigeon hole" in the Columbarium where bodies have been cremated and then "filed." If you search hard enough, you can find the tombs of that star-crossed pair, Abélard and Héloïse, the ill-fated lovers of the 12th century. At Père-Lachaise they have found peace at last. Other famous lovers also rest here: One stone is marked Alice B. Toklas on one side, Gertrude Stein on the other.

Spreading over more than 110 acres, Père-Lachaise was acquired by the city of Paris in 1804. Here, 19th-century sculpture abounds, each family trying to outdo the other in ornamentation and cherubic ostentation. Some French Socialists still pay tribute at the Mur des Fédérés, the anonymous gravesite of the Communards who were executed on May 28, 1871. Frenchmen who died in the Resistance or in Nazi concentration camps are also honored by several monuments. It was among the graves of the cemetery that these last-ditch fighters of the Paris Commune—the world's first anarchist republic—made their final desperate stand against the troops of the French government; overwhelmed, they were stood up against this wall and shot in batches. All died except a handful who had hidden in vaults and lived for years in the cemetery like wild animals, venturing into Paris at night to forage for food.

Note: A free map is available at the newsstand across from the main entrance. It will help you find the tombs.

Cimetière du Montparnasse. 3 bd. Edgar-Quinet, 6e. ☎ **01-44-10-86-50.** Free admission. Mon–Fri 8am–6pm, Sat 8:30am–6pm, Sun 9am–6pm. Métro: Edgar-Quinet.

In the shadow of the Tour Montparnasse, this debris-littered and badly maintained cemetery is a burial ground of *célébrités* of yesterday. A map (available to the left of the main gateway) will direct you to the most famous occupants, the shared gravesite of Simone de Beauvoir and Jean-Paul Sartre. Others resting here include Samuel

Beckett, Guy de Maupassant, editor Pierre Larousse (famous for his dictionary), and Alfred Dreyfus. The auto tycoon André Citroën is also interred here, as are sculptor Ossip Zadkine, composer Camille Saint-Saëns; Man Ray, the famous surrealist artist and familiar figure in the cafés of Montparnasse; and Charles Baudelaire, who had already written about "plunging into the abyss, Heaven or Hell."

Cimetière St-Vincent. Rue St-Vincent, 19e. ☎ **01-46-06-29-78.** Free admission. Mar 15–Nov 5, daily 8:30am–5:30pm; Nov 6–Mar 14, daily 8:30am–5pm. Métro: Lamarck-Caulaincourt.

Along this street lies the modest burial ground of St-Vincent, with a view of Sacré-Coeur on the hill. Because of the artists and writers who have their final resting place here, it's sometimes called "the most intellectual cemetery of Paris," but that epithet seems more apt for other graveyards. The artists Maurice Utrillo (1883–1955) and Théopile-Alexandre Steinien (1859–1923) were buried here, as was the musician Arthur Honegger. The writer Marcel Aymé came to rest here, too. In theory, the cemetery is open all day, but it would be foolish to disturb the caretaker's lunch any time from noon to 2pm—you'll regret it.

Cimetière de Passy. Av. G-Mandel, 16e. ☎ **01-47-27-51-42,** Free admission. Daily 8:30am–5:30pm. Métro: Trocadéro.

This cemetery runs along the old northern walls of Paris, south and southwest of Trocadéro. It's a small graveyard, sheltered by a bower of chestnut trees, but it contains many gravesites of the famous. A concierge at the gate will provide directions to some of the stellar locations. The painter Edouard Manet was buried here, as was Claude Debussy. Many greats from the world of literature since 1850 were interred here, including Tristan Bernard, Giraudoux, and Croisset. Also resting here are composer Gabriel Fauré, aviator Henry Farman, and actor Fernandel.

Cimetiére de Montmartre. 20 av. Rachel, 18e. ☎ **01-43-87-64-24.** Free admission. Mon–Fri 8am–6pm, Sat 8:30am–6pm, Sun 8am–7pm. Closes at 5:30pm in winter. Métro: La Fourche.

This cemetery, which opened in 1795, lies west of the Butte and north of boulevard de Clichy. The Russian dancer Nijinsky and novelist Alexandre Dumas the Younger are interred here. The great Stendhal was buried here, as were lesser literary lights, including novelists Edmond and Jules de Goncourt. The composer Hector Berlioz rests here, as does the poet and writer Heinrich Heine. The impressionist painter Edgar Degas still has fans who show up at his gravesite, as does the composer Offenbach. Alfred de Vigny, the poet and dramatist, is among those buried here; a more recent tombstone honors François Truffaut, the film director of the *nouvelle vague.* We like to pay our respects at the tomb of Alphonsine Plessis, the heroine of *La Dame aux camélias,* and Madame Récamier, who taught the world how to lounge. Originally, Emile Zola was interred here, but his corpse was exhumed and hauled off to the Panthéon in 1908. In the tragic year of 1871, the cemetery became the site of the mass burials of victims of the Siege and the Commune.

15 Especially for Kids

Boasting playgrounds with tiny merry-go-rounds and gondola-style swings, the large parks of Paris are always a treat for kids.

If you're staying on the Right Bank, take the children for a stroll through the **Tuileries** (see Section 3 of this chapter), where there are donkey rides, ice-cream stands, and a marionette show; at the circular pond, you can rent a toy sailboat. On the Left Bank, similar delights exist in the **Jardin du Luxembourg** (see Section 13 of this chapter). After a visit to the **Eiffel tower,** you can take the kids for a donkey ride in the nearby gardens of the **Champ-de-Mars** (see Section 4 of this chapter).

Attractions: The Père-Lachaise Cemetery

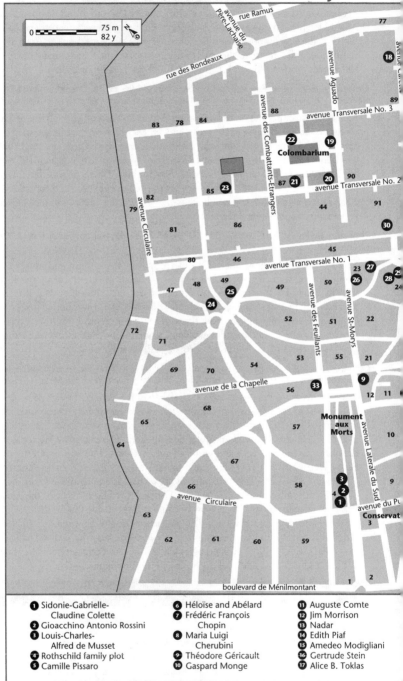

1. Sidonie-Gabrielle-
   Claudine Colette
2. Gioacchino Antonio Rossini
3. Louis-Charles-
   Alfred de Musset
4. Rothschild family plot
5. Camille Pissaro
6. Héloïse and Abélard
7. Frédéric François
   Chopin
8. Maria Luigi
   Cherubini
9. Théodore Géricault
10. Gaspard Monge
11. Auguste Comte
12. Jim Morrison
13. Nadar
14. Edith Piaf
15. Amedeo Modigliani
16. Gertrude Stein
17. Alice B. Toklas

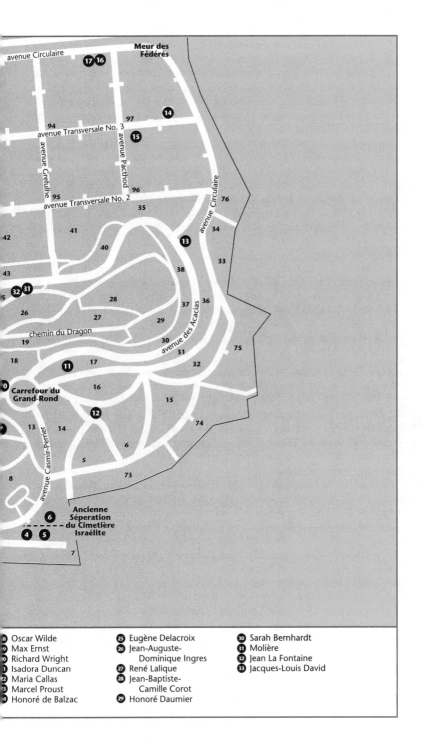

avenue Circulaire

Meur des Fédérés

17 16

avenue Transversale No. 3

94

97

14

avenue Gretilhe

avenue Pacthod

15

95

avenue Transversale No. 2

96

avenue Circulaire

76

35

42

41

34

40

13

33

38

43

32 31

36

5

28

37

avenue des Acacias

26

27

29

chemin du Dragon

19

30

75

18

31

11

17

32

0 **Carrefour du Grand-Rond**

16

15

7

13

14

12

74

avenue Casmir-Perrier

5

6

8

73

Ancienne Séperation du Cimetière Israélite

6

4 5

7

8 Oscar Wilde	25 Eugène Delacroix	30 Sarah Bernhardt
9 Max Ernst	26 Jean-Auguste-	31 Molière
0 Richard Wright	Dominique Ingres	32 Jean La Fontaine
1 Isadora Duncan	27 René Lalique	33 Jacques-Louis David
2 Maria Callas	28 Jean-Baptiste-	
3 Marcel Proust	Camille Corot	
4 Honoré de Balzac	29 Honoré Daumier	

A great Paris tradition, **puppet shows** are worth seeing for their enthusiastic, colorful productions—they're a genuine French child's experience. At the Jardin du Luxembourg, you'll see puppet productions with sinister plots set in Gothic castles and Oriental palaces; some young critics say that the best puppet shows are held in the Champ-de-Mars (performance times at the Luxembourg Gardens and Champ-de-Mars vary). In the Tuileries there are shows on Wednesday, Saturday, and Sunday at 3:15pm all summer long.

On Sunday afternoon, French families head up to the Butte **Montmartre** to bask in the fiesta atmosphere. You can join in the fun: Take the Métro to Anvers and walk to the Funiculaire de Montmartre (the silver cable car that carries you up to Sacré-Coeur). Once up top, follow the crowds to place du Tertre, where a Sergeant Pepper–style band will usually be blasting off-key and where you can have the kids' picture sketched by local artists. You can take in the views of Paris from the various vantage points and treat the kids to ice cream.

MUSEUMS

Set in the city's largest park, with special areas dedicated to children, the **Cité des Sciences et de l'Industrie** is one of the best museums for kids in Paris; for a full description, see Section 10, "More Museums," earlier in this chapter.

A Note for Parents: All the exhibits in Paris museums have only French explanations, so unless you've managed to struggle past your high school French lessons, or have some expertise on the display's subject matter, you aren't going to distinguish yourself with explanation.

Musée Grévin. 10 bd. Montmartre, 9e. ☎ **01-40-26-28-50.** Admission 42 F ($8.40) adults, 32 F ($6.40) children 12 and under. Daily 1–7pm; during French school holidays, daily 10am–7pm. Ticket office closes at 6pm. Métro: Montmartre or Richelieu-Drouot.

The desire to compare this place to Madame Tussaud's of London is almost irresistible. Grévin is the number-one waxworks of Paris. It isn't all blood and gore, and doesn't shock some, as Tussaud's might. Presenting a panorama of French history from Charlemagne to the mistress-collecting Napoléon III, it shows memorable moments in a series of tableaux.

Depicted are the consecration of Charles VII in 1429 in the Cathedral of Reims (Joan of Arc, dressed in armor and carrying her standard, stands behind the king); Marguerite de Valois, first wife of Henri IV, meeting on a secret stairway with La Molle, who was soon to be decapitated; Catherine de Médicis with the Florentine alchemist Ruggieri; Louis XV and Mozart at the home of the marquise de Pompadour; and Napoléon on a rock on St. Helena, reviewing his victories and defeats.

There are also displays of contemporary sports and political figures, as well as 50 of the world's best-loved film stars.

Two shows are staged frequently throughout the day. The first, called the *Palais des Mirages,* starts off as a sort of Temple of Brahma, and through magically distorting mirrors, changes into an enchanted forest, then a *fère* at the Alhambra at Granada. A magician is the star of the second show, *Le Cabinet Fantastique;* he entertains children of all ages.

Musée National d'Histoire Naturelle (Museum of Natural History). 57 rue Cuvier, 5e. ☎ **01-40-79-30-00.** Admission 40 F ($8) adults, 30 F ($6) ages 4–25, free for children 3 and under. Wed and Fri 10am–5pm, Thurs 10am–6pm, Sat 11am–6pm. Métro: Jussieu or Gare-d'Austerlitz.

In the Jardin des Plants, this museum has a wide range of science and nature exhibits that draw the children of Paris. It was founded in 1635 as a scientific research center by Guy de la Brosse, physician to Louis XIII. The museum's Grande Gallery of Evolution recently received a $90-million restoration. At the entrance, an 85-foot-long skeleton of a whale greets visitors. One display containing the skeletons of dinosaurs and mastadons is dedicated to endangered and vanished species. The museum also houses galleries that specialize in the fields of paleontology, anatomy, mineralogy, and botany. On the museum's grounds are tropical hothouses containing thousands of species of unusual plant life and a menagerie with small animal life in simulated natural habitats.

Musée de la Marine. In the Palais de Chaillot, place du Trocadéro. 16e. ☎ **01-45-53-31-70.** Admission 32 F ($6.40) adults, 22 F ($4.40) children 5–12 and seniors over 65, free for children 4 and under. Wed–Mon 10am–6pm. Métro: Trocadéro.

If your children have salt water in their veins, you may want to take them to this museum.

A lot here is pomp: gilded galleys and busts of stiff-necked admirals. There's a great number of old ship models, including, for instance, the big galley *La Réale,* the *Royal-Louis,* the rich ivory model *Ville de Dieppe,* the gorgeous *Valmy,* and a barge constructed in 1811 for Napoléon I which was used to carry another Napoléon (the Third) and his empress, Eugénie, on their first visit to the port of Brest in about 1858. The imperial crown is held up by winged cherubs.

There are many documents and artifacts concerning merchant fishing and pleasure fleets, oceanography, and hydrography, with films illustrating the subjects. Thematic exhibits explain, for instance, ancient wooden shipbuilding, the development of scientific instruments, merchant navy, fishing, steam, and sea traditions, and show some souvenirs of explorer Laperouse's wreck on Vanikoro Island in 1788. Important paintings include Joseph Vernet's *The Ports of France* during the 18th century.

AN AMUSEMENT PARK

Jardin d'Acclimation. Bois de Boulogne, 16e. ☎ **01-40-67-90-82.** Admission 10F ($2) for everyone. Daily 10am–6pm. Métro: A suitable itinerary, covering most of the park's sights, would involve arriving at Métro Sablons, walking across the park, and exiting at the far end (a distance of about half a mile), and then returning to central Paris from the Porte de Neuilly Métro station.

The definitive children's park in Paris is the Jardin d'Acclimation, a 25-acre amusement park on the northern side of the Bois de Boulogne. This is the kind of place that satisfies tykes and adults alike—but would make teenagers shudder in horror. The visit starts with a ride from Porte Maillot to the jardin entrance, through a stretch of wooded park, on a jaunty, green-and-yellow narrow-gauge train. Inside the gate is an easy-to-follow layout map. The park is circular—follow the road in either direction and it will take you all the way around and bring you back to the train at the end. (The train operates only on Wednesday, Saturday, and Sunday from 1:30pm until the park closes. A one-way fare is 5F-$1.) En route you'll discover a house of mirrors, an archery range, a miniature-golf course, zoo animals, an American-style bowling alley, a puppet theater (performances are only on Thursday, Saturday, Sunday, and holidays), a playground, a hurdle-racing course, and a whole conglomerate of junior-scale rides, shooting galleries, and waffle stalls.

You can trot the kids off on a pony or join them in a boat on a mill-stirred lagoon. Also fun to watch (and a superb idea for American cities to copy) is "La Prévention Routière," a miniature roadway operated by the Paris police. The youngsters drive through in small cars equipped to start and stop and are required by two genuine Parisian gendarmes to obey all street signs and light changes.

A ZOO

Parc Zoologique de Paris. In the Bois de Vincennes, 53 av. de St-Maurice, 12e. ☎ **01-44-75-20-00.** Admission 40 F ($8) adults, 20 F ($4) ages 4–25 and over 60, free for children 3 and under. May–Sept, Mon–Sat 9am–6:30pm, Sun 9am–6:30pm; Oct–Apr, Mon–Sat 9am–5pm, Sun 9am–5:30pm. Métro: Porte-Dorée or Château-de-Vincennes.

There's a modest zoo in the Jardin des Plantes, near the natural history museum, but without a doubt the best zoo this city has to offer is in the Bois de Vincennes, on the outskirts of Paris but quickly reached by Métro. This modern zoo displays its animals in settings as close as possible to their natural habitats. Here you never get that hunched-up feeling about the shoulders from empathizing with a leopard in a cage too small for stalking. The lion has an entire veldt to himself, and you can view each other comfortably across a deep protective moat. On a concrete mountain reminiscent of Disneyland's Matterhorn, lovely Barbary sheep leap from ledge to ledge or pose gracefully for hours watching the penguins in their pools at the mountain's foot. The animals seem happy here and are consequently playful. Keep well back from the bear pools or your drip-dries may be dripping wet.

16 Literary Landmarks

Countless Left Bank streets have literary tales to tell, so our list will necessarily be incomplete. There's **rue Monsieur-le-Prince,** 6e, in the Odéon section. During a famous visit in 1959, Martin Luther King, Jr., came to call on Richard Wright, the Mississippi-born African-American novelist famous for *Native Son.* King climbed to the third-floor apartment at no. 14, only to find that Wright's opinions on the civil rights movement conflicted with his own. Whistler rented a studio at no. 22, and, in 1826, Longfellow lived for a short time at no. 49. Oliver Wendell Holmes, Sr., lived at no. 55. After strolling along this street, you can dine at the former haunts of such figures as Kerouac and Hemingway. (See our recommendation of the **Crémerie-Restaurant Polidor,** 41 rue Monsieur-le-Prince, 6e, in Chapter 5.)

See also the listing for Victor Hugo's home in Section 8, "Le Marais."

Deux-Magots. 170 bd. St-Germain, 6e. ☎ **01-45-48-55-25.** Métro: St-Germain-des-Prés.

This long-established watering hole of St-Germain-des-Prés is where Jake Barnes meets Lady Brett in Hemingway's *The Sun Also Rises.*

Harry's New York Bar. 5 rue Daunou, 2e. ☎ **01-42-61-71-14.** Métro: Opéra or Pyramides.

F. Scott Fitzgerald and Ernest Hemingway were frequently seen on benders here, Gloria Swanson talked about her affair with Joseph Kennedy, and even Gertrude Stein showed up. And the place is still going strong. See also Chapter 9.

La Rotonde. 105 bd. Montparnasse, 6e. ☎ **01-43-26-68-84.** Métro: Raspail.

Americans tended to drink on the Right Bank, notably in the Ritz Bar, when they had money. When they didn't, they headed for one of the cafés of Montparnasse, which, according to Hemingway, usually meant La Rotonde.

Maison de Balzac. 47 rue Raynouard, 16e. ☎ **01-42-24-56-38.** Admission 27 F ($5.40) adults, 19 F ($3.80) children and seniors over 60. Tues–Sun 10am–5:45pm. Métro: Pasay or La-Muette.

In the residential district of Passy, near the Bois de Boulogne, sits a modest house. Here the great Balzac lived for 7 years beginning in 1840. Fleeing there after his possessions and furnishings were seized, Balzac cloaked himself in secrecy (you had to know a password to be ushered into his presence). Should a creditor knock on the Raynouard door, Balzac could always escape through the rue Berton exit.

The museum's most notable memento is the Limoges coffee pot (the novelist's initials are in mulberry pink) that his "screech-owl" kept hot throughout the night as he wrote *La Comédie humaine* to stall his creditors. Also enshrined here are Balzac's writing desk and chair. It also contains a library of special interest to scholars.

The little house is filled with reproductions of caricatures of Balzac. (A French biographer once wrote: "With his bulky baboon silhouette, his blue suit with gold buttons, his famous cane like a golden crowbar, and his abundant, disheveled hair, Balzac was a sight for caricature.")

The house is built on the slope of a hill, with a small courtyard and garden.

Shakespeare and Company. 37 rue de la Bûcherie, 5e. ☎ **01-43-26-96-50**. Daily 11am–midnight. Métro: St-Michel.

The most famous bookstore on the Left Bank was Shakespeare and Company, on rue de l'Odéon, home to the legendary Sylvia Beach, the "mother confessor to the Lost Generation." Hemingway, Fitzgerald, and Gertrude Stein were all frequent patrons. Anaïs Nin, the diarist noted for her description of struggling American artists in 1930s Paris, also stopped in often. At one point she helped her companion, Henry Miller, publish *Tropic of Cancer,* a book so notorious in its day that returning Americans trying to slip a copy through Customs often had it confiscated as pornography. (When times were hard, Ms. Nin herself wrote pornography for a dollar a page.)

Today the shop is located on rue de la Bûcherie, where expatriates still come to swap books and the latest literary gossip.

Le Procope. 13 rue l'Ancienne-Comédie, 6e. ☎ **01-43-26-99-20**. Métro: Odéon.

Dating from 1686, this is the oldest café in Paris. It's located in St-Germain-des-Prés and was the restaurant of choice for such historical figures as Franklin and Jefferson. Writers like Deiderot, Voltaire, George Sand, Victor Hugo, and Oscar Wilde all stopped by in their day as well. See Chapter 5.

17 Paris Underground

Les Catacombs. 1 place Denfert-Rochereau, 14e. ☎ **01-43-22-47-63**. Admission 17.50 F ($3.50) adults, 9 F ($1.80) children 7–18 and seniors over 60, free for children 6 and under. Tues–Fri 2–4pm, Sat–Sun 9–11am and 2–4pm. Métro: Denfert-Rochereau.

Every year an estimated 50,000 tourists explore some 1,000 yards of tunnel in these dank Catacombs to look at some six million skeletons ghoulishly arranged in artistic skull-and-crossbones fashion. It has been called the empire of the dead. First opened to the public in 1810, the Catacombs are now illuminated with overhead electric lights over their entire length.

In the Middle Ages the Catacombs were originally quarries, but in 1785 city officials decided to use them as a burial ground. So the bones of several million people were moved here from their previous resting places, since the overcrowded cemeteries were considered health menaces. In 1830 the prefect of Paris closed the Catacombs to the viewing public, considering them obscene and indecent. He maintained that he could not understand the morbid curiosity of civilized people who wanted to gaze upon the bones of the dead. Later, in World War II, the Catacombs were the headquarters of the French Resistance.

The Sewers of Paris (Les Egouts). Pont de l'Alma. 7e. ☎ **01-47-05-10-29**. Admission 25 F ($5) adults, 20 F ($4) students, free for children 9 and under and seniors over 60. May–Oct, Sat–Wed 11am–5pm; Nov–Apr, Sat–Wed 11am–4pm. Closed 3 weeks in Jan for maintenance. Métro: Alma-Marceau. RER: Pont-de-l'Alma.

The sophistication of a society can be judged by the way it disposes of its wastes, some sociologists assert. If that's the criteria, Paris receives good marks for its mostly invisible network of sewers.

In the early Middle Ages, drinking water was taken directly from the Seine and wastewater was poured onto fields or thrown onto the then unpaved streets, transforming the urban landscape into a sea of rather smelly mud.

Around 1200 the streets of Paris were paved with cobblestones, with open sewers running down the center of each. These open sewers helped spread the Black Death, which devastated the city. In 1370 a vaulted sewer was built on rue Montmartre, draining effluents directly into a tributary of the Seine. During the reign of Louis XIV improvements were made, but the state of waste disposal in Paris remained deplorable.

During the early 1800s, under the reign of Napoléon I, $18^1/_2$ miles of underground sewer were added beneath the Parisian landscape. By 1850, as the Industrial Revolution made the manufacture of iron pipe and steam digging equipment more practical, Baron Haussmann developed a system that utilized separate underground channels for both drinking water and sewage. By 1878 it was 360 miles long. Beginning in 1894, under the guidance of Belgrand, the network was enlarged, and new laws required that discharge of all waste and stormwater runoff be funneled into the sewers. Between 1914 and 1977 an additional 600 miles of sewers were added beneath the pavements of a burgeoning Paris.

Today the city known for its gastronomy boasts some memorable statistics regarding waste disposal: The network of sewers, one of the world's best, is 1,300 miles long. Within its cavities, it contains freshwater mains, compressed-air pipes, telephone cables, and pneumatic tubes. Every day, 1.2 million cubic meters of wastewater are collected and processed by a plant in the Parisian suburb of Achères. One of the largest in Europe, it's capable of treating more than two million cubic meters of sewage per day.

The *égouts* of the city, as well as telephone and telegraph pneumatic tubes, are constructed around four principal tunnels, one 18 feet wide and 15 feet high. It's like an underground city, with the street names clearly labeled. Further, each branch pipe bears the number of the building to which it's connected. These underground passages are truly mammoth, containing pipes bringing in drinking water and compressed air as well as telephone and telegraph lines.

That these sewers have remained such a popular attraction is something of a curiosity. They were made famous by Victor Hugo's *Les Misérables,* in which the character Jean Valjean, one of the best-loved heroes of narrative drama, takes desperate flight through the sewers of Paris, "All dripping with slime, his soul filled with a strange light."

Tours of the sewers begin at pont de l'Alma on the Left Bank. A stairway there leads into the bowels of the city. However, you often have to wait in line as much as half an hour. Visiting times might change when the weather is bad, as a storm can make the sewers dangerous. The tour consists of seeing a movie on sewer history, visiting a small museum, and then a short trip through the maze.

18 Organized Tours

ORIENTATION TOURS   The most popular way to get acquainted with Paris is on a 2-hour double-decker bus tour that takes you past the major attractions. No time is allotted to stop at any of the points of interest, but you'll get a panoramic view out of the large windows. The seats are comfortable, and individual earphones are distributed with a recorded commentary in 10 different languages. Contact **Cityrama,** 4 place des Pyramides, 1er (☎ **01-44-55-60-00**). A 2-hour "orientation tour" of Paris costs 150 F ($30). A morning tour with interior visits to Notre-Dame and the Louvre costs 260 F ($52). Tours to Versailles and Chartres are also offered. Métro: Palais-Royal or Musée-du-Louvre.

A separate tour of the nighttime illuminations leaves daily at 10pm in summer and 9pm in winter. The cost is 150 F ($30).

CRUISES ON THE SEINE   **Bateaux-Mouches** cruises on the Seine (☎ **01-42-25-96-10** for information and reservations; Métro: Alma-Marceau) depart frequently from pont de l'Alma on the Right Bank. Some boats have open sundecks, bars, and restaurants. All provide commentaries in six languages, including English. Tours depart daily every 30 minutes from 10am to 11:30pm (in good weather, boats leave every 15 minutes). Dinner cruises depart at 8:30pm; on these, ties and jackets are required for men. Fares are 40F ($8) for adults and 20 F ($4) for children for a ride lasting about 1$^1/_2$ hours; luncheon cruises cost 350 F ($70) Monday to Saturday; a deluxe dinner cruise costs 500 to 650 F ($100 to $130).

19 Special & Free Events

It won't cost you a franc to explore the streets of Paris. Walk along the quays of the Seine and browse through the shops and stalls; each street opens onto a new vista.

If you're an early riser, a walk through Paris at dawn can be memorable; you'll see the city come to life. Shopfronts are washed clean for the new day, cafés open, and vegetable vendors arrange their produce.

The spacious forecourt of the Centre Georges Pompidou, place Georges-Pompidou, is a free "entertainment center" featuring mimes, fire-eaters, would-be circus performers, and sometimes first-rate musicians. Métro: Rambuteau or Hôtel-de-Ville.

In the corridors of the Métro, classical music students (often from the Conservatoire National) perform; a hat (or violin case) is passed for donations.

If you're in Paris during one of the major festivals, you can join in the fun on the streets for free. On **Summer Solstice (June 21),** clowns, fire-eaters, and other performers roam the streets. On **Bastille Day (July 14),** the French traditionally drink wine and dance in the streets—fireworks are displayed, free concerts are given, and a parade of tanks heads down the Champs-Elysées.

Many **cultural events** (such as concerts, films, and lectures) in Paris are free; these events are often sponsored by foreign nations, such as the United Kingdom.

For free organ concerts in some of the city's old churches on Sunday afternoons, check *Pariscope,* the guide to entertainment events.

Free concerts featuring jazz, classical, and contemporary music from the Netherlands are held at the **Institut Neerlandais,** 121 rue de Lille, 7e (☎ **01-47-05-85-99**; Métro: Assemblée-Nationale).

At the **American Church,** 65 quai d'Orsay, 7e (☎ **01-47-05-07-99;** Métro: Invalides), free chamber-music concerts are presented.

20 A Day at the Races

Paris boasts an army of avid horse-racing fans who get to the city's eight racetracks whenever possible. Information on current races is available in such newspapers and magazines as *Tierce, Paris-Turf, France-Soir,* and *L'Equipe,* all sold at kiosks throughout the city.

The premier bastion of Paris horse-racing is the **Hippodrome de Longchamp,** Bois de Boulogne (☎ **01-44-30-75-00**). Established in 1855 during the autocratic but pleasure-loving reign of Napoléon III, it carries the most prestige, boasts the greatest number of promising Thoroughbreds, and awards the largest purse in France. The most important racing months at Longchamp are late June (Le Grand Prix de Paris) and early October (Prix de l'Arc de Triomphe). Métro: Auteuil; then one of the shuttle buses that operate on race days.

Another venue for horse racing is the **Hippodrome d'Auteuil,** also in the Bois de Boulogne (☎ **01-45-27-12-25**). Known for its steeplechases and obstacle courses, it sometimes attracts more than 50,000 Parisians at a time. These spectators appreciate the park's open-air promenades as much as they do the equestrian events. Established in 1870, the event is scattered over a sprawling 30 acres of parkland. It's designed to show to maximum advantage the skill and agility of both horses and riders. Métro: Auteuil.

Also popular, though rougher around the edges, is the **Hippodrome de Vincennes,** 2 route de la Ferme, Bois de Vincennes, 12e (☎ **01-49-77-17-77**). It holds most of its racing events under floodlights during evening hours in mid-winter. Métro: Château-de-Vincennes.

Strolling Around Paris 7

The best way to discover Paris is on foot, using your own shoe leather. This chapter highlights the attractions of Montmartre, the Latin Quarter, and the Grand Promenade.

WALKING TOUR 1
The Grand Promenade

Start: Arc de Triomphe.
Finish: Jardin des Tuileries.
Time: 3 leisurely hours; the distance is 2 miles.
Best Time: Sunday morning.
Worst Time: Rush hour.

In late 1995, after two hard, dusty, and hyperexpensive years of construction, Paris's most prominent triumphal promenade was reinaugurated with several important improvements. The *contre-allées* (side lanes that had always been clogged with parked cars) had been removed, new lighting added, the pedestrian sidewalks widened, new trees planted, and underground parking garages added to relieve what had been the neighborhood's curse—far too many parked cars. Now the Grand Promenade truly is grand again.

This is a lengthy walking tour, but it's the most popular walk in Paris. Start at the:

1. **Arc de Triomphe** (Métro: Charles-de-Gaulle–Etoile), from which 12 avenues radiate. Stand there for a moment (somewhere safe from traffic) and gaze down the long:

2. **Champs-Elysées,** which has been called "the highway of French grandeur." This street has witnessed some of the greatest moments in French history and some of its worst, such as when Hitler's armies paraded down the street in 1940. Louis XIV ordered construction of the 1.1-mile avenue in 1667. Originally called the Grand-Cour, and designed by Le Nôtre, it was renamed Champs-Elysées after the Elysian fields (the home of the virtuous dead) in 1709.

Stroll along the street. On one side it's a chestnut-lined park, on the other a commercial avenue of cafés, automobile showrooms, airline offices, cinemas, lingerie boutiques, and even hamburger joints. The Champs-Elysées has obviously lost the

The Grand Promenade

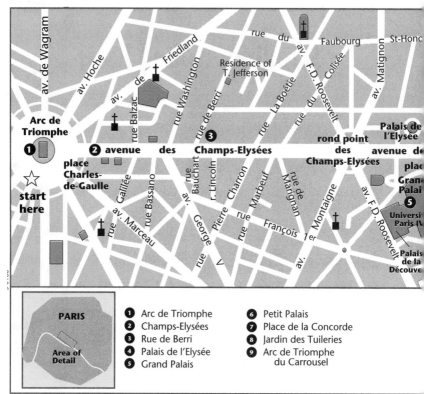

PARIS

Area of Detail

❶ Arc de Triomphe
❷ Champs-Elysées
❸ Rue de Berri
❹ Palais de l'Elysée
❺ Grand Palais

❻ Petit Palais
❼ Place de la Concorde
❽ Jardin des Tuileries
❾ Arc de Triomphe
    du Carrousel

fin-de-siècle elegance described by Proust in *Remembrance of Things Past.* Head down the avenue toward place de la Concorde, staying on the left-hand side.

When you reach:

3. Rue de Berri, turn left to no. 20, site of Thomas Jefferson's residence from 1785 to 1789. In its place today is a large modern apartment building. Back on the avenue again, continue to rond-point des Champs-Elysées. Close by is a philatelist's delight, the best-known open-air stamp market in Europe, held on Thursday and Saturday.

☕ **TAKE A BREAK**   Make it **Fouquet's**, 99 av. des Champs-Elysées (☎ **01-47-23-70-60**). Founded in 1901 and still serving coffee and food, this is an institution. In summer you can enjoy the flowers, and in winter the large glass windows will shelter you from the winds. Take plenty of money.

Continue down the avenue until you reach avenue Winston-Churchill on your right (from here there's a good panorama looking toward the Invalides). Ducking traffic and pausing for a view, cross to the other side of the avenue and go along avenue de Marigny. On your right will be the:

4. Palais de l'Elysée, the "French White House," whose main entrance is along fashionable Faubourg St-Honoré. Napoléon abdicated here. Now occupied by the president of France, it can't be visited without an invitation.

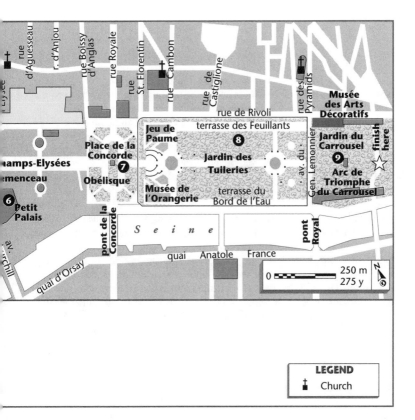

Back at rond-point and avenue Winston-Churchill, you come to the:

5. Grand Palais, which was constructed for the World Exhibition of 1900, as was the:

6. Petit Palais (whose entrance is on avenue Winston-Churchill), which now houses the Musée d'Art Moderne de la Ville de Paris (see Section 3 in Chapter 6 for details). Postponing a visit for the moment, continue along this avenue—now the garden district section—until you come to the landmark:

7. Place de la Concorde, an octagonal traffic hub built in 1757 to honor Louis XV. The statue of the king was torn down in 1792 and the name of the square was changed to place de la Révolution (following the Reign of Terror in 1795, it was named place de la Concorde). Floodlit at night, the square is dominated by an Egyptian obelisk from Luxor, considered the oldest man-made object in Paris. It was carved around 1200 B.C. and presented to France in 1829 by the viceroy of Egypt. During the Reign of Terror, the dreaded guillotine was erected at this spot and claimed the lives of thousands of people.

On each side of the obelisk are two fountains with bronze-tailed mermaids and bare-breasted sea nymphs. Gray-beige statues ring the square, honoring the cities of France. To symbolize France's loss of Alsace and Lorraine to Germany in 1871, the statue of Strasbourg was covered with a black drapery that wasn't lifted until the end of World War I (when the territory was restored). Two of the palaces on place de la Concorde are today the Ministry of the Navy and the deluxe Hôtel de

Crillon. They were designed in the 1760s by Ange-Jacques Gabriel. For a spectacular sight, look down the Champs-Elysées. The gateway of the Tuileries is flanked by the *Winged Horses* of Coysevox.

☕ **TAKE A BREAK** The **Bar of the Hôtel de Crillon**, 10 place de la Concorde (☎ **01-44-71-15-00**), is one of the best places in the world to have a drink. Fashion designer Sonia Rykiel has given it new luster, and the drinks, the setting, the ambience, and the atmosphere of "Paree" remain undiminished over the decades.

From place de la Concorde, you can enter the:

8. **Jardin des Tuileries,** as much a part of Paris as the Seine. These statue-studded gardens were designed by Le Nôtre, the gardener of Louis XIV. About 100 years before that, a palace was ordered built here by Catherine de Médicis, which was occupied by Louis XVI after he left Versailles. Napoléon I also called the palace home. Twice attacked by the people of Paris, it was finally burned to the ground in 1871 and never rebuilt. The gardens, however, remain, the trees arranged geometrically in orderly designs. Even the paths are straight, instead of winding as in English gardens. The fountains, though, soften the sense of order and formality.

The neoclassical statuary is often insipid and is occasionally desecrated by rebellious "art critics." Seemingly half of Paris is found in the Tuileries on a warm spring day, listening to the chirping birds and watching the daffodils and red tulips bloom. Fountains bubble, and parents push baby carriages around the grounds where 18th-century revolutionaries killed the king's Swiss guard.

At the end of your walking tour of the Tuileries—2 miles from place Charles-de-Gaulle–Etoile—you'll be at the:

9. **Arc de Triomphe du Carrousel,** at the cour du Carrousel. Accommodating three walkways and supported by marble columns, the monument honors the Grande Armée, celebrating Napoléon's victory at Austerlitz on December 5, 1805. The arch is surmounted by statuary, a chariot, and four bronze horses. At this point, you'll be at the doorstep of the Louvre.

WALKING TOUR 2
Montmartre

Start: Place Pigalle.
Finish: Place Pigalle.
Time: 5 hours—more if you break for lunch. It's a 3-mile trek.
Best Time: Any day that it isn't raining. Set out by 10am at the latest.
Worst Time: After dark.

The traditional way to explore Montmartre is on foot (see also Section 3 on Montmartre, in Chapter 6). Take the Métro to place Pigalle. Turn right after leaving the station and proceed down boulevard de Clichy, turn left at the Cirque Medrano, and begin the climb up rue des Martyrs. Upon reaching rue des Abbesses, turn left and walk along this street, crossing place des Abbesses. Walk uphill along rue Ravignan, which leads directly to place Emile-Goudeau, a tree-studded square in the middle of rue Ravignan. At no. 13, across from the Timhotel, stood the:

1. **Bateau-Lavoir** (Boat Washhouse), called the cradle of cubism. Although gutted by fire in 1970, it has been reconstructed by the city of Paris. Picasso once lived here, and in the winter of 1905–06 painted one of the world's most famous portraits, *The Third Rose* (Gertrude Stein). Other residents have included Kees van

Montmartre

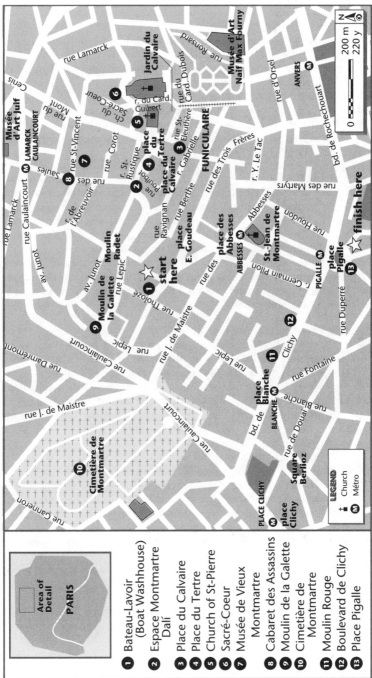

1. Bateau-Lavoir (Boat Washhouse)
2. Espace Montmartre Dalí
3. Place du Calvaire
4. Place du Tertre
5. Church of St-Pierre
6. Sacré-Coeur
7. Musée de Vieux Montmartre
8. Cabaret des Assassins
9. Moulin de la Galette
10. Cimetière de Montmartre
11. Moulin Rouge
12. Boulevard de Clichy
13. Place Pigalle

LEGEND
+ Church
Ⓜ Métro

Area of Detail
PARIS

233

Dongen and Juan Gris. Modigliani had his studio nearby, as did Rousseau and Braque.

Rue Ravignan ends at place Jean-Baptiste-Clément. Go to the end of the street and cross it onto rue Norvins (which will be on your right). This intersection, one of the most famous street scenes of Montmartre (and painted by Utrillo), is the meeting point of rues Norvins, St-Rustique, and des Saules. Turn right and head down rue Poulbot. At no. 11 you'll come to the:

2. **Espace Montmartre Dalí** (☎ **01-42-64-40-10**). This phantasmagorical world of Dalí features 300 original works by the artist, including his famous 1956 lithograph of *Don Quixote*. It's open daily from 10am to 6pm, charging 35 F ($7) for adults, 25 F ($5) for children.

☕ **TAKE A BREAK**   Chances are, you'll be in Montmartre for lunch. Many restaurants, especially those around place du Tertre, are unabashed tourist traps. You'll be asked eight times if you want your portrait sketched in charcoal. However, **La Maison-Rose,** 2 rue de l'Abreuvoir, is a good bargain. This was once the atelier of Utrillo, and the famous French singer Charles Aznavour used to perform here. The little pink house is about 300 yards from place du Tertre. But if you want better food, then leave the place du Tertre area and take a 12-minute walk down the *butte* to **Le Maquis,** 69 rue Caulaincourt. The prices are reasonable, and in sunny weather you can try for a seat on the tiny terrace. The restaurant is open Tuesday to Saturday.

Rue Poulbot crosses the tiny:

3. **Place du Calvaire,** which offers a panoramic view of Paris. On this square (a plaque marks the house) lived artist, painter, and lithographer Maurice Neumont (1868–1930). From here, follow the sounds of an oompah band to:

4. **Place du Tertre,** the old town square of Montmartre. Its cafés are overflowing, its art galleries (in and out of doors) always overcrowded. Some of the artists still wear berets, and the cafés bear such names as La Bohème—you get the point. Everything is so loaded with local color—applied as heavily as on a Seurat canvas—that it gets a little redundant.

Right off the square fronting rue du Mont-Cenis is the:

5. **Church of St-Pierre.** Originally a Benedictine abbey, it has played many roles— Temple of Reason during the French Revolution, food depot, clothing store, even a munitions factory. Nowadays it's back to being a church. In 1147 the present church was consecrated; it's one of the oldest in Paris. Two of the columns in the choir stall are the remains of a Roman temple. Note among the sculptured works a nun with the head of a pig, a symbol of sensual vice. At the entrance of the church are three bronze doors sculpted by Gismondi in 1980. The middle door depicts the life of St. Peter. The left door is dedicated to St. Denis, first bishop of Paris, and the right door to the Holy Virgin.

Facing St-Pierre, turn right and follow rue Azaïs to:

6. **Basilique du Sacré-Coeur,** overlooking square Willette (see Section 10 in Chapter 6 for a complete description). Facing the basilica, take the street on the left (rue du Cardinal-Guibert), then turn left onto rue du Chevalier-de-la-Barre and go to rue du Mont-Cenis, taking a right.

FROM MONT CENIS TO PLACE PIGALLE   Continue on this street to rue Corot, at which point turn left. At no. 12 is the:

7. **Musée de Vieux Montmartre** (☎ **01-46-06-61-11**), with a wide collection of mementos of *vieux Montmartre*. This famous 17th-century house was formerly

occupied by Dufy, van Gogh, and Renoir. Suzanne Valadon and her son, Utrillo, also lived here. It's open Tuesday to Sunday from 11am to 6pm. Admission is 25 F ($5) for adults, 20 F ($4) for students, free for children 11 and under.

From the museum, turn right heading up rue des Saules past a winery, a reminder of the days when Montmartre was a farming village on the outskirts of Paris. A grape-harvesting festival is held here every October.

The intersection of rue des Saules and rue St-Vincent is one of the most visited and photographed corners of the *butte.* Here, on one corner, sits the famous old:

8. Cabaret des Assassins, long ago renamed Au Lapin Agile (see Chapter 9 for details).

Continue along rue St-Vincent, passing the Cimetière St-Vincent on your right. Utrillo is just one of the many famous artists buried here. Take a left turn onto rue Girardon and climb the stairs. In a minute or two you'll spot on your right two of the windmills (*moulins*) that used to dot the *butte.* One of these:

9. Moulin de la Galette (entrance at 1 av. Junot), was immortalized by Renoir.

Turn right onto rue Lepic and walk past no. 54. In 1886 van Gogh lived here with Guillaumin. Take a right turn onto rue Joseph-de-Maistre, then left again on rue Caulaincourt until you reach the:

10. Cimetière de Montmartre, second in fame only to Père-Lachaise. The burial ground (Métro: Clichy) lies west of the *butte,* north of boulevard de Clichy. (See Section 14, "Cemeteries," in Chapter 6 for more information.)

From the cemetery, take avenue Rachel, turn left onto boulevard de Clichy, and go to place Blanche, where an even better-known windmill than the one in Renoir's painting stands, the:

11. Moulin Rouge, one of the most talked-about nightclubs in the world. It was immortalized by Toulouse-Lautrec.

From place Blanche, you can begin a descent down:

12. Boulevard de Clichy, fighting off the pornographers and hustlers trying to lure you into tawdry sex joints. With some rare exceptions—notably the citadels of the *chansonniers*—boulevard de Clichy is one gigantic tourist trap. Still, as Times Square is to New York, boulevard de Clichy is to Paris: Everyone who comes to Paris invariably winds up here. The boulevard strips and peels its way down to:

13. Place Pigalle, center of nudity in Paris. The square is named after a French sculptor, Pigalle, whose closest association with nudity was a depiction of Voltaire in the buff. Place Pigalle, of course, was the notorious "Pig Alley" of World War II. Toulouse-Lautrec had his studio right off Pigalle at 5 av. Frochot. When she was lonely and hungry, Edith Piaf sang in the alleyways, hoping to earn a few francs for the night.

WALKING TOUR 3
The Latin Quarter

Start: Place St-Michel.
Finish: The Panthéon.
Time: 3 hours, not counting stops.
Best Time: Any school day, Monday to Friday, from 9am to 4pm.
Worst Time: Sunday morning, when everybody is asleep.

This is the precinct of the Université de Paris (known for its most famous constituent, the Sorbonne), where students meet and fall in love over coffee and croissants. Rabelais named it the *quartier latin* after the students and the professors who spoke

The Latin Quarter

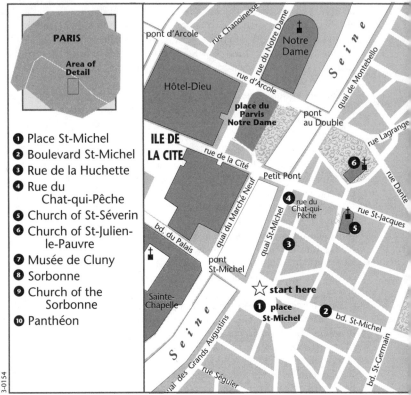

PARIS

Area of Detail

1. Place St-Michel
2. Boulevard St-Michel
3. Rue de la Huchette
4. Rue du Chat-qui-Pêche
5. Church of St-Séverin
6. Church of St-Julien-le-Pauvre
7. Musée de Cluny
8. Sorbonne
9. Church of the Sorbonne
10. Panthéon

pont d'Arcole — rue Chanoinesse — rue du Notre Dame — Notre Dame — Seine — quai de Montebello

Hôtel-Dieu — rue d'Arcole — place du Parvis Notre Dame — pont au Double — rue Lagrange

ILE DE LA CITÉ — rue de la Cité — Petit Pont — 6 — rue Dante

quai du Marché Neuf — bd. du Palais — quai St-Michel — 4 rue du Chat-qui-Pêche — rue St-Jacques — 5 — 3

pont St-Michel — Sainte-Chapelle — ☆ start here — 1 place St-Michel — 2 bd. St-Michel

Seine — quai des Grands Augustins — rue Séguier — bd. St-Germain

3-0154

Latin in the classrooms and on the streets. The sector teems with belly-dancers, exotic restaurants, sidewalk cafés, bookstalls, *caveaux,* and *clochards* and *chiffonniers* (bums and ragpickers). A good starting point for your tour is:

1. **Place St-Michel** (Métro: Pont-St-Michel), where Balzac used to get water from the fountain when he was a youth. This center was the scene of much Resistance fighting in the summer of 1944. The quarter centers around:

2. **Boulevard St-Michel** to the south, which the students call "boul Mich." From place St-Michel, with your back to the Seine, turn left down:

3. **Rue de la Huchette,** the setting of Elliot Paul's *The Last Time I Saw Paris.* Paul first wandered onto this typical street "on a soft summer evening, and entirely by chance," in 1923. Although much has changed since his time, some of the buildings are so old that they have to be propped up by timbers. Paul captured the spirit of the street more evocatively than anyone, writing of "the delivery wagons, makeshift vehicles propelled by pedaling boys, pushcarts of itinerant vendors, knife-grinders, umbrella menders, a herd of milk goats, and the neighborhood pedestrians." Branching off from this street to your left is:

4. **Rue du Chat-qui-Pêche** (Street of the Cat Who Fishes), said to be the shortest, narrowest street in the world, containing not one door and only a handful of windows. It's usually filled with garbage or lovers—or both.

Now, retrace your steps toward place St-Michel and turn left at the intersection with rue de la Harpe, which leads to rue St-Séverin. At the intersection, take a left to see the:

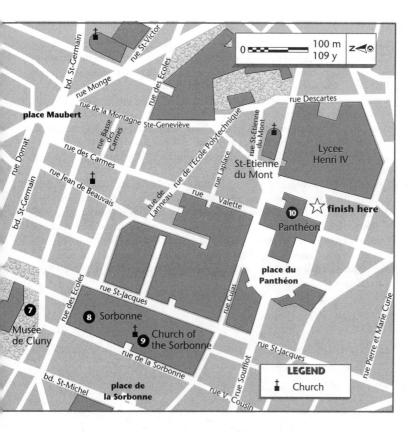

5. Church of St-Séverin (see Section 6 in Chapter 6 for details). After a visit to this flamboyant Gothic church, go back to rue St-Séverin and follow it to rue Galande. Stay on rue Galande until you reach the:

6. Church of St-Julien-le-Pauvre. First stand at the gateway and look at the beginning of rue Galande, especially the old houses with the steeples of St-Séverin rising across the way—one of the most characteristic and most painted scenes on the Left Bank. Enter the courtyard and you'll be in medieval Paris. The garden to the left of the entrance offers the best view of Notre-Dame.

Everyone from Rabelais to Thomas Aquinas has passed through the doors of this church. Prior to the 6th century a chapel stood on this spot. The present structure goes back to the Longpont monks, who began work on it in 1170 (making it the oldest existing church in Paris). In 1655 it was given to the Hôtel Dieu, and in time it became a small warehouse for salt. In 1889 it was given to the followers of the Melchite Greek rite, a branch of the Byzantine church.

☕ **TAKE A BREAK** At 14 rue St-Julien-le-Pauvre, **The Tea Caddy** (☎ 01-43-54-15-56) is perhaps one of the most charming tea salons in Paris. It serves light lunches, salads, omelets, quiches, and, of course, tea.

Return to rue Galande. Turn left at the intersection with rue St-Séverin. Continue on until you reach rue St-Jacques, then turn left and follow it to boulevard St-Germain. Turn right onto the boulevard and follow it until you reach rue de Cluny. Turn left and follow the street to the entrance to the:

7. Musée de Cluny (see Section 6 in Chapter 6 for details). Even if you're rushed, take time out to see *The Lady and the Unicorn* tapestry. After your visit to the Cluny Museum, exit onto boulevard St-Michel, but instead of heading back to place St-Michel, turn left and walk down to place de la Sorbonne and the:

8. Sorbonne, a constituent of the Université de Paris, one of the most famous academic institutions in the world. Founded in the 13th century, it had become the most prestigious university in the West by the 14th century, attracting such professors as Thomas Aquinas; subsequently, it was reorganized by Napoléon in 1806.

At first glance from place de la Sorbonne, the Sorbonne seems architecturally undistinguished. In truth, it was rather indiscriminately reconstructed at the turn of the century. The same cannot be said for the:

9. Church of the Sorbonne (Métro: St-Michel), built in 1635 by Le Mercier, which contains the marble tomb of Cardinal Richelieu, a work by Girardon based on a design by Le Brun. At his feet is the remarkable statue *Learning in Tears.*

From the church take rue Victor-Cousin south to the intersection with rue Soufflot. Turn left. At the end of this street lies place du Panthéon and the:

10. Panthéon (see Section 6 in Chapter 6). Sitting atop Mont Ste-Geneviève, this nonreligious temple is the final resting place of such distinguished figures as Hugo, Zola, Rousseau, and Voltaire.

Shopping

by Suzy Gershman

Suzy Gershman is the author of Frommer's Born
to Shop series. In Born to Shop Paris she offers
hundreds of sources, tips, and insider secrets
geared to the serious shopper.

Shopping is the local pastime of the Parisians; some would even say
it reflects the the city's very soul. The City of Light is one of the rare
places in the world where you don't go out to go shopping—instead,
shopping surrounds your very existence. Each walk you take im-
merses you in the legendary and uniquely French tradition of style.
The windows, the stores, the people (yes, and even their dogs), brim
with energy, creativity, and a sense of visual expression found in few
other cities.

You don't have to buy anything to appreciate shopping in Paris;
just soak up all the delicious consumerism as the true art form the
French have made it. Look in the *vitrines* (display windows), get
ideas, and gawk—and take home with you a whole new education
in style.

1 The Shopping Scene

It's traditional when you walk into a French store to greet the owner
or sales clerk with a direct address, not a fey smile or even weak
bonjour. Only "Bonjour, madame" (or "monsieur") will do.

BEST BUYS

Perfumes, Makeup & Beauty Treatments: A flat discount of 20%
to 30% makes these items a great buy; qualify for a détaxe refund
(see below) and you'll save 40% to 45% off the Paris retail price,
which can bring home goods at half the U.S. price. *Note:* So-called
duty free shops abound in Paris and are always less expensive than
the ones at the airport.

For bargain cosmetics, try out French dime store and drugstore
brands such as **Bourjois** (made in the Chanel factories), **Lierac,** and
Galenic. Vichy, famous for its water (not its government), has a
complete skin-care and makeup line. The newest retail trend in Paris
is the *parapharmacie,* a type of discount drugstore loaded with inexpensive brands, health cures, French beauty regimes, and diet plans.
These usually offer a 20% discount.

Foodstuffs: Nothing makes a better souvenir than a piece of France
brought home to savor later. Supermarkets are located in prime tour-
ist neighborhoods; stock up on coffee, designer chocolates (Lanvin!
Only $5!), mustards (try Maille brand), and for the kids, perhaps
American products in French packages. Mars, anyone? (That's Milky
Way to you Americans.)

Fun Fashion: Sure you can splurge for couture or prêt, but French teens and trendsetters have their own stores where the latest looks are affordable. Even the dime stores in Paris sell designer copies and hotshot styles.

In the stalls in front of the department stores on boulevard Haussmann you'll find some of the latest fashion contraptions, guaranteed for a week's worth of small talk once you get home.

Check out Le Pony, a wired fabric hair accessory with a hole stitched in (like a large button hole) to insert your ponytail before you twist and wrap. Voilà, for $10, now you are French!

VAT REFUNDS

The French tax is now a hefty 20.6%, but you can get most of that back if you spend 1,200 F ($240) or more in any store that participates in the VAT-refund program (see "Fast Facts: Paris," in Chapter 3). Most stores participate, although discount perfume shops usually peg the minimum at 1,200 F *net,* which is 1,600 or 1,700 F ($320 or $340).

This can get particularly confusing when you're buying perfume and makeup— among the best buys Paris has to offer—because some of the stores list their discounted price, which means all you need to do is run the bill up to 1,200 F. Other stores list the regular price and then take off 25% in front of your eyes—like magic— so that you can watch the discount being applied to your bill. In this case, you need to get the bill to 1,600 F or 1,700 F, which becomes 1,200 F when the price is recalculated.

Just because one perfume discounter tells you that you have to spend 1,600 to 1,700 F to get a refund and another tells you to spend 1,200 F doesn't mean that one is offering you a better deal than the other!

Once you meet your required minimum-purchase amount, you qualify for a tax refund. The amount of the refund varies with the way the refund is handled and the fact that some stores charge you a fee for processing it. So the refund amount at a department store may be 13%, while at a small shop it will be 15% or even 18%.

You'll receive détaxe papers in the shop (some stores, like Hermès, have their own; others provide a government form). Fill in the forms before you arrive at the airport, and expect to stand in line at the Customs desk for as long as half an hour. You're required by law to show the goods at the airport, so have them on you or visit the Customs office before you check your luggage. Once the papers have been mailed to the authorities, a credit will appear—often months later—on your credit- or charge-card bill.

All refunds are processed at the final point of departure from the European Union, so if you're going to another EU country, don't apply for the refund in France.

Be sure to mark the paperwork to request that your refund be applied to your credit or charge card so you aren't stuck with a check in francs that you can't cash. This also ensures the best rate of exchange. In some airports you're offered the opportunity to get your refund back in cash, which is tempting. If you accept cash in any currency other than francs, you'll be losing money on the conversion rate. You'll do far better with a credit/chrage-card conversion. Honest.

AIRPORT DUTY-FREE BOUTIQUES

Both airports have tons of shopping, but prices are often better in town, or a mere 2 to 3 F (40¢ to 60¢) better at the duty-free. Charles de Gaulle Airport has a virtual shopping mall, with crystal, cutlery, chocolates, luggage, wine, whisky, pipes and lighters, lingerie, silk scarves, perfume, knitwear, jewelry, cameras and equipment, cheeses, and even antiques. Both airports have a small branch of Virgin Megastore.

Best bets at the airport are goods from the deluxe French houses that cost less than 1,200 F (total), so while you forfeit the détaxe refund, you at least get a break on the actual VAT.

Note: A Hermès scarf costs 1,300 F in town but qualifies you for a 20% tax refund; the price at the airport is 1,040 F—exactly the same as the discounted in-town price—but the selection in town is far superior to what's at the airport.

BUSINESS HOURS

Shops are *usually* open Monday to Saturday from 10am to 7pm, but the hours vary greatly and Monday mornings in Paris don't run at full throttle. Small shops sometimes take a 2-hour lunch break, and may not open at all until after lunch on Monday.

Aside from Monday, while most stores open at 10am on weekdays and Saturday, some stores prefer to open at 9:30am or 11am. Thursday is the best day for late-night shopping, with stores open until 9 or 10pm. Monoprix, a French dime store (see below), is open until 9pm every night.

Sunday shopping is currently limited to tourist areas and flea markets, although there is growing demand for full-scale Sunday hours as in the States and the U.K. The big department stores are now open for the five Sundays prior to Christmas, but other than that, most Parisian stores are dead on *dimanche*.

Carrousel du Louvre, a mall adjacent to the Louvre, is open and hopping on Sunday, but closed Monday. The tourist shops that line rue Rivoli across from the Louvre are all open on Sunday. The antiques villages are all open, as are assorted flea markets and specialty events. There are several good food markets in the streets on Sunday. The Virgin Megastore on the Champs-Elysées pays a fine in order to stay open on Sunday. It's *the* teen hangout.

U.S. CUSTOMS

You're allowed to bring overseas purchases with a retail value of $400 back into the United States, providing you have been out of the country at least 48 hours and have claimed no similar exemptions within 30 days. After your duty-free $400 is exceeded, a tax of 10% is levied on the next $1,000 worth of items purchased abroad.

You pay no duty on antiques or art, if such items are 100 years old or more, even if they cost $4 million or more. In addition, you're allowed to send one gift a day to family or friends back home, providing its value does not exceed $50.

SHIPPING IT HOME

Shipping costs will possibly double your cost on goods. And you'll also pay U.S. Customs duties on the shipped items if they're valued at more than $50. The good news: Détaxe is automatically applied to any item shipped to an American—no need to worry about the 1,200 F minimum. Some stores have a $100 minimum for shipping. You can also walk into any PT&T (post office) and mail home a jiffy bag or small box of goodies. French do-it-yourself boxes cannot be reopened once closed, so pack carefully. The clerk at the post office will help you build the box (it's tricky), seal it, and send it off.

GREAT SHOPPING NEIGHBORHOODS

Paris neighborhoods are designated by their arrondissements (see Chapter 3). When you're planning a day of combined sightseeing and shopping, check a map to see how the arrondissements connect so that you can maximize your efforts. While the core of Paris is made up of 20 arrondissements, only a handful of them are prime real estate in terms of shopping. Here are the best of the shopping arrondissements:

1er & 8e arrondissements: These two *quartiers* adjoin each other (invisibly) and form the heart of Paris's best Right Bank shopping strip—together they're just one big hunting ground. This area includes the famed **rue du Faubourg St-Honoré,** where the big designer houses are, and the **Champs-Elysées,** where the mass market and teen scene is hot. At one end of the 1er is the **Palais Royal,** one of the best shopping secrets in Paris, where an arcade of boutiques flanks each side of the garden of the former palace.

The 1er also contains **avenue Montaigne,** the most glamorous shopping street in Paris, boasting 2 blocks of the fanciest shops in the world, where you simply float from big name to big name and in a few hours can see everything from **Louis Vuitton** to **Ines de la Fressange,** the model turned retailer. Avenue Montaigne is also the address of **Joseph,** a British design firm, and **Porthault,** makers of the fanciest sheets in the world.

2e arrondissement: Right behind the Palais Royal is the **Garment District** (Sentier), as well as a few very sophisticated shopping secrets such as **place des Victoires.** This area also hosts a few old-fashioned *passages,* alleys filled with tiny stores, such as **Galerie Vivienne,** on rue Vivienne.

3e & 4e arrondissements: The difference between these two arrondissements gets fuzzy, especially around **place des Vosges**—center stage of the **Marais.** No matter. The districts offer several dramatically different shopping experiences.

On the surface, the shopping includes the "real people stretch" (where all the nonmillionaires shop) of rue Rivoli and rue St-Antoine, featuring everything from **The Gap** and a branch of **Marks & Spencer** to local discount stores and mass merchants. Two "real people" department stores are in this area, **Samaritane** and **BHV;** there's also **Les Halles** and the **Beaubourg,** which is anchored by the Centre Georges-Pompidou.

Meanwhile, hidden away in the Marais is a medieval warren of twisting tiny streets all chock-a-block with cutting-edge designers and up-to-the-minute fashions and trends. Start by walking around place des Vosges for art galleries, designer shops, and fabulous little finds. Then dive in and simply get lost in the area leading to the Picasso Museum.

Finally, the 4e is also the home of the Bastille—an up-and-coming area for artists and galleries—where the newest entry on the retail scene, **Viaduc des Arts** (which actually stretches into the 12e), is situated.

6e & 7e arrondissements: While the 6th is one of the most famous shopping districts in Paris—it's the soul of the **Left Bank**—a lot of the really good stuff is hidden in the zone that becomes the wealthy residential district of the 7th. **Rue du Bac,** stretching from the 6e to the 7e in a few blocks, stands for all that wealth and glamour can buy.

8e arrondissement: See "1er & 8e arrondissements," above.

9e arrondissement: To add to the fun of shopping the Right Bank, the 9e sneaks in behind the 1er so that if you choose not to walk toward the Champs-Elysées and the 8e, you can instead head to the city's big department stores, all built in a row along **boulevard Haussmann** in the 9th. The department stores here include not only the two big French icons, **Au Printemps** and **Galeries Lafayette,** but a large branch of Britain's **Marks & Spencer** and a newly renovated branch of the Dutch answer to K-mart, the low-priced **C&A.**

ANTIQUES

Le Louvre des Antiquaires. 2 place du Palais-Royal, 1er. ☎ **01-42-97-27-00.** Métro: Palais-Royal.

Located directly across from the Louvre, with three levels of fancy knickknacks, many of them dripping with gilt, Le Louvre des Antiquaires is just the place if you're looking for 30 Baccarat crystal matching champagne flutes from the 1930s, a Sèvres tea service dated 1773, or maybe a small signed Jean Fouquet pin of gold and diamonds. Too stuffy? No problem. There's always the 1940 Rolex with the aubergine crocodile strap.

Prices can be high, but a few reasonable items are hidden here. What's more, the Sunday scene is fabulous, and there's a café with a variety of lunch menus beginning around 100 F ($20). Pick up a free map and brochure of the premises from the information desk. Open Tuesday to Sunday from 11am to 7pm (closed Sunday in July and August).

Mlinaric, Henry & Zervudachi. 54 Galerie de Montpensier, Palais Royal, 1er. ☎ **01-42-96-08-62.** Métro: Palais-Royal.

David Mlinaric, one of the three musketeers here, is the British interior designer who re-created Spencer House—Diana's ancestral manse in London—as well as all of Lord Jacob Rothschild's private residences. Tino Zervudachi is considered one of the hot young turks in Paris design. Hugh Henry, like Mlinaric, is English. Together they're considered the chicest antique dealers on the Right Bank. They specialize in museum-quality 18th-century items. Open Tuesday to Saturday from 11am to 7pm.

Village St-Paul. 23–27 rue St-Paul, 4e. No phone. Métro: St-Paul.

This isn't an antiques center but a cluster of individual dealers in their own hole-in-the-wall hideouts; the rest of the street, stretching from the river to the Marais, is lined with dealers, but most of them aren't open on Sunday. Village St-Paul *is* open on Sunday—and hopping. Bring your camera, because inside the courtyards and alleys are every dreamer's visions of hidden Paris: many dealers in a courtyard selling furniture and other decorative items in French country and formal styles. Open Thursday to Monday from 11am to 7pm.

ART

Carnavalette. 2 rue des Francs-Bourgeois, 3e. ☎ **01-42-72-91-92.** Métro: St-Paul.

Set adjacent to place des Vosges in the Marais, this historic shop sells unusual, one-of-a-kind engravings, plus a large collection of satirical 19th-century magazines and newspapers. Open daily from 10:30am to 6:30pm.

Galerie Adrien Maeght. 42 and 46 rue du Bac, 7e. ☎ **01-45-48-45-15**. Métro: Bac.

This art house is among the most famous names in galleries, selling contemporary art on a very fancy Left Bank street that's far more chic and fashionable than the bohemian Left Bank Picasso knew. Open Tuesday to Saturday from 9:30am to 1pm and 2 to 7pm.

Galerie 27. 27 rue de Seine, 6e. ☎ **01-43-54-78-54.** Métro: St-Germain-des-Prés.

This tiny closet of a store sells lithographs by some of the most famous artists of the early 20th century, including Picasso, Chagall, Miró, and Léger. Open Tuesday to Saturday from 10am to 1pm and 2:30 to 7pm.

Viaduc des Arts. 9–147 av. Daumensil, 12e. ☎ **01-43-40-80-80**. Métro: Bastille, Ledru-Rollin, Reuilly-Diderot, or Gare-de-Lyon.

This newly renovated establishment occupies a long, 2-block stretch from the Bastille Opéra to the Gare de Lyon, and features art galleries and artisans in individual boutiques created within the arches of an old train viaduct. As you can tell from the number of Métro stops that serve the address, you can start at one end and work your way to the other—or start in the middle. It's nothing spectacular, but it makes for interesting shopping. Open Tuesday to Saturday from 11am to 7pm.

BOOKS

Brentano's. 37 av. de l'Opéra, 2e. ☎ **01-42-61-52-50**. Métro: Opéra.

Brentano's is a large English-language bookstore selling guides, maps, novels, and nonfiction as well as greeting cards, postcards, holiday items, and gifts. It's conveniently located 1 block from the Opéra Garnier. Open Monday to Saturday from 10am to 7pm.

Tea and Tattered Pages. 24 rue Mayet, 6e. ☎ **01-40-65-94-35**. Métro: Duroc.

At this cute, cozy, adorable bookshop, you can take a break from browsing among the shelves to have tea at a little table provided. Though it's in a slightly out-of-the-way location, the shop's extra dose of charm makes it worth the trip. Open daily from 11am to 7pm.

The Village Voice

6 rue Princesse, 6e. ☎ **01-46-33-36-47**. Métro: Mabillon.

On a side street in the heart of the best Left Bank shopping district, this is a favorite venue for expatriate Yankees. The location is in the vicinity of some of the Left Bank gathering places described in Gertrude Stein's *The Autobiography of Alice B. Toklas*. The shop is a hangout for the literati of Paris. Open on Monday from 2 to 8pm and Tuesday to Saturday from 11am to 8pm.

W. H. Smith & Son. 248 rue de Rivoli, 1er. ☎ **01-44-77-88-99**. Métro: Concorde.

This bookstore stocks books, magazines, and newspapers published in English (most titles are from Britain). You can get the *Times* of London, of course, and the Sunday *New York Times* is available every Monday. There's a fine selection of maps and travel guides. There's also a special children's section that includes comics. Open Monday to Saturday from 9:30am to 7pm and on Sunday from 1 to 6pm.

CHILDREN: FASHION, SHOES & ASSORTED KID STUFF

Au Nain Bleu. 406 rue St-Honoré, 8e. ☎ **01-42-60-39-01**. Métro: Concorde.

This is the largest, oldest, and most centrally located toy store in all of Paris. More important, it's probably the fanciest toy store in the world. But don't panic—in addition to the elaborate and expensive fancy stuff, there are rows of cheaper toys in jars like penny candy on the first floor. Open Monday to Saturday from 9:45am to 6:30pm.

Bonpoint. 15 rue Royale, 8e. ☎ **01-47-42-52-63**. Métro: Concorde.

Grandparent alert! Bonpoint is part of a well-known *almost* haute couture chain. The clothing here is well tailored, traditional—and very expensive. The shop sells clothes for boys and girls ages 1 day to 16 years. Drool over formal party and confirmation dresses, and the long and elegant baptism robes, embroidered in France and edged in lace—and if you have the means, outfit your child or grandchild in the most sophisticated fashions. Open Monday to Saturday from 10am to 7pm.

Dipaki. 18 rue Vignon, 9e. ☎ **01-42-66-24-74.** Métro: Madeleine.

If you prefer clothes that have hip, hot style and color but are wearable, washable, and affordable, forget Bonpoint and try this small shop—it's a representative of a truly sensational French line of clothes for toddlers. And it's only a block from place de la Madeleine. Open Monday to Saturday from 10am to 7pm.

Natalys. 92 av. des Champs-Elysées, 8e. ☎ **01-43-59-17-65.** Métro: Franklin-D-Roosevelt.

This is part of a French chain with a dozen stores in Paris and many elsewhere—they're upscale mass marketers of children's wear, children's needs (layette, stroller), and maternity wear. They have just enough French panache without going over the top in design or price. Open Monday to Saturday from 10am to 7pm.

Nature et Decouvertes. In the Carrousel du Louvre, 99 rue Rivoli, 1er. ☎ **01-47-03-47-43.** Métro: Palais-Royal.

This French version of the Nature Company also has other addresses in Paris that are convenient for tourists. It doesn't matter where you go, but it's worth visiting a Nature et Decouvertes to find a gift for the kids, or to bring the kids to browse and buy. A small frog *cliquet* (a little toy noisemaker) for $3 is all it takes. Open Tuesday to Sunday from 10am to 8pm.

Pom d'Api. 28 rue du Four, 4e. ☎ **01-45-48-39-31.** Métro: St-Germain-des-Prés.

This adorable chain of kiddie shoes stores has other locations in Paris and all over France; it carries tiny gold woven sandals, patent leather high tops, and much more. Open Monday to Saturday from 10:15am to 7pm.

CHINA & CRYSTAL

Baccarat. 11 place de la Madeleine, 8e (☎ **01-42-65-36-26;** Métro: Madeleine), and 30 bis rue de Paradis, 10e (☎ **01-47-70-64-30;** Métro: Gare-de-l'Est).

Purveyor to kings and presidents of France since 1764, Baccarat produces world-renowned full-lead crystal in dinner wares, jewelry, chandeliers, and even statuary. The rue de Paradis address is the factory cum museum and store, but this is no discount factory shop; it's open Monday to Friday from 10am to 6:30pm and on Saturday from 10am to 5pm. The showroom on place de la Madeleine (open on Monday from 10am to 6:30pm, Tuesday to Friday from 9:30am to 6:30pm, and on Saturday from 10am to 6:30pm) is fancy, but the factory is incredible. Do it once in your lifetime!

Lalique. 11 rue Royale, 8e. ☎ **01-42-65-33-70.** Métro: Concorde.

Lalique is known around the world for its smoky frosted-glass sculpture, art deco crystal, and unique perfume bottles. The shop sells a wide range of merchandise, including gorgeous silk scarves meant to compete with Hermès and leather belts with Lalique buckles. There's also a tiny boutique in the Carrousel du Louvre. Open Monday to Saturday from 9:30am to 6:30pm.

Limoges-Unic. 12 and 58 rue de Paradis, 10e. ☎ **01-47-70-54-49** or 47-70-61-49. Métro: Gare-de-l'Est

Housed in two shops of more or less equal size, each within a 5-minute walk of the other along the same street, this store is crammed with Limoges china brands such as Céralène, Haviland, and Bernardaud, as well as anything else you might need for the table: glass and crystal, silver, etc. They will ship your purchases to you, but it will severely cut into your savings. Open Monday to Saturday from 10am to 6:30pm.

CHOCOLATE

Christian Constant. 26 rue du Bac, 7e. ☎ **01-47-03-30-00.** Métro: Rue-du-Bac.

Chef of the Les Ambassadeurs restaurant, where he holds three Michelin stars, Constant is a chocolatier in his heart—of Paris's chocolate dealers, he is most often named tops in town. The little shop is unprepossessing; the chocolates are not. Figure to spend $100 a kilo. Open Monday to Saturday from 8am to 9pm.

Debauve et Gallais. 30 rue des Saints-Pères, 7e. ☎ **01-45-48-54-67.** Métro: Sèvres-Babylone.

Lose yourself in deep dark wood, deep dark chocolate, and one of Paris's best-known status brands. Note that the counters are lined by gentlemen who are doing the buying; there are few women who will splurge for the luxury. Open Monday to Saturday from 10am to 7pm.

Jadis et Gourmande. 27 rue Boissy-d'Anglas, 8e. ☎ **01-42-65-23-23.** Métro: Madeleine.

This small chain of Parisian chocolatiers has a less lofty rep than Christian Constant and much more reasonable prices. It's best known for its chocolate blocks of the alphabet, which allow you to spell out any message you want, in any language. *Merci* comes prepackaged. Open Monday to Saturday from 10am to 1pm and 2 to 7pm.

La Maison du Chocolat. 225 rue du Faubourg St-Honoré, 8e. ☎ **01-42-27-39-44.** Métro: Ternes.

This chocolate shop has five other Paris locations. At each, racks and racks of chocolates are priced individually or by the kilo, although it costs near or over $100 for a kilo. Note the similarity to Hermès when it comes to wrap and ribbon (and prices). These stores offer a variety of chocolate-based products, including chocolate pastries, which are usually more affordable than the candy, and even chocolate milk! Open Monday to Saturday from 9:30am to 7pm.

DEPARTMENT & DIME STORES

Au Printemps. 64 bd. Haussmann, 9e. ☎ **01-42-82-50-00.** Métro: Havre-Caumartin. RER: Auber.

Before you even enter this landmark store, stand outside and take a look at the facade: They just don't make 'em like that anymore. When you've thoroughly appreciated the building's superb architecture, head for the stores that occupy the structure: Au Printemps, the famous department store, and an affiliated housewares shop, Maison. Don't be alarmed that they sell fragrance on Maison's first floor—upstairs you'll find floors and floors of merchandise devoted to the home.

Au Printemps, which competes with its neighbor, Galeries Lafayette (see below), by also selling every designer and brand available in France, is next door. Note that Au Printemps feels more modern and American in style than Galeries Lafayette (GL), especially now that the first floor of the main store has been renovated to match Maison.

Don't write this store off as too American: Check out the magnificent stained-glass dome, built in 1923, through which turquoise-colored light cascades into **Café Flo** on the 6th floor, where you can have a coffee or a full meal. (GL also has a dome, but you can't eat under that one!) Complete menus are available, with dishes and appetizers beginning around 60 F ($12); the menu is composed of pictures so you needn't worry about your French accent.

Behind the two main stores, there's **Brummell,** Au Printemps' men's clothing store, as well as a branch of **Prisunic,** the dime store owned by Au Printemps which competes with Monoprix. This Prisunic also has a grocery store in it upstairs. It's not as special as Gourmet Lafayette but it's worth a look.

Interpreters stationed at the Welcome Service in the basement will help you claim your détaxe, find departments, etc. Au Printemps also has a discount card for tourists offering a flat 10% discount. Open Monday to Wednesday and on Friday and Saturday from 9:35am to 7pm, and on Thursday from 9:35am to 10pm.

Bon Marché. 22 rue de Sèvres, 7e. ☎ **01-44-39-80-00.** Métro: Sèvres-Babylone.

Another two-part department store, this one is on the Left Bank in the midst of all the cutie-pie boutiques. One building houses a gourmet grocery store with a small flea market upstairs; the other building is a basic source for all your general shopping needs. Open Monday to Saturday from 9:30am to 7pm.

Galeries Lafayette. 40 bd. Haussmann, 9e. ☎ **01-42-82-34-56.** Métro: Chaussée-d'Antin or Opéra. RER: Auber.

Built in 1912, Galeries Lafayette, an almost legendary Paris department store, is now divided into several subdivisions: **Galfa** (which specializes in men's clothing), **Lafayette Sports** (sporting goods), and two other general merchandise stores, both known just as "GL," though the larger one is often called *"le magasin principal"* (the main store).

Typically, the Galeries complements its vast selection with world-class service: There's a welcome desk, multilingual help, and a free shopping tote if you turn in receipts totaling 200 F ($40) or more. Be sure to pick up a tourist discount card from your travel agent before you leave home, or from your hotel or the store itself after you arrive in Paris—the card provides a flat 10% discount for tourist shoppers that has nothing to do with the VAT détaxe program.

Galeries Lafayette and its neighbor, Au Printemps, have been competing for Parisian shoppers for nearly a century; you'll find France firmly divided into GL types and Printemps types, although the differences between the two stores fades with global trends and international imports.

Right now, Galeries Lafayette is more old-fashioned in the way it does business and therefore feels a little more staid . . . and French. Open Monday to Wednesday and on Friday and Saturday from 9:30am to 6:45pm, and on Thursday from 9:30am to 9pm.

Next door to GL is a branch of the dime store **Monoprix,** which the chain also owns. This isn't the best Monoprix in town, but it's convenient and can give you a taste of French dime store magic.

Above Monoprix is another affiliated store, **Gourmet Lafayette,** one of the fanciest grocery stores in Paris, with prices half those offered at the famous Fauchon, Paris's "supermarket for millionaires" (see below). This store has its own entrance next to Monoprix, and has extended hours.

FASHION
COUTURE

It's not that madame wants to buy a $20,000 dress—it's just that madame is, how you say . . . curious? Entrez-vous—step this way.

Okay, this is how it works. The world of handmade garments—haute couture—is still private and very much closed. After all, very few women can afford clothes that begin at $10,000 but average $25,000. And while new buyers do join the ranks every now and then, these women are either the daughters of members of the club or have been in appropriate financial and social positions long enough that they have the proper connections.

One does not merely pop into a couture house to see what's new. One is invited. These days, there are only live shows for a few days, first for the press at a hotel or public venue, then for store buyers at the mother house. For the most part the clothes are then shown only on videotape because no one can afford to mount those shows anymore, and only a few house models are on staff.

Properly, once madame has made her appointment, and is seated on the sofa sipping tea, the *vendeuse* (private sales woman) has decided which garments might be appropriate for madame's needs and has them shown on the house model. The entire collection is not shown, just a few pieces that seem to meet madame's specifications for the season.

Madame sits and sips. Sometimes a style number is written down or a husband nods approvingly. Sometimes the designer himself (kiss kiss, darling, you look marvelous) sits on the sofa, scratches madame's dog behind the ears, and makes the appropriate sounds for certain garments that would be proper for particular social occasions that madame will be attending.

A list, or a computer program, tells the vendeuse what the other ladies have bought so there are no embarrassing moments later. When the decision to buy has been made, the fitter arrives. Madame, of course, knows the fitter and kisses him on both cheeks. He, too, knows all her secrets. At least three fittings of the garment will be made.

The visit to the maison is a deadly serious event—not something the girls do after lunch. A woman may be accompanied by her mother, her husband, or maybe her lover, but it's not a party.

The Seriously Best Dressed shop alone. They have relationships with a particular vendeuse, who knows all their tastes and secrets, and possibly with a few couture houses. Designers fight between them to win the attention of a trend setter, style maker, or highly visible client—Princess Marie Chantal of Greece is the current preferred wealthy fashion plate.

Runway samples are sold at the end of the season; they're an unspecified size roughly equivalent to a size 6 or 8. Customers of the house are offered first pick. Unsold goods will go up for sale discreetly in the back rooms of the designer's boutique or maybe a shop like Anna Lowe (see below).

CUTTING-EDGE CHIC

Azzadine Alaia. 7 rue de Moussy, 2e. ☎ **01-42-72-19-19.** Métro: Hôtel-de-Ville.

Alaia, who became the darling of French fashion in the 1970s, is the man who brought body consciousness back to put the "oh la la" in Paris chic. If you can't afford the current collection, try the stock shop around the corner at 18 rue de Verrerie (☎ 01-40-27-85-58), where last year's leftovers are sold at serious discounts. Open Monday to Saturday from 10am to 7pm.

Jean-Charles de Castelbajac. 6 place St-Sulpice, 6e. ☎ **01-46-33-83-32.** Métro: Odéon or St-Sulpice.

Castelbajac is the bad boy of French fashion, known for flamboyant yet amusing gear in primary colors, often with big bold sayings scribbled across the clothes. His store is located in a cluster of designer shops that's great for gawking. Open Monday to Saturday from 11am to 7pm.

Courrèges. 40 rue François-1er, 8e. ☎ **01-47-20-70-44.** Métro: Franklin-D-Roosevelt.

Don't look now: André Courrèges is not only back in style but considered hot. Even those little white vinyl go-go boots are back. In Courrèges's collection, humor meets

1970s retro with bold color, plastic, and fun. There's another branch of his store in the Carrousel du Louvre mall, and a discount shop as well, upstairs at 7 rue Turbigo (☎ 01-42-33-03-57; Métro: Etienne-Marcel). Open Monday to Friday from 9:45am to 6:45pm and on Saturday from 9:45am to 1pm and 2 to 6:45pm.

Elle. 30 rue St-Sulpice, 6e. ☎ **01-43-26-46-10.** Métro: Odéon.

Elle magazine runs its own boutique that sells specific items as featured in the magazine, most of them hot, hip, and affordable. The store carries both housewares and clothing items. Open Monday to Saturday from 10am to 7pm.

Jean-Paul Gaultier. 6 rue Vivienne, 2e. ☎ **01-42-86-05-05.** Métro: Bourse or Palais-Royal.

Hidden in one of Paris's most famous *passages,* this large boutique features Gaultier's street fashion made high fashion, the typical fare of this master punk turned tailor. Open on Monday from 11am to 7pm and Tuesday to Saturday from 10am to 7pm.

Hervé Léger. 29 rue du Faubourg St-Honoré, 8e. ☎ **01-44-51-57-17.** Métro: Concorde.

This creator of the Band Aid Dress, a tightly wrapped concoction of stretch materials and color, has opened his own shop for those with curves to flaunt and cash to burn. Open Monday to Saturday from 10am to 7pm.

Lolita Lempicka. 14 rue du Faubourg St-Honoré, 8e. ☎ **01-49-24-94-01.** Métro: Concorde.

Lolita, formerly of the hidden Marais and the underground fashion scene, has gone mainstream with her own shop—tiny but quite visible—on the street of streets. The clothes continue to be inventive and creative, and, despite her new location, are hardly mainstream. Open Monday to Saturday from 10am to 7pm.

Claude Montana. 31 rue de Grenelle, 7e. ☎ **01-45-49-13-02.** Métro: Sèvres-Babylone.

The State of Claude Montana he calls it, making a lame pun and stunning you into wondering just what state that could be. Confusion? Undress? Or merely deconstructed chic? For rock 'n' roll stars and wannabes, Montana's is the place. Open Monday to Saturday from 10:15am to 7pm.

Thierry-Mugler. 10 place des Victories, 2e. ☎ **01-42-60-06-37.** Métro: Palais-Royal or Bourse.

Thierry-Mugler is most famous for body-hugging suits whose almost space-age construction makes for a "power look" that combines a serious fashion statement with whimsy and imagination. This closet-sized boutique designed by André Putnam is part of the whole shopping thrill of place des Victoires, and even though there's another Thierry-Mugler shop at 49 av. Montaigne, stick with this one for the authentic Parisian shopping experience. Open on Monday from 11am to 1pm and 2 to 7pm, and Tuesday to Saturday from 10am to 1pm and 2 to 7pm.

DISCOUNT & RESALE

Anna Lowe. 35 av. Matignon, 8e. ☎ **01-43-59-96-61.** Métro: Miromesnil.

Anna Lowe is one of the premier boutiques in Paris for the discriminating woman who wishes to purchase a little Chanel, or perhaps a Versace, at discount. Many clothes are runway samples; some have been gently worn. The boutique is only half a block from rue du Faubourg St-Honoré, where haute couture is much more expensive. Open Monday to Saturday from 10:30am to 7pm.

Mendès. 65 rue Montmartre, 2e. ☎ **01-42-36-83-32.** Métro: Les-Halles.

In the center of the French garment district, nowhere near Montmartre (don't let the street address throw you), this store mainly sells Yves Saint Laurent leftovers. The Variations line is downstairs; Rive Gauche, upstairs. Prices, even though discounted, can be quite steep and you have to get lucky to find anything worth sighing over. Open Monday to Thursday from 10am to 6pm and on Friday and Saturday from 10am to 5pm.

Réciproque. 89–123 rue de la Pompe, 16e. ☎ **01-47-04-30-28.** Métro: Pompe.

Forget about serious bargains but celebrate what could be your only opportunity to own designer clothing of this calibre; every major big name is carried here, along with some shoes, accessories, menswear, and wedding gifts. Everything has been worn, but some items only on runways or during photography shoots. Open Tuesday to Saturday from 10:30am to 7pm.

FASHION FLAGSHIPS

Chanel. 31 rue Cambon, 1er. ☎ **01-42-86-28-00.** Métro: Concorde or Tuileries.

If you can't have the sun, the moon, and the stars, at least buy something with Coco Chanel's initials on it, either a serious fashion statement (drop-dead chic) or something fun and playful (tongue in chic). Karl Lagerfeld's Chanel designs come in all different flavors and have him laughing all the way to the bank.

This store is adjacent to the Chanel couture house and behind the Ritz, where Mademoiselle Chanel once lived. Check out the beautiful staircase of the *maison* before you shop the two-floor boutique—it's well worth a peek. Open Monday to Friday from 9:30am to 6:30pm and on Saturday from 10am to 6:30pm.

Christian Dior. 26–32 av. Montaigne, 8e. ☎ **01-40-73-54-44.** Métro: Franklin-D-Roosevelt.

This famous couture house is set up like a small department store, selling men's, women's, and children's clothing, as well as affordable gift items, makeup, and perfume on the first floor as you enter. Unlike some of the other big-name fashion houses, Dior is very approachable. Open Monday to Friday from 9:30am to 6:30pm and on Saturday from 10am to 6:30pm.

Hermès. 24 rue du Faubourg St-Honoré, 8e. ☎ **01-40-17-47-17.** Métro: Concorde.

The single most important status item in France is a scarf or tie from Hermès. But the choices don't stop there. This large flagship store has beach towels and accessories, dinner plates, clothing for men and women, a large collection of Hermès fragrances, and even a saddle shop—a package of postcards is the least expensive item sold.

Ask to see the private museum upstairs. Once back outside, note the horseman on the roof with his scarf-flag flying. Open on Monday and Saturday from 10am to 1pm and 2:15 to 6:30pm, and Tuesday to Friday from from 10am to 6:30pm.

Louis Vuitton. 6 place St-Germain-des-Prés, 6e. ☎ **01-45-49-62-32.** Métro: St-Germain-des-Prés.

This Left Bank store is so gorgeous to look at that the famed merchandise becomes secondary. Not content to cover the world with little LVs (Vuitton's designs are typically covered with the "LV" logo), Vuitton has branched into assorted colored leather goods, writing instruments, various travel products, and even publishing. The *Carnet du Voyage,* a do-it-yourself scrapbook graced with watercolors and space in which to jot down your own memories, is a souvenir worth saving for and handing down in your family.

Don't just consider this a swanky overpriced store or an icon in which you have no interest: This store is a museum. Check it out—you might learn something. Open Tuesday to Saturday from 10am to 7pm.

INTERNATIONAL DESIGNER BOUTIQUES

There are two primary fields of dreams in Paris when it comes to showcases for the international big names in design—**rue du Faubourg St-Honoré** and **avenue Montaigne.** While the Left Bank is gaining in designer status with recent additions, including Christian Dior, Giorgio Armani, and Louis Vuitton, the heart of the international designer parade is on the Right Bank.

Rue du Faubourg St-Honoré is so famously fancy that it's simply known as "the Faubourg"; it was *the* traditional miracle mile until recent years, when the really exclusive shops shunned it for the wider and even more deluxe avenue Montaigne at the other end of the arrondissement. (It's a long but pleasant walk from one fashion strip to the other.)

While avenue Montaigne is filled with almost unspeakably fancy shops, a few of them have affordable **cafés** (try **Joseph,** at no. 14) and the sales help is almost always cordial to the well dressed. You needn't be decked out in fur to play the game: A good handbag and pair of shoes are all that matter. Leave *les baskets* (running shoes) at home, *s'il vous plaît.*

The mix is quite international—**Joseph** is British, **Jil Sander** is German, while **Krizia** is Italian. **Chanel, Christian Lacroix, Porthault, Nina Ricci, Christian Dior,** and **Ungaro** are just a few of the French big names. Also check out some of the lesser known creative powers that be: The whimsical boutique run by **Ines de la Fressange**, a former Chanel model, is a knockout. And don't miss a visit to **Caron.** Most of the designer shops sell men's and women's clothing.

The Faubourg hosts other traditional favorites: **Hermès, Lanvin, Jaeger, Sonia Rykiel,** and the upstart **Façonnable,** which sells preppy men's clothing in the United States through a business deal with Nordstrom's. Note that Lanvin has its own men's shop (**Lanvin Homme**) which has a café downstairs—perfect for a light (and affordable) lunch; a bowl of designer pasta at Café Bleu is about $10.

MENSWEAR

Charvet. 28 place Vendôme, 8e. ☎ **01-42-60-30-70.** Métro: Opéra.

The Duke of Windsor made Charvet famous, but Frenchmen of distinction have been having their shirts made here for years. The store offers ties, pocket squares, underwear, and pajamas as well, and women's shirts are also available, all custom-tailored or straight off the peg. Open Monday to Saturday from 9:45am to 6:30pm.

Favourbrook. In Le Village Royal, 25 rue Royale, 8e. ☎ **01-40-17-06-72.** Métro: Concorde or Madeleine.

This store is actually an English firm exploiting a French trend in a prime location that caters to visitors in search of cutesy souvenirs. The new rue Royale has been re-created to resemble an old-fashioned French village street—each boutique is cuter than the last. Favourbrook sells brocade vests and ties that would have made Louis XIV a happy man. Open Monday to Saturday from 10am to 7pm.

Alain Figaret. 21 rue de la Paix, 2e. ☎ **01-42-65-04-99.** Métro: Opéra.

Alain Figaret is one of France's foremost designers for men's shirts and women's blouses. Although this store has a broad range of fabrics, 100% cotton is its specialty. Also check out the silk neckties, which come in distinctively designed prints that can

Pamper Yourself Parisian Style

If there's one thing that international shoppers come to Paris for, it's cosmetics—after all, the City of Light is the world capital of fragrances and beauty supplies. These are a few of my favorite perfume and makeup shops.

While you can buy **Caron** scents in any duty-free or discount parfumerie, it's worth visiting the source of some of the world's most famous perfumes. The store is located at 34 av. Montaigne, 8e (☎ 01-47-23-40-82; Métro: Franklin-D-Roosevelt), and is a tiny shop with old-fashioned glass beakers filled with fragrances and a hint of yesteryear. Fleur de Rocaille, a Caron scent, was the featured perfume in the movie *Scent of a Woman*. Store hours are Monday to Saturday from 10am to 6:30pm.

While there are other branches of **Annick Goutal** (☎ 01-42-60-52-82; Métro: Concorde) in Paris—and while you can swipe Goutal bath amenities from any Concorde Hotel—the mosaic tile on the sidewalk at the 14 rue Castiglione store in the 1er arrondisement, and its unique and unearthly scents, make it a must-see. Try Hadrien for a unisex splash of citrus and summer. The shop is conveniently located near other fragrance landmarks, including **Guerlain** and **Catherine**, a duty-free shop. Store hours are Monday to Saturday from 10am to 7pm.

Off a small courtyard halfway between place de la Madeleine and the Champs-Elysées, **Makeup Forever,** 5 rue de la Boetie, 8e (☎ 01-42-65-48-57; Métro: St-Augustin), is known as *the* makeup resource for French models and actors. Aside from its theatrical products, it has fashion shades at reasonable prices. The purse-sized makeup zipper case, about $15, is a must-have for status seekers. Store hours are Monday from 2 to 7pm and Tuesday to Saturday from 10am to 7pm.

If you think you've seen/heard every perfume and aromatherapy gimmick known to man (and woman), this one will still impress you: At **Octée,** 53 rue Bonaparte, 6e (☎ 01-46-33-18-77; Métro: St-Germain-des-Prés or St-Sulpice), the collection of fragrances is color coded to match your personality, skin type, and mood. There's perfume, sprays, soaps, and body lotion, and you test everything on colored ribbons. Store hours are Monday to Saturday from 10am to 7pm.

Sheisido, 142 Galerie de Valois, Palais Royal, 1er (☎ 01-49-27-09-09; Métro: Palais-Royal), is the headquarters of fragrance master Serge Lutens, who creates his own perfumes in this hidden atelier. This is one of the most beautiful shops in Paris; don't be afraid to just wander in and ask for some scent strips.

Sephora, 50 rue Passy, 16e (☎ 01-45-20-03-15; Métro: Passy), is a chain of makeup stores that don't offer discounts, but do offer an enormous selection of big-name fragrance and makeup brands, its own brand of bath products, and a great assortment of hair accessories. You've simply never seen so much stuff that you want in your life. The bath products, including shampoo, conditioner, and foaming bath gel, come in tiny travel sizes. Store hours are Monday to Saturday from 10am to 7pm.

be quickly identified by the educated eye. (Figaret is half a block from Charvet, if you're comparison shopping.) Open Monday to Saturday from 10am to 7pm.

FOOD

Albert Menes. 41 blvd. Malesherbes, 8e. ☎ 01-42-66-95-63. Métro: St-Augustin or Madeleine.

About 2 blocks from the big-time food dealers, this small shop serves the Parisian upper crust with jams, confiture, sugared almonds, honey, and assorted packed gourmet foodstuffs, many from the provinces. Not only is this a chi-chi place for locals, but the owner is renowned in the French food industry for having rescued many regional specialties, packaging and distributing them to markets in order to carry on specific gourmet traditions. A specialty food basket for the holidays (and saints days) is a status treat. Open on Monday from 2 to 7pm and Tuesday to Saturday from 10am to 7pm.

Fauchon. Place de la Madeleine, 8e. ☎ **01-47-42-60-11.** Métro: Madeleine.

On place de la Madeleine stands one of the most popular sights in the city—not the church, but Fauchon, now a three-part store crammed with gastronomical goodies. One shop sells dry goods, one sells candy and pastry and bread, and one sells fresh fruits and veggies. A cafeteria and coffee bar (Brasserie Fauchon) are nestled in the basement of one shop, and a full restaurant, Le 30, is located above (see Chapter 5).

Even though prices are steep, it's easier than ever to pay for your goods because the store now employs its own electronic debit card. You're given the card when you first enter the store; when you finish shopping, head for the *caisse* (cash register), surrender the debit card, and pay the tally. Then return to the counters to pick up your groceries. Open Monday to Saturday from 9:40am to 7pm. A "Mini-Fauchon" is open Monday to Saturday from 7 to 9pm.

Hediard. 21 place de la Madeleine, 8e. ☎ **01-43-12-88-77.** Métro: Madeleine.

Although this temple to haute gastonomie opened in 1850, it has recently been completely renovated, perhaps to woo tourists away from Fauchon. The decor is now a series of salons filled with almost Disneyesque displays meant to give the store the look of a turn-of-the-century spice merchant. Upstairs, you can eat at the Restaurant de l'Epicerie. Open Monday to Saturday from 9:30am to 7:30pm.

Maison de la Truffe. 19 place de la Madeleine, 8e. ☎ **01-42-65-53-22.** Métro: Madeleine.

This tiny shop resembles a New York deli more than a Parisian boutique. This is your source not only for truffles but foie gras, caviar, and other gourmet foodstuffs. Food baskets for gifts are a house specialty. There are also a few tables and chairs so you can grab a quick bite. Open Monday to Saturday from 10am to 7pm.

La Maison du Miel. 24 rue Vignon, 9e. ☎ **01-47-42-26-70.** Métro: Madeleine.

"The House of Honey" has been a family tradition since before World War I. The entire store is devoted to products made from honey: honey oil, honey soap, and certainly various honeys to eat, including one made from heather. This store owes a tremendous debt to the busy honey bee. Open Tuesday to Saturday from 11am to 7pm.

Marks & Spencer. 35 bd. Haussmann, 9e. ☎ **01-47-42-42-91.** Métro: Chausée-d'Antin.

Okay, so it's a British department store. But the entire first floor is a giant supermarket devoted to the St. Michael's brand of English foodstuffs, and includes prepared foods for picnics. Open Monday to Saturday from 9:30am to 7pm.

JEWELRY

Cartier. 7 place Vendôme, 1er. ☎ **01-40-15-03-51.** Métro: Opéra or Tuileries.

Definitely one of the most famous jewelers in the world, Cartier has the prohibitive prices to go with its glamorous image. Go to gawk, and if your pockets are deep enough, pick up an expensive trinket. Open Monday to Saturday from 10am to 6pm.

Chaumet. 12 place Vendôme, 1er. ☎ **01-44-77-24-00.** Métro: Opéra or Tuileries.

This decidedly French establishment has long catered to old money. It's the kind of place where old respected *monsieurs* buy jewels for their wives and their mistresses and no one bats an eye. Open Monday to Saturday from 10am to 6:30pm.

Van Cleef & Arpels. 22 place Vendôme, 1er. ☎ **01-42-61-58-58.** Métro: Opéra or Tuileries.

This place markets the jewels of the rich and famous. Open Monday to Friday from 10am to 6:30pm.

KITCHENWARE

A. Simon. 48 rue Montmartre, 2e. ☎ **01-42-33-71-65.** Métro: Etienne-Marcel.

This large kitchenware shop, not in Montmartre but near the Forum Les Halles mall (half a block from Mendès, the Yves Saint Laurent outlet), supplies restaurants and professional kitchens. But it will also cover your table with everything from menu cards and wine tags to knives, and copper pots and pans. It also stocks white paper doilies and those funny little paper things they put on top of the tablecloth at bistros. Open on Monday from 2:30 to 7pm and Tuesday to Saturday from 10am to 7pm.

Dehillerin. 18 rue Coquellière, 1er. ☎ **01-42-36-53-13.** Métro: Les-Halles.

Dehillerin is the most famous cookware shop in Paris, located in the "kitchen corridor," alongside A. Simon and several other kitchenware stores. The shop has more of a professional chef feel to it than the layperson-friendly A. Simon, but don't be intimidated. Equipped with the right tools from Dehillerin, you, too, can learn to cook like a master culinary artist. Open on Monday from 8am to 12:30pm and 2 to 6pm, and Tuesday to Saturday from 8am to 6pm.

LEATHER GOODS

Didier Lamarthe. 219 rue St-Honoré, 1er. ☎ **01-42-96-09-90.** Métro: Tuileries.

A cult hero in France yet virtually unknown elsewhere, this designer is famous for his handbags and small leather goods in funky fashion shades like melon or mint. Sure, he does more conservative colors like navy and black, but if you want the world to know that you've been to Paris and that you're totally *branché* (plugged in), spring for the one of the more risqué shades. Open Monday from noon to 7pm and Tuesday to Saturday from 11am to 7pm.

Didier Lavilla. 15 rue Cherche-Midi, 6e. ☎ **01-45-48-35-90.** Métro: Sèvres-Babylone.

This darling of the French fashion press made his debut not in leather but in nylon—now he's branched into leather and suede. The look is color and texture in a tote bag–style handbag that smells of Paris and style and usually costs less than $100. Open Monday to Saturday from 10am to 7pm.

Longchamp. 390 rue St-Honoré, 1er. ☎ **01-42-60-00-00.** Métro: Concorde

Longchamp is a French brand known for high-quality leather and strong everyday durables that come in basic as well as fashion shades. Check out the pale-pink patent leather for a touch of Paris. Your best bet is a series of nylon handbags attached to leather handles that fold for storage or travel and unfold for shopping. Items are priced according to size but begin around $40. Open Monday to Saturday from 10am to 7pm.

Morabito. 1 place Vendôme, 1er. ☎ **01-42-60-30-76.** Métro: Tuileries.

While Hermès has the international rep, Morabito is the secret insider's source for chicer-than-thou handbags that begin at $1,000 and go up quickly. Open Monday to Saturday from 9:45am to 6:45pm.

LINGERIE

Cadolle. 14 rue Cambon, 1er. ☎ **01-42-60-94-94.** Métro: Concorde.

Herminie Cadolle invented the brassiere in 1889. Today the store she founded is managed by her family and they still make the specialty brassieres for the Crazy Horse Saloon. This is the place to go if you want made-to-order items or if you're hard to fit. Open Monday to Saturday from 9:30am to 1pm and 2 to 6:30pm.

Koba. In the Marché Saint Germain, 14 rue Lobineau, 6e. ☎ **01-46-33-91-17.** Métro: Odéon.

This small chain of lingerie shops are for real people who want French and fancy, but somewhat frugally. Koba has Chiffon garter belts with ruffled edges for $100, but it also has simpler (and cheaper) items: pantyhose, tights, and white cotton and plain lace panties. Open Monday to Saturday from 11am to 7pm.

Marie-Claude Fremau. 16 rue de la Paix, 2e. ☎ **01-42-61-61-91.** Métro: Opéra.

The French are big on shops that sell towels and bathrobes, as well as underwear. Naturally, French bathroom wear has characteristic flair and style—I'm talking about a yellow silk bathrobe with ruffled collar for about $300. Open Monday to Saturday from 10am to 7pm.

Sabbia Rosa. 73 rue des Sts-Pères, 6e. ☎ **01-45-48-88-37.** Métro: Sévres-Babylone.

Madonna shops here for $400 silk panties. Doesn't everyone? Open Monday to Saturday from 10am to 7pm.

MALLS

Le Carrousel du Louvre. 99 rue de Rivoli, 1er. No phone. Métro: Palais-Royal or Musée-du-Louvre.

If you want to combine an accessible location, a fun food court, handy boutiques, and plenty of museum gift shops with a touch of culture, don't miss Le Carrousel for the world. Always mobbed with locals and visitors, this is one of the few venues allowed to open on Sunday. There's a Virgin Megastore, a branch of the Body Shop, and several other terrific stores. Check out Diane Claire for the fanciest souvenirs of Paris you've ever seen. Open Tuesday to Sunday from 10am to 8pm.

Forum des Halles. 1–7 rue Pierre-Lescot, 1er. No phone. Métro: Etienne-Marcel, Les-Halles, or Châtelet.

Once the site of Paris's great produce market, Les Halles is now a vast crater of modern metal with layers of boutiques built around a courtyard. There's one of everything here, but the feel is very sterile—without a hint of the famous French *joie de vie*. Open Monday to Saturday from 10am to 7:30pm.

Marché Saint-Germain. 14 rue Lobineau, 6e. No phone. Métro: Odéon.

The Marché Saint-Germain used to be an open-air food market until it was transformed into a modern shopping mall. Now only a few food and vegetable stalls remain in one corner—the rest of the market is dominated by low ceilings, neon lights, and chain stores from mostly the States and the U.K. Yep, there's a Gap here. Open Monday to Saturday from 11am to 7pm.

Montparnasse Shopping Centre. Between rue de l'Arrivée and 22 rue de Départ, 14e. No phone. Métro: Montparnasse-Bienvenue.

This shopping center is sort of a quick-fix mini mall in a business center and hotel (Le Méridien) complex with a small branch of Galeries Lafayette and some inexpensive boutiques. Visiting it is really only worthwhile if you also take a trip across the street to Inno, a dime store division of Monoprix with a deluxe supermarket in the basement. You may want to play with the automatic train track for shopping carts. Open Monday to Saturday from 8:30am to 10pm.

Palais des Congrès de Paris Boutiques. 2 place de la Porte-Maillot, 17e. Métro: Porte-Maillot.

A shopping center for convention goers, located inside the Palais des Congrès building, this mall offers some 70 shops, including branch stores of many French big names. You'll also find a Japanese department store and hairdresser. Open Monday to Saturday from 10am to 7pm.

Les Trois Quartiers. 23 blvd. de la Madeleine, 8e. No phone. Métro: Madeleine.

This is a conveniently located modern mall with branch stores of many upscale designers and a large *parfumerie*, Silver Moon. Open Monday to Saturday from 10am to 7pm.

MARKETS

Marché aux Fleurs. Place Louis-Lépine, Ile de la Cité, 4e. Métro: Cité.

Artists and photographers love to capture the Flower Market on canvas or film. The stalls are ablaze with color, and each is a showcase of flowers, most of which escaped the perfume factories of Grasse on the French Riviera. The Flower Market is along the Seine, behind the Tribunal de Commerce. On Sunday this is a bird (oiseaux) market. Open daily from 8am to 4pm.

Marché aux Livres. Sq. Georges Brancion, 15e. No phone. Métro: Porte-de-Vanves.

This charming two-building market for used books, old books, rare books, and some ephemera is slightly in the middle of nowhere but nonetheless thronged by serious collectors. The market is covered but open, and doesn't close on a rainy day—the really valuable texts are draped in plastic. Open on Saturday and Sunday from 10am to 6pm (to 4pm in winter).

Marché aux Puces de Clignancourt. Av. de la Porte-de-Clignancourt. Métro: Porte de Clignancourt; From there, turn left and cross boulevard Ney, then walk north on avenue de la Porte de Clignancourt. Bus: 56.

The most famous flea market in Paris is actually a grouping of over a dozen different flea markets. This is a complex of 2,500 to 3,000 open stalls and shops on the fringe of Paris, selling everything from antiques to junk, from new to vintage clothing.

The first clues showing you're there will be the stalls of cheap clothing along avenue de la Porte-de-Clignancourt. As you proceed, various streets will tempt you. Hold on until you get to rue des Rosiers, then turn left. Vendors start bringing out their offerings around 9am and start taking them in around 6pm. Hours are a tad flexible depending on weather and crowds, but it's generally open Saturday to Monday from 9am to 6pm.

Monday is traditionally the best day for bargain seekers, as there's smaller attendance at the market and a greater desire on the part of the merchants to sell.

First-timers at the flea market always want to know two things: "Will I get any real bargains?" and "Will I get fleeced?" Actually, it's all comparative. Obviously, the best buys have been skimmed by dealers (who often have a prearrangement to have items held for them). And it's true that the same merchandise displayed here will sell for less in the provinces of France. But from the point of view of the visitor who has only a few days to spend in Paris—and only half a day for shopping—the flea market is worth the experience. Vintage French postcards, old buttons, and bistroware are quite affordable; each market has its own personality and sheds an aura on Paris glamour that can't be found elsewhere.

Dress casually; show your knowledge if you're a collector. The dealers in most of the markets are serious and only get into the spirit of things if you speak French or make it clear that you know what you're doing and have some expertise in their field. The longer you stay, the more you chat, the more you show your respect for the goods, the more room for negotiating the price.

Most of the markets have toilets; some have a central office to arrange shipping. There are cafés, pizza joints, and even a few real restaurants scattered throughout. Beware of pickpockets and teenage trouble makers.

Marché aux Puces de la Porte de Vanves. Av. Georges-Lafenestre, 14e. Métro: Porte-de-Vanves.

More a giant yard sale than anything serious, this weekend event sprawls along two streets and is actually the best flea market in Paris—dealers swear by it. There's little in terms of formal antiques, and few large pieces of furniture. You'll do better if you collect old linens, used Hermès scarves, toys, ephemera, costume jewelry, perfume bottles, and bad art. Asking prices tend to be high as dealers prefer to sell to non-tourists. On Sundays there's a food market one street over.

Marché aux Timbres. Av. Matignon (off the Champs-Elysées at rond-point), 8e. Métro: Franklin-D-Roosevelt or Champs-Elysées–Clemenceau.

This is where Audrey Hepburn figured it out in *Charade*, remember? At this stamp collector's paradise, nearly two dozen stalls are set up on a permanent basis under shady trees on the eastern edge of the rond-point. The variety of stamps is almost unlimited—some common, some quite rare. Generally open Thursday to Sunday from 10am to 7pm.

Marché Buci. Rue de Buci, 6e. No phone. Métro: St-Germain-des-Prés.

This traditional French food market is at the intersection of two streets and is only one block long, but what a block it is! Seasonal fruits and vegetables dance across table tops while chickens spin on the rotisserie. One stall is entirely devoted to big bouquets of fresh flowers. Open daily from 9am to 7pm (Monday mornings are light).

MUSEUM SHOPS

Boutique du Musée des Arts Decoratifs. 107 rue de Rivoli, 1er. ☎ **01-42-61-04-02.** Métro: Palais-Royal or Tuileries.

This two-part boutique is divided by the entryway to the museum—to the right is a fabulous bookstore. On the left is a boutique selling reproductions of many of the items on display in the museum: Giftables, knickknacks, and even a custom-made Hermès scarf. Open daily from 10:30am to 6:30pm.

La Comédie-Française. Place André-Malraux, Palais Royal. ☎ **01-40-15-00-15.** Métro: Palais-Royal.

This place is literary, chic, fun, and clever, a great source of gifts for snobs, actors, or theater buffs. Check out the snowdome (*baule de paillettes d'or*) with the bowing actor, or the earings with the faces of comedy and tragedy. While the theater itself is closed in August, the gift shop is not. Open daily from 11am to 8:30pm.

Musée de la Monnaie. 11 quai de Conti, 6e. ☎ **01-40-46-58-92.** Métro: Pont-Neuf or St-Germain-des-Prés.

Cute jewelry made from coins is sold in the museum gift shop, in addition to other souvenirs, including medals, reproductions of antique coins, and other gift items. Open Tuesday to Sunday from 1 to 6pm.

Musée et Compaigne. 49 rue Etienne-Marcel, 1er. ☎ **01-40-13-49-12.** Métro: Etienne-Marcel.

The museum shop features fancy reproductions of museum items, ranging from a vase pictured in a painting by Manet to jewelry from the 13th century. Daily from 10am to 7:30pm.

MUSIC

FNAC. 136 rue de Rennes, 6e. ☎ **01-49-54-30-00.** Métro: St-Placide.

This chain of large (by French standards) music and book stores is known for its wide selection and discounted prices. There are eight other locations in Paris. Open on Monday from 2 to 7pm, Tuesday to Friday from 10am to 7pm, and on Saturday from 10am to 1pm and 2 to 7pm.

Virgin Megastore. 52–60 av. des Champs-Elysées, 8e. ☎ **01-49-53-50-00.** Métro: Franklin-D-Roosevelt.

This is the largest music store in Paris, built into a landmark building that set the pace for the rejuvenation of the Champs-Elysées. There's also a bookstore and café downstairs. It's a worthwhile store to visit, if only to stare at the other customers. There are branch stores in the Carrousel du Louvre and at both airports. Open Monday to Thursday from 10am to midnight, on Friday and Saturday from 10am to 1am, and on Sunday from noon to midnight.

PERFUME & MAKEUP (DISCOUNT)

Catherine. 5 rue Castiglione, 1er. ☎ **01-42-61-02-89.** Métro: Concorde.

This tiny shop has the best détaxe plan in Paris—in most stores, you pay the final amount and wait for a détaxe refund; here you're given the discount up front. At Catherine, you sign two credit/charge-card chits—one for the final price of your purchases with all discounts applied, and one for the détaxe. When your détaxe papers clear, the second chit is destroyed. If you don't file for the refund, you are, of course, charged the VAT.

Even if you don't qualify for détaxe, you get a 30% discount on most brands of makeup and perfume, and a 20% discount on Chanel and Christian Dior. Spend 1,600 F ($320) to qualify for détaxe. You can also order items, tax free, by mail, with a $100 minimum order. Open Monday to Saturday from 9:30am to 7pm.

Michel Swiss. 16 rue de la Paix, 2e. ☎ **01-42-61-61-11.** Métro: Opéra.

This is tricky for a first-timer: You enter a courtyard and take an elevator to get upstairs to the shop. But once you get inside (there's no storefront window), you'll see the major brands of luxury perfumes, cosmetics, leather bags, pens, neckties, fashion accessories, and gifts. All items are discounted by varying degrees, plus an additional tax discount if you qualify for détaxe. In summer, don't be surprised if there's a line of people waiting to use the elevator. The minimum for détaxe refund is 1,700 F ($340), which is 1,200 F ($240) net. Open Monday to Saturday from 9am to 6:30pm.

Parfumerie de la Madeleine. 9 place de la Madeleine, 8e. ☎ **01-42-66-52-20.** Métro: Madeleine.

This shop offers good discounts, but the amount of the discount given varies with the brand—10% on Chanel, but 30% on Sisley. There are tons of fragrances and a few designer accessories in this light, bright, modern, chic shop. Prices are marked with the discount already applied, so it's hard to figure out what percent discount has been applied to which products and to comparison shop, but you get the détaxe refund when your total hits 1,200 F ($240). Open Monday to Saturday from 10am to 7pm.

SHOES

Maud Frizon. 81–83 rue des Sts-Pères, 7e. ☎ **01-45-49-20-59.** Métro: Sèvres-Babylone.

The collection of shoes here is among the most inventive in the city. If prices are too high, go to the Maud Frizon Club next door, where the shoes are machine-made and go for about one-third of the price. Open Monday to Saturday from 10:30am to 7pm.

Stéphane Kélian. 23 bd. de la Madeleine, 1er. ☎ **01-42-96-01-84.** Métro: Bourse.

Acclaimed as one of the most creative designers of women's shoes in Paris, Kélian attracts formidably chic and fashionable women from all over the city. A selection of men's shoes is also available. Open Monday to Saturday from 10am to 7pm.

SOUVENIRS & GIFTS

Au Nom de la Rose. 46 rue du Bac, 6e. ☎ **01-42-22-22-12.** Métro: Rue-du-Bac.

This theme store, which sells cute and kitschy gift items, has narrowly missed becoming a Disney cliché—each item sold is in some way related to roses, be it rose soap or rose-colored glasses. Nonetheless, the store radiates French *charme*. Part of its glory is the fact that it's on one of the best streets in town for cute little shops. Open Monday to Saturday from 10am to 7:30pm.

Galerie Architecture Miniature Gault. 206 rue de Rivoli, 1er. ☎ **01-42-60-51-17.** Métro: Tuileries.

This store features lilliputian town models complete with pint-sized houses, stores, and fountains—miniature versions of French country villages and Parisian neighborhoods, all built to scale. Collectors visit the galerie to buy models and kits for their own villages and towns. Open Monday to Saturday from 10am to 7pm and on Sunday from 11am to 7pm.

Hôtel de Crillon Gift Shop. 10 place de la Concorde, 8e. ☎ **01-49-24-00-52.** Métro: Concorde.

Now you don't have to steal the silverware and bathrobes when you stop by the most famous hotel in Paris—the Crillon's dishes, the napkin rings, the linen, and a whole lot more are now on sale in two specialty boutiques. For an affordable but high-status gift, consider the tasseled silk napkins. The shop is located inside the hotel lobby and is open on Sunday. It's the perfect opportunity to gawk and to shop. Open daily from 9am to 10pm.

La Tuile à Loup. 35 rue Daubenton, 5e. ☎ **01-47-07-28-90.** Métro: Censier-Daubenton.

One of the few regional handcrafts stores in Paris worth going out of your way to find, La Tuile à Loup carries beautiful pottery and faïence, and has all sorts of decorative notions and gift items. Drop by after visiting the Ile St-Louis or the Left Bank student quarter. Open Tuesday to Saturday from 10:30am to 7pm.

STATIONERY

Cassegrain. 422 rue St-Honoré, 8e. ☎ **01-42-60-20-08.** Métro: Concorde.

Nothing says elegance more than thick French stationery and note cards. Cassegrain offers beautifully engraved stationery, most often in traditional patterns; businesspeople can also get their business cards engraved to order. Several other items for the desk—many suitable for gifts—are for sale as well; there are even affordable pencils and small desk-top accessories. Open Monday to Saturday from 10am to 7pm.

Cassegrain also has a shop at 81 rue des Sts-Pères, 6e (☎ 01-42-22-04-76; Métro: Sèvres-Babylone).

TABLEWARE

Au Bain Marie. 10 rue Boissy-d'Anglas, 8e. ☎ **01-42-66-59-74.** Métro: Concorde.

The two floors of merchandise here include tableware of many different styles, inspired by many different eras. There's also a collection of books relating to food and wine, and a good selection of bathroom towels. Even if you don't buy anything, it's glorious just to look, and it's conveniently located right off rue du Faubourg St-Honoré. Open Monday to Saturday from 10am to 7pm.

The Conran Shop. 117 rue du Bac, 6e. ☎ **01-42-84-10-01.** Métro: Sèvres-Babylone.

Don't get the Conran Shop and Habitat confused, even though they look similar and were once associated with the same man. There are Habitat shops in Paris and they're okay, but the Conran Shop is a small piece of heaven, filled with color and style and all sorts of things to touch and take home—most of them for your home-decorating needs. What's so shocking is how very French this British resource is. It's situated next door to Bon Marché and at the top of a marvelous shopping street, so that from it, all the world is within your grasp. Open on Monday from noon to 7pm and Tuesday to Saturday from 10am to 7pm.

Geneviève Lethu. 95 rue de Rennes, 6e. ☎ **01-45-44-40-35.** Métro: St-Germain-des-Prés.

This Provençal designer has shops all over France—with several others in Paris—all selling her clever and colorful designs that seem to reflect what happens when Pottery Barn style goes French Mediterranean. Prices are moderate. Her goods, filled with energy, style, and charm, are also sold in the major department stores. Open Monday to Saturday from 10am to 7pm.

Paris After Dark

9

With five national theaters, including a new opera house, and 55 theaters of lesser renown, Paris is both the hub of French culture and host to all the best on the international circuit. Whatever the season, the choice is fantastic, with top pop stars, French classics, chamber concerts, and lavish music-hall spectaculars. An American singer might be belting out a standard to a packed crowd of Parisians in one cavernous hall, while on a shabby Left Bank lane, a young playwright anxiously watches his first work performed on the same small stage that launched Ionesco or Beckett.

Contemporary Paris has less nudity than London, less vice than Hamburg, and less drunkenness than San Francisco. Nevertheless, the quantity and variety of Paris's nocturnal pleasures still rival those of any metropolis on earth. Nowhere else will you find such a huge and mixed array of clubs, bars, discos, cabarets, jazz dives, music halls, and honky-tonks, ranging from the corniest tourist traps to the most sophisticated connoisseurs' fare.

Of course, the cafés are an important part of Paris nightlife, but since most of them are open all day serving coffee, tea, alcoholic beverages, fruit and chocolate drinks—not to mention sandwiches, snacks, and full meals—they are discussed in Chapter 5, "Dining."

1 The Performing Arts

The only limitation to your enjoyment of French theater is a language barrier. Those with modest French can still delight in some lively, sparkling Molière at the Comédie-Française. But those with no French at all might prefer an evening longer on melody and shorter on speech.

Announcements of shows, concerts, and opera programs are plastered on kiosks all over town. A better way to find out what's playing is to consult the English-language *Paris Passion* or *Pariscope, Une semaine de Paris,* a weekly entertainment guide that includes a section on the arts, with full listings of theaters, concerts, and more.

Although ticket agents are scattered all over Paris, they're heavily concentrated near the Right Bank hotels. Avoid them if possible, because you can get less expensive tickets at the theater box offices.

Performances tend to start later in Paris than in London or New York—sometimes as late as 9:30pm—and Parisians usually dine after the theater, but you may want to eat first, since many of the modest, less expensive restaurants are closed by 9pm. At the movies or the theater, remember to tip the usher who shows you to your seat.

DISCOUNT TICKETS   Several agencies sell tickets for cultural events and plays at discounts of up to 50%.

One outlet for discount tickets is the **Kiosque Théâtre,** at 15 place de la Madeleine, 8e (no phone; Métro: Madeleine), which offers leftover tickets for about half price on the day of the performance. Tickets for evening performances are sold Tuesday to Friday from 12:30 to 8pm and on Saturday from 2 to 8pm. If you'd like to attend a matinee, buy your ticket on Saturday from 12:30 to 2pm or on Sunday from 12:30 to 4pm.

For discounts of 20% to 40% on tickets for festivals, concerts, and theater performances, try two locations of the **FNAC** department store chain: 136 rue de Rennes, 6e (☎ **01-44-09-18-00**; Métro: Montparnasse-Bienvenue); or in the Forum des Halles, 1–7 rue Pierre-Lescot, 1er (☎ **01-40-41-40-00**; Métro: Châtelet–Les Halles). To obtain ticket discounts, you must purchase a *carte FNAC,* which costs 150 F ($30) and is valid for 3 years.

THEATER

Comédie-Française. 2 rue de Richelieu, 1er. ☎ **01-40-15-00-15.** Tickets 50–175 F ($10–$35). Métro: Palais-Royal or Musée-du-Louvre.

If you have a taste for fine theater but only speak halting French, don't let the language barrier scare you off—spend at least 1 night of your Paris stay at the Comédie-Française. Nowhere else will you see the French classics—by the likes of Molière and Racine—so beautifully staged in the original language. The Comédie-Française was established as a national theater to keep the classics in the cultural mainstream and to promote the most important contemporary authors. The box office is open daily from 11am to 6pm; the stage is dark from August 1 to September 15.

OPERA

✪ **L'Opéra Bastille.** Place de la Bastille, 120 rue de Lyon, 4e. ☎ **01-44-73-13-00.** Tickets 100–370 F ($20–$74). Métro: Bastille.

This giant and controversial showplace, inaugurated in 1989, was designed by Canadian architect Carlos Orr. On March 17, 1990, the curtain (created by the Japanese fashion designer Issey Miyake) rose on its first performance—Hector Berlioz's opera *Les Troyens.* The main hall is the largest of any opera house in France, with 2,700 seats. The building, which hosts operas and symphony concerts, also houses three additional concert halls, including an intimate room with only 250 seats. The box office is open Monday to Saturday from 11am to 6pm.

Several concerts are presented free, in honor of certain French holidays. Write ahead for tickets to the Opéra de Paris Bastille, 120 rue de Lyon, 75012 Paris.

Opéra-Comique. Place Boïeldieu, 2e. ☎ **01-42-66-45-45.** Métro: Richelieu-Drouot.

Originally constructed in 1840 but rebuilt in 1898 after a disastrous fire, this ornate music hall is classified as a historic monument. It was closed in 1995 during the renovation of the Opéra Paris Garnier, and since its reopening it has supplemented its usual fare, musical comedies, with more serious operas. If possible, make arrangements 2 weeks before the performance. The box office is open Monday to Friday from 11am to 6pm (closed July and August); prices vary depending on the performance.

Théâtre Musical de Paris (Théâtre du Châtelet). 1 place du Châtelet, 1er. ☎ **01-40-28-28-40.** Tickets: Opera, 80–580 F ($16–$116); concerts, 80–300 F ($16–$60); ballets, 80–200 F ($16–$40). Métro: Châtelet.

The Théâtre Musical de Paris, which presents less expensive opera and ballet performances than l'Opéra or l'Opéra Bastille, is known for its good acoustics. The performance season is September to June.

BALLET

✪ L'Opéra Paris Garnier. Place de l'Opéra, 9e. ☎ **01-40-01-17-89.** Tickets: Opera, 60–160 F ($12–$32); dance, 30–80 F ($6–$16). Métro: Opéra.

L'Opéra Garnier is Paris's premier stage for ballet and musical productions: Many of the world's great orchestral, operatic, and ballet companies have performed here. Because of the competition from the new Opéra at the Bastille, the Garnier has made great efforts to present more up-to-date works, including choreography by Jerome Robbins, Twyla Tharp, Agnes de Mille, and George Balanchine. The building, an imposing structure with a marble facade featuring elaborate and beautiful sculpture (including *The Dance* by Carpeaux), was designed as a contest entry by a young architect named Garnier during the heyday of France's empire. Years of neglect had taken their toll on the building, but now months of painstaking restorations have returned the Garnier to its former glory. The boxes and walls are lined with flowing red damask silk; the gilt is gleaming; the ceiling, painted by Marc Chagall, has been cleaned; and a new air-conditioning system has been added to the auditorium, to once again make the Garnier one of the best opera houses in Europe.

MAJOR CONCERT HALLS & AUDITORIUMS

In Paris, the concert-going public always has somewhere to go—every day the newspapers are filled with listings of performances in a variety of venues. Churches often feature organ recitals (the largest organ is in St-Sulpice), the city's modern art museum is often the site of jazz concerts, and there are countless music halls, auditoriums, and performance spaces throughout the city.

One of Paris's largest halls is the **Théâtre National de Chaillot,** located on place du Trocadéro, 16e (☎ **01-47-27-81-15;** Métro: Trocadéro), which hosts a variety of cultural events. Check the billboards in front of the theater to see what's playing. Tickets range in price from 50 to 160 F ($10 to $32).

Another venue for opera, ballet, and concerts is the **Théâtre des Champs-Elysées,** 15 av. Montaigne, 8e (☎ **01-49-52-50-00;** Métro: Alma-Marceau), an art deco theater that hosts national and international orchestras. The box office is open Monday to Saturday from 11am to 7pm. Events are held from September to July.

Classical music fans will want to check out the **Salle Pleyel,** at 252 rue du Faubourg St-Honoré, 8e (☎ **01-45-61-53-00;** Métro: Ternes), home of the

A Night on the Town

On a Paris night the cheapest entertainment, especially if you're young, is "the show" staged **behind Notre-Dame.** It might consist of just about anything—magicians, mimes, and music-makers from all over the world, performing against the backdrop of the illuminated cathedral—and the venue is the greatest place in Paris to meet other young people. Afterward, wander over to the **Café-Brasserie St-Regis,** 6 rue Jean-du-Bellay, 4e (☎ 01-43-54-59-41), for a drink. It's on the Ile St-Louis, across the street from the pont St-Louis. Here you can order a *plat du jour* or a coffee at the bar, or, like most of the Paris insiders here, just get a beer to go (*une bière à emporter*) in a plastic cup and take it with you on a stroll around Ile St-Louis. The little café is open daily from 7am to 11:30pm. Métro: Musée-du Louvre.

Want a Paris dive to hang out in until the Métro starts running again at 5am? The **Sous-Bock Tavern,** 49 rue St-Honoré, 1er (☎ 01-40-26-46-61; Métro: Pont-Neuf), at the corner of rue du pont-Neuf, a heady, two-level emporium of international consciousness and good times, is just the ticket. A mostly young crowd of beer drinkers from all over the world gathers here to sample 400 different varieties of beer. If you want a shot of whisky to accompany your brew, you can choose from 180 different kinds. Beer costs 18 to 40 F ($3.60 to $8), and the bar is open Monday to Saturday from 11am to 5am and on Sunday from 3pm to 5am. Our favorite dish here is a platter of mussels—curried, or with white wine or cream sauce. They go well with the brasserie-style french fries.

When it's time to get down and dirty and wander far from the tourist circuit, head for **Le Piano Show,** 20 rue de la Verrerie, 4e (☎ 01-42-72-23-81; Métro: Hôtel-de-Ville). This is one of those little offbeat cabarets that were popular in Berlin between the wars. There are only four *artistes* performing in this small, somewhat bedraggled cabaret. All of them happen to be stylish, carefully attired (with a fetching amount of décolletage) . . . and male. Variety acts change every month, but often include impersonations of hallowed French celebrities like the long-gone favorites Edith Piaf and Melina Mercouri. The spectacle comes complete with dinner for 200 F ($40), after which drinks are 80 F ($16). It's open Thursday to Tuesday; dinner begins at 8:30pm, followed by a show at 10:30pm.

Orchestre de Paris. Tickets vary in price from 105 to 320 F ($21 to $64). The concert season runs from September to Easter.

The **Radio France Salle Olivier Messian,** at 116 av. du Président-Kennedy, 16e (☎ 01-42-30-15-16; Métro: Passy-Ranelagh), is an even-better concert venue than the Salle Pleyel, offering top-notch concerts with guest conductors, and featuring performances by the Orchestre National de France (tickets are 50 to 190 F / $10 to $38), and the Orchestre Philharmonique (tickets are 120 F / $24). The box office is open from 11am to 6pm Monday to Saturday.

Cité de la Musique. 221 av. Jean-Jaurès, 19e. ☎ 01-44-84-45-00, or 01-44-84-44-84 for ticket sales and information. Concerts, 60–100 F ($12–$20) at 4:30pm, 100–160 F ($20–$32) at 8pm. Museum, 35 F ($7) adults, 24 F ($4.80) students and seniors over 60, 10 F ($2) children 17 and under; visits with commentary, 59 F ($11.80) adults, 48 F ($9.60) students and seniors over 60, 20 F ($4) children 17 and under. Tues–Wed and Fri–Sat noon–6pm, Thurs noon–9:30pm, Sun 10am–6pm. Métro: Porte-de-Pantin.

Of the half-dozen *grands travaux* conceived by the Mitterand administration, the Cité de la Musique has been the least criticized and most widely applauded. Set at the city's northeastern edge in what used to be a run-down and economically troubled

Remember the Marlon Brando film *Last Tango in Paris*? Relive it at **Le Tango,** 13 rue au Maire, 3e (☎ **01-42-72-17-78;** Métro: Arts-et-Métiers), a dance club devoted to Argentinian tango with pumping music and bordello decor. In addition to tango, this place features salsa and zouk from Africa and the French Caribbean islands such as Martinique. The club attracts revelers mostly in their 20s and 30s. The cover charge ranges from 50 to 60 F ($10 to $12), and it's open Thursday to Saturday from 11pm to 4am and on Sunday from 2 to 7pm.

Experience the best Brazilian samba and African music in Paris at **Chez Félix,** 23 rue Moffetard, 5e (☎ **01-47-07-68-78;** Métro: Monge). Sometimes watching the people who show up here is even more fun than dancing: It's often filled with colorful Latin expatriates, and is a gathering place for Paris's late-night hard-core party crowd. The cover charge, including your first drink, is 100 F ($20). Chez Félix is open Tuesday to Saturday from 11pm to 5am; closed August.

If salsa rhythms are in your blood and you want to go truly antillean, head for **La Plantation,** 45 rue Montpensier, 1er (☎ **01-49-27-06-21;** Métro: Palais-Royal), which doesn't really get hot until the wee hours of the morning. It's open Tuesday to Sunday from 11pm to dawn. While the French people in their 30s who frequent this place aren't the most impressive dancers, the club has a high energy level and everyone seems compelled to gyrate to the driving African rhythms. Admission, including your first drink, is 90 F ($18).

If you're more interested in watching scantily clad professionals dance than in dancing yourself, Pigalle's **Lili La Tigresse,** 98 rue Blanche, 9e (☎ **01-48-74-08-25;** Métro: Blanche), has the one of the hippest live revues in town. If you go, be sophisticatedly Parisian, not provincial.

On a rainy Paris evening, slip away for a revival showing of an oldie but goodie at **L'Arlequin,** 76 rue de Rennes, 6e (☎ **01-36-68-48-24;** Métro: St-Sulpice), our favorite *art-et-essai* movie house. Many films are shown in their *version originale,* which most often means English.

---

neighborhood, the Cité incorporates a network of concert halls, a museum, a library, and a musical research center.

Designed by the noted architect Christian de Portzamparc, this interconnected complex of bulky, post-cubist shapes is targeted at Paris's growing low-income, multicultural population. The Cité's directors envision it as one of the most democratic museums in Paris, a "Centre Beaubourg" of eclectic and multinational music, with archives documenting diverse musical forms like folk songs from Brittany and Siberia, classical music from North Africa, jazz, and unusual interpretations of French baroque musical forms. The complex serves as the nerve center for a series of educational programs aimed at grade- and high-school students throughout the Paris suburbs.

2 The Club & Music Scene

Paris today is still a nirvana for night owls, even though some of its once-unique attractions have become common. The fame of Parisian nights was established in those distant days of innocence when American visitors still gasped at the sight of a bare bosom in a chorus line and free love wasn't something you spoke of in polite circles.

Some of the best and most genuinely Parisian attractions are the *boîtes* in which *chansonniers* sing ballads and ditties intended only for local consumption. A few performers, like Edith Piaf and Juliette Greco, graduated to international fame from these places, but classic *boîte* fare is often inaccessible to non–French speakers, noted for its slang, innuendo, double-entendre, and sardonic French wit. To truly appreciate these places, your French would have to be more than good—it would have to be Pigalle-perfect. Luckily, there are hundreds of other establishments where linguistic limitations are of no consequence.

Many of the Right Bank—and a few of the Left Bank—hostelries are lavishly sprinkled with mademoiselles whose job it is to push a man's tab up to astronomical heights. They're incomparably skillful at it, and under their gentle touch you could be in for a staggering bill—including champagne, cigarettes, candy, and a teddy bear. An evening that might have cost you the equivalent of $25 can rapidly mount up to $300 and more—much more. Don't be afraid to respond with a firmly polite no to an unsolicited approach. The reaction is usually a regretful Gallic shrug, and she'll probably not try again.

One other general rule to remember is that the Right Bank, by and large, is plusher, slicker, and more expensive than the Left, which has more avant-garde entertainment and a younger clientele.

Also keep in mind that few spots in Paris begin swinging before 11pm, and most don't peak until midnight or later. Since the Métro stops running at 1am, be prepared to use taxis and to sleep late the next morning.

BOITES

In these traditional Paris music halls, the city's legendary *chansonniers* provide bombastic musical satire of the day's events. This combination of parody and burlesque is a time-honored Gallic amusement and a Parisian institution. The wit and ridicule these performers shower upon prostitutes and presidents alike make for an extravagant revue. Songs are often created on the spot, depending on current scandals and events for their inspiration. The best *boîtes* of the *chansonniers* are on boulevard de Clichy.

Au Caveau de la Bolée. 25 rue de l'Hirondelle, 6e. ☎ **01-43-54-62-20.** Cover 100 F ($20); free with fixed-price dinner at 230 F ($46). Métro: St-Michel.

To enter this boîte, you descend into the catacombs of the early 14th-century Abbey of St-André, once a famous literary café that attracted such personages as Verlaine and Oscar Wilde, who downed (or drowned in) glass after glass of absinthe here. The French songs are loud and bawdy, just the way the young student regulars like them. Occasionally the audience sings along.

A fixed-price dinner, which is served Monday to Saturday at 8:30pm, is followed by a series of at least four entertainers, usually comedians; you won't understand the jokes and references made in the show unless your French is extremely good. The cabaret starts at 10:30pm, and in lieu of paying admission, you can order dinner. If you've already had dinner, you can just order a drink, which will run 30 to 65 F ($6 to $13) each.

You'll find this establishment, which barely seats 70, on a tiny street near the western edge of place St-Michel, down a short flight of steps and under a giant archway beneath one of the square's grandiose buildings.

✪ **Au Lapin Agile.** 22 rue des Saules, 18e. ☎ **01-46-06-85-87.** Cover (including first drink) 110 F ($22). Métro: Lamarck.

This little cottage near the top of Montmartre, formerly known as the Café des Assassins, was once patronized by Picasso and Utrillo, who, like many other known and unknown artists, captured the boîte on canvas. For many decades it has been the heartbeat of French folk music, featuring folk songs, sing-alongs, and poetry readings. You'll sit at carved wooden tables in a low, dimly lit room with walls covered with bohemian memorabilia.

The music includes old French folk tunes, love ballads, army songs, sea chanteys, and music-hall ditties. You're encouraged to sing along, even if it's only the "*oui, oui, oui—non, non, non*" refrain of "Les Chevaliers de la Table Ronde." You can always hum along with songs like "Larilette" and "Madelon." Open Tuesday to Sunday from 9pm to 2am. Drinks cost 25 to 30 F ($5 to $6). No meals are served.

Caveau des Oubliettes. 11 rue St-Julien-le-Pauvre, 5e. ☎ **01-43-54-94-97.** Cover (including first drink) 70 F ($14). Métro: St-Michel.

It's hard to say what's more interesting in this place—the program or the environment. An *oubliette* is a dungeon with a trap door at the top as its only opening, and the name is quite accurate. Located in the Latin Quarter, just across the river from Notre-Dame, this nightspot is housed in a genuine 12th-century prison, complete with dungeons, spine-tingling passages, and scattered skulls, where prisoners were tortured and sometimes pushed through portholes to drown in the Seine. The caveau is beneath the subterranean vaults that many centuries ago linked it with the fortress prison of the Petit Châtelet.

Performers in medieval costumes sing French folk songs and tavern choruses—sentimental, comic, and bawdy—to exclusively tourist audiences. It's rather artificial and stagy, but charming nonetheless. There's nothing artificial, however, about the adjoining pub, which displays a working guillotine, chastity belts, and instruments of torture. Open Monday to Thursday from 9pm to 1am and on Friday and Saturday from 9pm to 2am. Drinks cost 15 to 50 F ($3 to $10) each.

Théâtre des Deux Anes. 100 bd. de Clichy, 18e. ☎ **01-46-06-10-26.** Tickets 200–210 F ($40–$42). Métro: Blanche.

Since around 1920 this theater has staged humorous satires of the foibles, excesses, and stupidities of various French governments. The current targets are President Jacques Chirac and assorted officials in *départements* scattered in all areas of the *héxagone française.* Cultural icons, both French and foreign, also receive a grilling that's sometimes very funny and sometimes harshly caustic. On the theater's door is a sign saying LEAVE YOUR CHEWING GUM AT THE DOOR, which helps to set the irreverent tone. The show, which lasts 2¹/₂ hours, is conducted entirely in rapid-fire, very colloquial French, so if your syntax isn't up to par, you might not fully appreciate its charms. Peformances are Tuesday to Saturday at 9pm, with a Sunday matinee at 3:30pm.

MUSIC HALLS

Paris music halls have thrived with the same familiar, time-tested formula for centuries: Sing a little, dance a little, juggle a few balls, and sprinkle generously with jokes. When this combination is slickly executed, it adds up to a top value in entertainment.

Olympia. 28 bd. des Capucines, 9e. ☎ **01-47-42-25-49.** Ticket prices vary depending on the show. Métro: Opéra.

Established a century ago, this first-rate city music hall offers packed programs of French professional talent and international stars. It's a cavernous hall devoted to a wide range of performances, where the French icons like Charles Aznavour make

---

La Miss & Maurice

Except for Edith Piaf, no figure has shone as brightly or as long in the French music hall as the legendary **Mistinguett.** Born in 1876 to a mattress-maker father and a feather-dresser mother who named her Jeanne Bourgeois, "Miss" went on to enchant Paris with her witty tongue and shapely legs that never seemed to grow tired or old, even after 60 years on stage. In time she became as much a symbol of Paris as the Eiffel Tower.

Her career was launched in 1893, and her final show was in 1950 at the age of 75, when she danced to bebop nightly for 12 minutes nonstop. Gifted with a natural sense of drama and showmanship, she would make grand entrances to her public appearance, walking down spiral staircases with 15 pounds of plumes on her head, 7 yards of feathers stretching behind her like a train. All the world learned the songs she introduced, ranging from "Valencia" to "Mon homme." She's been called "the true originator of the Spectacular Revue."

Mistinguett's male equivalent was **Maurice Chevalier,** who became far better known in America. Born in 1888 to a house-painter father and a braid-trimmer mother called *La Louque,* Maurice worked as a carpenter and metal engraver before he got his show business break at 13. The star of such films as *Ariane* and *Gigi,* he loved many women, none more so than Mistinguett. Wearing or carrying his famous straw hat, Chevalier enchanted audiences around the world. Though he never sang very well, he always pulled off a song with his familiar refrains, including "Thank Heaven for Little Girls" and "I Remember It Well," both from *Gigi.*

Both Chevalier and Mistinguett came from the streets, and although they later became sophisticated international travelers and stars, they never lost their ability to relate to the ordinary "street people" in their audiences. And they were adored by politicians, royalty, and millionaires as well. In the French music halls of the pre–World War II era, Maurice and La Miss reigned as king and queen.

---

frequent appearances. On one occasion the late Yves Montand appeared, but you had to reserve a seat 4 *months* in advance. A typical lineup would include an English rock duo singing its latest record hit, a showy group of Italian acrobats, a well-known French crooner, a talented dance troupe, a triple-jointed American juggling act/comedy team (doing much of their work in English), plus the featured "big name," all neatly laced together by a witty emcee and backed by an onstage band. Shows are given Tuesday to Saturday at 8:30pm and on Sunday at 5pm.

NIGHTCLUBS/CABARET

No Paris roll call would be complete without mention of the city's famous live revues. While decidedly expensive, they give you your money's worth by providing some of the most lavishly spectacular floor shows anywhere.

The hottest action in Paris today is at the Lido, the Moulin Rouge, most definitely at the Crazy Horse, and, to a lesser extent, the Paradis Latin. Once the most famous adult entertainment venue in the world, the Folies Bergère is now a conventional theater. And the former flesh clubs of the Latin Quarter are now more likely to host jazz bands than exotic dancers. The center of Paris's "sleazy" nightlife now focuses on boulevard de Clichy and the increasingly notorious place Pigalle, where sex clubs abound and where prostitutes, including transvestites and transsexuals, work the streets.

The clubs of the Pigalle, for the most part, are more interested in taking your money than entertaining you. The concierges of the leading Paris hotels no longer recommend these establishments, instead sending men with roving eyes to clubs like the Crazy Horse or the Lido. The nightclub areas around Pigalle, Gare St-Lazare and Beaubourg tend to be dangerous as well as seedy—in addition to hosting much of the city's prostitution, these areas are also the centers of Paris's drug trade.

Crazy Horse Saloon. 12 av. George-V, 8e. ☎ **01-47-23-32-32.** Cover (including the first two drinks) 220–620 F ($44–$124). Métro: George-V or Alma-Marceau.

Texans in 10-gallon hats and a host of international tourists are passionate fans of "le Crazy," the world's leading nude dancing venue. Alain Bernardin parodies the American West in the decor, but few patrons pay much attention to the western clichés on the walls, focusing all of their attention on the stage.

Two dozen dancers perform their acts entirely nude. The more sultry scenes are interspersed with three less provocative international variety acts. There are two shows Sunday to Friday, at 8:30 and 11pm, and three shows on Saturday, at 8pm, 10:35pm, and 12:50am. Drinks (beyond the first two included in the cover charge) begin at 100 F ($20).

Folies Bergère. 32 rue Richer, 9e. ☎ **01-44-79-98-98.** Cover 150–265 F ($30–$53), or 670 F ($134) for dinner and the show. Métro: Rue-Montmartre or Cadet.

According to legend, the first American GI to reach Paris during the liberation of 1944 asked for directions to the Folies Bergère. His son and grandson do the same today. And even the old man comes back for a second look.

A roving-eyed Frenchman would have to be in his second century to remember when the Folies began. Opened in 1886, the Folies Bergère has been associated with the unadorned female form since the turn of the century. Fresh off the boat, Victorians and Edwardians—starved for a glimpse of even an ankle—flocked to the Folies to get a look at much more. The show palace, after a multi-million-dollar refurbishment, opened again in 1993, and in some ways its new acts satirize its past extravagances.

In the modern climate of more sophisticated and permissive sexuality, the Folies Bergère has radically altered its program, abandoning much of its old fare for a less titillating, more conventional format. Today it often presents a bemused and light-hearted series of French-language comedies and musical comedies, many derived from shows that were successful on the stages of London or New York. Recent examples have included *Fou des Folies* (a coy memorial to the theater's raunchy old days) and *Les Années Twist* (a Gallic version of an American homage to rock 'n' roll). Performances are given Tuesday to Saturday at 9pm and on Sunday at 5pm. The restaurant opens at 7pm. Make your reservations at box-office window Tuesday to Sunday from 11am to 6pm.

Lido de Paris. 116 bis av. des Champs-Elysées, 8e. ☎ **01-40-76-56-10.** Cover (including a half bottle of champagne, service, and taxes) 540 F ($108), or 805–1100 F ($161–$222) for dinner and the show. Métro: George-V.

In a huge room with 1,200 seats and excellent visibility, this palatial nightspot puts on an avalanche of glamour and talent, combined with enough showmanship to make the late Mr. Barnum look like an amateur. The permanent attraction is the 60 Bluebell Girls, a fabulous ensemble of long-legged international beauties, and the 25 danseurs. The rest of the program changes frequently. One of its most recent shows, *C'est magique!*, presented the world of magic, complete with aerial ballets, astonishing aquatic dances, and various electrifying visual effects. Go at least once in your lifetime. The dinner dance begins at 8pm. La Revue is presented at 10pm and midnight.

Milliardaire. 68 rue Pierre-Charron, 8e. ☎ **01-42-89-88-09.** Cover (including the first two drinks) 450 F ($90). Métro: Franklin-D-Roosevelt.

The stylish, elegant Milliardaire is just off the Champs-Elysées, reached through a backyard that's not nearly as plush as the interior. The program includes comedians, jugglers, and first-rate dance numbers. Shows are nightly at 9:30 and 11:30pm. The place maintains a popular and discreet piano bar open every night after the last show (1:45 to 4am), where drinks cost 120 to 160 F ($24 to $32).

Moulin-Rouge. Place Blanche, Montmartre, 18e. ☎ **01-46-06-00-19.** Cover (including champagne) 495 F ($99), or 720 F ($144) for dinner and the show. Métro: Blanche.

Toulouse-Lautrec, who put this establishment on the map about a century ago, wouldn't recognize it today. The windmill is still there and so is the cancan. But the rest has become a super-slick, gimmick-ridden variety show with a heavy emphasis on the undraped female form. You'll see underwater ballets in an immense glass tank, young women in swings and on trick stairs, all interspersed with animal acts, comic jugglers, and singing trios. These are just a smattering of the acts usually found on the daily bill of fare—it's all expertly staged, but any connection with the old, notorious Moulin-Rouge is purely coincidental. Open nightly, with dinner at 8pm and the revue at 10pm. There's no minimum if you sit at the bar (where the view is not as good). Drinks cost around 90 F ($18).

Le Paradis Latin. 28 rue Cardinal-Lemoine, 5e. ☎ **01-43-25-28-28.** Cover (including a half bottle of champagne) 465 F ($93), or 680–1,260 F ($136–$252) for dinner and the show. Métro: Jussieu or Cardinal-Lemoine.

Built in 1889 on the site of an even earlier theatre from the age of Napoléon (1803), it's the only building in France to bear historic designations as both a building and as a theater. Le Paradis Latin, with its skeletal metallic structure that's reminiscent of the Eiffel Tower, is the only theater that architect Gustave Eiffel ever designed. Le Paradis helped to introduce vaudeville and musical theater to Paris in the late 19th century, before shutting down and becoming a warehouse in 1903. It was renovated and reopened in the 1970s, and quickly became host to one of the most successful cabarets in Paris. The emcee banters in French and English, and usually invites the audience to participate in the show. Open Wednesday to Monday, with the dinner revue at 8:30pm and the revue at 9:45pm. Drinks begin at 95 F ($19). In true Paris style, the revue ends with the cancan at 11:30pm.

Villa d'Este. 4 rue Arsène-Houssaye, 8e. ☎ **01-42-56-14-65.** Cover (inculding one drink) 150 F ($30); or 340–720 F ($68–$144) for dinner and the show (reservations required). Métro: Charles-de-Gaulle–Etoile.

A short stroll from the Champs-Elysées, the Villa d'Este has been around for a long time, and has retained a reputation for high-quality entertainment, featuring top singing talent from Europe and America. The place is a *dinner-dansant* club that mimics the style and atmosphere of a 1930s Big Band ballroom. The music emphasis here is beloved any Francophil, and includes duplications of the greatest hits of such grand names in French music of the postwar years as Piaf, Azanvour, Brassens, and Brel. The various fixed-price menus include wine, and if they don't want dinner, patrons can just order drinks, beginning at 150 F ($30). The place opens about 8pm and the orchestra begins playing about 8:30pm. The variety cabaret with comedians and magicians begins at 9:30pm and lasts until around midnight, after which there's dancing until 2am.

JAZZ & ROCK

You can probably listen and dance to more jazz in Paris than in any U.S. city, with the possible exception of San Francisco. The great jazz revival that long ago swept America is still going full swing in Paris, with Dixieland or Chicago-style jazz rhythms being pounded out in dozens of performance cellars called *caveaux*.

This is one city where you don't have to worry about being a self-conscious dancer. The locals, even young people, are not particularly good. The best dancers on any floor are usually American. And although Parisians take to rock with enthusiasm, their skill doesn't match their zest.

The majority of the jazz and rock clubs are crowded into the Left Bank near the Seine between rue Bonaparte and rue St-Jacques, which makes things easy for syncopation-seekers.

Le Bilboquet. 13 rue St-Benoît, 6e. ☎ **01-45-48-81-84.** No cover to either area. Métro: St-Germain-des-Prés.

This restaurant, jazz club, and piano bar offers some of the best music in Paris. In the heart of St-Germain-des-Prés, the site was famous during the heyday of existentialism. The film *Paris Blues* was shot here. Jazz is played nightly from 10:45pm to 2:45am on the upper level in Le Bilboquet restaurant, a wood-paneled room with a copper ceiling, a sunken bar with brass trim, and a Victorian candelabrum. The tables are on a raised tier and elevated balcony. The menu is limited but features classic French fare, specializing in carré d'agneau (roast lamb), fish, and beef. Appetizers include smoked salmon and terrines. Dinner runs 200 to 250 F ($40 to $50) and is served nightly from 8pm to 1am. Drinks begin at 120 F ($24).

Club St-Germain is a cellar-level disco with karaoke. It's also open Tuesday to Sunday from 11pm to 5am, and here drinks begin at 100 F ($20). You can walk from one club to the other, but you have to buy a new drink each time you change venues.

Caveau de la Huchette. 5 rue de la Huchette, 5e. ☎ **01-43-26-65-05.** Cover 60 F ($12) Sun–Thurs, 70 F ($14) Fri–Sat; for students with valid ID, 50 F ($10) Sun–Thurs, 60 F ($12) Fri–Sat. Métro: St-Michel. RER: St-Michel.

This celebrated jazz club, reached by descending a winding staircase, draws a young student crowd, who dance to the music of well-known jazz combos. In prejazz days, it was frequented by Robespierre and Marat. Open Sunday to Thursday from 9:30pm to 2:30am and on Friday, Saturday, and holidays from 9:30pm to 4am. Drinks cost 22 to 30 F ($4.40 to $6).

Jazz Club La Villa. In the Hôtel La Villa, 29 rue Jacob, 6e. ☎ **01-43-26-60-00.** Cover (including the first drink) 120–150 F ($24–$30). Métro: St-Germain-des-Prés.

This club is unusual in that it lies in the red-velour cellar of a small but chic four-star hotel in the Latin Quarter, but is much more upscale and elegant than most of the dives that this Left Bank area is known for. Don't expect backpackers or a scattering of impoverished painters—this place caters to hard-core jazz aficionados and famous artists. It specializes in Dixieland and other forms of New Orleans jazz, and features a new ensemble every week. No food of any kind is served, and the small, often claustrophobic venue includes a predictable array of tiny tables, banquettes, and armchairs crowded in front of a stage that has welcomed such artists as Joe Lovano, Josh Redman, and Shirley Horn. Open Monday to Saturday from 10:30pm to 2am; closed August. Drinks cost 60 F ($12).

Jazz Club Lionel Hampton. In the Hôtel Méridien, 81 bd. Gouvion-St-Cyr, 17e. ☎ **01-40-68-34-34.** Cover (including the first drink) 130 F ($26). Métro: Porte-Maillot.

This popular club in the outlying 17e arrondissement has a loyal following among club-goers from central Paris, who make the trip across town to hear and dance to jazz performed by prominent international musicians. Past acts have included Lionel Hampton (after whom the club was named), Fats Domino, and Nita Whitheker. It's open nightly from 10:30pm to 2am to later, depending on business.

New Morning. 7–9 rue des Petites-Ecuries, 10e. ☎ **01-45-23-51-41.** Cover 120–180 F ($24–$36). Métro: Château-d'Eau.

This club, which features jazz, salsa, and other dance music, was opened in 1981 and named after a 1969 album by Bob Dylan. In this high-ceilinged loft, which used to be the home of a daily newspaper, jazz maniacs dance, talk, flirt, and drink elbow to elbow at the bar. The dress code is relaxed, and concerts and musical soirées might feature practically every kind of music except disco. The only rule here seems to be that there are few rules. It's often impossible to predict if New Morning will be open on a given night, but when it is in business, it usually opens at 8:30pm and closes at 1:30 or 2am. And though it's usually closed Sunday, if a well-known performer can be booked for that night, it will stay open. A phone call will let you know what's going on the night of your visit. No food is served.

Slow Club. 130 rue de Rivoli, 1er. ☎ **01-42-33-84-30.** Cover 60 F ($12) Tues–Thurs, 75 F ($15) Fri–Sat and holidays. Métro: Châtelet.

One of the most famous jazz cellars in Europe, and Miles Davis's favorite jazz place in Paris, the Slow Club offers some of the best Dixieland this side of New Orleans in an atmosphere inspired by Harlem's legendary Cotton Club. Patrons tend to be in their 30s. The featured band changes regularly. Open Tuesday to Thursday from 10pm to 3am and on Friday, Saturday, and holidays from 10pm to 4am. Drinks cost 25 F ($5) without alcohol, 39 F ($7.80) with alcohol.

DANCE HALLS & DISCOS

Although Paris is supposedly the birthplace of the discothèque, nobody here seems to know anymore what, precisely, constitutes one. Originally the discos were small, intimate clubs where patrons danced to records—hence the term. Now, however, the tag is applied to anything from playground-sized ballrooms with full orchestras to tiny bars with taped tunes where they don't let you dance at all.

The area surrounding the Church of St-Germain-des-Prés is so packed with often short-lived dance clubs (some seem to have the life spans of sickly butterflies) that it's almost impossible to keep track of their comings and closings. What's hopping at the time of this writing might be a hardware store by the time you get there. But chances are two new happening places will have sprung into existence on the same block.

The samples below are a few of the hundreds of spots where people go chiefly to dance, as distinct from others where the main attraction is the music.

Les Bains. 7 rue du Bourg-l'Abbé, 3e. ☎ **01-48-87-01-80.** Cover (including the first drink) 140 F ($28). Métro: Réaumur.

This chic enclave has often slipped in and out of fashion, but lately it's a favorite among Paris's fickle club crowd. The club's name, Les Bains, refers to the building's former function as a Turkish bath that catered to Paris's gay community, back when Marcel Proust was a frequent client. Patrons often seem to dress more for show than for comfort, and the club seems to encourage this: If the bouncer at the door isn't impressed with your looks or attire, he might not let you in. Open daily midnight to 6am. Drinks run 100 F ($20).

Le Balajo. 9 rue de Lappe, 11e. ☎ **01-47-00-07-87.** Cover (including the first drink) 30–50 F ($6–$10) in the afternoon, 100 F ($20) in the evening. Métro: Bastille.

Established in 1936, this dance club is best remembered as the venue where Edith Piaf first won the hearts of thousands of Parisian music lovers. Today Le Balajo is hardly as fashionable as it once was, a hangout where older night owls usually feel comfortably nostalgic and where younger ones in their 20s can discover the hits their parents danced to. Though its glory days seem behind it, Le Balajo is still a good place to hear an often eclectic selection of dance music, including swing, be-bop, reggae, salsa, rock 'n' roll, rap, and, on Monday night, even American gospel. Open on Monday, Thursday, and Friday from 11:30pm to 5am, and on Sunday from 9pm to 5am. Also, the club features afternoon sessions on Saturday and Sunday from 3 to 6:30pm where a youthful older crowd dances to ballroom favorites of the Big Band era and dance standards of World War II.

Club Zed. 2 rue des Anglais, 5e. ☎ **01-43-54-93-78.** Cover (including the first drink) 50–100 F ($10–$20). Métro: Maubert-Mutualité.

Club Zed plays more rock 'n' roll, boogie-woogie, and danceable American tunes from the 1960s than any other club in Paris. It doesn't usually attract Paris's nocturnal "in" crowd, but it can be nostalgic, amusing, and fun. And if you were reared on the music that made the postwar years great, you just might love it. Open on Wednesday and Thursday from 10:30pm to 3am and on Friday and Saturday from 10:30pm to 5am. Drinks begin at 50 F ($10).

La Coupole. 102 bd. de Montparnasse, 14e. ☎ **01-43-20-14-20.** Cover 90 F ($18) evenings, 60 F ($12) Sat matinee, 80 F ($16) Sun matinee. Métro: Vavin.

One of the big Montparnasse cafés and a former bohemian stronghold, La Coupole is a throwback to the days when locals waltzed and tangoed to the the strains of a live orchestra. In addition to its upstairs café (reviewed separately in Chapter 5), La Coupole has a large basement ballroom reserved for dancing. Tuesday to Thursday night the venue features Antillean and Brazilian music and is devoted to dancing. Open Tuesday to Thursday from 9:30pm to 2am, on Friday from 9:30pm to 4am, on Saturday from 3 to 7pm and 9:30pm to 4am, and on Sunday from 3pm to 2am.

Le Palace. 8 rue du Faubourg-Montmartre, 9e. ☎ **01-42-46-10-87.** Cover 100 F ($20) evenings, 50 F ($10) after 6am Fri–Sun; 60 F ($12) gay men's Sun tea dance. Métro: Rue-Montmartre.

Originally conceived as a cabaret house in the 1930s, Le Palace was later a cinema and became a disco in the 1970s. It has retained much of its original eclectic decor, a mixture of vaguely Greek and Roman motifs with a good dose of Hollywood thrown in. The club has three bars scattered over three different levels, good acoustics, and plenty of room to dance. Drinks run 50 F ($10). Its clientele is among the most diverse in Paris, with a mixture of gay and straight clients. There's dancing Tuesday to Sunday from 11:30pm to 6am. On weekends Paris's hard-core club crowd parties here all night and on into the morning—in addition to its nighttime hours the club is open (and hopping) every Friday, Saturday, and Sunday from 6am till noon. On Sunday afternoons (from 5 to 11pm) the club hosts a tea dance reserved exclusively for gay men (no women are allowed).

Rex Club. 5 bd. Poissonière, 2e. ☎ **01-42-36-83-98.** Cover (including the first drink) 70 F ($14). Métro: Bonne-Nouvelle.

This is one of the many new dance clubs that have cropped up around Paris in recent years. Set in a deep cellar at the edge of the garment district, it welcomes a young clientele that seems to pride itself on its avant-garde weirdness. Come here to dance hectically to fast music, rub shoulders with jaded Parisian night owls, and sample the sense of hedonistic abandon and social anarchy for which Paris is famous. Different evenings feature different types of music, including rap, European disco, reggae, and acid rock, and the club often has performances by live bands. Open Thursday to Sunday from 11:30pm until dawn. Wednesday is sometimes reserved for special events.

Riverside Club. 7 rue Grégoire-de-Tours, 6e. ☎ **01-43-54-46-33.** Cover (including the first drink) 90 F ($18). Métro: St-Michel or Odéon.

This battered, cramped, and popular club in a Left Bank cellar attracts droves of jaded veteran club-goers. Its musical fare almost always includes the most popular songs of the 1970s, including electronic rock classics, and many hits by the Doors, which are played over and over and over. Women, especially when unaccompanied, are often let in free. Open daily from 11pm to 6am. Drinks begin at 60 F ($12).

3 The Bar Scene

WINE BARS

Instead of attending traditional cafés or bistros, many Parisians now prefer to patronize wine bars, where the food is often better and the ambience more inviting. Wine bars come in a wide range of styles, from old traditional places to more modern gathering centers, and have become increasingly popular venues on the Parisian nightlife scene.

Au Sauvignon. 80 rue des Sts-Pères, 7e. ☎ **01-45-48-49-02.** Glass of wine 21–42 F ($4.20–$8.40); all wines an additional 2 F (40¢) if consumed at a table. MC, V. Mon–Sat 8:30am–10:30pm. Closed major religious holidays, 2 weeks in Feb, and 3 weeks in Aug. Métro: Sèvres-Babylone.

Au Sauvignon is the best-known wine bar in Paris and enjoys a good reputation, but it's tiny and much of its seating overflows onto a covered terrace. The owner is from Auvergne, and when he's not polishing his zinc countertop or preparing a plate of charcuterie, he sells wines by the glass; beaujolais is the cheapest. He also serves Auvergne specialties, including goat cheese and terrines, if you'd like to have a snack with your wine. The fresh Poilane bread is ideal with the Auvergne ham, the country pâté, or the Crottin de Chavignol goat cheese. The decor boasts frescoes by Jean-Marie Philippe.

Ma Bourgogne. 19 place des Vosges, 4e. ☎ **01-42-78-44-64.** Coffee 14 F ($2.80); a glass of wine 18–30 F ($3.60–$6); *plats du jour*, 85–140 F ($17–$28); fixed-price menu 185 F ($37). No credig cards. Daily 8am–1am. Closed Feb. Métro: St-Paul or Bastille.

This fine brasserie has a good selection of wines and is situated in the recently improved place des Vosges, once the home of Victor Hugo. Sit under the arcades and contemplate this dreamy square, enjoying coffee or a glass of beaujolais. In the summertime you can sit at the rattan tables on the sidewalk tables; in harsher weather, retire to the cozy room inside. Customers come here from all over the city to sample the brasserie's famous steak tartare.

La Tartine. 24 rue de Rivoli, 4e. ☎ **01-42-72-76-85.** Glass of wine 7.50–15.50 F ($1.50–$3.10); sandwiches 14–40 F ($2.80–$8); plate of charcuterie 45 F ($9). Credit cards TK. Wed noon–10pm, Thurs–Mon 8:30am–10pm. Closed 2 weeks in August. Métro: St-Paul.

La Tartine, with a decor that hasn't changed since its installation in 1923, embodies the culture, style, and atmosphere of Old Paris. Decorative mirrors, brass details, a zinc bar, and frosted-globe chandeliers all contribute to this sense of time warp, and you expect to see Tito, Trotsky, or Lenin (all former patrons) walk in the door at any moment. At least 50 wines are offered at reasonable prices, and all categories of wine are served by the glass. You can choose from seven kinds of beaujolais and there's also a large selection of bordeaux. Sancerre, a light wine, is also very popular. Accompany your wine with some young goat cheese from the Loire Valley. Charcuterie, pâtés, terrines, and sandwiches are also available.

⊙ **Willi's Wine Bar.** 13 rue des Petits-Champs, 1er. ☎ **01-42-61-05-09.** Wine by the glass 26–30 F ($5.20–$6); main courses 78–110 F ($15.60–$22); fixed-price menu 155 F ($31). MC, V. Mon–Sat noon–2:30pm and 7–11pm. Métro: Bourse, Musée-du-Louvre, or Palais-Royal.

This wine bar in the center of the financial district is popular among journalists and stockbrokers. It's run by two Englishmen, Mark Williamson and Tim Johnston, and offers about 250 different kinds of wine (all sold by the glass) and several special deals every week.

Very crowded at lunchtime, it often settles down to a lower decibel level in the evening, when you can better admire the 16th-century architecture and the warm ambience. The dinner menu features a number of good dishes, including breast of quail with salad and balsamic vinaigrette, artichoke-and-onion salad, green beans, foie gras, brochette of lamb flavored with cumin, and such desserts as a chocolate terrine. A limited menu of platters, snacks, and wine is served throughout the afternoon as well.

BARS & PUBS

Parisian bars and pubs are imports from the United States and England, and as such tend to strike an alien chord in a landscape dominated by cafés and bistros, with a few notable exceptions. About half of them try to imitate Stateside cocktail bars and the other half pretend to be British pubs—and some go to amazing lengths in the process. Nonetheless, even the most blatant imitations can make for an enjoyable night of drinking and socializing.

Bar-hopping is fashionable with Paris's trendy set, as distinct from café-sitting, which is done by everyone. Bars, therefore, are generally a little more expensive than cafés, and can be quite costly if the place boasts a well-known bartender.

Le Bar. 10 rue de l'Odéon, 6e. ☎ **01-43-26-66-83.** Beer from 21 F ($4.20); drinks, from 40 F ($8). Daily 5:30pm—2am. Métro: Odéon.

Le Bar, a small and intimate hangout right off place de l'Odéon on the Left Bank, is permanently thronged with swarms of noisy, amorous, and argumentative university students, and is an ideal spot to meet Paris's college crowd. The walls are plastered with antique and popular posters, the place reverberates to the strains of an overworked jukebox, and the beer flows liberally. It just might remind you of your own college days. Open daily from 5:30pm to 2am. Beer begins at 21 F ($4.20); drinks, at 40 F ($8).

The China Club. 50 rue de Charenton, 12e. ☎ **01-43-43-82-02.** Métro: Bastille.

Situated close to the Opéra Bastille, this bar attracts the post-show crowd, as well as regulars from the fashion and arts communities. There's a Chinese restaurant on the street level, a calm and quiet bar upstairs (with a scattering of chess boards), and a more animated (and occasionally raucous) bar in the cellar. The red interior features decorative references to the French colonial empire in Asia. No one dances, but everyone seems to talk. The restaurant is open nightly from 7pm to 12:30am, serving meals beginning at 180 F ($36); there's a fixed-price menu at 155 F ($31). The bars are open Sunday to Thursday from 7pm to 2am and Friday to Saturday from 7pm to 3am; drinks begin at 45 F ($9).

Pub Saint-Germain-des-Prés. 17 rue de l'Ancienne-Comédie, 6e. ☎ **01-43-29-38-70.** Métro: Odéon.

With nine different rooms and 650 seats, this is the largest pub in France, offering 26 draft beers and 500 bottled international beers. The somewhat tacky decor consists of gilded mirrors on the walls, hanging gas lamps, and a stuffed parrot in a gilded cage. Leather booths render drinking discreet and the atmosphere is quiet, relaxed, and rather posh. Beer runs 20 to 80 F ($4 to $16), and popular beers featured include Genuine Whitbread and Pimm's No. 1. You can also order snacks or complete meals; fixed-price meals cost 88 to 158 F ($17.60 to $31.60) at lunch, 62 to 150 F ($12.40 to $30) at dinner. In the evening, a live band plays rock and a variety of popular music, and a piano bar is open from 10pm to 4am. The pub is open 24 hours daily.

Renault. 53 av. des Champs-Elysées, 8e. ☎ **01-42-25-28-17.** Métro: Franklin-D-Roosevelt.

This theme bar combines an auto showroom with a family-oriented bar serving beer and hamburgers. Cars and car motifs are everywhere, and you can order food from the fixed-price menu, an à la carte meal for 80 to 250 F ($16 to $50), or just a drink from the bar. A whisky starts at 43 F ($8.60). The free Musée de l'Automobile (automobile museum) is on the upper level. Open daily from 11:30am to 2:30am.

GRAND HOTEL BARS

If you want to recapture the elegance of the salons of 18th-century France, try one of the bars of Paris's grand hotels. Dress up, speak softly, and be prepared to spend a lot: You're not paying for the drink but for an ambience unmatched in most other places.

Bar Anglais. In the Hôtel Plaza Athénée, 25 av. Montaigne, 8e. ☎ **01-47-23-78-33.** Métro: Alma-Marceau.

On your way through this deluxe citadel, you'll pass a chattering telex machine, which carries recent quotes from the world's leading stock exchanges in case you want to check on your investment portfolio. In the rarefied atmosphere of this elegant bar, it would seem appropriate to do so. As its name would imply, the bar, located on the lower level of the hotel, has a decor that's vintage Anglo-Saxon, although the service is definitely French and the drinks are international. Every evening between 11pm and 1:30am a pianist and singer entertain an adult clientele in a medley of languages. The bar is open daily from 11am to 1:30am. Drinks start at 80 F ($16) before, or at 125 F ($25) after 11pm during the entertainment.

Bar du Crillon. In the Hôtel de Crillon, 10 place de la Concorde, 8e. ☎ **01-44-71-15-00.** Métro: Concorde. Drinks from 95 F ($19). Daily from 11am—2am.

Although some visitors consider the Bar du Crillon too stiff and self-consciously elegant to ever allow anyone to have a good time, the social and literary history of this bar is remarkable. Hemingway set a climactic scene of *The Sun Also Rises* here, and over the years it has attracted practically every upper-level staff member of the nearby American embassy, as well as a gaggle of visiting heiresses, stars, starlets, and wannabes. Under its new owner, the Concorde Group, the bar has been redecorated by Sonia Rykiel and no longer basks in the 1950s glow so favored by past clients such as Janet Flanner (legendary Paris correspondent of *The New Yorker*). The bar is open daily from 11am to 2am, serving drinks beginning at 95 F ($19). Drinks are also served in the Crillon's *salon de thé*, the Jardin d'Hiver.

George V Bar. In the Hôtel George V, 31 av. George-V, 8e. ☎ **01-47-23-54-00.** Métro: George-V.

Visit this elegant bar and experience firsthand the decadent atmosphere of one of Paris's most expensive and international hotels. If there's someone you're trying to avoid amid the tapestries and Regency antiques of the main lobby, this very *laissez-faire* watering hole provides a convenient hideaway. It's open daily from 11am to 1:30am. Mixed drinks begin at 85 F ($17).

Hemingway Bar. In the Hôtel Ritz, 15 place Vendôme, 1er. ☎ **01-42-60-38-30.** Métro: Opéra.

More than 50 years after Hemingway "liberated" the Ritz in 1945, the bar named after him is still going strong. The decor consists of warm wood paneling and leather chairs, providing a literary sort of atmosphere. Conferences on literature are frequently organized here, and daily newspapers, magazines, and a selection of books are always available. Black-and-white photographs of famous former patrons hang on the walls. Open Monday to Saturday from 6:30pm to 2am. Drinks run 100 F ($20) and up.

4 Specialty Bars & Clubs

GAY PARIS

Gay life in Paris is mainly centered around Les Halles and Le Marais, with the greatest concentration of gay clubs, restaurants, bars, and shops located between the Hôtel-de-Ville and Rambuteau Métro stops. Gay magazines that focus mostly on cultural and news events and are widely distributed within Paris include *Illico,* free within many gay bars, but priced around 12 F ($2.40) in sidewalk kiosks, and *Double-Face* (free and usually available in gay bars and bookstores). New and glossy gay magazines, in French, that focus on interviews and cultural developments, with a few porno pic inside, includ *Tetu* and *Idol,* both of which are sold at many, as is *Lesbia,* a national monthly lesbian magazine.

Banana Café. 13 rue de la Ferronnerie, 1er. ☎ **01-42-33-35-31.** No cover. Métro: Châtelet or Les-Halles.

This is the most popular gay bar in the Marais, a ritualized stopover for European homosexuals (mostly male but also female) visiting or doing business in Paris. Occupying two floors of a 19th-century building, it has walls the color of an overripe banana, dim lighting, and a well-known daily happy hour between 4:30 and 7pm when the price of drinks is reduced. There's a street-level bar and a dance floor in the cellar featuring a live pianist and recorded music, and, depending on the mood, clients sometimes dance. It's open daily from 4:30pm to 5am, but at its most crowded and animated every night after 11:30pm. On Thursday, Friday, and Saturday nights, go-go dancers perform from spotlit platforms in the cellar. Beer costs 10 to 35 F ($2 to $7); a whisky and soda, 20 to 60 F ($4 to $12).

Le Bar Central. 33 rue Vieille-du-Temple, 4e ☎ **01-48-87-99-33.** Métro: Hôtel-de-Ville.

Le Bar Central is one of the leading bars for men in the Hôtel de Ville area. In fact, it's the most famous gay men's bar in Paris today. The club has established a small hotel upstairs with a few facilities and only seven bedrooms. Both the bar and its little hotel are housed in a 300-year-old building in the heart of Le Marais. The hotel caters especially to gay men, less frequently to lesbians. The bar is open Sunday to Thursday from 2pm to 1am and on Friday and Saturday from 2pm to 2am. A beer will cost you 15 to 18 F ($3 to $3.60).

La Champmeslé. 4 rue Chabanais, 2e. ☎ **01-42-96-85-20.** Métro: Pyramides.

With dim lighting, background music, and comfortable banquettes, La Champmeslé offers a cozy meeting place for women. It is, in fact, the leading women's bar of Paris. The club is housed in a 300-year-old building, decorated with exposed stone and heavy ceiling beams, with retro 1950s-style furnishings. Every Thursday night one of the premier lesbian events of Paris—a cabaret—begins here at 10pm (no cover, and drinks cost the same as on any other day), and every month there's a photo exhibition. Open Monday to Saturday from 5pm until dawn. Drinks run 30 to 35 F ($6 to $7).

Madame Arthur. 75 bis rue des Martyrs, 18e. ☎ **01-42-54-40-21.** Cover (including the first drink) 165 F ($33), or for dinner and the show, 275 F ($55) Mon–Fri, 395 F ($79) Sat–Sun. Métro: Abbesses.

This famous place Pigalle showplace, which attracts both straight and gay people, is directed by Madame Arthur, who is no lady. The running joke is that this place has been around so long it welcomed the invading armies of Julius Caesar—and it's still going strong. You can visit just to drink or you can dine from a fixed-price menu. Reservations are a good idea. Open daily, with shows from 7:30 to 11pm. Drinks cost 95 F ($19).

Le New Monocle. 60 bd. Edgar-Quinet, 14e. ☎ **01-43-20-81-12.** Cover (including the first drink) 150 F ($30). Métro: Edgar-Quinet.

Although traditionally a lesbians-only hangout since the old Montparnasse days of Gertrude Stein and Alice Toklas, Le New Monacle recently relaxed its entrance policy and now admits well-behaved men. Inside is a bar, dim lighting, and a dance floor ringed with chairs, banquettes, and comfortably battered 1950s-inspired accessories. No self-respecting lesbian with a sense of literary history would dream of going to Paris without at least stopping by just once for a drink. Open Monday to Saturday from 3pm to 4am and on Sunday from 5pm to 4am. Drinks go for 150 F ($30).

Le Palace Gay Tea Dance. 8 rue du Faubourg-Montmartre, 9e. ☎ **01-42-46-10-87.** Cover (including the first drink) 100 F ($20). Métro: Rue-Montmartre.

If you're gay, this is *the* gathering place in Paris on Sunday afternoon from 4 to 11pm. Men—but not women—are welcomed into this chatty, gossipy, fun environment whether they've come to dance or not. It's an international crowd, and if you don't want to drink beer or liquor you can always sip coffee. For more details about Le Palace, see "Dance Halls & Discos" under "The Club & Music Scene," earlier in this chapter, and Le Privilège, below.

Le Piano Zinc. 49 rue des Blancs-Manteaux, 4e. ☎ **01-42-74-32-42.** No cover; one-drink minimum Fri–Sat. Métro: Rambuteau or Hôtel-de-Ville.

This ever-popular place was founded by a German-born Francophile named Jürgen about 13 years ago; it's both a piano bar and a cabaret, filled with singing patrons who belt out old French *chansons* with humor and gusto, or do versions of Madonna, Piaf, Liza, and the inevitable Judy Garland. It defines itself as a gay bar, "but you can happily bring your *grand-mère,* as some of our clients do," the management assured us. Le Piano Zinc occupies three floors of a building, and the free cabaret is presented in the basement at 10pm. Open Tuesday to Sunday from 6pm to 2am. Mixed drinks cost 45 F ($9); a beer, 35 F ($7).

Le Privilège. In the basement of Le Palace, 8 rue du Faubourg-Montmartre, 9e. ☎ **01-47-70-75-02.** Cover (including the first drink) 100 F ($20). Métro: Rue-Montmartre.

Set in the basement of Le Palace (see above), this bar is one of the most popular watering holes in Paris for lesbians, who arrive wearing everything from leather and sunglasses to silk scarves and lipstick. It's most popular with gay women between midnight and around 4am, after which it's usually relinquished to a crowd of mostly gay men. You may be rather intensely "screened" at the door before being allowed inside. Open daily from 11:30pm to dawn.

Le Queen. 102 av. des Champs-Elysées, 8e. ☎ **01-42-89-31-32.** Cover 50 F ($10) Mon, 80 F ($16) Fri–Sat. Métro: Franklin-D.-Roosevelt.

Should you miss gay life *à la* New York, follow the flashing purple sign on the "main street" of Paris, near the corner of avenue Georges V. The place is often mobbed, primarily with gay men and, to a much lesser degree, chic women (*photomannequins* and the like) who work in the fashion and film industries. Look for drag shows, muscle shows, strip tease from *danseurs* who gyrate atop the bars, and everything from 1970s-style disco nights (Monday) to Tuesday-night foam parties, when cascades of *mousse* descend onto the dance floor. Go very, very late, as the place is open daily from midnight to 6 or 7am.

LITERARY HAUNTS

La Closerie des Lilas. 171 bd. du Montparnasse, 6e. ☎ **01-43-26-70-50.** Métro: Port-Royal.

Hemingway, Picasso, Gershwin, and Modigliani all loved the Closerie, and it has once again become one of the hottest bars in Paris. Look for the brass nameplate of your favorite Lost Generation artist along the banquettes or at the bar. Open daily from 11am to 1:30am. A scotch and soda will set you back 75 F ($15); a beer, 36 F ($7.20).

Harry's New York Bar. 5 rue Daunou, 2e. ☎ **01-42-61-71-14.** Métro: Opéra or Pyramides.

Sank roo doe Noo, as the ads tell you to instruct your cab driver, is the most famous bar in Europe—quite possibly in the world. Opened on Thanksgiving Day in 1911, it's sacred to Hemingway disciples as the spot where Ernest did most of his Parisian imbibing. To others it's hallowed as the site where the white lady and sidecar cocktails were invented in 1919 and 1931, respectively. It's also the birthplace of the Bloody Mary and French '75, and the headquarters of the International Bar Flies (IBF).

The upstairs bar is popular among expatriates eager to unwind amid their fellow anglophones and their Gallic admirers. Here a dry martini costs 52 F ($10.40), and a whisky begins at 50 F ($10). The ambience is more lighthearted in the cellar, where a freewheeling cabaret is performed every night from 10pm to 2am, with whatever singer, actor, or comedian the management can arrange on any given evening. Prices in the cellar are 15 F ($3) higher, per drink, than those in the historic street-level bar. Open daily from 10:30am to 4am (snacks served from 11am to 5pm); closed December 24 and 25.

Rosebud. 11 bis rue Delambre, 14e. ☎ **01-43-35-38-54.** Métro: Vavin.

The name is taken from Orson Welles's greatest film, *Citizen Kane.* Rosebud is just around the corner from the famous cafés of Montparnasse, and once attracted such devotees as Jean-Paul Sartre and Simone de Beauvoir, Eugene Ionesco, and Marguerite Duras. Drop in at night for a glass of wine or a bite to eat, maybe a hamburger or chili con carne. Main-course platters run 72 to 136 F ($14.40 to $27.20), and drinks are 60 to 75 F ($12 to $15). Open daily from 7pm to 2am.

A HISTORIC TAVERN

Taverne Henri-IV. 13 place du pont-Neuf, 1er. ☎ **01-43-54-27-90.** Métro: Pont-Neuf.

The location of this *taverne* couldn't be more magnificent—in a 17th-century building at the Pont Neuf, on the Ile de la Cité. The host, Monsieur Cointepas, bottles his own wine, or at least some of it. His prize wines are listed on a chalkboard menu. You might order a special beaujolais or perhaps a glass of Chinon; a glass of wine will set you back 20 to 25 F ($4 to $5), and all drinks are cheaper at the bar. Snacks, at 25 to 30 F ($5 to $6), include wild-boar pâté; and 10 farmer's lunches are offered for 100 to 120 F ($20 to $24), with wine, including such delicacies as foie gras de canard (duckling) and escargots cooked in wine. Open Monday to Friday from noon to 9pm and on Saturday from noon to 4am; closed August.

Side Trips from Paris

10

Paris—the city that began on an island—is itself the center of a curious landlocked island known as the Ile de France.

Shaped roughly like a saucer, it lies encircled by a thin ribbon of rivers: the Epte, Aisne, Marne, and Yonne. Fringing these rivers are mighty forests with famous names—Rambouillet, St-Germain, Compiègne, and Fontainebleau. These forests are said to be responsible for Paris's clear, gentle air and the unusual length of its spring and fall. This may be a debatable point, but there's no argument that they provide the capital with a series of excursion spots, all within easy reach.

The forests were once the possessions of kings and the ruling aristocracy, and they're still sprinkled with the magnificent *châteaux* (palaces) of their former masters. Together with ancient hamlets, glorious cathedrals, and little country inns, they turn the Ile de France into a traveler's paradise. On a more modern note, Disneyland Paris attracts visitors from all over the world. Because of Paris's comparatively small size, it's almost at your doorstep.

The difficult question is deciding where to go. What we're offering in this chapter is merely a handful of the dozens of possibilities for 1-day jaunts.

1 Versailles

13 miles SW of Paris, 44 miles NE of Chartres

For centuries, the name of this Parisian suburb resounded through the consciousness of every aristocratic family in Europe. The palace built there outdistanced, outshone, and outdazzled every other kingly residence in Europe, a scandal because of its horrendous expense and a symbol to later generations of a corrupt and often frivolous régime obsessed with pretension and prestige.

Back in the *grand siécle,* all you needed was a sword, a hat, and a bribe for the guard at the gate. Providing you didn't look as if you had smallpox, you'd be admitted to the precincts of the Château de Versailles, there to stroll through salon after glittering salon— watching the Sun King at his banqueting table or dancing or flirting or even doing something far more personal. Louis XIV was acorded about as much privacy as an institution.

Ile de France

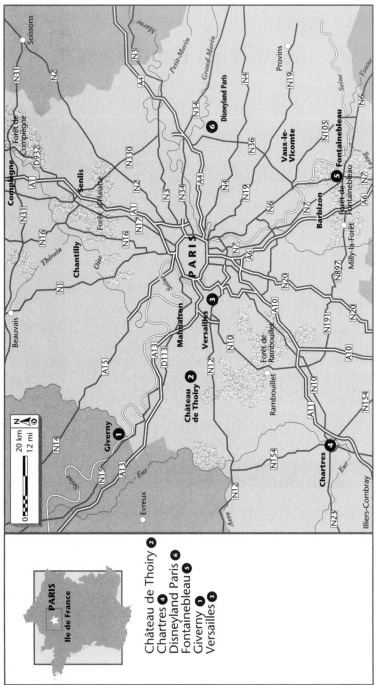

ESSENTIALS

GETTING THERE   By Train   To get to the palace at Versailles, catch RER Line C5 at the Gare-d'Austerlitz, St-Michel, Musée-d'Orsay, Invalides, Pont-de-l'Alma, Champ-de-Mars, or Javel station, and take it to the Versailles–Rive-Gauche station, where you can catch a shuttle bus to the château. The 35-F ($7) trip takes about half an hour. Eurailpass holders travel free. A regular train also leaves from the Gare St-Lazare for the Versailles–Rive-Gauche RER station.

By Métro   Get off at Pont-de-Sèvres and transfer to bus no. 171. The trip takes 15 minutes. To get there from Paris, it's cheaper to pay with three Métro tickets from a *carnet* packet. You'll be let off near the gates of the palace.

By Car   Head southwest from the center of Paris to the Place de la Porte de St-Cloud, or exit from the *périphéique* at Paris' southwestern edge, following the signs to Versailles. Follow the Avenue de Gen'l Leclerc straight through to Versailles.

ORIENTATION   The town is dominated by the palace. Three main avenues radiate from place d'Armes in front of the palace.

VISITOR INFORMATION   The **tourist office** is at 7 rue des Réservoirs (☎ **01-39-50-36-22**).

SEEING THE PALACE

The kings of France built a glittering private world for themselves, far from the grime and noise and bustle of Paris: the ✪ **Château de Versailles,** place d'Armes (☎ **01-30-84-74-00**). Seeing all the palace's rooms would take up an entire morning and leave you pretty exhausted, so you should probably skip some of them and save your energy for the park, which is the ultimate in French landscaping—every tree, shrub, flower, and hedge is disciplined into a frozen ballet pattern and spread among soaring fountains, sparkling little lakes, grandiose stairways, and hundreds of marble statues. It's more like a colossal stage setting than a park—even the view of the blue horizon seems like some ornately embroidered backdrop. It's a Garden of Eden for puppet people, a place where you expect the birds to sing coloratura soprano.

Inside, the **Grand Apartments, the Royal Chapel, and the Hall of Mirrors** (where the Treaty of Versailles was signed) can be visited without a guide Tuesday to Sunday between 9:45am and 5pm (it's closed on holidays). Admission costs 42 F ($8.40) for adults, 28 F ($5.60) for those ages 18 to 25, and free to children 17 and under and seniors over 60. On Sunday, admission for adults is reduced to 35 F ($7). Other sections of the château may be visited only at specific hours or on special days. Some of the sections are temporarily closed as they undergo restoration.

Try to save time to visit the **Grand Trianon,** which is a good walk across the park. In pink-and-white marble, it was designed by Hardouin-Mansart for Louis XIV in 1687. The Trianon is mostly furnished with Empire pieces. You can also visit the **Petit Trianon,** built by Gabriel in 1768. This was the favorite residence of Marie Antoinette, who could escape the rigors of court here. Once it was a retreat for Louis XV and his mistress, Madame du Barry. Both the Grand Trianon and the Petit Trianon are open Tuesday to Sunday from 10am to 5pm. Admission to the Grand Trianon is 23 F ($4.60) for adults, 15 F ($3) for ages 18 to 25, and is free for children 17 and under. Admission to the Petit Trianon is 13 F ($2.60) for adults, 9 F ($1.80) for those 18 to 25, and free for children 17 and under. Joint admission to both Trianons is 29 F ($5.80) for adults, 19 F ($3.80) for ages 18 to 25, and free for children 17 and under.

Peaches & Peas Fit for a King

Between 1682 and 1789, the Versailles palace housed a royal entourage whose population, except for 8 years during the minority of Louis XV, remained constant at 3,000. To feed them, the sprawling kitchens employed a permanent staff of 2,000. Without benefit of running water or electricity, they labored over the banquets that became day-to-day rituals at the most glorious court since the collapse of ancient Rome.

The fruits and vegetables that were arrayed on the royal tables were produced on site, in **Les Potagers du Roi** (King's Kitchen Garden). Surprisingly, the gardens have survived and can be found a 10-minute walk south of the château's main entrance, at 6 rue du Hardy, behind an industrial-looking gate. Here, 23 acres of fertile earth are arranged into parterres and terraces as formal as the legendary showcases devoted, during the royal tenure, to flowers, fountains, and statuary.

Meals at Versailles were quite a ritual. The king almost always dined in state, alone, at a table visible to hundreds of observers and, in some cases, other diners, who sat in order of rank. Fortunately for gastronomic historians, there are many detailed accounts about what Louis XIV enjoyed and how much he consumed: Devoted to salads, he ate prodigious amounts of basil, purslane, mint, and wood sorrel. He loved melons, figs, and pears. With him, apples were not particularly popular, but he found peaches so desirable that he rarely waited to cut and peel them, preferring to let the juices flow liberally down his royal chin. The culinary rage, however, was peas, imported from Genoa for the first time in 1660. According to Mme de Maintenon, Louis XIV's second wife, the entire court was obsessed with "impatience to eat them."

Today Les Potagers du Roi are maintained by about half a dozen gardeners under the direction of the Ecole Nationale du Paysage. It manages to intersperse the fruits and vegetables once favored by the monarchs with experimental breeds and hundreds of splendidly espaliered fruit trees.

EVENING SPECTACLES

The tourist office in Versailles offers a program of evening fireworks and illuminated fountains on several occasions throughout the summer. These 1¹/₂-hour spectacles, called the **Grande Fête de Nuit de Versailles,** are announced a full season in advance. They're usually on Saturday night, although the schedules change from year to year. Spectators sit on bleachers clustered at the boulevard de la Reine entrance to the Basin of Neptune. The most desirable front-view seats cost 185 F ($37), and standing room on the promenoir sells for 70 F ($14); it's free for children 9 and under. Gates that admit you to the Grande Fête open 1¹/₂ hours before show time.

Tickets can be purchased in advance at the tourist office in Versailles, or in Paris at **Agence Perroissier,** 6 place de la Madeleine, 8e (☎ **01-42-60-58-31**), and **Agence des Théâtres,** 78 av. des Champs-Elysées, 8e (☎ **01-43-59-24-60**). If you've just arrived in Versailles from Paris, you can take your chances and purchase tickets an hour ahead of show time at boulevard de la Reine.

From the beginning of May until the end of September, a less elaborate spectacle is staged each Sunday. Called **Grandes Eaux Musicales,** it's a display of fountains in the park and costs only 23 F ($4.60). Classical music is also played.

Versailles

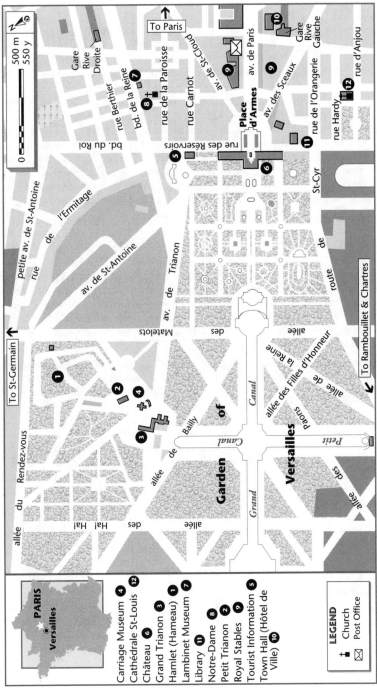

To Paris

Gare
Rive
Droite

Gare Rive
Gauche

av. de Paris

av. de St-Cloud

rue Berthier

rue de la Reine

bd. de la Reine

rue de la Paroisse

rue Carnot

av. des Sceaux

rue de l'Orangerie

rue d'Anjou

rue Hardy

Place
d'Armes

rue des Réservoirs

bd. du Roi

av. de St-Antoine

petite av. de St-Antoine

rue de l'Ermitage

av. de St-Antoine

av. de Trianon

rue des Matelots

St-Cyr

route de

To Rambouillet & Chartres

To St-Germain

allée du Rendez-vous

allée des Hal Hal

allée de Bailly

Garden of Versailles

Grand Canal

Petit Canal

allée de la Reine

allée des Filles d'Honneur

allée des Paons

Carriage Museum	4
Cathédrale St-Louis	6
Château	3
Grand Trianon	1
Hamlet (Hameau)	7
Lambinet Museum	11
Library	8
Notre-Dame	9
Petit Trianon	2
Royal Stables	5
Tourist Information	10
Town Hall (Hôtel de Ville)	12

PARIS

Versailles

LEGEND
Church
Post Office

500 m
550 y

WHERE TO DINE

Le Potager du Roy. 1 rue du Maréchal-Joffre. ☎ **01-39-50-35-34.** Reservations required. Main courses 85–175 F ($17–$35); fixed-price menu 120 F ($24) at lunch, 165 F ($33) at dinner. AE, DC, MC, V. Tues–Sat noon–2:30pm and 7:30–10:30pm, Sun noon–2:30pm. FRENCH.

Phillipe Le Tourneur used to work for the leading chef of Versailles, Gérard Vié, before setting up his own attractive restaurant on a busy street corner in the commercial part of town. Le Tourneur's restaurant may not have the culinary refinement of Vié's deluxe citadel, but he's a remarkable chef nevertheless, and his prices are a lot more democratic. Set behind a maroon facade, in a modern decor of three warmly decorated dining rooms, Le Tourneur offers a fixed-price menu or comparably priced à la carte meals. Each dish is perfectly prepared, including such courses as a lamb terrine with raisins and pistachio nuts as a starter. You might follow with an excellent duckling with baby turnips or a steamed filet of sole with fresh summer vegetables. Another delectable speciality is the roast lamb en paillote (parchment).

Le Quai No. 1. 1 av. de St-Cloud. ☎ **01-39-50-42-26.** Reservations recommended for dinner. Main courses 75–120 F ($15–$24); fixed-price menu 120–168 F ($24–$33.60). MC, V. Tues–Sat noon–2pm and 7:30–10:30pm, Sun noon–2pm. FRENCH.

Orléans-born Marc Le Loup and Compiègne-born Dominique de Ravel have breathed new life into this longtime favorite overlooking the château's western facade. Decorated with lithographs and wood paneling, the restaurant also has a summer terrace. Its fixed-price menus make dining a bargain in high-priced Versailles. Specialties include seafood sauerkraut, bouillabaisse, and home-smoked salmon. Care and imagination go into the cuisine, and the service is more than professional—it's also polite.

Les Trois Marchés. In the Hôtel Trianon Palace, 1 bd. de la Reine. ☎ **01-30-84-38-00.** Reservations required. Main courses 200–350 F ($40–$70); fixed-price menus 270 F ($54) (Tues–Fri at lunch) and 510–610 F ($102–$122). AE, DC, MC, V. Tues–Sat noon–2pm and 7:30–10pm. FRENCH.

For lunch you can dine in regal style at the Trianon Palace Hotel. Situated in a 5-acre garden, the hotel became world-famous in 1919 when it served as headquarters for the signers of the Treaty of Versailles. It still retains its old-world splendor, its dining room decorated with crystal chandeliers and fluted columns. The chef, Gérard Vié, is the most talented and creative chef feeding visitors to Versailles these days. He attracts a discerning clientele who don't mind paying the high prices. The *cuisine moderne* is subtle, often daringly conceived and inventive, the service smooth. Specialties are likely to include a flan of foie gras, roast pigeon in a garlic-and-cream sauce, a modern interpretation of a Toulouse-style cassoulet, and roasted turbot with a sauce made from meat drippings, wine, and beurre blanc (white butter).

Impressions

When Louis XIV had finished the Grand Trianon, he told [Mme de] Maintenon he had created a paradise for her, and asked if she could think of anything now to wish for. . . . She said she could think of but one thing—it was summer, and it was balmy France—yet she would like well to sleigh ride in the leafy avenues of Versailles! The next morning found miles and miles of grassy avenues spread thick with snowy salt and sugar, and a procession of those quaint sleighs waiting to receive the chief concubine of the gaiest and most unprincipled court that France has ever seen!
                                              —Mark Twain, *The Innocents Abroad* (1869)

2 Fontainebleau

37 miles S of Paris, 46 miles NE of Orléans

Set within the vestiges of a forest (*Forêt de Fontainebleau*) that bear its name, this suburb of Paris has offered refuge to French monarchs throughout the changing tides of French history. Kings from the Renaissance valued it because of its nearness to rich hunting grounds and its distance from the slums and smells of contemporary Paris, and Napoléon referred to the Palais de Fontainebleau, which he reembellished with his distinctive monogram and decorative style, as the house of the centuries. Many pivotal or decisive events have occurred within its walls, perhaps no moment more memorable than when Napoléon stood on the horseshoe-shaped exterior stairway and bade farewell to his shattered army before his departure to exile on Elba. That scene has been the subject of seemingly countless paintings, including Vernet's *Les Adieux*.

ESSENTIALS

GETTING THERE   By Train   Trains to Fontainebleau depart from the Gare de Lyon in Paris and take 35 minutes to an hour. The Fontainebleau station is just outside the town in Avon. The town bus makes the 2-mile trip to the château every 10 to 15 minutes (every 30 minutes on Sunday). A one-way ticket costs 8.70 F ($1.75).

By Car   Follow the A6 south of Paris, and exit at N191, then follow signs pointing toward Fontainebleau.

ORIENTATION   Dominated by its château, the town is surrounded by the dense Forêt de Fontainebleau. The main squares are place du Général-de-Gaulle and place d'Armes.

VISITOR INFORMATION   The **Office de Tourisme** is at 31 place Napoléon-Bonaparte (☎ 01-64-22-25-68).

SEEING THE PALACE

Napoléon called the ✪ **Château de Fontainebleau** (☎ 01-60-71-50-70) the house of the centuries. Much of French history has taken place within its walls, perhaps no moment more memorable than when Napoléon I himself stood on the horseshoe-shaped stairway and bade an emotional farewell to his army before his departure to Elba and exile. That scene has been the subject of countless paintings, including Vernet's *Les Adieux* of the emperor.

Napoléon's affection for Fontainebleau was understandable. He was following the pattern of a succession of French kings in the pre-Versailles days who used Fontainebleau as a resort and hunted in its magnificent forests. François I tried to turn the hunting lodge into a royal palace in the Italian Renaissance style—he brought several artists, including Benvenuto Cellini, to work for him.

Under the patronage of François I, the School of Fontainebleau, led by painters Rosso Fiorentino and Primaticcio, gained prestige. The artists adorned the 210-foot-long Gallery of François I. Stucco-framed panels depict such scenes as *The Rape of Europa,* and the monarch holding a pomegranate, a symbol of unity. The salamander, the symbol of the Chevalier King, is everywhere.

Sometimes called the Gallery of Henri II, the **Ballroom** is in the Mannerist style, with the interlaced initials H&D in the decoration, which referred to Henri and his mistress, Diane de Poitiers. You can also see the initials H&C, symbolizing Henri and his wife, Catherine de Médicis. At one end of the room is a monumental fireplace supported by two bronze satyrs, made in 1966 (the originals were melted down during the French Revolution). At the other side is the balcony of the musicians, with sculptured garlands. The ceiling displays octagonal coffering adorned with rosettes. Above the wainscoting is a series of frescoes, painted between 1550 and 1558, which depict such mythological subjects as *The Feast of Bacchus.*

An architectural curiosity is the richly and elegantly adorned **Louis XV staircase.** The room above it was originally decorated by Primaticcio for the bedroom of the duchesse d'Etampes, but when an architect was designing the stairway, he simply ripped out her floor. Of the Italian frescoes that were preserved, one depicts the queen of the Amazons climbing into Alexander's bed.

When Louis XIV ascended the throne, he neglected Fontainebleau because of his preoccupation with Versailles. However, he wasn't opposed to using the palace for house guests—specifically such unwanted ones as Queen Christina, who had abdicated the throne of Sweden. Under the assumption that she still had "divine right," she ordered one of the most brutal royal murders on record—that of her companion Monaldeschi, who had ceased to please her.

Louis XV and, later, Marie Antoinette also took an interest in Fontainebleau.

The château found renewed glory—and shame—under Napoléon I. You can walk around much of the palace on your own, but some of the **Napoleonic rooms** are accessible by guided tour only. His throne room and bedroom (look for his symbol, a bee) are equally impressive. You can also see where the emperor signed his abdication—the document exhibited is a copy. The furnishings in Empress Joséphine's *petits appartements* and the *grands appartements* of Napoléon evoke the imperial heyday.

After your long trek through the palace, visit the gardens and, especially, the carp pond; the gardens, however, are only a prelude to the Forest of Fontainebleau.

The interior is open Wednesday to Monday from 9:30am to 12:30pm and 2 to 5pm (in July and August, Wednesday to Monday from 9:30am to 5pm). A combination ticket allowing visitors to the *grands appartements,* the Napoleonic Rooms, and the Chinese Museum costs 31 F ($6.20) for adults, 20 F ($4) for students 18 to 20, and free for children 17 and under. A ticket allowing access to the *petits appartements* goes for 15 F ($3) for adults, 10 F ($2) for students 18 to 20, and free for children 17 and under.

WHERE TO DINE

Le Beauharnais. In the Grand Hôtel de l'Aigle Noir, 27 place Napoléon-Bonaparte. ☎ **01-64-22-32-65.** Fax 01-64-22-17-33. Reservations required. Main courses 110–160 F ($22–$32); fixed-price menu 180–450 F ($36–$90). AE, DC, MC, V. Daily noon–2pm and 7:30–9:30pm. FRENCH.

This is the leading restaurant of the town. Although it has been completely renovated, it still retains its old charm. Opposite the château, the building was once the home of Cardinal Dé Retz. It dates from the 16th century, but was converted into a hotel in 1720. The restaurant, the most beautiful in town, was installed in a former courtyard. The interior is filled with Empire furniture and potted palms.

The food has greatly improved here in recent years, and the only establishment to give it serious competition is the François 1er at 3 rue Royale. The refreshing menu includes such classics as roast duckling in the style of Rouen, but also dishes with more flair and subtlety, including sweetbreads with foie gras. The perfectly prepared grilled pigeon with pistachio nuts evokes Morocco. There's a changing variety of dishes, depending on seasonal availability.

Should you decide to stay the night, the hotel has 57 bedrooms and two suites, all with private bath, TV, radio, minibar, direct-dial phones, double windows, and electric heating. The hotel also boasts a swimming pool, sauna, and fitness center.

Fontainebleau

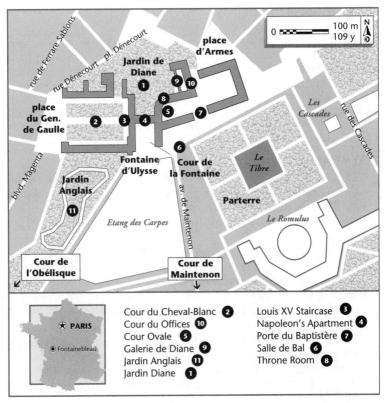

Cour du Cheval-Blanc ②
Cour du Offices ⑩
Cour Ovale ⑤
Galerie de Diane ⑨
Jardin Anglais ⑪
Jardin Diane ❶

Louis XV Staircase ③
Napoleon's Apartment ④
Porte du Baptistère ⑦
Salle de Bal ⑥
Throne Room ⑧

Each room is individually decorated, often with antiques and pleasantly tasteful colors. Doubles range in price from 750 to 1,200 F ($150 to $240), and suites are 1,200 to 2,000 F ($240 to $400), plus 85 F ($17) for breakfast.

Le Caveau des Ducs. 24 rue de Ferrare. ☎ **01-64-22-05-05.** Reservations recommended. Main courses 85–135 F ($17–$27); fixed-price menu 98–230 F ($19.60–$46). AE, MC, V. Daily noon–2pm and 7–10pm. FRENCH.

This reasonably priced restaurant occupies what was originally built in the 1600s as a storage cellar for the nearby château (a 5-minute walk). Candles flicker against the vaulted stone ceiling; the decor is traditional and the staff helpful. The restaurant is not in the same league as the grand cuisine leaders such as Le Beauharnais; it offers much simpler food, although the setting is dramatic. Each dish is competently prepared, but most are French clichés like snails in garlic butter or roast leg of lamb with garlic and rosemary sauce. The filet of rumpsteak is quite tasty, especially when it's served with Brie sauce, or you might prefer a platter of sole and salmon on a bed of pasta.

3 Disneyland Paris

20 miles E of Paris

After evoking some of the most enthusiastic as well as negative reactions in recent French history, the Euro Disney Resort opened its doors in 1992 to one of the most lavish theme parks in the world. In 1994 it unofficially changed its name to

"Disneyland Paris." Because the park was conceived on a scale rivaling that of Versailles, the earliest days of the project were not particularly happy. European journalists delighted in belittling it and accusing it of everything from cultural imperialism to sounding the death knell of French culture. But after financial jitters, and goodly amounts of public relations and financial juggling, the resort is on track, welcoming visitors at prices that have been reduced by around 20% from those at the resort's initial opening.

Situated on a 5,000-acre site (about one-fifth the size of Paris itself) in the Paris suburb of Marne-la-Vallée, east of the center, the park incorporates the most successful elements of its Disney predecessors—but with a European flair.

ESSENTIALS

GETTING THERE   By Train   The resort is linked to the RER commuter express rail network (Line A), which maintains a stop within walking distance of the theme park. Board the RER at such inner-city Paris stops as Charles-de-Gaulle–Etoile, Châtelet–Les Halles, or Nation. Get off at Line A's last stop, Marne-la-Vallée/Chessy, a 45-minute ride from central Paris. The round-trip fare from central Paris is 75 F ($15). Trains run every 10 to 20 minutes, depending on the time of day.

By Bus   Each of the hotels in the resort is connected by shuttle bus to and from both Orly Airport and Roissy–Charles de Gaulle. Buses depart from both airports at intervals of 30 to 45 minutes, depending on the time of day and day of the year. One-way transportation to the park from either airport costs 75 F ($15) per person.

By Car   Take the A4 highway east from Paris and get off at Exit 14 where it's marked PARC EURO DISNEYLAND. Guest parking at any of the thousands of parking spaces costs 40 F ($8) per day. An interconnected series of moving sidewalks speeds up pedestrian transit from the parking areas to the theme park's entrance. Parking is free for guests at any of the hotels in the resort.

VISITOR INFORMATION   All hotels listed below provide general information about the theme park, but for specific theme park information in all languages, contact the **Disneyland Paris Guest Relations Office,** located in City Hall on Main Street, U.S.A. (☎ 01-64-74-30-00).

FAST FACTS   Coin-operated lockers can be rented for 10 F ($2) per use, and larger bags can also be stored for 15 F ($3) per day. Children's strollers and wheelchairs can be rented for 30 F ($6) per day, with a 20-F ($4) deposit. Baby-sitting is available at any of the resort's hotels if 24-hour advance notice is given.

WHAT TO SEE & DO

The resort was designed as a total vacation package. Included in one enormous unit are the Disneyland Park with its five different entertainment "lands," six large hotels, a campground, an entertainment center (Festival Disney), a 27-hole golf course, and dozens of restaurants, shows, and shops.

One of the attractions, **Main Street, U.S.A.,** features horse-drawn carriages and street-corner barbershop quartets. From the "Main Street Station," steam-powered railway cars leave for a trip through a Grand Canyon Diorama to Frontierland, with its paddle-wheel steamers reminiscent of the Mississippi Valley of Mark Twain's era.

The park's steam trains chug past **Adventureland**—with its swashbuckling 18th-century pirates, the treehouse of the Swiss Family Robinson, and reenacted legends from the *Arabian Nights*—to **Fantasyland.** There you can see the symbol of the theme park, the Sleeping Beauty Castle (Le Château de la Belle au Bois Dormant), whose soaring pinnacles and turrets are an idealized (and spectacular) interpretation of the châteaux of France.

Visions of the future are displayed at **Discoveryland,** whose tributes to human invention and imagination are drawn from the works of Leonardo da Vinci, Jules Verne, H. G. Wells, the modern masters of science fiction, and the *Star Wars* series. Of all the areas, Discoveryland has proven among the most popular, and one of the few that was enlarged (in 1995) after the park's original inauguration.

Disney also maintains an entertainment center—**Festival Disney**—whose indoor/outdoor layout somewhat resembles a cross between a mall in California and the boardwalk at Coney Island. Scattered on either side of a pedestrian walkway, illuminated by an overhead grid of spotlights, it's set just outside the boundaries of the fenced-in acreage containing the bulk of Disneyland's attractions. The complex accommodates dance clubs, snack bars, restaurants, souvenir shops, and bars for adults who want to escape from the children for a while. Unlike the rest of the park, admission to Festival Disney is free, and consequently attracts night owls from Paris and its suburbs who wouldn't otherwise be particularly interested in the park itself.

Admission to the park for 1 day, depending on the season, is 150 to 195 F ($30 to $39) for adults and 120 to 150 F ($24 to $30) for children 3 to 12. Admission to the park for 2 days ranges from 285 to 370 F ($57 to $74) for adults and 230 to 285 F ($46 to $57) for children 3 to 12. Children 2 and under enter free. Admission prices vary according to the season; the peak season is from mid-June to mid-September, as well as Christmas and Easter weeks. Entrance to Festival Disney, the resort's consortium of shops, dance clubs, and restaurants, is free, although there's usually a cover charge for the dance clubs.

The park is open June 12 to September 12, daily from 9am to 11pm; September 13 to June 11, Monday to Friday from 9am to 7pm and on Saturday and Sunday from 9am to 11pm. Opening and closing hours, however, vary with the weather and the season. It's usually a good idea to phone the information office (see above).

Guided tours can be arranged for 50 F ($10) for adults and 35 F ($7) for children 3 to 11. Lasting 3¹/₂ hours and including 20 or more people, the tours offer an opportunity for a complete visit. In view of the well-marked paths leading through the park, and the availability of ample printed information in virtually any language once you get there, guided tours are not a particularly viable idea, and are not enthusiastically recommended either by Disneyland Paris or by these writers.

In 1995 Disneyland Paris, once infamous for its ability to lose money, reported its first profit since opening its doors in 1992. The park managed to slice operating costs through more stringent methods of management and record attendance. This combination has allowed the park to reduce admission prices, which in turn has attracted more visitors. With the construction of several new attractions and plans for a Planet Hollywood, Disneyland is currently facing a brighter future.

WHERE TO STAY

The resort has six hotels, each of which offers a different theme and shares a common reservations service. For more information call 407/W-DISNEY (934-7639) in North America, or 0171/753-2900 in London. For information or reservations in France, contact the **Central Reservations Office,** Disneyland Paris S.C.A., B.P. 105, F-77777 Marne-la-Vallée Cedex 4 (☎ **01-60-30-60-30**).

EXPENSIVE

Disneyland Hotel. Disneyland Paris, B.P. 105, F-77777 Marne-la-Vallée Cedex 4. ☎ **01-60-45-65-00.** Fax 01-60-45-65-33. 479 rms, 18 suites. A/C MINIBAR TV TEL. 1,650–1,995 F ($330–$399) room for one to four; 2,900–12,500 F ($580–$2,500) suite. AE, DC, MC, V.

Located at the entrance to the park, this flagship hotel is Victorian in style, with red-tile turrets and jutting balconies; some observers have likened it to the town hall of a major European city. The bedrooms are plushly and conservatively furnished. On the "Castle Club" floor, there are free newspapers, all-day beverages, and access to a well-equipped private lounge.

Dining/Entertainment: The hotel has three restaurants (the California Grill is recommended separately; see "Where to Dine," below) and two bars.

Facilities: Health club with indoor pool, whirlpool, sauna, private dining and banqueting rooms.

Services: Room service, laundry, baby-sitting.

Hotel New York. Disneyland Paris, B.P. 100, F-77777 Marne-la-Vallée Cedex 4. ☎ **01-60-45-73-00.** Fax 01-60-45-73-33. 538 rms, 31 suites. A/C MINIBAR TV TEL. 1,025–1,225 F ($205–$245) room for one to four; from 2,100 F ($420) suite. AE, DC, MC, V.

Inspired by the Big Apple at its best, this hotel was designed around a nine-story central "skyscraper" flanked by the Gramercy Park Wing and the Brownstones Wing. (The exteriors of both of these wings resemble row houses.) The bedrooms are comfortably appointed with art deco accessories and New York–inspired memorabilia.

Dining/Entertainment: The hotel has a diner, one restaurant, a cocktail and wine bar, and an art deco bar.

Services: Room service, laundry, baby-sitting.

Facilities: Indoor/outdoor pool, two outdoor tennis courts, health club.

MODERATE

Newport Bay Club. Disneyland Paris, B.P. 105, F-77777 Marne-la-Vallée Cedex 4. ☎ **01-60-45-55-00.** Fax 01-60-45-55-33. 1,083 rms, 15 suites. A/C MINIBAR TV TEL. 625–825 F ($125–$165) room for one to four; 1,400–2,000 F ($280–$400) suite. AE, DC, MC, V.

This hotel was designed with a central cupola, jutting balconies, and a blue-and-cream color scheme, reminiscent of a harborfront New England hotel. Each nautically decorated bedroom offers closed-circuit TV information and movies. The upscale Yacht Club and the less formal Cape Cod restaurants are the dining choices. Facilities include a lakeside promenade, a glassed-in pool pavilion, an outdoor pool, and a health club.

Sequoia Lodge. Disneyland Paris, B.P. 114, F-77777 Marne-la-Vallée Cedex 4. ☎ **01-60-45-51-00.** Fax 01-60-45-51-33. 997 rms, 14 suites. A/C MINIBAR TV TEL. 525–775 F ($105–$155) room for one to four; 1,500–1,700 F ($300–$340) suite. AE, DC, MC, V.

Built of gray stone and roughly textured planking, and capped by a gently sloping green copper roof, this hotel resembles a rough-hewn but comfortable lodge in a remote section of the Rocky Mountains. The hotel consists of a large central building with five additional chalets (each housing 100 bedrooms) nearby. The rooms are comfortably rustic. The Hunter's Grill serves spit-roasted meats carved directly on your plate. Less formal is the Beaver Creek Tavern. There's an indoor pool and health club.

INEXPENSIVE

Hotel Cheyenne and Hotel Santa Fé. Disneyland Paris, B.P. 115, F-77777 Marne-la-Vallée Cedex 4. ☎ **01-60-45-62-00** (Cheyenne) or ☎ **01-60-45-78-00** (Santa Fé). Fax 01-60-45-62-33 (Cheyenne) or 01-60-45-78-33 (Santa Fé). 2,000 rms. TV TEL. 400–695 F ($80–$139) room for one to four in the Hotel Cheyenne; 300–595 F ($60–$119) room for one to four in the Hotel Santa Fé. AE, DC, MC, V.

Located next door to one another, these two hotels are situated near a re-creation of Texas's Rio Grande and evoke different aspects of the Old West. The Cheyenne accommodates visitors in 14 two-story buildings along "Desperado Street," whereas the Santa Fé, sporting a desert theme, encompasses four different "nature trails" winding among 42 adobe-style pueblos. Accommodations in both are bare-boned and, except for the campgrounds, the least expensive at the entire resort. Their only disadvantage, according to some parents with children, involves their lack of a swimming pool.

Tex-Mex specialties are offered at La Cantina (Hotel Santa Fé), and barbecue and smokehouse specialties predominate at the Chuck Wagon Café (Hotel Cheyenne).

WHERE TO DINE

At the resort there are at least 45 different restaurants and snack bars, each trying hard to please millions of European and North American palates. Here are two recommendations:

Auberge de Cendrillon. In Fantasyland. ☎ **01-64-74-24-02.** Reservations not required. Main courses 98–130 F ($19.60–$26); fixed-price menu 140–260 F ($28–$52). AE, DC, MC, V. Fri–Tues 11:30am–11pm. FRENCH.

This is a fairy-tale version of Cinderella's sumptuous country inn, with a glass couch in the center. It's the major French restaurant at the resort. A master of ceremonies, in a plumed tricorne hat and wearing an embroidered tunic and lace ruffles, welcomes you. For an appetizer, try the warm goat-cheese salad with lardons or the smoked-salmon platter. If you don't choose one of the good fixed-price meals, you can order from the limited but excellent à la carte menu. Perhaps you'll settle happily for poultry in a pocket (puff pastry), loin of lamb roasted with mustard, or sautéed médaillons (medallion-shaped pieces) of veal.

The California Grill. In the Disneyland Hotel. ☎ **01-60-45-65-00.** Reservations required. Main courses 105–230 F ($21–$46); fixed-price menu 295 F ($59); children's menu from 85 F ($17). AE, DC, MC, V. Daily 7–11pm. CALIFORNIAN.

Focusing on the new and lighter recipes for which the Golden State has achieved recognition, this airy and elegant restaurant features such specialties as poached oysters with leeks and salmon as an appetizer, or oxtail consommé with crisp vegetables. Among the fish selections, grilled tuna appears with white beans and a soya sauce or you may prefer grilled shrimp with spicy rice. Main courses are likely to feature goat cheese tortellini with grilled vegetables, or glazed loin of veal with asparagus and fresh chives. The most expensive item on the menu is a squab and lobster fricassée. A number of dishes for children are named after everybody from Peter Pan to Goofy. The Napa Feast, one of the fixed-price menus, begins with home-cured smoked salmon, follows with roast rack of lamb scented with fresh thyme, and ends with crème brûlée (thick cream).

EVENING ENTERTAINMENT

Although you might find it hard to escape the presence of children and the props that were designed to entertain them, Disneyland Paris offers hideaways for adults as well. Here is one of the most visible:

Buffalo Bill's Wild West Show. In the Festival Disney Building. ☎ **01-60-45-71-00.**

This is the premier theatrical venue of Disneyland Paris, a twice-per-night stampede of entertainment that recalls the show that once traveled the West with Buffalo Bill and Annie Oakley. You'll dine at tables that ring, amphitheater style, a dirt-floored riding rink where sharpshooters, runaway stagecoaches, and dozens of horses and Indians ride very fast and perform some alarmingly realistic acrobatics. A Texas-style barbecue, served assembly-line style by waiters in 10-gallon hats, is part of the experience. Despite its cornpone elements, it's not without its charm and an almost mournful nostalgia for a way of life of another continent and another century. Wild Bill himself is suitably dignified and the Indians suitably brave. Two shows are staged nightly, at 6:30 and 9:30pm, costing (with dinner included) 300 F ($60) for adults and 200 F ($40) for children.

4 Chartres

60 miles SW of Paris, 47 miles NW of Orléans

Many observers feel that the architectural aspirations of the Middle Ages reached their highest expression in the Chartres cathedral. Come here to see its architecture, its sculpture, and—most important—its stained glass, which gave the world a new color, Chartres blue.

ESSENTIALS

GETTING THERE   By Train   Trains run directly to Chartres from Paris's Gare Montparnasse, taking less than an hour and passing through the sea of wheatfields that characterize Beauce, the granary of France.

By Car   Follow the A10/A11 southwest of Paris, following signs to Le Mans and Chartres. The exit for Chartres is clearly marked.

VISITOR INFORMATION   The **Office de Tourisme** is on place de la Cathédrale (☎ **01-37-21-50-00**).

SEEING THE CATHEDRAL

Reportedly, Rodin once sat for hours on the edge of the sidewalk, admiring the Romanesque sculpture of the ✪ **Cathédrale Notre-Dame de Chartres,** 16 Cloître Notre-Dame (☎ **01-37-21-58-65**). His opinion: Chartres is the French Acropolis. When it began to rain, a kind soul offered him an umbrella—which he declined, so transfixed was he by the magic of his precursors.

The cathedral's origins are uncertain; some have suggested that it grew up over an ancient Druid site that had later become a Roman temple. As early as the 4th century it was a Christian basilica. A fire in 1194 destroyed most of what had then become a Romanesque cathedral, but it spared the western facade and the crypt. The cathedral you see today dates principally from the 13th century, when it was built with the combined efforts and contributions of kings, princes, churchmen, and pilgrims from all over Europe. One of the greatest of the world's High Gothic cathedrals, it was the first to use flying buttresses. In size, it ranks fourth in the world, bowing to St. Peter's in Rome and the Canterbury Cathedral in Kent, England.

French sculpture in the 12th century broke into full bloom when the Royal Portal was added. A landmark in Romanesque art, the sculptured bodies are elongated, often formalized beyond reality, in their long flowing robes. But the faces are amazingly (for the time) lifelike, occasionally betraying *Mona Lisa* smiles. In the central tympanum, Christ is shown at the Second Coming, whereas his descent is depicted on the right, his ascent on the left. Before entering, you should stop to admire the Royal Portal and then walk around to both the north and south portals, each dating from the 13th century. They depict such biblical scenes as the expulsion of Adam and Eve from the Garden of Eden.

Inside is a celebrated choir screen; work on it began in the 16th century and lasted until 1714. The niches, 40 in all, contain statues illustrating scenes from the life of the Madonna and Christ—everything from the massacre of the innocents to the coronation of the Virgin.

But few of the rushed visitors ever notice the screen–they're too transfixed by the light from the stained glass. Covering an expanse of more than 3,000 square yards, the glass is without peer in the world and is truly mystical. It was spared in both world wars because it was painstakingly removed, piece by piece, and stored securely. Most of the stained glass dates from the 12th and 13th centuries.

See the windows in the morning, at noon, in the afternoon, at sunset—whenever and as often as you can. They constantly change like a kaleidoscope's images. It's difficult to single out one panel or window of special merit; however, an exceptional one is the 12th-century *Vierge de la belle verrière* (Our Lady of the Beautiful Window) on the south side. Of course, there are three fiery rose windows, but you couldn't miss those even if you tried.

The nave—the widest in France—still contains its ancient maze. The wooden *Virgin of the Pillar,* to the left of the choir, dates from the 14th century. The crypt was built over two centuries, beginning in the 9th. Enshrined within is *Our Lady of the Crypt,* a 1976 Madonna that replaced one destroyed during the Revolution.

Try to get a tour conducted by Malcolm Miller, an Englishman who has spent three decades studying the cathedral and giving tours in English. His rare blend of scholarship, enthusiasm, and humor will help you understand and appreciate the cathedral. He usually conducts tours at noon and 2:45pm Monday to Saturday. The cathedral is open daily from 7:30am to 7:30pm.

After your visit, stroll through the episcopal gardens and enjoy yet another view of this remarkable cathedral.

EXPLORING THE OLD TOWN

If time remains, you may want to explore the medieval cobbled streets of the **Vieux Quartiers** (Old Town). At the foot of the cathedral, the lanes contain gabled houses. Humped bridges span the Eure River. From the Bouju Bridge, you can see the lofty spires in the background. Try to find rue Chantault, which boasts houses with colorful facades; one is eight centuries old.

One of the highlights of your visit might be the **Musée des Beaux-Arts de Chartres,** 29 Cloître Notre-Dame (☎ **01-37-36-41-39**), which is open April to October, Wednesday to Monday from 10am to 1pm and 2 to 6pm; and November to March, Wednesday to Monday from 10am to noon and 2 to 5pm. Next door to the cathedral, this museum of fine arts charges 20 F ($4) for adults and 10 F ($2) for children. A former episcopal palace, the building at times competes with the exhibitions inside. One part dates from the 15th century and encompasses a courtyard. The permanent collection of paintings covers mainly the 16th to the 19th century, and includes the work of such old masters as Zurbarán, Watteau, and Brosamer. Of particular interest is David Ténier's *Le Concert.* Special exhibitions are often mounted.

WHERE TO STAY
MODERATE

Le Grand Monarque Best Western. 22 place des Epars, 28005 Chartres. ☎ **01-37-21-00-72,** or 800/528-1234 in the U.S. Fax 01-37-36-34-18. 49 rms, 5 suites. MINIBAR TV TEL. 555–665 F ($111–$133) double; 1,140 F ($228) suite. AE, DC, MC, V. Rates include continental breakfast. Parking 41 F ($8.20).

The leading hotel of Chartres is housed in a classical building enclosing a courtyard. Functioning as an inn almost since its original construction, and greatly expanded over the centuries, it still attracts guests who enjoy its old-world charm—such as art nouveau stained glass and Louis XV chairs in the dining room. The rooms are decorated with reproductions of antiques; most have sitting areas. The hotel also has an

To Taste a Madeleine

And suddenly the memory returns. The taste was that of the little crumb of madeleine which on Sunday mornings at Combray (because on those mornings I did not go out before church-time), when I went to say good day to her in her bedroom, my aunt Léonie used to give me, dipping it first in her own cup of real or of lime-flower tea.

—Marcel Proust, *Remembrance of Things Past*

Illiers-Combray, a small town 54 miles southwest of Paris and 15 miles southwest of Chartres, was once known simply as Illiers. Then tourists started to visit, and signs were posted: ILLIERS, LE COMBRAY DE MARCEL PROUST. Illiers was and is a real town, but Marcel Proust made it world famous as the imaginary Combray of his masterpiece, *A la recherche du temps perdu* (*Remembrance of Things Past*). So today the town is known as Illiers-Combray.

It was the taste of a madeleine that launched Proust on his immortal recollection. To this day hundreds of his readers from all over the world flock to the pastry shops in Illiers-Combray to eat a madeleine or two dipped in limeflower tea. Following the Proustian labyrinth, you can explore the gardens, streets, and houses he wrote about so richly and had frequently visited until he was 13. The town is epitomized by its Eglise St-Jacques, where, as a boy, Proust placed hawthorn on the altar.

Some members of Proust's family have lived in Illiers for centuries. His grandfather, François, was born here on rue du Cheval-Blanc. At 11 place du Marché, just opposite the church, he ran a small candle shop. His daughter, Elisabeth, married Jules Amiot, who ran a shop a few doors away. Down from Paris, young Marcel would visit his aunt at 4 rue du St-Esprit, which has been renamed rue du Docteur-Proust, honoring Marcel's grandfather.

The **Maison de Tante Léonie,** 4 rue du Docteur-Proust (☎ **01-37-24-30-97**), is a museum, charging 25 F ($5) for admission. In the novel this was Aunt Léonie's home; filled with antimacassars, it's typical of the solid bourgeois comfort of its day. Upstairs you can visit the bedroom where the young Marcel slept; today it contains souvenirs of key episodes in the novel. The house can be visited Tuesday to Sunday at 2:30, 3:30, and 4 or 4:30pm.

In the center of town, a sign will guide you to further Proustian sights.

---

anachronistic restaurant. One local critic found the kitchen trapped in an "*ancien régime* time warp."

Hôtel Châtlet. 6–8 av. Jehan-de-Beauce, 28000 Chartres. ☎ **01-37-21-78-00.** Fax 01-37-36-23-01. 48 rms. TV TEL. 420–490 F ($84–$98) double. AE, DC, MC, V. Third person 60 F ($12) extra. Free parking.

Though this 1982 hotel is one in a chain, it has many traditional touches, and the rooms are inviting, with reproductions of Louis XV and Louis XVI furniture. Most accommodations face a garden, and many windows open out to a panoramic cathedral view. In chilly weather, guests gather around the log fire. Breakfast is the only meal served, but there are numerous restaurants nearby.

INEXPENSIVE

🅢 **Hôtel de la Poste.** 3 rue du Général-Koenig, 28003 Chartres. ☎ **01-37-21-04-27.** Fax 01-37-36-42-17. 58 rms. TV TEL. 290–310 F ($58–$62) double. AE, DC, MC, V. Parking 39 F ($7.80).

A Logis de France, this hotel offers one of the best values in Chartres—even though it's short on charm when compared to the Hôtel Châtlet. It's in the center of town, across from the main post office. The rooms are soundproof and comfortably furnished and have wall-to-wall carpeting. There's an in-house garage.

WHERE TO DINE

Le Buisson Ardent. 10 rue au Lait. ☎ **01-37-34-04-66.** Reservations recommended. Main courses 98–122 F ($19.60–$24.40); fixed-price menu 118–218 F ($23.60–$43.60). MC, V. Mon–Sat 12:30–2pm and 7:30–9:30pm, Sun 12:30–2pm. FRENCH.

In a charming house in the most historic section of town, this establishment is one floor above street level in the shadow of the cathedral. You might expect it to be a tourist trap but it isn't, though the food rarely rises above bistro level. Dishes change every 3 weeks but might include stuffed mushrooms with garlic butter, followed by fresh codfish flavored with coriander and served with parsley flan. A dessert specialty is crispy hot apples with sorbet and a Calvados-flavored butter sauce.

NEARBY ACCOMMODATIONS & DINING

✪ **Château de Blanville.** Saint Luperce, 28190 Courville-sur-Eure. ☎ **01-37-26-77-36.** Fax 01-37-26-78-02. 5 rms, 2 suites. 700–800 F ($140–$160) double; 900 F ($180) suite. AE, MC, V. Rates include breakfast. From Chartres, head west along N23 for 6 miles, following the signs to Courville; then follow the signs to the Château de Blanville.

Built in the Louis XIII style in 1643 and acquired in 1738 by the ancestors of the present owners, this château is a testament to the accomplishments of many generations of the Cossé-Brissac family. Since 1992 they've rented some of their well-furnished rooms to visitors who announce their arrival in advance. Ringing the building are about 275 acres of forest and parkland, little changed since the building's construction. The guest rooms are high-ceilinged reminders of another age. None contains a TV or telephone, but shared facilities are available in one of three guest lounges.

An experience here is best appreciated during dinner, when your hostess, Lisa (a Cordon Bleu–trained chef), prepares three-course meals, with wine, coffee, and before-dinner drinks included. Reservations at least a day in advance are required, and few other experiences convey in as personal a way the preoccupations, grace, and problems of *la vie de château*.

Le Manoir des Prés du Roy. Saint-Prest, 28300 Chartres. ☎ **01-32-22-27-27.** Fax 01-37-22-31-26. 17 rms, 1 suite. MINIBAR TV TEL. 380–480 F ($76–$96) double; 580 F ($116) suite. MC, V. Free parking. From Chartres, take the road to Maintenon, following the vallée de l'Eure.

Lying 4¹/₂ miles north of Chartres and 50 miles south of Paris, this former private dwelling has lots of architectural character. It's a retreat for those wanting to escape touristy Chartres. The manor house is set in a 36-acre park along the River Eure with a private tennis court. The tile-roofed rustic building has been enlarged over the years and is covered with ivy and graced with gables and chimneys. The rooms are comfortably old-fashioned. Many Chartres residents visit to sample the cooking of Gilles Morel, who uses fresh products. Dinner is served nightly, costing 135 to 250 F ($27 to $50). The restaurant closes in winter on Sunday night and Monday.

5 Château de Thoiry

25 miles W of Paris

The Château et Parc Zoologique de Thoiry is a major attraction that in a year draws more visitors than the Louvre or Versailles.

GETTING THERE   By Car   Take the Autoroute de l'Ouest (A13) toward Dreux, exiting at Bois-d'Arcy. Then take N12, following the signs on D11 to Thoiry.

By Public Transport   It's so awkward to reach this place by public transport that the chateau itself doesn't publicize, promote, or recommend it. Isloted as it is, it's really a destination best visited by car.

SEEING THE CHATEAU & PARK

The 16th-century ✪ **Château et Parc Zoologique de Thoiry,** 78770 Thoiry-en-Yvelines (☎ **01-34-87-52-25**), owned by the vicomte de La Panouse family (now run by son Paul and his wife, Annabelle), displays two unpublished Chopin waltzes, antique furniture, and more than 343 handwritten letters of French or European kings, as well as the original financial records of France from 1745 to 1750. But these are not as much a draw as the game reserve.

The château's grounds have been turned into a game reserve with elephants, giraffes, zebras, monkeys, rhinoceroses, alligators, lions, tigers, kangaroos, bears, and wolves—more than 1,000 animals and birds roam at liberty. The reserve and park cover 300 acres, though the estate is on 1,200 acres.

In the French gardens you can see llamas, Asian deer and sheep, and many types of birds, including flamingos and cranes. In the tiger park a promenade has been designed above the tigers. In addition, in the *caveau* of the château is a vivarium. Paul and Annabelle are also restoring the 17th-, 18th-, and 19th-century gardens as well as creating new ones.

To see the animal farm you can drive your own car, providing it isn't a convertible (an uncovered car may be dangerous). Anticipating troubles, the owners carry thousands of francs' worth of insurance.

The park is most crowded on weekends, but if you want to avoid the crush, visit on Saturday or Sunday morning. The park is open from April to October, Monday to Saturday from 10am to 6pm and on Sunday from 10am to 6:30pm; and November to March, daily from 10am to 5pm. Admission is 97 F ($19.40) for adults, 77 F ($15.40) for children 3 to 12, and free for children 2 and under. The château is open daily from 2pm: to 6pm April to October, to 5pm November to March. Admission is 25 F ($5) for adults, 20 F ($4) for children 3 to 12, free for children 2 and under.

WHERE TO STAY & DINE

Hôtel de l'Etoile. 78770 Thoiry. ☎ **01-34-87-40-21.** Fax 01-34-87-49-57. 12 rms. TEL. 315 F ($63) double. AE, DC, MC, V. Free parking.

Built centuries ago, this rustic three-story inn has a stone-and-timber garden sitting room for guests. The guest rooms are comfortably furnished and well maintained. A dolphin fountain decorates one of the walls, and the pleasant restaurant has masonry trim. Meals consist of fairly routine homemade French dishes. Expect to pay 115 F ($23) for a fixed-price meal.

6 Giverny

50 miles NW of Paris

On the border between Normandy and the Ile de France, Giverny is home to the house—now the ✪ **Claude Monet Foundation,** rue Claude-Monet (☎ **01-32-51-28-21**)—where Claude Monet lived for 43 years. The restored house and its gardens are open to the public.

Impressions

I am entirely absorbed by these plains of wheat on a vast expanse of hills like an ocean of tender yellow, pale green, and soft mauve, with a piece of worked [farmed] land dotted with clusters of potato vines in bloom, and all this under a blue sky tinted with shades of white, pink, and violet.

—Vincent van Gogh, 1890

ESSENTIALS

GETTING THERE **By Train** Take the Paris–Rouen line (Paris–St-Lazare) to the Vernon station. A taxi can take you the 3 miles to Giverny.

By Bus Bus tours are operated from Paris by American Express and Cityrama.

By Car If you're driving, take the Autoroute de l'Ouest (Port de St-Cloud) toward Rouen. Leave the autoroute at Bonnières, then cross the Seine on the Bonnières Bridge. From there, a direct road with signs will bring you to Giverny. Expect about an hour of driving and try to avoid weekends.

Another way to get to Giverny is to leave the highway at the Bonnières exit and go toward Vernon. Once in Vernon, cross the bridge over the Seine and follow the signs to Giverny or Gasny (Giverny is before Gasny). This is easier than going through Bonnières, where there aren't many signs.

SEEING THE CLAUDE MONET FOUNDATION

Born in 1840, the French impressionist painter Claude Monet was a brilliant innovator, excelling in presenting the effects of light at different times of the day. In fact, some critics claim that he "invented light." His series of paintings of Rouen cathedral and of the water lilies, which one critic called "vertical interpretations of horizontal lines," are just a few of his masterpieces.

Monet came to Giverny in 1883. While taking a small railway linking Vetheuil to Vernon, he discovered the village at a point where the Epte stream joined the Seine. Many of his friends used to visit him here at Le Pressoir, including Clemenceau, Cézanne, Rodin, Renoir, Degas, and Sisley. When Monet died in 1926, his son, Michel, inherited the house but left it abandoned until it decayed into ruins. The gardens became almost a jungle, inhabited by river rats. In 1966 Michel died and left it to the Académie des Beaux-Arts. It wasn't until 1977 that Gerald van der Kemp, who restored Versailles, decided to work on Giverny. A large part of it was restored with gifts from American benefactors, especially the late Lila Acheson Wallace, former head of *Reader's Digest,* who contributed $1 million to the project.

You can stroll through the garden and view the thousands of flowers, including the *nymphéas.* The Japanese bridge, hung with wisteria, leads to a dreamy setting of weeping willows and rhododendrons. Monet's studio barge was installed on the pond.

The foundation is open only from April to October, Tuesday to Sunday from 10am to 6pm, charging 35 F ($7) for adults and 25 F ($5) for children. You can visit just the gardens for 25 F ($5). Reservations are a must.

WHERE TO DINE

Auberge du Vieux Moulin. 21 rue de la Falaise. ☎ **01-32-51-46-15.** Main courses 65–120 F ($13–$24); fixed-price menu 98–185 F ($19.60–$37). MC, V. Tues–Sun noon–3pm and 7:30–10pm. Closed Jan. FRENCH.

This is a convenient lunch stop for visitors at the Monet house. The Boudeau family maintains a series of cozy dining rooms filled with original paintings by the impressionists. Since you can walk here from the museum in about 5 minutes, leave your car in the museum lot. Specialties include appetizers like seafood terrine with baby vegetables. Main courses feature escalope of salmon with sorrel sauce and auiguillettes of duckling with peaches. The kitchen doesn't pretend that the food is any more than it is: good, hearty country fare. The charm of the staff helps a lot, too. The stone building is ringed with lawns and has a pair of flowering terraces.

Index

Queries:

Christian LaCroix s/b
    Christian Lacroix, 5
Jean-Claude Gaultier s/b
    Jean-Paul Gaultier, 5

FROMMER'S COMPLETE TRAVEL GUIDES

(Comprehensive guides to destinations around the world, with selections in all price ranges—from deluxe to budget)

FROMMER'S FRUGAL TRAVELER'S GUIDES
(The grown-up guides to budget travel, offering dream vacations at down-to-earth prices)

Australia from $45 a Day
Berlin from $50 a Day
California from $60 a Day
Caribbean from $60 a Day
Costa Rica & Belize from $35 a Day
Eastern Europe from $30 a Day
England from $50 a Day
Europe from $50 a Day
Florida from $50 a Day
Greece from $45 a Day
Hawaii from $60 a Day

India from $40 a Day
Ireland from $45 a Day
Italy from $50 a Day
Israel from $45 a Day
London from $60 a Day
Mexico from $35 a Day
New York from $70 a Day
New Zealand from $45 a Day
Paris from $65 a Day
Washington, D.C. from $50 a Day

FROMMER'S PORTABLE GUIDES
(Pocket-size guides for travelers who want everything in a nutshell)

Charleston & Savannah
Las Vegas

New Orleans
San Francisco

FROMMER'S IRREVERENT GUIDES
(Wickedly honest guides for sophisticated travelers)

Amsterdam
Chicago
London
Manhattan

Miami
New Orleans
Paris
San Francisco

Santa Fe
U.S. Virgin Islands
Walt Disney World
Washington, D.C.

FROMMER'S AMERICA ON WHEELS
(Everything you need for a successful road trip, including full-color road maps and ratings for every hotel)

California & Nevada
Florida
Mid-Atlantic
Midwest & the Great Lakes
New England & New York

Northwest & Great Plains
South Central &Texas
Southeast
Southwest

FROMMER'S BY NIGHT GUIDES
(The series for those who know that life begins after dark)

Amsterdam
Chicago
Las Vegas
London

Los Angeles
Miami
New Orleans

New York
Paris
San Francisco